ENCYCLOPEDIA OF THE UNITED STATES CONSTITUTION

ENCYCLOPEDIA OF THE UNITED STATES CONSTITUTION

VOLUME I
A–L

David Schultz

An imprint of Infobase Publishing

For Helene

Encyclopedia of the United States Constitution

Facts On File, Inc.
An imprint of Infobase Publishing
132 West 31st Street
New York NY 10001

Library of Congress Cataloging-in-Publication Data

Schultz, David A. (David Andrew), 1958–
Encyclopedia of the United States Constitution / David Schultz.—1st ed.
p. cm.
Includes bibliographical references and index.
ISBN 978-0-8160-6763-3 (hc : alk. paper) 1. Constitutional law—United States—Encyclopedias. I. Title.
KF4548.5.S38 2009
342.730203—dc22 2008023349

Text design by Annie O'Donnell
Cover design by Alicia Post
Illustrations by Sholto Ainslie

Printed in the United States of America

VB Hermitage 10 9 8 7 6 5 4 3 2 1

This book is printed on acid-free paper and contains 30 percent postconsumer recycled content.

Contents

List of Entries

List of Contributors

Jason Abel, Independent scholar
David Adamany, Temple University
Takeshi Akiba, University of California, Berkeley
Mark Alcorn, Independent scholar
Nedda Allbray, Independent scholar
Bruce E. Altschuler, SUNY Oswego
Ellen Ann Anderson, Indiana University–Purdue University Indianapolis
Kevin Anderson, Eastern Illinois University
Jennifer J. Ashley, Boise State University
Mary Welek Atwell, Radford University
John M. Aughenbaugh, Virginia Commonwealth University
Gordon A. Babst, Chapman University
Nancy V. Baker, New Mexico State University
Gregory Baldi, Georgetown University
Thomas J. Baldino, Wilkes University
Jeremy D. Ball, Boise State University
Daniel Baracskay, Valdosta State University
Matthew W. Barber, University of Florida
Tim J. Barnett, Jacksonville State University
Elizabeth Beaumont, University of Minnesota
Valerie Bell, Boise State University
Michael John Berry, University of Colorado, Boulder
Ryan Black, Washington University in St. Louis
Karen Blackistone, Holtzman Vogel PLLC
Neil Bradley, American Civil Liberties Union
Aaron-Andrew P. Bruhl, University of Houston
Brigette J. Bush, Northern Arizona University
Winston E. Calvert, Armstrong Teasdale LLP
Raymond V. Carman, Jr., Binghamton University
Walter F. Carroll, Bridgewater State College
Peter A. Collins, Boise State University
Frank J. Colucci, Purdue University Calumet
Michael Comiskey, Pennsylvania State University
Miles A. Cooper, Georgia Southwestern State University
Erika N. Cornelius, Purdue University
Nathan H. Cristler, Charles W. Hanor, P.C.
Caitlin F. Currie, Florida Atlantic University
Robert Davidow, George Mason University
Julian M. Davis , University of Michigan
Katherine J. Davis, Monmouth College
Lorna M. Dawson, Lynchburg University
Robert DeWees, Louis D. Brandeis School, University of Louisville
Steve Diamond, University of Miami
Amanda DiPaolo, Middle Tennessee State University
Graham G. Dodds, Concordia University (Montreal, Canada)
Scott Dodson, University of Arkansas
Steven B. Dow, Michigan State University
Philip A. Dynia, Loyola University New Orleans
Thomas C. Ellington, Wesleyan College
James Ely, Jr., Vanderbilt University
JeDon Emenhiser, Humboldt State University
Francene M. Engel, University of Maryland
Sean Evans, Union University
Stefano Fait, University of St. Andrews
Cleveland Ferguson III, Florida Coastal School of Law
James Daniel Fisher, Edinboro University of Pennsylvania
Joel Fishman, Duquesne University
Michael P. Fix, University of Kentucky
John Fliter, Kansas State University
James C. Foster, Oregon State University, Cascades
Alaina Fotiu-Wojtowicz, University of Michigan Law School
James R. Fox, Dickinson School of Law
Amanda Freeman, New Mexico State University
Barry D. Friedman, North Georgia College and State University

Mark A. Fulks, Tennessee State University
Cheryl Crozier Garcia, Hawai'i Pacific University
Alison Gash, University of California, Berkeley
Scott D. Gerber, Ohio Northern University
Tobias T. Gibson, Monmouth College
Laura Gimeno-Pahissa, Universitat Autonoma de Barcelona
Ernest Gomez, University of Notre Dame
Timothey Gordinier, State University of New York, Potsdam
Paul Gowder, Stanford University
J. David Granger, Georgetown University
Jensen Grant, Florida Atlantic University
Scott E. Graves, Georgia State University
William Crawford Green, Morehead State University
Robert Drew Grey, Morehead State University
Ellen Grigsby, University of New Mexico
Martin Gruberg, University of Wisconsin, Oshkosh
Kevin R. C. Gutzman, Western Connecticut State University
Randy W. Hagedorn, University of Minnesota
Michael W. Hail, Morehead State University
Richard J. Hardy, Western Illinois University
Robin A. Harper, Wellesley College
Brian M. Harward, Southern Illinois University
Barbara J. Hayler, University of Illinois, Springfield
Craig Hemmens, Boise State University
John Allen Hendricks, Southeastern Oklahoma State University
Ryan C. Hendrickson, Eastern Illinois University
Johanna Hickman, Georgetown University
Arthur Holst, Widener University
Charles Howard, Tarleton State University
Bruce Huber, University of California, Berkeley
Marianne Hudson, Boise State University
Steven F. Huefner, Ohio State University
Brian Iannacchione, Boise State University
Nathan M. Ingebretson, University of Minnesota
Randa Issa, University of Southern California
Jim Jacobson, Independent scholar
Aaron Jones, Morehead State University
Robert M. Kahn, University of St. Thomas School of Law
Daniel M. Katz, University of Michigan
C. Woodward Kaupert, San Antonio College
Sheila Suess Kennedy, Indiana University–Purdue University Indianapolis
Joshua A. Kimsey, Porter Wright Morris & Arthur LLP
Kyle L. Kreider, Wilkes University
Dan Krejci, Jacksonville State University
Dylan R. Kytola, University of Minnesota
Stephen J. Lange, Morehead State University
Julie Lantrip, Georgetown University
R. Reid LeBeau, Lockridge, Grindal, Nauen, PLLP
William Lester, Jacksonville State University
Justin Levitt, Brennan Center for Justice, New York University School of Law
Steven B. Lichtman, Shippensburg University
Jinee Lokaneeta, Drew University
Jacqueline M. Loubet, University of Florida
Kim Mac Innes, Bridgewater State College
Patrick Malcolmson, St. Thomas University, Canada
Wendy L. Martinek, Binghamton University
David A. May, Eastern Washington University
Mark A. McGinnis, Independent scholar
Virginia Mellema, U.S. Equal Employment Opportunity Commission, San Francisco
Jesse R. Merriam, Center for Constitutional Litigation
Susan Gluck Mezey, Loyola University Chicago
Dennis B. Miles, Southeastern Oklahoma State University
Mark C. Milewicz, Gordon College
Katherine M. Miller, Radford University
Dale Mineshima-Lowe, Center for International Relations
Melanie K. Morris, Ball State University
Sharon L. Morrison, Southeastern Oklahoma State University
David Mueller, Boise State University
Andre Mura, Center for Constitutional Litigation
Caryn E. Neumann, Ohio State University
Daniel G. Ogbaharya, Northern Arizona University
Michael Paris, City University of New York
Matthew J. Parlow, Chapman University School of Law
William D. Pederson, Louisiana State University, Shreveport

George Peery, Mars Hill College
Steven A. Peterson, Pennsylvania State University, Harrisburg
Jason Pierceson, University of Illinois, Springfield
Mark W. Podvia, Dickinson School of Law, Pennsylvania State University
Vincent Kelly Pollard, University of Hawai'i, Manoa
Norman Provizer, Metropolitan State College
Marc G. Pufong, Valdosta State University
Jane G. Rainey, Eastern Kentucky University
Kirk A. Randazzo, University of Kentucky
Michael Reese, North Georgia College and State University
Ann D. Reynolds, Southeastern Oklahoma State University
William W. Riggs, Texas A & M International University
Phyllis Farley Rippey, Western Illinois University
William Rose, Albion College
Bertrall Ross, Independent scholar
Marc Ruffinengo, Boise State University
Patrick Schmidt, Macalester College
David Schultz, Hamline University
Christopher E. Smith, Michigan State University
Jinney S. Smith, Lycoming College
Mark S. Stein, University of Missouri, St. Louis
Jerry E. Stephens, U.S. Court of Appeals for the Tenth Circuit
Ryane McAuliffe Straus, College of St. Rose
Ruth Ann Strickland, Appalachian State University
Rick A. Swanson, University of Louisiana, Lafayette
Martin J. Sweet, Florida Atlantic University
Marshall Tanick, Mansfield, Tanick & Cohen PA
Douglas C. Telling, Framingham State College
K. Thirumaran, National University of Singapore
Lydia Brashear Tiede, University of California, San Diego
Jocelyn Tipton, Eastern llinois University
Jurij Toplak, University of Maribor
Jason Torchinsky, Holtzman Vogel PLLC
Margaret Tullai, State University of New York, Albany
John Vile, Middle Tennessee State University
Carol Walker, Georgia State University
Bryan H. Ward, Ohio Northern University College of Law
Maria Collins Warren, University of North Carolina, Wilmington
Andrew J. Waskey, Dalton State College
Brian Weber, Morehead State University
Stephen Wermiel, American University, Washington College of Law
Rebecca Wiggins, New Mexico State University
William R. Wilkerson, State University of New York, Oneonta
April Willeford, New Mexico State University
Gwyneth I. Williams, Webster University
R. Owen Williams, Yale University
Loretta M. Young, NCC Family Court Wilmington, Delaware

Acknowledgments

Encyclopedia of the United States Constitution is more than the product of one person's efforts. As editor, I have had the pleasure of working with more than 200 authors who composed the hundreds of essays in these volumes. Together, we have done our best to produce a reference book that readers should find informative and enjoyable. Mere words cannot begin to describe the gratitude I have toward all who contributed to this project. I have benefited immensely from all who participated in this project, both intellectually and in a spirit of friendship. In doing a project like this, one learns of the great genius, knowledge, and passion so many others share for the Constitution. I am a better person for having worked with all the contributors and leave this project with lifelong friends.

Finally, while all effort has been made to acknowledge personally and individually everyone who contributed, no doubt I have missed a few people. To those unintentionally forgotten or passed over, I apologize for this error and any others in this encyclopedia.

Preface

"We the People." These three words elegantly grace the opening sentence of the U.S. Constitution. For many, these three words say it all when it comes to understanding the document that the constitutional framers wrote back in 1787. It is a constitution written for all in the United States by noble, selfless patriots and meant to endure forever. It is a document whose meaning is fixed in time, meant to provide for personal freedoms, a representative government, and an effective government that was to be a vast improvement over the weak and decentralized Articles of Confederation that it replaced. However, this interpretation is not shared by everyone.

Former Supreme Court justice Thurgood Marshall, in reflecting during the bicentennial in 1987 on the Constitution and its opening three words remarked:

> I do not believe that the meaning of the Constitution was forever "fixed" at the Philadelphia Convention. Nor do I find the wisdom, foresight, and sense of justice exhibited by the Framers particularly profound. To the contrary, the government they devised was defective from the start, requiring several amendments, a civil war, and momentous social transformation to attain the system of constitutional government, and its respect for the individual freedoms and human rights, we hold as fundamental today. When contemporary Americans cite "The Constitution," they invoke a concept that is vastly different from what the Framers barely began to construct two centuries ago.
>
> For a sense of the evolving nature of the Constitution we need look no further than the first three words of the document's preamble: "We the People." When the Founding Fathers used this phrase in 1787, they did not have in mind the majority of America's citizens. "We the People" included, in the words of the framers, "the whole Number of free Persons." On a matter so basic as the right to vote, for example, Negro slaves were excluded, although they were counted for representational purposes at three-fifths each. Women did not gain the right to vote for over a hundred and thirty years.

Marshall's comments are as challenging as they are disturbing. They challenge us to ask what the words of the Constitution really mean and what this document was meant to accomplish. For Federalists such as James Madison and the other authors of the *Federalist Papers* (a collection of 85 letters that many consider to be the definitive statement of the framers regarding what the Constitution is supposed to mean), their goal was to protect liberty, preserve popular government, and limit the threats of what we would now call the tyranny of the majority. It would secure these goals by setting up an elaborate machine that would use checks and balances, separation of powers, bicameralism, federalism, and self-interest to check political power. Yet for the Anti-Federalists, they saw the words of the proposed constitution of 1787 as saying something else. They spoke of a threat to personal liberty and the values inherent in the American Revolution and the 1776 Declaration of Independence.

Justice Marshall's comments are also disturbing because in many respects he is correct. The Constitution of today is very different from the one written by the framers. The document of 1787 was born of the politics of the times. It was a constitution written for an agrarian society fearful of central power. It was a constitution that provided for slavery and failed to guarantee explicitly the right to vote, and it was a document produced in an era well before the advent of the Internet, cell phones, cars, airplanes, and nuclear bombs. Moreover, as the historian Richard Hofstadter contended in *The American Political Tradition*, the men who wrote the Constitution went to Philadelphia with value-laden assumptions about human nature and theories of politics and economics that may be very different from the ones that many of us hold today.

In the course of the more than 220 years since the Constitution was written, a Bill of Rights has been attached to it, in addition to 17 other amendments, with literally hundreds of other efforts to amend it. The United States has been though a civil war, two world wars, a civil rights revolution, and dramatic cultural changes in how its citizens view women and racial, ethnic, and political minorities, as well as those who adopt different religions (or no faith) and have differing sexual orientations.

America has also experienced dramatic technological changes, as well as seen a world transformed so much that it is not isolated from others as it once was but instead is enmeshed in an interdependent global economy. The world of the 21st century is vastly different from the one the constitutional framers experienced. Given all this, what did the U.S. Constitution mean in 1787? What does it mean today? And how has an understanding of it (and the document itself) evolved to respond to all the changes that have occurred throughout U.S. history? This is what the *Encyclopedia of the United States Constitution* seeks to explain.

This encyclopedia is not meant to be the definitive last word on what the Constitution means. In fact, given the evolving nature of the document, persistent efforts to amend it, and scores of new Supreme Court decisions every year seeking to interpret it, there can be no definitive last word. Instead, this encyclopedia, written primarily for students, the general public, and perhaps even some legal specialists, seeks to explain some of the major clauses, amendments, court decisions, personalities, issues, and challenges that have affected the Constitution over its history. It is an effort to respect the spirit of Chief Justice John Marshall's words in *McCulloch v. Maryland,* 17 U.S. 316 (1819), in which he stated: "We must never forget that it is a constitution we are expounding." The goal here is, thus, to expound on the history of the Constitution. After all, the history of the United States is interconnected with the Constitution, and one can see how the challenges that America faced are played out in this document.

Battles over the power of states versus the national government, prayer in public school, abortion, gay rights, censorship, peace, war, the death penalty, and a host of other issues inevitably reach the Constitution. Here one finds that, over time, some issues once dominant in their day, such as slavery, have long since faded, but new ones, such as how to respond to international terrorism since the events of September 11, 2001, continue to challenge the Constitution. But throughout all these challenges, there is the assumption, as best captured by Chief Justice Salmon P. Chase in *Texas v. White,* 74 U.S. 700 (1869), that "[t]he Constitution, in all its provisions, looks to an indestructible Union, composed of indestructible States." The document that the framers created over 220 years ago, despite all the changes in it and in the world, is at its core supposed to represent something timeless and permanent about how the United States wishes to govern itself.

Inasmuch as the Constitution is supposed to be permanent in one respect, some claim that it is outdated, despite all the changes Thurgood Marshall described. Some would argue that in a world of terrorist threats, the framework of the Constitution is inadequate, necessitating either abandoning it in time of crisis or giving its clauses new meanings, much in the same way some claim the Supreme Court did during the New Deal, World War II, or during the cold war. In response, as Chief Justice Charles Evans Hughes stated so eloquently in *Home Bldg. & Loan Ass'n v. Blaisdell,* 290 U.S. 398 (1934),

> Emergency does not create power. Emergency does not increase granted power or remove or diminish the restrictions imposed upon power granted or reserved. The Constitution was adopted in a period of grave emergency. Its grants of power to the federal government and its limitations of the power of the States were determined in the light of emergency, and they are not altered by emergency. What power was thus granted and what limitations were thus imposed are questions which have always been, and always will be, the subject of close examination under our constitutional system.

The *Encyclopedia of the United States Constitution* aims to assist its readers in undertaking a closer examination of the Constitution, a document that has endured well for many years and with little indication that it will soon disappear or become irrelevant to an understanding of U.S. government and history.

—David Schultz
Hamline University

NOTE

When a case has been decided, but not yet published in the case reporter, the citation may note the volume but leave blank the page of the case reporter until it is determined. For example, *Meredith v. Jefferson,* 551 U.S. ___ (2007).

Abington Township v. Schempp 374 U.S. 203 (1963)

In *Abington Township v. Schempp,* the second landmark "SCHOOL PRAYER" case, the Supreme Court, in an 8-1 decision, invalidated state-sponsored devotional Bible reading and Lord's Prayer recitation in public schools as a violation of the ESTABLISHMENT CLAUSE of the FIRST AMENDMENT, placing in jeopardy the laws and policies of many states and school districts and prompting efforts to contravene the Court's ruling or amend the Constitution and verbal attacks on the Court as antireligion. In fact, the justices took great pains to explain both what they were and were not doing and to show that they were not hostile to religion.

The Schempps, a Unitarian family, objected to Abington High School's morning devotionals consisting of Bible verses and recitation of the Lord's Prayer. Students could leave or not participate, but the Schempps worried that leaving during the devotional could endanger relations with teachers and other students. Along with the *Schempp* case, the Court addressed the similar complaint of Madalyn Murray O'Hair, an outspoken atheist from Baltimore, who welcomed the notoriety associated with ending the religious exercises.

In his majority opinion, Justice Thomas Clark reviewed the history of the establishment clause that led to a standard of government neutrality toward religion and the relation of the establishment clause to the free exercise clause that guaranteed the right of all to choose their religions without state coercion. (Unlike the free exercise clause, however, coercion need not be a factor in establishment clause cases.) Clark distilled the precedent of previous Court decisions into two criteria: a law or government action must have both a secular purpose and a primary effect that neither promotes nor restricts religion. These later became two elements of the three-pronged Lemon test used to decide many major establishment clause cases. In response to charges that the Court was creating a "religion of secularism" in the schools, Clark reiterated that this decision did not forbid objective study of the Bible in school for its literary and historic qualities. Finally, he rejected the idea that the free exercise clause gave members of the majority religion the right to have their school devotionals: "While the free exercise clause clearly prohibits the use of state action to deny the rights of free exercise to anyone, it has never meant that a majority could use the machinery of the State to practice its beliefs."

Several justices wrote concurring opinions to augment Clark's analysis. Justice WILLIAM O. DOUGLAS focused on the impropriety of the expenditure of any public money to fund a religious exercise. Justice WILLIAM J. BRENNAN, JR.'s lengthy concurrence expanded on Clark's discussion of the relation of *Schempp* to the whole scope of the Court's establishment clause jurisprudence. He cataloged the futility of trying to apply the "original intent" of the Founding Fathers to *Schempp.* While acknowledging the long tradition of prayer and Bible reading in U.S. schools, he amassed ample evidence that even in the 19th century, school devotionals were not universally considered appropriate by state governments. Brennan, however, also suggested situations in which government ACCOMMODATION of religion should not be affected by *Schempp.*

Justice Potter Stewart, the sole dissenter, said the Court's rigid reading of the establishment clause posed a threat to the free exercise of children wanting morning devotionals.

The *Schempp* ruling met with substantial public criticism. Some school districts stubbornly continued religious exercises, and others started them. Yet, many religious leaders endorsed the Court's position.

For more information: Alley, Robert S. *Without a Prayer: Religious Expression in Public Schools.* Amherst, N.Y.: Prometheus Books, 1996; Ivers, Gregg. *Redefining the First Freedom.* New Brunswick, N.J.: Transaction Publishers, 1993; Morgan, Richard E. *The Supreme Court and Religion.* New York: Free Press, 1972.

—Jane G. Rainey

abortion

Abortion, a procedure used to remove an embryo or fetus from its mother's womb, is a hotly contested political issue. In addition, abortion and its regulation implicates numerous legal questions, most particularly, whether the Constitution protects a woman's decision to terminate a pregnancy and the rules the government may place on a woman who makes this choice.

Throughout much of the 19th century, the United States placed no national legal restrictions on obtaining an abortion in the first few months of pregnancy. Not until the 1830s did state governments begin to enact bans on abortion after quickening (the first notice of fetal movement during a pregnancy). In the Civil War era, the American Medical Association (AMA) lobbied and persuaded most state governments to outlaw abortions, based on fears that abortions were not being performed safely. In 1873, Congress passed the Comstock Act, which banned any mail or mail advertisements about objects used for abortion or contraceptive purposes as well as drugs or medicines.

Throughout the first half of the 20th century, little attention was devoted to abortion politics; however, in the mid-1960s, in response to back-alley deaths and unsanitary, illegal abortion procedures, pro-choice groups began to push for abortion law reform. In response, many states started allowing therapeutic and elective abortion procedures. These early reformers argued for abortion reforms on health grounds such as saving the life or preserving the mental or physical health of the mother. However, the political discourse on abortion was headed for a dramatic change with the filing of *ROE V. WADE.*

One of the most controversial cases of the 20th century, *Roe v. Wade,* 410 U.S. 113 (1973), involved the constitutionality of the 1857 Texas statute that banned abortion except to save the mother's life. The U.S. Supreme Court declared the Texas law unconstitutional, claiming that state laws outlawing or restricting access to abortion violated a constitutional right to PRIVACY. Justice Harry Blackmun, writing for the majority, devised a trimester formula to balance a woman's right to end her pregnancy and a valid state interest in protecting potential human life. In the first trimester (first three months) of pregnancy, the abortion decision is left to the medical judgment of the woman and her assisting physician. In the second trimester, the state may regulate the abortion procedure in the interest of the mother's health. During the third trimester, the state may regulate or even prohibit abortions to protect the life of a fetus, and late-term abortions would be allowed only when necessary to protect the life or health of the mother.

With this sweeping decision, the Supreme Court renewed the abortion debate. Now, every year on January 22, the anniversary of the *Roe* decision, antiabortion proponents protest on the U.S. Capitol steps by calling for the protection of the lives of the unborn, and pro-choice advocates make speeches about maintaining the right to reproductive freedom for women. Since *Roe,* abortion politics has become more polarized and contentious than ever. In a 2006 CNN–*USA Today*–Gallup poll, about half of Americans labeled themselves "pro-choice," while 42 percent called themselves "pro-life." Almost 60 percent of Americans favor keeping abortion legal by supporting the laws as they currently stand or by making access to abortions less cumbersome. A large majority of Americans favor keeping abor-

On the anniversary of *Roe v. Wade,* thousands of antiabortion protesters gather outside the White House before the start of a rally in Washington, D.C. *(Jamal Wilson/Getty)*

tion legal if necessary to preserve the mother's life, when the mother's mental health is threatened, or when the pregnancy occurred due to rape or incest. Support drops off when women seek elective abortions for reasons such as financial hardship or a genetic defect of the fetus. An extraordinary majority of Americans support legislation to ban the controversial "partial-birth" late-term abortion procedure unless the procedure is necessary to save the mother's life. Despite the controversy over abortion since the *Roe* ruling, most Americans oppose efforts to overturn the decision and return to the pre-*Roe* era.

Since *Roe,* the U.S. Supreme Court has been embroiled in numerous abortion disputes about when and under what circumstances a woman may obtain an abortion. One major challenge to *Roe* came in *PLANNED PARENTHOOD V. CASEY,* 505 U.S. 833 (1992). In *Casey,* the state of Pennsylvania enacted a series of abortion restrictions requiring parental consent, informed consent, a 24-hour waiting period, and spousal notification prior to obtaining an abortion. Antiabortion advocates hoped that this case would result in the overturn of *Roe.* Although the Court did not overturn *Roe,* it abandoned the trimester formula by holding that any abortion restriction that placed an undue burden on a woman's right to an abortion would be struck down. An undue burden was defined as one which put a substantial obstacle in a woman's path who sought to have an abortion of a nonviable fetus. Of Pennsylvania's abortion restrictions, only the spousal notification requirement was struck down as unconstitutional under the UNDUE BURDEN STANDARD.

Many states, heartened by the *Casey* ruling, developed laws regulating and limiting access to abortion, such as requiring that an abortion be performed by a licensed physician or in hospitals, prohibiting partial-birth abortions and abortions when the fetuses are viable except when necessary to protect a woman's life, disallowing use of public funds to provide abortions, allowing individual health-care providers to refuse to insure or perform abortion procedures, mandating counseling for women considering an abortion, mandating waiting periods for women who seek an abortion, and requiring some kind of parental involvement in a minor's decision to get an abortion. Most of these state restrictions have passed constitutional muster, except for the bans on partial-birth or late-term abortion.

In *Stenberg v. Carhart*, 530 U.S. 914 (2000), the U.S. Supreme Court examined a Nebraska law that criminalized partial-birth abortions. The term, *partial-birth abortion*, generally refers to the dilation and extraction (D & X) procedure in which a physician pulls all of the fetus's body except the head from the uterus and into the vaginal canal. The fetus is then killed by extracting the contents of the skull, and finally the entire fetus is delivered. The Court held that the Nebraska law was unconstitutional because it placed an undue burden on a woman's right to choose, it did not provide for allowing the D & X procedure if the woman's life or health were at stake, and it was too broad, possibly encompassing other abortion procedures aside from the D & X. In February 2006, the Court indicated a willingness to revisit this issue by reviewing a case in which a lower federal court blocked the enforcement of the Partial-Birth Abortion Ban Act. Yet, in a closely divided 5-4 opinion, the Court, in *GONZALEZ, ATTORNEY GENERAL V. CARHART*, 550 U.S. ___ (2007), reversed the lower court and upheld the law. This decision was the first one ever to uphold the banning of a specific abortion procedure.

Since the turn of the 21st century, both Congress and the president have shared antiabortion tendencies and have used their legislative and executive powers to restrict access to abortion. In 2001, President George W. Bush reinstated the global gag rule, stopping 430 organizations in 50 countries from performing or speaking about abortion if they wish to qualify for U.S. foreign aid. In 2003, he signed the Partial-Birth Abortion Ban Act, the first federal ban on abortion since *Roe v. Wade* was decided. Bush supported and signed into law the Unborn Victims of Violence Act in early 2004, which recognizes the embryo's rights as a person, separate and apart from the mother. This law makes it a federal crime to harm an embryo or fetus. Later in 2004, Congress enacted and the president signed legislation that allows health-care companies to deny insurance coverage to women who seek abortion services. In 2005, the House of Representatives passed the Child Interstate Abortion Notification Act, which makes it a crime for any relative or counselor other than the parents to accompany a minor across state lines to obtain an abortion. Bush indicated his support for this should it pass in the Senate. In addition, President Bush nominated and the Senate confirmed two new Supreme Court justices on the bench—Chief Justice JOHN G. ROBERTS, JR., and Justice SAMUEL ALITO—who have demonstrated hostility toward *Roe v. Wade* in their writings.

In *Gonzales, Attorney General v. Carhart*, the Supreme Court upheld the Partial-Birth Abortion Ban Act in a 5-4 decision, with Justice ANTHONY M. KENNEDY writing the majority opinion. This was the first abortion procedure ban the Supreme Court had upheld since it decided *Roe*.

Antiabortion and pro-choice groups remain on high alert. Since the 1973 *Roe* ruling, all nine of the original *Roe* justices have died or retired. Thus, the abortion question is far from settled, and *Roe v. Wade* could be significantly modified or even overruled. The abortion controversy divides people into seemingly irreconcilable camps of those who sponsor family values and the rights of the unborn versus those who champion women's individual rights and choice. Because the abortion issue has been framed as a "rights" issue rather than a matter of public health, common ground and compromise in the political arena have been almost impossible to attain.

For more information: Burns, Gene. *The Moral Veto: Framing Contraception, Abortion, and Cultural Pluralism in the United States*. New York:

Cambridge University Press, 2005; Herring, Mark Y. *The Pro-Life/Choice Debate.* Westport, Conn.: Greenwood Press, 2003; Hull, N. E. H., William James Hoffer, and Peter Charles Hoffer, eds. *The Abortion Rights Controversy in America: A Legal Reader.* Chapel Hill and London: University of North Carolina Press, 2004; Jost, Kenneth. "Abortion Debates." *CQ Researcher* 13 (2003): 249–272; Nossif, Rosemary. *Before Roe: Abortion Policy in the States.* Philadelphia: Temple University Press, 2001; Smith, T. Alexander, and Raymond Tatalovich. *Cultures at War: Moral Conflicts in Western Democracies.* Peterborough, Canada: Broadview Press, 2003; Strickland, Ruth Ann. "Abortion: Pro-Choice versus Pro-Life." In *Moral Controversies in American Politics,* 3d ed., edited by Byron W. Danes and Raymond Tatalovich, 3–35. Armonk, N.Y.: M. E. Sharpe, 2005.

—Ruth Ann Strickland

abstention doctrine

Abstention denotes a collection of judicially created rules under which a federal court that has jurisdiction over a case will decline to exercise its jurisdiction out of deference to ongoing or anticipated proceedings in state court. This doctrine is supposedly rooted in the constitutional concept of FEDERALISM, which requires the federal courts to respect litigation already occurring in state legal proceedings.

Abstention represents an exception to normal principles of judicial administration. The usual practice is that parties may file overlapping lawsuits in both the state and federal courts. Each court can proceed with its case rather than staying its hand in favor of the other, at least until one of the cases concludes. (Once one case concludes, doctrines of preclusion may require the second court to honor the first judgment rather than reexamining the same issues.) Abstention is accordingly reserved for special circumstances. Several distinct varieties of abstention have developed and merit discussion.

One doctrine, named Pullman abstention, requires federal courts to refrain from deciding difficult or controversial federal constitutional questions when the constitutional ruling could be rendered unnecessary by future state proceedings. The doctrine takes its name from *Railroad Commission of Texas v. Pullman Co.,* 312 U.S. 496 (1941), which involved a challenge to a state regulation that required trains with sleeping cars to be staffed by white employees instead of only black employees. The railroad and some black employees sued in federal court, contending that the regulation both exceeded the state agency's authority as a matter of state law and violated the U.S. Constitution.

The Supreme Court determined that the federal district court should abstain from deciding the case so that the unsettled state law question could first be litigated in the state courts. If the state court decided that the agency had exceeded its authority, then it would be unnecessary for the federal court to decide the constitutional questions. The Supreme Court believed this rule would serve the goal of avoiding rulings on difficult and divisive constitutional questions and would reduce friction between state and federal courts. One disadvantage, of course, is that the plaintiffs might have to go through two lawsuits to get relief. Pullman abstention has become increasingly rare in recent decades, as many states have established procedures allowing federal courts to "certify" questions to state courts (that is, send a formal request for an opinion on a matter of state law), thus eliminating the need for a separate lawsuit in state court.

Other abstention precedents require federal courts to abstain in favor of pending state proceedings when the federal case would interfere with a complex state administrative scheme or involves unsettled and especially sensitive questions of state law. Unlike the case of Pullman abstention, in these circumstances abstention is not motivated by a desire to avoid a federal constitutional ruling but is rather more directly concerned with respecting state interests. Like Pullman abstention, these types of abstention are rare.

A more consequential abstention doctrine is Younger abstention, which takes its name from *Younger v. Harris,* 401 U.S. 37 (1971). The Younger doctrine generally forbids federal courts from interfering with a pending state court prosecution. Thus, a criminal defendant with a potential federal defense must present it to the state court rather than filing a separate federal case trying to stop the prosecution. (It should be noted that a federal statute, the Anti-Injunction Act, also restricts the federal courts' authority to halt state lawsuits; the judicially created Younger doctrine applies even when the statute does not.) Younger abstention reflects notions of respect for state courts as well as the thought that an extraordinary remedy such as an anti-suit INJUNCTION should not be granted when the federal defense can be heard in the due course of the state criminal proceedings. Later cases have applied Younger abstention principles to certain civil cases that resemble criminal proceedings.

The various abstention doctrines are controversial because Congress defines the jurisdiction of the federal courts by statute (within the bounds set out by the Constitution). Therefore, just as it would be improper for a court to expand its own jurisdiction by hearing cases that it is not empowered to hear, some argue that it is equally improper for a court to refuse to act when it has been given jurisdiction.

For more information: Chemerinsky, Erwin. Chapters 12–14 in *Federal Jurisdiction*. 4th ed. New York: Aspen, 2003; Redish, Martin H. "Abstention, separation of powers, and the limits of the judicial function." *Yale Law Journal* 94 (1984): 71–115.

—Aaron-Andrew P. Bruhl

accommodation

Accommodation in the parlance of modern jurisprudence is the interpretation of the U.S. Constitution's religion clauses in deference to traditional views of religious liberty. This involves concessions for limited nonpreferential governmental assistance of religion. Court allowances for neutrally based encouragement of religion reflect an enduring American tradition of facilitating religious expression while separating church and state.

The FIRST AMENDMENT declares: "Congress shall make no law respecting an establishment of religion, or prohibiting the free exercise thereof . . ." The U.S. Supreme Court understood these clauses at face value for decades. In its first case involving the free exercise clause—*Permoli v. First Municipality of New Orleans,* 44 U.S. (3 How.) 589 (1845)—the Court declared that the Constitution "makes no provision for protecting the citizens of the respective states in their religious liberties; that is left to the state constitutions and laws. . . ."

Permoli continued to be the Court's lens for viewing the First Amendment's religion clauses until a litigious environment concerning religious practices was well under way in the 1940s. World Wars I and II elevated issues pertaining to religious oaths, religiosity in flag salutes, and religiously based draft exemptions. Industrialization and the nationalization of commerce pushed society to define the nature of employers' and workers' rights in matters pertaining to Sunday closing laws, employment benefits, and religious observances. The expansion of publicly funded education raised questions about state aid to parochial schools, released time from school for religious studies, SCHOOL PRAYER, and compulsory education—each of these matters putting government and religion on overlapping territory. Likewise, government initiatives in medicine produced controversy about vaccinations, blood transfusions, and life-saving measures. Finally, ethnically diverse immigration produced urbanization patterns that heightened controversies over religious solicitation, religious displays in public places, and coercive religious expression in government-sponsored PUBLIC FORUMS.

The expansion of religiously fueled conflicts made the situation ripe for federal court intervention, especially in instances where the coercive powers of state governments were effectively advantaging some sects at the expense of others. Consequently, the U.S. Supreme Court found pragmatic value in adjusting its longstanding jurisprudence, finding cause to incorporate the DUE PROCESS clause of the FOURTEENTH AMENDMENT against the religion clauses of the

First Amendment. Initially, this jurisprudential adjustment was not viewed as hostile to religion since the Court was in the process of applying the due process clause to other parts of the BILL OF RIGHTS, an endeavor highlighted by Justice Benjamin N. Cardozo in *PALKO V. STATE OF CONNECTICUT*, 302 U.S. 319 (1937). The purpose of the Court's adjustment was to make the religion clauses binding upon state and local governments as well as the federal government. As a consequence, religion began losing its place of policy privilege in the states; however, the trend stabilized in the 1980s and has since readjusted slightly toward accommodation.

Accommodationists generally seek to prevent the secular state from encroaching on the place of religion in the public square. They argue that courts ought to give equal treatment or even preferential treatment to religious free exercise and expression in circumstances where religious rights clash with other private rights. Many accommodationists—legal scholars, political scientists, and government officials—believe that the modern state threatens the church more than the church threatens the state; hence, where roles overlap, they believe religion ought to be shown deference on a nonpreferential basis except in instances where state interests have compelling value. Traditional accommodationists recognize that purely theoretical arguments can put the interests of atypical religions on equal footing with traditional Western religions; as a result, some of these accommodationists elevate the historic role of culturally embedded religion (de facto religion) in America, creating, in essence, a bias or preference for Christianity.

The ideal of separationism exists in contrast to notions of accommodation. Separationists aspire not only to separate the affairs of church and state but to prevent public religion from impinging on freedom of choice and a wide range of possibilities for private conduct. Separationists, while not monolithic in their philosophy, tend to believe that the autonomy of the individual is of overriding importance in establishing the relative priority of competing rights. Freedom of the individual usually therefore trumps preferences or claims of religious community—a libertarian ideal. However, separationists tend to affirm the rights of nontraditional religious communities against the establishment power of Western traditional religions, demonstrating that an affinity for separation can be strategic as well as philosophical. Strict separationists claim both theoretical and empirical support for state-constructed barriers between religion and the state.

Interestingly, separationism sometimes accommodates traditional religious practices, especially where state government compels religionists to compromise their traditional religious practices. This accommodationist form of separationism is evident in some Supreme Court decisions, most visibly in *WISCONSIN V. YODER*, 406 U.S. 205 (1972).

It is difficult to construct a constitutionally viable and politically feasible jurisprudence of pure accommodation or definitive separation. The Court's landmark rulings as well as pedestrian decisions have bounced between the two poles, reflecting the change of personnel on the Court, the idiosyncrasies of the selected cases, political pressures, and the emergence of new interpretive tools. Overall, the trend has been for the high court to hybridize accommodation and separation, producing a middle way that fits most Americans.

Some scholars assert that if there is a Jeffersonian wall of separation it has become a serpentine wall of varied height, well riddled with breeches and constructed from assorted materials. From all appearances, the Court has rationalized a set of principles that regards the vulnerabilities, traditions, relative power, and fashionableness of competing claims. Such assessments are hardly derogatory to the work of the Court, the observations admitting the enormous challenges that accompany the nationalization of religious, private, corporate, and governmental rights.

Supreme Court cases that figure prominently in accommodation jurisprudence would include *Cantwell v. Connecticut*, 310 U.S. 296 (1940), and *EVERSON V. BOARD OF EDUCATION*, 330 U.S. 1 (1947): The former case nationalized free exercise at the expense of the states, and the latter accomplished the same for disestablishment. *Zorach v.*

Clauson, 343 U.S. 306 (1952), is viewed as one of the earliest Supreme Court decisions articulating a principle of accommodation; in this instance, the accommodation of a narrowly constructed school released-time program for religious studies. It was in this case that Justice WILLIAM O. DOUGLAS constructed a conceptual divide between permissible and impermissible accommodation, stating that Americans are "a religious people" for whom the accommodation of religion "follows the best of our traditions."

Sherbert v. Verner, 374 U.S. 398 (1963), is important because it stood for three decades as the central precedent in free exercise law. *Sherbert* was a separationist decision with elements of accommodation, since it held that government must show a compelling interest in any law or governmental practice that puts a burden on religious exercise. *Widmar v. Vincent*, 454 U.S. 263 (1981), is noteworthy because it put the accommodation of religious speech on the same footing as the protection of secular speech.

EMPLOYMENT DIVISION V. SMITH, 494 U.S. 872 (1990), is widely viewed as a landmark case and one founded on a tactical change by the Court in its religion clause jurisprudence. In *Smith*, FEDERALISM is substituted for exemptions when generally applicable laws are neutral toward religion. This approach reduces the burden on government to show a compelling state interest when its actions touch religious practice. The effect of this jurisprudence is to place greater responsibility on state legislatures and less burden on courts in working out conflicts that involve religious free exercise.

Since *Smith*, other Court decisions such as *CITY OF BOERNE V. FLORES*, 521 U.S. 507 (1997), have upheld the *Smith* logic, notwithstanding the efforts of the U.S. Congress in the early 1990s to resurrect a pre-*Smith* approach to accommodation by means of the now largely unconstitutional RELIGIOUS FREEDOM RESTORATION ACT (1993). While the long-term future of accommodation will reflect the evolution of American culture, the near-term prospects for accommodation are favorable. This is owed to the ideologically conservative disposition of the emerging Court majority and the tendency of America to place religion in its abiding self-image.

For more information: Finkleman, Paul, ed. *Religion and American Law: An Encyclopedia*. New York: Garland Publishing, 2000; Perry, Michael J. *Under God? Religious Faith and Liberal Democracy*. New York: Cambridge University Press, 2003.

—Timothy J. Barnett

Adams, John (1735–1826) *first U.S. vice president, second U.S. president*

John Adams was the second president of the United States and was one of the Founding Fathers and Revolutionary War heroes who had an enormous influence upon the Constitution, especially in his 1776 booklet *Thoughts on Government* and his 1787 book *A Defence of the Constitutions of Government of the United States*.

Adams was a blunt-speaking politician and brilliant political philosopher who rose to become the second president of the United States of America, and his impact on the formation of the country was as profound as THOMAS JEFFERSON's, George Washington's, and JAMES MADISON's. Adams was born to a Massachusetts Bay family in 1735 and obtained a law degree from Harvard. He served nobly at the First (1774) and Second (1777) Continental Congresses as a delegate from Massachusetts while furthering his career as international statesman while representing the emerging democracy abroad.

The Revolutionary War had earlier taken him overseas, during which time he mastered the foreign service both in Holland and then in France. Through his leadership and efforts, he forged a peace TREATY with Britain and then returned home from his post at the English court of St. James's. When Washington was elected president in 1788, he was by his side as the duly elected VICE PRESIDENT for the first term. His ego drove him to restlessness, and his lust for action and creation in contrast to the boredoms of his double-termed vice presidency shine through in several of his personal writings of the period.

Adams rose to the presidency in 1797, and Jefferson, who lost the popular election by three electoral votes to Adams, became the vice president. Adams served with ALEXANDER HAMILTON in his corner and Jefferson in the other through the turbulent times of the war between France and Britain that challenged both American trade and loyalties. The difficulties of the relationship with France became evident politically when the country suspended trade relations with the United States and refused to receive the American diplomatic corps. Adams seized the opportunity and used the French alienation to high degree when he exposed the French request for what amounted to a bribe in order to begin commercial negotiations. As a spokesman for his party, he stood the test of scrutiny, gaining a fervent group of followers, which allowed him unparalleled political success within the Congress and the emerging democracy, as well as voracious challengers from the Republican Party. Adams successfully obtained powers to create a provisional army, build warships (with the power to add more), impose taxes, and even get the foreigner unfriendly Alien and Sedition Acts passed.

Adams's contributions to the Constitution are varied. His *Thoughts on Government* is considered a classic of American political thought. In it, he defends a mixed theory of government that calls for several distinct national institutions to form the basis of a national government. Many attribute the eventual development of the BICAMERAL LEGISLATURE and separation of powers idea to Adams. *A Defence of the Constitutions of Government of the United States* criticized the weakness of state governments and paralleled Madison's call for a stronger national government. Adams's support for the Alien and Sedition Acts facilitated the development of free speech and FIRST AMENDMENT ideas. The acts prompted Madison and Jefferson to write the Virginia and Kentucky Resolutions in opposition, laying the groundwork for those who viewed these acts as unconstitutional violations of free speech.

For more information: McCullough, David. *John Adams.* New York: Simon & Schuster, 2001; Ryerson, Richard Alan, ed. *John Adams and the Founding of the Republic.* Boston: Massachusetts Historical Society, 2001.

—Ernest Gomez

Adarand Constructors, Inc. v. Peña 515 U.S. 200 (1995)

In *Adarand Constructors, Inc. v. Peña,* the Supreme Court ruled on the issue of the proper level of scrutiny for analyzing governmentally imposed racial classifications, including remedial measures such as AFFIRMATIVE ACTION. In a 5-4 plurality opinion, Justice SANDRA DAY O'CONNOR wrote that all racial classifications imposed by any federal, state, or local governmental actor must be analyzed by the reviewing court under a STRICT SCRUTINY standard.

Adarand Constructors, Inc., was the low bidder on the guardrail portion of a highway construction project that a division of the U.S. Department of Transportation had awarded to prime contractor Mountain Gravel & Construction Company. However, because the prime contract's terms provided that Mountain Gravel would receive additional compensation if it hired subcontractors certified as small businesses controlled by "socially and economically disadvantaged individuals," Adarand lost the subcontract to Gonzales Construction Company. Federal law required that a comparable subcontracting clause be included in most federal agency contracts, and the clause had to state that "[t]he contractor shall presume that socially and economically disadvantaged individuals include Black Americans, Hispanic Americans, Native Americans, Asian Pacific Americans, and other minorities. . . ." Adarand claimed that this presumption discriminated on the basis of race in violation of the Fifth Amendment. Both the district court and the Tenth Circuit upheld the contract provision as constitutional, the court of appeals holding that the Supreme Court's decision in *FULLILOVE V. KLUTZNICK* (1980), further developed in *METRO BROADCASTING, INC. V. FCC* (1990), established "a lenient standard, resembling intermediate scrutiny" for evaluating federal race-based action.

However, the Court plurality now repudiated *Fullilove* and *Metro Broadcasting* to the extent that they differentiated between federal and state racial classifications. Noting that the Court had already held in *CITY OF RICHMOND V. J. A. CROSON CO.* (1989) that the FOURTEENTH AMENDMENT requires strict scrutiny of all race-conscious action by state and local governments, Justice O'Connor wrote that three general principles compel a similar outcome for federally imposed classifications: 1) skepticism, based on the concept that "any preference based on racial or ethnic criteria must necessarily receive a most searching scrutiny"; 2) consistency, which requires that the standard of EQUAL PROTECTION review should not depend "on the race of those burdened or benefited by a particular classification"; and 3) congruence, which dictates that Fifth Amendment equal protection analysis should mirror that under the Fourteenth Amendment.

In so holding, the Court finally resolved an issue in contention since the plurality decision in *REGENTS OF THE UNIVERSITY OF CALIFORNIA V. BAKKE* (1978), namely, the proper level of analysis for remedial race-based governmental action. Regardless of whether imposed by the federal or a state or local governmental actor, any racial classification, whether arguably benign or not, must be narrowly tailored to serve a COMPELLING GOVERNMENTAL INTEREST.

Not surprisingly, in light of the fact that the Court had been unable for almost two decades to reach a consensus on the appropriate level of analysis for racial distinctions made for remedial purposes, the concurring and dissenting opinions in *Adarand* were highly charged. Justice ANTONIN GREGORY SCALIA opined in his concurrence (contradicting Justice O'Connor's claim that strict scrutiny was not necessarily "strict in theory, but fatal in fact") that governments could "never have a 'compelling interest' in discriminating on the basis of race in order to 'make up' for past racial discrimination in the opposite direction. Justice CLARENCE THOMAS in his concurrence went even further and claimed that there was a constitutional and moral equivalence between "laws designed to subjugate a race and those that distribute benefits on the basis of race in order to foster some current notion of equality." Justice JOHN PAUL STEVENS, joined in his dissent by Justice Ruth Bader Ginsburg, offered a particularly stinging rebuke, asserting that while one might reasonably dispute the efficacy of affirmative action programs, "[i]t is another thing altogether to equate the many well-meaning and intelligent lawmakers and their constituents—whether members of majority or minority races—who have supported affirmative action over the years, to segregationists and bigots."

Ultimately, it appears for the most part that Justice O'Connor's, not Justice Scalia's viewpoint, has prevailed. At least some lower courts have found that some governmental programs, primarily federal, have met the strict scrutiny test by showing the existence of private-sector discrimination that a congressional affirmative action provision was intended to address. However, although strict scrutiny may not always be "fatal in fact," there can be no denying that setting the constitutional bar at the highest level has had a profound impact on the once ambitious affirmative action programs of local, state, and federal governments.

For more information: Spann, Girardeau A. *The Law of Affirmative Action: Twenty-Five Years of Supreme Court Decisions on Race and Remedies.* New York: New York University Press, 2000.

—Virginia Mellema

Adderley et al. v. Florida 385 U.S. 39 (1966)

In *Adderley v. Florida,* the Supreme Court upheld the conviction of the defendants on a charge of trespassing at the county jail. In a 5-4 decision, the Court ruled that the Florida trespass statute was not void on the grounds of vagueness, an infringement on the CIVIL RIGHTS ACT OF 1964, or a denial of DUE PROCESS, and that the convictions did not unconstitutionally deprive the defendants of their rights to freedom of speech, press, assembly, or petition.

Harriet Adderley and 31 other students at Florida A & M University left the school and proceeded to the jail to protest the arrest of other

Florida A & M students demonstrating against racial segregation, including at the county jail in Tallahassee. The students gathered on a nonpublic jail driveway and the adjacent county jail property and demonstrated against the arrest of their classmates by singing, clapping, and dancing. The sheriff advised the students that they were trespassing and would have to leave or be arrested; those students who did not leave were arrested and charged with "trespass with a malicious and mischievous intent." The students were tried and convicted by a jury in Leon County, Florida, and the convictions were affirmed by the Florida circuit court and the Florida district court of appeals. The case was then appealed and granted certiorari by the U.S. Supreme Court.

Justice HUGO BLACK, writing for the five-person majority, found that the conviction should be upheld because the students gathered at a facility that has a primary public function of security and the public protest at the jail compromised that essential function. The students argued that their case was similar to *Edwards v. South Carolina,* a case in which a number of students were arrested after a protest at the South Carolina State House, yet the court had found the function of the jail to be a mitigating factor in this circumstance. The Court also found in *Adderley* that no services or accommodations were being denied by the actions of the sheriff, thus the complaint of violation of the Civil Rights Act of 1964 did not apply. The Court ruled that the actual charges did not signal a clear violation of due process and that the restriction on assembly hereby ordered did not infringe upon the speech, press, petition, or assembly rights of the students.

The importance of this case emanates from the legitimate restrictions that can be placed on the freedom to assemble in order to protect the public good. In this case, the Court found reasons to place limits on the protest in order to protect the larger public good of security for the community. The guidelines for granting a permit for picketing and parading are spelled out as follows: 1) The permit must be reasonable, 2) it must be precisely drawn (including the time, date, and location of the march), and 3) it must be applied fairly. These guidelines help to balance the right to assemble with the broader concern of a peaceful community.

For more information: Emerson, Thomas. *The System of Freedom of Expression.* New York: Random House, 1971; Stone, Geoffrey. "Fora Americana: Speech in Public Places." *Supreme Court Review* 233 (1974): 233–279.

—Kevin Anderson

Adkins v. Children's Hospital 261 U.S. 525 (1923)

In *Adkins v. Children's Hospital,* the Supreme Court struck down a federal statute fixing minimum wages for women and children employed within the DISTRICT OF COLUMBIA. The Court ruled Congress had violated the Fifth Amendment by interfering with a "LIBERTY OF CONTRACT" protected by the Fifth's DUE PROCESS clause. This case both discarded the decision set forth in *Muller v. Oregon,* 208 U.S. 412 (1908), which had allowed legislatures to provide special protections for female employees, and began a 14-year period in which the notion of SUBSTANTIVE DUE PROCESS reached its zenith.

In the latter part of the 19th century, the nation's rapid industrialization created political pressures on both state legislatures and Congress to restrain a multitude of business practices. When governments responded with various types of regulations on businesses, corporations challenged the regulations in court, arguing that this use of POLICE POWER unconstitutionally deprived them of the "liberty" guaranteed by the due process clauses of the Fifth and FOURTEENTH AMENDMENTS. This doctrine, known as substantive due process, included the concept that employers and employees have a constitutionally protected liberty to form an employment contract free from legislative interference. The Supreme Court first announced the liberty of contract in *Allgeyer v. Louisiana,* 165 U.S. 578 (1897), but did not hold that this liberty was absolutely protected from governmental regulation. For the next two decades, the Court struck down some pieces of labor legislation and upheld others, depending on whether it deemed the government's use of police power as "reasonable." It was most apt to find legislation "reasonable" if it was seen to protect public health, safety, or morals rather than individual workers.

A strong restatement of the liberty of contract doctrine occurred in *Lochner v. New York*, 198 U.S. 45 (1905), when the Court struck down a New York statute prohibiting bakers from working more than 60 hours per week. The Court maintained bakers had a liberty to determine how many hours they chose to work and that public health was not endangered by bread baked by those who worked longer hours. However, just three years later, the Court exempted women from this liberty of contract. In *Muller v. Oregon*, all nine justices agreed that states were indeed reasonable in limiting the hours that women could work. *Lochner* did not apply to them, said Justice David Josiah Brewer, because women are physically weaker than men, as well as legally and economically unequal. Because of these differences between the sexes, public health and safety concerns justified the use of police power to protect women from unscrupulous employers. After the *Muller* decision, legislation that "protected" women in the workforce proliferated, as legislatures freely regulated the hours, wages, and conditions of women's employment.

In 1923, *Adkins v. Children's Hospital* discarded the logic of *Muller*. In a 5-3 decision (Justice Louis D. Brandeis, who had argued *Muller* before the Court in 1908, did not participate), the Court ruled that minimum wage laws unconstitutionally interfered with women's liberty of contract. Writing for the majority, Justice George Sutherland argued that women "are legally as capable of contracting for themselves as men." In distinguishing this case from *Muller*, he pointed out that "great—not to say revolutionary—changes which have taken place since that utterance, in the contractual, political and civil status of women, culminating in the Nineteenth Amendment" greatly diminished the need to protect women. Furthermore, the majority rejected the argument that minimum wage laws protected women's morals by ensuring them a decent standard of living. "It cannot be shown that well paid women safeguard their morals more carefully than those who are poorly paid," wrote Sutherland.

Chief Justice William Howard Taft's dissent argued that legislatures had concluded employees were not on equal footing with employers and "in their necessitous circumstances are prone to accept pretty much anything that is offered." Whether the Court agreed with this economic view, Taft wrote, it should defer to legislative judgment in this arena. Futhermore, he said, despite the Nineteenth Amendment, women were not on equal footing with men either physically or economically. Justice Oliver Wendell Holmes, Jr., wrote a separate dissent, attacking the notion of liberty of contract as lacking any moorings in the text of the Constitution. Congress had used its police powers constitutionally to "remove conditions leading to ill health, immorality, and the deterioration of the race," he wrote. Holmes also agreed with Taft that the Nineteenth Amendment had not erased significant differences between the sexes and that Congress could indeed "take those differences into account."

Adkins did not result in the abolition of all protectionist legislation, but it did signal the beginning of a period in which the Court eagerly struck down numerous statutes that interfered with the liberty of contract and the notion of a laissez-faire economic system. With the advent of the Great Depression in the 1930s, this put the Court on a collision course with a Democratic Congress and the New Deal policies of President Franklin D. Roosevelt. As the composition of the Court changed and the public support for the New Deal remained steady, support for *Adkins* eroded. It was directly overruled by the Court in 1937 in *West Coast Hotel v. Parrish*, 300 U.S. 379 (1937), under Chief Justice Charles Evans Hughes. In the majority opinion, Hughes reiterated many of the points made by Taft and Holmes in their *Adkins* dissents, while Sutherland, now a dissenter, clung to a defense of liberty of contract. Sutherland was fighting a lost battle, however, for the reasoning in *Adkins* and the doctrine of liberty of contract were now completely defunct.

For more information: Cushman, Barry. *Rethinking the New Deal Court: The Structure of a Constitutional Revolution.* New York: Oxford University Press, 1998; Gillman, Howard. *The Constitution Besieged: The Rise and Demise of Lochner-Era Police Powers Jurisprudence.* Durham, N.C.: Duke University Press, 1993; Phillips, Michael J. *The Lochner Court, Myth and Reality: Substantive Due Process from the 1890s to the 1930s.* Westport, Conn.: Praeger, 2001.

—Gwyneth I. Williams

affirmative action

Affirmative action is a legal concept that refers to the use of race, gender, or nationality in employment decisions and schools admissions in order to diversify schools and workplaces. The use of affirmative action is subject to significant criticism, with many claiming that the use of race, for example, for any purpose is prohibited by the Constitution by way of the EQUAL PROTECTION clause of the FOURTEENTH AMENDMENT. The Constitution, in effect, is "color-blind," prohibiting the use of race for any purpose. Conversely, others contend that the remedial use of race or gender in employment or school admissions decisions is constitutionally permitted and necessary in order to achieve racial and gender integration.

Race has occupied an ambiguous place in America and in the U.S. Constitution from its earliest days. Slavery dominated much of America's early history, and the original text of the 1787 Constitution addressed the topic in terms of how African Americans were counted for representation and in the census, for example. In *DRED SCOTT V. SANDFORD*, 60 U.S. 393 (1857), Justice ROGER TANEY indicated that it was clear from the original intent of the Constitution that African slaves could not be citizens, and therefore, they did not have the right to sue for their freedom in federal court. Subsequently, the THIRTEENTH, FOURTEENTH, and FIFTEENTH AMENDMENTS overturned this decision and sought to expand the CIVIL RIGHTS of the freed slaves. However, in *PLESSY V. FERGUSON*, 163 U.S. 537 (1896), the Court upheld segregation with the "separate but equal" doctrine. It was not until *BROWN V. BOARD OF EDUCATION OF TOPEKA*, 347 U.S. 43 (1954), that the Court declared school segregation unconstitutional, thereby beginning the process of dismantling legally sanctioned, or de jure, discrimination against blacks.

Some argued that merely dropping the laws that formally discriminated was not enough; instead, efforts needed to be undertaken to undo past discrimination. Executive Order 10925, for example, was issued by President John F. Kennedy in 1961 to bar discrimination in the executive branch, and it urged "affirmative action" to diversify the federal workforce. Executive Order 11246, issued by President Lyndon B. Johnson in 1965, reinforced this order and again called for steps to diversify the workforce by reaching out to women and individuals of color.

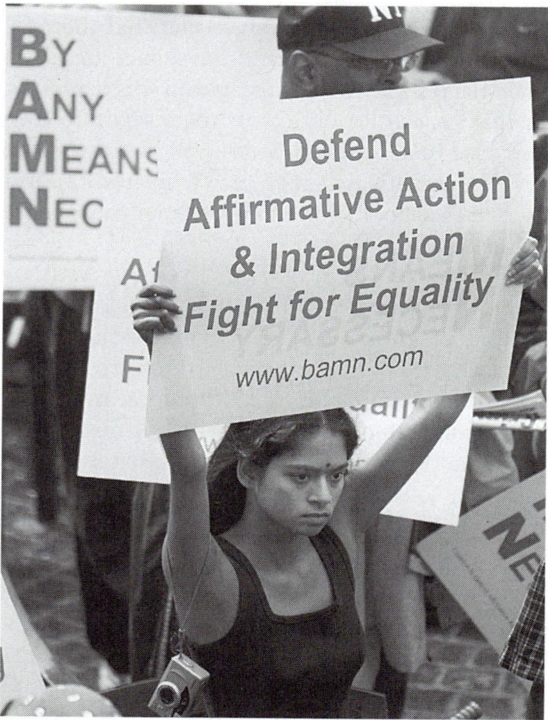

University of Cincinnati student Survi Parvatiyar gathers with several hundred other protesters from the group By Any Means Necessary to rally in favor of affirmative action, on October 23, 2001, in downtown Cincinnati. *(Getty Images)*

In 1972, the employment practices of both public and private employers began to change due to the methodology being used to determine racial inequalities. Statistics were reported to the Office of Federal Contract Compliance as to racial makeup of those responsible to comply with Title VII of the CIVIL RIGHTS ACT OF 1964 and then proposals as to how they might correct race-defined statistical inequalities. The resultant effect was that employees were often hired based on racial and ethnic origin rather than only their paper qualifications. Schools also began to consider race and gender in admissions decisions. In *REGENTS OF THE UNIVERSITY OF CALIFORNIA V. BAKKE*, 438 U.S. 265 (1978), the Court upheld the use of affirmative action in admissions policies but established that although race may be one factor to consider when conducting employment and application searches, the school's program was unconstitutional owing to the fact that the program amounted to a quota, because race appeared to be the only factor in some admissions decisions. Justice LEWIS POWELL, writing a separate concurrence in a Court otherwise split 4-4, held that the Fourteenth Amendment permitted the use of race in school admissions in order to promote diversity.

Subsequently, in *UNITED STEELWORKERS OF AMERICA V. WEBER*, 443 U.S. 193 (1979), the Court upheld voluntary use of affirmative action in employment. In *FULLILOVE V. KLUTZNICK*, 448 U.S. 448 (1980), the Court upheld federal programs setting aside money for minority business enterprises, and in *JOHNSON V. TRANSPORTATION AGENCY OF SANTA CLARA, CALIFORNIA*, 480 U.S. 616 (1987), it upheld a gender-based affirmative action hiring program. In *METRO BROADCASTING, INC. V. FCC*, 497 U.S. 547 (1990), the Court upheld the use of race in the awarding of broadcast licenses.

Yet, by the end of the 1980s and as the justices changed, the Supreme Court began to rethink its views on the use of race or gender in employment and hiring decisions. In a series of decisions in 1989, the Court made it more difficult to prove racial discrimination yet was overturned by the 1991 Civil Rights Act. But in *ADARAND CONSTRUCTORS, INC. V. PEÑA*, 515 U.S. 200 (1995), the Court invalidated a set-aside program using racial preferences when awarding federal contracts. The decision effectively overturned *Metro Broadcasting.* In *GRUTTER V. BOLLINGER*, 539 U.S. 306 (2003), the Court upheld a law-school admissions program that was narrowly tailored to ensure a critical mass of minority students at the school as permitted under the Fourteenth Amendment. In writing for the Court, Justice SANDRA DAY O'CONNOR indicated hope that in 25 years affirmative action would no longer be needed. However, in a companion case challenging the University of Michigan's undergraduate admissions policy, the Court invalidated it in *GRATZ V. BOLLINGER*, 539 U.S. 244 (2003), claiming the school's more rigid use of race was the type of quota that the Court had struck down in *Bakke.*

Finally, in *Parents Involved in Community Schools v. Seattle School District No. 1*, 551 U.S. ___ (2007), decided together with *Meredith v. Jefferson*, 551 U.S. ___ (2007), the Supreme Court invalidated the use of race in school assignments. These two cases, along with *Gratz*, suggest that the Supreme Court under Chief Justice JOHN G. ROBERTS, JR., is moving away from support for affirmative action as a remedial tool to diversify and toward a "color blind" view of the Constitution that prohibits all use of race and gender in employment and school admissions decisions.

For more information: Anderson, Terry H. *The Pursuit of Fairness: A History of Affirmative Action.* New York: Oxford University Press, 2005; Wise, Tim J. *Affirmative Action.* New York: Taylor & Francis, 2005.

—Ernest Gomez and David Schultz

age and the Constitution

The U.S. Constitution makes several references to age, specifically to minimum age requirements for members of the HOUSE OF REPRESENTATIVES and the SENATE. Members of the House of Representatives must be at least 25 years of age; senators must be at least 30 years of age. The Constitution further dictates that the president and VICE PRESIDENT must be at least 35 years of age and establishes citizenship and residency requirements on members of the House and Senate, as well as the president and vice president.

Courts throughout the United States have upheld the constitutionality of laws that afford citizens and residents special privileges, responsibilities, and special protections based on their age. Chief among the privileges based on age is the RIGHT TO VOTE, which is afforded to U.S. citizens age 18 or older who are not convicted felons, as granted by the TWENTY-SIXTH AMENDMENT.

At the age of 18, U.S. citizens and residents reach the "age of legal majority"; that is, they become adults in the eyes of the law. Thus, they are able to enter into contracts and own property in their own names, live independently of their parents, marry without parental consent, establish credit and incur debt in their own names, and enjoy all the rights of adulthood. Upon reaching the age of legal majority, U.S. citizens and residents are also subject to the full penalties of civil and criminal law; they can be convicted of crimes and imprisoned or fined, as appropriate. Male citizens of the United States reaching age 18 are obliged to register for selective service (the draft). Registered voters rolls and selective service rolls are used to summon people to jury duty, as under the SEVENTH AMENDMENT, accused persons have the RIGHT TO TRIAL BY JURY. Despite reaching legal majority, adults in the United States may not purchase, possess, or drink alcoholic beverages until they reach 21 years of age.

Another legal aspect of age is called the "age of consent." This is the age at which the law states that people have the moral agency to consent to sexual activity. Age of consent laws are intended to protect children from sexual exploitation by adults. Prior to reaching the age of consent, a person may agree to engage in sexual activity, but in the eyes of the law, such behavior is illegal. A person older than the age of consent who engages in sexual activity, even if the activity is consensual, with someone under the age of consent may be charged with statutory rape, child molestation, or sexual abuse of a minor. The age of consent varies across states, but the average age of consent is 16. Age of consent laws pertain to heterosexual and homosexual activity, and the definition of sexual activity is broader than sexual intercourse or penetration.

The Fair Labor Standards Act prohibits children and youth from working under certain conditions and during specific hours. Children age 14 through 17 may work between 7 A.M. and 7 P.M. (up to 9 P.M. between June 1 and Labor Day) for three hours per school day and eight hours per non–school day, up to 18 hours per week. Generally, children age 14 and 15 may work in clerical and retail positions, as long as their working conditions are not hazardous as defined by law. Children age 16 and 17 may work in any jobs that are not deemed hazardous by the U.S. Department of Labor; generally, jobs in driving, excavation, heavy machinery operations, meatpacking and processing, mining, paper manufacturing, and roofing are considered hazardous. These laws pertain until the age of 18. After age 18, that is, upon reaching the age of legal majority, adults may work in any type of jobs they wish, even if those jobs are deemed hazardous.

People over age 40 also enjoy special protection under the law, specifically from discrimination associated with employment. The Age Discrimination in Employment Act (ADEA), passed in 1967, makes it illegal to discriminate against workers age 40 and over in any term, condition, or benefit of employment. Hiring, termination, promotion, layoff, pay and benefits, job assignments, and training are specifically covered by the act. Furthermore, it is illegal to discriminate based on age in admission to apprenticeship programs unless the Equal Employment Opportunity Commission (EEOC) grants a specific exemption. Age limits may be imposed only when the employer can prove a bona fide occupational qualification (BFOQ). While the ADEA does not specifically prohibit inquiries about a person's age or date of birth, such requests tend to be closely scrutinized to ensure that the inquiry was made for a legal purpose rather than for the purpose of discrimination. Asking a person's age or birth date may prevent certain older workers from applying for employment or may indicate an intentional attempt to discriminate based on age.

In 1990, passage of the Older Workers Benefit Protection Act (OWBPA) expanded the ADEA to prohibit employers from denying benefits to older workers. Employers may reduce benefits based on age only if the cost of providing the benefits to older workers is the same as that associated with providing benefits to younger workers.

For more information: MacNichol, John. *Age Discrimination: An Historical and Contemporary Analysis.* New York: Cambridge University Press, 2006; Schwartz, Bernard. *A History of the Supreme Court.* New York: Oxford University Press, 1993.

—Cheryl Crozier Garcia

airline passenger searches

Searches of airline passengers, like other searches, must comply with the FOURTH AMENDMENT, which guarantees the right to be secure against "unreasonable searches and seizures." The normal requirement for "reasonableness" is particularized suspicion and probable cause to support that suspicion. Search warrants are the strongest evidence of reasonableness but are rarely used in airline passenger searches.

Routine searches of airline passengers and their luggage began in response to the hijackings of the 1960s and 1970s. Their primary purpose was to prevent hijackings by preventing weapons from being carried on board. Since these searches were not intended to gather evidence in criminal cases, they were approved under an administrative search exception to the warrant requirement recognized by the Supreme Court in *Camara v. Municipal Court of San Francisco,* 387 U.S. 523 (1967). Under this exception, neither particularized suspicion nor probable cause is required.

The California Supreme Court case of *People v. Hyde,* 12 C3d 158 (1974), analyzed these issues in detail and concluded:

> The fact that airport searches . . . will inevitably lead to the detection of some individuals involved in criminal conduct unrelated to the commandeering or destruction of aircraft does not alter the fundamentally administrative character of the screening procedure. If the initial intrusion is justifiable as part of a regulatory effort to prevent the hijacking of airplanes, the incidental discovery of contraband does not offend the Fourth Amendment.

Some states, such as California, permitted evidence found in these searches to be used in criminal cases; others, such as Illinois, allowed contraband to be seized but prohibited its use in criminal prosecutions.

Some courts concluded that these searches were reasonable when they balanced the government interest in airline security—preserving both lives and property—against the relatively limited intrusion of a routine search (for example, *United States v. Epperson,* 454 F.2d 769 [4th Cir. 1972]). Others ruled that they were permitted under the consent exception, that passengers implicitly consented to the search when they chose to travel by plane (for example, *United States v. Pulido-Baquerizo,* 800 F.2d 899 [9th Cir. 1986]). Other courts acknowledged the limited options available to travelers and questioned whether this could properly be considered voluntary consent, but they consistently rejected the argument that passenger searches violated the constitutionally protected freedom to travel. Some parties also argued that airline passengers no longer had a reasonable expectation of PRIVACY from magnetometers and X-ray scanners, since they are now so common. If there is no reasonable expectation of privacy, then the searches are not subject to the Fourth Amendment.

September 11, 2001, changed the nature of airport searches and the legal context in which they take place. After 9/11, it was clear that these were not routine administrative searches but intended to identify and incapacitate potential threats to national security. The searches became more intrusive, and the costs of noncooperation, higher. With not just the security of the airplane but the security of the nation at stake, the balance has shifted. Courts continue to uphold intrusive searches, authorizing the Transportation Security Administration (TSA) to search luggage randomly

(*Torbet v. United Airlines, Inc.*, 298 F.3d 1087 [9th Cir. 2002]), review the contents of laptop computers, and even seize suspect persons. By 2008, the Supreme Court had not yet handed down a decision specifically dealing with the TSA's authority to search passengers and luggage, but its decisions have deferred to other executive authority claims based on national security.

For more information: *Airline Passenger Security Screening: New Technologies and Implementation Issues.* Washington, D.C.: National Academy Press, 1996; Lawson, Deborah. "Casenote: Fourth Amendment Searches with Liberty and Justice for All . . . Unless You Choose to Fly: *Torbet v. United Airlines, Inc.*" *Journal of Air Law and Commerce* 68 (2003): 647–654; Miller, Eric J. "Comment: The 'Cost' of Securing Domestic Air Travel." *John Marshall Journal of Computer and Information Law* 21 (2003): 405–436; Rochow-Leuschner, Deborah von. "CAPPS II and the Fourth Amendment: Does It Fly?" *Journal of Air Law and Commerce* 69 (2004): 139–172.

—Barbara J. Hayler

Alabama v. Shelton 535 U.S. 654 (2002)

In *Alabama v. Shelton*, the U.S. Supreme Court, in a 5-4 decision, with the opinion of the majority being delivered by Justice Ruth Bader Ginsburg, upheld the decision rendered in the Alabama Supreme Court that a lawyer must be provided for the accused in criminal cases that may result in imprisonment even if it is for a short period of time. This case, like *GIDEON V. WAINWRIGHT*, 372 U.S. 335 (1963), involved the SIXTH AMENDMENT to the U.S. Constitution and the right of an indigent defendant to have the assistance of a court-appointed counsel. The Shelton case took the concept of RIGHT TO COUNSEL a step further by indicating that the right to counsel also extends to defendants who receive a suspended sentence.

The defendant was LeReed Shelton, who took it upon himself to be his own representative at a bench trial in the District Court of Etowah County, Alabama. He was convicted by this court of third-degree assault. The charge carried a maximum penalty of one-year imprisonment and a $2,000 fine. Shelton invoked his right to a new trial before a jury in the circuit court. He appeared before the circuit court and again represented himself and was convicted a second time. Even though the court warned Shelton of the dangers of representing himself, the court at no time offered to provide Shelton with legal counsel. The circuit court sentenced Shelton to 30 days, suspended his sentence, and then placed him on two years probation.

Shelton appealed this court's decision on the tenets of the Sixth Amendment, and the Alabama Court of Criminal Appeals initially affirmed this, yet when the case was returned for remand, the appeals court reversed itself and noted: "a suspended sentence . . . does not trigger the Sixth Amendment right to appointed counsel unless there is 'evidence in the record that the [defendant] has actually been deprived of liberty.'" The Alabama Supreme Court reversed the appeals court decision, noting "that a defendant may not be 'sentenced to a term of imprisonment' absent provision of counsel." The Alabama Supreme Court found that a suspended sentence constituted a "term of imprisonment" even though imprisonment was taking place immediately after the verdict.

The U.S. Supreme Court majority opinion noted:

> We think it plain that a hearing so timed and structured cannot compensate for the absence of trial counsel, for it does not even address the key Sixth Amendment inquiry: whether the adjudication of guilt corresponding to the prison sentence is sufficiently reliable to permit incarceration. Deprived of counsel when tried, convicted, and sentenced, and unable to challenge the original judgment at a subsequent probation revocation hearing, a defendant in Shelton's circumstances faces incarceration on a conviction that has never been subjected to the "crucible of meaningful adversarial testing," *United States v. Cronic* 466 U.S. 648, 656 (1984).

The Supreme Court held that a prison term, even though suspended, is still a prison term.

For more information: Bodner, Polina R. "Imposition of a Suspended Sentence in a Misdemeanor Case Invokes a Defendant's Sixth Amendment Right to Counsel." *Suffolk University Law Review* 37, no. 1 (2004): 211–217; Kitai, Rinat. "What Remains Necessary Following *Alabama v. Shelton* to Fulfill the Right of a Criminal Defendant to Counsel at the Expense of the State?" *Ohio Northern University Law Review* 30, no. 1 (2004): 30–58; Lewis, Anthony. *Gideon's Trumpet.* New York: Vintage Books, 1989; Young, Adam D. "An Analysis of the Sixth Amendment Right to Counsel As It Applies to Suspended Sentences and Probation: Do Argersinger and Scott Blow a Flat Note on Gideon's Trumpet?" *Dickinson Law Review* 107, no. 3 (2003): 699–722.

—Dan Krejci

Alden v. Maine 527 U.S. 706 (1999)

In *Alden v. Maine,* the Supreme Court ruled that the ELEVENTH AMENDMENT barred a suit against a state involving enforcement of the Fair Labor Standards Act (FLSA), a law requiring employers to pay their workers minimum wages and overtime pay. Although the FLSA had initially exempted federal, state, and local governments, by 1974, it had been amended to include most government employees.

In 1992, John Alden and other state probation officers filed suit in a Maine federal district court, claiming that the state had violated the FLSA and owed them overtime pay. The court agreed and ordered the state to pay them, but the parties did not agree on the amount. In the interim, the U.S. Supreme Court had ruled that the principle of state sovereignty, as stated in the Eleventh Amendment, barred federal courts from exercising jurisdiction over states. Alden et al.'s case was dismissed.

Shortly thereafter, they filed suit in state court, which also dismissed their case, ruling that the doctrine of sovereign immunity incorporated the principles of the Eleventh Amendment and that the states cannot be sued in state court, either. The Maine Supreme Court affirmed, holding that if states are immune from suit by private individuals in federal court, they are also immune in state court. The court concluded that if plaintiffs cannot sue states in federal court, they cannot simply bring their actions to state court to achieve their ends.

The probation officers' principal argument was that Article VI of the U.S. Constitution, known as the SUPREMACY CLAUSE, requires state courts to enforce valid federal laws such as the FLSA. Citing Congress's power to regulate the national economy, they emphasized that the state must enforce the federal law in its courts. The U.S. government entered the case to urge the Supreme Court to reverse the state court, declaring that the supremacy clause prevails over a state's sovereign immunity. The brief for the United States noted that the FLSA specifies that any government may be sued by their employees in any state or federal court and the supremacy clause requires the state courts to enforce the law.

In announcing the decision for the Court, Justice ANTHONY M. KENNEDY strongly defended the principle of state sovereign immunity, quoting from the writings of the nation's founders to demonstrate how deeply they felt about the importance of immunity from private lawsuits as an attribute of state sovereignty. The Court held that the plaintiffs must show that states had been required to relinquish their immunity as part of the original constitutional compromise. But there was no evidence of this in the constitutional text, he said, rejecting the plaintiffs' argument that the supremacy clause in Article VI required the state to enforce federal laws. Kennedy concluded that Congress lacked the authority to revoke state sovereign immunity through regulatory laws such as the FLSA.

Justice DAVID H. SOUTER dissented, quoting extensively from the constitutional debates and arguing that there was no clear consensus among the founders on the breadth of sovereign immunity. Moreover, states should not be allowed to violate federal rights with impunity, and this ruling, he charged, would allow them to engage in illegal wage and hours practices.

For more information: Mezey, Susan Gluck. "The U.S. Supreme Court's Federalism Jurisprudence: *Alden v. Maine* and the Enhancement of State Sovereignty." *Publius: The Journal of Federalism* 30 (2000): 21–38; Royer, Christine. "Paradise Lost? State Employees' Rights in the Wake of New Federalism." *Akron Law Review* 34 (2001): 637–688.

—Susan Gluck Mezey

Alito, Samuel (1950–) *Supreme Court justice*
Samuel Anthony Alito, Jr., member of the U.S. Supreme Court and former U.S. Court of Appeals judge, was born on April 1, 1950, in Trenton, New Jersey. Strong academically, Alito posted excellent results at Steinert High School in Hamilton Township, New Jersey, and was able to attend Princeton University, where he graduated from the Woodrow Wilson School of Public and International Affairs in 1972. He continued his studies at Yale Law School, where he served as editor of the school's prestigious legal journal and graduated with a J.D. in 1975.

Enlisted by Selective Service in 1970, Alito was able to continue his studies while being assigned to ROTC and a summer boot camp. He served on active duty in 1975 following his graduation but thereafter was assigned to inactive reserves until he left the military in 1980.

From the start of his career, Alito has constructed an impressive record of employment in the legal sector. He began as a legal clerk on the Third Circuit and went on to work as an assistant U.S. attorney in New Jersey. He argued numerous cases concerning drugs and the Mafia. In 1985, Alito became deputy assistant to Attorney General Edwin Meese during the second term of the Reagan administration. In his post, he established himself as an active conservative, stating that William F. Buckley, ALEXANDER MORDECAI BICKEL, and Barry Goldwater inspired him. He also expressed his views on the Constitution and current affairs at the time, stating that he did not believe in racial or ethnic quotas nor in a constitutional protection for the right to have an ABORTION.

From 1987 to 1990, Alito was a U.S. attorney in New Jersey, before being nominated by President George H. W. Bush on February 20, 1999, to the U.S. Court of Appeals for the Third Circuit, where he remained until 2006. During some of this time, he worked as a professor of law at Seton Hall University.

In late 2005, Alito's dream of becoming a member of the U.S. Supreme Court began to come to fruition. On October 31, 2005, he was nominated by President George W. Bush to the Supreme Court seat formerly occupied by SANDRA DAY O'CONNOR. The nomination was officially submitted to the U.S. SENATE on November 10, 2005, and Alito's confirmation hearing took place in January 2006.

Alito received a "well-qualified" rating from the American Bar Association, and his nomination was approved in committee by a vote broken along party lines, 10 to 8. Although a filibuster by the Democratic opposition threatened his confirmation in the Senate, Alito was confirmed by a vote of 58 to 42. He was sworn in to his post shortly after by Chief Justice JOHN G. ROBERTS, JR. Alito joined the Court midterm.

As a result of Alito's ascension, the U.S. Supreme Court has become majority–Roman Catholic for the first time ever in its history. Alito's religion, Italian-American roots, and conservative views have resulted in comparisons with fellow justice ANTONIN GREGORY SCALIA. Notably, Alito is a member of the Federalist Society, a conservative and libertarian group. He is married and has two children.

In his first two years on the Supreme Court, he has aligned himself with Chief Justice Roberts, voting with him almost 90 percent of the time. He has supported the conservative wing of the Court in ruling that bans on partial-birth abortions do not violate a woman's right to terminate a pregnancy, and he has also voted in cases such as *Hein v. Freedom from Religion Foundation,* 127 S.Ct. 2553 (2007), and *Lance v. Coffman,* 127 S.Ct. 1194 (2007), to tighten the rules of STANDING and make it more difficult for plaintiffs to be able to present their cases in federal court.

For more information: CNN.com. "Bush Nominates Alito to the Supreme Court." Available online. URL: http://www.cnn.com/2005/POLITICS/10/31/

scotus.bush/index.html. Downloaded November 1, 2005; Federal Judicial Center. "Alito: Judges of the Federal Courts." Available online. URL: http://www.fjc.gov/public/home.nsf/hisj. Downloaded May 6, 2008.

—Arthur Holst

Allen v. State Board of Elections 393 U.S. 544 (1969)

In *Allen v. State Board of Elections*, the Supreme Court ruling, consistent with SOUTH CAROLINA V. KATZENBACH (1966), upheld the constitutionality of Section 5, affirming a broad range of voting practices for which preclearance is required under the VOTING RIGHTS ACT OF 1965.

The four cases that constitute *Allen* involve the application of the 1965 Voting Rights Act to state election laws and regulations in both Mississippi and Virginia. The Mississippi cases were consolidated on appeal and argued together, and because of the grounds on which the Supreme Court decides these cases, the appeal in a Virginia case was also disposed by the Court's opinion in the case. Thus, in all four cases, both states passed new laws in which the central issue is whether the provisions of these laws fell within the Section 5 prohibitions that prevent the enforcement of "any voting qualification or prerequisite to voting, or standard, practice, or procedure with respect to voting" unless the state first complies with one of the section's approval procedures as provided under the Voting Rights Act.

In *Allen v. State Board of Elections*, the Supreme Court ruled that provisions of both the Mississippi and Virginia state laws violate the Voting Rights Act of 1965. Specifically, in a 7-2 opinion by Chief Justice Earl Warren, the Court interpreted Section 5 of the Act broadly to require preclearance for a wide range of election practices and therefore against state prerogatives. According to the Court, states are prohibited by Section 5 from enacting or seeking "to administer any voting qualification or prerequisite to voting, or standard, practice, or procedure with respect to voting different from that in force or effect on November 1, 1964," without first submitting their intended change to the U.S. Office of the Attorney General to obtain consent or secure a favorable declaratory judgment from the District Court for the DISTRICT OF COLUMBIA.

In cases titled Nos. 25 (*Fairley v. Patterson*), 26 (*Bunton v. Patterson*), and 36 (*Whitley v. Williams*), the Mississippi parties who brought suits sought declaratory judgments in the District Court for the Southern District of Mississippi, alleging that certain amendments to the Mississippi Code were subject to the provisions of Section 5 and therefore not enforceable until the state has complied with the approval requirements established by the Voting Rights Act. Dismissing the complaints in all three cases, a three-judge district court ruled for the state of Mississippi and held that its amendments did not come within the purview of Section 5 of the Voting Rights Act. Appellants brought direct appeal, and the Supreme Court consolidated the cases and postponed consideration of jurisdiction to a hearing on the merits. In *Allen*, appellants were functionally illiterate, duly registered voters of the Fourth Congressional District of Virginia. They brought a declaratory judgment action in the U.S. District Court for the Eastern District of Virginia claiming that a Virginia statute modifying voting bulletin violates the EQUAL PROTECTION clause of the FOURTEENTH AMENDMENT and the Voting Rights Act of 1965. After the three-judge court dismissed their complaint, a direct appeal was lodged, and the Supreme Court similarly postponed consideration of jurisdiction questions to a hearing on the merits.

Remanding all four cases to the district courts with instructions to issue INJUNCTIONs restraining the further enforcement of the enactments until such time as both states adequately demonstrated compliance with Section 5 of the Voting Rights Act, Chief Justice Warren ruled that "what a fair interpretation of the Voting Right Act requires is that States in some unambiguous and recordable manner submit any legislation or regulation directly to the Attorney General with a request for his consideration." The term *voting*, the Court observed, included

> all action necessary to make a vote effective in any primary, special, or general election, includ-

ing, but not limited to, registration, listing . . . or other action required by law prerequisite to voting, casting a ballot, and having such ballot counted properly and included in the appropriate totals of votes cast with respect to candidates for public or party office and propositions for which votes are received in an election.

Further, the Court noted that "the Voting Rights Act was aimed at the subtle, as well as the obvious, state regulations which have the effect of denying citizens their RIGHT TO VOTE because of their race." Citing *REYNOLDS V. SIMS,* the Supreme Court observed that the act gives a broad interpretation to the right to vote, recognizing that voting includes "all action necessary to make a vote effective." The legislative history on the whole, according to the Court, "supports the view that Congress intended to reach any state enactment which altered the election law of a covered State in even a minor way."

Thus, according to the Court, Section 5 suits may be brought in at least three ways. First, the state may institute a declaratory judgment. Second, an individual may bring a suit for declaratory judgment and injunctive relief, claiming that a state requirement is covered by 5 but has not been subjected to the required federal scrutiny. Third, the office of the Attorney General may bring an injunctive action to prohibit the enforcement of a new regulation because of the state's failure to obtain approval under Section 5. Finally, a three-judge district court is required for all actions challenging provisions of the Voting Rights Act.

Recently, in *Presley v. Etowah County Comm'n,* 502 U.S. 491 (1992), while reaffirming *Allen,* the Supreme Court emphasized that changes covered under Section 5 must have a direct relation to voting. Seemingly retreating from its more expansive position with *Allen,* the Supreme Court provided a nonexclusive list of four categories in which voting changes covered under Section 5 would normally fall: 1) changes in the manner of voting, 2) changes in candidacy requirements and qualifications, 3) changes in the composition of the electorate that may vote for candidates for a given office, and 4) changes affecting the creation or abolition of an elective office.

For more information: Hasen, Richard. *The Supreme Court and Election Law: Judging Equality from* Baker v. Carr *to* Bush v. Gore. New York: New York University Press, 2003.

—Marc G. Pufong

Ambach v. Norwick 542 U.S. 507 (1979)

In *Ambach v. Norwick,* the Supreme Court narrowly upheld the constitutionality of a New York statute that restricted the permanent certification of public school teachers to U.S. citizens or aliens who intend to apply for citizenship. The Court ruled that because public classroom teachers are agents of the government and have a significant influence over students, the state has compelling interest in refusing to certify aliens who express no interest in becoming U.S. citizens. In applying the "rational basis" test, the Court rejected claims that the law violated the FOURTEENTH AMENDMENT's EQUAL PROTECTION clause.

Susan M. W. Norwick was born in Scotland, moved to the United States in 1965, and married a U.S. citizen. Norwick was eligible to apply for U.S. citizenship but expressed no intention of renouncing her British citizenship. In 1973, after graduating from college, Norwick applied to become an elementary teacher in the state of New York. Although otherwise qualified, her application for certification was denied by the New York Commission on Education solely on the basis of Section 3001(3) of the New York Education Law, which bars aliens from teaching in public schools unless they manifest intention to become U.S. citizens. Norwick sued Gordon M. Ambach, New York State commissioner of education, and others in U.S. district court, asserting that the law violated her right to equal protection under the Fourteenth Amendment.

The three-judge federal district court, applying STRICT SCRUTINY, ruled for Norwick. Under "strict scrutiny," a law that on its face distinguishes between people in part because of their nationality is presumed to be unconstitutional, and the heavy burden is upon the government to demonstrate a rational and compelling interest in making such a distinction. More specifically, the trial court held that the state's blanket ban on public school teaching by aliens was unconstitutionally "overbroad" because it did not take into account the subjects being taught, the relationship of the alien's home country to the United States, and the possibility of including an alien's loyalty statement in lieu of declaring his or her intent to become a citizen.

Ambach appealed to the U.S. Supreme Court asserting that the law was "rational" and that the lower court had inappropriately applied strict scrutiny. Writing for a five-person majority, Justice LEWIS FRANKLIN POWELL, JR., reversed the district court ruling, holding that the New York law was indeed rational and that the lower court had erred in applying the stricter standard. Powell noted that while aliens living in the United States are entitled to many of the rights of citizens, states nevertheless have the right to restrict aliens where there is a compelling interest in doing so. According to Powell, teachers are uniquely suited to serve as role models for children. They instill attitudes toward government, the political processes, and the responsibility of citizenship. Given this unique relationship and government's demonstrated interest in promoting good citizens, Powell stated it is indeed rational for New York State to restrict public school teaching to U.S. citizens or those who have expressed a desire to become one. Joining Powell were Chief Justice WARREN BURGER and Justices Byron White, WILLIAM HUBBS REHNQUIST, and SANDRA DAY O'CONNOR.

Justices Harry Blackmun, Thurgood Marshall, JOHN PAUL STEVENS, and WILLIAM J. BRENNAN, JR., dissented. Justice Blackmun argued in part that the law in question "sweeps indiscriminately" against aliens and is not rational because it fails to cover aliens teaching in New York's private and parochial schools. Blackmun then compared *Ambach* to *In re Griffiths* (1973), a case in which the U.S. Supreme Court ruled that qualified aliens have a right to take the state bar and practice law. According to Blackmun, "If an attorney has a constitutional right to take a bar examination and practice law, despite being an alien, it is impossible for me to see why a resident alien, otherwise completely competent and qualified . . . is constitutionally disqualified from teaching in the public schools of the great State of New York."

Ambach was one in a series of cases where the U.S. Supreme Court grappled with constitutionality of state laws restricting alien actions. Examples are *Sugarman v. Dougall*, 413 U.S. 634 (1973)—in which the Supreme Court struck down a New York law that banned aliens from civil service employment—and *Foley v. Connelie*, 435 U.S. 291 (1978)—where the Supreme Court upheld a New York regulation restricting employment of state troopers to U.S. citizens.

For more information: Aleinikoff, Thomas Alexander, David A. Martin, and Hiroshi Motomura. *Immigration and Citizenship: Process and Policy*. 4th ed. St. Paul, Minn.: West, 1998; Bosniak, Linda. "Membership, Equality, and the Difference That Alienage Makes." *New York University Law Review* 69 (1994): 1,047; Gordon, Charles, Stanley Mailman, and Stephen Yale-Loehr. *Immigration Law and Procedure*. New York: Matthew Bender, 2001; Neuman, Gerald L. *Strangers to the Constitution: Immigrants, Borders, and Fundamental Law*. Princeton, N.J.: Princeton University Press, 1996.

—Richard J. Hardy

amending the Constitution

Amending the U.S. Constitution refers to the formal process of changing the document's language or provisions. When the Founding Fathers framed the Constitution in 1787, they included in Article V a process to make amendments to it. The amending process is a means for enabling the government to keep the Constitution ready to meet challenges, both present and future, striking a balance between entrenchment and flexibility.

The Founding Fathers believed that amending a written constitution was just as much an exercise of constituent power as framing and adopting

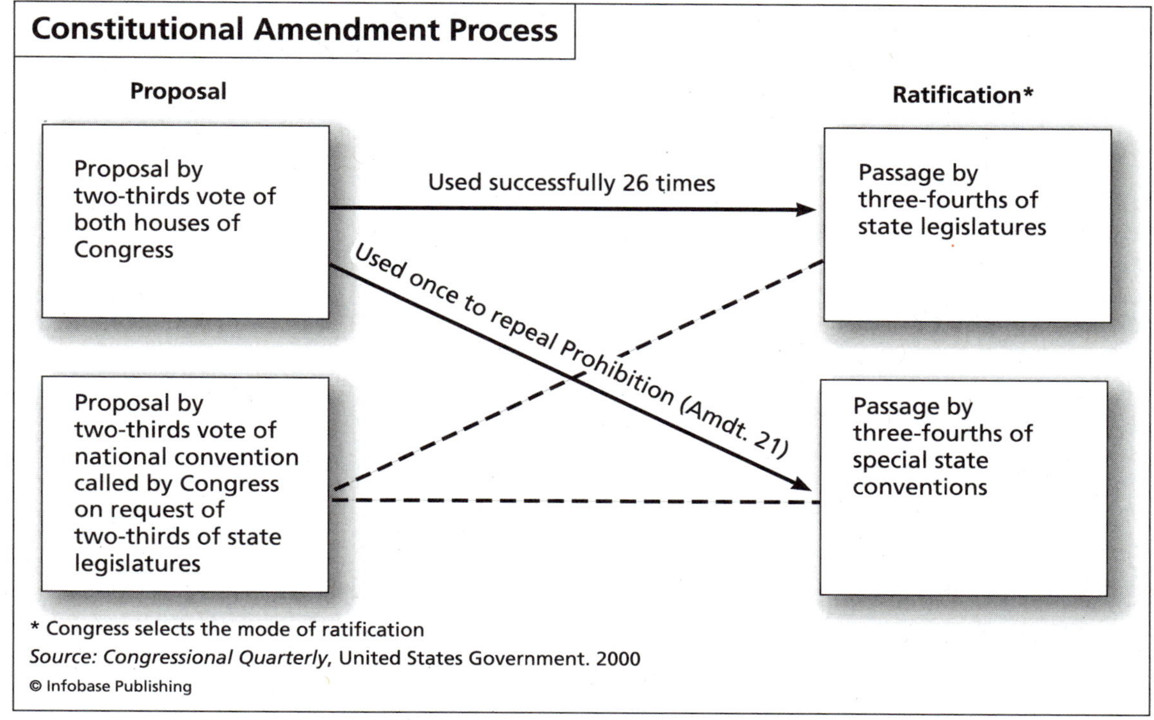
Constitutional Amendment Process
Proposal
Ratification*
Proposal by two-thirds vote of both houses of Congress
Used successfully 26 times
Passage by three-fourths of state legislatures
Used once to repeal Prohibition (Amdt. 21)
Proposal by two-thirds vote of national convention called by Congress on request of two-thirds of state legislatures
Passage by three-fourths of special state conventions

* Congress selects the mode of ratification
Source: Congressional Quarterly, United States Government. 2000

one and that the people had an inalienable right to alter or abolish an inadequate government. This revolutionary generation also believed that the act of revising a written constitution required corresponding formality and difficulty. Formal changes to the Constitution should be made only when the problem to be solved cannot be done so at the administrative, statutory, or judicial level.

Article V was included to correct defects as they became apparent or to adapt the Constitution to changing circumstances. According to Article V, there are two ways to propose an amendment. The first method is for a bill to pass both houses of the legislature by a two-thirds majority in each. Once the bill has passed both the HOUSE OF REPRESENTATIVES and the SENATE, it goes to the states. The second method prescribed is for a constitutional convention to be called by two-thirds of the legislatures of the states and for that convention to propose one or more amendments. This method has never been used. Of the 17 amendments that have followed the BILL OF RIGHTS, all have originated in Congress. Regardless of which proposed route is taken, the amendment must be approved by three-fourths of the states. The amendment as passed may specify whether the bill must be passed by the state legislatures or by a state convention. The TWENTY-FIRST AMENDMENT is the only one thus far to be ratified by specifically selected state conventions, not state legislatures. At no time does the president have a role in the amendment process. The president cannot VETO an amendment proposal or ratification.

Because the amending process was intentionally made to be difficult, of the 10,000 amendments proposed, only 33 have received approval by both the House and Senate, and just 27 have been ratified by the states. The amendments make a statement to the world and to posterity about what governmental principles the United States most cherishes. They represent a kind of political symbol of who Americans believe themselves to be and ought to be. Twelve of the 27 amendments (the Bill of Rights, the THIRTEENTH AMENDMENT, and the FOURTEENTH AMENDMENT) address individual rights.

The amendments that were adopted fall into two categories: (1) defining or redefining the fundamental principles at the heart of the nation's constitutional system and (2) correcting defects in the mechanism of government established by the Constitution. Amendments to the Constitution have come in separated clusters that have arisen during four periods. The period from 1789 to 1804 produced what are referred to as the Anti-Federalist amendments. The first 10—the Bill of Rights—adopted in 1791, were ratified immediately and have been instrumental in protecting basic liberties in the United States. These changes were promises fulfilled by the Federalists, who made them to win RATIFICATION OF THE CONSTITUTION itself. For all intents and purposes, they are part of the original. The ELEVENTH AMENDMENT of 1795 protected universal loyalty to states' rights. It forbade lawsuits against a state by citizens of another. The TWELFTH AMENDMENT, adopted in 1804, provided for the separate election of the president and VICE PRESIDENT, which was a reaction to the 1800 electoral college tie between THOMAS JEFFERSON and Aaron Burr. It became a "fix" of an unanticipated problem.

Sixty years elapsed before the Thirteenth, Fourteenth, and FIFTEENTH AMENDMENTs were passed. Known as the post–Civil War, or Reconstruction, amendments, they sealed nationalism by making U.S. citizenship the source of equal rights and of protections that the states could not deny. The Thirteenth Amendment, adopted in 1865, abolished slavery. In 1867, the Fourteenth Amendment granted all citizens PRIVILEGES AND IMMUNITIES, DUE PROCESS, EQUAL PROTECTION under the law, apportionment of representatives, and Civil War disqualification and debt. The Fifteenth Amendment, adopted in 1870, guaranteed that the rights of an individual could not be denied because of race.

Another half-century intervened before the ratification of the Sixteenth through Nineteenth Amendments. The SIXTEENTH AMENDMENT, adopted in 1913, provided for an income tax. The SEVENTEENTH AMENDMENT, in 1913, provided for the direct election of senators by the people. In 1919, the EIGHTEENTH AMENDMENT called for the prohibition of alcohol, and in 1920, the NINETEENTH AMENDMENT provided women's suffrage. These four amendments were part of the progressive and populist movements to curb the power of corporations and political bosses and restore government to the people.

The TWENTIETH AMENDMENT proposed in 1932 and ratified in 1933, ended the custom of a "lame duck" Congress having an extra session after an election that may have thrown out many of its members. The TWENTY-FIRST AMENDMENT, which was ratified in 1933 and was the only amendment to be ratified by state conventions, repealed Prohibition. The TWENTY-SECOND AMENDMENT and TWENTY-FIFTH AMENDMENT, ratified in 1951 and 1967, respectively, reflected mid-20th century concern with presidential succession. They limited a president to two terms and provided for his replacement in case of disability. These are the only amendments that do not fall into the four clusters.

The last cluster—which includes the TWENTY-THIRD, TWENTY-FOURTH, and TWENTY-SIXTH AMENDMENT—gave the vote in presidential elections to the disenfranchised and predominantly black citizens of the DISTRICT OF COLUMBIA, to men and women too poor to pay poll taxes or any other kinds of levy as a prerequisite to suffrage, and to 18-year-olds, respectively. These three reflect the egalitarian strains of the 1960s and might also be called the modern era of constitutional amendment.

The most recent, TWENTY-SEVENTH AMENDMENT provided that any pay raise that Congress votes for itself may not take effect until after another election, thus giving voters a chance to express their displeasure. This was sent to the states in 1789 and ratified two centuries later.

The exact wording of the Constitution can only be changed by using the formal amendment process; however, the meaning or the interpretation of the Constitution can change over time. When circumstances change, the meaning or interpretation can change as well. As the ultimate arbiter of how the Constitution is interpreted, the judiciary wields more actual power than the Constitution alludes to. For example, before the PRIVACY cases, it was perfectly constitutional for a state to forbid married couples from using contraception, for a state to forbid blacks and whites to marry, and for a state to abolish ABORTION. Because of judicial changes in the interpretation of the Constitution, the nation's outlook on these issues changed. In these examples, the Constitution was not altered but rather, the way people viewed the Constitution. These changes are significant because they can occur by a judge's ruling; therefore, since they are not a part of the written Constitution, they can be changed later. Historically, the Supreme Court has interpreted the original document and its formal amendments with considerable latitude, enabling adaptation to new circumstances and to changes in social understanding without formal amendments.

The Founding Fathers created a process that provided an almost ideal balance between stability and change. Constitutional amendments have enduring and lasting importance in a system that prizes America's distinctive conception of sovereignty. The inclusion of Article V and its powerful mechanisms are at the very core of the Constitution's existence and survival.

For more information: Bernstein, R. B., and J. Angel. *Amending America: If We Love the Constitution So Much, Why Do We Keep Trying to Change It?* New York: Times Books, 1993; Chism, K. "The Constitutional Amendment Process." *Social Education* 69 (November 2005): 373–375; Kaplan, D. A., and G. Cerio. "Tinkering with the Constitution." *Newsweek* (June 5, 1990), 115; Kyvig, D. E. *Explicit and Authentic Acts: Amending the U.S. Constitution, 1776–1995.* Lawrence: University of Kansas Press, 1996; Weisberger, B. A. "Amending America." *American Heritage* (May/June 1995), 24–25.

—Sharon L. Morrison

American Civil Liberties Union

The American Civil Liberties Union (ACLU) is a major national nonprofit organization devoted to protecting individual rights against unconstitutional exercises of government power. It is best known for bringing lawsuits, but it also monitors and testifies on legislation and offers public education programming. The ACLU has approximately 500,000 members nationwide and affiliates (chapters) in all 50 states and is financed through membership dues, private donations, and legal fees awarded when one of its lawsuits is successful and such fees are available.

The organization that became the ACLU was organized in 1917, during the height of the now infamous Palmer Raids, "roundups" and deportations of resident aliens suspected of holding unorthodox or unpatriotic opinions. It was then called the National Civil Liberties Bureau and provided legal advice and aid for conscientious objectors and people being prosecuted under the Espionage Act of 1917 and the Sedition Act of 1918. In 1920, the organization changed its name to the American Civil Liberties Union.

Sometimes called "liberty's lawyer," the ACLU supports the individual liberties protected by the BILL OF RIGHTS: separation of church and state, freedom of speech and of the press, racial equality, reproductive rights for women, full CIVIL RIGHTS for gays and lesbians, the FOURTH AMENDMENT rights of criminal defendants and other citizens, immigrants' rights, the right to PRIVACY, and many others. Over the years, ACLU lawsuits have had an enormous influence on U.S. constitutional law. Some of the organization's most famous cases have included the 1925 *Scopes* case (Tennessee's prosecution of a science teacher who taught about evolution despite a Tennessee law forbidding it); *KOREMATSU V. UNITED STATES,* 323 U.S. 214 (1944); *BROWN V. BOARD OF EDUCATION OF TOPEKA,* 347 U.S. 483 (1954); and *ROE V. WADE,* 410 U.S. 113 (1973). More recently, it has vigorously opposed several provisions of the PATRIOT ACT and National Security Agency (NSA) efforts to monitor the communications of ordinary Americans.

As influential as its lawsuits have been, many people (including many who often disagree with the ACLU) believe the organization's most important function has been the mere fact that it exists as a watchdog against abuses of government power. Often, improper state and federal behavior is averted simply because the ACLU sends a warning letter to the official or agency involved.

The organization is very controversial. To some extent, this is inevitable, because the Bill of Rights that it protects was specifically designed to protect minority beliefs and unpopular people from the passions of popular majorities. There is also confusion about the difference between protecting people's rights and agreeing with them. Arguing for an individual's right to express an opinion is not agreement with that opinion (the ACLU has defended the rights of Nazis, for example, to express opinions and take positions with which the organization strenuously disagrees). When the ACLU brings a lawsuit against prayers in public schools, what the organization is opposing is not religion but the right of government to dictate citizens' religious beliefs or observances.

For more information: Kennedy, Sheila Suess. *What's a Nice Republican Girl Like Me Doing at the ACLU?* Amherst, N.Y.: Prometheus Books, 1997; Walker, Samuel. *In Defense of American Liberties: A History of the ACLU.* Carbondale: Southern Illinois University Press, 1999.

—Sheila Suess Kennedy

American Indians and the Constitution

The Constitution, in its expressed language and through interpretation and application of several of its provisions, has always treated American Indians differently from any other group of people.

Three-fifths Compromise

Section 2 of ARTICLE I OF THE U.S. CONSTITUTION provides that representation in the HOUSE OF REPRESENTATIVES and direct taxes shall be apportioned among the states according to their respective populations. These numbers were to "be determined by adding the whole Number of free Persons, including those bound to Service for a Term of Years, excluding Indians not taxed, three-fifths of all other persons." The term *other persons* was a euphemism for slaves, and the compromise was designed to accommodate the competing concerns of southern and northern states regarding an acceptable distribution of the direct tax burden and representation in the House. Often overlooked in this compelling debate about slavery was the complete omission of Native Americans in this calculation. American Indians as a whole were not taxed at the time, and consequently, they had neither a representative link to nor a particular stake in the new republic.

Commerce Clause

Article I, Section 8, provides that Congress shall have the power to "regulate Commerce with foreign Nations, and among the several States, and with the Indian Tribes." Delegates to the CONSTITUTIONAL CONVENTION approached this issue against a backdrop of years of hostilities with American Indians on the one hand counterbalanced by a comparably long period of trade and commerce with them on the other. Fractured approaches to these issues by states had been largely unsuccessful in producing lasting solutions. These experiences informed the delegates that uniform regulation, administered by a centralized federal authority, was essential. The resulting commerce clause was utilized quickly with the passage, between 1790 and 1834, of several Trade and Intercourse Acts (for example, 1 Stat. 137, 1790; 1 Stat. 329, 1793; 1 Stat. 469, 1796; 1 Stat. 743, 1799; and 4 Stat. 729, 1834). But the significance of the commerce clause as it relates to Native Americans advanced far beyond its original parameters of trade and intercourse, for over time it became a stepping-stone to the development of the tremendous federal power over Indian affairs. Conversely, it has in many respects served to preclude state intrusion into Indian affairs.

Fourteenth Amendment

The Thirteenth, Fourteenth, and Fifteenth Amendments, ratified during the Reconstruction era after the Civil War, were designed to establish and protect the rights of black Americans. Accordingly, Section 2 of the FOURTEENTH AMENDMENT revisited the Three-fifths Compromise by providing as follows: "Representatives shall be apportioned among the several States according to their respective numbers, counting the whole number of persons in each State, excluding Indians not taxed." Thus, the three-fifths component regarding slaves in the apportionment computation for representation in the House was abolished; however, the exclusion of most Indians in this computation continued.

Citizenship

Section 1 of the Fourteenth Amendment provides as follows: "All persons born or naturalized in the United States and subject to the jurisdiction thereof, are citizens of the United States and of the State wherein they reside." By design, this provision extended national and state citizenship to former slaves, but its broad language could certainly be construed to extend the same rights and privileges to American Indians. The U.S. Supreme Court rejected this position in *Elk v. Wilkins,* 112 U.S. 94 (1884), ruling that the "Indians not taxed" exclusion retained in Section 2 of the amendment reflected a congressional intent to exclude Native Americans from the grant of citizenship. This exclusion was not a mere formality, for citizenship was a prerequisite for other constitutional rights, such as voting. Although the Fourteenth Amendment did not extend blanket citizenship, many American Indians attained citizenship status under the provisions of various treaties and statutes. These selective grants of citizenship required some condition precedent on the part of the Indians; for example, the General Allotment Act, 24 Stat. 388 (1887), conferred citizenship to American Indians who complied with the statutory provisions and received an allotment. Another piece of legislation bestowed citizenship on Indian women who married non-Indian citizens (25 U.S.C. Section 182 [1888]). These issues and the impediments associated with them were rendered moot with the passage of the Citizenship Act of 1924 (8 U.S.C. Section 1401 (b)), which extended citizenship to all Native Americans born in the United States.

Treaty Making

Pursuant to Section 2 of ARTICLE II OF THE U.S. CONSTITUTION, the president has the power, with the advice and consent of the SENATE, to make treaties. Although this provision makes no specific mention of American Indians, there was in fact a long history of treating with tribes that predated the Constitution. This policy was pursued by the various colonial powers because Indian allies were advantageous in their competition to establish dominance in the New World. After RATIFICATION OF THE CONSTITUTION, the new and vulnerable United States continued this policy in order to cultivate trade, facilitate the acquisition of land needed for white settlement, and avoid the burdens, economic and otherwise, that would accompany prolonged hostilities with the tribes. For nearly 100 years thereafter, treaties were the preferred national policy in dealing with Native Americans, addressing a range of issues from hunting and fishing rights to removal and relocation, as well as reservations. This prolific treaty-making era ended in 1871, when Congress, in a rider attached to an appropriations bill, declared that the United States would no longer contract with Indian tribes by TREATY (16 Stat. 566; 25 U.S.C. Section 71). One enduring legacy of this period was that tribes were viewed as separate and sovereign entities.

Tribal Sovereignty

As suggested above, the constitutional bases for tribal sovereignty are anchored in the commerce clause of Article I and in the treaty-making power of Article II. The commerce clause, by grouping American Indian tribes with foreign nations and the states, suggested that tribes were imbued with a degree of inherent sovereignty comparable to that of states and other nations. Similarly, the national policy of making treaties with tribes, conducted in much the same way as the nation entered into treaties with foreign governments, reinforced this attribute of tribal sovereignty. The parameters of tribal sovereignty were first addressed by the Supreme Court in *Cherokee Nation v. Georgia,* 30 U.S. (5 Pet.) 1 (1831), a case in which the tribe sought an INJUNCTION to prevent state incursions into tribal territory. The Cherokee filed their action directly with the Supreme Court, invoking the Court's ORIGINAL JURISDICTION as provided in Article III, Section 2, of the Constitution. The propriety of this tactic depended on whether the tribe was a "foreign state." The Court concluded that, while the tribe was a separate entity with distinctive attributes of sovereignty, it was not a foreign state. Rather, Chief Justice JOHN MARSHALL characterized tribes as "domestic dependent states." Despite this and other setbacks, tribal sovereignty continues as a viable, albeit limited concept in today's America.

Many tribes have their own governments, for example, with legislative, executive, and judicial branches. Some have their own police forces and fire departments and operate their own schools. Also, some federal courts have ruled that violations of tribal law and federal law in one transaction amounted to two different offenses for purposes of dual sovereignty and the DOUBLE JEOPARDY clause of the Fifth Amendment (*Ramos v. Pyramid Tribal Court*, 621 F. Supp. 967, D. Nev. [1985]). Consequently, those violations can be prosecuted in both tribal and federal courts. It must be remembered, however, that the extent of tribal sovereignty must be measured against a backdrop of tremendous federal power over Indian affairs. In fact, this plenary power of the federal government is the counterbalance to tribal sovereignty, as well as to state efforts to intrude into that sovereignty.

The federal government has wielded this power to erode tribal sovereignty on some occasions and to reinforce it on others. Erosion of tribal sovereignty occurred, for example, with the passage of Public Law 280, whereby the federal government granted several states broad criminal and civil jurisdiction over reservations located within those states (18 U.S.C. Section 1162 and 28 U.S.C. Section 1360 [1953]). On the other hand, official federal policy for the past 40 years or so has been one of promoting tribal sovereignty and self-determination. This endeavor, which almost always includes governmental reinforcement of tribal economic development, is often at odds with the competing interests of state and local governments. One emerging conflict in this context involves tribal gaming activities, an issue addressed by the Supreme Court in *California v. Cabazon Band of Mission Indians*, 480 U.S. 202 (1987). In that case, the tribe, pursuant to federally approved ordinances, operated high-stakes bingo and card games. These activities were open to the public and played mostly by non-Indians. State and local officials sought to prevent or restrict these gaming activities via application of various regulatory statutes and ordinances. They argued that unregulated high-stakes bingo and card games were susceptible to infiltration by organized crime. The competing federal-tribal interests focused on promoting tribal self-determination, providing employment opportunities for tribal members, and generating revenue for the tribe. The state maintained that it had jurisdiction because the gaming activities occurred on Public Law 280 reservations. The Court rejected this contention, ruling that while P.L. 280 ceded jurisdiction over criminal cases and private civil litigation, it did not grant the state general civil regulatory authority.

The Court added that the state laws and local ordinances were preempted by federal policy. This PREEMPTION in turn reinforced tribal sovereignty. In the aftermath of *Cabazon*, Congress passed the Indian Gaming Regulatory Act, 25 U.S.C. Sections 2701–2721 (1988), which established a comprehensive framework for the regulation of Indian gaming activities. By its express language, the act is designed to strengthen tribal government and promote tribal economic development and self-sufficiency (25 U.S.C. Section 2702). On the other hand, the act does recognize that states have legitimate interests that must be considered; for example, it provides that tribes have the exclusive right to regulate gaming activities that are neither specifically prohibited by federal law nor prohibited by the particular state's criminal law or public policy (25 U.S.C. Section 2701[5]). This area of inquiry and the accompanying interplay among federal, tribal, and state interests will most certainly command attention in the future.

Bill of Rights

The BILL OF RIGHTS protected CIVIL LIBERTIES by limiting the powers of the federal government. Most of those same protections were made applicable to state action via the DUE PROCESS clause of the Fourteenth Amendment and the judicially created concept of selective INCORPORATION. In their relationships with the federal and state governments, Native Americans enjoy these rights and protections. Regarding these FUNDAMENTAL RIGHTS, one area of prolific litigation has centered on Indian use of peyote. The FIRST AMENDMENT's free exercise clause protects religious freedom, and, in the exercise of that freedom, members of the Native American Church have long used peyote as a sacrament in religious ceremonies. More recently, many states have added peyote to their lists of controlled substances and proscribed its use. One illustrative case involving these competing interests was *EMPLOYMENT DIVISION V. SMITH,* 494 U.S. 872 (1990), in which two of the church's practitioners were terminated from their employment and denied unemployment benefits because they had used peyote in religious services.

At the time, there was longstanding precedent to the effect that governmental action that substantially burdens religious practice must be justified by a COMPELLING GOVERNMENTAL INTEREST (*Sherbert v. Verner,* 374 U.S. 398 [1963], and *WISCONSIN V. YODER,* 406 U.S. 205 [1972]). The U.S. Supreme Court departed from this compelling interest test in *Smith,* holding instead that there was no violation of the First Amendment if the impediment to the exercise of religion was not the object of the law in question but "merely the incidental effect of a generally applicable and otherwise valid provision" (402 U.S. 872, 878). Congress responded to *Smith* by passing the RELIGIOUS FREEDOM RESTORATION ACT (RFRA), which prohibits government from substantially burdening the free exercise of religion unless it can demonstrate that the burden is in furtherance of a compelling governmental interest and is the least restrictive means of furthering that interest (42 U.S.C. Section 2000bb-1). As originally enacted, this prohibition applied to all federal and state laws, with Congress relying on Section 5 of the Fourteenth Amendment in extending RFRA's coverage to the states.

Section 5 empowers Congress to enforce, by appropriate legislation, the amendment's other provisions, most notably the due process and EQUAL PROTECTION clauses. This is critical because, as mentioned above, the Bill of Rights originally limited the federal government but had no application to the states. The Fourteenth Amendment provides in pertinent part that no "State shall deprive any person of life, liberty, or property, without due process of law. . . ." Over time, most of the liberties contained in the Bill of Rights, including the free exercise clause, were selectively incorporated into the due process clause and made applicable to the states. In *CITY OF BOERNE V. FLORES,* 521 U.S. 507 (1997), the Supreme Court ruled that RFRA was unconstitutional insofar as it purported to bind the states. The Court determined that Congress in applying RFRA to state action, had exceeded its enforcement power under Section 5 and had in fact altered the meaning of the free exercise clause. According to the Court, this infringed on the interpretive power of the judiciary and, thereby, violated the principle of separation of powers and the federal-state balance. RFRA's scope was subsequently narrowed to cover only federal actions, and its application to federal legislation was upheld in *Gonzales v. O Centro Espirita Beneficente Uniao Do Vegetal,* 546 U.S. 418 (2006).

Indian Civil Rights Act

As noted above, Native Americans, in their relationships with federal and state governments, enjoy constitutional rights and protections. Until 1968, however, there was no similar vehicle for safeguarding fundamental rights against actions by tribal governments. In *Talton v. Mayes,* 163 U.S. 376 (1896), the Supreme Court ruled that the Bill of Rights did not apply to tribal governments, and other courts have held that the Fourteenth Amendment does not limit tribal authority (*Barta v. Oglala Sioux Tribe,* 259 F.2d 533, 6th Cir. [1958]). Consequently, American Indians, vis-à-vis their relationship with tribal governments, had no guarantees relative to these basic rights. Congress addressed this discrepancy with the passage of the Indian Civil Rights Act of 1968 (ICRA; 25 U.S.C. Sections 1301–1323).

ICRA prevents tribes, in the exercise of their powers of self-government, from denying to individuals most of the rights contained in the First, Fourth, Fifth, Sixth, Eighth, and Fourteenth Amendments. These statutory rights, while comparable to their constitutional counterparts, are not exactly the same; for example, the First Amendment guarantees the free exercise of religion and prohibits the establishment of religion. ICRA includes a free exercise clause but contains no ESTABLISHMENT CLAUSE (25 U.S.C. Section 1302 [1]). Consequently, tribal governments may endorse a particular religion. In addition, the SIXTH AMENDMENT has been interpreted to require appointed counsel for indigent defendants for all felonies (*GIDEON V. WAINWRIGHT,* 372 U.S. 335 [1963]) and for many misdemeanors (*Argersinger v. Hamlin,* 407 U.S. 25 [1972], and *ALABAMA V. SHELTON,* 535 U.S. 654 [2002]). ICRA, on the other hand, provides that a criminal defendant has the right "at his own expense to have the assistance of counsel for his defense" (25 U.S.C. Section 1302 [6]).

For more information: Getches, David H., Charles Wilkinson, and Robert Williams, Jr. *Federal Indian Law: Cases and Materials.* St. Paul, Minn.: West Publishing, 1993; Reese, Michael. "The Indian Civil Rights Act: Conflict Between Constitutional Assimilation and Tribal Self-Determination." *Southeastern Political Review* 20: 29–61.

—Michael Reese

appellate jurisdiction

Appellate jurisdiction is the power of one court or other entity to review the actions of another body. The power to hear cases regarding federal constitutional and statutory issues is allocated to the U.S. Supreme Court, the inferior (or lower) federal courts, and the various state court systems. The actual authority over any particular matter may derive from either federal constitutional provisions or the statutory enactments of Congress.

ARTICLE III OF THE U.S. CONSTITUTION assigns the judicial power of the United States to the Supreme Court and those inferior federal courts created by Congress. Article III specifically defines the judicial power by two criteria: subject matter and class of litigants. The subject matter of the federal judicial power includes the ability of the federal courts to hear all cases arising under the Constitution, federal laws or treaties, or admiralty or maritime authority. Article III also extends the judicial power to cases involving ambassadors and other public ministers or officers and cases that involve a controversy between two or more states or between parties of differing states.

The actual exercise of appellate jurisdiction by the Supreme Court is one characterized by significant statutory discretion. Such discretionary flexibility is not the rule for all other federal courts. The appellate jurisdiction of the Supreme Court and the other federal courts is, furthermore, subject to the "Exception and under such Regulations" clause of Article III. Through the operation of this constitutional provision, Congress has on occasion acted to control the ability of the federal courts to hear certain classes of cases; for example, recent congresses have sought to limit the power of the federal courts over such diverse matters as busing for school integration purposes, ABORTION, prayer in the public schools, and the recitation of the Pledge of Allegiance.

The question of the extent of the appellate jurisdiction of the Supreme Court and other federal courts is one as old as the nation itself. The heart of the controversy lies in whether Congress has the authority to determine which cases the federal courts may hear under the judiciary's constitutional grant of appellate jurisdiction. The first act of Congress addressing the judicial power of the federal courts, the JUDICIARY ACT OF 1789, 1 Stat. 73, did not provide authority for the inferior federal courts to exercise all of the judicial power identified in Article III. This statutory basis for the view that Congress is not required to grant to the lower federal courts all the jurisdiction authorized by Article III was somewhat affirmed by Supreme Court in the case of *Sheldon v. Still,* 49 U.S. 441 (1850). The Supreme Court held that Congress has the power to establish the federal courts and to define the jurisdiction these courts may exercise. The action by the Supreme Court in the appeal in *EX PARTE MCCARDLE,* 74 U.S. 506

(1869), in which the Court accepted the congressional withdrawal of jurisdiction over HABEAS CORPUS appeals, would also seem to support that view of the extensive authority of the Congress to control boundaries of appellate jurisdiction.

The extent of the appellate jurisdiction of the federal courts may be a somewhat unresolved issue. The actual practice is much less complicated. Three basic methods of securing JUDICIAL REVIEW by the Supreme Court are now statutorily authorized: certiorari review pursuant to 28 U.S.C. sec. 1254 (1), appeals pursuant to 28 U.S.C. sec. 1253, and certification of questions pursuant to 28 U.S.C. sec. 1254 (2). The mandatory appeals jurisdiction of the Supreme Court was eliminated by statute in 1988, P.L. 100-352, 102 Stat. 662.

The United States courts of appeal were created by the Circuit Courts of Appeals Act in 1891, 26 Stat. 826. These courts were created to be an intermediate step between the federal district courts and the Supreme Court. This is the essential character of the courts of appeal today. The courts of appeal are expressly courts of limited appellate jurisdiction. The basic authority of the courts of appeal is set out in 28 U.S.C. sec. 1291, where jurisdiction is granted for "appeals from all final decisions of the district courts of the United States."

Specific rules of procedure, promulgated by the Supreme Court through the work of its advisory committees, provide in great detail how appellate litigants are to seek judicial review through the federal courts' appellate jurisdiction. The procedural details are contained in the various editions of the *Rules of the Supreme Court of the United States* and the *Federal Rules of Appellate Procedure.* These rules are subject to congressional review, which extends, to a certain degree, congressional authority over the actual practice of appellate jurisdiction in the United States.

For more information: Fallon, Richard H., Daniel J. Meltzer, and David L. Shapiro. *Hart and Wechsler's the Federal Courts and the Federal System.* 4th ed. New York: Foundation Press, 2003; Stern, Roger J., Eugene Gressman, Stephen M. Shapiro, and Kenneth S. Geller. *Supreme Court Practice.* 8th ed. Washington, D.C.: Bureau of National Affairs, 2002.

—Jerry E. Stephens

Apprendi v. New Jersey 530 U.S. 466 (2000)

In *Apprendi v. New Jersey,* the Supreme Court ruled that a judge could not set a sentence above the statutory maximum without a jury determination of the facts beyond a reasonable doubt supporting such a decision. The significance of this decision is to remove more sentencing discretion from the judge and to ensure the protection of the RIGHT TO TRIAL BY JURY and the right to DUE PROCESS of the defendant.

Charles Apprendi, Jr., fired shots into the home of an African-American family. He pled guilty to two counts of second-degree possession of a firearm for an unlawful purpose, which carried a minimum of five years and a maximum of 10 years in prison, and third-degree possession of an antipersonnel bomb, which carried a minimum of three years and a maximum of five years in prison.

After Apprendi pled guilty, the prosecutor filed a motion to enhance the sentence under the hate crime statute. An enhancement to an existing sentence is a statutorily determined increase of a sentence for a particular reason. For a hate crime enhancement, the sentence can be increased when the committed crime is completed with a racially discriminatory purpose. In the *Apprendi* case, the judge alone heard evidence on the hate crime enhancement and found, by a preponderance of the evidence, that the crime was completed with a racially biased purpose. The judge, therefore, sentenced Apprendi to a prison term of 12 years for one of the counts of second-degree possession of a firearm for an unlawful purpose.

Apprendi appealed his case to the U.S. Supreme Court, claiming that any fact determined by the judge alone that increased the statutory maximum for which a defendant was charged and convicted violated his SIXTH AMENDMENT right to jury trial. The grounds of his claim were based on FOURTEENTH AMENDMENT rights of due process and Sixth Amendment rights to jury trial. The Supreme Court held that any fact that raises the sentence above the statutory maximum must be submitted to a jury and be proved beyond a reasonable doubt—the "elements rule" (Bibas 2001). The only exception to this rule was the judicial consideration of prior convictions during a sentencing hearing; that is, after conviction, the judge could raise the sentence after considering prior convictions without a jury determination.

Although the state argued that the facts supporting the enhancement penalty were merely "sentencing factors," the Supreme Court ruled that these facts were more akin to "element factors"—that is, factors attributed to the elements of the underlying crime—to which the Sixth Amendment right to jury trial attached. In this case, the facts given during the sentencing hearing went toward the defendant's biased purpose, which went toward proving the defendant's state of mind—that is, the mental element of the crime. Therefore, the defendant's biased purpose was an element factor that necessitates protection of the defendant's Sixth Amendment right to jury trial. The jury is therefore required to determine the facts beyond a reasonable doubt to support the enhanced sentence.

For more information: Bibas, S. "Judicial Factfinding and Sentence Enhancements in a World of Guilty Pleas." *Yale Law Journal* 110 (2001): 1,097–1,185; Levine, A. M. "The Confounding Boundaries of '*Apprendi*-land': Statutory Minimums and the Federal Sentencing Guidelines." *American Journal of Criminal Law* 29 (2002): 377–454; Priester, B. J. "Structuring Sentencing: *Apprendi,* the Offense of Conviction, and the Limited Role of Constitutional Law." *Indiana Law Journal* 79 (2004): 863–935; Yellen, D. "Saving Federal Sentencing Reform after *Apprendi, Blakely* and *Booker.*" *Villanova Law Review* 50 (2005): 163–187.

—Jeremy D. Ball

Arizonans for Official English v. Arizona

520 U.S. 43 (1997)

In *Arizonans for Official English v. Arizona,* the Supreme Court avoided ruling on whether a law that mandated all state business be conducted in English violated either the FIRST AMENDMENT or FOURTEENTH AMENDMENT of the Constitution.

Arizonans for Official English v. Arizona originated in October 1987 when a group named Arizonans for Official English began a petition drive to amend Arizona's constitution. The organization aimed to prohibit all government officials and employees from using languages other than English in the performance of government business. In practice, the legislation targeted Spanish speakers, a substantial proportion of the state's population. Advocates for the measure stated that record levels of immigration into the United States threatened to overwhelm assimilation. They argued that a common language brought political unity and stability. Opponents viewed the measure as an attack on illegal immigrants out of frustration for the nation's failed immigration policy.

In November 1988, voters approved the amendment, entitled "English as the Official Language," as Article 28 of the Arizona Constitution. The amendment permitted the use of languages other than English only to protect public health and safety, protect the rights of crime victims and criminal defendants, and comply with federal law, such as English as a Second Language (ESL) classes for schoolchildren. Any Arizona resident or person doing business in Arizona had STANDING to bring a suit for enforcement. Arizona thus became the 21st state to declare English as its official language.

Maria-Kelly Yniguez, a first-year law student who evaluated medical malpractice claims against state hospitals for the Arizona Department of Administration, promptly sued to stop the law. Yniguez spoke in Spanish to claimants who spoke only Spanish, and she spoke in a combination of English and Spanish with bilingual claimants. Yniguez maintained that she had a First Amendment right to fill out release-of-claim forms in Spanish. The state supreme court found that the amendment violated the Fourteenth Amendment's guarantees of EQUAL PROTECTION by impinging upon both the fundamental right to participate equally in the political process and the RIGHT TO PETITION THE GOVERNMENT for redress. Article 28 unconstitutionally inhibited the free discussion of governmental affairs by depriving limited- and non-English-speaking persons from access to government information and by depriving elected officials and public employees of their ability to communicate with their constituents and with the public.

Both the U.S. district court in Phoenix and the Ninth Circuit majority struck down Article 28 in its entirety. The courts held that the choice of language alone, independent of any content, was protected speech that the state could not regulate. Meanwhile, Yniguez resigned from her state job to accept a private-sector position.

In 1997, the U.S. Supreme Court vacated the Ninth Circuit decision. It held that the case should have been dismissed when Yniguez quit her job because the amendment pertains only to government employees. Public employees have constitutional protections such as those providing freedom of speech, but private employees do not have constitutional protections. With this decision, the Court avoided the hotly contested issue of the constitutionality of English-only laws.

For more information: Smith, Zachary A. *Politics and Public Policy in Arizona*. Westport, Conn.: Praeger, 2002.

—Caryn E. Neumann

Article I of the U.S. Constitution

Article I of the U.S. Constitution establishes the legislative branch (known as Congress) of the federal government. Congress consists of the HOUSE OF REPRESENTATIVES and the SENATE. The article establishes the composition, conditions, and requirements for members of the legislative branch and their role, powers, and limits. In addition to outlining the role and scope of powers of members of each congressional house, Article I outlines the legislative procedures and delineates the limits of legislative power at both the federal and state levels of government.

The House of Representatives

Section 2 of Article I establishes the House of Representatives, often referred to as the "lower house," despite its powers being roughly equivalent to those of the Senate. In some areas, the powers of the House of Representatives are actually superior to those of the Senate; for example, the House of Representatives has sole responsibility and power to generate REVENUE BILLS.

It is within this section of Article I that the term for office holders, the electoral process for elections to this congressional house, qualifications for those elected, apportionment (the number of representatives per state), and specific offices within the House of Representatives itself are established. The article provides for the election of members to the House of Representatives every second year by the people, with the provision that if vacancies should occur during a term, it is left to the governor of the affected state to issue a writ of election calling for a special election to be held to ensure representation for that congressional district. The Constitution also provides a minimum-age requirement for those seeking to hold office within the House; the minimum age is set at 25 years. In addition to this age requirement, the Constitution's Article I also outlines other qualifications, such as residency of the state that the individual is representing (although, technically, one does not need to be a resident of the district one represents, this is mostly the case in practice), and the representative must also have been a U.S. citizen for a minimum of seven years prior to his or her election to the House of Representatives.

With regard to apportionment, the number of representatives for each state is dependent on the size of its population, although each state is entitled to at least one representative. Originally, the population of a state was determined according to the following guidelines: all "free persons," three-fifths of "other persons" (that is, slaves), and excluding Native Americans. Women were not excluded but they could not vote. This "formula" was not necessarily meant to deny the humanity of slaves but rather served as a means of limiting the political power of slave-holding states by reducing their representation within the House of Representatives. However, the Fourteenth Amendment, passed after the Civil War, changed this apportionment provision by removing the three-fifths clause, as slavery had been abolished. Today, all persons of a state—whether voters or not—are counted with regard to calculating the population of a state for the purposes of selecting members to the House of Representatives. This is done through a population census conducted every 10 years, as provided for by the Constitution.

Section 2 of Article I provides for the House of Representatives to select the Speaker and other officers. In this regard, although the Constitution does not mandate that the Speaker of the House of Representatives be a member of the House, this has always been the case. Finally, Section 2 designates the House of Representatives as having sole power of IMPEACHMENT, although impeachments are tried in the Senate, as discussed in the next section.

The Senate

Section 3 of Article I establishes the Senate, also known as the "upper house," although it is roughly equal in terms of powers bestowed upon it by the Constitution. However, the Senate is traditionally viewed as the upper house because there are fewer senators than representatives and a senator's term in office is longer than that of a representative's, thereby providing the average senator with more influence than perhaps the average representative.

As in Section 2 for the House of Representatives, Section 3 outlines the composition, selection process, and qualifications for members of the Senate. With regard to the composition and selection process, each state is entitled to two senators to be chosen for a term of six years, provided for by the Constitution. During the very first meeting of the Senate, senators were divided into three classes of near-equal size, as each had a different length of term in office to allow for staggered rotation in the future: The first class had a two-year term; the second class, a four-year term; and the third class, a six-year term. Thereafter, all senators had six-year terms. This first-meeting "class system" successfully ensured that every two years, about one-third of the Senate would be up for election, thereby preserving stability and continuity within the chamber.

Originally, senators were selected by state legislatures, and in cases of vacancies during a recess of the legislature, the legislatures could authorize the state's governor to make temporary appointments to the Senate. However, this selection process changed with the passing of the SEVENTEENTH AMENDMENT, which provides for the direct election of senators by their state's voters.

There are few stipulations regarding qualifications for becoming a senator, as is the case for representatives. The three qualifications to become a Senator are a minimum age of 30 years, U.S. citizenship for at least nine years prior to winning an election, and residency in the state that the or she will represent at the time of winning the election.

In addition to outlining the establishment of the Senate, Section 3 also includes clauses that cover the selection by the Senate of officers such as the president pro tempore, the majority and minority leaders, and the majority and minority whips. Section 3 also provides that the VICE PRESIDENT is to serve as the president of the Senate but without a voting right unless a vote is equally divided. In the absence of the vice president presiding over the Senate, the president pro tempore takes over the duties as necessary. The last two clauses of Section 3 cover impeachment trials and judgments, whereby the Senate is granted the sole power to try impeachments, and in judgments, the Senate may also disqualify a defendant from holding any future public office.

The last six sections of Article I establish further guidelines with regard to elections and meetings, procedures, and compensation, privileges, and restrictions on holding civil office. Section 7, referred to as the PRESENTMENT CLAUSE, establishes the method of making acts of Congress (congressional bills becoming law). While Sections 8 and 9 enumerate the powers and limits of Congress, respectively, the final section, Section 10, outlines the limits on the powers of states.

For more information: Burnham, James. *Congress and the American Tradition.* Chicago: H. Regnery Co., 1959; English, Ross M. *The United States Congress.* Manchester, England: Manchester University Press, 2003; Galloway, George B. *History of the House of Representatives.* New York: Thomas Y. Crowell, 1962; Grant, Alan. *The American Political Process.* New York: Routledge, 2003; Posner, Richard A. *An Affair of State: The Investigation, Impeachment, and Trial of President Clinton.* Cambridge, Mass.: Harvard University Press, 1999; Stark, Jack. *Prohibited Government Acts: A Reference Guide to the United States Constitution.* Westport, Conn.: Praeger, 2002.

—Dale Mineshima-Lowe

Article II of the U.S. Constitution

Article II of the U.S. Constitution establishes the executive branch (consisting of the president and other executive officers) of the federal government. The article is divided into four sections covering areas relating to the president and the executive branch, such as the election and term of the president, the role of the VICE PRESIDENT, presidential powers and responsibilities, and the issue of IMPEACHMENT.

The President and Vice President

Section 1 states that executive power shall be vested in the office of the president during his term of four years and that the president and a vice president are to be elected by the ELECTORAL COLLEGE. This section also outlines how members of the electoral college are chosen and about their voting. The electoral college is made up of individuals selected according to the state legislatures' procedures, with each state allowed to choose as many electors to the college as the total number of representatives and senators the state has in U.S. Congress. Electors may not include senators, representatives, or other federal officers.

With regard to the electoral college's voting procedures, originally, electors from each state were required to make a list of all persons voted for, listing the number of votes each had received, and then deliver this list to Congress, where the president of the SENATE would count it before both houses of Congress. The individual with the most votes would then be selected president, with the individual with the next highest number of votes as the vice president. In the event of a tie, the Senate would then select between the tied candidates, their choice for vice president. This procedure was replaced (implicitly) by the TWELFTH AMENDMENT in 1804. The Twelfth Amendment introduced key changes to the electoral college voting procedure, endowing each elector now with one vote for president and another vote for the vice president. In the case where there is no clear presidential candidate receiving a majority of the votes, the House then selects from among the top three. The Senate, in cases where vice presidential candidates have an equal number of electoral votes, selects from the two with the highest number of votes. In addition to the electoral college selection and voting procedures, Article II also dictates the date on which electors are chosen: the Tuesday following the first Monday in November, in the year before the president's term is due to expire.

Other aspects covered in detail in Section 1 are qualifications for office, salary, the oath or affirmation of the office, and contingency plans in cases of vacancies or disabilities during a term in office. Qualifications for the president and vice president are that both must be natural-born citizens, at least 35 years of age by the time of their inauguration, and inhabitants of the United States for at least 14 years. The TWENTY-SECOND AMENDMENT also prevents the president from serving more than two terms in office.

With regard to salaries, although there is no specific amount set for the president or vice president, Article II states that the president (and by implication the vice president) shall be compensated for services rendered; however, the amount of compensation shall remain constant during the term of office and that no other compensations may be received during this period.

Before taking office, the president pronounces the oath of office: "I do solemnly swear [or affirm] that I will faithfully execute the Office of the President of the United States, and will to the best of my Ability, preserve, protect and defend the Constitution of the United States." And by convention established by George Washington, the president ends the oath with ". . . so help me God." Normally, the chief justice of the Supreme Court presides and administers the oath of office. The vice president also has an oath of office, but unlike the presidential oath, it is not mandated by the Constitution but rather is prescribed for by statute. The oaths taken by both the president and vice president are significant, especially in the event of vacancy or disability.

The wording of Clause 6 has in the past caused controversy regarding succession in these events, the quandary being whether the vice president became the president or was more of an acting president until an election could be held to determine a new president. However, the death of President William Henry Harrison while in office and Vice President John Tyler's assumption that he had the right to become president in the wake of Harrison's death set the precedent that has since been used by other vice presidents (such as Andrew Johnson, Harry Truman, and Lyndon Johnson) to take up the mantle and assume the role of president for the remainder of the term. This precedent became solidified with the passing of the TWENTY-FIFTH AMENDMENT, which explicitly set out that in cases where the presidency became vacant due to death, illness, resignation, or inability, the vice president would then become the president. In the case of a vice presidential vacancy, the Twenty-fifth Amendment also allows for the president to appoint, with the approval of both the HOUSE OF REPRESENTATIVES and the SENATE. The amendment also outlines that when the president is unable to discharge his duties, the vice president then becomes acting president. This allows the president to take control back at a later point unless two-thirds of both houses of Congress vote to uphold the finding of the vice president and cabinet.

Presidential Powers

The president is the COMMANDER IN CHIEF of the armed forces in the United States. Although presidents have often deployed troops, the president cannot declare war—a congressional power covered in ARTICLE I OF THE U.S. CONSTITUTION—and needs congressional support for deployment. In addition to his or her role as commander in chief, the president, implicitly through the Constitution, can create a cabinet that includes principle officers from different executive departments for the purpose of providing the president with advice when called upon to do so. Other presidential powers provided for by Article II include the ability to grant pardons or reprieves (although not in impeachment cases) and the ability to ratify treaties and make senior-level and judicial appointments upon the advice and consent of the Senate; the power to remove individuals from office (although this is a power that Congress has, over time, sought to limit in various ways). Lastly, the president has the power to make appointments filling vacancies that may occur during a Senate recess, thereby granting a commission that would expire at the end of the next Senate session. A recent example of presidential use of this particular power was George W. Bush's appointment of John Bolton as ambassador to the United Nations in 2005.

Presidential Responsibilities

The president must deliver regular addresses to Congress about the "State of the Union," making recommendations about measures and issues that representatives and senators should be aware of and consider. In addition to his regular addresses, the president can call Congress into extraordinary sessions as well as call for its adjournment when both Houses cannot agree upon a date for adjournment. The president is also the country's representative and is responsible for receiving all foreign ambassadors. Regarding the execution of the law, the president is responsible for ensuring its faithful execution. Lastly, the president is responsible for commissioning all United States officers, including those of the military and foreign services.

Impeachment

The final section of Article II provides for the involuntary removal from office of the president, the vice president, civil officers, and executive officers. It stipulates that the House of Representatives may impeach these officers, and the Senate tries them.

For more information: Applewood Books. *U.S. Constitution by Founding Fathers.* Carlisle, Mass.: Applewood Books, 2006; Crenson, Matthew, and Benjamin Ginsberg. *Presidential Power: Unchecked and Unbalanced.* New York: W. W. Norton, 2007; Grant, Alan. *The American Political Process.* New York: Routledge, 2003; Posner, Richard A. *An Affair of State: The Investigation, Impeachment, and Trial of President Clinton.* Cambridge, Mass.: Harvard University Press, 1999; Stark, Jack. *Prohibited Government Acts: A Reference Guide to the United States Constitution.* Westport, Conn.: Praeger, 2002; Sunstein, Cass R. *The Declaration of Independence and the Constitution of the United States of America.* Washington, D.C.: Georgetown University Press, 2003.

—Dale Mineshima-Lowe

Article III of the U.S. Constitution

Article III of the U.S. Constitution specifies the authority given to the judicial branch. Section 1 states:

> [T]he judicial Power of the United States shall be vested in one supreme Court, and in such inferior Courts as the Congress may from time to time ordain and establish. The Judges, both of the supreme and inferior Courts, shall hold their Offices during good Behavior, and shall, at stated Times, receive for their Services, a Compensation, which shall not be diminished during the Continuance in Office.

This section describes the general structure of the federal judiciary: one supreme court that oversees the decisions of several lower courts, with the actual number of lower courts determined by Congress. Section 1 also stipulates that all federal judges possess life tenure, provided they serve during good behavior. Thus, federal judges can be removed from office only by IMPEACHMENT, which is spelled out in ARTICLE II OF THE U.S. CONSTITUTION, Section 4. Additionally, federal judges shall receive monetary compensation for their work, and these salaries cannot be reduced while the judges remain in office. Taken together, these last two provisions (life tenure and no reduction in salary) are designed to provide federal judges with a certain degree of independence to insulate them from external political influences.

Section 2 describes the types of jurisdictions (in other words, legal authority) available to the federal courts and, in particular, the U.S. Supreme Court. It states that judicial authority shall extend to all cases, in law and equity, arising under the Constitution, the laws of the United States, and any obligations imposed by international treaties. Cases involving the "law" of the United States are relatively self-explanatory, since they occur most frequently and exemplify the typical court action. The term *law* essentially refers to a norm, rule, or regulation governing society that, if violated, is punishable by a recognized authority (such as the government). Cases arising under equity are similar with the primary exception pertaining to the type of legal remedy involved. In an equity suit, litigants can request judges to issue orders (writs) telling other individuals to perform a specific action or cease performing a specific action. Thus, suits of equity can be used to prevent a potential wrong from occurring, such as asking a judge to issue an INJUNCTION to stop the demolition of a house. In contrast, suits in law involve determining the appropriate remedy for events that have already occurred, such as suing for financial compensation after a house has been demolished.

Section 2 also describes the difference between ORIGINAL JURISDICTION and APPELLATE JURISDICTION and specifies which cases belong in which category (for the Supreme Court). *Original jurisdiction* refers to the legal authority to conduct a trial (that is, where the case is heard originally). In contrast, appellate jurisdiction refers to the legal authority to review a decision from a lower court (that is, to hear a case on appeal). Section 2 indicates that in cases affecting foreign officials (such as ambassadors or consuls) and suits between two or more states, to name just a few categories, the

Supreme Court will possess original jurisdiction. In all other instances, the Supreme Court will possess appellate jurisdiction. Though Congress possesses the authority to alter the Supreme Court's appellate jurisdiction through the passage of specific statutes, only a constitutional amendment can change the Supreme Court's original jurisdiction. This important distinction and clarification of law was handed down in the case *MARBURY V. MADISON*, 5 U.S. (1 Cranch) 137 (1803), by Chief Justice JOHN MARSHALL. At issue in this case was the nomination of William Marbury to a position as justice of the peace for the DISTRICT OF COLUMBIA.

According to the JUDICIARY ACT OF 1789, which helped establish the first lower federal courts, the Supreme Court was provided with the authority to issue writs of mandamus (an order directing the government to do something) to government officials under its original jurisdiction. In writing one of the most important and widely recognized opinions for the Supreme Court, *Marbury v. Madison*, Chief Justice Marshall stated that, since the original jurisdiction of the Supreme Court was specified in Article III of the Constitution, Congress could not alter this jurisdiction through the passage of an ordinary statute; rather, a constitutional amendment was required. In stipulating this provision, Marshall declared unconstitutional Section 13 of the Judiciary Act of 1789—the section including the writ of mandamus in the Court's original jurisdiction—and consequently established the power of JUDICIAL REVIEW.

While *Marbury* establishes relatively clear definitions for the Court's original jurisdiction, its appellate jurisdiction is somewhat less clear, in particular regarding the circumstances under which Congress may limit or remove appellate jurisdiction. Perhaps the leading decision outlining Congress's authority over the Supreme Court's jurisdiction is *EX PARTE MCCARDLE*, 74 U.S. (7 Wall.) 506 (1869). This case, arising in the aftermath of the U.S. Civil War, involved the arrest of McCardle for publishing libelous materials. McCardle filed a petition for HABEAS CORPUS to challenge his trial before a military commission. Fearing that the Supreme Court might declare the Reconstruction Acts unconstitutional, Congress revoked the Court's appellate jurisdiction—in a somewhat controversial manner—one year prior to McCardle's case reaching the justices.

Speaking on behalf of a unanimous Court, Chief Justice Salmon P. Chase stated that the justices "are not at liberty to inquire into the motives of the legislature. We can only examine into its power under the Constitution; and the power to make exceptions to the appellate jurisdiction of this Court is given by express words." Yet, the Court acknowledged three years after *McCardle* that Congress's authority to make exceptions to its appellate jurisdiction was not without limits. In *United States v. Klein*, 80 U.S. (13 Wall.) 128 (1872), the Supreme Court countered an attempt by Congress to eliminate the president's authority to issue pardons. Since this authority is explicitly granted to the president by the Constitution, the justices stated that Congress's attempt to limit his jurisdiction was unconstitutional because it was a "means to an end" for an impermissible action.

Currently, several attempts exist in Congress to limit the appellate jurisdiction of the Supreme Court and the general jurisdiction of the lower courts. The Defense of Marriage Act (2004) contains language that states: "No court created by Congress shall have any jurisdiction, and the Supreme Court shall have no appellate jurisdiction, to hear or decide any question pertaining to the interpretation of [marriage]." Additionally, the HOUSE OF REPRESENTATIVES has passed legislation that includes language limiting the jurisdiction of federal courts in hearing cases involving the phrase *under God* in the Pledge of Allegiance, in response to the initiatives leading to the case *Elk Grove Unified School District v. Newdow*, 542 U.S. 1 (2004).

Also linked to this section of Article III are additional requirements that must be met before federal judges will hear cases. First, there must be an actual case or controversy. This means that courts will not decide cases in the abstract (and will not issue advisory opinions). Instead, a specific event or action is necessary that caused a particular injury (either in law or equity) to one of the litigants (parties to the case). Second, the case must be brought under the appropriate jurisdiction, either original or appellate. Third, the case must be appropriate for a judicial resolution (in other words, the case must be justiciable). Some issues are better left to the legislative or executive branches of government, and the judiciary is hesitant to issue decisions in cases that present a political question. If a court states that an issue presents a political question, it will dismiss a case and not rule on the merits of the dispute.

In the case *BAKER V. CARR*, 369 U.S. 186 (1962), Justice WILLIAM J. BRENNAN, JR., specifically identified examples of issues that present political questions: foreign affairs (reserved for the executive branch), the duration of hostilities (reserved for the legislative branch), validity of enactments (reserved for the legislative branch), status of American Indian tribes (reserved for the executive branch), and the appropriate form of government (reserved for the legislative and executive branches). Finally, the litigant bringing the dispute must be able to demonstrate legal STANDING. This is a requirement that the party must show the occurrence of a specific injury that is linked to the litigant being sued. If any of these requirements, called "threshold issues," are not met, then the case will be dismissed and the federal court will not rule on the merits of the dispute.

Article III also specifies several requirements for criminal trials: "The Trial of all Crimes, except in Cases of Impeachment, shall be by Jury; and such Trial shall be held in the State where said Crimes shall have been committed; but when not committed within any State, the Trial shall be at such Place or Places as the Congress may by Law have directed." This statement requires jury trials for all crimes except impeachment. Though the jury requirement is also listed in the SIXTH AMENDMENT, the framers of the Constitution felt so strongly about the RIGHT TO TRIAL BY JURY that they originally placed the requirement in Article III. This clause also stipulates that criminal trials will be held in the state where the offense occurred. Consequently, courts in Ohio, for example, cannot hold trials for crimes committed in Kentucky. However, if the criminal offense cannot be isolated to a particular state (such as smuggling drugs across multiple state lines), then Congress has the authority to stipulate where the trial will occur.

The final section of Article III—Section 3—specifies the requirements necessary to bring charges of TREASON against individuals. The framers of the Constitution were concerned that the charge of treason could be used to imprison political opponents, and they therefore provided a specific definition of treason and listed particular requirements that must be met in order to bring this charge.

For more information: Rakove, Jack N. *Original Meanings: Politics and Ideas in the Making of the Constitution.* New York: Knopf Publishing, 1997; Simon, James F. *What Kind of Nation: Thomas Jefferson, John Marshall, and the Epic Struggle to Create a United States.* New York: Simon and Schuster Adult Publishing, 2003.

—Kirk A. Randazzo

Ashcroft v. ACLU 542 U.S. 656 (2004)

Ashcroft v. ACLU was the last in a series of cases seeking to protect children from OBSCENITY on the Internet. The decision blocked enforcement of the Child Online Protection Act (COPA), 47 U.S.C. Section 231 (1998).

The development of the Internet permitted information and pictures to be published on any computer anywhere in the world and made available to anyone. Pornographers quickly established themselves as a major presence on the Internet, making obscenity available to unsupervised children. Congress, in response, adopted the COMMUNICATIONS DECENCY ACT (CDA) of 1996, which was signed by President Bill Clinton. CDA made the "knowing" transmission of "obscene or indecent" messages to any recipient under 18 years of age a felony with fines and/or a prison sentence. The CDA provided that access for adults could be allowed by several mechanisms including the use of a credit card as adult identification. Attorney General Janet Reno was enjoined, however, from enforcing the act in *Reno v. ACLU,* 521 U.S. 844 (1997), which became known as *Reno I.*

In response, Congress passed COPA the following year, which was signed by President Clinton. Again the law was challenged by the AMERICAN CIVIL LIBERTIES UNION (ACLU) and others. A case was begun in Philadelphia that led to a federal district judge declaring COPA unconstitutional. On appeal, the U.S. Court of Appeals for the Third Circuit also declared COPA unconstitutional, but on different grounds. The Supreme Court issued its opinion in 2002 by which time *Reno II* had been renamed *Ashcroft v. ACLU,* or *Ashcroft I,* for the new attorney general, John Ashcroft. Supporting the government's case were conservative groups such as the Center for Law and Justice.

The Supreme Court returned *Ashcroft I* to the U.S. court of appeals for further decisions in light of several issues. Among these were the fact that the law was drawn close to the decision in *MILLER V. CALIFORNIA,* 413 U.S. 15 (1973), and other similar decisions. However, on remand, the court of appeals upheld the district court's INJUNCTION on the grounds that COPA was not tailored tightly enough to prevent adults from being denied access to lawful material, even if objectionable for children and for other reasons.

The case then returned to the Supreme Court, which issued its ruling on June 29, 2004. The Court held COPA to be unconstitutionally broad. The decision stressed the use of adult-controlled filters for blocking access to adult-content materials. The Court's position was that the least restrictive means of access were those needed, otherwise there might be a chilling effect upon freedom of speech on the Internet.

For more information: Drucker, Susan J. J. *Real Law @ Virtual Space: The Regulation of Cyberspace.* Cresskill: New Jersey Hampton Press, 2005; Thomas, Lisa M. *Children's Online Protection Act (Copa) and an Overview of Select Cases: The Over-Arching Issues You Need to Know.* Boston: Aspatore Books, 2006.

—Andrew J. Waskey

Ashwander v. Tennessee Valley Authority

297 U.S. 288 (1936)

In *Ashwander v. Tennessee Valley Authority,* the Supreme Court ruled that Congress had not exceeded its constitutional authority in establishing the Tennessee Valley Authority (TVA).

The TVA was initially a government-led corporation established to better the lives of the denizens of the Tennessee Valley, a region of rivers that flowed through the state of Tennessee. The original mission of the TVA was to aid in national defense, specifically through the production of munitions materials. Soon the TVA was simultaneously developing enough hydroelectric power to support the region while supplying the energy needed to perform the munitions production. In addition, the TVA and its presence provided control and navigational assistance to river traffickers as well as control and implementation of new engineering models to alleviate the dangerous yearly flooding that was plaguing the lower river plains.

The TVA entered into a contract with the Alabama Power Company for transmission lines from the area of the Wilson Dam—where the United States owned the underlying territory, substations, and auxiliary properties, some of which are the basis for the construction of the Wheeler Dam—and for the excess supply of power that the TVA had available. The Alabama Power Company, a privately owned public company, had its preferred stockholders bring suit on behalf of the overall shareholders against the TVA so as to block the TVA from acquiring a large portion of the Alabama Power Company's plant and equipment. The claim was that the actions entitled within the contract were injurious to the corporate interests of the company as a whole and should be annulled. The plant and equipment that was purchased would result in allowing the TVA to provide electricity to the region and to the private companies thereby creating a disadvantage for the privately held companies to compete against the larger and better-funded Tennessee Valley Authority.

Chief Justice Charles Evans Hughes, who delivered the opinion for the Court, offered that the rights observed and understood within the Constitution allowed for the Congress to alter the service offerings of the TVA irrespective of its original intentions and mission. Specifically, the Court ruled that the authority to sell the electricity produced by the dams was supported by Article IV, Section 3 of the Constitution. This clause of the Constitution gives Congress the power to dispose of property belonging to the United States.

For more information: *Does Congress Delegate Too Much Power to Agencies and What Should Be Done About It?* Washington, D.C.: U.S. Government Printing Office, 2001; Hargrove, Erwin C. *Prisoners of Myth: The Leadership of the Tennessee Valley Authority, 1933–1990.* Knoxville: University of Tennessee Press, 2001.

—Ernest Gomez

Atkins v. Virginia 536 U.S. 304 (2002)

In *Atkins v. Virginia,* the Supreme Court ruled that executing mentally retarded individuals violated the CRUEL AND UNUSUAL PUNISHMENT clause of the Eighth Amendment. *Atkins* thus reversed an earlier decision, *PENRY V. LYNAUGH,* 492 U.S. 302 (1989), which had permitted the execution of mentally retarded individuals.

At around midnight on August 16, 1996, Daryl Atkins and William Jones entered a convenience store, where, at gunpoint, they robbed, abducted, and murdered Eric Nesbit. For his part in the crime, the Virginia supreme court sentenced Atkins to death. The defense argued that because Atkins was mentally retarded, he could not receive the death penalty. The Virginia supreme court rejected this argument, consistent with a previous U.S. Supreme Court ruling in *Penry v. Lynaugh* that stated that the Eighth Amendment did not prohibit the execution of mentally retarded persons.

The U.S. Supreme Court granted certiorari in order to set the standard regarding mental disabilities and the death penalty. In a 6-3 decision based on the Eighth Amendment's prohibition against cruel and unusual punishment, the Court ruled against the use of the death penalty in cases involving mentally disabled individuals. The Court's ruling dealt with the "evolving standards of decency" approach to Eighth Amendment claims, proportionality, and changes in societal attitudes.

Historically, the Supreme Court has held that the Eighth Amendment requires that "punishment for a crime must be graduated and proportioned to the offense," referred to by the Court as the "proportionality precept." In recent years, the Court has employed three standards to determine if the punishment is proportionate, the first addressing "whether the mode of punishment was cruel or unusual when the BILL OF RIGHTS was adopted," the second addressing if the "evolving standards of decency that mark the progress of a maturing society have been violated," and the third addressing if the punishment is "excessive."

These "evolving standards" help to inform courts of a national consensus regarding the form of punishment and are arrived at through established objective measures. Simply, with time comes change, and in order for a principle rooted in a statute or constitution to be capable of wider application, it needs to be developed within a broad and nonconstrictive framework, otherwise "rights declared in words might be lost to reality," as stated in *Weems v. United States,* 217 U.S. 349 (1910). Evolving standards represent a resolution to the predicament of static definitions within the Eighth Amendment (as exemplified in *Trop v. Dulles,* 356 U.S. 86 [1958]).

In *Atkins,* the Supreme Court observed a historical trend in state legislation favoring the elimination of the death penalty as a punishment for offenders with mental disabilities. This trend began in 1986, with Georgia enacting a statute prohibiting the execution of such offenders. In the following years, 18 more states enacted legislation forbidding the execution of the mentally disabled. The Court did not, however, rely on the "raw numbers" as the significant factor in their ruling; rather, they justified their decision by reasoning that the "consistency and direction of change" was the most significant factor in gauging a national consensus.

For more information: Church, Lori M. "Mandating Dignity: The United States Supreme Court's Extreme Departure from Precedent Regarding the Eighth Amendment and the Death Penalty [*Atkins v. Virginia,* 122 S. CT. 2242 (2002)]." *Washburn Law Journal* 42, no. 305 (2003): 1–24; Hall, Joanna. "*Atkins v. Virginia*: National Consensus or Six-Person Opinion?" *American University Journal of Gender, Social Policy and the Law* 12, no. 361 (2004): 1–26.

—Peter A. Collins

attorney advertising

Interpreting the FIRST AMENDMENT and generally following the path of increasing protection for "COMMERCIAL SPEECH" as a whole, the Supreme Court has protected much advertising by attorneys as essential freedom of speech. But that protection is not absolute, and in recent years the Supreme Court has refused to give complete protection to lawyers seeking clients through solicitation and targeted advertising.

Prior to the 1970s, the Supreme Court gave less protection to commercial speech than political speech and other forms of expression, leaving attorney advertising open to virtually any restrictions imposed by state bar associations. State bar associations, which operate under the authority of state governments, have long argued that advertising—especially that conducted by "ambulance chasers" acting for individual plaintiffs and criminal defense lawyers—is unprofessional, unseemly, and demeaning to the judicial system. Bar associations have also argued that advertising can be misleading, can "stir up" litigation, and can lead to unhealthy competition among lawyers that ultimately hurts clients.

The landmark decision in this area is *Bates v. State Bar of Arizona,* 430 U.S. 350 (1977). Coming one year after *VIRGINIA STATE BOARD OF PHARMACY V. VIRGINIA CITIZENS CONSUMER COUNCIL,* 425 U.S. 748 (1976), in which the Court defended the right of pharmacists to advertise the prices of prescription drugs, *Bates* involved a challenge to a blanket ban on advertising by lawyers of their prices for routine services. The Supreme Court's 5-4 decision held that the bar's concerns were not sufficient to justify a total ban on lawyers' ads, especially those that were not fraudulent, deceptive, or misleading.

For the next 20 years, the Supreme Court further protected attorneys' ads in a variety of cases, extending the protection to various media, including targeted print advertisements. These decisions have had a significant effect on lawyer advertising in the United States, which now can be found on television, in print, and on billboards.

A unanimous Court did allow a ban on the personal solicitation of potential clients in a case concerning an attorney who visited an automobile accident victim who was still in the hospital (*Ohralik v. Ohio State Bar Association,* 436 U.S. 447 [1978]). Yet, the boundary between protected speech and regulable solicitation remains unclear. While the Court has given some protection to direct-mail solicitation of clients (*Shapero v. Kentucky Bar Association,* 486 U.S. 466), in the 1995 case of *Florida Bar v. Went For It, Inc.,* 515 U.S. 618, the Supreme Court allowed a ban on direct-mail solicitations to accident victims within 30 days of their accidents. Now with the advent of Internet and e-mail advertising, states continue to test the boundaries that the Court will set on regulations.

A number of the justices of the Supreme Court, themselves elite members of the legal profession, have echoed the bar's concern with the special ethical role required by attorneys, making the attorney advertising a unique, distinctive area of commercial speech.

For more information: American Bar Association. *Lawyer Advertising at the Crossroads: Professional Policy Considerations.* Chicago: American Bar Association, Commission on Advertising, 1995.

—Patrick Schmidt

Avery v. Midland County 390 U.S. 474 (1968)

In *Avery v. Midland County,* the Supreme Court ruled that the principle of ONE PERSON, ONE VOTE applied to the apportionment of local governments. This ruling extended the principle of equal voting rights first articulated in *REYNOLDS V. SIMS,* 377 U.S. 533 (1964).

When it comes to representation, especially equal representation, how much representation is enough? How do we measure the equality of representation? The Court addressed these important questions in the 1960s. In the case *Reynolds v. Sims,* the Court ruled that apportionment is based on the logic of "one person, one vote." This ruling implied that congressional districts must be equal in population based on the most recent census. This is in line with Article I, Section 2, of the U.S. Constitution.

The Texas Constitution, Article V, Section 18, mandates that Texas counties be divided into four commissioner precincts (four county commissioners), with a county judge serving as the presiding officer. In *Avery v. Midland County,* allegedly one district of Midland County had a population of 67,906, while the other three had populations of 852; 414; and 828. The petitioner in this case alleged that the population disparity of the four precincts violated the EQUAL PROTECTION clause of the FOURTEENTH AMENDMENT. The Supreme Court ruled: "That the state legislature may itself be properly apportioned does not exempt subdivisions from the Fourteenth Amendment." In addition, the Court noted:

> While state legislatures exercise extensive power over their constituents and over the various units of local government, the States universally leave much policy and decisionmaking to their governmental subdivisions. . . . What is more, in providing for the governments of their cities, counties, towns, and districts, the States characteristically provide for representative government—for decisionmaking at the local level by representatives elected by the people.

Based on the concept that a state's governmental subdivisions are representative in nature, the Court concluded: "We therefore, see little difference, in terms of the application of the Equal Protection Clause and the principles of *Reynolds v. Sims* between the exercise of state power through legislatures and its exercise by elected officials in cities, towns, and counties."

Midland County, by this ruling, was denying equal protection by not affording the voters of Midland County equal representation. In other words, subdivisions of a state's government are also susceptible to the provisions of the Fourteenth Amendment, and even if the counties have large administrative and judicial roles, they also have a role as a judicial body as well as a legislative body, and as such, each county commissioner needs to be representative of the people. Therefore, a county must follow the adage of "one person, one vote" as espoused in *Reynolds v. Sims*: The apportionment of Midland County's precincts must have equal populations.

For more information: Hasen, Richard. *The Supreme Court and Election Law: Judging Equality from* Baker v. Carr *to* Bush v. Gore. New York: New York University Press, 2003.

—Dan Krejci

B

bail

Bail refers to a process through which an individual who is arrested and awaiting trial may be released if he or she or someone else provides an amount of money meant to guarantee that the charged person will show up for trial. While the Eighth Amendment to the Constitution does not mandate a right to bail, it contains a prohibition against excessive bail.

The legal connotation for the word *bail* is "one who holds something or someone for another" (Goldfarb). The etymology of the word reaches back to the Old French word *baille,* which means to "deliver." A modern definition, according to Goldfarb, is a "means or a process of getting out." The bail system allows individuals accused of criminal offenses to be released prior to their court appearances. Bail is set in an amount deemed by the court to be sufficient to deter flight and enforce compliance with the court's orders.

The roots of the American bail system can be traced to English law. One theory proposes that *bail* derives its meaning from the ancient English institution of "hostageship," which was developed in England by Germanic Angles and Saxons. Used as a war tactic, the hostage was held until the promise of a certain person was fulfilled or a certain consequence achieved. Another theory suggests that modern bail comes from old English laws governing debt, or the primitive concept of *wergeld.* Under this scheme, the one accused of committing a wrong had to guarantee a payment to reimburse that wrong, should he or she later be found at fault.

During the years 1000 to 1300, these customs and procedures gradually developed into a more formal, institutionalized system. In 1275, the Statute Westminster I was passed, under which, for the first time, bail practices were made a matter of specific articulated law. In 1689, the ENGLISH BILL OF RIGHTS included a provision that forbade excessive bail. The U.S. Constitution, while not guaranteeing bail, contains a similar provision in its Eighth Amendment, which states "Excessive bail shall not be required."

The American system has developed into several different types of bail. Fully secured bail most resembles the original common law system. This procedure requires the defendant to deposit with the court the full bond amount or collateral worth the full bond amount. Once the amount has been met, the defendant is freed from custody.

Because many defendants lack the necessary funds to post bond, alternative bail systems have been developed. The most common of these is privately secured bail, in which a defendant hires a bail bondsman to post the full amount for a fee, usually 10 percent. Most bondsmen require collateral in addition to their fee before agreeing to post the bond. If the bailee appears for trial, the bond is returned.

Another type of bail is percentage bail, in which defendants post a percentage, typically 10 percent, of the total bail bond amount. This amount is returned in full if the defendant returns for trial. Those who fail to appear lose their deposits and are liable for the remainder of the bond.

The fourth type of bail is unsecured bail, which does not require defendants to post any money or collateral in order to be released from custody but still holds them responsible for the full amount set by the judge. Defendants charged with minor offenses are released on their own recognizance (ROR) rather than being required to post a bond. These defendants promise to return to court for trial; however, if they fail to appear, a warrant for their arrest may be issued.

Some defendants are put on conditional release, meaning that they must agree to abide by certain restrictions before they are allowed to post bond. Typical conditions include submitting to random drug testing and/or participating in a substance abuse or other treatment program. Finally, some defendants are released into third-party custody. A third party, typically a family member or friend, agrees to ensure that the accused will appear for trial.

Widespread criticism for the system arose when it became evident that judges had broad discretion in setting bail. Decisions were supposed to be based on criminal characteristics, such as seriousness of the crime committed and prior appearances history; however, racial groups and male offenders became targets for high bail. Because wealthy defendants are better positioned to post bail or provide collateral, the American bail system has been criticized as being biased against the poor. Additionally, the bail system has been criticized for the practice of preventive detention, which uses exorbitant bail to keep accused offenders from committing crimes while awaiting trial.

The Bail Reform Act of 1966 was an attempt to limit judicial discretion and remove discrimination from the bail process. The issue of preventive detention was addressed in the Bail Reform Act of 1984. This act gave judges the power to assess defendants on their level of dangerousness to the community if released, and it gave judges the legal right to use preventive detention. This reform act permitted judges to deny bail to those offenders who were judged to be at extremely high risk for nonappearance.

The Bail Reform Act of 1984 was challenged in *United States v. Salerno,* 481 U.S. 739 (1987), where opponents argued that the idea of preventive detention or the incarcerating of alleged offenders violates their right to DUE PROCESS of law. They argued that preventive detention violates the PRESUMPTION OF INNOCENCE to which every arrestee is entitled. The Supreme Court upheld the judicial right to preventive detention as long as judges have convincing evidence that the offender is likely to commit a crime while awaiting trail.

For more information: "Bail Reform Act." *St. John's Law Review* (2002): 492–493; Carr, James G. "Bail Bondsmen and the Federal Courts." *Federal Probation* (1993): 9–16; Goldfarb, Ronald. *Ransom: A Critique of the American Bail System.* New York: Harper & Row, 1965; "Preventive Detention Before Bail." *Harvard Law Review* (1966): 1,489–1,510.

—Sharon L. Morrison

Bailey v. Drexel Furniture Company 259 U.S. 20 (1922)

In *Bailey v. Drexel Furniture Company,* the U.S. Supreme Court held that Congress could not use its power of taxation as a means to regulate activities within the purview of state governments. In striking down a congressional attempt to regulate CHILD LABOR, the Court's *Bailey* decision added to a line of early 20th-century Supreme Court cases that limited the power of Congress to regulate the activities of business.

Shortly after the Supreme Court struck down the first congressional attempt to regulate child labor in *HAMMER V. DAGENHART,* 247 U.S. 251 (1918), Congress passed the Child Labor Tax Law. This statute imposed an excise tax of 10 percent of the yearly net profits on any business that employed children within certain age limits at any point during the tax year.

One of the businesses affected by this statute, the Drexel Furniture Company, was assessed taxes in excess of $6,000 by the Bureau of Internal Revenue for employing a boy under the age of 14. After paying the tax under protest and having its claim for a refund rejected, the company brought suit in the U.S. District Court for the Western District of North Carolina. It its suit, the company argued that the statute was designed solely to punish businesses for using child labor. The government, in contrast, argued that the statute was an excise tax legitimately within the taxation power of Congress and supported by Supreme Court precedent. The district court ruled in favor of Drexel, holding the tax to be invalid.

Writing for an 8-1 majority (Justice John Hessin Clarke dissenting), Chief Justice William Howard

Taft affirmed the decision of the lower court. In his opinion, Chief Justice Taft argued that the statute in question was clearly an attempt to penalize the use of child labor, a regulatory function that is within POLICE POWER reserved for the states under the Tenth Amendment. Taft went further to equate this case with *Hammer v. Dagenhart* in that both cases represented congressional attempts to use legitimate constitutional powers outside their proper scope to regulate activity under state authority.

Chief Justice Taft also addressed the claim that precedent mandated upholding the tax even if it had purposes other than raising revenue. Taft distinguished this case from previous cases, noting that this tax was not on any specific item but punishment for deviating from a specific "course of business." While acknowledging that a statute could be valid even with motives other than taxation, Taft cautioned that this still required that the law be designed for the purpose of collecting taxes and "not solely to the achievement of some other purpose."

The greatest impact of the *Bailey* decision was its success in delaying regulation of child labor in the United States for nearly 20 years. After an unsuccessful attempt to pass a constitutional amendment, it was not until 1938 that Congress was able to successfully regulate child labor with the passage of the Fair Labor Standards Act. The *Bailey* decision also stands as a significant deviation from previous Supreme Court rulings on congressional tax power.

For more information: Hall, Kermit L. *The Magic Mirror: Law in American History*. Oxford: Oxford University Press, 1989; Wood, Steven B. *Constitutional Politics in the Progressive Era: Child Labor and the Law*. Chicago: University of Chicago Press, 1968.

—Michael P. Fix

Baker v. Carr 369 U.S. 186 (1962)

Baker v. Carr is a landmark in the history of voting rights in which the Supreme Court ruled that reapportionment cases could be heard by the federal courts. This case opened the door for future litigation on voting rights, especially state legislative district apportionment. The decision allowed the Court to later consider the particulars of legislative districts and to offer to disenfranchised citizens the hope of a judicial solution to problems that defied political remedy.

The case originated in Tennessee, which had seen significant migration of its citizens from rural to urban areas in the 20th century. Despite several attempts to redistrict, no alteration of the electoral map had managed to make it through the state legislature. In 1961, the state of Tennessee had the same electoral district boundaries that it had drawn in 1901.

This created a large disparity in the power of individual citizens in state elections. Urban areas contained far more voters in 1961 than in 1901 but elected no additional representatives. In effect, an individual voter in a rural area exercised about 19 times as much influence in the election of a state representative as did his or her urban counterpart.

Charles Baker and residents from cities including Memphis, Knoxville, and Nashville sued the secretary of state, Joseph Carr. Baker alleged that the failure to redraw legislative districts denied him his FOURTEENTH AMENDMENT rights to EQUAL PROTECTION of the laws. He asked a federal district court to order an at-large election for state representatives or to order that the state redistrict based on the 1960 census.

The district court agreed that Baker's rights were being denied but, believing that it could provide no relief, dismissed the case. The court was bound by the decision in *Colgrove v. Green*, 382 U.S. 549 (1946), which stated that apportionment questions were "political questions" and therefore not justiciable. The obvious problem for citizens was that the political process would not deal with the issue, which is exactly why Baker turned to the courts.

The Supreme Court agreed to hear an appeal and faced two contentious questions. The first was whether questions of redistricting in states were truly political and nonjusticiable. The second spoke to the merits of individual plans for apportionment and equal representation within states.

The case was held over for a year as the Court struggled with the issues raised. Two possible answers emerged. The first, championed by Justices Felix Frankfurter, JOHN HARLAN, Tom C. Clark, and Charles Evans Whittaker, held to the *Colgrove* position that the Court should avoid "this political thicket." Progressive justices Earl Warren, HUGO BLACK, WILLIAM O. DOUGLAS, and WILLIAM J. BRENNAN, JR., believed that the issues ought to be decided. The ninth justice, Potter Stewart, believed that the issue was justiciable but in extending its jurisdiction, the Court should not address the question of specifics. The position of Justice Stewart ultimately became the opinion of the Court.

The most significant effects of this case were felt in the federal suits begun in two-thirds of the states over apportionment and in subsequent cases such as *REYNOLDS V. SIMS*, 377 U.S. 533 (1964). This case resulted in 20 states reapportioning or putting reapportionment plans on ballots by 1962. Many states in the South continued to resist redistricting, and a three-judge federal panel stepped in to redistrict Alabama after it failed to change its 60-year-old districts. In the state of Georgia, after redistricting, an African-American legislator was elected, the first time since Reconstruction.

The majority opinion in *Baker v. Carr* was limited to the questions of jurisdiction and did not reach the specifics of Tennessee's districts, requiring only that districts within states be "fair." The case's importance, however, stretches far beyond Tennessee and Baker's position. By redefining what types of cases could be brought to the Court and what constitutes a "political question," the Supreme Court indicated how far it was willing to go to protect individual rights, particularly in matters related to the ballot box.

For more information: Hasen, Richard. *The Supreme Court and Election Law: Judging Equality from* Baker v. Carr *to* Bush v. Gore. New York: New York University Press, 2003; Mann, Thomas E., and Bruce E. Cain, eds. *Party Lines: Competition, Partisanship, and Congressional Redistricting.* Washington, D.C.: Brookings Institution Press, 2005.

—David A. May

balanced budget amendment

The balanced budget amendment (BBA) was a proposed amendment to the Constitution that would have required that the president submit and the Congress pass a budget in which net revenues equal net expenditures, with different stipulations concerning when an unbalanced budget may be passed or how and when a budget may become unbalanced during a fiscal year. A BBA to the U.S. Constitution has never passed the Congress, but there have been many proposed by members of Congress since 1936, with the number increasing since 1980. Any amendment to the Constitution must pass both houses with a two-thirds vote before it is sent to the states for ratification. Three-fourths of the states must approve it.

A BBA is proposed by a member of Congress who believes that the legislature or the executive or both lack the political will to balance the budget. A sponsor, therefore, wishes to compel the branches by constitutional mandate to make the necessary but difficult decisions of reducing spending (shrinking or eliminating programs) or raising revenue (increasing taxes or eliminating tax expenditures, tax breaks for special interests).

Congress was first presented with a BBA by Republican representative Harold Knutson of Minnesota in 1936, but it died in the Judiciary Committee. Several BBAs were introduced in 1947, and though hearings were held and the amendments reported out of the SENATE Appropriations Committee, the amendments languished for lack of additional support. The first hearing in the Senate Judiciary Committee on a BBA took place in 1956, but the amendment was not voted on. It was not until 1980 that the Judiciary Committee voted on a BBA proposed by Senator Dennis DeConcini, a Democrat from Arizona, but it failed to pass. DeConcini's amendment required that the president submit a balanced budget and that the Congress adopt it each year, unless three-fifths of both houses voted to waive the requirement. A somewhat modified BBA did pass the Senate Judiciary Committee the next year that included, among other things, a waiver for a balanced budget in times of war. The amendment never went to the full Senate for debate.

A major advance for BBA proponents occurred in 1982 when the Republican senator of South Carolina Strom Thurmond's amendment passed in the Senate 69-31, but the House vote of 236-187 failed to attain the necessary two-thirds vote. A BBA was passed by the Senate Judiciary Committee in 1983, but it was not brought to the Senate floor. In 1985, the committee again passed the amendment but was rebuffed 66-34 in March 1986, one vote short of two-thirds.

By 1984, movement for a BBA at the state level found 32 states that had passed resolutions calling for a constitutional convention to debate a BBA, two shy of the required 34 states. Critics warned that, if convened, a constitutional convention could consider amendments other than a BBA, and interest in a convention dissipated. Three states—Alabama, Florida, and Louisiana—have rescinded their resolutions since 1990.

Beginning in 1990, Democratic representative Charles Stenholm of Texas and Democratic senator Paul Simon of Illinois worked to have a BBA passed in their respective houses. Stenholm's HJ Res. 268 had somewhat similar language to DeConcini's earlier proposal, but it could not muster the necessary 286 votes, failing 279-150. The Simon amendment survived the Senate Judiciary Committee but was not brought to the full Senate for a vote. Stenholm's BBA was considered again in 1992, but it failed again to receive the required two-thirds vote. In 1994, 26 BBAs were introduced. Simon joined with Orrin Hatch, a Republican from Utah, in proposing SJ Res. 41, but it too failed. Stenholm's HJ Res. 103 also was rejected, this time by 12 votes.

The odds for successfully passing a BBA in Congress improved markedly following the 1994 congressional elections in which the Republican Party gained control of Congress. As part of their successful campaign, Republicans, led by Georgia representative Newt Gingrich, promised in their platform, Contract with America, to pass a BBA. In 1995, Speaker Gingrich made the BBA the first order of business in the House. The amendment required that the president submit and Congress pass a balanced budget each fiscal year unless three-fifths of both houses voted to incur a deficit. The resolution also waived the balanced budget requirement whenever the United States was engaged in a declared war or there was an "imminent and serious threat to national security." To invoke the waiver, a joint resolution had to be passed by majority vote in both houses and be signed by the president. To increase the public debt or to raise taxes, the BBA required a three-fifths roll-call vote in both chambers. The BBA would have taken effect in fiscal year 2002 or the second fiscal year after it was ratified, whichever was later. Despite a relatively quick passage by a vote of 300-132 in the House on January 26, 1995, the resolution died in the Senate, 65-35, on March 2.

The Congress considered a BBA again in early 1997. While the House Judiciary Committee debated the measure, its counterpart in the Senate was defeated on the floor 65-35. Many of the provisions in this BBA were similar to the 1995 version, but there was greater concern for the treatment of the Social Security Trust Fund, which contributed to its defeat.

Republican representative Ernest Istook of Oklahoma sponsored a BBA in 2003 that appeared much like the 1995 and 1997 measures. The BBA was debated in the Judiciary Committee, but it was never brought up for a vote before the full committee. A very similar BBA was debated in the Judiciary Committee in 2004, but again, no vote was taken.

It appears likely, especially in light of the rising annual budget deficits and the dramatic increases in the national debt, that there will be future BBAs introduced and debated in Congress. The likelihood that any BBA will pass will remain a function of how dire the economic future appears for the United States and whether the BBA accommodates the concerns of lawmakers worried about financing entitlement programs such as Social Security and Medicare and tying the hands of the president or Congress should a national emergency arise that would necessitate deficit spending.

For more information: Savage, James D. *Balanced Budgets and American Politics.* Ithaca, N.Y.: Cornell University Press, 1988; Schier, Steve. "Deficits Without End: Fiscal Thinking and Budget Failure in Congress." *Political Science Quarterly* 107, no. 3 (1992): 411–433.

—Thomas J. Baldino

Barenblatt v. United States 360 U.S. 109 (1959)

In *Barenblatt v. United States,* the Supreme Court held that when national security is at stake, Congress possesses authority to compel relevant testimony of recalcitrant witnesses. A bare majority ruled that a witness could not withhold information about his or her previous ties to the Communist Party on grounds of the FIRST AMENDMENT.

Oversight is an important function of Congress, and from the earliest days of the republic, witnesses have been called to testify before congressional committees. However, the authority to compel witness testimony is not specifically mentioned in the Constitution. What happens when a person refuses to testify before a congressional committee on grounds that it may violate his or her First Amendment rights of expression and association?

In 1954, Lloyd Barenblatt, a psychology professor at Vassar College, was called before the House Un-American Activities Committee to answer questions concerning his alleged membership in the Communist Party. Barenblatt first objected to a line of questioning concerning his religious and political beliefs, then refused to answer questions about his personal "associational activities." The committee held Barenblatt in contempt. He was later tried, convicted, and sentenced to six months in jail and given a $250 fine. Barenblatt appealed, contending that the government's actions amounted to an unconstitutional BILL OF ATTAINDER and violated his First, Ninth, and Tenth Amendment rights. The federal court of appeals sustained the conviction, and the U.S. Supreme Court affirmed.

The central issue before the high court was "whether the Subcommittee's inquiry into petitioner's past or present membership in the Communist Party transgressed the provisions of the First Amendment, which of course reach and limit congressional investigations." Speaking for a narrow majority, Justice JOHN HARLAN first noted: "Where First Amendment rights are asserted to bar governmental interrogation, resolution of the issue always involves a balancing by the courts of the competing private and public interests at state in the particular circumstances shown." Harlan then noted that the Communist Party is no ordinary party in that it advocates the overthrow of the U.S. government. In striking a balance between Barenblatt's individual interests and the government's compelling interest in stopping communism, the scale "must be struck in favor of the latter, and that therefore the provisions of the First Amendment have not been offended." Joining Harlan in the majority were Justices Felix Frankfurter, Tom C. Clark, Charles Evans Whittaker, and Potter Stewart.

In a strongly worded dissent, Justice HUGO BLACK wrote: "Congress shall pass no law abridging freedom of speech, press, assembly and petition, unless Congress and the Supreme Court reach the joint conclusion that on balance the interests of the Government in stifling these freedoms is greater than the interest of the people having them exercised." Black then concluded: "Ultimately all the questions in this case really boil down to one—whether we as a people will try fearfully and futilely to preserve democracy by adopting totalitarian methods, or whether in accordance with our traditions and our Constitution we will have the confidence and courage to be free." Also in dissent were Justices WILLIAM O. DOUGLAS, WILLIAM J. BRENNAN, JR., and Chief Justice Earl Warren.

Barenblatt is one in a series of cases where the Supreme Court attempted to define the efficacy and limits of congressional hearings and witnesses' rights; for example, one can compare and contrast the Court's decisions in *McGrain v. Daugherty* (1927), *Watkins v. United States* (1957), and *Senate Select Committee on Ethics v. Packwood* (1994).

For more information: Aberbach, Joel D. *Keeping a Watchful Eye: The Politics of Congressional Oversight.* Washington, D.C.: Brookings Institution Press, 1990; Devins, Neal, and Keith E. Whittington, eds. *Congress and the Constitution.* Durham, N.C.: Duke University Press, 2005.

—Richard J. Hardy

Barron v. Mayor and City Council of Baltimore 7 Pet (32 U.S.) 243, 8 L.Ed. 672 (1833)

In *Barron v. Mayor and City Council of Baltimore,* the Supreme Court ruled that the BILL OF RIGHTS applies only to the federal government and not to the governments of the states. In his opinion, Chief Justice JOHN MARSHALL stated that the question was "not of much difficulty," but future amendments to the Constitution, most notably the DUE PROCESS clause of the FOURTEENTH AMENDMENT, have made the issue much more complex.

The plaintiff in this case, John Barron, was the part-owner of a profitable wharf in Baltimore harbor. Between 1815 and 1821, the city of Baltimore passed a series of ordinances aimed at making the parts of the city near the wharf more suitable for development. Included in these plans was the rerouting of certain streams in the area. Just as soon as the changes were made, earth and sand began to build up where the streams met the harbor, causing the water near the plaintiff's wharf to become increasingly shallow. By 1822, the water had become so shallow that the land was no longer usable as a wharf.

The plaintiff brought suit on behalf of himself and his partner John Craig, who was deceased by the time the final opinion was written, for damages resulting from the city's actions. The plaintiff claimed that the city owed him compensation under the TAKINGS CLAUSE of the Fifth Amendment.

The trial court ruled in favor of Barron and awarded him $4,500. The appellate court reversed the judgment and finalized it in favor of the city without remand. Barron appealed to the Supreme Court.

Ultimately, the Supreme Court dismissed the case for lack of jurisdiction. Chief Justice Marshall, writing on behalf of a unanimous Court, ruled that the Bill of Rights applied only to the national government and could not be used against the city of Baltimore. He reasoned that the primary purpose of the framers in drafting the Bill of Rights was to protect the public from unwarranted intrusion by the federal government. He also noted that if the framers of the Bill of Rights had intended for the Fifth Amendment to apply to the states, they would have explicitly stated so, just as the original framers did when drafting Section 10 of ARTICLE I OF THE U.S. CONSTITUTION.

Today, this case would most likely yield a different result. After the Civil War, Congress passed a series of amendments aimed at protecting individuals, especially newly freed blacks, from state governments. Relying on the due process clause of the FOURTEENTH AMENDMENT, the Supreme Court incorporated most of the Bill of Rights, to the governments of the states. The most notable exception is the Second Amendment, which has not been incorporated.

For more information: Langran, Robert W. *The Supreme Court: A Concise History.* New York: Peter Lang, 2004; Smith, Jean Edward. *John Marshall: Definer of a Nation.* New York: Henry Holt & Co., 1996.

—Dylan R. Kytola

Batson v. Kentucky 476 U.S. 79 (1986)

In *Batson v. Kentucky,* the U.S. Supreme Court ruled that excluding jurors on account of their race is unconstitutional and violates a criminal defendant's right to EQUAL PROTECTION.

On one occasion, after a judge at the trial court level had questioned the jurors and excused several for cause, the state used its PEREMPTORY CHALLENGES to remove four African Americans from the jury. Defendant James Kirkland Batson was an African American charged with second-degree burglary and receipt of stolen goods. The state's four challenges resulted in an entirely white jury. Batson's attorney moved to have a new jury for SIXTH AMENDMENT (right to a fair trial) and FOURTEENTH AMENDMENT (right to equal protection) reasons. His motion was denied on the grounds that only the venire need be racially diverse and that peremptory strikes may be used however the parties wish. Batson was convicted on both charges. He appealed to the Kentucky Supreme Court, which affirmed the conviction.

Upon appeal to the U.S. Supreme Court, the decision was reversed and remanded. Justice LEWIS FRANKLIN POWELL, JR., delivered the opinion of the Court. He largely relied on equal protection grounds. Two earlier cases were especially significant. *Strauder v. West Virginia,* 100 U.S. 303 (1880), held that a person does not have a fair trial when he or she must go before a jury from which his or her own race was purposefully excluded. *Swain v. Alabama,* 380 U.S. 202 (1965), stated that African Americans could not be denied participation on juries. *Swain* was upheld as to that part. The high court, however, reduced the defendant's burden of proof as to the wrongful actions of the state, as it had been too high in the *Swain* decision. *Swain* had required that the defendant show a pattern by the state over more than just the case at hand, which was declared inconsistent with equal protection in *Batson.* Now a prima facie case could be shown for discrimination based solely on the defendant's own trial.

Justice Powell further decided that equal protection principles apply to the venire as well. The defendant is not entitled, however, to any certain number (or even any) jurors of his own race on the jury.

As noted, the burden of proof is initially on the defendant to show a prima facie case of discrimination. At this point, the burden shifts to the state to explain that its peremptory challenges all had a race-neutral purpose.

Justice Powell was joined by Justices WILLIAM J. BRENNAN, JR., Byron Raymond White, Thurgood Marshall, Harry Andrew Blackmun, JOHN PAUL STEVENS, and SANDRA DAY O'CONNOR. Justices White and Marshall wrote concurring opinions. Of particular interest was Justice Marshall's opinion. He stated that the only way to truly eliminate racial discrimination from jury selection would be to eliminate peremptory challenges entirely. Chief Justice WARREN EARL BURGER and Justice WILLIAM HUBBS REHNQUIST dissented. Among other reasons, the dissent was based on the feeling that peremptory challenges would be too restricted by this ruling.

Of note, the term *Batson challenge* or *Batson motion* has entered the trial lawyer's lexicon as a result of this case. It is typically shorthand for when the lawyer is raising the issue of his or her client's right to a jury from which people of his or her own race have been improperly removed through peremptory challenges, though it can be in reference to the jury venire as well.

Cases have emerged from related issues. Among others, *Edmonson v. Leesville Concrete Co.,* 500 U.S. 614 (1991), applied *Batson* to juries in civil trials, and *J.E.B.* v. ALABAMA, 511 U.S. 127 (1994), applied *Batson* to gender.

For more information: Mauet, Thomas A. *Trial Techniques.* 4th ed. Frederick, Md.: Aspen Publishing, 1996.

—Maria Collins Warren

Beard, Charles Austin (1874–1948) *scholar*
Charles Austin Beard was an influential historian and scholar who wrote numerous books in the early half of the 20th century. His most important book is *An Economic Interpretation of the Constitution of the United States,* which argued that the Constitution was an antidemocratic document meant to protect the economic interests of the wealthy, including those who wrote and signed it.

Much of Beard's research examined the disciplines of American history, government and politics, and economics. Beard contended that economic factors had previously been ignored in historical studies and instead offered his cross-disciplinary approach as an alternative to the mainstream historical methods of the era. Deemed radical at the time, Beard's pinnacle work, *An Economic Interpretation of the Constitution of the United States,* was published in 1913. In it, Beard critiqued three schools of interpretation that had dominated historical research. The first school was associated with the name Bancroft and advanced an interpretation of history that viewed humankind as being driven by a higher will, suggesting a morality guided by providence.

The second school of historical interpretation referenced by Beard and that followed Bancroft was termed *Teutonic.* This school was derived from the political talents and genius of the Teutonic tribes who invaded England and destroyed the older Roman and British cultures. Their example of free government became a model for the world, and Teutonic knowledge has served as a foundation for the creation of the federal constitution. The third school was not characterized by a unique phrase or title and lacked a central hypothesis. This school was narrowly empirical and turned away from historical interpretation to critical analysis of documents and facts.

Beard's critique of these classical interpretations of history proved influential in the development of his own interpretations and his decision to ally himself instead to some degree with the Turner school (named for Frederick Jackson Turner), given its affinity for economic interpretation. Beard's *Economic Interpretation of the Constitution of the United States* examined numerous historical documents, including unpublished records from the U.S. Department of the Treasury and records from the debates at the CONSTITUTIONAL CONVENTION. An investigation of these sources and the documented observations of ALEXANDER HAMILTON led Beard to conclude that the convention was composed of five distinct upper-class groups. In his own words, Beard argued that "the overwhelming majority of members, at least five-sixths, were immediately, directly, and personally interested in the outcome of their labors at Philadelphia, and were to a greater or less extent economic beneficiaries from the adoption of the Constitution" (149). Each group represented a different economic interest in society.

The first group was composed of public security interests such as creditors, financiers, bankers, and moneylenders. Beard was able to identify at least 40 of the 55 delegates at the convention as falling in this category. A second category of economic interests was represented by merchants and manufacturers and those in shipping lines. This grouping consisted of 11 of the 55 delegates at the convention, who were ultimately influential in designing Article I, Section 9, of the U.S. Constitution dealing with the INTERSTATE COMMERCE clause. This clause centralized control of commerce at the national level and prevented state tariffs on imports. The third category identified by Beard consisted of bankers, debtors, and investors. Of the delegates there were 24 who fell in this group and represented economic interests in areas of business law and contracts. This interest influenced the design of Congress's powers to formulate bankruptcy laws, coin money, and regulate some of the more financially driven elements of the new nation.

A fourth category of convention delegates was composed of western land speculators and promoters, men like George Washington, BENJAMIN FRANKLIN, Robert Morris, James Wilson, William Blount, and others of wealth who had purchased large parcels of land. This group included 14 of the 55 delegates and was influential in bolstering the constitutional powers of the chief executive and U.S. militia to fight American Indian tribes who populated western territories. The final category was composed of slaveowners. Beard's research identified 15 of the 55 delegates in this category, which mainly consisted of southern slave owners who were influential in propagating slavery until ratification of the THIRTEENTH AMENDMENT. In all, Beard argued that the gathering of interest-driven delegates who convened to draft the U.S. Constitution was composed of practical men who "were able to build the new government upon the only foundations which could be stable: fundamental economic interests" (151).

Beard's categorical typology has served as a reference for historians, political scientists, and economists. While he places many of the 55 delegates into one or more of the five categories, the typology still provides an idea for what motivated the delegates and how the U.S. Constitution may have consequently been designed to consider such economic interests. Beard was a champion of the progressive school of history, writing during an era of tremendous economic growth and industrial development. His unorthodox economic interpretations of key historical eras and political events questioned traditional modes of writing and have in turn been challenged by numerous academicians over time, such as Edward S. Corwin, Robert Brown, and Richard Hofstadter. Beard himself acknowledged that his research was fragmentary in nature but contended that it was "designed to suggest new lines of historical research rather than to treat the subject in an exhaustive fashion" (v). Even so, his historical interpretation that the Constitution was an economic document has survived criticism and has earned a place in the literature as an interesting, if not unorthodox, perspective on the Founding Fathers.

For more information: Beale, Howard K., ed. *Charles Beard: An Appraisal.* New York: Octagon Books, 1976; Beard, Charles. *An Economic Interpretation of the Constitution of the United States.* New York: Macmillan, 1925; Benson, Lee. *Turner and Beard: American Historical Writing Reconsidered.* New York: Free Press, 1960; Brown, Robert E. *Charles Beard and the Constitution: A Critical Analysis of "An Economic Interpretation of the Constitution."* Princeton, N.J.: Princeton University Press, 1965; Hofstadter, Richard. *The Progressive Historians: Turner, Beard, Parrington.* New York: Alfred A. Knopf, 1968.

—Daniel Baracskay

Beauharnais v. Illinois 343 U.S. 250 (1952)

In *Beauharnais v. Illinois,* the U.S. Supreme Court upheld an Illinois group libel statute by a 5-4 vote, ruling that it did not violate the FIRST AMENDMENT. While *Beauharnais* has never been explicitly overruled, many legal scholars question whether it is still good law.

Joseph Beauharnais, president of the White Circle League, distributed a leaflet, set forth as a petition of grievances, that called on Chicago's mayor and city council "to halt . . . the further encroachment . . . [of] white people . . . by the Negro." The leaflet added that if "persuasion" would not unite the white race, "the aggressions . . . rapes, robberies, knives, gins and marijuana of the negro . . . surely will."

Beauharnais was convicted under an Illinois statute banning public distribution of materials portraying "depravity, criminality, unchastity or lack of virtue of a class of citizens" on the basis of "race, color, creed, or religion" when it exposes the group in question to "contempt, derision or obloquy" or causes a "breach of the peace or riots." Although Beauharnais offered to present evidence that statements in the pamphlet were true, the trial judge restricted the jury to the issue of whether Beauharnais published the pamphlet. The Illinois Supreme Court affirmed the conviction.

U.S. Supreme Court justice Felix Frankfurter, affirming the Illinois Supreme Court, relied on *CHAPLINSKY V. NEW HAMPSHIRE,* 315 U.S. 568 (1942), which held that certain types of speech—including libel—fell outside the First Amendment. He buttressed this point by noting that in 1952 most states punished criminal libel by common law or statute. He then discussed the history of race relations in Illinois, a history that could have led the state to conclude that conveying falsehood about "racial and religious groups" tends to "obstruct the manifold adjustments required for free, ordered life in a polyglot community." Therefore, the Illinois legislature was not "without reason" in trying to curb "false and malicious DEFAMATION of racial and religious groups," especially given the "powerful emotional impact" on those exposed to it. While Justice Frankfurter admitted the Illinois statute could be used in a discriminatory manner, he would not strike it down based on the mere possibility of abuse.

There were four dissents. Justice HUGO BLACK, laying great emphasis on the RIGHT TO PETITION THE GOVERNMENT, accused the Court of wanting to "degrade First Amendment freedoms to a rational basis level." He also worried that the statute could be used against proponents of racial integration, a concern shared by Justice WILLIAM O. DOUGLAS in his dissent. The remaining dissents were narrower. Justice Stanley Reed, conceding that Illinois could ban group libel, argued that terms such as *virtue* made the Illinois law unconstitutionally vague. Finally, Justice Robert Jackson argued that the states had great leeway in punishing speech but faulted the Illinois statute because it did not let the accused present the defense of truth to the jury.

Beauharnais has not aged well. In 1961, Illinois removed the group libel statute. Three years later, in NEW YORK TIMES V. SULLIVAN, 376 U.S. 254 (1964), the Court outlawed criminal libel, weakening one of the mainstays of Justice Frankfurter's argument. Later, in *Collin v. Smith,* 578 F.2d 1197 (7th Cir. 1978), the case growing out of the Skokie affair, the Seventh Circuit questioned whether *Beauharnais* remains good law. Interestingly, *Beauharnais* has fared better outside the United States, where foreign courts use it as an example of a constitutionally valid HATE SPEECH law.

For more information: Kalven, Harry, Jr. *The Negro and the First Amendment.* Chicago: University of Chicago Press, 1965; Walker, Samuel. *Hate Speech: The History of an American Controversy.* Lincoln: University of Nebraska Press, 1994.

—Robert A. Kahn

Betts v. Brady 316 U.S. 455 (1942)

In *Betts v. Brady,* the Supreme Court ruled that an individual facing criminal charges in state court was not entitled to a attorney provided by the government if he or she could not afford one of his own.

Betts, an unemployed farmhand on welfare and with little formal education, was charged with robbery in Maryland. As he could not afford to hire a defense lawyer, he asked the court to appoint one. When his request was denied, Betts pleaded not guilty and attempted to conduct his own defense in a bench trial. He questioned the state's witnesses and called his own witnesses in an effort to establish an alibi. The judge found him guilty and sentenced Betts to eight years in prison. Betts sought a writ of HABEAS CORPUS claiming he had been denied his RIGHT TO COUNSEL under the FOURTEENTH AMENDMENT DUE PROCESS guarantee.

Justice Owen Roberts delivered the opinion of the Court, which found that Betts was not denied due process of law. They held that the SIXTH AMENDMENT of the Constitution, providing for assistance of counsel, applied only in federal courts and was not applicable to the states. Rather they found that due process is measured by a totality of the circumstances in a given case. They distinguished Betts's situation from their holding in *Powell v. Alabama,* 287 U.S. 45 (1932), where the Court held that depriving the Scottsboro boys of adequate counsel was a due process violation. To the *Betts* majority, it was significant that the *Powell* defendants faced capital charges and additionally that they were considered incapable of making their own defense because of "ignorance, feeblemindedness, illiteracy, or the like." Betts did not face the death penalty, and, they claimed, he was not helpless but a 43-year-old man of average intelligence. Therefore, requiring states to provide counsel in situations like his would force them to afford attorneys in "every criminal case, whatever the circumstances."

The majority opinion also drew on the original intent of the writers of the Constitution. They noted that when the BILL OF RIGHTS was adopted, the founders intended the Sixth Amendment to allow defendants only the privilege of hiring private counsel. If individual states wished to provide attorneys for indigent defendants, that was their choice rather than a constitutional requirement.

Justice HUGO BLACK wrote the dissent, joined by Justices WILLIAM O. DOUGLAS and William Francis Murphy. They argued that the right to counsel was fundamental to a fair trial and that the Sixth Amendment was applicable to the states through the Fourteenth Amendment's due process guarantee. They further claimed that the circumstances in Betts's case constituted a denial of procedural protection. To deny a request for an attorney and to subject someone to a greater likelihood of conviction merely because of the defendant's poverty was not consistent with "common and fundamental ideas of fairness and right." It contradicted a democratic society's promise of equal justice under law. *Betts v. Brady* was overturned in 1963 in GIDEON V. WAINWRIGHT, 372 U.S. 335.

For more information: Lewis, Anthony. *Gideon's Trumpet.* New York: Random House/Vintage, 1966; Uelmen, Gerald F. "A Train Ride: A Guided

Tour of the Sixth Amendment Right to Counsel." *Law and Contemporary Problems* 58 (2001): 13–29.

—Mary Welek Atwell

bicameral legislature

Bicameralism is the principle that describes the division of power in the U.S. legislative branch between the HOUSE OF REPRESENTATIVES and the SENATE. Bicameralism is provided for in ARTICLE I OF THE U.S. CONSTITUTION and is one of the many checks placed upon legislative power.

Bicameralism describes any legislature composed of two distinct chambers. The chambers, or houses, are often differentiated on the basis of their constituencies or method(s) of election or selection. A so-called lower house is normally directly elected by the general voting-age population, while the upper house may be appointed, directly elected, or indirectly elected. Bicameralism, in the U.S. Constitution, provides for CHECKS AND BALANCES of legislative authority by dividing its powers between the two houses, requiring concurrence in the passage of legislation while assigning unique authority to one chamber or the other, for example, ratification of treaties, confirmation of appointments, and origination of REVENUE BILLS. The governments of many countries utilize bicameral parliaments, though some democratic nations operate under a unicameral (single chamber) parliament, an example being the Knesset in Israel. The lengths of members' terms differ by chamber, with lower-house delegates serving shorter terms (normally two years) and upper-house delegates serving longer ones (normally four to six years).

When applied to governments in the United States, the U.S. Congress and 49 of the 50 states operate with bicameral legislatures. Only Nebraska maintains a unicameral legislature, a feature it implemented in 1937, championed by U.S. senator George W. Norris. The vast majority of local governments in the United States—cities, towns, boroughs, school districts, etc.,—employ unicameral bodies, such as city councils, boards, or commissions.

Dividing a parliament into two chambers establishes an internal check on legislative powers. To pass a law, both chambers must agree on exactly the same language, which requires compromise between the houses, thereby greatly reducing extremist legislation. Critics of bicameral legislatures argue that they are inefficient and easily stalemated by partisan politics.

The bicameral tradition in the United States may be traced to the British Parliament, which itself is a bicameral institution. As each of the thirteen colonies in America established its government, many adopted the English model, although several, such as Pennsylvania, opted for a unicameral body. The first U.S. constitution—the Articles of Confederation—created a unicameral legislature in which each state, regardless of the size of its population or delegation to the congress, received one vote.

The Convention of 1787 drafted a new constitution, one that included, out of political necessity, a bicameral legislature. One of the most contentious issues faced by the CONSTITUTIONAL CONVENTION's delegates was the matter of representation, in particular, whether states or citizens or both should be reflected in a new legislature. Those states with small populations favored a unicameral body similar to that under the Articles of Confederation, while heavily populated states argued for parliamentary representation based on population. The convention assigned the problem to a committee, and from that group emerged the Great Compromise, which struck a balance between the demands of the large and small states, finally settling the matter. The U.S. Congress consists of the House of Representatives, in which representation is based on a state's population, and the Senate, in which each state is treated equally, receiving two votes.

Who should be counted in the population of a state divided the convention's delegates as well. The framers reached another compromise in the matter, the odious Three-fifths Compromise, which counted each slave as three-fifths of a person.

Recently, the question of how to count the population was brought before the Supreme Court. At issue was the use of statistical sampling to predict more accurately the census of the United States as opposed to the traditional, actual head count. In *Department of Commerce v. U.S. House of Representatives,* 525 U.S. 316 (1999), the majority, in a 5-4 vote, ruled that the U.S. Census Bureau must use an actual enumeration for the purpose of determining the total population to be used for apportioning representatives in the House. However, in *Utah v. Evans,* 535 U.S. 452 (2002), with another 5-4 vote, the Court approved the U.S. Census Bureau's use of "hot-deck imputation," a statistical technique that Congress had earlier approved, which estimates how many people the actual count is missing.

For more information: Pitkin, Hanna Fenichel. *The Concept of Representation.* Berkeley: University of California Press, 1967; Tsebelis, George, and Jeannette Money. *Bicameralism.* Cambridge: Cambridge University Press, 1997.

—Thomas J. Baldino

Bickel, Alexander Mordecai (1924–1974)
scholar

Alexander Mordecai Bickel was a renowned commentator and scholar who studied and wrote about the role of the U.S. Supreme Court in American life.

Bickel was born in Bucharest, Romania, but immigrated to the United States with his parents in 1939. He received his undergraduate degree from City College of the City University of New York in 1947 and graduated in 1949 from Harvard Law School with highest honors after serving as editor of the school law review. Bickel then went on to serve as a law clerk to Supreme Court justice Felix Frankfurter from 1952 to 1953. While working for Frankfurter, Bickel was involved in assisting the justice as the Court debated the historic school DESEGREGATION decision, *BROWN V. BOARD OF EDUCATION OF TOPEKA,* 347 U.S. 483 (1954).

In 1956, Bickel accepted a position as a professor at Yale Law School, where he taught until his death. It was during this time that Bickel had his most enduring impact on the scholarly community. One of Bickel's contributions was his coining of the phrase *countermajoritarian difficulty,* a phrase still widely in use today (see COUNTERMAJORITARIANISM). This phrase represented the concept that there is an inherent tension between the exercise of JUDICIAL REVIEW and the democratic principles on which the United States is founded. Judicial review is the idea that the federal courts can strike down legislation passed by Congress if it violates the Constitution.

Bickel also presented a solution to lessen the tension between these two ideas that was at the core of his main scholarly contribution. Unlike many at the time, Bickel did not believe the Supreme Court should be an unimportant part of the government. At the same time, however, Bickel believed that in many regards the Supreme Court had extended itself too far in major national controversies such as school desegregation and AFFIRMATIVE ACTION. The Court's main role, for Bickel, was one where its wisdom and isolation from elections allowed it to defend historic moral virtues from the short-term desires of the public and elected officials.

Another contribution made by Bickel was his theory of the *passive virtues* of judicial decision making. Under this logic, the Supreme Court should decide cases on the narrowest grounds possible. Justice Byron R. White, who served on the Court from 1962 to 1993, is an example of a judge whose legal beliefs were generally supportive of Bickel's viewpoint. Justice White would frequently admonish his colleagues who used broad constitutional reasoning in an opinion when a much narrower approach would suffice.

Bickel was also involved in several Supreme Court cases while he was a law professor. The most important was a Supreme Court case involving free speech and national security. Bickel represented the *New York Times* at oral argument in *New York Times v. United States,* 403 U.S. 713 (1971), which addressed whether the government could prohibit newspaper publication of allegedly sensitive war materials during the Vietnam War (Bickel's side prevailed). Just three years later, in 1974, Bickel died of cancer at the age of 50 in New Haven, Connecticut.

For more information: Ward, Kenneth D., and Cecilia R. Castillo, eds. *The Judiciary and American Democracy: Alexander Bickel, the Countermajoritarian Difficulty, and Contemporary Constitutional Theory.* Albany: State University of New York Press, 2005.

—Ryan C. Black

bill of attainder

A bill of attainder is a specific law naming an individual guilty of a crime. Bills of attainder are prohibited by the U.S. Constitution.

Article I, Section 9, Clause 3 of the Constitution states: "No Bill of Attainder or ex post facto Law shall be passed." Section 10, Clause 1 additionally states: "No State shall enter into any TREATY, Alliance, or Confederation; grant LETTERS OF MARQUE AND REPRISAL; coin Money; emit Bills of Credit; make any Thing but gold and silver Coin a Tender in Payment of Debts; pass any Bill of Attainder, ex post facto Law, or Law impairing the Obligation of Contracts, or grant any Title of Nobility." Therefore, neither the federal government nor any state government shall be able to pass a law that equates to a bill of attainder.

A bill of attainder is defined in *United States v. Brown,* 381 U.S. 437, 448–49 (1965), as "legislative acts, no matter what their form, that apply either to named individuals or to easily ascertainable members of a group in such a way as to inflict punishment on them without a judicial trial." An act is a bill of attainder when the punishment is death, and it is a bill of pains and penalties when the punishment is less severe. Both kinds of punishment fall within the scope of the constitutional prohibition.

The prohibitions covered in both Sections 9 and 10 are best illustrated by *United States v. Lovett,* 328 U.S. 303 (1946). In *Lovett,* Congress passed a law that prohibited the payment of salaries to three named federal government employees. Congress did this because the employees were engaged in subversive activities. Lovett and two other named defendants were government employees working in government agencies that had lawfully employed them. Their employers were fully satisfied with the quality of their work and wished to keep them employed in their jobs. Congress provided in Section 304 of the Deficiency Appropriation Act of 1943 that no salary should be paid to these three named individuals. Congressman Martin Dies spoke on the floor of the House and attacked, among others, Lovett, naming him as an "irresponsible, unrepresentative, crackpot, radical bureaucrat" and an affiliate of "Communist front organizations." The U.S. Supreme Court said that Section 304 was designed to apply to particular individuals, and it thus operated "as a legislative decree of perpetual exclusion" from a chosen vocation. The Court went on to declare the act invalid as a bill of attainder since it applied to named individuals and punishes them through nonpayment for services rendered without a judicial trial in front of a neutral and detached magistrate.

For more information: Cohen, William, and David J. Danelski. *Constitutional Law: Civil Liberty and Individual Rights.* 5th ed. New York: Foundation Press, 2002.

—Kelli Styron

Bill of Rights (1791)

The Bill of Rights refers to the first 10 amendments to the U.S. Constitution introduced in the HOUSE OF REPRESENTATIVES by JAMES MADISON in 1789 and ratified in 1791 after three-quarters of the then 14 states adopted them. The Bill of Rights are perhaps the most important amendments to the Constitution, including some of the most FUNDAMENTAL RIGHTS and liberties regarding free expression, religion, rights of the accused, and property rights. Throughout U.S. history these rights have been the subject of countless Supreme Court constitutional law decisions.

The idea of a bill of rights dates back to the MAGNA CARTA of 1215. This document, signed by King John, forced him to recognize certain fundamental rights such as HABEAS CORPUS and a RIGHT TO TRIAL BY JURY of one's peers. In 1689, Parliament adopted the ENGLISH BILL OF RIGHTS, which protected many religious liberties and granted individuals the right to petition the monarch to address grievances. Together, the Magna Carta and the Bill of Rights placed limits on governmental power in an effort to protect individual rights.

The need for a bill of rights in the new American nation surfaced during the ratification debates in the states following the drafting of the Constitution in Philadelphia in 1787. Critics of the proposed con-

Congress of the United States,
begun and held at the City of New-York, on
Wednesday the fourth of March, one thousand seven hundred and eighty nine.

The Bill of Rights *(National Archives)*

stitution were known as the Anti-Federalists, and they were fearful of the new national government that it created because in part they saw it as too powerful. Anti-Federalists such as Patrick Henry asserted the need for a bill of rights. One of the Anti-Federalist publications known as the *Letters from a Federal Farmer* noted the importance of a bill of rights in England: "The country from which we have derived our origin, is an eminent example of this. Their magna charta and bill of rights have long been the boast, as well as the security, of that nation." For Anti-Federalists, a bill of rights listing the basic liberties of individuals was necessary to restrain the new national government.

In response, Federalists such as ALEXANDER HAMILTON, Madison, and James Wilson, who were defenders of the new constitution, generally rejected calls for a bill of rights. Hamilton, in *Federalist* 84 (of *The Federalist Papers*), sought to respond to Anti-Federalist demands for a bill of rights by dismissing the need for one. First he pointed out that the Constitution already contained numerous provisions protecting individual rights. Second, he asserted: "I go further, and affirm that bills of rights, in the sense and to the extent in which they are contended for, are not only unnecessary in the proposed Constitution, but would even be dangerous. They would contain various exceptions to powers not granted; and, on this very account, would afford a colorable pretext to claim more than were granted." For Hamilton, no bill of rights was needed since the Constitution did not grant the national government the power to limit individual rights.

Eventually, the Federalists held the day, and the Constitution was adopted; however, to secure its confirmation, Madison conceded the arguments of the Anti-Federalists and promised introduction of a bill of rights in Congress if the new constitution was adopted. In 1789, he introduced 17 amendments. Of these 17, 12 were adopted by Congress, and of these, 10 of them were ratified by 1791 and became what is now known as the Bill of Rights. Originally, Madison's plan was to have them directly incorporated into the text of the Constitution, but he later changed his mind and opted to add them as a separate document.

The Bill of Rights contains numerous provisions. The FIRST AMENDMENT contains clauses guaranteeing rights to free speech, press, exercise of religion, and right to assembly and petition for grievances. It also prevents the establishment of religion.

The Second Amendment refers to a RIGHT TO BEAR ARMS. In *DISTRICT OF COLUMBIA V. HELLER*, the Supreme Court resolved a long-running debate and held that this amendment protects an individual's right to bear arms. The THIRD AMENDMENT protects against quartering of troops in one's home. The FOURTH AMENDMENT is protection against unreasonable seizures, and the Fifth Amendment protects a right to an indictment by a grand jury, protection against DOUBLE JEOPARDY, and a RIGHT AGAINST SELF-INCRIMINATION. The Fifth Amendment also contains the TAKINGS CLAUSE, which regulates the use of EMINENT DOMAIN, as well as a DUE PROCESS clause.

The SIXTH AMENDMENT provides for a right to a speedy trial, to defend oneself with witnesses and to confront witnesses and question them, and to be represented by a lawyer. The SEVENTH AMENDMENT provides for a jury trial in some civil matters. The Eighth Amendment proscribes CRUEL AND UNUSUAL PUNISHMENT and excessive BAIL. Finally, the NINTH AMENDMENT and Tenth Amendment serve as catch-all protections of rights, with the former stating that the enumeration of specific rights shall not deny people of all their other rights and the latter reserving to the states powers not delegated to the national government nor prohibited to them.

The Bill of Rights was originally written to limit the power of the national government, not the state governments. The significance of the point was emphasized by Chief Justice JOHN MARSHALL in *BARRON V. MAYOR AND CITY COUNCIL OF BALTIMORE*, 32 U.S. 243 (1833). In this case, he rejected claims that a state violated the Fifth Amendment rights of an individual who had had property taken without compensation. He held that the "Fifth Amendment must be understood as restraining the power of the general government, not as applicable to the States." Thus, the Bill of Rights did not apply to the states or limit their authority.

This view of the Bill of Rights as inapplicable to the states changed with the adoption of the FOURTEENTH AMENDMENT in 1868. Section 1, containing the due process clause, has been used to apply many of the provisions of the Bill of Rights to the states. Starting first in *Chicago, B. & Q. R. Co. v. City of Chicago,* 166 U.S. 226 (1897), which reversed *Barron* and stipulated that the Fifth Amendment's JUST COMPENSATION applied to the states, and then in *GITLOW V. PEOPLE OF THE STATE OF NEW YORK,* 268 U.S. 652 (1925), where the Court stated that the First Amendment free speech clause limited states, the Supreme Court has ruled that most of the major provisions of the Bill of Rights are applicable and enforceable against states by way of the due process clause of the Fourteenth Amendment.

The process of applying the Bill of Rights to the states by way of the due process clause is known as INCORPORATION. The Court, with the notable exception of Justice HUGO BLACK, has never adopted the argument that the entire Bill of Rights was incorporated through the Fourteenth Amendment to limit states. Instead, it has opted for selective incorporation of parts of the Bill of Rights. Most of the Bill of Rights was incorporated after World War II and under the WARREN COURT. Except for the Second and Third Amendments, the Grand Jury provision of the Fifth Amendment, the right to jury trial provision in the Seventh Amendment, and the excessive bail provision of the Eighth, the rest of the Bill of Rights has been incorporated.

The adoption of the Bill of Rights represented a major change in the way rights were to be protected in the United States. Instead of relying on FEDERALISM, separation of powers, and CHECKS AND BALANCES to protect individuals, the Bill of Rights takes certain issues out of the political process, leaving it up to the courts to protect them. Beginning with *United States v. Carolene Products Co.,* 304 U.S. 144 (1938), the Supreme Court subjected legislation implicating Bill of Rights protections to STRICT SCRUTINY, demanding that the government demonstrate a compelling interest that is narrowly tailored before permitting their restriction or limitation. Generally, the Court has not been supportive of limits on Bill of Rights protections since *Carolene Products.*

While Bill of Rights provisions are generally supported, it is often difficult to ascertain what the amendments mean today, and many are controversial. For example, in 1791, the World Wide Web and the Internet did not exist, and many other technologies of today were absent. Determining how to apply the First and Fourth Amendments to these new technologies is difficult. In addition, since the terrorist attacks of September 11, 2001, some have argued for the need to relax some of the search and seizure and other criminal law protections of the Bill of Rights in order to facilitate the "war on terrorism." In response, defenders of individual liberties such as the AMERICAN CIVIL LIBERTIES UNION oppose this, arguing that the Bill of Rights is supposed to apply at all times, including during periods of war.

Overall, the Bill of Rights is one of the major constitutional law documents in the United States. Its adoption has had a significant impact on the protection of rights and the operation of the different levels of government.

For more information: Kelly, Alfred, Winfred A. Harbinson, and Herman Belz. *The American Constitution: Its Origins and Development.* New York: W. W. Norton & Co., 1991; Levy, Leonard W. *Original Intent and the Framers' Constitution.* New York: Macmillan Publishing, 1989; Perry, Michael J. *We the People: The Fourteenth Amendment and the Supreme Court.* New York: Oxford University Press, 1999; Schwartz, Bernard. *A History of the Supreme Court.* New York: Oxford University Press, 1993; Stone, Geoffrey R., and Richard A. Epstein. *The Bill of Rights in the Modern States.* Chicago: University of Chicago Press, 1992; Storing, Herbert J. *What the Anti-Federalists Were For.* Chicago: University of Chicago Press, 1981.

—David Schultz

Bivens v. Six Unknown Named Agents of Federal Bureau of Narcotics 403 U.S. 388 (1971)

In *Bivens v. Six Unknown Named Agents of Federal Bureau of Narcotics,* the U.S. Supreme Court established a civil remedy for individuals who had been allegedly wronged by illegal action by the federal government.

Traditionally, individuals who had been subject to illegal activity by police officers, such as the use of excessive force, could sue them and the federal government under the Federal Tort Claims Act. However, in *Bivens*, the Court ruled that the Constitution provided for civil remedies to compensate for wrongs committed against them by federal law-enforcement agents who violate their rights.

Webster Bivens was arrested without warrant and had his house searched without warrant. No charges were brought against him, whereupon Bivens brought suit that his FOURTH AMENDMENT right to protection from unreasonable searches and seizure was violated. The Supreme Court, with the opinion delivered by Justice WILLIAM J. BRENNAN, JR., ruled that the Fourth Amendment provided for financial damages or remedy to citizens for every wrong committed by the government where a remedy did not exist or where one could have been recovered if the violation had been committed by a private citizen and suit was then brought against that person.

For more information: Langran, Robert W. *The Supreme Court: A Concise History.* New York: Peter Lang, 2004.

—Ernest Gomez

Black, Hugo (1886–1971) *Supreme Court justice*
Hugo Black was nominated to serve as a U.S. Supreme Court associate justice by President Franklin Roosevelt in 1937. After confirmation in 1937, Black served on the Supreme Court until 1971. Associate Justice Black left a lasting legacy on the judiciary. Serving more than 34 years on the Supreme Court, Black is one of the longest-serving Supreme Court justices, along with Associate Justices WILLIAM O. DOUGLAS and Stephen Johnson Field and Chief Justice JOHN MARSHALL. Justice Black is best known as one of the liberals on the Roosevelt Supreme Court and for his insistence that the FOURTEENTH AMENDMENT served to incorporate all of the BILL OF RIGHTS provisions to apply to the states.

Hugo Black came from humble beginnings to national prominence. He was born on February 27, 1886, in a poor farming community in Alabama and was the youngest of eight children of Hugo and Martha Black. After attending medical school for a year, Black decided to pursue law instead. In 1906, Hugo Black graduated from the University of Alabama law school. In February 1921, Black married Josephine Foster, and the couple had three children. Josephine died in 1951, and Black married Elizabeth DeMeritte in 1957.

In 1927, Black was sworn in as a senator representing the state of Alabama. An eloquent speaker and a loyal Democrat, Black quickly won the admiration of leaders of his party and gained the attention of President Roosevelt. This admiration earned Black a nomination for the U.S. Supreme Court. Since Black was serving as a senator when he was nominated, it seemed his confirmation would be quick and easy; however, this was the first appointment that President Roosevelt made after his court-packing plan. For the first time since 1888, instead of receiving a quick confirmation with little debate, Senator Black's nomination was sent to the SENATE Judiciary Committee. Black was placed under much scrutiny, and his confirmation seemed in doubt when his former membership in the Ku Klux Klan (KKK) came into question. A radio speech on October 1, 1937, in which Black denied any present affiliation with the KKK helped sway public support. Ultimately, the Senate confirmed Black's nomination with a vote of 63-13. On his first day of service to the Supreme Court, on October 4, 1937, demonstrators protesting Black's appointment to the Court crowded the Supreme Court building.

As a justice, the rulings of Black would be labeled "activist" because of his willingness to review laws and strike them down as unconstitutional. On the Court, Black's rulings distanced his image as a Klan member. In one of his early rulings as justice, the unanimous opinion of the Supreme Court in *Chambers v. Florida,* 309 U.S. 227 (1940), written by Black, favored three African-American defendants in a question of unjust convictions. Generally considered a liberal on the Court, Black often sided with the defendants or with those seeking protection of their constitutional rights.

With such a long tenure on the Supreme Court, Black had the opportunity to participate in many influential rulings, such as *United States v. Carolene Products Co.*, 304 U.S. 144 (1938), and *Korematsu v. United States*, 323 U.S. 214 (1944). In the latter, while writing the majority opinion upholding the Japanese internment program, he also described the use of racial classifications as inherently suspect. This concept of suspect classifications would eventually became a constitutional principle under the WARREN COURT and subsequent courts to strike down racially discriminatory legislation. Black sided with the majority in major cases such as *Brown v. Board of Education of Topeka* 349 U.S. 294 (1955); *Baker v. Carr*, 369 U.S. 186 (1962); *Engel v. Vitale*, 370 U.S. 421 (1962); *Gideon v. Wainwright*, 372 U.S. 335 (1963); *Escobedo v. Illinois*, 378 U.S. 478 (1964); and *Miranda v. Arizona*, 384 U.S. 436 (1966). Some cases in which he was in the minority opinion include *Roth v. U.S.*, 354 U.S. 476 (1957), and *Griswold v. Connecticut*, 387 U.S. 479 (1965). During a 1968 interview, Black placed his dissent in *Adamson v. California*, 332 U.S. 46 (1947), as the best work he had done while on the Supreme Court.

Constitutionally, Black's other major legacy was his insistent support of the total INCORPORATION doctrine. This doctrine states that the DUE PROCESS clause of the Fourteenth Amendment incorporates all of the Bill of Rights provisions to be limits on states. This theory has never received a majority of the Court's support, with it instead opting for selective incorporation.

Black resigned from the Supreme Court on September 17, 1971, due to health problems as the result of a stroke. He died just eight days later.

For more information: Black, Hugo L., and Elizabeth Black. *Mr. Justice and Mrs. Black: The Memoirs of Hugo L. Black and Elizabeth Black.* New York: Random House, 1986; Dunne, Gerald T. *Hugo Black and the Judicial Revolution.* New York: Simon & Schuster, 1977; Magee, James J. *Mr. Justice Black: Absolutist on the Court.* Charlottesville: University Press of Virginia, 1980; Newman, Roger K. *Hugo Black.* New York: Fordham University Press, 1997.

—Carol Walker

Blackstone, William (1723–1780) *lawyer and jurist*

William Blackstone was an important English writer, attorney, judge, university lecturer, and member of Parliament whose *Commentaries on the Laws of England* significantly influenced the Founding Fathers and the writing of the U.S. Constitution.

Blackstone published his four-volume treatise *Commentaries on the Laws of England* between 1765 and 1769. Blackstone's *Commentaries* represented the most comprehensive and accessible analysis of English law available to 18th- and early 19th-century English and American audiences, and while Blackstone himself opposed the American Revolution, his *Commentaries* helped shape American political and legal theory. Indeed, generations of American political thinkers and leaders, from THOMAS JEFFERSON to ABRAHAM LINCOLN, were familiar with Blackstone and made reference to his *Commentaries.*

Born in London, Blackstone was educated at Oxford. In 1737, he was awarded a prize for his proficiency in Latin. He studied a variety of disciplines, most notably logic, mathematics, science, and classics. His intellectual interests were wide ranging and included—in addition to law—subjects such as architecture and Greek poetry. Blackstone graduated from Oxford in 1741, was elected a fellow at Oxford's All Souls College in 1743, was awarded a Doctor of Civil Law in 1750, and was named to the first chair at Oxford for the study of English law in 1758. Blackstone served as a member in the House of Commons of Parliament from 1761 to 1770, during which time he had occasion to articulate his support for the Stamp Act (1765), a piece of legislation so loathsome to American colonists that they used tactics ranging from street protests to the calling by nine American colonies of the Stamp Act Congress in New York City in 1765 in order to pressure England to repeal the act in 1766. In addition to his academic and parliamentary pursuits, Blackstone practiced law and in 1770, assumed a position of justice of the Court of Common Pleas.

Blackstone's continuing relevance stems, however, from neither his service in Parliament nor his work as a lawyer and judge but rather his authorship of *Commentaries on the Laws of England.* In the preface, Blackstone informed the reader that his work grew out of a lecture series he had presented while teaching at Oxford, and he lamented what he referred to as "prejudice" against innovative educational ideals. Blackstone proceeded to argue that an understanding of law should not be limited to lawyers; on the contrary, an informed understanding of the principles and practices of law, Blackstone contended, would enhance civic life generally.

While Blackstone embraced the 18th-century class-based perspectives held by many of the privileged members of his own generation (for example, he called specifically for the propertied "gentlemen" of his day to become well versed in law), his larger aim of expanding access to legal doctrine was translatable to contexts much less aristocratic than his own (for example, the United States). Numerous signers of the U.S. DECLARATION OF INDEPENDENCE (1776) owned copies of the *Commentaries*; moreover, analyses of 20th-century U.S. Supreme Court decisions reveal that the *Commentaries* were cited by the Court an average of 10 times per year.

What were the major ideas that American readers of Blackstone's *Commentaries* encountered? Drawing upon ancient theorists such as Cicero (106–43 B.C.E.) and modern ones such as JOHN LOCKE (1632–1704), Blackstone argued that NATURAL LAW (also known as the laws of nature) is the basis of human-made laws, that God is the author of natural law and that human beings can know natural law by virtue of human reason. Natural law teaches that humans should be free to pursue happiness. Blackstone also upheld the natural rights of liberty, security, and property. With respect to governmental organization, he theorized that legislative authority is the highest ("supreme") authority of government, and he advocated a separation of powers and a system of CHECKS AND BALANCES. Blackstone was adamant that governmental systems that failed to separate executive and legislative authority were nothing short of tyrannical, regardless of whether citizens could be construed to have consented to such arrangements. It is important to keep in mind, however, that Blackstone's discussion was grounded in a concept of legislative authority modeled according to the English parliamentary system in which the executive was considered a member of the legislature.

A prominent and recurring theme of the *Commentaries* is the thesis that the English legal system—in both its common law (unwritten, customary) traditions and its government-enacted laws—had successfully protected natural rights and liberties. This position—along with Blackstone's argument in favor of property requirements for voting and his opposition to the American Revolution—have led some readers to see in Blackstone an apologist for the status quo and an enemy of progress. More recently, however, scholars have challenged one-dimensional interpretations of the *Commentaries* and have called attention to Blackstone's support for natural rights, his suggestions that cultural variations in common-law traditions merit a respect for relativism, and his appreciation of the role of human reason and discernment (and thus flexibility) in interpretative decision making.

For more information: Alschuler, Albert W. "Rediscovering Blackstone." *University of Pennsylvania Law Review* 145 (1996): 1–55; Blackstone, William. *Commentaries on the Laws of England.* Vol. 1. Edited by Stanley N. Katz. Chicago: University of Chicago Press, 1979; Prest, Wilfrid. "Blackstone as Architect: Constructing the Commentaries." *Yale Journal of Law and the Humanities* 15 (2003): 103–133; Schultz, David. "Political Theory and Legal History: Conflicting Depictions of Property in the American Political Founding." *American Journal of Legal History* 37 (1993): 464–495.

—Ellen Grigsby

blogs and free speech

A blog is a form of Internet Web site created by one or more users with entries made in a journal style. In many respects, the blog resembles an online diary. The journal format, however, is one that is intended to foster personal communication between readers of the blog and the blog's creator. The term is a shortened form of *Weblog.*

Recent studies and surveys have shown that the portion of the Internet devoted to blogs, an area commonly known as the blogosphere, is large and rapidly growing. The Internet authority Technorati, in a February 2006 survey titled *State of the Blogosphere,* estimated that there were 27.2 million blogs. The blogosphere is believed to double in size every five and one-half months. A more recent report by the Pew and American Life Project, *Bloggers: A Portrait of the Internet's New Storytellers,* estimated that 12 million Americans were regular contributors to blogs. The number of U.S. blog readers was estimated to be around 57 million adults, or about 39 percent of the American population who use online resources.

Blogs are a prime example of the FIRST AMENDMENT in action. The author of the blog entry exercises the right to speak as freely as possible by writing in the online journal. Readers of the blog exercise a mirror-image right to receive all of the information posted on the blog. Some commentators have observed that the idea of a blog is somewhat akin to a "virtual soapbox" providing both creators and readers a relatively unrestricted place in which to express ideas and opinions.

There are, however, significant legal issues surrounding the creation and existence of blogs. These include not only the questions of how unrestricted is the freedom to write as much as one chooses in the blog and to read what others have written. Other legal issues that have arisen include concerns over liability that may attach to the inclusion of certain materials deemed by others to be either harmful or offensive and copyright issues that frequently arise when other resources are republished or when links to other Internet materials are provided in the blog.

One frequent source of contention over blog sites and entries involves blogs maintained by employees who feel compelled to discuss their own employers and employers' conduct and affairs. An influential Delaware Supreme Court decision in the case of *John Doe v. Patrick Cahill and Julia Cahill,* 884 A.2d 451 (Oct. 5, 2006), addressed the issue of whether specific blog comments were defamatory to local public officials. The legal analysis in the Delaware decision joined a significant number of other court decisions that have upheld provisions of the 1996 federal COMMUNICATIONS DECENCY ACT, P.L. 104-104, 110 Stat. 56 (Feb. 8, 1996), a measure that protects Web site owners from legal liability in libel or DEFAMATION lawsuits. A more recent decision from the California Supreme Court, in *Stephen J. Barrett v. Ilena Rosenthal,* 146 P.3d 510 (Nov. 20, 2006), held that the federal act's immunity to liability applied to distributors of Internet information as well.

Copyright controversies arise frequently. One source of conflict is a popular perception that blog creators and writers are free to use any material found online without securing prior permission or a grant of a license to legally use the material from the copyright owner. One reason for this belief is that many bloggers feel they are free to use copyrighted material as long as they are not themselves making money from its use.

For more information: Hewitt, Hugh. *Blog: Understanding the Information Revolution That's Changing Your World.* Nashville, Tenn.: Thomas Nelson, 2005; Lenhart, Amanda, and Susannah Fox. *Bloggers: A Portrait of the Internet's New Storytellers.* Washington, D.C.: Pew Internet and American Life Project, 2006; Technorati Web site. Available online. URL: http://www.technorati.com.

—Jerry E. Stephens

BMW of North America, Inc. v. Gore 517 U.S. 559 (1996)

In *BMW of North America, Inc. v. Gore,* the U.S. Supreme Court held that a $2 million punitive damages award against BMW for selling a paint-damaged car violated the DUE PROCESS clause in the FOURTEENTH AMENDMENT. This case was an important decision in recent efforts by the Supreme Court to decide if the Constitution places limits on punitive damages.

The case arose after Dr. Ira Gore discovered that his recently purchased BMW had been repainted. Furthermore, Gore was not the only one who had bought a damaged BMW believing it to be in perfect condition: BMW had a nationwide policy of selling damaged cars as new if the damage could be fixed for less than 3 percent of the car's suggested retail price. To compensate Gore for the lost value of his car, an Alabama jury awarded him $4,000 in compensatory damages. And to punish BMW for its egregious conduct, the jury awarded Gore $4 million in punitive damages. After BMW appealed the punitive damages award, the Alabama Supreme Court reduced that award to $2 million, a judgment that BMW then appealed to the U.S. Supreme Court, arguing that even this reduced award violated BMW's due process right to be free from excessive penalties.

Writing for the majority, Justice JOHN PAUL STEVENS found the award unconstitutional. In reaching this decision, the Court announced three guideposts that states must consider in awarding punitive damages: (1) the reprehensibility of the defendant's conduct, (2) the proportionality between the punitive damages and the compensatory damages awarded, and (3) the comparability of the punitive damages award to civil or criminal penalties that the state could have imposed for the defendant's misconduct. Because Gore's injury was purely economic, because the punitive damages award was 500 times the amount of Gore's compensatory damages, and because the maximum penalty available for similar conduct was limited to $2,000, the Court reversed the Alabama Supreme Court decision. Incidentally, on the ultimate remand to the trial court, the punitive damages awarded against BMW were $50,000.

Justice ANTONIN GREGORY SCALIA wrote a dissenting opinion, in which Justice CLARENCE THOMAS joined, arguing that the due process clause does not require these three guideposts but merely some judicial determination that the jury award is "reasonable." Justice Ruth Bader Ginsburg also wrote a dissenting opinion, in which Chief Justice WILLIAM HUBBS REHNQUIST joined, claiming that the Court should not get involved in limiting punitive damages, a matter traditionally controlled by the several states.

Gore is an important case for the business community because it means that, absent a constitutional amendment or a Supreme Court decision overruling the decision, all punitive damages awards against corporate wrongdoers must comport with the three guideposts. Some business interests, however, argue that the *Gore* ruling does not go far enough, because the proportionality guidepost is a loosely defined relational guideline, rather than a binding numeric ratio. So far, the Court has resisted announcing a numeric requirement and in fact has suggested it will not move in that direction. Most likely, the Court will continue to permit states to consider the reprehensibility of the defendant's conduct as the most important factor in awarding punitive damages.

For more information: Sunstein, Cass. *Punitive Damages: How Juries Decide.* Chicago: University of Chicago Press, 2003.

—Jesse R. Merriam

Board of Education of Kiryas Joel Village School District v. Grumet 512 U.S. 687 (1989)

In *Board of Education of Kiryas Joel Village School District v. Grumet,* the U.S. Supreme Court held that a statute creating a special school district based on the lines for a village incorporated by a religious sect to exclude all but its followers violated the ESTABLISHMENT CLAUSE of the FIRST AMENDMENT.

The state of New York created a school district based on the lines of a village named Kiryas Joel, established by followers of a strict form of Judaism. Residents of Kiryas Joel were religiously conservative and avoided assimilation into what they saw as the modern world by, among other things, segregating individuals by sex, speaking primarily Yiddish, and rejecting popular culture. Taxpayers and an association of school boards brought suit, challenging the constitutionality of this new school district.

In Justice DAVID H. SOUTER's opinion for the Court, he explained that the religion clauses require neutrality toward religion; thus, government may not favor one religion or its adherents over another religion or nonadherents. On the other hand, government may accommodate the religious needs of students by alleviating special burdens placed upon those students without violating the religion clauses.

In light of this neutrality requirement, the Court held that the creation of the Kiryas Joel school district was unconstitutional. When the state created the school district, it improperly delegated its discretionary authority over public schools to a religiously defined group. The Court explained that because the group with control over the schools was religiously defined, there is no guarantee that it will remain neutral toward religion.

However, because government may accommodate the religious needs of students to a certain extent, the Court held that the state and the parents from the Kiryas Joel school district may seek other means of addressing the unique issues inherent in such a religiously isolated community. For example, the school district of which Kiryas Joel was part before the creation of their own district could have accommodated the religious needs of the sect through bilingual or bicultural special education for the Kiryas Joel children.

Justice ANTONIN GREGORY SCALIA dissented, arguing that the creation of the Kiryas Joel school district did not violate the establishment clause. In his view, the school district was based on the diverse and unique cultural needs of the students, not on their religious affiliation.

For more information: Bagyi, John. *Board of Education of Kiryas Joel v. Grumet*: Misconstruing the Status Quo as a Neutral Baseline." *Albany Law Review* 60 (1996): 541; Epps, Garrett. "What We Talk About When We Talk About Free Exercise." *Arizona State Law Journal* 30 (1998): 563.

—Winston E. Calvert

Board of Education Pottawatomie County v. Earls 536 U.S. 822 (2002)

In *Board of Education Pottawatomie County v. Earls,* the U.S. Supreme Court upheld a policy requiring all middle and high school students to consent to urinalysis testing for drugs in order to participate in any extracurricular activity. Here, the Court ruled that the test did not violate the FOURTH AMENDMENT or the FOURTEENTH AMENDMENT.

In 1998, the public school district in Tecumseh, Oklahoma, adopted the Student Activities Drug Testing Policy. The policy permitted mandatory, suspicionless drug testing of students participating in extracurricular activities such as the debate team, band, or drama club. Lindsay Earls, a high school student and member of Tecumseh's choir, the marching band, and the academic team, alleged that the policy violated her Fourth Amendment rights.

Supreme Court precedents have placed student drug testing under a "special needs" exception to the Fourth Amendment warrant requirement, because such testing is considered to be an administrative rather than a criminal search. In *Vernonia School District v. Acton,* 515 U.S. 646 (1995), the Supreme Court upheld random, suspicionless drug testing for student athletes in a school where athletes were the leaders of a pervasive drug culture. The Court reasoned that athletes are often involved in contact sports, and it is important for player safety to ensure that no participant is using drugs. The Court also argued that student athletes, given the nature of their activities, have a reduced expectation of PRIVACY and that the testing did not lead to criminal prosecution but merely probation from school for repeated violations.

Applying *Vernonia,* the district court in *Earls* ruled in favor of the school district. The Tenth Circuit reversed, holding that the testing policy violated the Fourth Amendment. It concluded that before imposing a suspicionless drug-testing program, a school must demonstrate some identifiable drug abuse problem among a sufficient number of those tested. The court determined that the school district had failed to demonstrate such a problem among Tecumseh students participating in competitive extracurricular activities.

Justice CLARENCE THOMAS's majority opinion in *Earls* (joined by Chief Justice WILLIAM HUBBS REHNQUIST and Justices ANTONIN GREGORY SCALIA, ANTHONY M. KENNEDY, and STEPHEN G. BREYER) applied a fact-specific balancing test between the special needs of the school in promoting a safe educational environment and the Fourth Amendment rights of students. Justice Thomas concluded that the testing policy did not violate the Fourth Amendment because any privacy invasion was insignificant given the minimally intrusive nature of the testing. The Court also noted that the testing did not lead to criminal prosecution but merely exclusion from the group and probation from school for repeated offenses. Like the *Vernonia* decision, the Court argued that students involved in extracurricular activities have a reduced expectation of privacy. Justice Thomas cited the nationwide epidemic of drug use and evidence of increased drug use in the schools as reasonable bases for the drug-testing policy.

Justice Ruth Bader Ginsburg authored the dissenting opinion, joined by Justices DAVID H. SOUTER, SANDRA DAY O'CONNOR, and JOHN PAUL STEVENS. The dissenters distinguished the facts of the case from *Vernonia.* Justice Ginsburg argued that the Tecumseh policy was "capricious, even perverse" in that it "targets for testing a student population least likely to be at risk from illicit drugs and their damaging effects." The dissenters gave greater weight to a student's privacy expectation and argued that the Tecumseh policy is counterproductive because it steers students at greatest risk for substance abuse away from extracurricular involvement that potentially may reduce drug problems.

Following the *Earls* decision, a few schools implemented a policy of random drug testing for all students, regardless of participation in sports or extracurricular activities. These broad testing programs are still being litigated in the courts.

For more information: Donovan, Courtney. "*Board of Education v. Earls*: Has the Supreme Court Gone Too Far on Student Drug Testing?" *Georgetown Journal of Law and Public Policy* 2 (2004): 337; Higbee, Kari L. "Student Privacy Rights: Drug Testing and Fourth Amendment Protections." *Idaho Law Review* 41 (2005): 361.

—John Fliter

Board of Education v. Pico 457 U.S. 853 (1982)

In *Board of Education v. Pico,* a plurality of the U.S. Supreme Court found that a school board may not remove a book from the school library because of the viewpoint expressed in the book.

In *Pico,* the school board for the Island Trees Union Free School District in New York had ordered the removal of several books, including *Slaughterhouse-Five, The Naked Ape,* and *Soul on Ice,* from the school library for being "anti-American, anti-Christian, anti-Semitic, and just plain filthy." Justices WILLIAM J. BRENNAN, JR., Thurgood Marshall, JOHN PAUL STEVENS, and Harry Andrew Blackmun contended that once a library acquires a book, the FIRST AMENDMENT prohibits denying students such a book because of the ideas contained in the book. Justice Byron Raymond White, concurring in judgment, did not reach the First Amendment question but instead found that the original trial court should have let the matter proceed to trial. The four dissenting justices, WARREN E. BURGER, WILLIAM HUBBS REHNQUIST, LEWIS FRANKLIN POWELL, JR., and SANDRA DAY O'CONNOR, argued, to no avail, that the school board's actions should not be overturned by the courts.

Local school boards and school officials generally possess wide latitude in organizing and administering public education, yet the Constitution still imposes limits. In ruling that students may not be compelled to recite the Pledge of Allegiance (*West Virginia Board of Education v. Barnette,* 319 U.S. 624 [1943]), the Supreme Court famously stated: "If there is any fixed star in our constitutional constellation, it is that no official, high or petty, can prescribe what shall be orthodox in politics, nationalism, religion, or other matters of opinion or force citizens to confess by word or act their faith therein." And in reviewing a case involving the suspension of high school students who wore black armbands to protest the government's actions in Vietnam (*Tinker v. Des Moines School District,* 393 U.S. 503 [1969]), the Court illustriously declared: "Neither students nor teachers shed their constitutional rights to freedom of speech or expression at the schoolhouse gate." The *Pico* plurality similarly bristled at the censorship of the Island Trees Union Free School District: "Our Constitution does not permit the official suppression of *ideas.*"

In the quarter-century following the Supreme Court's ruling in *Pico,* censorship efforts still persist, including efforts to remove library books about voodoo, homosexuality, and even Harry Potter. While these efforts to remove library books have generally been stymied, *Pico* has been limited sometimes in its application to the school library setting. Efforts to remove works such as Aristophanes' *Lysistrata* and Chaucer's *The Miller's Tale* from the classroom have on occasion been successful.

For more information: Peltz, Richard J. "Pieces of Pico: Saving Intellectual Freedom in the Public School Library." *Brigham Young University Education and Law Journal* 103, no. 2 (2005): 103–158.

—Martin J. Sweet and Caitlin F. Currie

Board of Regents v. Roth 408 U.S. 564 (1972)

The constitutional rights of public-sector employees whose jobs are terminated were limited by the decision of the U.S. Supreme Court in *Board of Regents v. Roth.* The *Roth* ruling restricts most public-sector employees from challenging their discharge under the DUE PROCESS clause of the FOURTEENTH AMENDMENT of the U.S. Constitution, which provides that a person may not be deprived of property or liberty without due process of law. But the *Roth* case and its progeny give public-sector employees a right to a "name-clearing" hearing for aspersions cast on their character when fired.

The *Roth* case arose out of the termination of a nontenured college professor in Wisconsin. He was informed, after one year, that he would not be rehired, without any explanation or reasons. He sued the school officials, claiming that nonretention without any reasons violated his right to procedural due process under the Fourteenth Amendment. He based his claim on cases that had required government to provide a hearing before depriving anyone of their property rights. The U.S. Supreme Court rejected his claims, however, holding that although he had an "abstract concern in being rehired," his expectation did not constitute a "property interest" requiring a hearing.

The *Roth* ruling presaged subsequent cases that did expand the rights of terminated employees. In *Cleveland Board of Education v. Loudermill,* 470 U.S. 532 (1985), the Supreme Court held that public-sector employees must be given at least a minimal opportunity to respond to allegations before they are fired. The *Loudermill* hearing supplemented other reports of terminated governmental employees that may exist in state laws, civil service rules, governmental personnel policies, or collective bargaining agreements.

The *Roth* case also created another right for public-sector employees. In *Roth,* the Court alluded to rights that employees may have to a hearing if aspersions are cast about them in connection with their discharge. Subsequent cases fleshed out the name-clearing right established in *Roth.* The right applies to public-sector employees who, when terminated, are subject to public charges that impute serious misconduct, including immoral or illegal behavior. If so, they may be entitled to a hearing to respond to the charges.

The failure of a government entity to provide a name-clearing hearing can entitle a discharged employee to money damages for the harm caused to the individual's reputation. The procedure an employee must follow to activate the right to a name-clearing hearing is uncertain. Some courts require that the employee make a formal request for a name-clearing hearing, while others dispense with that obligation.

For more information: Schwartz, Bernard. *A History of the Supreme Court.* New York: Oxford University Press, 1993.

—Marshall Tanick

Bob Jones University v. United States 461 U.S. 574 (1983)

In *Bob Jones University v. United States,* the Supreme Court held that denial of tax-exempt status for a charitable organization on the ground that its policies were racially discriminatory and therefore violated public policy was consistent with the Constitution.

This opinion involves two separate cases that the Court consolidated as they both involved the same issue. In the first case, Bob Jones University, an evangelical Christian school, maintained a policy that denied admission to any person who was involved in or advocated interracial marriage or dating. The second case involved Goldsboro Christian Schools, which maintained other racially discriminatory admissions policies whereby it admitted almost exclusively Caucasian students. Both institutions claimed that their admissions policies were based on the respective institutions' religious beliefs.

Although both institutions previously enjoyed tax exemption under Section 501(c)(3) of the Internal Revenue Code, which provides tax exemption to religious, charitable, and educational organizations, the Internal Revenue Service (IRS) amended its regulations to provide that institutions would not qualify for tax exemption unless they adopted nondiscriminatory policies. Because both Bob Jones University and Goldsboro Christian Schools maintained racially discriminatory policies after adoption of this regulation, the IRS withdrew tax-exempt status from both institutions.

The Supreme Court held that the denial of tax-exempt status did not violate the Constitution. Writing for the Court, Chief Justice WARREN EARL BURGER explained that Section 501(c)(3) included the common law concept of "charity." Thus, an organization must show not only that it is a religious, charitable, or educational institution but also that its practices and mission do not offend public policy. In light of the important public policy of eliminating racial discrimination, the Court held that denial of tax exemption to religious or educational institutions whose policies discriminate on the basis of race was not constitutionally suspect.

Moreover, the Court held, denial of tax exemption does not violate the rights of the institutions under the religion clauses of the FIRST AMENDMENT. The Court held that the fundamental, overriding interest of eliminating racial discrimination in education substantially outweighs the burden placed upon the institutions by denying tax exemption.

The sole dissenter, Justice WILLIAM HUBBS REHNQUIST, agreed with the majority that there is a strong national policy against racial discrimination but argued instead that Section 501(c)(3) did not require institutions to abide by such important public policies. In his view, the language of the statute clearly did not require what the majority asserted. And any change to the effect of the statute should be enacted by Congress rather than required by a judicial opinion.

For more information: Edwards, John. "Democracy and Delegation of Legislative Authority: *Bob Jones University v. United States.*" *Boston College Law Review* 26 (1985): 745.

—Winston E. Calvert

Bolling v. Sharpe 347 U.S. 497 (1954)

In *Bolling v. Sharpe,* the Supreme Court applied the school DESEGREGATION ruling of the landmark companion case *BROWN V. BOARD OF EDUCATION OF TOPEKA,* 347 U.S. 483 (1954), to the public schools of Washington, D.C. The Court also suggested that the guarantee of DUE PROCESS in the Fifth Amendment included an implicit guarantee of "EQUAL PROTECTION" similar to the equal protection clause of the FOURTEENTH AMENDMENT.

The case began in 1950 when Spottswood T. Bolling, Jr., and other black junior high school students, led by a group of local parents, were turned away from the newly built, all-white John Philip Sousa Junior High School. The junior high school the students were instead forced to attend was nearly 50 years old and lacked many facilities and resources. A lawsuit was filed for Bolling and several other students, challenging segregation in the D.C. schools. After the case was dismissed in federal district court, the Supreme Court agreed to hear the appeal, before a ruling by a federal appeals court, in order to consider it along with four other cases that made up *Brown v. Board of Education*.

The *Bolling* case, however, had to be handled separately because the other cases involved a claim that segregation was unconstitutional in violation of the equal protection guarantee of the Fourteenth Amendment, which applies only to state governments and not to the federally controlled D.C. school board. At the time, the Fifth Amendment due process guarantee had not been interpreted to include the same antidiscrimination ideal as the Fourteenth Amendment.

Bolling v. Sharpe was decided unanimously on the same day, May 17, 1954, as the *Brown* decision and was also written by Chief Justice Earl Warren. The Court said the concepts of equal protection and due process both are derived "from our American ideal of fairness." The Court said that the kind of discrimination involved in the case was "so unjustifiable" as to violate the liberty guaranteed by due process in the Fifth Amendment. Chief Justice Warren thought the Constitution had to be understood to impose the same nondiscrimination ideal on all levels of government. "In view of our decision that the Constitution prohibits the states from maintaining racially segregated public schools, it would be unthinkable that the same Constitution would impose a lesser duty on the Federal Government," Warren wrote.

The Court's reading of an equal protection component into the Fifth Amendment has served as the basis for many discrimination lawsuits against the federal government in the decades since the ruling. Cases involving race or gender discrimination in federal programs and AFFIRMATIVE ACTION in federal programs were decided under this Fifth Amendment principle.

The Sousa Junior High School, which accepted its first black students in the fall of 1954, is still in use and has been designated a National Historic Landmark. At the start of the 21st century, however, the student population at Sousa was almost entirely black due to the shifting nature of the District of Columbia's population and neighborhoods.

For more information: Kluger, R. *Simple Justice: The History of* Brown v. Board of Education *and Black America's Struggle for Equality.* New York: Knopf, 1975; Rubin, Peter J. "Taking Its Proper Place in the Constitutional Canon: *Bolling v. Sharpe, Korematsu,* and the Equal Protection Component of Fifth Amendment Due Process." *Virginia Law Review* 92 (2006): 1,879.

—Stephen Wermiel

book burning

Book burning is the destruction of books or the written word by fire. It is ordinarily a public and often ceremonial practice aimed at a particular person or group of persons. The practice is most often an expression of moral, political, or religious objection to the specifically targeted material. The term, however, presently includes items of writing other than books. Thus, for example, CDs, videotapes, and other recordings have also been destroyed through "book" burning. In some situations, especially if it involves a government entity, book burning may implicate FIRST AMENDMENT issues.

Despite the dramatic nature of the actions taken, book burning is merely one form of the attempted suppression or censorship of ideas. A wide range of books—from the works of William Shakespeare to John Steinbeck's *Grapes of Wrath*—have been the targets of action by opponents of these books. The more extreme form of suppression may, on occasion, take the form of the physical destruction of the book itself. Ironically enough, one book often targeted by would-be book burners is the classic science fiction novel by Ray Bradbury, *Fahrenheit 451*. The novel tells the story of a futuristic totalitarian society in which firemen are used to burn unapproved literature. The novel begins, appropriately enough, with "It was a pleasure to burn."

The history of book burning is almost as extensive as the history of writing itself. Notable examples of the ceremonial destruction of the printed word have occurred in many places and at many times. One of the most significant, and still little understood historically, was the destruction of the Library of Alexandria in A.D. 391 following encouragement from the Roman emperor Theodosius I, who had ordered the destruction of all pagan temples. Other notable book burning incidents include the destruction of supposedly heretical texts after the First Council of Nicaea in A.D. 325, the destruction of the royal library of the Persian Samanid dynasty at the turn of the 11th century following the invasion by the Turks, and the burning of Arabic and Hebrew texts, on the instructions of the archbishop of Granada, in Andalusia, Spain, in about 1400. The 20th century witnessed many book burning incidents including the destruction by the Bolsheviks in 1917 Russia of works deemed to be contrary to communism and the burning of works by Jewish authors in the 1930s and 1940s in Nazi Germany.

The United States has not been immune to book burning fervor. In 1953, Senator Joseph McCarthy submitted a list of books by supposedly procommunist authors found in U.S. Department of State libraries in Europe. The State Department acquiesced in McCarthy's demands that the books and any other "material by controversial persons, communists, fellow travelers" and others were to be removed. To his credit, President Dwight D. Eisenhower urged Americans not to burn books and instead turn to libraries and read.

A more contemporary target of book burners has been the various Harry Potter novels by the Scottish author J. K. Rowling. The boy wizard has inspired many, particularly the more fundamental religionists in the United States, to attack the ideas and writings in the popular book series.

As a practice, book burning is contrary to the fundamental principles of the First Amendment itself. The constitutional amendment protects not only acceptable, conventional, and noncontroversial ideas and writings but those ideas and writings that are not as popularly received in any community. The First Amendment establishes a powerful presumption in support of the free expression of ideas. These ideas and their written forms are furthermore afforded a reasonable process in order to determine whether the ideas and writings are to be constitutionally protected.

A set of constitutional standards has been developed for when challenged ideas and writings are alleged to contain merely prurient content. For example, a standard for a definition of pornography was developed in the U.S. Supreme Court decision of *MILLER V. CALIFORNIA*, 413 U.S. 15 (1973). This standard assures that suppression efforts do not encroach upon those constitutionally protected forms of speech and writing. A single community standard forms the basis of this constitutional test. In addition, in cases such as *BOARD OF EDUCATION V. PICO*, 457 U.S. 853 (1982), a plurality of the Court ruled that it was a violation of the First Amendment for a school board to remove a book from the school library because of the viewpoint expressed in it. While neither *Miller* nor *Pico* addressed book burning, were such a practice pursued by a governmental agency or office as a way of suppressing speech, it would violate the First Amendment. Otherwise, private citizens who wish to burn books as a form of protest may do so as they wish.

For more information: *Book Burning.* American Library Association, Office of Intellectual Freedom. Available online. URL: http://www.ala.org/oif/bannedbooks-week/bookburning/bookburning.htm; Center for Media Literacy Web site. Available online. URL: http://www.medialit.com/about_cml.html.

—Jerry E. Stephens

Bork, Robert H. (1927–) *legal scholar*
Born March 1, 1927, Robert H. Bork is a renowned legal scholar. He earned a law degree at the University of Chicago in 1953, joined a Chicago law firm, and then became a faculty member of Yale Law School before serving as solicitor general from 1973 until 1977. During this period, he also served as acting attorney general in 1974. He taught at Yale from 1977 to 1979 and served as a U.S. court

of appeals judge from 1982 to 1988. He became a fellow at the American Enterprise Institution for Public Policy Research in 1988. His many publications include *Slouching Towards Gomorrah* (1997), *The Tempting of America* (1997), and *Coercing Virtue* (2003).

He is first known for his dark role in the Watergate scandal and his willingness to carry out President RICHARD NIXON's order to fire Watergate special prosecutor Archibald Cox following Cox's request of tapes of Oval Office conversations, the existence of which had been revealed by Nixon presidential assistant Alexander Butterfield. Nixon's attorney general, Elliot Richardson, and deputy attorney general, William Ruckleshaus, resigned rather than carry out that order. Bork, as next in line promptly fired Cox. Public reaction to the chain of events became popularized as the "Saturday Night Massacre." The subsequent appointment of Leon Jaworski as another special prosecutor ultimately led to public knowledge of Nixon's role in the Watergate cover-up when the Supreme Court ordered the tapes to be reviewed. Rather than confront IMPEACHMENT proceedings stemming from his role in the Watergate cover-up, Nixon resigned the presidency thus averting a possible constitutional crisis.

Bork's second foray into the public spotlight involved his 1987 nomination to the Supreme Court by President Ronald Reagan. Throughout his career, Bork has remained critical of the judicial activism practiced by the Supreme Court in landmark cases involving ABORTION, CIVIL RIGHTS, and AFFIRMATIVE ACTION. A self-proclaimed strict constructionist in interpreting the Constitution, Bork remains critical of judges applying broad interpretations of constitutional intent and has vowed to exercise judicial restraint and not be complicitous in Supreme Court decisions that thwart the will of popularly elected lawmakers. Bork believes judges should not substitute their values for the original INTENT OF THE FRAMERS of the Constitution. Bork's contrary public position in cases such as *GRISWOLD V. CONNECTICUT,* 318 U.S. 479 (1965), which provided the constitutional foundation for the right to PRIVACY, and *ROE V. WADE,* 410 U.S. 113 (1973), which established a woman's right to an abortion, was characterized by Bork as "a serious and wholly unjustified usurpation of state legislative authority." Bork also criticized the public accommodation provision in the CIVIL RIGHTS ACT OF 1964 for being a violation of the proprietor's freedom of association, and its principle, one of "unsurpassed ugliness." Comments like these ignited a firestorm of controversy at his confirmation hearings and placed him at the center of a jurisprudence maelstrom when he appeared before the 14-member judiciary committee. Throughout his five days of testimony, the longest confirmation hearing since hearings began in 1939, Bork surprised everyone by providing testimony that revealed a moderation of his controversial views.

However, despite Bork's attempt at conciliatory and nonideological testimony, his confirmation hearings became so vituperative and vitriolic that his ultimate defeat in the judiciary committee (9-5) and a floor vote in the SENATE (58-42) has possibly forever scarred, politicized, and tainted the advice-and-consent role of the Senate. The Bork confirmation experience established a new verb, *bork,* to describe the rough treatment of presidential nominees at congressional hearings.

Bork has had two major influences on the Constitution. In his articles and especially in his book *The Tempting of America,* he has developed many of the ideas of Herbert Wechsler and has argued that the Court must use NEUTRAL PRINCIPLES as a guide to interpreting the Constitution. Bork's arguments have taken him to arguing for a limited Court role in resolving constitutional disputes if it cannot apply neutral principles of law that were given to it by Congress. Second, Bork's writings on antitrust law, such as *The Antitrust Paradox* (1978), have been tremendously influential. In that book, he advocated that the Supreme Court adopt a more economic approach to understanding and interpreting antitrust law. To a large extent, the Court has done that in part because of the arguments made by Bork.

For more information: Vieira, Norman, and Leonard Gross. *Supreme Court Appointments* *and the Politicization of Senate Confirmations.* Carbondale: Southern Illinois University Press, 1998.

—William W. Riggs

Boumediene v. Bush, ___ U.S. ___ 128 S.Ct. 2229 (2008)

In *Boumediene v. Bush,* the Supreme Court issued a 5-4 decision declaring that aliens detained as enemy combatants at the U.S. Naval Station at Guantánamo Bay, Cuba, could use HABEAS CORPUS to challenge the legality of their detention. *Boumediene* is an important decision because it represents the fifth case the Bush administration lost before the Supreme Court regarding presidential authority to prosecute individuals involved with terrorism and the events of 9/11.

As a result of terrorist attacks against the United States on September 11, 2001, Congress authorized the president to use all "necessary and appropriate force" against any persons, organizations, and nations that aided or supported those acts of terrorism. To fight the "War on Terror" President George W. Bush used this authorization to send troops to Afghanistan against al-Qaeda and the Taliban regime that had supported them. He also used this authority and the power granted to him under ARTICLE II OF THE U.S. CONSTITUTION to create a detainment facility at the Naval Station at Guantánamo Bay to incarcerate individuals who were suspected of involvement in the events of 9/11 or other acts of terrorism. These individuals were declared by the president as "enemy combatants," not entitled to protections under international law, such as the Geneva Convention Relative to the Treatment of Prisoners of War, and were ordered held in confinement without HABEAS CORPUS protection. Habeas corpus refers to a right of individuals found in Article I, Section 9 of the Constitution that allows persons to challenge in court their detention, unless the right has been suspended by Congress for reasons of rebellion, invasion, or public safety. This section of the Constitution is often referred to as the suspension clause.

Prior to *Boumediene,* several cases had tested the scope of Bush's presidential power to fight terrorism. In *RASUL V. BUSH,* 545 U.S. 466 (2004), the U.S. Supreme Court ruled that aliens being held in confinement at the U.S. military base at Guantánamo Bay were entitled to have a federal court hear challenges to their detention under the federal habeas corpus statute. In *Hamdan v. Rumsfeld,* 548 U.S. ___, 126 S.Ct. 2749 (2006), the Supreme Court ruled that a Yemeni national held at Guantánamo Bay was entitled to habeas review of his detention and trial before a special military commission.

As a result of *Rasul* and *Hamdan,* Congress sought to limit the rights of detainees at Guantánamo Bay. First it adopted the Detainee Treatment Act (DTA) of 2005, which sought to deny habeas review to any alien detained at this facility. In *Hamdan,* the Court declared this act inapplicable to cases pending when it was passed. Congress then adopted the Military Commissions Act (MCA) of 2006, which sought to preclude courts from having habeas jurisdiction over detained aliens determined to be enemy combatants. Lakhdar Boumediene, an alien designated as an enemy combatant detained at Guantánamo Bay, challenged the law and his confinement by seeking habeas review of his incarceration. The lower courts ruled against Boumediene, holding that they lacked jurisdiction as a result of the MCA. The Supreme Court reversed the rulings.

In a 5-4 opinion written by Justice ANTHONY M. KENNEDY, the majority noted that neither aliens nor individuals designated as enemy combatants were precluded by the suspension clause from raising a habeas claim. Second, the Court ruled that the clause was applicable to the facility at Guantánamo Bay. Third, the provisions for trials set up in the MCA were inadequate substitutes for habeas review. Finally, the narrow exceptions that past precedents had established for when habeas review may be limited did not exist in this case.

The dissenters criticized the majority opinion on several counts. First, they criticized them for second guessing Congress and the president regarding the adequacy of protections that ought to be offered to enemy combatants. Second, it was unclear if the provisions of MCA were insufficient, because no one had tried to avail himself fully of them. Finally, the majority failed to describe what procedures had to be in place to comply with the suspension clause requirements.

Boumediene v. Bush was considered a major victory for individual rights and a blow to presidential and congressional power. Many saw it as a rejection of the way President Bush had conducted the war on terrorism. The case is an important statement about the scope of habeas rights for any individuals detained by the government in facilities located in areas under United States' control.

For more information: Adler, David Gray, and Robert George, eds. *The Constitution and the Conduct of American Foreign Policy.* Lawrence: University Press of Kansas, 1996; Fisher, Louis. *Presidential War Power.* Lawrence: University Press of Kansas, 2004; Henkin, Louis. *Foreign Affairs and the United States Constitution.* Oxford: Clarendon Press, 1996; ———. *Constitutionalism, Democracy, and Foreign Affairs.* New York: Columbia University Press, 1990; Schultz, David. "Democracy on Trial: Terrorism, Crime, and National Security Policy in a Post 9-11 World," *Golden Gate Law Review* 38 (2008): 195–248.

—David Schultz

Bowers v. Hardwick 478 U.S. 186 (1986)

In *Bowers v. Hardwick,* the U.S. Supreme Court ruled 5-4 that a Georgia statute that criminalized consensual sodomy was constitutional. Michael Hardwick, a homosexual man accused of consensual sodomy, challenged the Georgia statute in federal district court claiming that it violated his FUNDAMENTAL RIGHTS because "his homosexual activity is a private and intimate association that is beyond the reach of state regulation." The district court granted the Georgia attorney general's motion to dismiss for failure to state a claim, and a short time later, the U.S. Court of Appeals for the Eleventh Circuit reversed and remanded, stating that the statute violated certain rights guaranteed under the NINTH AMENDMENT and the DUE PROCESS clause of the FOURTEENTH AMENDMENT.

The issue the Supreme Court addressed was framed by Justice Byron White, in his majority opinion, as whether "the Federal Constitution confers a fundamental right upon homosexuals to engage in sodomy," along with addressing the Court's reach or role in altering historically longstanding state laws that criminalize such behavior. Justice White answered this question in the negative. First, the Court noted that prior cases conferring rights within family relationships, child rearing, procreation, and ABORTION had no resemblance to the rights claimed by Hardwick, as sodomy between two homosexual males was not part of the traditional familial relationship. Second, in granting certain substantive rights heightened judicial protection, the Court must show that the right to engage in homosexual sodomy is "deeply rooted in this Nation's history and tradition" and that this right is "implicit in the concept of ordered liberty," which the Court found that it did not (*PALKO V. STATE OF CONNECTICUT* [1937]).

This decision is no longer good law, however. The Supreme Court in *Lawrence et al. v. Texas* (2003), overturned the ruling in *Bowers* and declared that making it a crime for two persons of the same sex to engage in certain intimate sexual conduct violated the due process clause of the Fourteenth Amendment.

For more information: Pinello, Daniel R. *Gay Rights and American Law.* New York: Cambridge University Press, 2003; Richards, David A. J. *The Case for Gay Rights: From* Bowers *to* Lawrence *and Beyond.* Lawrence: University Press of Kansas, 2005.

—Peter A. Collins

Bowsher v. Synar 478 U.S. 714 (1986)

The Supreme Court, in *Bowsher v. Synar,* ruled that the provision in the Balanced Budget and Emergency Deficit Control Act of 1985 (commonly known as GRAMM-RUDMAN-HOLLINGS ACT) that gave authority to the U.S. Office of the Comptroller General to order the president to cut funds from the federal budget violated the separation of powers doctrine and was, therefore, unconstitutional.

The purpose of Gramm-Rudman-Hollings was to eliminate the annual budget deficits that had been increasing sharply since 1980 and to forestall the projected, steep increases of the next 10 years. The budget crisis came about with the election of Ronald Reagan, who campaigned in 1980 promising to cut income-tax rates, increase defense spending, and significantly reduce discretionary domestic spending. Reagan delivered on two of his pledges, cutting taxes and increasing defense spending; however, his reluctance to call for drastic cuts in domestic spending, coupled with a Congress more willing to spend than save, caused the national debt (the accumulated annual deficits) to more than double in four years.

Faced with two branches that appeared incapable of willfully making the decisions necessary to resolve the problem, Republican senators Phil Gramm of Texas and Warren Rudman of New Hampshire, with assistance from Democratic senator Ernest (Fritz) Hollings of South Carolina, proposed the act, which essentially took budget decisions away from both branches and gave them to the Comptroller General's office (CG).

The law established shrinking deficit targets for each year from 1986 to 1991, at which point the deficit would reach zero. If Congress and the president were unable voluntarily to attain the targeted figures, then automatic, across-the-board cuts were to be imposed, with half made in the military budget and the other half made equally across the remaining budget categories. Exempted from any reductions were Social Security, veterans, health, and several antipoverty programs. There were also provisions that protected the budget in case of national emergency, economic recession, or war.

The automatic budget cuts were to occur each year after the directors of the Office of Management and Budget (OMB), an executive agency, and the Congressional Budget Office (CBO) independently estimated the size of the budget deficit. If the deficit exceeded the target figure, the directors independently were to calculate, on a program-by-program basis, the reductions needed to ensure the target was met (Section 251). The directors' reports were then submitted to the CG for review. The comptroller general next sent his own recommendations to the president (Section 251[b]). The president was then to issue a sequestration order (in other words, a mandatory spending reduction order) using the CG's figures (Section 252 [a][3]). Congress was given some additional time to make spending cuts of its choice to meet the target, but failing that, the sequestration order was to take effect.

The law was immediately challenged by Ohio representative Michael Synar, a Democrat, and the case was first heard by a three-judge district court appointed for the purpose. That court, in *Synar v. U.S.* (626 F.Supp. 1374), ruled that the deficit reduction process violated the separation of powers because Congress had effectively legislated itself a role in the implementation of the act by placing authority to cut budgeted funds in the hands of the comptroller general, an officer of the Congress. The appeal was made in an expedited process to the Supreme Court.

In writing for the majority, Chief Justice WARREN EARL BURGER drew heavily on the reasoning of the lower court. By assigning the authority to the comptroller general to issue essentially sequestration orders and thus carry out the provision of the act, Congress had violated the separation of powers doctrine. Central to the majority's decision was the relationship of the comptroller general to the Congress.

As head of the Government Accountability Office (then called the General Accounting Office), an agency Congress created to assist it in overseeing the executive branch, the comptroller general is nominated by the president from a list of three people recommended by the Speaker of the HOUSE OF REPRESENTATIVES and president pro tempore of the SENATE, is confirmed by the Senate, but may be removed only at the discretion of Congress by a joint resolution or by IMPEACHMENT. While a president could VETO a joint resolution, such a veto may be overridden by Congress; therefore, the comptroller general is not removable by the president alone. Congress, declared the majority, may not "retain the power of removal over an officer performing executive functions" and cited the cases of *MYERS V. UNITED STATES*, 272 U.S. 52 (1926) and *HUMPHREY'S EXECUTOR V. UNITED STATES*, 295 U.S. 602 (1935):

> By placing the responsibility for execution of the Balanced Budget and Emergency Deficit

> Control Act in the hands of an officer who is subject to removal only by itself, Congress in effect has retained control over the execution of the Act and has intruded into the executive function. The Constitution does not permit such intrusion.

Justices JOHN PAUL STEVENS and Thurgood Marshall concurred with the majority, but instead of basing their reasoning on which branch can remove the comptroller general, they focused on his "longstanding statutory responsibilities" as an agent of Congress. The act empowered the comptroller general, an agent of the legislature, to make policy (decide budget cuts) without going through the full legislative process. Such delegation of power to the comptroller general violated the separation of powers doctrine.

Dissenting in the case were Justices Byron White and Harry Blackmun. White found the removal of the comptroller general argument "insignificant," while Blackmun would have restricted the Court's ruling to the invalidation only of those provisions of the act that concerned the sequestration order.

Bowsher, Immigration and Naturalization Service v. Chadha, 462 U.S. 919 (1983), and *Clinton v. New York,* 524 U.S. 417 (1998), remain important as cases that sustain the Supreme Court's interpretation of the separation of powers doctrine. Moreover, should questions be brought to the Court about the constitutionality of PRESIDENTIAL SIGNING STATEMENTS, the justices are likely to seek direction from these decisions.

For more information: Clayton, Cornell W. "Separate Branches, Separate Politics: Judicial Enforcement of Congressional Intent." *Political Science Quarterly* 109, no. 5 (1994): 843–872; Shepsle, Kenneth A. "Representation and Governance: The Great Legislative Trade-Off." *Political Science Quarterly* 103, no. 3 (1988): 461–484; West, William F., and Joseph Cooper. "Legislative Influence v. Presidential Dominance: Competing Models of Bureaucratic Control." *Political Science Quarterly* 104, no. 4 (1989): 581–606.

—Thomas J. Baldino

Boy Scouts of America v. Dale 530 U.S. 640 (2000)

In its 5-4 decision in *Boy Scouts v. Dale,* the Supreme Court reversed the lower New Jersey court decision and held that the Boy Scouts of America (BSA) was a private, not-for-profit organization, as well as an expressive organization, protected under the FIRST AMENDMENT from having to comply with state regulations concerning antidiscrimination on the basis of sexual orientation in public accommodations.

Earlier, in the New Jersey state court, the BSA had been found to be a public accommodation and hence within the purview of the regulations. As such, it could not discriminate against James Dale—an adult volunteer assistant scoutmaster who had been in the BSA since 1978, had been admitted to the Order of the Arrow and also awarded the rank of eagle scout, and had earned 25 merit badges along the way—because he was gay, as he had expressed on his college campus. At the time his membership was revoked, however, BSA had no publicly expressed standard specifically regarding gay members.

The resolution of this case in the favor of the BSA mirrors other rulings involving the BSA and discrimination on the basis of sexual orientation or atheism. These cases present a conflict between a large, national organization that relies on public support or government gratuities and makes use of public accommodations, which are governed by various nondiscrimination statutes, and the organization's claim nonetheless to be private and values based in such a way that to require it to adhere to these local statutes would compromise its identity and infringe on its mission and ability to interpret it.

The Court found that the BSA's stated policy and mission constituted it as an expressive association within the ambit of the First Amendment. Here, both its freedom of speech and FREEDOM OF RELIGION rights were implicated, given the nature of its mission, which included the BSA oath to be "morally straight" and the BSA policy INJUNCTION to be "clean," interpreted here to exclude all gay persons from any field position with the BSA as "unfit role models." An internal policy memo clari-

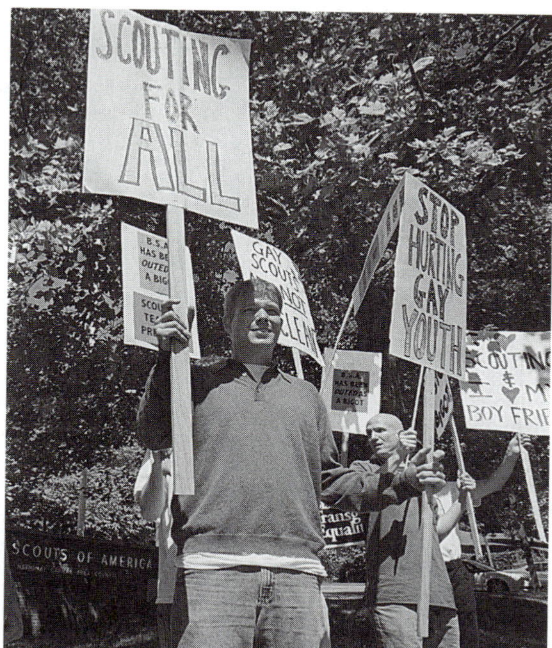

Demonstrators protest outside the National Capital Area Council for the Boy Scouts of America, August 21, 2000, in Bethesda, Maryland. *(Michael Smith/Getty)*

fying the meaning of *morally straight* to exclude gay persons had been only recently distributed to a few within the BSA's national leadership hierarchy and not disseminated to any lower or field levels prior to this case. Nonetheless, the Court gave deference to the BSA's assertions regarding its expression of values and found that to be required to retain Dale would burden the BSA's right to oppose or disfavor homosexual conduct as a legitimate form of behavior. The forced inclusion of Dale would probably significantly affect the BSA's ability to advocate public or private viewpoints, and so the New Jersey antidiscrimination statute had to give way to the right of expression as protected under the First Amendment.

The dissent in *Boy Scouts* argued that the BSA's contentions regarding its goals and the values it teaches warranted examination. In his dissenting opinion Justice DAVID H. SOUTER expressed skepticism at BSA claims and expressed concern that the right of expressive association not become a convenient trump of antidiscrimination law, itself a valuable state interest. Justice JOHN PAUL STEVENS's dissent focused attention on the BSA's lack of any specific language regarding the terms *morally straight* and *clean* in reference to sexual orientation, as well as the BSA injunction against any discussion of sexual matters with a boy scout, referring any inquiring boy scout to the religious leader of his choice, who might well not interpret those terms as in any way prejudicial to gay persons.

The general issues raised by cases involving the BSA have included whether the United Way should donate money to it if it is a private organization, whether a city should make public school facilities available to it as it can discriminate on the basis of sexual orientation, whether it may recruit members on public property given both its status as private and its stated views and policies regarding homosexuality and atheism, and whether public agencies governed by state and federal antidiscrimination statutes should abrogate charters with the BSA.

For more information: Babst, Gordon A. *Liberal Constitutionalism, Marriage, and Sexual Orientation.* New York: Peter Lang Publishing, 2002; Pinello, Daniel R. *Gay Rights and American Law.* New York: Cambridge University Press, 2003; Richards, David A. J. *The Case for Gay Rights: From* Bowers *to* Lawrence *and Beyond.* Lawrence: University Press of Kansas, 2005.

—Gordon A. Babst

Bradwell v. State of Illinois 83 U.S. 130 (1872)

The Supreme Court held, in *Bradwell v. Illinois*, that the state of Illinois could deny Myra Bradwell a license to practice law because she was a married woman without violating the PRIVILEGES AND IMMUNITIES clause of the FOURTEENTH AMENDMENT. The reasoning of this decision was couched in historical notions regarding the female sex, notions ultimately grounded in a religious perspective, the assumption of which would trouble today's jurists. Hence, what *Bradwell* is most known for is its now iconic statement regarding women and women's role in society.

Bradwell, whose application to practice law in the state of Illinois, where she had been residing for several years, was denied by that state's supreme court, appealed the decision to the U.S. Supreme Court. Both courts relied on traditional views about women and legal practices that reflected them. For example, it was submitted that, as in the earlier era in which the law was rooted, no one contemplated women's employment outside the domestic sphere, so there was no reason to suspect that, although never explicitly stated, the law ever contemplated the inclusion of women. In addition, it was believed that married women who practiced law were limited in that they would have difficulty enforcing contracts for their clients, as they were themselves limited in their own ability to enter into binding contracts separate from their husbands.

On behalf of Bradwell, it was argued that she was fully qualified to practice law, a point that was never in doubt regarding her professional training, extensive legal experience in her native state of Vermont, and success as a legal scholar. It was further argued that the Fourteenth Amendment applies to each state and so protected a member of a class of citizens when she emigrates from one state to another within the Union and so, too, the privileges and immunities she enjoyed in her former state of residence. The issue before the Court became whether admission to the bar in one state constituted a class of privileges that a state may not abridge or whether it belongs to a class of political rights in which the state may discriminate between citizens.

The Court answered the question of whether Bradwell had an enforceable right to employment by practicing at the bar of a judicial court in the negative, stating that this right is in no sense dependent on national citizenship and is not an avocation open to all citizens as a matter of right. The Court held that the privileges and immunities enjoyed by citizens in their state of residence applied only there and may not pertain to other states. The Court, then, gave this clause a narrow reading, one that was being explicated in the *Slaughterhouse Cases*, and rejected the analogy urged on it between discrimination against a class of people because of race and because of sex. Women, presumably regardless of their race, stood in a different relation to the law than did men, against whom it would be unlawful to discriminate on the basis of race.

The opinion of Justice Joseph P. Bradley was especially pointed as regards women's place in society "from time immemorial" and the ultimate source of that wisdom, before which the civil law must bend. He stated that the "paramount destiny and mission of woman are to fulfill the noble and benign offices of wife and mother" and that this is "the law of the Creator" to which "humane movements of modern society" as regards women's advancement must be adapted. Furthermore, he opined that it is the POLICE POWER of the state to comprehend the law of nature in order to ordain which honorable professions and offices women may be permitted entry as a matter of right and which are reserved for men.

For more information: Friedman, Jane M. *America's First Woman Lawyer: The Biography of Myra Bradwell.* Buffalo, N.Y.: Prometheus Books, 1993; Mezey, Susan Gluck. *Elusive Equality: Women's Rights, Public Policy, and the Law.* Boulder, Colo.: Lynne Rienner Publishers, 2003.

—Gordon A. Babst

Brandeis brief

When first presented in 1908, the Brandeis brief was a revolutionary approach to elaborating legally before the U.S. Supreme Court. It is named for Louis D. Brandeis (1856–1941), who argued before the Court against the removal of labor restrictions related to the number of hours a woman could work in the state of Oregon.

The seminal report for *Muller v. Oregon*, 208 U.S. 412 (1908), incorporated economic, statistical, and psychosocial data, within the disciplines of sociology and psychology. The reliance on factual data allowed Brandeis to successfully make his point that the restriction of hours upon female workers was both reasonable and within the underpinnings of the protections covered by the Constitution. His brief pursuant to this arguing before the Court resulted in a new manner of argument based upon data, not just legal thought.

Brandeis had a history of defending the public welfare and was hired in 1907 to represent the state of Oregon in a case before the U.S. Supreme Court that involved the constitutionality of limiting hours for female laundry workers. This effort by Brandeis to argue before the high court a cause championed by the Progressive movement resulted in a legal brief that retained the typical identity of a brief on the first two pages and then moved into more than 100 pages of data. At the time, the political climate had begun to turn against industrialists, and the regulation of industries began to be battled out in the courts. When the state of Oregon established a 10-hour workday, businesses challenged the law.

The Progressive movement was meanwhile picking battles across the United States to push its agenda, and Oregon was ripe for change. The Progressives claimed that businesses had long been operating in manners that furthered the exploitation of women, children, and the environment. Brandeis believed that private property rights of employers were subject to regulation by the government, and, thus, he acted as counsel and argued cases where he believed the courts did have a place in affirming the power of Congress to regulate industry through the acknowledgment of the need to manage the health and welfare of the populace. His lasting legacies were both the style of brief he created in *Muller* and its melding of facts with jurisprudence precedent to answer a previously unanswered challenge by the Supreme Court in the 1905 *LOCHNER V. NEW YORK* case. In a first, Justice David Josiah Brewer acknowledged the brief, which was the highest of compliments, but also admitted that he agreed with the approach that women were in fact different from men and consequently needed labor protections. As the FOURTEENTH AMENDMENT was not absolute, Brewer stated, the government retained a compelling right to limit the citizen's power of contract for his or her and others' benefit.

For more information: Strum, Philippa. *Louis D. Brandeis: Justice for the People.* Cambridge, Mass.: Harvard University Press, 1984.

—Ernest Gomez

Brandenburg v. Ohio 395 U.S. 444 (1969)

In *Brandenburg v. Ohio,* the U.S. Supreme Court defined the modern standard for when speech that may incite illegal action is protected by the FIRST AMENDMENT and when such speech goes too far and may be punished. The Court ruled that speech advocating illegal action may be punished only if it is "directed to inciting or producing imminent lawless action and is likely to incite or produce such action."

The decision was a monumental one in free speech law. It moved the Court away from the decades-old CLEAR AND PRESENT DANGER TEST first developed in *SCHENK V. UNITED STATES,* 249 U.S. 47 (1919). That test, developed by Justice OLIVER WENDELL HOLMES, JR., had launched a 50-year struggle in the Court to try to define when words create a "clear and present danger" of unlawful action that Congress thus has a right to prohibit. Critics said this standard restricted far too much speech that posed no real threat and punished dissent because it was effective.

In *Brandenburg,* the Court moved to a standard that was much more protective of free speech. The test requires both an intent by the speaker to provoke illegal action immediately and circumstances in which such action is likely to occur.

The case involved a Ku Klux Klan rally in Ohio. Clarence Brandenburg was a Klan leader who was convicted under Ohio law for advocating violence for political change; he was sentenced to one to 10 years in prison and $1,000 fine. According to evidence at his trial, Brandenburg called a local television reporter who arrived with a cameraman and recorded the rally. In a speech at the rally, Brandenburg warned that if the federal government did not stop acting against white Americans, "there might have to be some revengeance

[sic] taken." He challenged his conviction as violating the First Amendment as applied to the states through the FOURTEENTH AMENDMENT, but the Ohio courts rejected the constitutional arguments.

The Supreme Court reversed the ruling of the Ohio courts and also overruled an earlier decision, *WHITNEY V. CALIFORNIA*, 274 U.S. 357 (1927), which had upheld a California law similar to Ohio's. The Court said the Ohio law punished simple advocacy and did not require any evidence of imminent lawless action. As a result, the Court said the Ohio statute was unconstitutional.

The Court ruled in an unsigned opinion labeled *per curiam*, meaning "for the court." Researchers have determined that the opinion was started by Justice Abe Fortas, but when he resigned from the Court in a scandal in May 1969, Justice WILLIAM J. BRENNAN, JR., completed the decision.

Justice WILLIAM O. DOUGLAS wrote a concurring opinion, as did Justice HUGO BLACK. Since the Supreme Court did not expressly overrule the clear and present danger test but rather simply did not mention it, the two justices wrote to make sure the Court was no longer relying on the old test, which they believed did not properly reflect the values of the First Amendment. Douglas wrote: "I see no place in the regime of the First Amendment for any 'clear and present danger' test."

For more information: Linde, Hans A. "Clear and Present Danger Reexamined: Dissonance in the Brandenburg Concerto." *Stanford Law Review* 22 (1970): 1,163; Smolla, Rodney A. *Smolla & Nimmer on Freedom of Speech.* New York: Clark Boardman Callaghan, 1996; Wirenius, John F. "The Road to Brandenburg: A Look at the Evolving Understanding of the First Amendment." *Drake Law Review* 43 (1994): 1.

—Stephen Wermiel

Branzburg v. Hayes 408 U.S. 665 (1972)

In *Branzburg v. Hayes,* the U.S. Supreme Court ruled that the FIRST AMENDMENT guarantees of freedom of speech and FREEDOM OF THE PRESS do not shield journalists from the legal obligation to testify before grand juries about their confidential sources or other information.

In a 5-4 decision, written by Justice Byron R. White, the Court said that when a law is generally applicable (that is, it applies in the same manner to everyone), the First Amendment does not require that an exception be made to protect journalists. In this case, the generally applicable legal principle is that everyone has the same legal obligation to comply with subpoenas to appear before a grand jury or to testify at a trial.

The ruling was intended to settle an important legal question, yet the issue has remained the focus of controversy and debate for numerous reasons. First, lawyers representing news organizations have successfully taken advantage of ambiguity in the *Branzburg* ruling. Second, state legislatures have created various forms of privilege for journalists and their sources. Third, there have been periodic high-profile cases in which reporters have gone to jail rather than reveal their sources, calling dramatic attention to the question of whether lawyers can protect their confidential providers of information.

The *Branzburg* ruling was actually four consolidated cases. Paul Branzburg, a *Louisville Courier-Journal* reporter, was called to testify before a grand jury after he wrote a story in 1969 about two local hashish makers whose identity he had promised not to reveal. He also was called to testify before a second grand jury based on a 1971 story about drug use in Frankfort, Kentucky, in which he did not identify the names of users. The Kentucky courts ordered him to testify and rejected his claims of a First Amendment privilege.

A third case involved Paul Pappas, a reporter-photographer for a New Bedford, Massachusetts, television station who in 1970 spent several hours inside a Black Panther headquarters that was barricaded to protect against a rumored police raid that never materialized. Pappas refused to tell a grand jury about what he had observed and recorded, and the Massachusetts courts ruled against his claims of privilege.

The fourth case centered on *New York Times* reporter Earl Caldwell who was subpoenaed to tell a grand jury what he had learned from interviews with leaders of the Black Panther Party. A federal judge found that Caldwell had a First Amendment privilege to protect confidential informants but had to testify about anything he was told for purposes of publication. When the grand jury expired, the process was repeated with a new grand jury and judge. When Caldwell did not appear, he was held in contempt. But the U.S. Court of Appeals for the Ninth Circuit reversed and said Caldwell had a right not to appear before the grand jury because testifying would interfere with the flow of news to the public.

The U.S. Supreme Court ruled against all of the journalists. "It is clear that the First Amendment does not invalidate every incidental burdening of the press that may result from the enforcement of civil or criminal statutes of general applicability," Justice White wrote. Although White was clear in his decision, Justice LEWIS FRANKLIN POWELL, JR., wrote a concurrence that seemed to create some ambiguity. "The asserted claim to privilege," Powell wrote, "should be judged on its facts by the striking of a proper balance between freedom of the press and the obligation of all citizens to give relevant testimony with respect to criminal conduct." When compared to the dissent of Justice Potter Stewart, supported by Justices WILLIAM J. BRENNAN, JR., and Thurgood Marshall, and that of WILLIAM O. DOUGLAS, Powell's words left the impression that five justices favored a First Amendment privilege under some circumstances. Urged on by news media lawyers, numerous federal appeals courts agreed in the decades that followed.

Also in the years that followed, many states passed shield laws, recognizing some degree of privilege for reporters to protect confidential sources. In others, state supreme courts found the privilege to exist in state law or state constitutions. Some offer an absolute privilege; others attach qualifications. Only the U.S. Congress and Wyoming have refrained from recognizing a reporter's privilege.

High-profile jailings of journalists have also kept the issue in focus. In 2005, *New York Times* reporter Judith Miller refused to identify a source in the case involving the disclosure of covert CIA agent Valerie Plame's identity. Miller spent almost three months in jail before saying her confidential source had given her permission to reveal his identity. A freelance blogger and journalist spent seven months in prison in 2006 and 2007 for refusing to turn over to police video outtakes of a San Francisco protest in 2005 during an economic summit. In 1978, *New York Times* reporter Myron Farber spent more than a month in jail for refusing to turn over notes and interviews in a high-profile New Jersey murder case.

For more information: Dienes, C. Thomas, Lee Levine, and Robert C. Lind. "Newsgathering and the Law Section 14-1–Section 14-6, 720–765." Charlottesville, Va.: Lexis Law Publishing, 1999; Smolla, Rodney A. *Smolla & Nimmer on Freedom of Speech.* New York: Clark Boardman Callaghan, 1996.

—Stephen Wermiel

Bray v. Alexandria Women's Health Clinic

506 U.S. 263 (1993)

In *Bray v. Alexandria Women's Health Clinic*, the Supreme Court held that anti-ABORTION rights protesters could not be sued as a private conspiracy to deny women their constitutional rights.

As a result of controversy stemming from the decision in *ROE V. WADE*, 410 U.S. 113 (1973), which had legalized abortion across the country, individuals and organizations who opposed abortion rights protested outside abortion clinics. The protesters occasionally trespassed on the clinics' property, obstructed access to the clinics, and, in some instances, even took violent action against the clinics, doctors, and women seeking abortions. Several abortion clinics brought suit against the protesters, arguing that the protesters were engaged in a private conspiracy to deprive women seeking abortions of their constitutional right to interstate travel.

The Supreme Court held, in an opinion by Justice ANTONIN GREGORY SCALIA, that the abortion clinics could not bring suit against the protesters because the federal statute under which the clinics had brought suit did not provide a private cause of action against people obstructing access to abortion clinics. The federal statute required that the protesters discriminate against the women seeking an abortion because of their sex. The Court determined that the protesters did not have a generalized animus toward women but instead intended to protect fetuses by preventing women from seeking abortions. Furthermore, the Court explained that the protesters' activities were not aimed specifically at the women's right to travel across state lines to receive an abortion but were rather aimed at all women who sought an abortion.

In a dissent, Justice JOHN PAUL STEVENS argued that the federal statute under which the abortion clinics brought suit provided a private cause of action to the abortion clinics. In his view, the anti-abortion rights protesters were engaged in exactly the kind of "massive, organized, lawlessness" that the statute was originally enacted to punish. Rather than accepting what he saw as Justice Scalia's too "abstract question of logical deduction," Justice Stevens argued that the majority's decision ignored Congress's intent to protect "this Nation's citizens from what amounts to the theft of their constitutional rights by organized and violent mobs across the country." Because the abortion clinics were merely asserting the private cause of action that Congress sought to provide private litigants, the clinics should have been permitted to proceed with their suit.

For more information: Eisenstein, Laurence J., and Semeraro, Steven. "Abortion Clinic Protest and the First Amendment." *Saint Louis University Public Law Review* 13 (1993): 221; McCammond, Lisa. "Bray v. Alexandria's Women's Clinic: Narrowing the Scope of 42 U.S.C. 1985(3)." *Gonzaga Law Review* 29 (1994): 645.

—Winston E. Calvert

Brennan, William J., Jr. (1906–1997)

Supreme Court justice

William Joseph Brennan, Jr., was an associate justice of the U.S. Supreme Court from 1956 until 1990. He was one of the most influential liberal forces on the high court of the 20th century.

Brennan was born in Newark, New Jersey, on April 25, 1906, the second of William and Agnes McDermott Brennan's eight children. His parents were both Irish immigrants who met and married in the United States. William Brennan, Sr., was initially a laborer but rose to the position of Newark's director of public safety. He was an active labor leader at a time when many signs still hung on shop doors indicating that "no Irish need apply." Brennan, Sr., would play an enormously influential role in Brennan, Jr.'s life. It was his father's idea, in fact, that young William become a lawyer. This pro-labor, pro–common man influence of his father would help Brennan to become a leader of constitutional revolution on the Supreme Court.

Brennan graduated from Barringer High School in Newark in 1924, capturing most of the academic awards that were available. He then went on to the University of Pennsylvania's undergraduate Wharton School of Finance and Commerce. Although he graduated with honors in economics in 1928, his academic career was solid but somewhat unremarkable. He eloped with Marjorie Leonard right before his college graduation but made sure to have a Catholic wedding in Baltimore Cathedral. They remained married and deeply devoted to one another for 54 years, until her death. They had three children (William Brennan III, Hugh, and Nancy).

Marjorie stayed and worked in Newark to help pay tuition while Brennan attended Harvard Law School. His father died of pneumonia in 1930 during Brennan's second year. He nearly was forced to drop out but was granted a scholarship and supplemented by waiting tables and working odd jobs. Brennan was a member of Harvard's Legal Aid Society and represented the poor in various civil cases. He hoped to represent unions after his graduation in 1931, but with his wife, mother, and six siblings to support, he opted instead for a position with Pitney, Hardin & Skinner, Newark's premier law firm. He had clerked there during law school and became their first Catholic lawyer. He would later go on to become a partner in 1937. During his time with the firm, he represented management in labor affairs—180 degrees from his inclinations. He became an expert labor negotiator, and as an associate justice of the U.S. Supreme Court, he would become one of the most famous legal negotiators of all time. He would also end up becoming a great proponent of the individual worker through his Supreme Court opinions.

In 1942, Brennan accepted a post in the U.S. Army to help with labor issues during World War II. He eventually became chief of the Ordinance Department's Civilian Personnel Division and retired from the army in 1946 as a full colonel. He then headed back to his old law firm. In 1949, he acquiesced and agreed to become a trial judge and was appointed by the Republican governor of New Jersey. Brennan took a substantial pay cut with this position but still managed to support his extended family. After two other judicial promotions, he was quickly appointed to the New Jersey Supreme Court in 1952 by the same governor.

The year 1956 held a number of fortuitous events for Brennan. Associate Justice Sherman Minton resigned, which opened a seat on the high court. Several important supporters of Brennan suggested to President Dwight D. Eisenhower that he appoint him to the Supreme Court. It was an election year, and having an Irish Catholic Democrat appointed seemed to be a shrewd political move for Eisenhower. Later, President Eisenhower would say that appointing Justice Brennan was one of the worst mistakes he had made as president. At the time of Brennan's appointment, there were certainly inklings of his later clear liberal leanings, but his real influence would be on the Supreme Court.

Justice Brennan was characterized by a love of humanity. He was deeply religious and extremely close to his family. Notably, he was just as interested in the life of the Supreme Court's janitor as he was in the lives of the other justices. Even his critics noted his great warmth, charm, and ability to come up with a compromise if at all possible. He was driven by a desire to protect human dignity through democracy, the BILL OF RIGHTS, and the Fifth, THIRTEENTH, and FOURTEENTH AMENDMENTS. The increasingly liberal WARREN

Associate Justice William Joseph Brennan, Jr. *(U.S. Supreme Court)*

COURT, which was headed by Chief Justice Earl Warren from 1953 to 1969, was the perfect soil in which Justice Brennan's ideals could be planted. He masterfully drafted compromise opinions and authored the second most opinions of any Supreme Court justice: 1,360 in all.

Justice Brennan's long career on the Court includes many landmark and controversial cases. It is impossible to recite a full listing here, but some of his opinions particularly stand out. In *BAKER V. CARR*, 369 U.S. 186 (1962), Brennan's opinion of the Court stated that apportionment (voting distributions) was an appropriate question for federal courts. This set the stage for later cases ensuring "one person, one vote."

In *Jencks v. United States*, 353 U.S. 657 (1957), he wrote the majority opinion, which required prosecutors to release statements that would be used by witnesses at trial. He continued to fight for the constitutional rights of criminal defendants throughout his career.

Justice Brennan also was very involved in protecting the rights of free speech and the FIRST AMENDMENT. Brennan took his seat on the Supreme Court around the time of the McCarthy era and fought to keep Americans free to voice their political opinion. He also penned the opinion of the Court in *NEW YORK TIMES V. SULLIVAN*, 376

U.S. 254 (1964), which pushed back politicians' ability to stifle free press through libel laws.

Brennan is most remembered as a bulwark of CIVIL RIGHTS (and one of the most activist judges of all times). In *GREEN V. COUNTY SCHOOL BOARD OF NEW KENT COUNTY, VIRGINIA,* 391 U.S. 430 (1968) and *Keyes v. School District No. 1,* 413 U.S. 189 (1973), Justice Brennan furthered the cause of school DESEGREGATION. In *PLYLER V. DOE,* 457 U.S. 202 (1982), his well-negotiated majority opinion ensured access to public schools for undocumented alien children. He also staunchly supported the rights of women. He remained adamantly pro-choice and voted with the majority in *ROE V. WADE,* 410 U.S. 113 (1973).

After the death of his wife, Marjorie, in 1982, he married his secretary of 25 years. Brennan was 77 at the time. The marriage came as a surprise to others at the Supreme Court, who found out about it after the fact. Justice Brennan sent out a memo that simply said, "Mary Fowler and I were married yesterday and we have gone to Bermuda." They remained married until Justice Brennan's death.

The more conservative REHNQUIST COURT decisions were challenging for a liberal, but Brennan remained a bridge builder between liberals and conservatives. He continued to write important opinions until the end of his career as a Justice in 1990, when he retired due to failing health. For example, in *TEXAS V. JOHNSON,* 491 U.S. 397 (1989), and *United States v. Eichman,* 496 U.S. 310 (1990), Justice Brennan wrote powerful majority opinions protecting free speech rights. After his retirement, his seat on the Supreme Court was filled by Associate Justice DAVID H. SOUTER.

After his retirement from the Court, he taught seminars on constitutional law and theory and often visited his friends in the Court. He died in an Arlington, Virginia, nursing home, where he was recuperating from a broken hip.

The core, if not all, of his constitutional philosophy is likely to be a lasting legacy in constitutional law as society and civil rights continue to evolve.

For more information: Eisler, Kim Isaac. *The Last Liberal: Justice William J. Brennan, Jr. and the Decisions That Transformed America.* Frederick, Md.: Beard Books, 2003; Sepinuck, Stephen L., ed. *The Conscience of the Court: Selected Opinions of Justice William J. Brennan, Jr. on Freedom and Equality.* Carbondale: Southern Illinois University Press, 1999.

—Maria Collins Warren

Breyer, Stephen G. (1938–) *Supreme Court justice*

Stephen G. Breyer has been an associate justice of the U.S. Supreme Court since August 3, 1994, after a distinguished career that included lengthy tenure as a professor at Harvard Law School and a judge on the U.S. Court of Appeals for the First Circuit.

He was born on August 15, 1938, in San Francisco, earned his undergraduate degree from Stanford University, and obtained his law degree from Harvard Law School. He served as a law clerk to Supreme Court justice Arthur Goldberg and then as an assistant in the Antitrust Division of the U.S. Department of Justice before joining the Harvard Law School faculty in 1967, where he became an expert in regulation and administrative law. In the 1970s, he did stints as an assistant prosecutor on the staff of the Watergate Special Prosecutor and as special counsel and then chief counsel to the Senate Judiciary Committee. In 1980, he was sworn in as a federal appeals court judge on the First Circuit and served as chief judge from 1990 to 1994. While on the appeals court, he also served as a founding member of the U.S. Sentencing Commission, which rewrote the federal criminal SENTENCING GUIDELINES. He was nominated to the Supreme Court by President Bill Clinton to replace Justice Harry A. Blackmun.

On the bench, Breyer generally slipped into the liberal or moderate wing of the Court that regularly included Justices JOHN PAUL STEVENS, DAVID H. SOUTER, and Ruth Bader Ginsburg. He wrote the Court's 5-4 decision in *Stenberg v. Carhart,* 530 U.S. 914 (2000), striking down a Nebraska law banning a form of late-term ABORTION. Although his decision was eclipsed by *GONZALES, ATTORNEY GENERAL V. CARHART,* ___ U.S. ___ (2007), which upheld a similar federal law, Breyer made his position on abortion clear that governments should not impose obstacles in the path of women seeking abortions.

His decisions are often described as pragmatic and not as predictable as some other liberal justices. When the Supreme Court upheld one display of the TEN COMMANDMENTS and struck down another, it was Breyer alone who saw all-important factual distinctions between the unlawful Kentucky display, *MCCREARY COUNTY, KENTUCKY V. AMERICAN CIVIL LIBERTIES UNION,* 545 U.S. 844 (2005), and the lawful Texas one, *VAN ORDEN V. PERRY,* 545 U.S. 677 (2005).

He was a solid member of the liberal wing that dissented from the Court's several rulings curtailing the powers of Congress in relation to the states. He wrote a dissent in *UNITED STATES V. LOPEZ,* 514 U.S. 549 (1995), when the Court invalidated a federal restriction on guns near schools. Breyer offered a list of reasons why it was appropriate for Congress to feel that guns near schools had a substantial effect on INTERSTATE COMMERCE.

Breyer has had unusual visibility for at least two reasons. First, in 2005, he wrote *Active Liberty: Interpreting Our Democratic Constitution,* a book in which he analyzed his own judicial decision-making patterns and concluded that the Constitution must be understood as promoting active citizen participation in democracy. He also engaged in a series of debates with Justice ANTONIN GREGORY SCALIA, first in 2005 over the relevance of foreign law to decisions of the U.S. Supreme Court and then in 2006 over the differences in their approaches to CONSTITUTIONAL INTERPRETATION. Breyer argued in the first instance that foreign courts could influence the evolution of U.S. court decisions, while Scalia was adamant that foreign law has no relevance to interpreting the U.S. Constitution. In the second engagement, Breyer took the position that the Constitution must be understood not just as a set of words but also as a set of goals and ideals; Scalia argued that it was the words of the Constitution that mattered when it was drafted in 1787 and that still matter today.

For more information: Breyer, Stephen G. *Active Liberty: Interpreting Our Democratic Constitution.* New York: Alfred A. Knopf, 2005; Gewirtz, Paul. "The Pragmatic Passion of Stephen G. Breyer." *Yale Law Journal* 115 (2006): 1,675; Urofsky, Melvin I., ed. *Biographical Encyclopedia of the Supreme Court.* Washington, D.C.: CQ Press, 2006.

—Stephen Wermiel

Broadrick v. Oklahoma 413 U.S. 601 (1973)

In *Broadrick v. Oklahoma,* the Supreme Court issued an important FIRST AMENDMENT ruling that clarified what is known as the "overbreadth" doctrine.

Broadrick v. Oklahoma involved three appellants who were employees of the state of Oklahoma. Charges were filed against these state employees for having violated Section 818 of the Oklahoma Merit System of Personnel Administration Act. According to paragraph six of this act, no classified state employee "shall directly or indirectly, solicit, receive, or in any manner be concerned in soliciting or receiving any assessment . . . or contribution for any political organization, candidacy or other political purpose." Paragraph seven of this act states that no employee shall be a member of "any national, state or local committee of a political party." In other words, an Oklahoma state employee may not be involved in politics "except to exercise his right as a citizen privately to express his opinion and . . . vote."

In 1970, employees of the Oklahoma Corporation Commission had been actively involved in the reelection campaign of a state corporation commissioner who was their superior. They allegedly asked other employees to take part in the campaign. One individual was charged with distributing campaign posters, and two of the appellants were charged with soliciting campaign contributions from commission employees. The appellants claimed in the federal district court that the act was overly broad when applied; therefore, the act may deprive people of protected forms of free speech, such as using campaign button or bumper stickers. The district court upheld the law, and the case made its way to the U.S. Supreme Court.

In a 5-4 decision, written by Justice Byron White, the Court upheld the law under the First Amendment of the Constitution. The Court noted the following:

> Although such laws, if too broadly worded, may deter protected speech to some unknown extent there comes a point where that effect—at best a prediction—cannot, with confidence, justify invalidating a statute on its face and so prohibiting a State from enforcing the statute against conduct that is admittedly within its power to proscribe. . . . To put the matter another way, particularly where conduct and not merely speech is involved, we believe that the *overbreadth* [emphasis added] of a statute must not only be real, but substantial as well, judged in relation to the statute's plainly legitimate sweep. . . . It is our view that 818 is not substantially overbroad and that whatever overbreadth may exist should be cured through case-by-case . . . analysis of the fact situations to which its sanctions, assertedly, may not be applied.

The Court noted two key points to this doctrine of overbreadth. A law that focuses on conduct and not just mere speech must (1) be real and (2) be substantial. In this case, the Court determined the law focused on conduct and not merely speech and that the law was not substantial enough to be overbroad. However, the Court appears to have left the issue open with the comment, "that whatever overbreadth may exist should be cured through case-by-case . . . analysis."

For more information: Farber, Daniel A., William N. Eskridge, Jr., and Philip P. Frickey. *Cases and Materials on Constitutional Law: Themes for the Constitution's Third Century*. St. Paul, Minn.: West Publishing, 1993.

—Dan Krejci

Brown v. Board of Education of Topeka

347 U.S. 483 (1954)

In *Brown v. Board of Education of Topeka,* the Supreme Court struck down the "separate but equal" doctrine as it applied to primary and secondary education. The 1954 decision was the culmination of decades of work by CIVIL RIGHTS activists including the National Association for the Advancement of Colored People (NAACP), which had been working in the federal courts for decades to desegregate the nation's schools. Arguably, the *Brown* decision is one of the most important cases and opinions ever issued by the Supreme Court.

In the 1930s and 1940s, some progress was made toward DESEGREGATION in higher education. Then, in 1950, the Supreme Court held in *Sweatt v. Painter,* 339 U.S. 629, that the EQUAL PROTECTION clause of the FOURTEENTH AMENDMENT required a black man, Herman Marion Sweatt, be admitted to the University of Texas Law School because the available schooling for blacks was grossly unequal to that for whites. Also in 1950, in *McLaurin v. Oklahoma,* 339 U.S. 637, the Court held that allowing blacks into the school for whites (the University of Oklahoma) and providing them with separate spaces within that school created an unequal situation.

About the time those decisions were being handed down, in the early 1950s, Linda Brown, a third grader in Topeka, Kansas, was walking six blocks to her school bus stop to ride to Monroe Elementary, her segregated black school one mile away, while Sumner Elementary, a white school, was only seven blocks from her house. Her father contacted a local attorney, who, in turn, referred him to the local chapter of the NAACP. It asked parents of black students to attempt enrolling their children in the closest neighborhood school in the fall of 1951. Each was refused enrollment and directed to segregated schools.

A class-action suit was filed against the Board of Education of the City of Topeka, Kansas, in the U.S. District Court for the District of Kansas on behalf of these parents and their children. Eventually, the case made its way to the Supreme Court, which combined five cases under the heading of *Brown v. Board of Education* because each sought the same legal remedy. The combined cases originated in Delaware, Kansas, South Carolina, Virginia, and Washington, D.C.

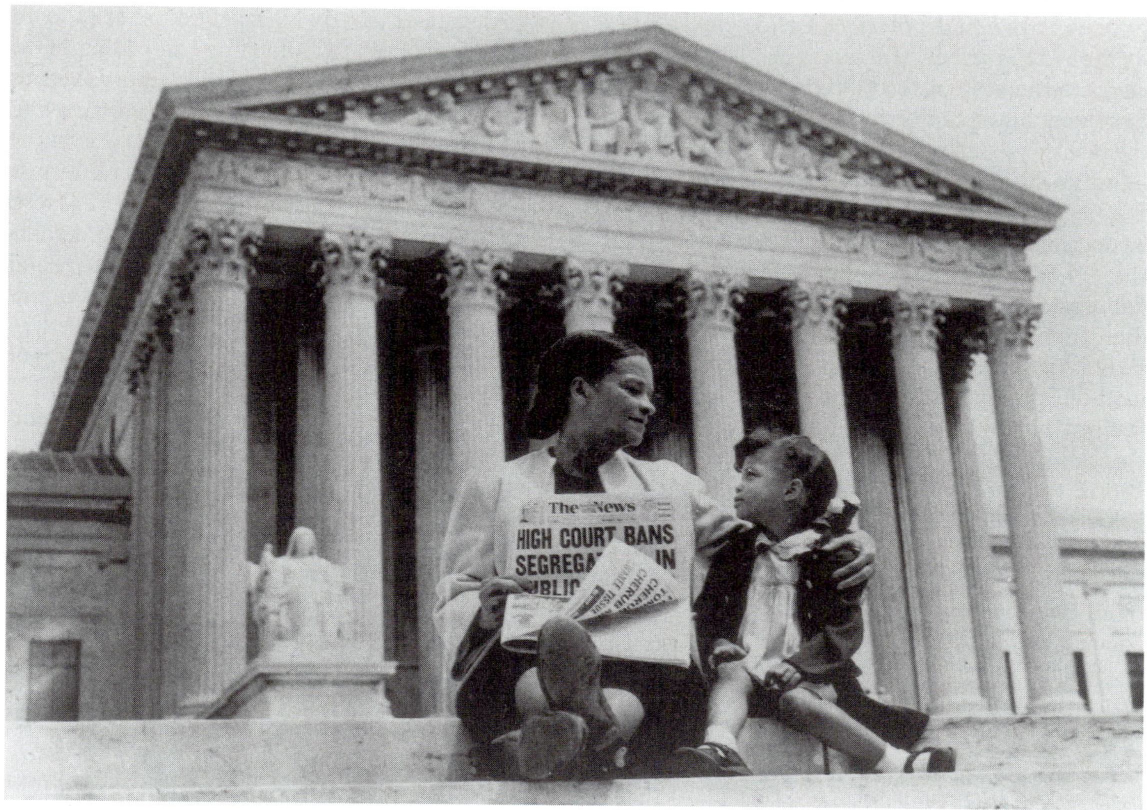

A newspaper headline announcing that the U.S. Supreme Court has abolished segregation in public schools *(Schomburg Center for Research in Black Culture)*

Four of the cases were to be argued on the basis of the equal protection clause of the Fourteenth Amendment. The DISTRICT OF COLUMBIA case, *BOLLING V. SHARPE,* was covered by the equal protection clause of the Fifth Amendment, not of the Fourteenth.

The cases were initially argued in December 1952, but a decision was never handed down because, under Chief Justice Frederick Moore Vinson's leadership, the Court attempted to decide the case both on the merits and remedy. The Court was divided not on the merits but on relief. In summer 1953, Vinson died and President Dwight D. Eisenhower appointed Earl Warren to succeed him. The case was reargued on December 8, 1953, and the Court handed down a unanimous decision on May 17, 1954.

Warren had convinced the members of the Court to decide the case on just the merits and defer the question of relief to a second opinion following reargument. It was the decision on the merits that was handed down in May 1954. The decision was just 11 pages: Warren wanted an opinion that the layperson could read and understand and one that the newspapers could print in its entirety. The decision did not expressly overturn *PLESSY V. FERGUSON* as it applied only to primary and secondary education. It stated that segregation of children in public schools solely on the basis of race deprives the children of the minority group of equal educational opportunities and that the separate but equal doctrine had no place in the field of public education. When the state undertook to provide education, it had to do so on equal terms to all.

A controversial portion of the opinion was footnote 11 in which Warren applied sociological views to the case instead of interpreting the law. Northern newspapers, for the most part, hailed the decision as "momentous," while the black community took a mixed wait-and-see reaction.

One year after *Brown,* the Court handed down its decision dealing with relief. The decision states that school districts should desegregate "with all deliberate speed." This ambiguous decision muddied the waters more than it cleared them, and it took many years for consistent progress to be made in the implementation of *Brown.* With no federal leadership, implementation of *Brown* was deliberately slow and uneven. By the mid-1960s, the Departments of Justice and Health, Education, and Welfare had assumed leadership in implementing *Brown.* But whatever the weaknesses were in the *Brown* decision, it was still a significant step toward attempting to bring about equality among the races.

For more information: Klarman, Michael J. *From Jim Crow to Civil Rights.* New York: Oxford University Press, 2004; Kluger, Richard. *Simple Justice: The History of* Brown v. Board of Education *and Black America's Struggle for Equality.* New York: Vintage Books, 2004; Urofsky, Melvin, and Paul Finkelman. *A Constitutional History of the United States.* Vol. 2: *A March of Liberty.* New York: Oxford University Press, 2002.

—Mark Alcorn

Buchanan v. Warley 245 U.S. 60 (1917)

In *Buchanan v. Warley,* the Supreme Court ruled that residential segregation laws violated the property rights of individuals. Such laws were enacted in a number of communities in the upper South during the second decade of the 20th century. These measures were justified as an exercise of POLICE POWER to prevent racial conflict by mandating separate residential areas for blacks and whites.

In 1914, Louisville, Kentucky, passed an ordinance prohibiting whites and blacks from living in houses on blocks where a majority of homes were occupied by individuals of the other race. To arrange a test case challenging the ordinance, a white seller and a black purchaser entered a contract for the sale of property on a majority white block. The purchaser then refused to complete the transaction on grounds that he could not occupy the premises under the ordinance. The Kentucky Court of Appeals sustained the ordinance as a valid police power regulation to promote racial harmony and safeguard racial purity. It therefore ruled that the ordinance constituted a defense to an action for specific performance of the contract by the seller.

The Supreme Court, in a unanimous opinion by Justice William R. Day, held that the ordinance amounted to a deprivation of property without DUE PROCESS of law in violation of the FOURTEENTH AMENDMENT. Justice Day declared: "Property is more than the mere thing which a person owns. It is elementary that it includes the right to acquire, use and dispose of it." He was skeptical about the racial purity rationale, pointedly observing that "the employment of colored servants in white families [was] permitted." Day was also unconvinced that racial segregation would preserve property values. He noted that nearby property might be acquired "by undesirable white neighbors." Cutting to the heart of the matter, Justice Day asserted: "The right which the ordinance annulled was the civil right of a white man to dispose of his property if he saw fit to do so to a person of color and of a colored person to make such disposition to a white person." It followed that this restriction on the right to alienate land constituted an unconstitutional deprivation of an essential attribute of property. Day concluded that the goal of racial harmony could not be accomplished by destroying the right to dispose of property.

Decided in an era when segregationist attitudes were widely shared, *Buchanan* linked judicial solicitude for the rights of property owners with concern for racial minorities. This landmark decision halted the movement to enact residential segregation laws in American cities and was the most significant victory for CIVIL RIGHTS in the early decades of the 20th century. Justice Day's opinion rested squarely on the premise that the due process clause of the Fourteenth Amendment imposed substantive limits on state governments. *Buchanan* was a powerful reminder that a principled defense of individual property rights may safeguard the interests of vulnerable segments of society.

For more information: Ely, James W., Jr. "Reflections on *Buchanan v. Warley,* Property Rights, and Race." *Vanderbilt Law Review* 51 (1998): 953; Klarman, Michael J. *From Jim Crow to Civil Rights: The Supreme Court and the Struggle for Racial Equality.* New York: Oxford University Press, 2004.

—James W. Ely, Jr.

Buck v. Bell 274 U.S. 200 (1927)

In *Buck v. Bell,* the U.S. Supreme Court upheld a Virginia statute providing for compulsory sterilization of the mentally retarded for the protection and general welfare of the state. The effect of the case was to legitimize eugenic sterilization in the United States. While many states already had sterilization statutes in effect at the time of the ruling, the Court's decision led many other states to create new sterilization statutes or update their current ones to resemble more closely the Virginia statute upheld by the Court.

The case began when, on September 10, 1924, the superintendent of the Virginia State Colony for Epileptics and Feebleminded petitioned to the board of directors of the Virginia State Colony to have Carrie Buck, an 18-year-old patient at the institution, sterilized. The statute required that a hearing be conducted prior to the sterilization procedure to determine whether it was necessary. The board of directors granted the petition and the guardian of Buck appealed the case to the Circuit Court of Amherst County, which upheld the decision of the board. The case then moved to the Supreme Court of Appeals of Virginia, where the board's decision was again upheld. Following the decision of the lower courts to uphold the sterilization statute as compliant with both state and federal constitutions, the case moved to the U.S. Supreme Court. The question presented by the case was whether the Virginia statute that called for compulsory sterilization denied Buck the DUE PROCESS of law as guaranteed under the FOURTEENTH AMENDMENT.

The Supreme Court held, in an 8-1 ruling, that the statute did not violate the due process clause of the Fourteenth Amendment. The Court determined that given the fact that before the sterilization procedure could take place a hearing, at which the patient and a parent or guardian could be present, must be conducted and the fact that the appeals process allowed the case to reach the circuit court of the county as well as the supreme court of appeals of the state, Buck's Fourteenth Amendment rights had not been violated. Writing for the majority, Justice OLIVER WENDELL HOLMES, JR., stated that the interests of the state in preventing the birth of mentally underdeveloped children was sufficient to justify the statute and added, in words that have become infamous, "Three generations of imbeciles are enough."

For more information: Kevles, Daniel J. *In the Name of Eugenics: Genetics and the Uses of Human Heredity.* New York: Knopf, 1985; Lombardo, Paul A. "Three Generations, No Imbeciles: New Light on *Buck v. Bell." New York University Law Review* 60, no. 1 (1985): 50–62.

—Marc Ruffinengo

Buckley v. American Constitutional Law Foundation 525 U.S. 182 (1999)

In *Buckley v. American Constitutional Law Foundation* (ACLF), the Supreme Court held that portions of Colorado's restrictions on initiative petition circulators violated the FIRST AMENDMENT. The case demonstrates the Supreme Court's delicate balance between First Amendment protections and proper regulations to ensure fair elections.

Colorado's initiative process allows its residents to add proposed laws to the ballot by submitting petitions with a required number of valid signatures. In *Meyer v. Grant,* 486 U.S. 414 (1988), the Supreme Court had struck down Colorado's ban on paid initiative petition circulators, finding that initiative petitioning was "core political speech." The state's subsequent limitations on petition circulators were challenged in federal court by the ACLF and several individuals. The district court upheld requirements that circulators submit affidavits with their names and addresses, a six-month time limit for petitions, and requirements that circulators be 18 years or older and be registered to vote. However, the court held the requirement that circulators wear name badges, as well as portions of the requirements for reporting the names of payors and payments made to circulators, to be in violation of the First Amendment in *ACLF v. Meyer,* 870 F. Supp. 995 (Colo. 1994). The Tenth Circuit agreed but added that the voter registration requirement unduly limited political expression (*ACLF v. Meyer,* 120 F.3d 1092 [1997]).

The Supreme Court's majority decision, written by Justice Ruth Bader Ginsburg and joined by Justices JOHN PAUL STEVENS, ANTONIN GREGORY SCALIA, ANTHONY M. KENNEDY, and DAVID H. SOUTER, affirmed the Tenth Circuit's balance between valid ballot-access regulations and undue limitations on First Amendment rights, noting that there can be "no litmus paper test." The Court found that the state's interest in policing circulators who might break election laws was fulfilled by the affidavit requirement and, therefore, did not justify the voter registration or name badge requirements. The Court found that voter registration requirements substantially decreased the number of eligible circulators and noted that the refusal to register to vote might be an act of political expression. The Court argued that the name badge requirement overly burdened the circulator's interest in anonymous speech at the moment of contact, which might limit the number of people willing to circulate petitions on volatile issues. The Court also found that the state's interest in disclosure of special interest influence was served by reporting the names and amounts of payors of petition circulators, but requiring disclosure of payments to individual circulators failed to survive the "exacting scrutiny" required by *BUCKLEY V. VALEO,* 424 U.S. 1 (1976).

Justice CLARENCE THOMAS concurred but argued that the Court should have used STRICT SCRUTINY analysis to find that the requirements were not narrowly tailored to serve the state's interests. Chief Justice WILLIAM HUBBS REHNQUIST, dissenting, argued that voter registration and residency requirements were not unduly burdensome and that states should be able to limit those circulating petitions to those who can ultimately vote on them. SANDRA DAY O'CONNOR and STEPHEN G. BREYER, concurring in part and dissenting in part, agreed with Rehnquist's analysis of voter registration requirements but argued that the disclosure requirements reasonably advanced state interests in public disclosure and deterring fraud, similar to campaign contributor requirements previously upheld under *Buckley v. Valeo.*

The effect of *Buckley v. American Constitutional Law Foundation* was to affirm that direct democracy petition campaigns are "core political speech" that cannot be unduly burdened and to distinguish these undue burdens from necessary election regulations, as in *Storer v. Brown,* 415 U.S. 724 (1974); *Anderson v. Celebrezze,* 460 U.S. 780 (1983); and *TIMMONS V. TWIN CITIES AREA NEW PARTY,* 520 U.S. 351 (1997).

For more information: Braunstein, Richard. *Initiative and Referendum Voting: Governing Through Direct Democracy in the United States.* New York: LFB Scholarly Publishing, 2004; Ryden, David. *The U.S. Supreme Court and the Electoral Process.* 2d ed. Washington, D.C.: Georgetown University Press, 2002; Urofsky, Melvin I. *Money and Free Speech: Campaign Finance Reform and the Courts.* Lawrence: University Press of Kansas, 2005; Zimmerman, Joseph F. *The Initiative: Citizen Law-Making.* Oxford: Praeger, 1999.

—Julie Lantrip

Buckley v. Valeo 424 U.S. 1 (1976)

Buckley v. Valeo is the key CAMPAIGN FINANCE ruling of the U.S. Supreme Court. At its broadest level, *Buckley v. Valeo* held that limits on spending by candidates are unconstitutional but that campaign contributions could be limited to prevent corruption or the appearance of corruption. The issues raised in *Buckley* continue to be litigated in federal courts and before the Supreme Court, and campaign finance remains an emerging and changing area of constitutional law.

In 1974, in the wake of the Watergate scandal, the U.S. Congress passed the Federal Election Campaign Act (FECA). The primary provisions of the FECA imposed expenditure limits for candidates, established contribution limits set at $1,000 per election, created public disclosure requirements, established the Federal Election Commission (FEC), and created the presidential campaign public financing system.

The Court addressed the constitutionality of the contribution limits and upheld them. The Court found that contribution limits implicate both the freedom of association and freedom of expression provisions of the FIRST AMENDMENT. Despite the infringement on protected rights, the Court held that the prevention of corruption or the appearance of corruption was a sufficient and constitutional justification for limiting campaign contributions from an individual to a candidate for federal office to $1,000. On balance, the Court concluded, the $1,000 contribution limit was allowed to stand; however, the Court created an exemption from the contribution limit for contributions from the candidate's own personal funds. The Court reasoned that a candidate's own money could not corrupt the candidate.

Litigation has continued to challenge the constitutionality of contribution limits, and such limits were upheld in cases such as *NIXON V. SHRINK MISSOURI GOVERNMENT PAC*, 528 U.S. 377 (2000), which dealt with candidates for state office in Missouri, but were ruled unconstitutional in *Randall v. Sorrell*, 126 S. Ct. 1184, 163L. Ed. 2d 1126 (2006), which dealt with candidates for state office in Vermont.

In contrast to the contribution limits, the Court found that expenditure limits imposed "direct and substantial restraints on the quantity of political speech." These limits, the Court held, did not address the "corruption or appearance of corruption" that justified contribution limits because there is no legitimate government interest in reducing the quantity of political speech.

The Court did uphold, however, expenditure limits contained within the voluntary public financing system established by the FECA for candidates for president. The Court reasoned that the exchange of government money for restrictions on spending did not violate the First Amendment. The Court upheld the public disclosure provisions of the FECA, which required that both contributions and expenditures by candidates, political parties, and political committees be publicly disclosed.

The Court, nonetheless, appeared to narrow the scope of the FECA so that "expenditures" for public communications were covered by the FECA only if they contained words of "express advocacy" such as *elect, support, defeat,* or *vote for.* This led to the rise of so-called issue ads that were run by political parties and other interest groups that would say "Call candidate Smith and tell him to support lower taxes" and, as a result, were outside of the regulation of the FECA.

This apparent narrowing of the FECA has been at issue since that time. The FEC litigated numerous cases against speech it felt was covered by the FECA, but the courts, with one exception, have uniformly rejected the FEC's view of the scope of the FECA. However, in 2002, the U.S. Congress passed the Bi-Partisan Campaign Reform Act (BCRA), which sought to limit so-called issue advocacy by requiring disclosure and limiting the source of funds that could be used to air broadcast advertisements mentioning or referring to federal candidates within a certain period of time before an election. The Supreme Court ultimately upheld this limitation and cast doubt on the validity of the apparent narrowing construction of *Buckley* when the Court decided *MCCONNELL V. FEC*, 540 U.S. 93 (2003).

Buckley v. Valeo continues to be the most important of the Supreme Court's campaign finance opinions. When legislatures consider creating or modifying campaign finance schemes, the Supreme Court's ruling in *Buckley* must be reviewed and incorporated into the legislation or the scheme risks invalidation under the First Amendment. Litigation over the meaning of *Buckley* continues to this day and is expected to continue for years to come.

For more information: Bauer, B. *More Soft Money Hard Law.* 2d ed. Washington, D.C.: Perkins Coie, 2004; Malbin, M. J. *The Election After Reform: Money, Politics, and Bipartisan Campaign Reform Act.* Lanham, Md.: Rowman & Littlefield, 2006.

—Jason Torchinsky

Burdick v. Takushi 504 U.S. 428 (1992)

In *Burdick v. Takushi,* the U.S. Supreme Court considered a Hawaii election law that barred write-in voting on election day. Alan B. Burdick challenged the statute, arguing that it unconstitutionally restricted the casting, tabulation, and publication of write-in votes. Specifically, the registered voter asserted the limitations constituted an infringement of his FIRST and FOURTEENTH AMENDMENTS rights. The district court upheld the voter's position, but the Court of Appeals for the Ninth Circuit disagreed. The U.S. Supreme Court, in an opinion authored by Justice Byron White, held that Hawaii's prohibition of same-day write-in voting is constitutional.

The Court began by noting that voting is of fundamental significance. At the same time, it noted states are permitted to make reasonable regulations to administer elections. When states impose severe restrictions, they must justify the interference by a compelling interest, but if the restrictions are reasonable and nondiscriminatory, Justice White noted, a lower degree of justification would be necessary.

With that basic understanding, the Court turned to classifying the regulation at hand. In Hawaii, there exist three methods to secure access to the ballot: a party petition, an established party nomination, or nonpartisan nominating papers. In each case, there exist time limits, nominating papers, and sometimes a required number of voter signatures. The Court argued the burdens from these requirements are limited and do not seriously restrict the right to make free choices. Every requirement, to some degree, restricts the individual RIGHT TO VOTE and, as such, interferes with the right to associate for political reasons; however, outlawing reasonable, nondiscriminatory limitations would tie the hands of the states. Justice White thus argued write-in candidates have no inherent superior right to await the 11th hour and thereby avoid those requirements imposed by the traditional ballot access.

The Court raised a series of legitimate policy concerns that favored this state regulation; for example, write-ins could be a sore-loser device to further challenge the winner of the primary. This could create factionalism in the general election. States have a recognized legitimate concern against this. Additionally, Hawaii conducts an open primary in which voters from one party can vote for primary candidates from another party. However, the candidates for a particular nomination must certify their membership in that party. Write-ins could undermine this principle. This write-in procedure would allow individuals to run for a party nomination without certifying membership in that party.

In sum, the Court felt the state's overall ballot access scheme provided ample opportunities for participation by would-be candidates. Thus, prohibitions against write-in voting are presumptively valid. In many instances, the write-ins are mere protests against the nominated candidates, and, for Justice White, the state need not finance the counting and publishing of such protest votes.

For more information: Hasen, Richard. *The Supreme Court and Election Law: Judging Equality from* Baker v. Carr *to* Bush v. Gore. New York: New York University Press, 2003.

—Daniel M. Katz

Burger, Warren E. (1907–1995) *Supreme Court chief justice*

Warren E. Burger was appointed by President RICHARD NIXON in 1969 to succeed Earl Warren and become the 15th chief justice of the U.S. Supreme Court. Burger served in that capacity until 1986, when he resigned and was replaced by WILLIAM HUBBS REHNQUIST. While Burger himself tended to vote more conservatively than his predecessor, his legacy as a chief justice was one as an able administrator but not as a leader who dramatically turned the Court toward a new ideological and legal direction as many had hoped.

Burger was born in St. Paul, Minnesota, in 1907. He was a boyhood friend of Harry Blackmun, who would eventually serve with him on the Supreme Court with the latter's appointment to the Court in 1970. Burger attended and graduated John A. Johnson High School in 1925, lettering in four sports. He attended the University of Minnesota and then the St. Paul College of Law, now known as William Mitchell College of Law. Upon graduation from law school, in 1931, he worked in a local law firm and also taught for several years at the St. Paul College of Law.

Active in Minnesota Republican Party politics, Burger helped Harold Stassen in his successful gubernatorial bid of 1948. Burger gained prominence in the 1952 presidential convention by arranging for Stassen's delegates (from his unsuccessful presidential bid) to be transferred to Dwight D. Eisenhower. This political maneuvering caught the attention of Herbert Brownell, Eisenhower's campaign manager. After Eisenhower's election, Burger was appointed to head the civil division of the Justice Department. He was then offered a position, in 1955, to serve on the Court of Appeals for the District of Columbia Circuit. As a judge there, he voted conservatively, especially on criminal DUE PROCESS matters, and was very critical of WARREN COURT decisions such as *MIRANDA V. ARIZONA*, 384 U.S. 436 (1966).

Burger's elevation to chief justice of the Supreme Court was the product of luck and circumstance. When President Lyndon B. Johnson announced in 1968 that he was not running for reelection, Chief Justice Warren announced his retirement, hoping that the outgoing president would be able to replace him before leaving office. Johnson sought to elevate Justice Abe Fortas to Chief Justice, but his liberal views, close friendship with the president, and personal financial improprieties doomed his appointment, giving Nixon the opportunity to nominate Burger when he took office in 1969. Burger was quickly confirmed and took office the same year.

Burger served as chief justice from 1969 to 1986. Burger was acknowledged to be an excellent administrator for the Court and brought many reforms to it, including the introduction of photocopiers. A tireless advocate for pay raises for federal judges, he often spoke out in support of the judiciary. The latter led him to help found the National Center for State Courts in 1971. However, his major idea to create an intermediate court of appeals between the Supreme Court and the federal courts of appeals, to address the exploding workload of the former and handle what he saw as more mundane appeals, was rejected.

While Burger was considered a good administrator, few if any consider him an intellectual leader for the Court in the mold of other chief justices such as JOHN MARSHALL or even Earl Warren. Burger presided over what can be described as a transitional Court—one that stood between the liberal Court of Warren and then the more conservative Court of Rehnquist. Nixon had hoped that his four appointments to the Court—Blackmun, LEWIS FRANKLIN POWELL, JR., Rehnquist, and Burger—would turn the Court in a more conservative direction and reverse many Warren Court precedents, especially those dealing with the rights of the accused. However, while the Burger Court may have limited some precedents, such as *Miranda* or even *Mapp v. Ohio*, 367 U.S. 643 (1961), which upheld the application of the EXCLUSIONARY RULE to the states, ultimately the Court did not overturn them. In addition, in criminal matters, the Court both invalidated and then upheld death penalty statutes in *FURMAN V. GEORGIA*, 408 U.S. 238 (1972), and *GREGG V. GEORGIA*, 428 U.S. 153 (1976), respectively.

Under Burger, the Court issued many important opinions. For example, in *ROE V. WADE*, 410 U.S. 113 (1973), it upheld a woman's right to an ABORTION. The Court in cases such as *Frontiero v. Richardson*, 411 U.S. 677 (1973) struck down laws discriminating against women. In *REGENTS OF THE UNIVERSITY OF CALIFORNIA V. BAKKE*, 438 U.S. 265 (1978), it upheld the use of AFFIRMATIVE ACTION, and in *BUCKLEY V. VALEO*, 424 U.S.

1 (1976), it upheld many provisions of a federal law imposing contribution limits on candidates for federal office, while rejecting expenditure caps.

Among Burger's most notable decisions is the unanimous *UNITED STATES V. NIXON*, 418 U.S. 683 (1974), where the Court ordered the president to turn over to a special prosecutor his taped White House conversations. This decision led to the president's resignation. He also wrote the majority opinion in *BOWSHER V. SYNAR*, 462 U.S. 919 (1983), invalidating the one-house LEGISLATIVE VETO, and in *SWANN V. CHARLOTTE-MECKLENBURG BOARD OF EDUCATION*, 402 U.S. 1 (1971), he upheld the use of mandatory busing to achieve integration.

In 1986, Burger resigned from the Supreme Court to oversee activities surrounding the American Bicentennial of the Constitution. He died in 1995.

For more information: Maltz, Earl M. *The Chief Justiceship of Warren Burger, 1969–1986*. Columbia: University of South Carolina Press, 2000; Trowbridge, Ronald L. *With Sweet Majesty: Warren E. Burger*. Washington, D.C.: Trust for the Bicentennial of the United States Constitution, 2000; White, G. Edward. *The American Judicial Tradition: Profiles of Leading American Judges*. New York: Oxford University Press, 1988.

—David Schultz

Bush v. Gore 531 U.S. 98 (2000)

In *Bush v. Gore*, the Supreme Court settled the disputed recount of votes in Florida for the presidential election of 2000. The Court's decision ultimately resulted in George W. Bush winning the state's electoral votes and the presidency.

Following one of the closest elections in U.S. history, presidential candidates George W. Bush (Republican) and Albert Gore (Democrat) looked to the courts for assistance in determining the ultimate outcome of the election. The U.S. Supreme Court played a major role in determining the outcome of the election, despite many criticisms that the Court had forgotten the separation of power tenet of American democracy. *Bush v. Gore*, 531 U.S. 98 (2000) played a decisive role in determining who would become the next president.

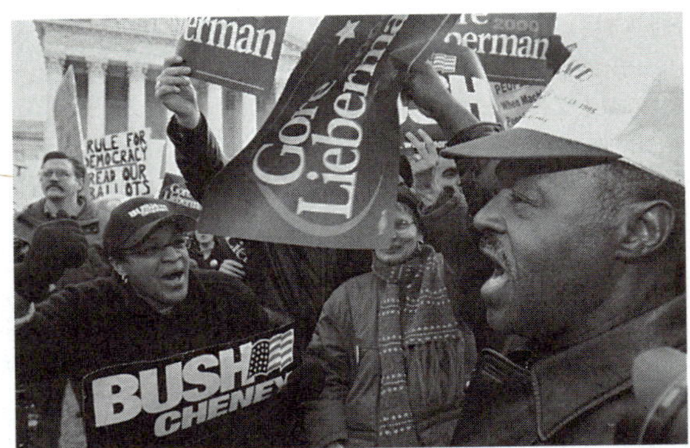

Gore and Bush supporters face off during a protest outside the U.S. Supreme Court in Washington, D.C., December 11, 2000. *(Wong/Newsmakers)*

Bush v. Gore actually involves a series of three cases that came before the Supreme Court following the 2000 presidential election. The first of these cases was *Bush v. Palm Beach County Canvassing Board*, 531 U.S. 70. This case was remanded to the Florida Supreme Court to determine if the postelection decision of the Florida court violated the DUE PROCESS clause due to the ballot certification process. The next two opinions came in *Bush v. Gore*.

The electoral votes in the state of Florida were in question, and these votes would determine the election outcome. Days after the election, many voting precincts scrambled to recount their votes. When the date for election results certification established by Florida law arrived, the precinct votes favored Bush; however, Gore contested the results of the election, and the case went before the Florida Supreme Court. On December 8, 2000, the Florida Supreme Court ordered that the Circuit Court of Leon County hand-count about 9,000 contested ballots from Miami-Dade County, while it required all other districts in the state to recount by hand any ballot that did not indicate a vote for president. Bush and vice presidential running mate Dick Cheney wanted a stay or a delay of the Florida Supreme Court decision and filed an emergency petition to the U.S. Supreme Court the next day. The Supreme Court accepted the emergency petition, granting certiorari, or review, to the case. Oral arguments began for *Bush v. Gore* in the U.S. Supreme Court on December 11, 2000.

The question of the law that the Supreme Court sought to answer in *Bush v. Gore* was whether the Florida Supreme Court violated Article II, Section 1, Clause 2, of the Constitution by allowing the manual recounts. Were the recounts in violation of the EQUAL PROTECTION and due process clauses of the Constitution?

By a majority of 7-2, the Court ruled that the Florida recount was unconstitutional because it violated the equal protection clause owing to the significant problems in the uneven way the votes were being recounted throughout the state of Florida. Some counties had to do partial recounts, while others had to perform full manual recounts of the ballots. In addition, in the second opinion in *Bush v. Gore,* a 5-4 majority ruled that the state of Florida would not be able to complete a constitutionally valid recount that could be completed by the December 12 deadline. As there was no formal statewide standard for certifying the votes, the recount was ceased since it was determined that it was a violation of the equal protection clause.

The decision was very controversial because the justices' decisions were mainly along party lines. The decision was also written so that it was very specific to the current circumstances, suggesting the justices knew this decision would never become precedent.

For more information: Dionne, E. J., and William Kristol, eds. Bush v. Gore: *The Court Cases and Commentary.* Washington, D.C.: Brookings Institution Press, 2001; Jarvis, Robert. Bush v. Gore: *The Fight for Florida Vote.* New York: Kluwer Law International, 2001; Urofsky, Melvin I., ed. *The Public Debate over Controversial Supreme Court Decisions.* Washington, D.C.: CQ Press, 2006.

—Carol Walker

Butchers' Benevolent Association of New Orleans v. Crescent City Live-Stock Landing and Slaughter-House Co. 16 Wall. (83 U.S.) 36 (*Slaughterhouse Cases*) (1873)

In *Butchers' Benevolent Association of New Orleans v. Crescent City Live-Stock Landing and Slaughter-House Co.*, or the *Slaughterhouse Cases,* the Supreme Court upheld a Louisiana statute that gave a 25-year monopoly to a single slaughterhouse for the city of New Orleans and surrounding parishes (counties). The purpose of the statute was to control and limit slaughterhouse waste polluting the Mississippi River and spreading cholera. The Butchers' Benevolent Association, a group of independent butchers, challenged the statute as an abridgement of their PRIVILEGES AND IMMUNITIES, EQUAL PROTECTION, and DUE PROCESS rights under the FOURTEENTH AMENDMENT and as a form of involuntary servitude under the THIRTEENTH AMENDMENT. In this landmark case, in which the Supreme Court offered its interpretation of the Thirteenth and Fourteenth Amendments for the first time, the Court rejected the independent butchers' argument on all points, upholding the authority of Louisiana to enact the statute. The significance of this case comes not from the majority opinion but instead from the seed of an idea of a new conception of Fourteenth Amendment due process protections that the dissenting justices on the Court planted in this case.

The 5-4 majority argued that the purpose of the Thirteenth and Fourteenth Amendments was to bring freed slaves and "Negroes" as a class within the fold of constitutional protections already enjoyed by other Americans. The majority opinion rejected the argument that these amendments applied broadly to all citizens or that new rights were established for anyone under them. The majority held that the Fourteenth Amendment's privileges and immunities clause required no more than that states treat their own citizens and those from other states the same. The Court also rejected summarily the argument that equal protection and due process rights were abridged by the statute or that awarding a monopoly butchering license to some and not others imposed involuntary servitude on anyone under the provisions of the Thirteenth Amendment.

The dissenting justices, however, embraced the argument put forward by the lawyer for the independent butchers. This argument asserted that the Fourteenth Amendment does offer new constitutional protections against government interference in business. Under this reading of the Fourteenth Amendment, the due process clause could be understood to be a check on state regulation of business when such regulation amounts to a deprivation of the liberty of individuals to participate in their chosen profession or limits other economic choices.

The interpretation of due process by the dissenting justices in this case came to be the majority opinion in future cases and served to introduce a framework of analysis of the Fourteenth Amendment due process clause that evolved into the doctrine of SUBSTANTIVE DUE PROCESS. This doctrine, still utilized by the Supreme Court today, enables the Court to review the substance of duly enacted legislation and strike it down when, in the Court's judgment, it unconstitutionally infringes an individual right under the BILL OF RIGHTS and the Fourteenth Amendment.

For more information: Corwin, Edwin S. *The Higher Law Background of American Constitutional Law.* Ithaca, N.Y.: Cornell University Press, 1955; O'Brien, David M. *Storm Center: The Supreme Court in American Politics.* 7th ed. New York: W.W. Norton & Co., 2005.

—Phyllis Farley Rippey

C & A Carbone, Inc., et al. v. Town of Clarkstown, New York 511 U.S. 383 (1994)

In *C & A Carbone, Inc., et al. v. Town of Clarkstown, New York*, the Supreme Court ruled that a law mandating all contractors handling solid waste had to use a specific facility for disposal violated the COMMERCE CLAUSE. The case is important because it affected the ability of local governments to regulate waste and garbage.

Clarkstown, New York, permitted a contractor to construct and operate a waste processing facility within city limits. In order to assist the facility financially, the town made a promise that the plant would receive 120,000 tons of solid waste each year and allowed the contractor to charge a special fee for each ton of solid waste received for processing. In order to ensure that the facility met the 120,000-ton quota, Clarkstown passed a flow control ordinance that required all solid waste flowing into and originating in the town to pass through the new facility.

C & A Carbone operated a similar facility in Clarkstown and in an attempt to avoid paying the $81 fee per ton of solid waste, decided that it would truck its processed waste via trucks to a landfill in another state (Indiana). In 1991, a C & A Carbone truck crashed, spilling its illegal cargo, exposing C & A Carbone's violation of the flow control ordinance. Clarkstown sued C & A Carbone in a New York supreme court, and in return, C & A Carbone sued Clarkstown in a federal district court, claiming that the flow control ordinance violated the commerce clause of the Constitution. The New York supreme court ruled in favor of Clarkstown.

The case was appealed to the U.S. Supreme Court. The question before the Court in this case was whether the Clarkstown flow control ordinance violated the commerce clause of the Constitution by impeding commerce for waste processing plants in other states. In a 6-3 decision delivered by Justice ANTHONY M. KENNEDY, the Court concluded that the ordinance did violate the commerce clause. According to Kennedy,

> The flow control ordinance does serve a central purpose that a nonprotectionist regulation would not: It ensures that the town-sponsored facility will be profitable, so that the local contractor can build it and Clarkstown can buy it back at nominal cost in five years. In other words, as the most candid of amici and even Clarkstown admit, the flow control ordinance is a financing measure. By itself, of course, revenue generation is not a local interest that can justify discrimination against INTERSTATE COMMERCE. Otherwise States could impose discriminatory taxes against solid waste originating outside the State. See *Chemical Waste Management, Inc. v. Hunt*, 504 U.S. 334 (1992), (striking down Alabama statute that imposed additional fee on all hazardous waste generated outside the State and disposed of within the State); *Oregon Waste Systems, Inc. v. Department of Environmental Quality of Ore.*, (striking down Oregon statute that imposed additional fee on solid waste generated outside the State and disposed of within the State).

Clarkstown maintained that special financing was necessary to ensure the long-term survival of the designated facility. If so, the town could have subsidized the facility through general taxes or municipal bonds (as in *New Energy Co. of Ind. v. Limbach,* 486 U.S. 269 [1988]). But having elected to use the open market to earn revenues for its project, the town could not employ discriminatory regulation to give that project an advantage over rival businesses from out of state.

For more information: Langran, Robert W. *The Supreme Court: A Concise History.* New York: Peter Lang, 2004; Waltenburg, Eric N., and Bill Swinford. *Litigating Federalism: The States Before the U.S. Supreme Court.* Westport, Conn.: Greenwood Press, 1999.

—Dan Krejci

Calder v. Bull 3 U.S. 386 (1798)

In *Calder v. Bull,* the Supreme Court issued an opinion clarifying what constituted ex post facto law in Article I, Section 9, of the Constitution.

An ex post facto law is a law that makes illegal behavior or actions that were previously legal and thus now subject to legal ramifications due to the change in interpretation of the behavior or actions. This is the underlying principle of retroactive laws, or laws that look backward with their interpretations.

In *Calder v. Bull,* the rights to an estate were in dispute, and the original inheritor, Calder, was given the property and the Bull family was denied the ability to appeal. The Bulls were unhappy with the decision and were successful in having the Connecticut legislature overturn the restrictions. Calder then pushed the case to the Supreme Court for resolution and to interpret the Constitution as it related to ex post facto laws. Calder's position offered that the Connecticut law should be considered void because the law had violated Section 9 of ARTICLE I OF THE U.S. CONSTITUTION. The EX POST FACTO CLAUSE in this article prohibited states from enacting any ex post facto laws.

The Supreme Court upheld the Connecticut law, ruling that the constitutional prohibition against ex post facto laws applied only to criminal and not civil laws. Thus, as the state had retroactively changed a civil law regarding property rights, the Constitution did not prevent it.

Calder v. Bull is important for two reasons. First, its clarification of the ex post facto clause is significant, and second, it is one of the important Supreme Court opinions prior to Chief Justice JOHN MARSHALL's Court (1801–35).

For more information: Bork, Robert H. *The Tempting of America: The Political Seduction of the Law.* New York: Free Press, 1990; Langran, Robert W. *The Supreme Court: A Concise History.* New York: Peter Lang, 2004.

—Ernest Gomez

Calhoun, John C. (1782–1850) *secretary of state, secretary of war, U.S. vice president*

John C. Calhoun was a famous statesman, writer, and VICE PRESIDENT of the United States who advocated and developed an important concept of CONSTITUTIONAL INTERPRETATION that gave states the right to VETO federal legislation. This theory is known as his concurrent majority thesis.

Calhoun was born in 1782 and served as a senator of South Carolina (1832–43; 1845–50). He was vice president from 1825 to 1832 and an original War Hawk at the outbreak of the War of 1812. He is also one of the more interesting political thinkers in American history. His work contributed to a discussion of the proper relationship of the states to the national government and to the protection of rights. Hence, whatever one thinks of his motivation (protecting sectional interests, including slavery), his voice must be considered as a part of the ongoing constitutional discussion in the United States regarding the allocation of constitutional power between states and the national government. Two major works of his on this subject are his well-known *A Disquisition on Government* and *A Discourse on the Constitution and Government of the United States.* Both were published in 1853, after Calhoun's death in 1850.

Calhoun's key concern was the threat of an oppressive national government. He argued: ". . . government, although intended to protect and preserve society, has itself a strong tendency to disorder and abuse of its powers, as all experience and almost every page of history testify" (1953, 7). Calhoun claimed that societies are made up of numerous groupings, each with its own interest. In Calhoun's estimation, "[There is] nothing more easy than to pervert its powers into instruments to aggrandize and enrich one or more interests by oppressing and impoverishing the others. . . ." (1953, 13). Somehow or another, then, some instrumentality must be developed ". . . to prevent any one interest or combination of interests from using the powers of government to aggrandize itself at the expense of others" (1953, 20). Furthermore, he wrote: "There is but one certain mode in which this result can be secured, and that is by the adoption of some restriction or limitation which shall so effectively prevent any one interest or combination of interests from obtaining the exclusive control of the government as to render hopeless all attempts directed to that end" (1953, 20).

Use of the "numerical majority" to make decisions essentially can suppress minorities, and Calhoun argued that the use of numerical majorities as the mechanism of decision making forces a country "to regard the numerical majority as in effect the entire people; that is, the greater part as the whole, and the government of the greater part as the government of the whole" (1953, 24). He believed that the idea of the "concurrent majority" would reduce the possibility of tyranny. In Calhoun's own words, the essence of the concurrent majority is:

> The necessary consequence of taking the sense of the community as the concurrent majority is . . . to give each interest or portion of the community a negative on the others. It is this mutual negative among its various conflicting interests which invests each with the power of protecting itself, and places the rights and safety of each where only they can be securely placed, under its own guardianship (1953, 28).

The concurrent majority gave an absolute veto power over national government legislation to any territorial or regional majority or the majority of any large nonterritorial interest.

Numerically, absolute majorities would not be able to exercise tyrannical power over minorities that were, however defined, fairly large and substantial. Again, in Calhoun's terms, ". . . the government of the concurrent majority . . . excludes the possibility of oppression by giving to each interest, or portion, or order . . . the means of protecting itself by its negatives against all measures calculated to advance the peculiar interests of others at its expense" (1953, 30). The use of the veto was termed *nullification,* the right of states (or other interests) to veto national laws.

Critics, of course, would contend that the concurrent majority would make it very difficult to take any significant action; however, Calhoun felt that this plan would actually foster unity rather than making it impossible to accomplish anything. In a key passage, Calhoun stated:

> The concurrent majority . . . tends to unite the most opposite and conflicting interests and to blend the whole in one common attachment to the country. By giving to each interest, or portion, the power of self-protection, all strife and struggle between them for ascendancy is prevented, and thereby not only every feeling calculated to weaken the attachment to the whole is suppressed, but the individual and the social feelings are made to unite in one common devotion to country. Each sees and feels that it can best promote its own prosperity by conciliating the good will and promoting the prosperity of the others (1953, 37–38).

Calhoun's relevance for constitutional principles in the United States is that it directly addresses the Constitution's concept of FEDERALISM. Calhoun's vision was far different from that enunciated by the Supreme Court over time. Whereas the Supreme Court emphasized the SUPREMACY CLAUSE, Calhoun rejected that concept as violating his understanding of the Constitution and its origins. His conclusion was that the United States was a confederation, as quoted from his *Discourse*: ". . . I have thus established, conclusively, that these States, in ratifying the Constitution, did not lose the confederated character which they possessed when they ratified it" (1953, 99). His vision was one that did not carry the day, but it offers an alternative perspective to the issue of the division of power between states and the national government.

For more information: Bartlett, Irving H. *John C. Calhoun: A Biography.* New York: W.W. Norton, 1993; Calhoun, John C. *A Disquisition on Government and Selections from the Discourse.* Edited by G. Gordon Post. Indianapolis, Ind.: Bobbs-Merrill Co., 1953; Current, Richard N. *John C. Calhoun.* New York: Washington Square Press, 1963.

—Steven A. Peterson

campaign finance

Campaign finance refers to the ways campaigns and elections are funded in the United States. Efforts to limit or regulate political contributions and candidate, party, or independent expenditures by third-party groups raise important FIRST AMENDMENT free speech issues.

Fair and honest elections serve as a vehicle for promoting values of democracy and give meaning to the notion of "consent of the governed." Political campaigns have become the means by which candidates run for office in elections and disseminate information, positions, and ideas to the American public. Campaign financing has been an integral part of the election process and a documented phenomenon since the pre-Constitution days. For instance, George Washington, long before becoming the first U.S. president, was chastised for exchanging whiskey for votes during the 1757 race for the Virginia House of Burgesses. The trend was even more blatantly apparent throughout the 1800s, but political parties were miniscule in the late 18th and early 19th centuries when compared to today. Campaigns have become increasingly complex, larger in size and scope, and more expensive over time. The costs associated with political campaigning have risen dramatically, and television advertising is the medium of choice, particularly for national office seekers.

The framers of the U.S. Constitution did not address the role that political parties would play, let alone campaign finance, in the system of politics. This has resulted in varying interpretations over what the Founding Fathers had intended for these elements and has given new significance to viewing the Constitution as a living document. The trend toward raising and spending money in an election cycle has prompted both lawmakers and citizens to scrutinize more carefully the campaign finance environment. Americans have always been wary that contributions may buy influence in the government, and lawmakers have over time been forced to respond to these valid concerns voiced by their constituents.

Until the Watergate Scandal (1972), which toppled the presidency of Republican RICHARD NIXON, campaign finance was controlled by political parties and "fat cats" who raised large sums of money for their war chests. However, secret donations and other events surrounding Nixon's 1972 reelection campaign became catalysts for the creation of the Federal Election Commission (FEC). The FEC is the primary enforcer of election procedures and laws and was specifically created to enforce the provisions of the Federal Election Campaign Act (FECA) of 1971. Amendments to the act in 1974 placed limits on the amounts that could be contributed by nonparty groups and created the federal matching criteria used in presidential elections. The contribution limits were set so that individuals could give up to $1,000 to federal candidates for both the primary and general elections and up to $25,000 in all contributions in a single calendar year, with sublimits of $20,000 per year to national party committees and $5,000 per year to a political action committee (PAC) or any other party committee. Limits up to $5,000 in both the primary and general elections were also set for PACs and other party committees ($10,000 total for the election cycle).

One of the leading constitutional challenges to individual spending limits came in the U.S. Supreme Court case *BUCKLEY V. VALEO*, 424 U.S. 1 (1976). In this case, the Court ruled that candidates (and associated independent organizations) have the right to express their views and run campaigns without being constrained by spending limits. This landmark case associated unlimited spending with freedom of speech and the protections afforded under First Amendment rights protected by the U.S. Constitution. The Court's ruling struck down several of the individual spending limits established in the 1974 FECA amendments. Since then, the courts have tended to scrutinize and deem many types of campaign finance restrictions as inherent threats to the First Amendment.

Contemporary political campaigns have moved from being party centered to candidate centered. Election costs have grown to approximately $900,000 for candidates seeking a seat in the House of Representatives, and from $5 to $6 million for candidates for the Senate. While this average depends on individual spending patterns and geographic location, it still suggests that a large sum of money is used to campaign for a congressional seat. Spending in presidential races has also grown. Spending by all presidential candidates was more than $500 million in 2000 and more than $700 million in 2004.

The lobbying power of PACs, along with the increase in "soft money" contributions, which have been largely unregulated, have stifled many reform efforts over time, as have other loopholes in the system. So has the U.S. Supreme Court's inclination to view certain restrictions as violations of the First Amendment. However, the most recently successful reform initiative was implemented with the Bipartisan Campaign Finance Reform Act (BCRA), passed in 2002. The BCRA raised the old limits on individual spending set by the FECA amendments of 1974 from $1,000 to $2,000 for hard money. Other limits included $5,000 per year for each party or political committee, $20,000 per year to a national party, and a limit of $95,000 over a two-year cycle for contributions to individual candidates and committees. The $5,000 limit for PACs to a candidate remained the same, but consideration is now granted for inflation rates when determining limits for future elections. The BCRA was challenged but deemed constitutional by the U.S. Supreme Court in 2003. Irrespective, campaign finance will undoubtedly continue to be an issue of contention in times to come.

For more information: Alexander, Herbert E. *Campaign Money: Reform and Reality in the States.* New York: Free Press, 1976; Magleby, David B. *Financing the 2000 Election.* Washington, D.C.: Brookings Institution Press, 2002; Malbin, Michael J., ed. *Money and Politics in the United States.* Chatham, N.J.: Chatham House Publishers, 1984; Sorauf, Frank. *Inside Campaign Finance.* New Haven, Conn.: Yale University Press, 1992.

—Daniel Baracskay

Camps Newfound/Owatonna, Inc. v. Town of Harrison 520 U.S. 564 (1997)

In *Camps Newfound/Owatonna, Inc. v. Town of Harrison,* the Supreme Court ruled that a state tax exemption for the use of a park that favored organizations incorporated in the state was found to be a violation of the commerce clause.

An operator of a children's church camp in Maine, Camps Newfound/Owatonna, Inc., financed its camp operations using a $400 per week camper tuition charge. Most of the campers who used the facilities were from out of state. Maine created a tax scheme that allowed an exemption for charitable organizations that were incorporated in the state yet provided a limited benefit to those organizations that catered to nonresidents as long as their fee did not exceed $30 per person. Camps Newfound/Owatonna, Inc., due to catering to nonresidents and charging a $400 fee, did not qualify for any exemptions. Camps Newfound/Owatonna filed suit in a Maine superior court, which sided with Camps Newfound/Owatonna, yet the Maine Supreme Judicial Court reversed the lower court's decision.

Camps Newfound/Owatonna appealed to the Supreme Court, and in a 5-4 decision delivered by Justice John Paul Stevens, the Court concluded that the Maine tax exemption did violate the commerce clause of the Constitution. The Court noted that the exemption was a violation because it was selective in nature when awarding tax benefits. In effect, Maine was engaging in a form of protectionism that favored local consumers and business operators over those consumers and business operators who were from out of state. This, the Court ruled, was a violation of the commerce clause.

For more information: Langran, Robert W. *The Supreme Court: A Concise History.* New York: Peter Lang, 2004.

—Dan Krejci

candidate filing fees

Candidate filing fees are fees that individuals running for office have to pay to gain access to the ballot. The Supreme Court has declared these fees to be unconstitutional as they are in violation of the FIRST AMENDMENT.

The payment of a candidate filing fee has long been recognized as a way for a candidate to gain ballot access. This form of ballot access provides relatively easy access to those qualified candidates seeking ballot access. At the same time, the candidate filing fee has received criticism for blocking access to the ballot for qualified but low- and middle-income candidates.

Generally, ballot access can be gained by paying a filing fee, gathering enough valid signatures on a petition, or by having the prospective candidate sign an affidavit stating that there is a lack of funds for paying a filing fee. Alternative forms of ballot access are not standard throughout all political jurisdictions. However, alternatives to the payment of a candidate filing fee are necessary if a system of ballot access is to be found constitutional. Though candidacy is not mentioned in the Constitution, the framers did stress the importance of keeping electoral restrictions to a minimum. It was recognized by many of the founders that a democratic republican form of government necessitates ballot access for both voters and candidates. While the early concerns with ballot access were voiced, the early debates on the topic did not result in its inclusion in the Constitution.

The debate and ratification of the Fifth Amendment (1870) brought ballot access back to the forefront. Both the HOUSE OF REPRESENTATIVES and the SENATE proposed versions of the amendment that placed the RIGHT TO VOTE alongside a right to hold public office. Ultimately, the language dealing with the right to hold public office was stripped from the Fifth Amendment in the House-Senate conference committee. When the amendment was presented to the states, there were even more debates about whether a right to hold public office should have been included in the language of the amendment. Still, the fact that there was such debate demonstrates the significance given to the issue of ballot access at this point in American history.

The U.S. Supreme Court held in *Bullock v. Carter,* 405 U.S. 134 (1972), and in *Lubin v. Panish,* 415 U.S. 709 (1974), that a candidate filing fee is constitutional only if an alternative form of filing is available. Not providing alternative ballot access was found to deprive a potential candidate of his or her right to EQUAL PROTECTION under the FOURTEENTH AMENDMENT and the right of the candidate to freedom of expression and association guaranteed by the First and Fourteenth Amendments. Constitutionally accepted alternatives are most often the gathering of a requisite number of valid petition signatures or the signing of an affidavit stating that the prospective candidate cannot pay the filing fee.

Candidate filing fees have generally opened up ballot access to a larger candidate pool. Even with this basically positive outcome, a problem arises when there is no alternative for a potential candidate who cannot pay the filing fee or would be severely hampered by doing so. Hence, an alternative must always be in place in order to gain ballot access outside of the payment of a filing fee, if a state's ballot access system is to pass constitutional muster.

For more information: Gordon, Nicole A. "The Constitutional Right to Candidacy." *Political Science Quarterly* 91 (Autumn 1976): 471–487.

—William Lester

capital punishment

Capital punishment refers to the use of the death penalty as the punishment for the commission of a crime. While death has been imposed as a penalty for numerous crimes since the early days of colonial America, its use is subject to the limits imposed by the Fifth, Sixth, Eighth, and Fourteenth Amendments to the Constitution.

The original Constitution, written in 1787, considered with the nearly contemporaneous BILL OF RIGHTS, shows that the drafters of both assumed that the practice of imposing the death penalty, derived from English law, on those convicted of serious crimes would be continued. The issue of the constitutionality of aspects of the death penalty was not first considered until the latter part of the 19th century, and it was not until the 1970s that the U.S. Supreme Court began to impose some limits on its imposition.

In England, before the American Revolution, the death penalty was prescribed for all serious crimes, called "felonies," as contrasted with minor offenses, called "misdemeanors." Most crimes were felonies, including murder, robbery, burglary, rape, arson, and larceny. Death was usually by hanging. In the thirteen colonies, the death penalty was similarly prescribed, as it was in the new nation around the time of the ratification of the original Constitution. In Virginia, for example, a 1788 statute punishing bigamy (marrying for a second time without a divorce from the first live spouse) stated that "every such offense shall be felony, and the person or persons, so offending, shall suffer death as in cases of felony" (12 *Henning's Statutes at Large* (Va) 691 [1823]).

The Constitution of 1787 makes no mention of the death penalty, but the Fifth Amendment, ratified along with the rest of the Bill of Rights

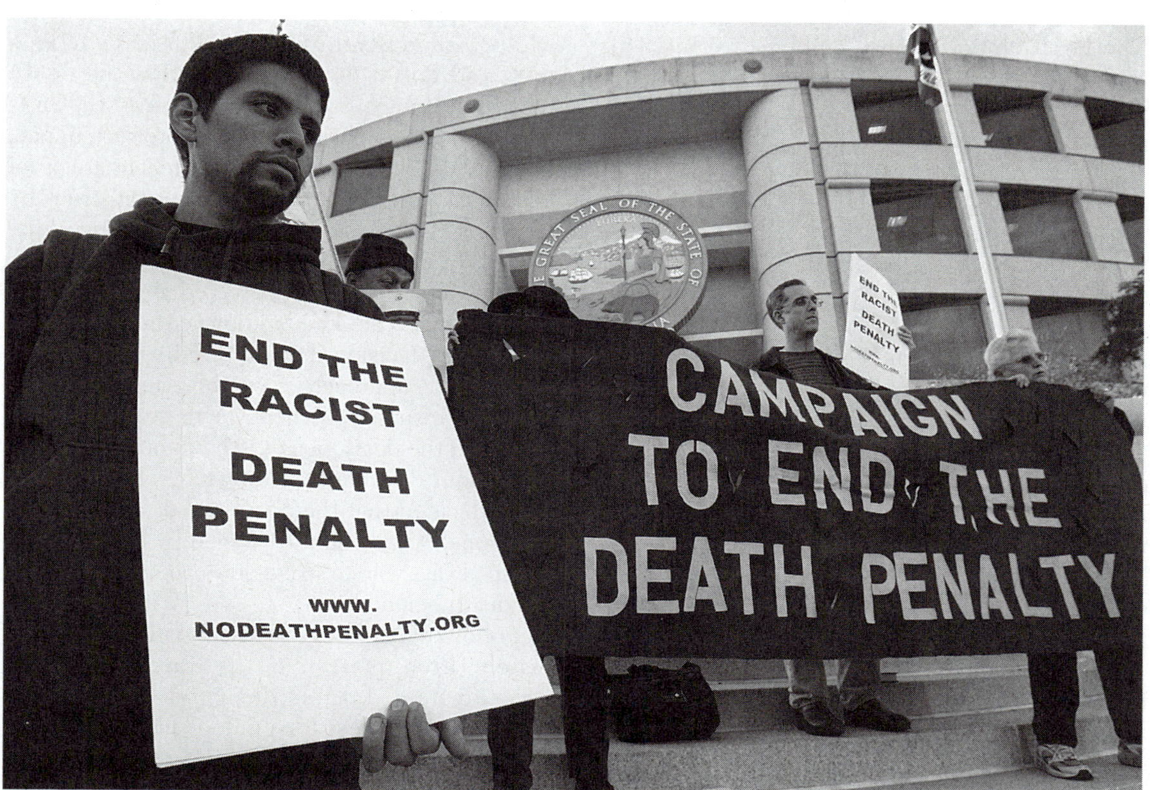

Opponents of the death penalty carry signs during a rally, January 12, 2005, on the steps of a California State building in San Francisco. *(Justin Sullivan/Getty)*

in 1791, presupposes the existence of capital punishment in that it guarantees, among others, the right to indictment by a grand jury in cases in which a person is "held to answer for a capital or otherwise infamous crime," freedom from being "twice put in jeopardy of life or limb" for the same offense, and the right not to be "deprived of life, liberty, or property without DUE PROCESS of law." Because the original Constitution would probably not have been ratified without an assurance in the ratifying conventions of a number of key states that one of the first orders of business of the first Congress would be the adoption of amendments including a bill of rights, it is proper to think of the Bill of Rights as functionally part of the original Constitution.

In general, the death penalty continued to be imposed in the 19th and 20th centuries but by a gradual process became possible for only some felonies; moreover, juries were given discretion whether to impose it in specific cases. In 1846, Michigan became the first state to abolish capital punishment.

In a federal case in the late 19th century, the U.S. Supreme Court ruled that execution by shooting was not a violation of the Eighth Amendment's proscription of CRUEL AND UNUSUAL PUNISHMENT (*Wilkerson v. Utah*, 99 U.S. 130 [1879]). In another case, *In re Kemmler*, 136 U.S. 436 (1890), the Court concluded that the FOURTEENTH AMENDMENT's guarantee of due process (again with a reference to "life, liberty, or property") was not inconsistent with execution by electrocution. (In the latter case, a state case, the Court did not consider the possible effect of the Eighth Amendment's proscription of cruel and unusual punishment because of a much earlier decision that the Bill of Rights limited the federal government but not the states.) In the middle of the 20th century, the Court upheld a second effort at electrocution of a condemned person, the first attempt having failed, against a claim that this second attempt constituted cruel and unusual punishment (*Louisiana ex rel. Francis v. Resweber*, 329 U.S. 459 [1947]).

In *McGautha v. California*, 402 U.S. 183 (1971), the U.S. Supreme Court upheld the imposition of the death penalty and in so doing rejected a claim that the death penalty violated the due process clause of the Fourteenth Amendment because the jury that imposed it had totally unlimited discretion whether to impose it. A year later, in *FURMAN V. GEORGIA*, 408 U.S. 238 (1972), the Court struck down the death penalty as then administered on the ground that it violated the Eighth Amendment (the Court having decided 10 years previously that the Eighth Amendment did apply to the states after all because it was "incorporated" into the due process clause of the Fourteenth Amendment). There were 10 opinions in *Furman*: a per curiam opinion (that is, an unsigned opinion expressing the ruling of the Court, in this instance that the death penalty was unconstitutional), and nine separate opinions, one by each of the justices.

Two members of the Court, Justices WILLIAM J. BRENNAN, JR., and Thurgood Marshall, expressed the view that the death penalty was in all circumstances cruel and unusual punishment, while Justices Byron White, WILLIAM O. DOUGLAS, and Potter Stewart stated that the death penalty was unconstitutional because of the arbitrariness of its imposition. (Justice Stewart, in particular, said that "[t]hese death sentences are cruel and unusual in the same way that being struck by lightning is cruel and unusual.") Four justices dissented, in part because they said that the issue, in substance, had been resolved the other way the previous year. The holding of the Court (the part of the decision that was binding precedent) was thus the approach of the three justices in the middle: Presumably, whenever these three voted to uphold the death penalty, they would be joined by the four dissenters; presumably, whenever, the three decided that the death penalty was unconstitutional, they would be joined by the two who would always vote to strike down the imposition of the death penalty.

Following the decision in *Furman*, approximately three-quarters of the state legislatures enacted new statutes designed to meet the requirement of less (or guided) jury discretion set forth by the three middle justices. Some opponents of the death penalty thought that the Supreme Court would strike down all of these statutes, but such was not to be. Four years after

Furman, the Court decided a series of cases, in three of which the Court upheld the death penalty under new statutes: GREGG V. GEORGIA, 428 U.S. 153 (1976); *Proffitt v. Florida*, 428 U.S. 242 (1976); and *Jurek v. Texas*, 428 U.S. 262 (1976). The Court as a whole concluded that the new statutes were constitutional because they required a jury to find facts that distinguished the murder being prosecuted from the "ordinary" murder, for example, that the victim was a police officer acting in the line of duty, and thus limited the jury's discretion. The statutes contained lists of such factors, referred to as aggravating factors, at least one of which the prosecution had to prove at a hearing separate from, and subsequent to, the hearing at which the jury was to decide whether the defendant was guilty or not guilty of the crime charged. The person convicted in *Gregg* argued that unconstitutional arbitrariness was still present because the prosecutor, as contrasted with the jury, still had complete discretion whether to try a case as a capital case. The majority rejected this claim. Also in *Gregg*, the Court concluded that a desire for retribution could properly be considered by the jury. In two cases decided on the same day as *Gregg*—*Woodson v. North Carolina*, 428 U.S. 280 (1976), and *Roberts v. Louisiana*, 428 U.S. 325 (1976)—the Court ruled that statutes could not provide for automatic imposition of the death penalty when a defendant was convicted of first-degree murder.

Since 1976, the U.S. Supreme Court has declared unconstitutional the imposition of the death penalty for some crimes and has also invalidated certain procedures, but also on occasion has changed its mind. The Supreme Court has ruled, under the Eighth Amendment, that the punishment of death cannot be imposed for the crime of rape when no victim was killed (*Cooker v. Georgia*, 433 U.S. 584 [1977]). Similarly, the Court has held that the death penalty cannot be imposed on a defendant who was insane at the time of the scheduled execution (*Ford v. Wainwright*, 477 U.S. 399 [1986]). The Court concluded that it was unconstitutional to execute a juvenile who was only 15 at the time of the commission of the murder (*Thompson v. Oklahoma*, 487 U.S. 815 [1988]). The Court initially reached the opposite conclusion regarding juveniles over 15 (STANFORD V. KENTUCKY, 492 U.S. 361 [1989]), but recently, the Court has overruled *Stanford*, concluding that the death penalty cannot be imposed on juveniles (*Roper v. Simmons*, 543 U.S. 551 [2005]). At first, the Court held that there was no blanket prohibition of capital punishment for the mentally retarded (PENRY V. LYNAUGH, 492 U.S. 302 [1989]), but the Court has now ruled to the contrary (ATKINS V. VIRGINIA, 536 U.S. 304 [2002]). Also, according to the Court, to be eligible for the death penalty, a defendant in a murder case must have had a state of mind at the time of the killing that can be described as at least a reckless indifference to human life (simple negligence will not do), and where codefendants are involved, the defendant's participation in the crime must have been major (*Tison v. Arizona*, 481 U.S. 137 [1987]).

Although 12 states and the DISTRICT OF COLUMBIA do not have statutes providing for the death penalty, the federal death penalty statute can be applied to any capital offense committed within a U.S. territorial jurisdiction that is itself located within any of the 50 states (18 U.S.C.S. sec. 1111 [2006]). The Supreme Court cases dealing with procedure in capital cases are numerous and complex. For example, the Court has held that if the defendant demands a jury, a judge cannot make a factual finding about the existence of an aggravating factor that would make the defendant eligible for the death penalty; in so doing, the Court has relied on the SIXTH AMENDMENT's guarantee of trial by jury (RING V. ARIZONA, 536 U.S. 584 [2002]). Because the Supreme Court has held that the sentencing decision must be an individualized one, the sentencer must consider any potentially mitigating evidence offered by the defense, such as that the defendant had a troubled childhood (*Eddings v. Oklahoma*, 455 U.S. 104 [1982]).

The Supreme Court has upheld the practice of "death-qualifying" juries. This refers to the process of selecting jurors in capital cases. To understand this practice, one must first note that there are at least two stages in a death penalty case. In the first stage, the jury decides whether it is convinced beyond a reasonable doubt that the defendant has committed the crime charged. If the jury finds the defendant not guilty, that finding, of course, ends the case. If the jury finds the defendant guilty of murder, the jury then must decide at a separate hearing whether to impose the death penalty. The states that have the death penalty use the same jury for both purposes, and that is where a problem has been said to arise. Clearly, if a state has chosen to have the death penalty, it cannot permit prospective jurors who are unalterably opposed to capital punishment to sit on the jury during the second, or penalty, phase.

However, the Supreme Court has allowed states to disqualify from the first (guilt-determination) stage prospective jurors who would never impose the death penalty regardless of the quantity or quality of aggravating circumstances, even if those prospective jurors said that they could impartially judge whether the defendant was guilty or not guilty of the crime (and thus could serve at the first stage of the trial). Some social science studies have shown that when these prospective jurors are excluded from the guilt-determination stage, the resulting jury is somewhat more likely to convict than is a jury from which such prospective jurors are not excluded.

In *Lockhart v. McCree,* 476 U.S. 162 (1986), the defendant argued, among other things, that this disqualification violated his Sixth Amendment right to an impartial jury. The Supreme Court first questioned the validity of the social science studies just mentioned but ultimately was willing to assume that they were valid. The Court, nevertheless, rejected the defendant's argument, concluding, in part, that the state's interest in having a single jury, rather than two juries, outweighed the defendant's interest in having the sort of jury to which the defendant would have been entitled in any noncapital case, for example, a case involving robbery.

Federal review of state capital cases is possible in two ways: direct review of the decision of a state's highest court upholding imposition of the death penalty, and HABEAS CORPUS proceedings, beginning in a federal district court. As a practical matter, such review is difficult to obtain. In the first situation, the problem is that the Supreme Court chooses to hear fewer than 100 cases each year, whereas more than 8,000 petitions for review have been filed each year in the recent past. In the second situation, a 1996 federal statute has placed a number of obstacles in the path of someone seeking habeas corpus review (28 U.S.C. sec. 2254). For example, a petitioner (originally the defendant) in a federal district court cannot win by showing that the state court was wrong; the petitioner must show that the state court was clearly wrong on the basis of cases previously decided by the U.S. Supreme Court. Cases previously decided in the lower federal courts cannot help the petitioner.

No member of the present Supreme Court has shown a willingness to use the Eighth Amendment's proscription of cruel and unusual punishment to declare the death penalty unconstitutional under all circumstances, as the late Justices Brennan and Marshall did. Substantial differences among members of the Court continue to exist, however. There continues to be a basic disagreement over whether the Eighth Amendment, like other provisions of the Constitution and Bill of Rights, should be interpreted according to the original understanding at the time of its adoption, or whether its meaning can evolve over time. The latter approach was adopted by a majority of the Court in the early part of the 20th century (*Weems v. United States,* 217 U.S. 349 [1910]). The former approach is taken by two members of the present Court, Justices ANTONIN GREGORY SCALIA and CLARENCE THOMAS. Members of the present Court are also divided, for example, over the issue whether, in judging the constitutionality of a death penalty provision, the Court should take into account the practices in other countries.

For the foreseeable future, the U.S. Supreme Court is likely to continue on its present path, tinkering with procedural aspects of the death penalty, while refusing to declare it unconstitutional as a whole. There will be no shortage of death penalty cases reaching the Supreme Court since defense attorneys in capital cases will seek to save the lives of their clients regardless of whether their clients have been properly found guilty of the offenses charged. With broad public support for capital punishment as an abstract matter, it is probable that a majority of states will not abandon it, at least in the near term.

For more information: Bedau, Hugo Adam, and Paul G. Cassell, eds. *Debating the Death Penalty: Should America Have Capital Punishment? The Experts on Both Sides Make Their Best Case.* Oxford and New York: Oxford University Press, 2004; LaFave, Wayne R. *Criminal Law.* 4th ed. St. Paul, Minn.: West-Thomson, 2003; LaFave, Wayne R., Jerold H. Israel, and Nancy J. King. *Criminal Procedure.* Vol. 5. 2d ed. St. Paul, Minn.: West Group, 1999; Latzer, Barry. *Death Penalty Cases: Leading U.S. Supreme Court Cases on Capital Punishment.* Woburn, Mass.: Butterworth-Heinemann, 1998.

—Mary Welek Atwell and Robert Davidow

Carter v. Carter Coal Company 298 U.S. 238 (1936)

In *Carter v. Carter Coal Company,* the Supreme Court declared unconstitutional a federal law seeking to regulate the coal industry. The Court said that the law was a violation of the COMMERCE CLAUSE because Congress's power under this clause did not allow for the type of regulation found in this law. The decision in this case is significant because it was one of several important cases testing the constitutional limits of the New Deal.

Carter v. Carter Coal is perhaps most significant for the politics it reflected and engendered rather than for any lasting contribution to constitutional law. This case was generated from a lawsuit brought by a stockholder in the Carter Coal Company that challenged the company's submission to the Bituminous Coal Conservation Act passed by Congress in 1935 (also known as the Guffey Coal Act, so-named for the senator who was its primary sponsor). Because shareholder James Carter and Carter Coal Company both had the same desire of seeing this act of Congress declared unconstitutional, the suit was without adverseness and on that ground, alone, should not have been heard by the Supreme Court, given its own threshold requirement rules. In spite of the lack of adverseness, the Court took the case because it presented the opportunity for the Court to strike down, yet again, Roosevelt administration legislation that sought to bring the country out of the Great Depression through government regulation of business.

Between 1877 and 1936, the Supreme Court had constitutionalized laissez faire economic theory, as it developed lines of doctrine under the FOURTEENTH AMENDMENT'S DUE PROCESS clause and Article I's commerce clause, effectively reading the Constitution as barring the regulation of business by both the states (under the Fourteenth Amendment) and Congress (under Article I, Section 8, Clause 3).

By the time *Carter* reached the Court, in 1936, the Court's interpretation of the commerce clause had come down to the question of whether the subject of the regulatory act was directly or indirectly tied to INTERSTATE COMMERCE. Here, the mining of coal was deemed to be a local matter, since the mines themselves were situated in localities. The Court reasoned that even if the product of the mines was intended for the national market, extraction itself and regulations surrounding its extraction were only indirectly related to interstate commerce. Congress's purpose in enacting the Bituminous Coal Conservation Act of 1935 was to stabilize coal prices and encourage fair competition, production, wages, hours, and labor relations. To fund the program, Congress imposed a tax on coal producers whose participation in the program was voluntary. Participating coal companies would be rewarded, however, with a rebate of 90 percent of the tax paid. Carter Coal did not want to participate, nor did it wish to pay the tax and, consequently, challenged the constitutionality of the legislation.

Although, in this case, the Court did embrace the Carter Coal Company's argument that Congress could not regulate local aspects of production, within a year, a new majority had formed on the Court that returned to the broad understanding of Congress's commerce clause powers originally laid down in 1824 in *GIBBONS V. OGDEN,* 9

Wheat. (22 U.S.) 1 (1824). *Carter v. Carter Coal* was one of the last cases heard by the Supreme Court when it was dominated by activist justices of the so-called Lochner era who saw their role on the Court as that of "correcting the misguided policies" of Congress. Within a year of handing down this decision, the Court had not only returned to its original, broad interpretation of congressional powers but had also repudiated the judicial activism that the Lochner era represented.

For more information: Benson, Paul R., Jr. *The Supreme Court and the Commerce Clause, 1937–1970.* New York: Dunellen Publishing, 1970; Schwartz, Bernard. *A History of the Supreme Court.* New York: Oxford University Press, 1993.

—Phyllis Farley Rippey

case and controversy

Case and controversy refers to a constitutional mandate that every issue the federal courts hear must refer to a real and not a hypothetical issue or claim.

Section 2 of ARTICLE III OF THE U.S. CONSTITUTION states:

> [J]udicial Power shall extend to all Cases, in Law and Equity, arising under this Constitution, the Laws of the United States, and Treaties made, or which shall be made, under their Authority; —to all Cases affecting Ambassadors, other public Ministers and Consuls; —to all Cases of admiralty and maritime Jurisdiction; —to Controversies to which the United States shall be a Party; —to Controversies between two or more States; —between a State and Citizens of another State; —between Citizens of different States; —between Citizens of the Same State claiming Lands under Grants of different States, and between a State, or the Citizens thereof, and foreign States, Citizens or Subjects.

The "case and controversy" requirement therefore mandates that all federal courts deal with real, actual disputes. As such, the U.S. courts must have parties with STANDING disputing their rights before a court can enter a binding judgment. Standing is a concept utilized to determine if a party is sufficiently affected so as to ensure that a justiciable controversy is presented to the court. It is the right to take the initial step that frames legal issues for ultimate adjudication by a court or jury (*State ex rel. Cartwright v. Oklahoma Tax Commission,* Okl., 653 P. 2d 1230, 1232). These federal courts may consider only questions arising in a case or controversy that equates to a "justiciable case." The phrase *justiciable controversy* refers to real and substantial controversies that are appropriate for judicial determination, as distinguished from dispute or difference of contingent, hypothetical, or abstract character (*State v. Nardini,* 187 Conn. 109, 445 A. 2d 304, 307). Therefore, the federal courts are prohibited from giving advisory opinions. Advisory opinions are opinions that give advice about areas involving the legislative or executive branches of the government when no party is before the court who has suffered true injury or faces actual future injury.

As such, judges have no "self-starting capacity" in that they may not see a current issue and then issue an opinion giving legal advice regarding how to best solve the problem the way a president, legislators, a governor, or a mayor might approach the same issue. An actual issue between two parties with rights at stake must bring their case to the court in a format where they are asking for a judicial remedy (court action) to be handed down. The actual issue must be "ripe" and cannot be moot. RIPENESS refers to the fact that the issue has completely come to a point where it is necessary for legal action to be undertaken and where there is nothing left to do but for a court to render a judgment. Mootness, on the other hand, refers to a case where the issue has ceased to exist and is no longer a factor in need of a court-rendered decision.

For more information: Murphy, Walter F., James E. Fleming, Sotirios A. Barber, and Stephen Macedo. *American Constitutional Interpretation.* 3d ed. New York: Foundation Press, 2003.

—Kelli Styron

Chaplinsky v. New Hampshire 315 U.S. 568 (1942)

In *Chaplinsky v. New Hampshire,* a unanimous Supreme Court held that freedom of speech does not extend to "fighting words."

The case grew out of a confrontation between Jehovah's Witnesses and police in Rochester, New Hampshire. The Witnesses were holding a public meeting to proselytize the masses during which the crowd became unruly. Marshal Bowering of the Rochester police confronted Walter Chaplinsky, one of the leaders of the meeting, who called Bowering a "damned racketeer" and "a damned Fascist."

Chaplinsky was convicted under a New Hampshire law making it illegal to utter "any offensive, derisive, or annoying word" to a person in a public place. On appeal, Chaplinsky argued that the statute violated his freedom of speech and religion. The New Hampshire Supreme Court affirmed the conviction, construing the statute as only involving those words having "a direct tendency to cause acts of violence by the person to whom, individually, the remark is addressed." These were words that would "likely . . . cause an average addressee to fight."

The U.S. Supreme Court affirmed. Writing for the Court, Justice Frank Murphy rejected Chaplinsky's FREEDOM OF RELIGION argument, holding that the Constitution would not immunize Chaplinsky "from the legal consequences of concomitant acts committed in violation of a valid criminal statute." Justice Murphy then observed that "free speech is not absolute at all times and under all circumstances." Instead, there are "certain well-defined and narrowly limited classes of speech" whose banning does not raise a constitutional problem. In addition to "the lewd and obscene" and "the libelous," this category included "insulting or fighting words," which Justice Murphy defined as "those words which by their very utterance inflict injury or tend to incite an immediate breach of the peace." Such words play "no essential part of any exposition of ideas" and "are of such slight social value" that any benefit gained from protecting them "is outweighed by the social interest in order and morality." Turning to Chaplinsky's remarks, Justice Murphy held the terms *damn racketeer* and *damn Fascist* would "provoke the average person to retaliation and thereby cause a breach of the peace."

Over time, *Chaplinsky* has been narrowed considerably. In *COHEN V. CALIFORNIA,* 403 U.S. 15 (1971), the Court held that a jacket bearing the phrase "Fuck the Draft" did not constitute fighting words because the phrase was not directed at a specific person. For similar reasons, in *Collin v. Smith,* 578 F.2d 1197 (7th Cir. 1978), the Seventh Circuit held that the city of Skokie's ban on Nazi symbols fell outside the fighting words doctrine. Finally, in *R.A.V. v. ST. PAUL,* 505 U.S. 377 (1992), the Court held that the government could not ban a subset of fighting words that offend on the basis of "race, color, creed, religion or gender." However, *R.A.V.* reaffirmed the government's general power to proscribe fighting words, provided it did so in a content-neutral manner.

Chaplinsky is also significant because, for the first time, the Court explicitly stated that some speech did not merit full FIRST AMENDMENT protection, an idea the Court would later extend to the areas of group libel, OBSCENITY, and COMMERCIAL SPEECH.

For more information: Kalven, Harry, Jr. *A Worthy Tradition: Freedom of Speech in America.* New York: Harper & Row, 1974; Walker, Samuel. *Hate Speech: The History of an American Controversy.* Lincoln: University of Nebraska Press, 1994.

—Robert A. Kahn

Chase Court (1864–1873)

The Chase Court could also be called the Reconstruction Court. Only months before the end of the Civil War, President ABRAHAM LINCOLN appointed Salmon P. Chase (1808–73) as chief justice of the U.S. Supreme Court. During the decade that followed, Americans reevaluated and redesigned most aspects of their society. Even the U.S. Constitution came under close scrutiny; it was amended three times in just five years. The task of interpreting those amendments and the newly empowered national government essentially created by them fell to the Chase Court.

The previous chief justice, ROGER TANEY, presided over the Court from 1836 until his death in October 1864. He wrote the majority opinion in the most notorious decision in Supreme Court history, the 1857 case of *DRED SCOTT V. SANDFORD.* In that case, Taney held that Congress lacked the power to prohibit slavery in a territory, much less a state, and that African Americans were "a subordinate and inferior class of beings" who had "no rights which the white man was bound to respect." That decision unleashed a fury among Northerners that hastened the Civil War; it also caused Lincoln to fear how the Court, in the wrong hands, might undermine his war measures. Prior to the Civil War, the Supreme Court always consisted of Democrats, most of them Southerners.

In just two years, from 1862 to 1864, the passing of old Jacksonians enabled President Lincoln to appoint five justices, thus transforming the Supreme Court to a fully Republican majority, which is how it remained for more than a generation. Indeed, between 1862 and 1882, five Republican presidents appointed 14 justices to the Supreme Court. Although the justices were expected to be nonpartisan, their politics often informed their decisions on the bench. More important, their political ambitions led four of Lincoln's five appointees—the bulk and backbone of the Chase Court—to run for president while members of the Supreme Court.

The number of justices on the bench vacillated between six and 10, due to bad health and the struggle between the branches. Noah Swayne, Lincoln's first appointee, was a Quaker who moved from Virginia to Ohio out of opposition to slavery. Dr. Samuel Miller practiced medicine in his home state of Kentucky before becoming Iowa's most successful advocate for small farmers. David Davis, a judge who presided over many cases argued by Lincoln the backwoods lawyer, became Lincoln's campaign manager in the presidential election of 1860 and served as his third appointment to the Supreme Court. Exhausted by Reconstruction, Davis resigned from the bench when elected to the U.S. SENATE seat Lincoln failed to secure in 1858.

Stephen Field, regarded as Lincoln's finest addition to the Court, filled the new federal Tenth Circuit that Congress created in California and Oregon, intended to shore up the pro-Union majority on the bench. With this appointment, Lincoln became the first president to nominate a justice from another party, since Field was a pro-Union Democrat. Field supported Lincoln's war measures and later buoyed business in most of the 620 opinions he wrote in his record-setting 34 years on the bench.

The best known of Lincoln's justices, of course, was Chase, who ran against Lincoln for president in 1860. After graduating from Dartmouth College and gaining a reputation as an antislavery lawyer, Chase helped form the Free Soil Party. He served Ohio as both U.S. senator and governor before becoming Lincoln's secretary of the treasury, a post from which he rather petulantly resigned (for the fourth time) just prior to being made chief justice. Chase tried hard to create a socially amicable environment within the Court, but those efforts failed as most of the justices tended to dislike and distrust each other, Chase most of all. That Lincoln's justices were highly regarded is best demonstrated by the fact that all were confirmed within days of nomination. Three more justices joined the Chase Court when President Ulysses S. Grant appointed William Strong and Joseph Bradley in 1870 and Ward Hunt in 1873. Grant's fourth appointee, Morrison Remick Waite, replaced Chase as chief justice in 1874.

From 1860 to 1935, the U.S. Supreme Court met in the old Senate chamber, on the first floor of the Capitol building. The case docket grew from 360 cases per year at the start of the Chase Court—more than three times the current load—to 623 in 1891 when Congress finally provided relief by creating an intermediary tribunal called the Circuit Court of Appeals. That same legislation, the Judiciary Act of 1891, also eliminated the dreaded task of "circuit riding" that consumed three-quarters of the justices every year. The Court was in session from December to March each year, 11 A.M. to 3 P.M. Monday through Friday and 11 A.M. to 4 P.M. on Saturday. The justices received a salary of $6,000 and lived in a boardinghouse at No. 23 Four-and-a-half Street, though they upgraded their lodgings to hotels when their salaries were increased in 1871.

The Court's bulging docket consisted of mostly quotidian and uninteresting cases pertaining to commercial matters of banking, state taxes, and government bonds that waited two to three years to be heard. During the Civil War, the Court contended with the constitutionality of Lincoln's suspension of HABEAS CORPUS and Congress's issuance of legal tender, but by the early years of the Chase Court, maritime cases—addressing the law of prize regarding enemy property captured at sea—provided the greatest excitement.

The Chase Court remained divided along partisan lines regarding several issues, not least the proper reach of federal military authority. The Freedmen's Bureau, a federal agency responsible for assimilating the 4 million recently freed slaves, was often accused of operating unconstitutionally. Whereas the Court upheld Lincoln's ability to curtail CIVIL LIBERTIES in wartime in the 1864 case of *Ex parte Vallandigham*, by 1866, in *EX PARTE MILLIGAN*, the Court cast doubt on the notion that "military necessity" excused the abridgment of civil liberties and rights such as habeas corpus.

The postwar concern for amnesty and pardon of secessionists gave rise to oaths of allegiance in various occupations. When a lawyer balked at the iron-clad oaths required to practice law before the Supreme Court and a priest resisted such oaths in Missouri, the Court ruled against such oaths as unconstitutional, in *Ex parte Garland* and *Missouri v. Cummings*, both in 1867. The Democrats, including Field, provided the majority in those decisions, while the Republicans dissented. Congress, upset by the test oath decisions, granted itself the authority to decide such matters in the FOURTEENTH AMENDMENT, ratified in 1868.

Later that same year, the Court somewhat surprisingly accepted Congress's fiat, as demonstrated in *EX PARTE MCCARDLE*, yet another habeas corpus case. The Court knocked heads with Congress again in the *Legal Tender Cases*, in which paper money (first issued under Chase's watch as secretary of treasury) was ironically ruled unconstitutional by Chase and the Democrats, then two years later deemed appropriate by the Republican majority made stronger by President Grant's appointments to the Court. On the thorniest issue of all, rights for blacks, the Court at first supported a broad conception of their freedom, as seen in *United States v. Rhodes*, which struck down a lower court opinion barring black testimony in cases involving whites. But by *Blyew v. United States*, five years later, in 1871, the Court oddly reversed itself. In the most famous decision of the Chase Court, the *Slaughterhouse Cases* of 1873, the justices seemed to support blacks but actually narrowed their rights in a manner that lasted well into the 20th century. That decision laid the seed of "state action" jurisprudence by holding that the federal government could prohibit only state, not private, acts of discrimination.

The standard textbook treatment suggests that the Supreme Court grew steadily in stature from the founding era until the *Dred Scott* case of 1857, at which point the bench suffered a blow to its power and prestige that lasted late into the 19th century. Other historians insist the Court was quite weak until Reconstruction, when the justices stepped in to help decide how secessionist states would be readmitted and to determine the scope of the Thirteenth, Fourteenth, and Fifteenth Amendments (the THIRTEENTH AMENDMENT abolished slavery, the FOURTEENTH AMENDMENT reversed *Dred Scott* by granting citizenship to African Americans, and the FIFTEENTH AMENDMENT extended the franchise to all American males).

There can be little doubt but that the Supreme Court participated in the war between the branches that was so important a part of Reconstruction. Historians tend to focus more on the conflicts between the executive and the legislative branches of the federal government, in particular the efforts by radicals to impeach President Andrew Johnson. But the members of Congress made several efforts to alter or contain the Court as well; some congressmen even spoke of eliminating the Supreme Court altogether. Witness the four Judiciary Acts within the 1860s that reshaped the size and composition of the Court.

Yet Lincoln's justices were a forceful and ambitious lot who subtly yet consciously elevated the profile of the Supreme Court. It is important to note that the Supreme Court overturned only two federal and 30 state acts of legislation throughout its pre–Civil War history, whereas the Chase Court overturned 10 federal and 46 state acts of legislation in just eight years. There can be little doubt that Chase and his fellow justices sat through the most challenging chapter in American and Supreme Court history.

For more information: Fairman, Charles. *Reconstruction and Reunion: History of the Supreme Court.* New York: Macmillan, 1971; Kutler, Stanley. *Judicial Power and Reconstruction Politics.* Chicago: University of Chicago Press, 1968; Niven, John. *Salmon P. Chase.* New York: Oxford University Press, 1995; Wyman, Harold, and William Wiecek. *Equal Justice Under Law: Constitutional Development, 1835–1875.* New York: Harper & Row, 1982.

—Owen Williams

checks and balances

Checks and balances refers to a constitutional system of limiting the political and legal power of the three branches of government by giving the executive, judicial, and legislative branches some control over one another.

Checks and balances are absolutely basic to the American constitutional structure. The most fundamental of our checks and balances is the separation of powers—the assignment of executive, legislative, and judicial authority to distinct branches of government. The Founding Fathers wanted to avoid concentrating power in a single institution so as to foster, as JOHN ADAMS famously put it, "A government of laws and not of men." Their concept of checks and balances begins with this separation of powers, but it also includes a number of other elements that were built into our constitutional structure.

Those who drafted the Constitution recognized that the central government needed enough authority to govern effectively. The fatal defect of the Articles of Confederation, which the Constitution replaced, had been the weakness of the federal government. The Constitution attempted to remedy that defect without endangering America's newly won liberties. Accordingly, the entire system was designed to check, or limit, use of the increased authority being delegated to the federal government.

In addition to separation of powers, drafters of the Constitution opted for a representative, rather than a direct, democracy. Representative government was intended to provide a buffer between public passions and government action; the founders believed that the process of electing representatives who would then cast the actual votes on public issues would encourage deliberation and compromise. A federalist structure, in which state and local governments each retained significant powers, was intended to act as a check on the authority of both. A BICAMERAL LEGISLATURE and a requirement that laws be approved by both the HOUSE OF REPRESENTATIVES and the SENATE was designed to slow further the legislative process and encourage deliberation.

These decisions about our constitutional architecture grew out of a view of human nature firmly rooted in the philosophy of the Enlightenment. It was a view that differed in important respects from the Puritan beliefs of most of the early settlers. The Puritans had come to America for religious liberty; however, the Puritan definition of *liberty* was freedom to "do the right thing." The government would still decide what the right thing was. To these early colonists, religious freedom had simply meant establishing governments that would require the "right" religion. The philosophy of the Enlightenment, which flowered in the period between those early settlements and the American Revolution, dramatically changed that view. Enlightenment philosophers believed humans were entitled to personal autonomy—the right to make their own political, moral, and religious decisions. They defined liberty as freedom from government interference in the rights of the individual unless and until that individual was harming the person or property of a nonconsenting other. It was the Enlightenment understand-

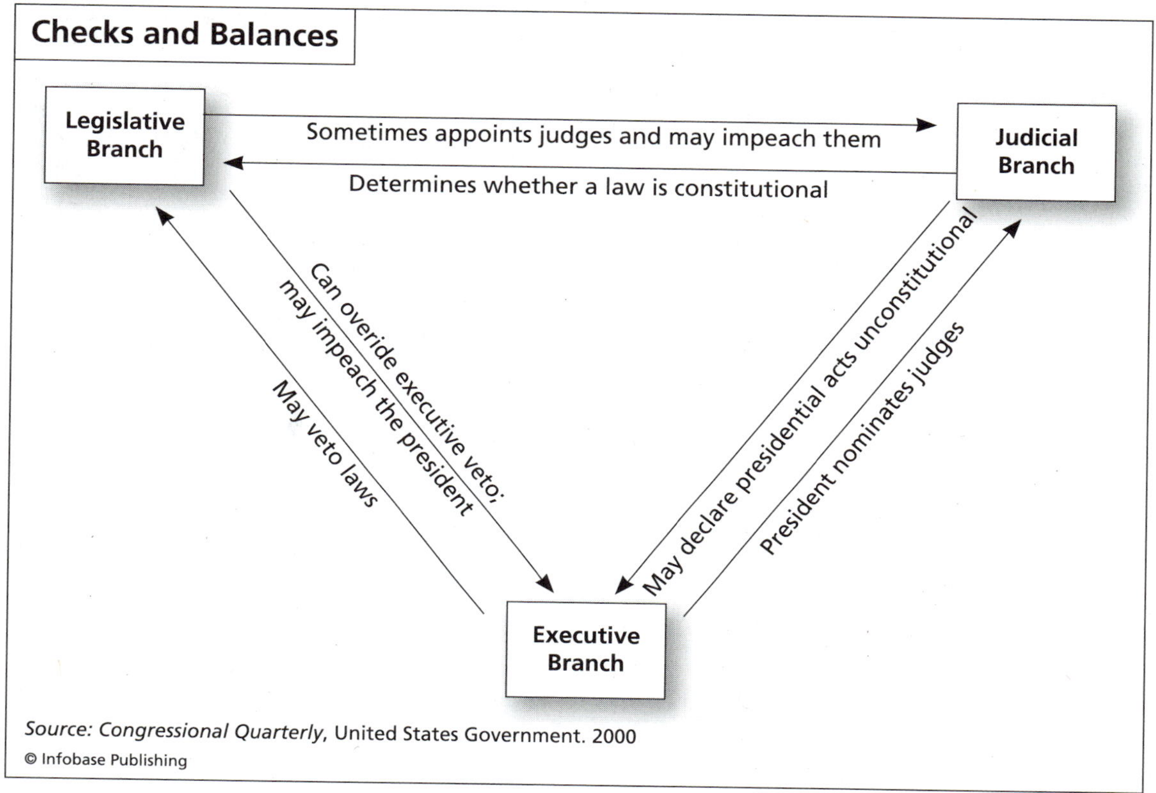
Checks and Balances
Legislative Branch
Judicial Branch
Executive Branch
Sometimes appoints judges and may impeach them
Determines whether a law is constitutional
Can overide executive veto; may impeach the president
May veto laws
May declare presidential acts unconstitutional
President nominates judges

Source: Congressional Quarterly, United States Government. 2000

ing of liberty—not the earlier Puritan one—that inspired America's constitutional system.

The founders believed that the proper role of the state was to protect individual liberty, not to impose "right" behavior. This role requires checks and balances, mechanisms that, as JAMES MADISON put it in *Federalist 10*, will set "faction against faction" and thus avoid the tyranny which is unavoidable when too much power is concentrated in one person or institution. In the Founding Fathers' worldview, protection of individual liberty and the creation of an empowered citizenry were necessary to the cultivation of our true nature as human beings. Protecting liberty required the establishment of a state in which no one would be above the law and government would be accountable to its citizens, rather than the other way around. Checks and balances were intended to provide that accountability.

Individual liberty—newly defined as limited state power—was also seen as essential to the emerging system of capitalism. It was no accident that belief in limiting state power first took root in a nation with no feudal history, a nation composed primarily of bourgeois, property-owning small businessmen and farmers—people who understood the importance of property rights and the dangers that arbitrary exercises of power posed to private property.

The founders also believed that effective checks and balances would create the sort of open and accountable system that would be likely to attract people of integrity and substance to public service. Just as the new Constitution required American trials to be public in a way that European trials had never been, U.S. government was to be public and accountable in ways that European monarchs had never been.

Ultimately, a fair election process in which citizens had the RIGHT TO VOTE officeholders out of power was designed to be the most important check and balance of all.

For more information: Amar, Akhil Reed. *America's Constitution: A Biography.* New York: Random House, 2005; Hamilton, A., J. Madison, and J. Jay. *The Federalist Papers.* New York: New American Library, 1961.

—Sheila Suess Kennedy

child labor

Child labor refers to the use of minors or individuals under the age of 18 at work. Regulations banning or limiting child labor were the subject of many lawsuits in the 19th and early 20th centuries because of concerns that neither states nor the federal government had the constitutional authority to regulate it.

By the early part of the 20th century, only three states placed no restrictions on the employment of children. Progressives, who had succeeded in enacting child-protective legislation in most states, turned their attention to Congress to establish national child labor standards, achieving this goal with the enactment of the Federal Child Labor Act of 1916. Using its COMMERCE CLAUSE powers that gave Congress authority over all INTERSTATE COMMERCE, Congress barred from shipment in interstate commerce the products of factories that employed children under the age of 14 or allowed children between the ages of 14 and 16 to work more than eight hours a day, more than six days a week, or at night. Congress had been pressed to enact such legislation both as a protective measure for children and to equalize competition among states, some of which enjoyed a price advantage through the use of low-cost child labor. Court challenges to the act came swiftly, reaching the Supreme Court within two years of its enactment.

In *HAMMER V. DAGENHART*, 247 U.S. 251 (1918), the Supreme Court declared the act an unconstitutional usurpation of state power by Congress. This case was one of a long line of cases handed down by the Supreme Court between 1877 and 1937 in its effort to use the Tenth Amendment to limit congressional action in the regulation of business. This line of cases narrowing Congress's powers under the commerce clause amounted to the Court's constitutionalizing laissez faire economics.

Thwarted in its first attempt to protect children from, in the words of Justice OLIVER WENDELL HOLMES, JR., in dissent in *Hammer*, "ruined lives," Congress passed the Child Labor Tax Law under its taxing authority in 1919. In 1922, the Supreme Court struck down this act as an unconstitutional "penalty" against child labor and, thus, an unconstitutional intrusion on the reserved powers of the states. Consequently, children were left unprotected by the national government until 1938, when Congress enacted the Fair Labor Standards Act, which established a minimum wage for all workers. Without the ability to pay child labor considerably less than adult labor, the desire for child labor waned. In 1941, the Supreme Court reversed course once again on Congress's interstate commerce clause powers, reverting to its broad interpretation of the power first articulated in *GIBBONS V. OGDEN*, 9 Wheat. (22 U.S.) 1 (1824), and upholding the Fair Labor Standards Act in *UNITED STATES V. DARBY LUMBER CO.*, 312 U.S. 100 (1941).

For more information: Wood, Stephen. *Constitutional Politics and the Progressive Era: Child Labor and the Law.* Chicago: University of Chicago Press, 1968.

—Phyllis Farley Rippey

child pornography

Child pornography generally refers to the use or depiction of individuals under the age of 18 in sexually explicit materials, such as films or magazines. The Supreme Court has declared that child pornography is not a form of speech protected by the FIRST AMENDMENT.

The definition of child pornography varies from country to country. Most prohibit visual depictions of sexual activities involving actual children under a specified age. Some countries go further and prohibit any nude pictures of minors, whether or not the minor is depicted in an erotic pose or engaging in a sex act. Historically, according to British rule, reactions to child pornography were based on moral grounds, the claim being that consumers' minds would be corrupted. By distinction, child pornography in the United States is prohibited not by moral infraction but as a form of child abuse.

Child pornography is not protected by the First Amendment. Three landmark rulings—*Ginzburg v. United States,* 383 U.S. 463 (1966); *MILLER V. CALIFORNIA,* 413 U.S. 15 (1973); and *New York v. Ferber,* 458 U.S. 747 (1982)—illustrate this lack of protection. Regarding *Ginzburg v. New York,* the Supreme Court held that the government can constitutionally prohibit children from accessing certain types of sexually explicit material that it cannot constitutionally ban for adults. In *Miller v. California,* the Supreme Court established that material can be judged obscene by community standards; in other words, the Supreme Court left it up to communities to decide what they felt was obscene.

In *New York v. Ferber,* the Supreme Court upheld the constitutionality of a state statute that prohibited anyone from knowingly producing, promoting, directing, exhibiting, or selling any material showing a sexual performance by a child under the age of 16. This case also established that child pornography does not have to meet all of the requirements of the Miller test. Additionally, the U.S. Supreme Court found a New York law criminalizing child pornography as a form of child abuse to be constitutional under the First Amendment in *New York v. Ferber.* As amended in 1996, Congress defined the pornography it prohibited as

> any visual depiction, including photography, film, video, picture, or computer, or computer-generated image or picture, whether made or produced by electronic, mechanical, or other means, of sexually explicit conduct, where (A) the production of such visual depiction involves the use of a minor engaging in sexually explicit conduct; (B) such visual depiction is, or appears to be, of a minor engaging in sexually explicit conduct; (C) such visual depiction has been created, adapted or modified to appear that an identifiable minor is engaging in sexually explicit conduct; or (D) such visual depiction is advertised, promoted, presented, described or distributed in such a manner that conveys the impression that the material is or contains a visual depiction of a minor engaging in sexually explicit conduct.

Sexually explicit conduct in this context was defined as actual or simulated sexual intercourse. This includes genital-genital, oral-genital, anal-genital, and oral-anal acts whether between persons of the same or opposite sex. This also includes bestiality, masturbation, sadistic or masochistic abuse, and the lascivious exhibition of the genitals and/or pubic area of any person. The Court found that a work deemed to be child pornography could be outlawed even if it is not obscene and that child pornography ought to be banned because it contributes to the sexual abuse of children.

The idea of protecting children from sexual exploitation is relatively recent. As late as the 1880s in the United States, the age of consent for girls was just 10 years. In 1977, only two states had legislation specifically outlawing the use of children in obscene materials. The first federal law concerning child pornography was passed in 1978, and the first laws that specifically referred to computers and pornography were passed in 1988. The 1978 law referred to minors under the age of 16. Age of a minor covered by child pornography legislation was raised to 18 in 1984.

Legally, morally, and socially, pornography is difficult to define and classify, as it is a very complex cultural process. Pornography is produced by people and consumed by customers. Pornography derives most of its meaning from the social context in which it exists. The United States struggles with consistent and unquestionable definitions of child pornography. Although the above definition of child pornography appears expansive, there is no clear legal definition in federal or state law as to what constitutes *lascivious* exhibition. This term is to be interpreted according to "contemporary community standards." Additionally, the term *obscene* is difficult to define. OBSCENITY has moral connotations that the federal law does not recognize as child abuse. Debate arose in the late 1990s as to whether the depiction of nudity of minors could constitute obscenity. As a result of this debate and the seizure of nude depictions of minors from Europe, an appellate court ruled in 2000 that depictions of nude minors engaging in activities otherwise normal for their age cannot be held obscene. The idea is that nudity in and of itself does not constitute obscenity.

The final decision as to whether an image is pornographic is made by a judge. In the United States, the production and sale of child pornography is illegal. The United States also outlaws the possession of child pornography. There are many arguments against the production and distribution of child pornography. The main argument is that a child cannot consent to participating in pornographic activities if the child is under a certain age. This age varies according to state, but for the most part it is under the age of 18. Federal and state governments classify child pornography as a form of child abuse including physical, sexual, and emotional abuse. Additionally, child pornography harms children because materials that capture the child in pornography are permanent and that permanent record increases the harm to the child when it is circulated. The continued distribution of such material contributes to the demand of child pornography thus requiring the exploitation of more children.

The Internet is currently the most popular avenue for pornography and caused explosive growth for the pornography industry. It has escalated the problem of child pornography by increasing the amount of material available, the efficiency of its distribution, and the ease of its accessibility. Some estimate there are more than 300,000 pornographic Web sites on the Internet. At any one time, there are estimated to be more than 1 million pornographic images of children on the Internet, with 200 new images posted daily. It has been reported that a single child pornography site received a million hits in one month. This means that pornography is instantly available. It has been estimated that child pornography on the Internet is an industry worth $20 billion a year. The most dangerous aspect of the Internet is its use by pedophiles. It has been estimated that there are between 50,000 and 100,000 pedophiles involved in organized pornography rings around the world and that one-third of these operate in the United States. Many child molesters use the Internet to view pornographic images of children and may also pose as youngsters themselves to communicate with other children, in chats, for example. Many child molesters expose children to pornography and arrange to meet them in person.

The National Center for Missing and Exploited Children found that one in five children age 10–17 who regularly use the Internet have received invitations to meet supposed adults posing as youngsters. Sociologists often point to a supply-and-demand argument regarding pornography. There is a demand for pornography because of the existence of pedophiles. The only way one can produce pornography is to molest a child. Child pornography exists primarily for the consumption of pedophiles; if there were no pedophiles, there would be no child pornography.

Many pornographic images of children on the Internet involve very young children. Specifically, 83 percent of pornographic material confiscated by the Federal Bureau of Investigation (FBI) in the past three years consisted of children between the ages of six and 12, 12.4 percent had material involving children between the ages of three and five, and 19 percent had images of infants or toddlers under the age of three. It has become increasingly difficult to eradicate child pornography on the Internet because of sophisticated technology and security; for example, adults can own their own servers, change the site of the server, or use proxy servers to hide the identification of members. The first case in the United States involving the conviction of a pedophile who made contact with his victim on the Internet occurred in 2002. The body of 13-year-old Christine Long was discovered in Greenwich, Connecticut. Police allege that she was strangled by a 25-year-old man she met online.

The Internet makes finding child pornography much easier. Someone who wishes to view child pornography can do so without asking someone else to locate such images. The Internet thus makes accessing child pornography much more anonymous. The user of this material can access it from the PRIVACY of his or her home 24 hours a day, 365 days a year. The Internet also provides legitimization. In online communities, users of child pornography and pedophiles can join a virtual world where the use of child pornography and the abuse of children are considered acceptable. In the physical world, most people view child pornography as repugnant.

In the United States, since 1995, there has been a special unit of the FBI called Innocent Images. This unit is devoted to tracking down those who use the Internet to sexually exploit children. This is now a $10 million a year operation.

For more information: Gillespie, A. A. "Indecent Images of Children: The Ever-Changing Law." *Child Abuse Review* 14 (2005): 430–443; MacKinnon, Catharine. *Sex Equality*. New York: Foundation Press, 2001; Quinn, James F., and Craig J. Forsyth. "Describing Sexual Behavior in the Era of the Internet: A Typology for Empirical Research." *Deviant Behavior* 26 (2005): 191; Wortley, Richard, and Stephen Smallbone. *Child Pornography on the Internet*. Washington, D.C.: U.S. Department of Justice, 2006.

—Kim MacInnis

Chimel v. California 395 U.S. 752 (1969)

In *Chimel v. California*, the U.S. Supreme Court drew clearer boundaries for law-enforcement officials in the area of search and seizure. The Court held that an officer may search only the area "within the immediate control" of a person following a lawful arrest.

On September 13, 1965, California police arrested Ted Chimel on burglary charges. At the time of their arrival, Chimel was not home, but his wife permitted the officers to wait in the living room. Immediately upon entering the home, the arrest warrant was executed, and Chimel was taken into custody in connection with numerous burglaries. The officers sought consent to "look around the house," but Chimel and his wife declined their requests. The police then proceeded to conduct a room-by-room search, turning up numerous items that had been reported stolen in several burglaries. The evidence seized during the search was admitted into evidence at trial and resulted in a conviction for the state.

Chimel is a landmark constitutional law case. The Constitution is the document that defines and shapes the relationship between the government and the people of the United States. The first 10 amendments to the Constitution are known as the BILL OF RIGHTS and were adopted to address the concerns of citizens that the rights of the people were not clearly or adequately covered in the Constitution. The FOURTH AMENDMENT addresses search and seizure and guarantees "the right of the people to be secure in their persons, houses, papers, and effects against unreasonable searches and seizures." It requires that no search and/or seizure shall take place absent a warrant based on probable cause and that the warrant describe with specificity the place to be searched and what items or persons are being searched for.

The trial court held that the search was constitutional because it was conducted immediately following the arrest of Chimel. On certiorari, the Supreme Court reversed the finding of the trial court.

Whenever the Court is asked to make a determination of the constitutionality of a search and seizure, it must address whether the actions of the government were reasonable under the circumstances. In *Chimel*, the Court found that a warrantless search of the area immediately surrounding the arrestee would be justified by the need to remove any weapon the arrestee might seek to use to resist arrest or escape and the need to prevent the concealment and destruction of evidence. However, the evidence seized from Chimel's house was taken from rooms and other areas outside his immediate control. Chimel was arrested as soon as he entered his home; his access to other areas was limited. There was no testimony that raised concerns about the officer's safety,

Chimel's escape, or the possible destruction of evidence. The conduct of the police was found to be unreasonable and a violation of Chimel's constitutional rights.

For more information: Allen, Ronald J. *Criminal Procedure: Investigation and Right to Counsel.* New York: Aspen Publishers, 2005; Schwartz, Bernard. *A History of the Supreme Court.* New York: Oxford University Press, 1993.

—Loretta M. Young

Chisholm v. Georgia 2 U.S. 419 (1793)

In *Chisholm v. Georgia,* the Supreme Court ruled that a state was not immune from suit from citizens of other states or foreign nations. As a result of the decision, the ELEVENTH AMENDMENT was adopted to overturn the ruling.

This case is important because it is about sovereignty and the idea that a state was immune from suit from citizens of other states or foreign nations. The concept of sovereign immunity had its roots in the English maxim "the sovereign could not be sued without his consent."

Chisholm began as a claim for the repayment of money the state of Georgia owed to a citizen from South Carolina, Robert Farquhar. Farquhar tried to bring suit against Georgia in the federal circuit court, but to no avail. When Farquhar died, Alexander Chisholm, one of the executors of his estate, appealed the ruling and brought suit against Georgia in the Supreme Court.

Georgia was so adamant in assertion of sovereign immunity that it refused to even appear in Court to plead its case against Edmund Randolph, attorney general for the United States and also Chisholm's counsel. In a 4-1 decision, the Court ruled in favor of Chisholm. Justice William Cushing found that the Constitution expressly granted the Court jurisdiction over controversies between a "State and citizens of another state." Therefore, when a citizen of one state has a dispute with another state, the Court is presented with a real controversy that is no different than the state having the dispute with the citizens of another state.

Chief Justice JOHN JAY invoked Section 2 of ARTICLE III OF THE U.S. CONSTITUTION, which provides that the judicial power extends to all cases under the Constitution, including controversies between a "State and citizens of another state." Jay rejected the contention that Article III, Section 2, covered states only as plaintiffs, not defendants, instead focusing simply on the language of the Constitution extending to the Court ORIGINAL JURISDICTION in all cases arising between a state and a citizen of another state.

Another theme resonating among the justices was the rejection of state sovereignty and an emphasis on popular sovereignty, the idea that the United States was a union of people. Justice James Wilson asserted that sovereignty rested with the people of the United States, not with the states, which meant that states were subordinate to the people and therefore could be sued by them.

The *Chisholm* decision was met with quick and considerable outrage considering that there were a number of similar suits pending against the states. The Georgia House of Representatives tried to pass a bill declaring that anyone who attempted to bring suit against the state would be guilty of a felony punishable by death. The Massachusetts and Virginia legislatures proposed amendments to the Constitution removing any clause that could be construed as forcing the states to be subject to federal suit by citizens of other states. In Congress, efforts to curtail federal judicial power produced variations of an amendment that was supported by both sides of the aisle.

On March 4, 1794, Congress passed the Eleventh Amendment, and by February 7, 1795, the amendment was ratified. It provided that: "the judicial power of the United States shall not be construed to extend to any suit in law or equity, commenced or prosecuted against one of the United States by citizens of another state, or by citizens or subjects of any foreign state."

For more information: Jacobs, Clyde E. *The Eleventh Amendment and Sovereign Immunity.* Westport, Conn.: Greenwood Press, 1972; Mathis, Doyle. "*Chisholm v. Georgia*: Background and Settlement." *Journal of American History* 54

(1967): 19–29; Orth, John V. *The Judicial Power of the United States: The Eleventh Amendment in American History.* New York and Oxford: Oxford University Press, 1987; Swindler, William F. "Mr. Chisholm and the Eleventh Amendment." *Supreme Court Historical Society, Annual Yearbook.* Washington, D.C.: Supreme Court Historical Society, 1981; Wintersteen, A. H. "The Eleventh Amendment and the Nonsuability of the State." *American Law Register* 39 (1891): 1–15.

—Randa Issa

Church of the Lukumi Babalu Aye, Inc. v. City of Hialeah 508 U.S. 520 (1993)

In *Church of the Lukumi Babalu Aye, Inc. v. City of Hialeah,* the Supreme Court ruled that a law forbidding a religion from performing animal sacrifices was unconstitutional because the law was specifically targeted at the religion.

This case involved practitioners of Santeria. One of the religion's practices involved animal sacrifice, in which practitioners would kill, cook, and eat an animal. A Santeria church purchased land in the city of Hialeah, Florida, and announced plans to worship there. In response, the city passed ordinances prohibiting animal sacrifice but permitting the killing of animals in a number of other contexts, such as in slaughterhouses. Church members sued, claiming that the ordinances violated their rights under the free exercise clause of the FIRST AMENDMENT.

The Supreme Court reversed, in an opinion by Justice ANTHONY M. KENNEDY, holding that the ordinances violated the free exercise clause. Applying the framework established in *EMPLOYMENT DIVISION V. SMITH,* 494 U.S. 872 (1990), Justice Kennedy determined that the ordinances were not neutral because the city singled out the Santeria religion for suppression. In other words, the ordinances were enacted because of, rather than in spite of, their suppression of Santeria religious practice. Justice Kennedy also determined that the ordinances were not generally applicable under *Smith* because the city only pursued its governmental interest in protecting the health and safety of animals and the community when it related to conduct with a religious motivation; that is, the ordinances did not apply to killing animals for purely secular reasons.

Because the resolutions were not neutral or generally applicable, Justice Kennedy applied STRICT SCRUTINY. Although the governmental interests at issue, protecting public health and preventing cruelty to animals, may be a COMPELLING GOVERNMENTAL INTEREST, the ordinances were not narrowly tailored to these interests. The Court held that each of the ordinances were either overly broad or underinclusive; therefore, the Court invalidated each of the ordinances.

In Justice ANTONIN GREGORY SCALIA's concurrence, with which Chief Justice WILLIAM HUBBS REHNQUIST joined, he argued that the terms *neutral* and *generally applicable* in *Smith* were not only interrelated but that they substantially overlapped. They further argued that a legislative body's motive in enacting an ordinance should be irrelevant: There is no way to determine the single motivational force behind a piece of legislation, and the First Amendment does not refer to the purposes for which legislators enact laws but to the effects of the laws enacted.

For more information: O'Brien, David. *Animal Sacrifice and Religious Freedom:* Church of the Lukumi Babalu Aye v. City of Hialeah. Lawrence: University of Kansas Press, 2004.

—Winston E. Calvert

citizenship and alienage

Citizenship and alienage refer to the legal status and rights and privileges of individuals in the United States. The national government has the constitutional authority to regulate both.

Immigration and naturalization remain an important component of nation building since the founding of the United States. The DECLARATION OF INDEPENDENCE cites the lack of free migration and establishment of a system of naturalization as rationales for declaring independence. However, there has always been tension between the need for people and the rights accorded to those

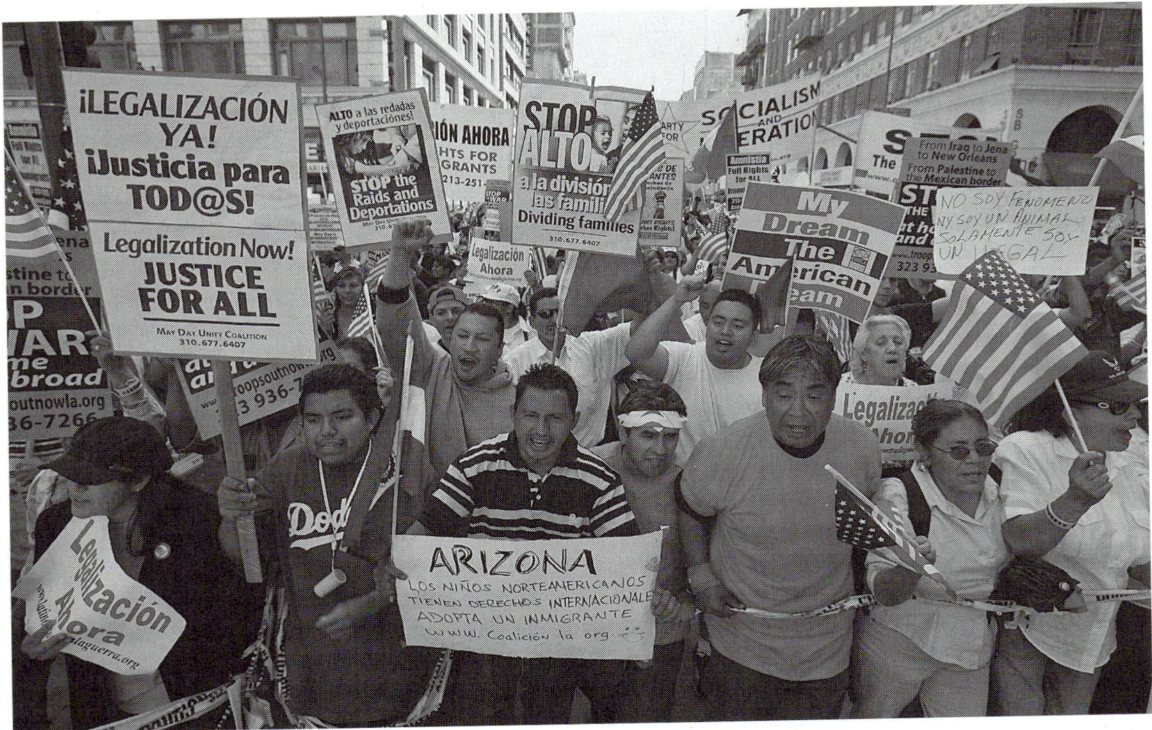

Demonstrators for immigrants' rights march May 1, 2008, in Los Angeles, California. *(David McNew/Getty Images)*

people. The Supreme Court maintains the Constitution relegates immigration and naturalization to congressional control (plenary power), precluding JUDICIAL REVIEW. Constitutional matters still permit judicial review.

From the early days of the republic, it has been easy to naturalize; however, the founders feared instant naturalization of foreigners and concomitant antidemocratic sentiment in the new nation. They therefore imposed a waiting period to give aliens time to acculturate politically. One of the first acts of the first Congress was a naturalization law (March 26, 1790, 1Stat. 103) providing the opportunity to apply for naturalization to any free white person who had been a resident in the United States for two years and in his own state for one year, showed good moral character, and was willing to swear an oath of allegiance to the state. If the state deemed him worthy, he could naturalize. Few requirements have changed since. Most notably, race requirements on people of African descent were lifted in the 1870s and on Asians in the 1940s. Women gained equal access to citizenship in the 1990s. The Immigration and Naturalization Act currently requires that permanent residents maintain continuous residency for five years (three years if married to a U.S. citizen); file in their own state; prove literacy, basic English, and U.S. history competence; have good moral character; pay taxes; register for the draft (if male); and take the oath of naturalization. Armed service members have fewer requirements for naturalization.

The FOURTEENTH AMENDMENT (1868) clarified many citizenship issues left unclear in the Constitution as part of the compromise over slavery. It established an *ius soli* system of citizenship, granting citizenship to anyone born in U.S. territory, thus conferring citizenship to all former slaves and to the native-born children of immigrants. It extended U.S. citizenship to citizens of any state. It made all citizens, native born or naturalized, equal under the law. Practically, citizens and noncitizens may be treated differently in many areas. There are more than 30 different classes of aliens, each with different rights and responsibilities; however, the Fourteenth Amendment includes a DUE PROCESS clause mandating due process for all people, not just citizens. The Supreme Court has held that due process extends to all of the rights to "people" stated in the Bill of Rights and does not limit those rights to citizens.

Citizenship traditionally conferred few legal, economic, or social advantages. The major advantage of citizenship is the right to enter, exit, and remain permanently without possibility of deportation. Aliens remain in the United States at the pleasure of the government and may be removed in accordance with law. Citizens may vote, serve on juries, hold elected office, and join political parties. All residents regardless of status maintain the rights enumerated in the Bill of Rights including (but not limited to) the right to speech, association, press, religion, petition, protection from government intrusion, and due process. The law permits political participation but limits campaign donations to citizens and legal permanent residents (LPRs). Only citizens may get federal jobs, certain national security positions, and some public welfare benefits. Citizens hold U.S. passports, which may facilitate easier travel and protection of the U.S. government when abroad. Citizens may sponsor overseas relatives for immigration. Only LPRs may also sponsor a more limited list of relatives for immigration. Noncitizens may join the armed forces and, like citizens, must (if male) register for the draft. Everyone is entitled to emergency health care, public education, and public services such as fire and police protection.

The longer an immigrant remains in the United States, the more likely he or she will naturalize. There are, however, large discrepancies between naturalizations based on country of origin.

As of the 2000 census, more than 31 million immigrants resided in the United States. Forty percent had naturalized, and the remaining 60 percent were aliens of different statuses. There are more than 30 government-defined noncitizen statuses. Even as naturalization is expected, the government has traditionally treated naturalization as a policy-neutral event, assuming that immigrants want to naturalize. This changed in 1996 when the government encouraged naturalization as a way to move vast blocks of immigrants from alien to citizen status. The policy, coming in conjunction with burgeoning national anti-immigrant sentiment and a change in benefit eligibility rules that conditioned eligibility on citizenship status and the achievement of five years' residency for immigrants amnestied in 1986 (Immigration Reform and Control Act, Pub. L. No. 99-603, 100 Stat. 3359), resulted in the largest number of naturalizations in the history of the country. Almost all citizenship-based benefit eligibility requirements have since been overturned.

For more information: Aleinikoff, T. Alexander. "United States." In T. Alexander Aleinikoff and Douglas Klusmeyer, *From Migrants to Citizens: Membership in a Changing World,* 137–147. Washington, D.C.: Carnegie Endowment for International Peace, 2000; Bosniak, Linda. *The Citizen and the Alien: Dilemmas of Contemporary Membership.* Princeton, N.J.: Princeton University Press, 2006.

—Robin A. Harper

City of Boerne v. Flores 521 U.S. 507 (1997)

In *City of Boerne v. Flores,* the Supreme Court held that the RELIGIOUS FREEDOM RESTORATION ACT (RFRA) of 1993 was unconstitutional because it exceeded Congress's powers under Section 5 of the FOURTEENTH AMENDMENT. The *Boerne* decision was the final nail in the coffin of the STRICT SCRUTINY test as it applied in religion cases prior to *EMPLOYMENT DIVISION V. SMITH,* 494 U.S. 872 (1990), and it introduced the "congruence and proportionality" test into the Court's jurisprudence under Section 5 of the Fourteenth Amendment.

For several decades prior to *Employment Division v. Smith,* the Supreme Court applied strict scrutiny to all laws that had the effect of burdening a religious practice. In *Smith,* the Court reversed course, holding that neutral and generally applicable laws that burden particular religious practices need not be justified by a COMPELLING GOVERNMENTAL INTEREST. A bipartisan Congress responded to *Smith* by passing RFRA, which reestablished the strict scrutiny standard. Specifically, RFRA prohibited government from "substantially burdening" a person's exercise of religion unless the government could show that the restriction is in furtherance of a compelling governmental interest and that it is the least restrictive means of furthering that interest.

At the same time that Congress was debating RFRA, the city of Boerne, in Texas, enacted an ordinance creating historical districts within the town. When a church applied for a permit to enlarge its building, the city denied the permit because it was within one of the newly created historical districts. The church then challenged the permit denial, arguing that it violated RFRA.

The Supreme Court, in an opinion by Justice ANTHONY M. KENNEDY, held that RFRA was unconstitutional as it applied to state governments because it was not a proper exercise of Congress's power under Section 5 of the Fourteenth Amendment. Although Section 5 delegates to Congress the power to enforce certain rights, its power is limited to enforcing the constitutional rights as recognized by the Supreme Court. Congress may not "decree the substance of the Fourteenth Amendment's restrictions on the States." In one often-quoted line from Justice Kennedy's opinion, he states that "Congress does not enforce a constitutional right by changing what the right is."

The Court announced that it would apply a new test to Section 5 legislation, requiring that there be a "congruence and proportionality between the injury to be prevented or remedied and the means adopted to that end." The Court held that RFRA did not survive this congruence and proportionality test because it attempted to substantively change the scope of constitutional protections for religious freedom.

In their dissent, Justices SANDRA DAY O'CONNOR and STEPHEN G. BREYER directly challenged the Court's holding in *Smith.* They argued that if the Court would only correct its holding in *Smith,* it would put "our FIRST AMENDMENT jurisprudence back on course" and be in accord with the "legitimate concerns of a majority of Congress who believed that *Smith* improperly restricted religious liberty."

Justice JOHN PAUL STEVENS concurred, arguing that RFRA is a law "respecting an establishment of religion" and therefore violates the ESTABLISHMENT CLAUSE. In his view, RFRA provides the religiously devout with a legal weapon that no atheist or agnostic can obtain. This governmental preference for religion, as opposed to irreligion, is forbidden by the First Amendment.

For more information: Berg, Thomas C. *Religious Freedom After* Boerne. *NEXUS: A Journal of Opinion.* (1997); 91–102; Paisner, Michael. "*Boerne* Supremacy: Congressional Response to *City of Boerne v. Flores* and the Scope of Congress's Article I Powers." *Columbia Law Review* 105 (2005): 537–582.

—Winston E. Calvert

City of Chicago v. Morales 527 U.S. 41 (1999)

In *City of Chicago v. Morales,* the Supreme Court declared unconstitutional a city law that made it illegal for gang members to congregate. The Supreme Court determined from the facts that the FIRST, FOURTH, Eighth, and FOURTEENTH AMENDMENTS were either directly violated or indirectly contradicted by the Chicago city ordinance that was the underlying tenet of the case.

At issue in this case was whether or not the city ordinance that forbade gang members or their associates from loitering after responding police officers advised them to disperse and move away from the immediate area violates their constitutional rights. The Illinois courts held that the vagaries in the ordinance allowed for too much power on the police's part in making determinations as to who was, in fact, practicing his or her right to congregation and who was engaged in discussion of ill refute or criminal conspiracy. If the police officer believed the group to be part of a gang, then the officer could direct them to leave, and if they did not comply with the order, the officer could then arrest the persons. The police department in Chicago did establish some restrictions on the officers' discretion to arrest by defining the potential offender's behavior. Adding to this restriction, the respective areas where this ordinance could be enforced further restricted the ability for the officers to operate at whim.

The Illinois Supreme Court decided that the ordinance violated the DUE PROCESS clause of the Constitution in that the vagaries associated with the law placed an arbitrary burden upon the freedoms of the person. On appeal to the U.S. Supreme Court, Justice JOHN PAUL STEVENS declared the law unconstitutional. He stated that the definition of gang member was vague and that the type of practice or activity that the law sought to prohibit was also unclear, thereby failing to give individuals sufficient notice regarding what the law required. Finally, the Court stated that the law gave law-enforcement officials too much discretion to stop and order individuals to move. Overall, *City of Chicago v. Morales* is an important case that limits the government's ability to regulate gangs and loitering.

For more information: Cassack, Lance, and Milton Heumann. *Good Cop, Bad Cop: Racial Profiling and Competing Views of Justice.* New York: Peter Lang, 2003; Langran, Robert W. *The Supreme Court: A Concise History.* New York: Peter Lang, 2004.

—Ernest Gomez

City of Cuyahoga Falls, Ohio, et al. v. Buckeye Community Hope Foundation, et al. 538 U.S. 188 (2003)

In *City of Cuyahoga Falls, Ohio, et al. v. Buckeye Community Hope Foundation, et al.*, the Supreme Court ruled that allowing citizens to vote on whether a low-income housing project could be built in a city did not violate the EQUAL PROTECTION clause of the FOURTEENTH AMENDMENT.

The city of Cuyahoga Falls, in Ohio, passed a city ordinance allowing Buckeye Community Hope Foundation, a nonprofit organization, to build a low-income housing development. Some citizens of Cuyahoga Falls organized and drew up and presented a petition to the city requesting that the ordinance be repealed or the matter sent to the voters in the form of a referendum (a process of referring a public issue to voters for approval).

The foundation filed a suit claiming that the city violated the equal protection clause and DUE PROCESS clause of the Fourteenth Amendment to the Constitution, as well as the Fair Housing Act, when the city submitted the foundation's site plan to the voters for approval. The Ohio Supreme Court, applying Ohio's constitution to the case, declared the referendum invalid. In the meantime, district court found for the city, and the case was appealed to the U.S. Court of Appeals for the Sixth Circuit. The appeals court reversed the decision of the lower court noting that the foundation had made a valid claim under the Fair Housing Act and violated due process.

The case was appealed to the Supreme Court. The question before the Court was whether the decision by the court of appeals was correct. Did the Buckeye Community Hope Foundation have a valid claim against the city of Cuyahoga Falls? In a 9-0 decision, delivered by Justice SANDRA DAY O'CONNOR, the Court concluded that the court of appeals erred in its decision and the foundation's claims were not valid. The Court stated that lacking clear evidence of discriminatory intent, the vote on housing was not unconstitutional.

City of Cuyahoga Falls, Ohio, et al. v. Buckeye Community Hope Foundation, et al. is an important case clarifying what constitutes discrimination and also what options cities have when it comes to placing housing for individuals who may be unpopular.

For more information: Bonelli, David M. "If You Build It 'They' Will Come: Intentional Discrimination and Disparate Impact Theory in

Buckeye Community Hope Foundation v. City of Cuyahoga Falls." *Hamline Law Review* 26, no. 3 (Spring 2003): 631–678.

—Dan Krejci

City of Ladue v. Gilleo 512 U.S. 43 (1994)

In *Ladue v. Gilleo,* the Supreme Court held that the tradition of individuals expressing their views by placing signs on their yards or in their windows has a special place in American culture and law.

The Court invalidated an ordinance adopted by the city of Ladue, in Missouri, that prohibited homeowners from displaying signs on their property. The Court termed yard signs "a venerable means of communication that is both unique and important." Ladue resident Margaret P. Gilleo placed a two-by-three foot sign in her yard printed with the words "Say No to War in the Persian Gulf, Call Congress Now." The sign disappeared; she replaced it, and that one was knocked down. When Gilleo reported these incidents to the police, they told her that her signs were illegal. She then placed an 8.5-by-11 inch sign in her second floor window that read "For Peace in the Gulf." The city responded by replacing its ordinance with a new one that specifically prohibited window signs. Gilleo sued under the FIRST AMENDMENT.

In striking down this ban on signs placed by residents on their own property, the Supreme Court emphasized the unique role displaying signs at one's residence serves in the expression of ideas. The Court held that "[a] special respect for individual liberty in the home has long been part of our culture and our law." The Court noted that "[d]isplaying a sign from one's own residence often carries a message quite distinct from placing the same sign somewhere else." It gave examples of a peace sign on the lawn of a retired general or decorated war veteran or a sign espousing socialism on the lawn of a stately mansion provoking different reactions or carrying different implications than similar signs placed elsewhere. The Court also noted that yard signs are "often intend[ed] to reach *neighbors,* an audience that could not be reached nearly as well by other means." Additionally, the Court held that yard signs convey information about the speaker and quoted Aristotle to support its view that the identity of the speaker can be an important aspect in the attempt to persuade. In short, there was no satisfactory alternative for yard signs.

The city ordinance spelled out what the city thought were its interests in regulating signs, including its belief that signs "would create ugliness, visual blight and clutter," diminish property values, and "may cause safety and traffic hazards." Though the Court noted that residents had strong incentives not to diminish their property values with "visual clutter," the Court accepted the validity of regulating signs, just as cities may, within reasonable bounds, regulate noise. But totally foreclosing this mode of communication to political, religious, or personal messages violated the First Amendment.

The Court's ruling was consistent with its ruling 18 years earlier that struck down a ban on house "for sale" signs in residential areas (*Linmark Associates, Inc. v. Willingboro,* 431 U.S. 85 [1977]). That ordinance by a New Jersey city had been defended as necessary to maintain stable, integrated neighborhoods. The Court held that regardless of the importance of that or any other goal, the city violated the First Amendment by "achieving its goal by restricting the free flow of truthful information."

For more information: Langran, Robert W. *The Supreme Court: A Concise History.* New York: Peter Lang, 2004; Volokh, Eugene. *The First Amendment: Problems, Cases and Policy Arguments.* New York: Foundation Press, 2001.

—Neil Bradley

City of Los Angeles v. Alameda Books, Inc. 535 U.S. 425 (2002)

In *City of Los Angeles v. Alameda Books, Inc.,* the Supreme Court upheld the use of a study on crime and the adult entertainment industry to support a zoning ordinance that limited the location and placement of these types of establishments within the city. This case is important because it rejected FIRST AMENDMENT arguments in favor of giving governments more authority to regulate the secondary effects of adult entertainment.

In 1977, in an effort to curb crime, Los Angeles conducted a study in order to identify the entities or factors that affect crime rates. This 1977 study demonstrated that there is an apparent association between high crime rates and the presence of adult entertainment establishments. Based on this study, the Los Angeles city government enacted a municipal code (Section 12.70 (C) [1978]). This code prohibited adult entertainment enterprises from operating within 1,000 feet of each other or within 500 feet of "a religious institution, school, or public park." Los Angeles failed to note a weakness in the ordinance, that more than one establishment could occupy the same structure. This oversight was amended in 1983 to include "more than one adult entertainment business in the same building."

Two adult entertainment establishments, Alameda Books, Inc., and Highland Books, Inc., sued the city of Los Angeles claiming that the ordinance violated their First Amendment right to free speech. Their claim was that the ordinance was not content neutral. The Court had provided a definition of *content neutral* in *Ward v. Rock Against Racism,* 491 U.S. 781 (1989):

> The principal inquiry in determining content neutrality, in speech cases generally and in time, place, or manner cases in particular, is whether the government has adopted a regulation of speech because of disagreement with the message it conveys. The government's purpose is the controlling consideration. A regulation that serves purposes unrelated to the content of expression is deemed neutral, even if it has an incidental effect on some speakers or messages but not others.

The district court sided with the plaintiffs, noting that the 1977 study failed to provide a reasonable connection between adult entertainment establishments and crime rates. The court of appeals affirmed the district court ruling, stating that the city failed to provide sufficient evidence that "its regulation of multiple use establishments was designed to serve its substantial interest in reducing crime."

The city of Los Angeles appealed the decision, and the Court decided in favor of the city of Los Angeles. The question before the Court was whether the city of Los Angeles could use a study it conducted to "demonstrate whether an ordinance serves a substantial government interest." In a plurality decision (5-4) written by Justice SANDRA DAY O'CONNOR, the Court determined that the city of Los Angeles, "may reasonably rely on a study it conducted years before enacting the present version of section 12.70 (C) to demonstrate that its ban on multiple-use adult establishments serves its interest in reducing crime." In a concurring opinion, Justice ANTHONY M. KENNEDY concluded "that Los Angeles may impose its regulation in the exercise of the zoning authority, and that the city is not, at least, to be foreclosed by summary judgment."

For more information: Baradaran-Robison, Shima. "Viewpoint Neutral Zoning of Adult Entertainment Businesses." *Hastings Constitutional Law Quarterly* 31, no. 4 (Summer 2004): 447–497; Jelsema, Mindi M. "Zoning Adult Businesses." *Saint Louis University Law Journal* 47, no. 4 (Summer 2003): 117–150; Prygoski, Philip J. "Content Neutrality and Levels of Scrutiny in First Amendment Zoning Cases." *Whittier Law Review* 25, no. 1 (Fall 2003): 79–111.

—Dan Krejci

City of Richmond v. J. A. Croson Company 488 U.S. 494 (1989)

In *City of Richmond v. J. A. Croson Co.,* the Supreme Court ruled that a city program that awarded a fixed percentage on all city construction contracts to minority business enterprises (MBEs) was a violation of the FOURTEENTH AMENDMENT EQUAL PROTECTION clause. The significance of this decision was to call into question the authority of the federal, state, and local governments to create programs to assist minority-owned businesses to overcome past discrimination in securing contracts to perform work.

Even after African Americans were emancipated from slavery and given equal rights to those of whites under the THIRTEENTH, Fourteenth, and FIFTEENTH AMENDMENTS, they continued to face discrimination in numerous ways, including in the realm of employment. Blacks, for example, faced many difficulties in forming their own businesses and in being successful bidders in the awarding of government contracts to perform services, such as for construction projects. While laws were adopted in the 1960s to end discrimination, such as the CIVIL RIGHTS ACT OF 1964, some contended that the government needed to provide additional support to help blacks overcome historical discrimination. Among those developed were AFFIRMATIVE ACTION and MBEs.

MBE programs were developed at the federal, state, and local levels during the 1960s. Governments, acting in their capacity as employers, would arrange to set aside a certain percentage or dollar amount of all their contracts to companies with majority ownership of minorities (MBEs) or women (WBEs). However, some contended that these programs were illegal, citing a violation of the Fourteenth Amendment's equal protection clause.

In *FULLILOVE V. KLUTZNICK*, 448 U.S. 448 (1980), the Supreme Court upheld an MBE program in the 1977 Public Works Employment Act. Here, the Court had ruled that a 10 percent set-aside for MBEs was not unconstitutional; however, the ruling was a 6-3 decision. Subsequently, several justices, including Chief Justice WARREN EARL BURGER, departed, and as a result of appointments by President Ronald Reagan, the Court shifted right. The REHNQUIST COURT was less supportive of affirmative action and MBE programs and decided to hear the *Croson* case.

The city of Richmond, in order to overcome historical discrimination against blacks and to encourage more minority businesses, enacted a law requiring that at least 30 percent of the dollar value of all city-awarded construction contracts be awarded to businesses owned by minorities. "Owned by minorities" meant that at least 51 percent of the business had to be controlled by people of color. The program was not limited to defining MBEs as blacks but also included those who were Spanish-speaking, Asian, Indian, Eskimo, or Aleut. When the law was adopted, its supporters noted that while 50 percent of the city's population was African American, less than 1 percent of the contracts awarded by Richmond in the previous five years had been awarded to blacks. J. A. Croson, Inc., was a heating and plumbing contractor that objected to the MBE set-aside program. The company challenged it in court, and after it had prevailed in the lower courts, the Supreme Court agreed to hear the case.

Writing for a divided majority in a 6-3 opinion, Justice SANDRA DAY O'CONNOR ruled that the Richmond MBE program violated the Fourteenth Amendment's equal protection clause. The basis of her argument was that it was not narrowly tailored. She first contended that because there was no documented history of discrimination against Spanish-speaking, Asian, Indian, Eskimo, or Aleut individuals, their inclusion in the MBE program was improper. Second, O'Connor noted that there was no documentation that supported evidence of discrimination in the construction industry in the city. Third, given that Richmond was half African American and that a majority of its city council was black, these facts boded against the idea that individuals of this race were a minority lacking representation and in need of special protection. Fourth, the Court also noted that the MBE program, especially with the 30 percent set-aside, appeared to be more than a remedial measure meant to overcome past discrimination. If the goal of the city was to be remedial, O'Connor suggested that other race-neutral programs were available. Finally, Justice O'Connor asserted that the Richmond program denied some the ability to compete for contracts based on their race and therefore, under a STRICT SCRUTINY analysis, such a program was unconstitutional. In concurrence, Justice ANTONIN GREGORY SCALIA ruled that race-based programs such as MBEs were unconstitutional under strict scrutiny.

In dissent, Justice Thurgood Marshall contended that the use of race for remedial purposes should not be examined under strict scrutiny but under a more relaxed standard. Moreover, he chided the majority for its claims that there was no history of discrimination in Richmond, noting that at one time during the Civil War, it was the capital of the Confederacy.

Critics of MBEs, affirmative action, and race-based programs thought *Croson* was the end of set-aside programs; however, one year later, in *Metro Broadcasting, Inc. v. FCC*, 497 U.S. 547 (1990), Justice William J. Brennan, Jr., wrote a 5-4 opinion upholding the constitutionality of a Federal Communications Commission policy that considered race when awarding radio station licenses. It was not until *Adarand Contractors, Inc. v. Peña*, 515 U.S. 200 (1995), that the Court appeared to rule finally that MBE-type programs were unconstitutional because of their use of race.

For more information: Drake, W. Avon, and Robert D. Holsworth. *Affirmative Action and the Stalled Quest for Black Progress.* Urbana: University of Illinois Press, 1996.

—Martin J. Sweet and David Schultz

civil liberties

Civil liberty is the right of an individual to be free of unjustified government interference with his or her person, property, beliefs, or decisions. In the United States, the Bill of Rights sets limits on the sorts of government interference that can be legally justified. Understanding what those limits are, why they were put in place, and how they compare to rights of citizens in other countries is central to understanding American civil liberties.

Those who drafted the nation's foundational documents were profoundly influenced by the philosophy of the Enlightenment, especially the writings of John Locke. They believed that the state had a moral obligation to respect individual autonomy, defined as the right of individuals to set and pursue their own moral ends. Accordingly, our constitutional system begins with the premise that government is not entitled to interfere with an individual's behaviors unless that individual is harming the person or property of a nonconsenting other. This is sometimes called the "libertarian principle."

The U.S. Bill of Rights protects fundamental civil liberties: freedom of speech and the press, freedom to assemble and "petition the government for redress of grievances" (that is, dissent), religious liberty, freedom from unreasonable searches and seizures, and a variety of other procedural protections that together constitute basic American due process guarantees. More recently, equal protection of the laws has been added as a fundamental right.

Civil liberties (and human rights generally) are based on the beliefs that individuals have inherent dignity and status simply by virtue of being human and that government has the obligation to recognize and respect that personhood. In the U.S. legal system, unlike some other countries, civil liberties are individual in nature. The American constitutional system does not recognize group rights; ethnic and other minorities do not have rights separate and apart from those enjoyed by individual members of the group.

At their base, all civil liberties disputes revolve around finding the proper balance between the power of the state and the right of individuals to live as they choose. This is primarily a procedural issue: Who shall decide? Who, in other words, has the authority to make any particular decision, the government or the individual?

Citizens frequently fail to recognize that the essential characteristic of our constitutionally protected liberties is this restraint on the government's power to decide certain matters, and they therefore fail to distinguish between the act of limiting government's power and the endorsement of a particular outcome. When a court refuses to allow an agency of government to censor a particular book, for example, the court is not endorsing the content of that book; it is upholding the principle that citizens have a right to choose their own reading material, free of government interference. When courts refuse to allow official prayer in public schools, it is not because the judges are hostile to religion; it is because parents have a right to control the religious upbringing of their children, free of government interference. The emphasis is upon how decisions are made rather than what decisions are made. In the

American legal system, good ends cannot be used to justify improper means.

The procedural nature of the U.S. constitutional system is often criticized by communitarians who believe that citizens should be more "embedded" in a shared moral framework. The negative nature of U.S. civil liberties, where liberty is envisioned as freedom from government control, is also criticized by those who favor the addition of so-called positive rights, or entitlements, to the American conception of FUNDAMENTAL RIGHTS, much as is the case with the United Nations Declaration of Human Rights and many European constitutions that give citizens a government-insured right to adequate housing, medical care, or education. Whatever the merits or flaws of those arguments, the U.S. constitutional structure was built upon a commitment to individual choice and respect for the integrity and inviolability of the individual conscience. Partially as a result, America has one of the most individualistic cultures in the world, and its legal system both reflects and reinforces that individualism.

It is instructive to note that there was no disagreement between the Federalists and Anti-Federalists about the proper role of government and the nature of the so-called inalienable rights, or civil liberties, that each citizen was entitled to enjoy. Their great debate was not a dispute about the importance of guaranteeing individuals freedom from government interference; rather, these founders disagreed about the proper method of insuring that personal freedom. Anti-Federalist critics of the new constitution wanted a Bill of Rights, specifying the liberties that would be insulated against official action. Federalists such as ALEXANDER HAMILTON, on the other hand, argued that the new national government was a creature of "delegated powers" only and that it therefore lacked any authority to invade personal liberties. Hamilton worried about the dangers of "enumerating" or listing protected rights. He and others feared that the existence of a written Bill of Rights would lead future government officials to argue that if a right was not specifically listed, it was not protected. The compromise between these two arguments was the language of the NINTH and Tenth AMENDMENTS, sometimes called the "rights and powers" amendments. Read together, they provide that enumeration of certain rights is not to be construed as denial of others, and any powers not specifically given to the federal government remain with the states or the people.

Originally, the Bill of Rights restrained only the federal government. Many states continued to have "established" religions until the early 1800s and continued to enforce a variety of other laws that were inconsistent with civil liberty. It was not until after the passage of the FOURTEENTH AMENDMENT, in the wake of the Civil War, that the Bill of Rights would be "incorporated" into the Fourteenth and made binding on all levels of government.

Civil liberties are not protected against private infringements. The Bill of Rights limits government only; unless there is "state action" (that is, action by a unit or agency of government), there is no violation of civil liberties. CIVIL RIGHTS, on the other hand, are rights to be free of discrimination by private parties. Civil rights are creatures of statute, not products of the Constitution. The first federal law establishing a legally enforceable right to be free of private discrimination in employment, housing, or education was the CIVIL RIGHTS ACT OF 1964.

When the Constitution was first drafted, civil liberties were enjoyed by free, white male property owners. Over the years, despite some "detours," the American idea of liberty has expanded. Today, women and racial and ethnic minorities are entitled to the same fundamental rights as white males, and since the 1990s, great strides toward equality have been made by members of other minorities, notably gays and lesbians.

For more information: Amar, Akhil Reed. *The Bill of Rights: Creation and Reconstruction.* New Haven, Conn.: Yale University Press, 2000; Kennedy, Sheila Suess. *What's a Nice Republican Girl Like Me Doing at the ACLU.* New York: Prometheus Books, 1992; Kersch, Ken I. *Constructing Civil Liberties: Discontinuities in the Development of American Constitutional Law.* New York: Cambridge University Press, 2004.

—Sheila Suess Kennedy

civil rights

Civil rights refer to protections against discrimination by the government and private parties. The basis of most civil rights laws is found in the Constitution and under federal law, although many states and local governments also have enacted their own antidiscrimination provisions.

Civil rights laws stand in contrast to CIVIL LIBERTIES. Civil liberties, which generally include the first eight amendments to the Constitution, include the rights to free speech and FREEDOM OF THE PRESS and against self-incrimination and CRUEL AND UNUSUAL PUNISHMENT. These are rights citizens have against the government. Civil rights generally are rights against discrimination by the government or nongovernmental actors, and in some cases they may require government action. While, in general, civil rights laws in the United States have been aimed toward protecting African Americans from discrimination, women, other people of color, and, increasingly, gays and lesbians have been and are the recipients of civil rights protection.

Prior to their emancipation from slavery, African Americans lacked basic civil rights. These rights included the RIGHT TO VOTE, to secure housing and employment, to travel freely inter- or intrastate, or to sign and enter into contracts. Once African Americans were freed from slavery with the adoption of the THIRTEENTH AMENDMENT after the Civil War, the Reconstruction Congress passed the 1866 Civil Rights Act in order to protect the rights of the freed slaves. This act barred discrimination against blacks by the government or by private parties in many areas, such as in employment. Subsequently, as a result of some concern in Congress that the legislature lacked the authority to prohibit private discrimination as described in the 1866 Civil Rights Act, Congress adopted the FOURTEENTH and FIFTEENTH AMENDMENTS in 1868 and 1869, respectively. In adopting these two amendments, Sections 5 and 2 each stated that "Congress shall have power to enforce this article by appropriate legislation." These enforcement provisions appeared to grant Congress the authority it needed to adopt civil rights legislation.

But in the *CIVIL RIGHTS CASES*, 109 U.S. 3 (1883), the Supreme Court ruled that despite the enforcement language of the Fourteenth Amendment, Congress lacked the constitutional authority to ban private discrimination. After Reconstruction ended in 1876 with the removal of federal troops from the South, discrimination reemerged with the adoption of Jim Crow and other laws that denied African Americans the right to vote or otherwise permitted both the government and private parties to deny them the same privileges that whites had. This new discrimination can be best seen in *PLESSY V. FERGUSON*, 163 U.S. 537 (1896), where the Supreme Court upheld laws that mandated separate provisions for blacks and whites. Here, the Court stated that separate but equal facilities for members of different races were permitted. As result of *Plessy*, African Americans were segregated into separate school districts and otherwise were denied equal treatment when it came to housing, employment, and a host of other actions.

In an effort to overturn *Plessy* and the separate but equal doctrine, the National Association for the Advancement of Colored People (NAACP) was formed in 1909. In a series of court cases over the next five decades, the NAACP challenged *Plessy*. Representing the NAACP, future Supreme Court justice Thurgood Marshall successfully argued for the overturning of the separate but equal doctrine in *BROWN V. BOARD OF EDUCATION OF TOPEKA*, 347 U.S. 483 (1954). After *Brown*, and as a result of civil rights protests across the country that were led by Martin Luther King, Jr., and acts of civil disobedience by individuals such as Rosa Parks, Congress passed the 1957 Civil Rights Act, which aimed at strengthening the voting rights of African Americans. However, it was the passage of the CIVIL RIGHTS ACT OF 1964, especially Title VII, that dramatically enlarged civil rights. This act, like its 1866 predecessor, barred private discrimination, but it also extended the protection to include women and other people of color. Concerned that the act would meet the same fate as the 1866 act, Congress based its authority to enact this legislation both on Section 5 of the Fourteenth Amendment and on the COMMERCE

CLAUSE. In *HEART OF ATLANTA MOTEL V. UNITED STATES*, 379 U.S. 241 (1964), the Supreme Court upheld it under both clauses.

After the passage of the 1964 Civil Rights Act, Congress adopted the VOTING RIGHTS ACT OF 1965 in order to strengthen the ability of African Americans to register and vote. Adoption of the TWENTY-FOURTH AMENDMENT in 1964, which outlaws poll taxes, and numerous Supreme Court decisions after *Brown* all helped to strengthen civil rights in America. Since the 1960s, Congress has reauthorized the Voting Rights Act several times and has adopted additional civil rights acts.

Despite the passage of these laws, critics argue that women, African Americans, people of color, and gays, lesbians, and transsexuals still face discrimination. They point to further need either for more antidiscrimination laws or for more aggressive enforcement by the Equal Employment Opportunity Commission (EEOC) or other government agencies.

For more information: Kluger, Richard. *Simple Justice: The History of* Brown v. Board of Education *and Black America's Struggle for Equality*. New York: Vintage, 2004; Woodward, C. Vann. *The Strange Career of Jim Crow*. New York: Oxford University Press, 2001.

—David Schultz

Civil Rights Act of 1964

The Civil Rights Act of 1964 was the most far-reaching law of its kind since Reconstruction. At the heart of this landmark legislation is the section guaranteeing equal access to public accommodations for all.

Prior to this, there were CIVIL RIGHTS bills passed in 1957 and 1960. The Civil Rights Act of 1957 had set up a commission with power to investigate violations of racial discrimination and authorized suits to protect voting rights. The 1960 act had emphasized protection of voting rights and authorized judges to appoint referees to help African Americans register and vote. While the two acts were the first time since Reconstruction that Congress had attempted to protect the rights of black people, they gave relatively little aid to the progress in civil rights.

In June 1963, President John F. Kennedy announced he would ask Congress for legislation to provide the kind of equal treatment that "we would want ourselves." He stated that the measure would promote civil rights on two broad fronts, including banning discrimination in public accommodations. Black leaders immediately hailed the president's speech as a "Second Emancipation Proclamation." This announcement led to a massive march on Washington, D.C., in August 1963 supporting legislation, which may be best known for Martin Luther King, Jr.'s "I Have a Dream" speech. Then, on November 22, 1963, Kennedy was assassinated, and Lyndon B. Johnson became president. Few who supported the legislation had much hope for Johnson, as he was a southerner, and it was presumed he would be pursuing the Democratic Party's nomination in 1964.

President Johnson, in his speech to Congress five days after the assassination, singled out the civil rights bill and made it clear that he was determined to see this become law. Passage of this bill required all of Johnson's abilities, which were plentiful, as demonstrated when he was a leader in Congress and secured passage of tax cuts and legislation regarding the war on poverty. Johnson had several reasons to support this cause. Growing up in Texas, he had seen firsthand the viciousness of racial discrimination and empathized with the victims. Furthermore, as a congressman he had battled to ensure that federal agricultural programs treated blacks and whites equally.

Johnson recognized a great effort would be needed if the bill was to become law. In February 1964, the bill passed the HOUSE OF REPRESENTATIVES 290-130. The White House knew that the southern senators would try to filibuster the bill to death. To the president, the key to getting the 67 votes needed for cloture (to end the filibuster) would be SENATE Minority Leader Everett Dirksen, a Republican from Illinois. To lobby senators, Johnson used liberal labor union leaders, civil rights activists, church leaders, and VICE PRESIDENT Hubert H. Humphrey. The filibuster did take place and lasted three months, during which

President Lyndon Johnson signs the Civil Rights Act of 1964, as Martin Luther King, Jr., looks on. *(Johnson Library)*

time opponents of the bill grew more emphatic in their opposition. The cloture vote was 71-29, and the vote on the actual bill was 73-27. President Johnson signed the bill into law on July 2, 1964.

The bill contained several strong provisions. It banned racial discrimination in privately run accommodations for the public, such as theaters, movie houses, restaurants, gas stations, and hotels. The U.S. attorney general was authorized to eliminate de jure racial segregation in public schools, hospitals, playgrounds, libraries, museums, and other public places. It stated that schools, as well as other federally assisted institutions, would face loss of federal funds if they continued to discriminate. Finally, it authorized the attorney general to bring suits on behalf of parents complaining of discrimination in the schools and declared that the government would assume their legal costs.

Within six months of the president signing the bill into law, the Supreme Court heard challenges seeking to prevent enforcement of the public accommodations section of Title II. In *HEART OF ATLANTA MOTEL V. U.S.*, 379 U.S. 241 (1964), the Court unanimously rejected the claim that a motel located in a city did not fall within the meaning of INTERSTATE COMMERCE. In *KATZENBACH V. MCCLUNG*, 379 U.S. 294 (1964), the Court unanimously sustained the law as it applied to restaurants.

The Civil Rights Act of 1964 had a significant effect in many areas but was lacking in voting rights. Thus, Congress produced the VOTING RIGHTS ACT OF 1965. In areas that the 1964 Civil Rights Act did cover, many employers and unions were able to evade portions regarding job discrimination. Particularly in housing and schooling, de facto racial discrimination remained widespread in the North. Many school districts, primarily in the deep South, continued to employ deceptions of one sort or another to circumvent DESEGREGATION in public education. Finally, the law did nothing to improve the dreadful economic condition of blacks in the country. Its focus was on legal issues, not those of social or economic equality.

The Civil Rights Act of 1964, though not perfect, is arguably the most important piece of legislation in the history of American race relations, and without President Johnson, it would not have happened.

For more information: Klarman, Michael J. *From Jim Crow to Civil Rights.* Oxford and New York: Oxford University Press, 2004; Patterson, James T. *Grand Expectations: The United States, 1945–1974.* Oxford and New York: Oxford University Press, 1996; Urofsky, Melvin, and Paul Finkelman. *A March of Liberty: A Constitutional History of the United States.* Vol. II. Oxford and New York: Oxford University Press, 2002.

—Mark Alcorn

Civil Rights Cases 109 U.S. 3 (1883)

The *Civil Rights Cases* were five cases (*U.S. v. Singleton, U.S. v. Stanley, U.S. v. Nichols, U.S. v. Ryan,* and *U.S. v. Robinson*) consolidated into one and mark the end of 19th-century efforts to achieve CIVIL RIGHTS for African Americans. The Supreme Court held that Congress lacked the constitutional authority under the FOURTEENTH AMENDMENT to prohibit racial discrimination by private individuals, despite whatever power Congress had over state governments.

Except for the TWELFTH AMENDMENT, ratified in 1804, the U.S. Constitution was amended only three times in the 19th century, all in the five years just after the Civil War. The THIRTEENTH AMENDMENT formally abolished slavery; the Fourteenth made African Americans citizens and prohibited the states from depriving "all persons" of life, liberty, or property without DUE PROCESS of the law; and the FIFTEENTH AMENDMENT made it illegal to deprive anyone of the RIGHT TO VOTE "on account of race, color, or previous condition of servitude."

During the early 1870s, there was not a single state in the country whose laws required the separation of whites from blacks. In fact, the trend in the North and West was toward acceptance of black patrons in most public facilities. Furthermore, most state and federal courts upheld state statutes mandating black rights.

Senator Charles Sumner of Massachusetts proposed the Civil Rights Act of 1875, which was passed a year after his death, partly as a tribute to his tireless devotion to equal rights. The act expanded upon the civil and political rights ensured by the Reconstruction amendments to include social rights as well; it stated, thus, that all people, regardless of race, were entitled to the same treatment in "public accommodations." In five separate lower court cases, African Americans sued theaters, hotels, and transit companies that had denied them the access to "white-only" facilities.

Justice Joseph P. Bradley delivered the opinion for the Court. The Thirteenth Amendment, he observed, had nothing to do with "social" injustices, and the Fourteenth Amendment limited only state actions but had no relevance or application to private acts of discrimination. Bradley was nothing if not direct: Blacks could not expect to be coddled by the government nor "the special favorite of the laws." Bradley insisted that Congress had no affirmative powers to ensure freedmen's rights but could only act in a remedial manner by blocking unconstitutional state legislation. Congress could not initiate civil rights legislation. By this decision, the Court essentially put private acts of discrimination beyond the reach of Congress.

Justice JOHN MARSHALL HARLAN of Kentucky, a Southerner and former slaveholder, was the lone dissenter to the majority opinion. Justice Harlan—one-time conservative slavery supporter turned uncompromising black rights advocate—proudly wrote his dissent with the very same pen Chief Justice ROGER TANEY had used to write the infamous *DRED SCOTT V. SANDFORD* opinion of 1857, one of the more important events leading up to the Civil War. Harlan correctly pointed out that the majority opinion deprived the Fourteenth Amendment of all its meaning. The violence and vigilantism spreading throughout the South convinced Harlan that federal government guarantees were imperative for the establishment of civil rights.

In the aftermath of the *Civil Rights Cases,* Southern states provided no protection against a burgeoning number of assaults against African Americans. The delicate balance that was gradually shifting toward assimilation of blacks ground to a halt. The U.S. Supreme Court essentially removed any and all prospects for civil rights, which would not begin to be realized until another, very different Supreme Court case—BROWN V. BOARD OF EDUCATION OF TOPEKA—several decades later.

For more information: Urofsky, Melvin I., and Paul Finkelman. *A March of Liberty: A Constitutional History of the United States.* Oxford and New York: Oxford University Press, 2002; Westin, Alan F. "The Case of the Prejudiced Doorkeeper." In John A. Garraty, ed., *Quarrels That Have Shaped the Constitution.* New York: Harper & Row, 1962.

—R. Owen Williams

civil service and the Pendleton Act

Civil service refers to employment within a governmental agency, particularly within the federal bureaucracy. Civil service employees are protected by the Civil Service Act. The first Civil Service Act was adopted in 1883. It was sponsored by Ohio senator George Pendleton and came to be known as the Pendleton Act. Although the Pendleton Act ended the practice of awarding government jobs based on political patronage for most civil servants, the U.S. Supreme Court was eventually asked to address the impact of political patronage on the FIRST AMENDMENT rights of government employees. The Court held that the hiring practices of administrative agencies could not be based on patronage unless political party affiliation is directly related to effective job performance.

The Pendleton Act created the U.S. Civil Service Commission and instituted hiring practices based on job qualifications rather than social status, political patronage, or scholarly achievement. It was adopted in response to two periods of favoritism in government employment. During the first period (1789–1829), employment in the federal government was based on social status. Jobs were reserved for upper-class "gentlemen" or "aristocrats," who were almost exclusively white, educated male landowners.

During the second period (1829–83), government jobs were awarded according to the "spoils system," which was implemented by President Andrew Jackson after his election in 1829. Under the spoils system, government jobs were awarded based on political support rather than competence or ability. Political parties recruited government employees and job seekers alike to work on political campaigns and required them to pay a percentage of their salary, called a "political assessment," to support the party and the campaign. In exchange, the employees received job security; the job seekers received a promise of future employment. This practice was accepted by government employees because they risked being replaced by party activists after the election if they did not participate. The practice was accepted by job seekers because of the promise of future employment. At that time, the spoils system was considered a democratic employment process because it removed control of employment in the bureaucracy from the aristocracy and opened government employment to ordinary citizens.

The spoils system, however, was criticized for politicizing government employment and rendering administrative agencies ineffective. The system caused high rates of employee turnover and low employee morale, because every presidential election placed jobs at risk and resulted in the replacement of large numbers of employees. Additionally, the system led to the hiring of some incompetent employees, as competence was not required for appointment. Finally, the system also led to corruption, as government employees used their positions for personal profit through bribes and graft. In response to these problems, reform-minded citizens began to call for the implementation of a merit-based hiring system and the end of political assessments. According to advocates, a merit-based system would increase the efficiency and effectiveness of the federal government by creating a politically neutral, professional administrative staff.

The civil service reform movement did not take hold, however, until the election of President James A. Garfield, in 1881. Although President Garfield supported civil service reform, he was in the process of awarding jobs to his supporters when he was shot by a disgruntled and demented aspiring civil servant who had demanded a consul position in exchange for his political support. Garfield died several months later and became the symbol of the civil service reform movement. The Pendleton Act was adopted two years later.

The Pendleton Act created the U.S. Civil Service Commission to administer the newly created civil service system. The act required open, competitive examinations that focused on the practical skills required for effective job performance. It also required the hiring of applicants with the highest test scores, apportioned civil service jobs among the states, protected civil service employees from political assessments, prohibited government officials from soliciting campaign contributions from employees, and prohibited anyone from soliciting or receiving political contributions in a government-owned building. It also created job classifications and allowed employees to enter at the level of their competence, rather than limiting entry to the lowest level. Finally, although the act initially extended protection to a limited number of civil servants, it empowered the president to extend that protection by executive order. Within 20 years, employment protection was expanded from 10 percent to 50 percent of civil servants.

Employees affected by political patronage soon began to claim that the practice violated their First Amendment rights to freedom of speech and freedom of association. The First Amendment states: "Congress shall make no law . . . abridging the freedom of speech." This amendment has been construed to protect the right of the people to engage in the political activity of their choosing, including associating with the political party of their choice. Accordingly, the continuing practice of political patronage on a limited basis in the federal government and on a broad basis in state and local governments eventually drew the U.S. Supreme Court into the debate. In a series of cases, the Court ruled in favor of employees who claimed that political patronage violated their First Amendment rights to freedom of speech and association. In doing so, the Court rejected the government's arguments in favor of patronage. Consequently, civil servants may not be denied a benefit or discharged for exercising their constitutional rights. Personnel decisions based on patronage, including the hiring, firing, promoting, and transferring of employees and independent contractors, must be based on a demonstrable effect that political party affiliation has on performance of the job itself. Generally, patronage decisions are limited to policy-making positions, such as department or agency leadership posts.

The Pendleton Act effectively separated the administration of governmental programs from the political process, and it governed the civil service from its enactment in 1883 until it was replaced by the Civil Service Act of 1978.

For more information: Hoogenboom, Ari. *Outlawing the Spoils: A History of Civil Service Reform Movements, 1865–1883*. Westport, Conn.: Greenwood Press, 1961; Schultz, David, and Robert Maranto. *The Politics of Civil Service Reform*. New York: Peter Lang Publishing, 1998; Van Riper, Paul. *History of the United States Civil Service*. Westport, Conn.: Greenwood Press, 1958.

—Mark A. Fulks

Civil War and the Constitution, the

The U.S. Civil War was one of the most challenging and contentious eras in American history. The war, which spanned from 1861 through 1865, resulted from numerous disagreements and disputes. Sectional tensions between Northern and Southern states had noticeably surfaced in the middle of the 19th century. One such tension involved the institution of slavery, which existed long before the CONSTITUTIONAL CONVENTION convened in 1787. However, slavery was only one issue that caused Southern states to secede from the Union.

The Constitution that was drafted in 1787 created a system of separation of powers, CHECKS

AND BALANCES, and FEDERALISM. Despite the addition of the first 10 amendments to the U.S. Constitution, known as the BILL OF RIGHTS, only a fraction of the population enjoyed fundamental protections or rights such as voting. The disagreement and debate that engulfed the United States during the first half of the 19th century grew in small stages until it exploded into the Civil War.

Numerous leaders for both the Northern and Southern states emerged to debate controversial issues and advance their own political and cultural perspectives. For instance, in the South, an influential politician named JOHN C. CALHOUN (from South Carolina) became one of the principal supporters of the Southern secessionist movement. Calhoun served several terms in Congress and was also VICE PRESIDENT under John Quincy Adams from 1825 to 1829 and Andrew Jackson from 1829 to 1832. He was best known as a staunch advocate of states' rights. Initially, Calhoun was a nationalist and proponent of a strong central government during his service in Congress.

After Calhoun was elected vice president for a second time during Jackson's presidency, several personal and political differences surfaced to cause extensive conflict between Jackson and Calhoun. During this time, Calhoun began to support more aggressively the doctrine of nullification, derived from constitutional theory, under which states could individually override legislation passed by the federal government that they deemed unconstitutional. The antecedents for the nullification doctrine were found in arguments forwarded by THOMAS JEFFERSON and JAMES MADISON, who drafted resolutions in the Kentucky and Virginia legislatures, respectively, from 1798 to 1799 to justify a nullification of the Alien and Sedition Acts by the states.

Calhoun resigned the vice presidency in 1832 to protest the stagnating effects that the "tariff of abominations" had on states' economies. He used the ideas offered by Jefferson and Madison and the Tenth Amendment to develop further the theory of nullification. He viewed nullification as a middle ground between submitting to an overly aggressive federal government and outright secession, which ultimately came with the Civil War. The doctrine also became a political statement that indicated the South's discontentment with economic conditions and the fact that it was feeling isolated from national policy, which was perceived as falling under the influence of Northern states. Further, Calhoun viewed any successful attempts by abolitionists either to curtail or to end slavery as acts that would permanently weaken the power of Southern states in relation to the North. Jackson's perspectives were much different. Jackson stated that any attempt to support nullification would be considered treasonous and forced a bill through Congress that permitted the president to deploy military troops to enforce federal laws.

Calhoun's ideas for supporting states' rights were relatively popular within the state of South Carolina and selected portions of the South. Residents had come to perceive the federal government as a source of friction and suppression, and tariffs had disillusioned many farmers and traders who had been struggling economically. But Jackson and others, such as Senator Henry Clay, worked toward averting the nullification crisis by proposing a tariff reduction to appease Southern frustrations. Calhoun's support of slavery became a catalyst for the eventual secession of Southern states from the Union and the commencement of the Civil War.

In the years just before the Civil War began, ABRAHAM LINCOLN was also growing in political notoriety. After a short interlude to practice law, Lincoln reentered the political scene in the early 1850s to protest the KANSAS-NEBRASKA ACT of 1854. President Franklin Pierce was a supporter of the act, which intensified the slavery issue and split the Whig Party apart. It reorganized as the Republican Party later that year, but the issue of slavery persisted, particularly after the *DRED SCOTT V. SANDFORD* (1857) decision. Lincoln was opposed to slavery but was not an abolitionist.

Lincoln won the presidential election in fall 1860. Soon after, the American Civil War erupted when Calhoun's home state of South Carolina became the first to secede. Several other states in the South followed suit over the next several months, and the nation was divided between Union forces in the North and Confederate forces in the South. The beginning of the Civil War was marked by an attack by the Confederate Army on Fort Sumter in Charleston, South Carolina, on April 12, 1861.

Also in April 1861, Lincoln suspended the writ of HABEAS CORPUS, a fundamental right that was derived from English common law and was incorporated into ARTICLE I OF THE U.S. CONSTITUTION. The writ requires that public officials bring all prisoners before the court to present their reason(s) for detainment. Lincoln's suspension of the writ instigated an unprecedented use of presidential power. Prior to this, only a select few presidents used the latitude of the office to make decisions that were generally considered beyond the scope of what the Founding Fathers had likely intended for the chief executive. (Prior examples, would be George Washington's issuance of the Proclamation of Neutrality during the war between France and Britain after the French Revolution, Thomas Jefferson's use of presidential power to conduct the Louisiana Purchase, and Andrew Jackson's decision to remove federal funds from the national bank and his dismissal of the treasury secretary from his administration.)

Even though the nation was torn apart by civil war, the U.S. Supreme Court ruled in *EX PARTE MILLIGAN*, 4 Wallace 2 (1866), that the president did not have the authority to suspend the writ. This decision set a precedent under which presidents were afforded extensive powers, particularly in times of crisis, but not to the extent that they could suspend FUNDAMENTAL RIGHTS provided for in the U.S. Constitution. Further, the case reinforced the power of the Court to check the executive branch and curtail presidential actions that are perceived as exceeding the boundaries of executive authority. This Civil War–era case precedent was a poignant consideration when the U.S. Supreme Court later became a check on several 20th-century presidents, most notably Franklin D. Roosevelt, Harry Truman, and RICHARD M. NIXON.

As the Civil War continued, the number who were either wounded and/or died grew to staggering numbers on both sides. Lincoln's antislavery stance intensified during the war, and in June 1862, he signed a law that banned slavery in the United States. The Emancipation Proclamation, issued by Lincoln on January 1, 1863, proclaimed that all slaves living on Confederate soil were free. Lincoln delivered the Gettysburg Address, one of the more famous speeches in American history, on November 19, 1863. He won a second term in office in the presidential election of 1864. Shortly thereafter, the Confederate Army had endured casualties so great that it was forced to surrender on April 9, 1865. General Robert E. Lee surrendered to General Ulysses S. Grant at Appomattox Courthouse, in Virginia. On April 11, Lincoln spoke publicly for the final time. He was assassinated on April 14, 1865, by John Wilkes Booth, while attending a play in Washington, D.C.

Despite the divisive nature of the Civil War, the nation reunited and the Constitution remained intact, although not without amendments. Lincoln's legacy, the changing political culture of the nation, and the Reconstruction policies after the war all became catalysts for change. The post–Civil War era introduced a series of constitutional amendments in the Reconstruction era that were ratified to promote universal suffrage and human rights. For instance, ratified on December 6, 1865, the THIRTEENTH AMENDMENT was designed to end slavery in the United States and any associated territories falling under its jurisdiction. The FOURTEENTH AMENDMENT, ratified on July 9, 1868, provided that freed slaves are U.S. citizens. It also guarantees that citizens will be afforded "EQUAL PROTECTION of the laws" and prohibits states from depriving "any person of life, liberty, or property, without DUE PROCESS of law." The FIFTEENTH AMENDMENT was the last of the post–Civil War era. Ratified on February 3, 1870, the Fifteenth Amendment extended voting rights to all citizens, irrespective of "race, color, or previous condition of servitude."

These amendments did not guarantee that such safeguards would be aggressively enforced, and their implementation in U.S. society has often been a slow and incremental process. Opposition against efforts to end racial and prejudicial behavior was apparent, particularly in the South where an agricultural economy had traditionally relied extensively on slave labor. It was not until the middle of the 20th century, when the CIVIL RIGHTS movement finally saw Congress pass various acts and pieces of legislation culminating in the landmark Supreme Court decision in *BROWN V. BOARD OF EDUCATION OF TOPEKA* (1954), that the issue of equality was championed on a national level.

For more information: Belz, Herman. *Reconstructing the Union: Theory and Policy During the Civil War.* Ithaca, N.Y.: American Historical Association/Cornell University Press, 1969; Degler, Carl N. *The Other South.* New York: Harper & Row, 1974; Donald, David. *The Politics of Reconstruction, 1863–1867.* Baton Rouge: Louisiana State University Press, 1965; Freehling, William W. *The Road to Disunion.* Vol 1: *Secessionists at Bay.* Oxford and New York: Oxford University Press, 1990; Harmon, M. Judd, ed. *Essays on the Constitution of the United States.* New York: National University Publications, 1978; Randall, J. G., and David Donald. *The Civil War and Reconstruction.* 2d ed. Boston: D.C. Heath & Co., 1961.

—Daniel Baracskay

Clayton Antitrust Act (1914)

The Clayton Antitrust Act of 1914 together with the Sherman Act of 1890 are major pieces of congressional legislation regulating anticompetitive behavior of corporations and businesses.

Among the focal points of President Woodrow Wilson's "New Freedom" was trust busting, and one of his answers to this problem was legislation that became the Clayton Antitrust Act. The Sherman Act of 1890 notwithstanding, the centralization of economic power continued to grow through the end of the 19th century and into the 20th century, something that greatly troubled Wilson and his supporters. This piece of legislation exempted trade unions and agricultural groups from antitrust laws, and it reined in the use of court INJUNCTIONS during strikes. There were business practices that it prohibited as well as an expansion of permitted labor activities.

Alabama representative Henry D. Clayton, a Democrat, drafted an antitrust bill that would prohibit practices such as price discrimination and agreements that restricted the right of dealers handling the products of competing manufacturers. The debate was fairly lengthy with much of the focus on the sections involving LABOR UNIONS and their activities. Despite the amount of debate, the legislation passed both houses of congress fairly easily. The SENATE vote was 46-16, and the vote in the HOUSE OF REPRESENTATIVES was 277-54, with 102 not voting. The Federal Trade Commission (FTC) was established at roughly the same time as the Clayton Act to enforce the provisions of the antitrust legislation but was passed in a weakened form because conservatives from the North and South amended the act to provide for broad JUDICIAL REVIEW of the FTC's decisions.

Since passage of the Sherman Antitrust Act, Samuel Gompers and his American Federation of Labor had been lobbying for labor groups to be exempt from antitrust laws. The new law stated that unions should not be considered illegal combinations as applied to the restraint of trade. It also denied federal courts the authority to issue injunctions against striking unions unless required to prevent irreversible damage to property. It legalized strikes and peaceful picketing while exempting union and agricultural groups from antitrust prosecution. Furthermore, it increased the list of objectionable business practices to include price discrimination and interlocking directorates.

Labor groups were so thrilled with the Clayton Act that Gompers called the legislation the "MAGNA CARTA of Labor." At the time of its passage, the bill signaled a change in the relationship between management and labor, but future court decisions weakened the legislation. For example, in *Duplex Printing Co. v. Deering*, 254 U.S. 443 (1921), the Supreme Court held, 6-3, that the Clayton Antitrust Act did not insulate labor unions engaged in illegal activities, such as the conduct of a secondary boycott. Because of the narrow interpretation of the act, lower courts found it easier to issue injunctions against organizing activities of unions.

On the other hand, there were Court decisions suggesting that the Clayton Antitrust Act had significant power. In the dissenting opinion in *U.S.*

v. E. I. du Pont, 353 U.S. 586 (1957), there is the suggestion that if a corporation has acquired stock in another corporation and has business dealings with that corporation, they are in violation of Section 7's prohibition of interlocking directorates.

The Clayton Antitrust Act remains in effect today as the nation's basic antitrust law. Later, amendment to the legislation strengthened its provisions against unreasonable price reductions and intercorporate stockholdings.

For more information: Harbeson, Robert W. "The Clayton Act: Sleeping Giant of Antitrust?" *American Economic Review* 48, no. 1 (March 1958): 92–104; Hovenkamp, Herbert. *The Antitrust Enterprise: Principle and Execution.* Cambridge, Mass.: Harvard University Press, 2006; Posner, Richard A. *Antitrust Law.* 2d ed. Chicago: University of Chicago Press, 2001.

—Mark Alcorn

clear and present danger test

The clear and present danger test began as an attempt to balance free speech under the FIRST AMENDMENT and national security during wartime. In *Masses Publishing Co. v. Patten,* 244 F. 535 (1917)—a prosecution of a Socialist magazine under the Espionage Act—Judge LEARNED HAND, then a district court judge, held that government could punish only speech that offers "direct incitement to violent resistance." Applying the test narrowly, Judge Hand found no incitement.

Two years later, however, in *SCHENCK V. UNITED STATES,* 249 U.S. 47 (1919), Supreme Court justice OLIVER WENDELL HOLMES, JR., held that the key question was whether the words, and their surrounding circumstances, "create a clear and present danger that they will bring about the substantive evils that Congress has a right to prevent." Applying the test, Justice Holmes upheld the conviction of a Socialist Party official charged with distributing anticonscription leaflets.

Six months later, in *Abrams v. United States,* 250 U.S. 616 (1919), Justice Holmes, now writing in dissent, used the test to oppose the conviction of a man charged under the Espionage Act with promoting the Bolshevik revolution. Over the next decade, Justice Holmes, joined by Justice Louis Brandeis, issued a series of dissenting opinions in which they used the clear and present danger test to defend speech. The most notable of these dissents was *WHITNEY V. CALIFORNIA,* 274 U.S. 357 (1927), in which Justice Brandeis linked the test to libertarian values of "[t]hose who won our independence." He added that "no danger flowing from speech can be deemed clear and present, unless the incidence of the evil . . . is so imminent that it may befall before there is opportunity for full discussion."

Eventually, as the Court took a more libertarian turn during the 1940s, the clear and present danger test became the law of the land. During this period, the Court used it to protect speech in a wide variety of cases ranging from labor picketing to denaturalization proceedings. But the test's heyday was short-lived. *Dennis v. United States,* 341 U.S. 494 (1952), a case involving prosecutions of Communists at the height of the cold war, added a new factor to the test—the gravity of the evil. This meant that a very grave danger (such as a Communist takeover of the United States) could justify restrictions on speech even if it was not likely in the immediate future.

While its potential damage to free speech was mitigated by the *United States v. Yates* ruling, 354 U.S. 298 (1957), which took the first steps back toward a broader protection of speech, *Dennis* marked the end of the clear and present danger test. When the Supreme Court issued its broad protection of speech in *BRANDENBURG V. OHIO,* 395 U.S. 444 (1969), there was no mention of the clear and present danger test. Instead, the Court held that the state could restrict only speech that directly incites imminent lawless action.

The test survives in other areas of law, however. In particular, it is used in cases involving contempt of court and in cases involving attacks on the integrity of the judicial process.

For more information: Hentoff, Tom. "Note, Speech, Harm, and Self-government: Understanding the Ambit of the Clear and Present Danger Test." *Columbia Law Review* 91 (October 1991):

1,453–94; Kalven, Harry, Jr. *A Worthy Tradition: Freedom of Speech in America.* New York: Harper & Row, 1974.

—Robert A. Kahn

Clinton v. City of New York 524 U.S. 417 (1998)

In *Clinton v. City of New York*, the Supreme Court declared unconstitutional a federal law giving the president of the United States line-item VETO authority.

In 1997, President Bill Clinton used the Line Item Veto Act of 1996 to remove or delete individual items that were contained within bills, resolutions, and other budgetary items that he would otherwise have vetoed. Through the new act, the president basically had the power to cancel three major types of financially defined items. The range of his authority to veto began at one end with the ability to challenge the dollar amount of discretionary budget authority. This allowed for the limitations of several constituent or lobbyist rewards that derived from a potential quid pro quo format that was common within the congressional ranks. Thus, in order to get approval for the item, the president retained an ability to alter the political scheme in an effort to gain concession for his party or from the congressperson.

The president also retained the ability to veto an item that was of newer direct spending, which allowed him to challenge the size of government to limit the operational expansion of agencies. This could serve as the ability to bring agency heads under his control and limit their independence. Third, the president was able to veto potential tax changes that would be established solely as reward for political lobbyists and thus limit the congressional power to trade supportive laws for their respective constituencies for political support, thereby stemming the tide of opposing power growth by limiting what these leaders could do for their followers.

The major question in this case was whether the President had violated the PRESENTMENT CLAUSE of ARTICLE I OF THE U.S. CONSTITUTION. The decision by the high court affirmed that he did in fact violate that component of the Constitution and thus exceeded his presidential authority. In the opinion of the Court, the presentment clause requires any legislation to pass both houses of Congress, and if this is accomplished, then the president must approve or veto the legislation in its entirety. It was here that the Court stood its ground, interpreting that the line-item veto actions amounted to a tailoring of the law and thus fundamentally altered the meaning of the legislation in sum created by the legislative bodies. This "amending" as granted in the act was without authority and incongruent with the spirit of the Constitution, according to the Court. The Court argued that the negotiations enjoyed though the legislative creation process that had existed for 200-some years, based on constant compromise, was now a useless concept and endeavor.

The actual repeal of the act has never occurred, but the unconstitutionality of the operational endeavor makes the pulling it off the books, in a matter of speaking, highly likely.

For more information: Brownell, Roy E. "The Unnecessary Demise of the Line Item Veto Act: The Clinton Administration's Costly Failure to Seek Acknowledgement of 'National Security Rescission.'" *American Law Review* 1,273–1,351, no. 47 (1997–98): 357–373; Kennedy, J. Stephen. "How a Bill Does Not Become Law: The Supreme Court Sounds the Death Knell of the Line Item Veto." *Mississippi College Law Review* 357, no. 20 (1999–2000); Langran, Robert W. *The Supreme Court: A Concise History.* New York: Peter Lang, 2004.

—Ernest Gomez

Clinton v. Jones 520 U.S. 681 (1997)

In *Clinton v. Jones*, the Supreme Court ruled that the Constitution does not provide the president immunity from civil suits for misconduct that occurred before he took office. The significance of the case is that it reaffirmed the principle that no one is above the law and set the stage for President Bill Clinton's IMPEACHMENT.

On May 8, 1991, then-governor Bill Clinton gave a speech at an official conference at the Excelsior Hotel in Little Rock, Arkansas, where Paula Jones, a state employee, was working the registration desk. That afternoon, Jones alleged that Danny Ferguson, an Arkansas state trooper, persuaded her to visit the governor in a hotel suite where he made unwanted sexual advances that she immediately rejected. Due to her rejection of the governor, she claims that her superiors punished her by creating a hostile working environment and changing her job duties.

Three years later, Jones sued President Clinton for sexual harassment. Clinton's attorney filed a motion to dismiss Jones's suit until after the president left office, claiming that presidential immunity prevents the judicial branch from interfering with the performance of the president's constitutional duties by subjecting him to litigation. The district court rejected the motion but did extend temporary immunity by postponing the trial until the end of Clinton's presidency. The U.S. Court of Appeals for the Eighth Circuit reversed the postponement, and on appeal, the Supreme Court held for Jones, ordering the trial to proceed.

Writing for a unanimous court, Justice JOHN PAUL STEVENS rejected the presidential immunity claim because the Constitution provides no immunity for unofficial acts. Moreover, impairment of duties is unlikely because history shows that presidents are rarely sued and the time it takes to resolve these cases is minimal. Further, Justice Stevens argued that the Court was not violating the separation of powers by interfering with the performance of executive duties by ordering the trial to proceed. Rather, the Court was merely pursuing its authority under ARTICLE III OF THE U.S. CONSTITUTION to resolve cases and controversies. Finally, the Court ruled that deferring the trial was an abuse of discretion by the district court because delay would increase the probability of denying justice to Jones due to a loss of evidence, the inability of witnesses to recall specific facts, or the possible death of one of the parties.

Concurring in the judgment, Justice STEPHEN G. BREYER expressed skepticism that litigation would not impair presidential performance. He preferred a narrower ruling that allowed the Court to consider temporary immunity if the president could prove impairment.

As a result, the case went to trial and was dismissed as groundless. Eventually, Clinton settled the case with Jones out of court for $850,000 but no admission of guilt. However, Clinton's legal and political troubles continued as he was found in contempt of court for misleading and evasive testimony in the Jones case. This led to a fine, the voluntary surrender of his law license, and the basis for two articles of impeachment that the HOUSE OF REPRESENTATIVES approved in 1998, making Clinton only the second president in history to be impeached. Overall, *Clinton v. Jones* is an important case both in terms of its impact upon the Clinton presidency and in terms of ruling that in many cases sitting presidents could face civil judgments.

For more information: Conasan, Joe, and Gene Lyons. *The Hunting of the President.* New York: St. Martin's Press, 2001; Miller, Randall K. "Presidential Sanctuaries After the Clinton Sex Scandal." *Harvard Journal of Law and Public Policy* 22, no. 2 (1999): 647–735; Turley, Jonathan. "From Pillar to Post: The Prosecution of American Presidents." *American Criminal Law Review* 37 (Summer 2000): 149–217.

—Sean F. Evans

Coe v. Town of Errol 116 U.S. 517 (1886)

In *Coe v. Town of Errol,* the Supreme Court ruled that goods may be taxed by a state as "the general mass of property of that state" prior to the actual commencement of the goods' journey toward another state. The significance of this decision is that it established a point of time after which goods become INTERSTATE COMMERCE. *Coe v. Town of Errol* is of particular importance to states whose primary exports are natural resources; such goods are often subject to storage or holdover for a period of time prior to actual shipment to other states or foreign countries.

Edward Coe owned an operation that cut trees for export as timber in New Hampshire. Coe banked logs along a stream within the jurisdiction of the town of Errol, New Hampshire, in the winter of 1879 with the intention of shipping the logs down the Androscoggin River toward Maine in the spring of 1880. The town of Errol assessed taxes on the logs as they awaited transit, during the winter months, toward Maine. Coe argued before the New Hampshire Supreme Court that the logs were not subject to taxation in the state of New Hampshire on the grounds that the Androscoggin River constituted an interstate waterway, that the goods were in transit while in New Hampshire, and that this transit route was long established. The New Hampshire Supreme Court upheld the town of Errol's assessment of taxes on the logs.

The case was heard by the U.S. Supreme Court, and Justice Joseph P. Bradley wrote the majority opinion. Justice Bradley argued that the intention to export goods does not provide immunity from state taxation. The point of commencement for goods intended for export does not necessarily start at the earliest stage of activity. In this case, the felling of timber would not constitute the point at which the timber became interstate commerce. The timber became interstate commerce when it began its actual journey down the Androscoggin River toward Maine. Justice Bradley made an important point by noting that the owner's intention to export cannot always be taken for granted; the owner can change his mind. The goods are considered the general mass of property in the state "until [goods are] actually put in motion for some place out of state, or committed to the custody of a carrier for transportation to such place."

Justice Bradley made another point by noting that the economies of some states, particularly those in the West and South, depend primarily on the exportation of agricultural goods. Precluding agricultural goods from state taxation prior to the point of their commencement along a shipping route or prior to their custody by a carrier would have a significant impact on the economies of these states. Justice Bradley cited the case of *The Daniel Ball,* 10 Wall. 565 (1870), in discerning the boundaries of interstate commerce. In *The Daniel Ball,* it was argued that a ship did not need a federal license, because it was engaged only in the internal commerce of a state even if the river it sailed on was considered to be a navigable waterway of the United States. The Supreme Court found that a navigable waterway was one that allowed for a continuous movement between states and that goods being transported along it could be considered interstate commerce even if the ship carrying them did not leave the state. The decision of the Supreme Court in *The Daniel Ball* is reflected in Justice Bradley's opinion.

Whenever a commodity has begun to move as an article of trade from one state to another, commerce in that commodity between the states has commenced, but this movement does not begin until the articles have been shipped or started for transportation from one state to the other. The carrying of them in carts or other vehicles, or even floating them to the depot where the journey is to commence, is not part of that journey. That is all preliminary work, performed for the purpose of putting the property of a state in preparation and readiness for transportation. Until actually launched on its way to another state, or committed to a common carrier for transportation to such state, its destination is not fixed and certain.

The case examines one final question: Can special taxes be assessed by a state on goods intended for exportation? Justice Bradley argues that goods intended for export are not subject to special taxation on the grounds that such goods are exports. The manner of taxation of the goods, prior to the commencement of their actual journey, is to be one that would be applied to such goods as the general mass of property of that state and not as goods intended for export.

Coe v. Town of Errol was important in establishing a point in time at which goods begin to be considered interstate commerce. Goods are subject to state taxation, as products of the state and not as exports. Once the journey toward another state actually commences, the goods become interstate commerce and are subject to regulation by the federal government. This case is particularly relevant for states whose economies depend primarily on the export of natural resources because it allows the state a means of procuring revenue that could be precluded if goods were considered exports from the beginning of the process.

For more information: Schwartz, Bernard. *A History of the Supreme Court.* New York: Oxford University Press, 1993.

—J. David Granger

Cohens v. Virginia 19 U.S. 264 (1821)

In *Cohens v. Virginia,* the U.S. Supreme Court upheld the state convictions of two individuals arrested for selling lottery tickets in defiance of Virginia state law. The case had strong nationalistic overtones that angered Virginia, even though the decision was in its favor.

In an effort to fund the building of the DISTRICT OF COLUMBIA's infrastructure, Congress had authorized a national lottery. In response, Virginia enacted a law banning out-of-state lotteries. Brothers Philip and Mendes Cohen, who were citizens of Maryland, were arrested and convicted in the Virginia state court for selling national lottery tickets in defiance of state law. The Cohen brothers appealed their conviction to the state supreme court and then to the U.S. Supreme Court. The main point of contention was whether the U.S. Supreme Court had the authority to review the decision of the Virginia Supreme Court.

Counsel for Virginia argued that the Constitution did not provide for a tribunal to be the final arbiter of disputes between the states and the federal government. Counsel further argued that the ELEVENTH AMENDMENT's prohibition of judicial power over matters between citizens and other states precluded the Court from asserting jurisdiction between Virginia and the citizens of another state. Rather, such power would be found only in the states; therefore, the Court had no jurisdiction to even entertain the matter, let alone decide it.

Chief Justice JOHN MARSHALL wrote for the unanimous Court, rejecting this claim and, instead, arguing that ARTICLE III OF THE U.S. CONSTITUTION and Section 25 of the JUDICIARY ACT OF 1789 authorized the Court to review state criminal proceedings. Marshall argued that Article III, Section 2 of the Constitution provided that the judicial power extends to all cases under the Constitution, including controversies between states as well as between a state and individuals. He also argued that Section 25 of the Judiciary Act provided for review of state supreme court decisions by the U.S. Supreme Court in cases where a federal law—in this case, the national lottery—or the Constitution were involved. Marshall's decision to uphold the convictions was not based on the assumption that Virginia's law was correct. Rather, it was based on upholding the sanctity of federal law, in particular the Constitution. Indeed, according to Marshall, the sanctity of the Union was dependent on it. Accordingly, the American people came together as one to form the Union and a government for the Union. The exercise of APPELLATE JURISDICTION over the decisions of state courts that violated federal law or the Constitution was essential to the supremacy of the Constitution and the Union. Marshall gave a strongly worded defense of national power, and, more specifically, judicial power, and made it clear that any state constitution or state law that was repugnant to the U.S. Constitution or federal law was "absolutely void." It was the U.S. Supreme Court, not the Virginia Supreme Court, that had the final say over the Constitution.

Although the Court upheld the convictions of the Cohen brothers, Virginia was angered by the Court's assertion of jurisdiction over the decision of the state supreme court that it considered it to be void. The *Cohens* decision was one in a series of pre–Civil War nationalistic decisions that invoked outrage from the states.

For more information: Graber, Mark. "The Passive-Aggressive Virtues: *Cohens v. Virginia* and the Problematic Establishment of Judicial Power." *Constitutional Commentary* 12 (1995): 67–92; Warren, Charles. "Legislative and Judicial Attacks on the Supreme Court of the United States: A History of the Twenty-fifth Section of the Judiciary Act." *American Law Review* 47 (1913): 1–47 and 161–189.

—Randa Issa

Cohen v. California 403 U.S. 15 (1971)

In *Cohen v. California,* the U.S. Supreme Court held that offensive language, including profanity, is protected FIRST AMENDMENT speech and thus may not be suppressed under a statute that regulates the manner in which profane words are used.

Paul Robert Cohen was convicted in the Los Angeles Municipal Court in 1968 for wearing a jacket that read "Fuck the Draft." The statute under which he was convicted was the California Penal Code Section 415, which prohibited "maliciously and willfully disturbing the peace or quiet of any neighborhood or person . . . by . . . offensive conduct." Cohen stated that he wore the jacket as a means of informing the public of his feelings against the Vietnam War and the draft. Although women and children were present in the hall where Cohen was observed wearing the jacket, Cohen himself did not engage in or threaten to engage in, nor did anyone else as the result of his conduct commit or threaten to commit, any act of violence. In fact, Cohen did not utter any sound at all prior to his arrest, and no one voiced a protest to the jacket.

While the state attempted to influence the Supreme Court's decision by arguing that the members of society in the hall where the jacket was worn were a "captive audience" forced to view an "obscene statement," and as such the state had a right to ban certain expletives in order to complete its duty as "guardians of public morality," all such arguments failed.

In the majority opinion, authored by Justice JOHN MARSHALL HARLAN and joined by Justices WILLIAM O. DOUGLAS, WILLIAM J. BRENNAN, JR., Potter Stewart, and Thurgood Marshall, Justice Harlan struck down all three arguments of the state. He explained that while the First Amendment and FOURTEENTH AMENDMENT "have never been thought to give absolute protection to every individual to speak whenever or wherever he pleases, or to use any form of address in any circumstances that he chooses," none of the nonprotected forms of speech (that is, fighting words) occurred in Cohen's case regarding the jacket. The jacket was not obscene as case law defines *obscene* because the reference to the war and draft were in no way erotic. Secondly, Harlan argued that no one present in the corridor could reasonably have regarded the words on Cohen's jacket as a "direct personal insult." Harlan concluded by explaining that the group in the corridor were by no means a captive audience as that term is commonly used, and anyone viewing the jacket could have simply averted his or her eyes if the person did not want to see it.

The Court went through several analogies for free speech, concluding that the right of free expression is "powerful medicine," and as such, "one man's vulgarity is another's lyric." Justice Harlan stated emphatically that to allow a statute such as Section 415 stand would create the risky situation of allowing the government to potentially seize upon the "censorship of particular words as a convenient guise for banning the expression of unpopular views." The Court concluded that without a compelling state reason, the state may not make the simple public display of a specific four letter word a criminal offense.

For more information: Kalven, Harry, Jr. *A Worthy Tradition: Freedom of Speech in America.* New York: Harper & Row, 1988; Shiffrin, Steven. *The First Amendment, Democracy, and Romance.* Cambridge, Mass.: Harvard University Press, 1990.

—Kelli Styron

Coker v. Georgia 433 U.S. 584 (1977)

In *Coker v. Georgia,* the Supreme Court held that imposing the death penalty for the rape of an adult woman was disproportionate and unconstitutional under the Eighth Amendment's CRUEL AND UNUSUAL PUNISHMENT clause. As a result of this decision, no one has been sentenced to death or executed since 1977 except for crimes involving death.

Ehrlich Anthony Coker was not a sympathetic defendant. After escaping from prison while serving consecutive life sentences, he robbed the victim's husband at knife point, raped the 16-year-old victim, and abducted her in the family's car. At trial, the jury convicted him of rape and recommended a sentence of death based on two aggravating factors: Coker had previously been convicted of a capital felony, and the rape had been committed in the course of another capital felony (the armed robbery of the husband).

The *Coker* case tested the use of the law to impose a death sentence in a rape case in which the victim was neither killed nor physically injured beyond the rape itself. Although the Supreme Court decided the case by a vote of 7-2, there was no single majority opinion. Justice Byron White, writing for a four-member plurality, concluded that the death penalty was "grossly disproportionate and excessive punishment" for the crime of raping an adult woman. White stated that although rape was a serious crime, it did not compare with murder in terms of moral depravity or injury to the victim or the public. His comment that rape "does not include . . . serious injury" prompted much criticism from feminists and rape victim supporters at the time.

Justice White first analyzed the "objective" evidence of public opinion and legislative decisions and concluded that death was becoming less acceptable as a penalty for rape. While 18 states had authorized the death penalty for rape in 1925, and 16 of these still had the provision on the books at the time of the *FURMAN V. GEORGIA* decision in 1972, only three had reenacted that provision after state death penalty laws were struck down by the Supreme Court. By 1977, Georgia was the only state to punish the rape of an adult woman by death. Of those rape cases tried in Georgia under the new law, juries had chosen not to impose the death penalty in at least 90 percent of the cases.

Turning from factual data to logical analysis, Justice White expressed the plurality's "abiding conviction" that death was an excessive and therefore disproportionate punishment for a rapist who did not kill, particularly when a deliberate killer would not receive a capital sentence unless additional aggravating factors were present.

The dissent, filed by Chief Justice WARREN EARL BURGER, which Justice WILLIAM HUBBS REHNQUIST joined, was longer than the plurality opinion. It accused the Supreme Court of "substituting its policy judgment for that of the state legislature." The chief justice argued that states should have the flexibility to experiment within the criminal justice system, an argument that had frequently been made in the 1940s and 1950s but was becoming less persuasive as the Supreme Court moved to establish national standards of DUE PROCESS and criminal procedure.

Chief Justice Burger pointed out that the decision could have implications for other crimes that were also punishable by death, a point that is even more significant today. While states generally responded to the *Coker* decision by limiting the death penalty to homicide cases, Louisiana extended the death penalty to child rapists in 1995, and several other states have since followed suit. Since 1977, the federal government has greatly expanded the number of crimes for which death may be imposed; some crimes that do not result in death, such as running a large-scale drug enterprise, are eligible under the 1994 Omnibus Crime Bill. Although death sentences are still rare at the federal level, the existence of more than 60 death penalty crimes creates the potential for conflict with the standard of proportionality developed in *Coker.* The context for this debate will include an international community that increasingly rejects the death penalty as an appropriate penalty for any crime.

For more information: Fleming, Annaliese Flynn. "Louisiana's Newest Capital Crime: The Death Penalty for Child Rape." *Journal of Criminal Law and Criminology* 89, no. 2 (1999): 717–750; Foster, Burk. "Struck by Lightning: Louisiana's Electrocutions for Rape in the Forties and Fifties." In *Death Watch: A Death Penalty Anthology*. Upper Saddle River, N.J.: Prentice Hall, 2001; Schaaf, David W. "What If the Victim Is a Child? Examining the Constitutionality of Louisiana's Challenge to *Coker v. Georgia.*" *University of Illinois Law Review* 1 (2000): 347–378.

—Barbara J. Hayler

Colegrove v. Green 328 U.S. 549 (1946)

In *Colegrove v. Green*, the Supreme Court held that the redistricting cases were not within the

Court's jurisdiction. The decision established a long-standing precedent that, on the grounds of nonjusticiability, U.S. courts could not enter matters of legislative districting.

At the time of the case, congressional districts in Illinois had not been redrawn for more than four decades, and huge inequities—an eightfold difference ranging from a low of 112,116 to a high of 914,053—existed in their sizes. Despite the variation in populations, each district had but one representative in Congress. A resident of the biggest district sued on the grounds that this inequity rendered his vote less effective than one in the smallest district.

In a sharply divided (4-3) decision, the Supreme Court justices found the issue of legislative districting to be beyond the jurisdiction of the Court. Justice Felix Frankfurter, joined by Justices Stanley Forman Reed and Harold H. Burton, delivered the opinion. He argued that, according to Section 4 of ARTICLE I OF THE U.S. CONSTITUTION, "The Times, Places and Manner of holding Elections for . . . Representatives, shall be prescribed in each State by the Legislature thereof; but the Congress may at any time by Law make or alter such Regulations." According to the Court's decision, therefore, the obligation to fairly apportion congressional districts rested squarely with Congress:

> [T]he appellants ask of this Court what is beyond its competence to grant. This is one of those demands on judicial power which cannot be met by verbal fencing about "jurisdiction" . . . it is hostile to a democratic system to involve the judiciary in the politics of the people. . . .
>
> [T]he Constitution has conferred upon Congress exclusive authority to secure fair representation by the States in the popular House, and left to that House determination whether States have fulfilled their responsibility. If Congress failed in exercising its powers, whereby standards of fairness are offended, the remedy ultimately lies with the people. . . .
>
> To sustain this action would cut very deep into the very being of Congress. Courts ought not to enter this political thicket.

Frankfurter relied on the so-called political question doctrine, according to which certain issues are viewed as constitutional issues committed to some branch of government other than the judicial branch. As was later shown, the Court was asking for the impossible, namely, that the urban residents in underrepresented districts should expect relief from a legislature or a congressional delegation that was elected by and firmly in the hands of rural populations in overrepresented districts. As it has been observed by scholar Richard K. Shur,

> [i]t was absurd or naive or both to expect members of a legislature who had been successfully elected to office under one system of districts to throw that system over in favor of another that did not provide them with any assurances of electoral success. Naturally, nothing happened as a result of *Colegrove* to correct the growing malapportionment of state legislative and congressional districts.

Colegrove's principle of nonjusticiability of redistricting issues was followed by the courts until the early 1960s. In *GOMILLION ET AL. V. LIGHTFOOT, MAYOR OF TUSKEGEE, ET AL.*, 364 U.S. 339 (1960), the Supreme Court admitted for the first time that the redistricting plan can be a tool for discrimination on the basis of race. *BAKER V. CARR*, 369 U.S. 186 (1962), and *REYNOLDS V. SIMS*, 377 U.S. 533 (1964), finally overruled *Colegrove* and developed the "ONE PERSON, ONE VOTE" rule.

For more information: Scher, Richard K., et al. *Voting Rights and Democracy: The Law and Politics of Districting.* Chicago: Nelson-Hall Publishers, 1997.

—Jurij Toplak

Collector v. Day 78 Wall. 113 (1871)

In *Collector v. Day,* the Supreme Court ruled 8-1 that the Tenth Amendment bars the U.S. government from taxing income of state workers. This was one of the first Supreme Court cases involving the constitutionality of the federal income tax, and it fostered the principle of INTERGOVERNMENTAL TAX IMMUNITY, that the national government must not tax state government workers and the state government cannot tax federal workers.

The decision in *Collector* was eventually reversed in 1939. Congress established the first income tax in 1862 to help defray the enormous debt incurred by the Civil War. Americans paid taxes on the amount of income they derived from wages, salaries, property, interest, dividends, and other sources. For example, a person earning between $600 and $10,000 annually was taxed at a rate of 3 percent. To ensure compliance, Congress also created the Commission of Internal Revenue, the forerunner of the modern Internal Revenue Service (IRS). Congress modified the law and the rates several times over the following decade. In 1871, the tax was set at 5 percent on all yearly income over $1,000.

J. M. Day was a Massachusetts probate court judge, and his salary was set by law and paid from the state treasury. A federal tax collector assessed Day's income and set his tax at $61.50. Judge Day paid the tax and then sued the collector to recover the amount paid. The suit averred that the U.S. government had no constitutional authority to tax income derived from state governments. The circuit court ruled for Day, and the federal government asked the U.S. Supreme Court to review the case on a writ of error.

Supreme Court justice Samuel Nelson, affirming the lower court ruling, delivered the majority opinion. He noted that while Congress has authority under Section 8 of ARTICLE I OF THE U.S. CONSTITUTION to lay and collect uniform taxes to pay the public debts, it is nevertheless restricted by the reserved powers of the Tenth Amendment. Under the Tenth Amendment, states may possess all powers that are neither given to the national government nor prohibited to the states under the Constitution. Citing Chief Justice JOHN MARSHALL's famous quotation in *MCCULLOCH V. MARYLAND* (1819), "the power to tax involves the power to destroy," Nelson reasoned that state judges are instruments of the state governments, and if the national government could place an income tax on the states, it had the potential for destroying the very state powers permitted under the reserve powers of the Tenth Amendment. Nelson concluded that state governments and their agents are not the proper subjects of federal taxation. Joining in the opinion were Justices Robert Grier, Nathan Clifford, Noah Swayne, Samuel F. Miller, David Davis, Stephen Field, and Chief Justice Salmon P. Chase. The lone dissent, offered by Justice Joseph Bradley, asserted: "No man ceases to be a citizen of the United States by being an officer under the State government."

The decision in *Collector* was eventually overturned in *Graves v. New York ex rel. O'Keefe* (1939). In *Graves,* the Supreme Court ruled 6-2 that the state tax on the income of a federal employee did not place an undue burden upon the federal government. Today, the federal government may tax income of state workers, and the state governments may tax the income of federal workers.

For more information: Brownlee, W. Elliot. *Federal Taxation in America.* New York: Cambridge University Press, 1996; Fairman, Charles. *Reconstruction and Reunion, 1864–1868.* New York: Macmillan, 1971; Witte, John F. *The Politics and Development of the Federal Income Tax.* Madison: University of Wisconsin Press, 1985.

—Richard J. Hardy

commander in chief

The title of commander in chief refers to the powers of the president found in Section 1 of ARTICLE II OF THE U.S. CONSTITUTION. One of the major constitutional issues is determining what powers the president has as commander in chief and how they compare to the authority of Congress in the area in foreign affairs and national defense. Determining the lines of authority between the president and Congress has been a historical point of controversy, especially since the Vietnam War and more recently with President George W. Bush and the "war on terrorism."

When the framers wrote the Constitution in 1787, they textually committed certain powers both to the president and Congress in the areas of foreign policy and national defense. Section 8 of

ARTICLE I OF THE U.S. CONSTITUTION includes the power to declare war, organize an army and navy, and regulate the armed forces, among other powers. Conversely, Article II declares the president to be commander in chief of the armed forces, and this section also gives the president and SENATE joint powers in approving treaties and nominating ambassadors. Thus, in some cases, the Constitution textually commits some powers to Congress, the president, or jointly. Historically, the division of power between the legislative and executive branches has been to treat the president as commander in chief as the person responsible for taking emergency action, such as deploying troops if the United States is attacked or to commit troops for a variety of short-term missions. Throughout U.S. history, there are numerous examples of this. The real question, though, that has emerged is where do the powers of Congress end in the area of military and foreign affairs, and where do the powers of the president pick up?

In *UNITED STATES v. CURTISS-WRIGHT EXPORT CORP.*, 299 U.S. 304 (1936), the Supreme Court suggested that presidents potentially have more power to depart from the normal constitutional arrangements in foreign affairs as opposed to domestic matters. However, one effort to clarify the lines of constitutional authority between the president and Congress was made in *YOUNGSTOWN SHEET & TUBE v. SAWYER*, 343 U.S. 579 (1952). In that case, President Harry S. Truman stepped in via executive order and had the steel mills of the nation seized in order to avert a strike during the Korean War. The Supreme Court overturned the seizure. Justice Robert Jackson's concurrence in the case suggested that the president's, or commander in chief's, authority is limited in scope, and he cannot act on his own without the consent of Congress on most matters that offer other methods for recourse. Jackson described three categories of presidential power: 1) "When the President acts pursuant to an express or implied authorization of Congress, his authority is at its maximum"; 2) "When the President acts in absence of either a congressional grant or denial of authority, he can only rely upon his own independent powers, but there is a zone of twilight in which he and Congress may have concurrent authority, or in which its distribution is uncertain"; and 3) "When the President takes measures incompatible with the expressed or implied will of Congress, his power is at its lowest ebb, for then he can rely only upon his own constitutional powers minus any constitutional powers of Congress over the matter."

Jackson's concurrence has become the touchstone for understanding the president's power as commander in chief. It suggests that there is some inherent executive authority to act in foreign and military affairs, yet that line was not defined in that case. It was further blurred during the Vietnam War when Presidents Lyndon Johnson and RICHARD NIXON deployed hundreds of thousands of troops without a formal declaration of war by Congress. They instead relied upon the Gulf of Tonkin Resolution, which was adopted by Congress on August 7, 1964, in response to an alleged attack on the United States by North Vietnam. The resolution stated: "Congress approves and supports the determination of the President, as commander in chief, to take all necessary measures to repel any armed attack against the forces of the United States and to prevent further aggression."

In 1973, Congress sought to address the gap between the lines of authority of Congress to make war versus the president's power as commander in chief by adopting the WAR POWERS ACT. This act provides for limited presidential engagement of troops for up to 60 days, and it also mandates that the president must consult with Congress when possible before deploying troops. Congress, by joint resolution, could also require the president to bring the troops home sooner. However, the act has thus far been invoked by the president only once—in 1975 when Gerald Ford sent troops in to rescue members of the *Mayaguez* who had been captured by Cambodia—and the constitutionality of it is in question since it relies on a LEGISLATIVE VETO. In *INS v. Chada*, 462 U.S. 919 (1983), the Supreme Court declared unconstitutional a one-house legislative veto, leaving open whether even a two-house VETO would be upheld.

The terrorist attacks of September 11, 2001, on the United States have yet again raised questions about what powers the president has as commander in chief. Similar to what happened in Vietnam, Congress authorized the president to respond to the attacks with the authorization to use military force (AUMF) on September 14, 2001: "to use all necessary and appropriate force against those nations, organizations, or persons he determines planned, authorized, committed or aided the terrorist attacks that occurred on September 11, 2001, . . . in order to prevent any future acts of international terrorism against the United States by such nations, organizations, or persons." As a result of AUMF, President Bush has invoked it, as well as claims of inherent executive authority as commander in chief, to undertake a variety of actions including electronic surveillance of overseas communications without warrants issued by the courts and the detaining of suspected terrorists without arraignments. In a series of cases including *HAMDI V. RUMSFELD*, 542 U.S. 507 (2004), *RASUL V. BUSH*, 545 U.S. 466 (2004), *RUMSFELD V. PADILLA*, 542 U.S. 426 (2004), and *Hamdan v. Rumsfeld*, 126 S.Ct. 2749 (2006), the Supreme Court has not ruled on the inherent powers of the president as commander in chief, and it has generally followed the dicta of Justice Jackson from *Youngstown* in describing whether Bush was given congressional authority to undertake the activities at issue in these cases.

Overall, the power of the president as commander in chief is significant in his being the civilian head of the military, but the Constitution remains silent on how much authority is vested in that office.

For more information: Adler, David Gray, and Robert George, eds. *The Constitution and the Conduct of American Foreign Policy*. Lawrence: University Press of Kansas, 1996; Henkin, Louis. *Constitutionalism, Democracy, and Foreign Affairs*. New York: Columbia University Press, 1990; Henkin, Louis. *Foreign Affairs and the United States Constitution*. Oxford and New York: Clarendon Press, 1996.

—Ernest Gomez and David Schultz

commerce clause

The commerce clause is one of the most important clauses in the entire Constitution in terms of granting powers to Congress. Throughout American history, various interpretations have been at the center of many disputes between the power of the national versus state governments.

The commerce clause, which appears in Section 8 of ARTICLE I OF THE U.S. CONSTITUTION, is quite brief: "The Congress shall have Power . . . To regulate Commerce with foreign Nations, and among the several States, and with the Indian Tribes." Despite its brevity, the commerce clause has been an important source of authority for Congress. The legislative branch has used this clause to regulate both commercial and noncommercial activities, though the Supreme Court has not always approved of all usages to which Congress has attempted to put this authority. In determining the permissible scope of congressional power under the clause, the Court has dealt primarily with INTERSTATE COMMERCE, but its explicit language also gives Congress prerogatives with regard to foreign commerce and commerce concerning Native American tribes.

The impetus for including the commerce clause in the Constitution was the economic turmoil that prevailed under the Articles of Confederation. Prior to the RATIFICATION OF THE CONSTITUTION, the central government had virtually no effective tools at its disposal to regulate the economic conditions of the nation. Individual states, however, were largely unconstrained in the pursuit of their own independent economic policies, even if those policies were harmful to the national economy. Among the most harmful were trade barriers intended to protect businesses native to particular states, barriers that interfered with interstate trade. The commerce clause firmly removed such power from the states and lodged it in the new federal government.

As the Court made clear in the 1824 case of *GIBBONS V. OGDEN*, 22 U.S. 1, congressional commerce clause authority is not strictly limited to commerce in the sense of buying and selling goods. Rather, it includes such things as navigation and anything else related to commercial intercourse.

In this seminal case, the Court also distinguished between interstate commerce and intrastate commerce, with the latter falling outside the purview of Congress. Though it asserted that commerce commencing within the confines of one state may nonetheless be part of interstate commerce if it is part of a larger transaction that ends in another state, the Court subsequently struggled with determining exactly when something intrastate rose to the occasion of being interstate in nature and thereby fell within the purview of Congress.

One distinction the Court originally relied on to make this determination was that between the manufacture of goods within a state and the subsequent transportation of such goods across state lines. For example, in *UNITED STATES v. E. C. KNIGHT CO.*, 156 U.S. 1 (1895), the Court declined to find that the commerce clause gave Congress the authority to take steps to bar monopolistic control over sugar refining. In adjudicating this case, the Court said that while the manufacture of a good did give the manufacturer influence on the good's later disposition (including possible disposition in interstate commerce), manufacturing is not the same as commerce and such incidental effects on interstate commerce did not bring manufacturing within the reach of Congress under the commerce clause.

The Court held similarly in *HAMMER v. DAGENHART*, 247 U.S. 251 (1918), when it found Congress had exceeded its authority under the commerce clause when it attempted to regulate CHILD LABOR. The challenged legislation prohibited the interstate shipment of goods made by children under the age of 14. It further prohibited the shipment of such goods across state lines if they were manufactured using children 14 to 16 years of age who worked more than eight hours a day. In rendering its decision, the Court expressed the view that permitting Congress to regulate local manufacturing conditions, even when what is manufactured ends up shipped interstate, would artificially enhance commerce clause authority at the expense of traditional state authority reserved to the states under the Tenth Amendment.

The Court developed a much more liberal understanding of congressional commerce clause authority through its stream of commerce doctrine. First articulated in *SWIFT & CO. v. UNITED STATES*, 196 U.S. 375 (1905), the stream of commerce doctrine was fully developed in the 1922 case of *Stafford v. Wallace*, 258 U.S. 495. Both of these cases dealt with challenges to the federal regulation of stockyards, which served as important conduits for the movement of livestock from farm to consumer. When a group of meatpacking companies joined forces to control stockyard prices, the federal government sought to break the alleged monopoly through the use of, first, the Sherman Antitrust Act of 1890 and, second, the Packers and Stockyards Act of 1921. In upholding these laws, the Court characterized the stockyards as "but a throat through which the current [of commerce] flows, and the transactions which occur therein [such as those between and among the ranchers, brokers, and meatpacking companies] are only incident to this current." In other words, though any given stockyard is located within the confines of a particular state, it is not the endpoint of the commercial transaction. Instead, the stockyards are part of a stream of commerce that is interstate in character and, accordingly, is properly within the authority of Congress to regulate under the commerce clause.

Through the early years of the New Deal, the Court reined in congressional authority under the commerce clause, striking down a wide range of legislation intended to address the dreadful economic conditions left in the wake of the Great Depression. For example, the Court struck down key provisions of the National Industrial Recovery Act (NIRA) as exceeding the confines of the commerce clause in *SCHECHTER POULTRY CORPORATION v. UNITED STATES*, 295 U.S. 495 (1935). At issue were codes intended to regulate working conditions and provide for sanitary slaughtering conditions in New York's chicken market. The Schechter Poultry Corporation did purchase large quantities of chickens from out of state through poultry dealers, but, according to the Court, that was an insufficient connection to interstate commerce to bring to bear congressional authority under the commerce clause. The Court found similarly in *CARTER v. CARTER COAL COMPANY*, 298 U.S. 238 (1936), a case challenging the regulation of working conditions and labor relations in the coal industry under the Bituminous Coal Conservation Act, the successor to the NIRA's coal codes.

Angered by what he saw as the Court's dogged determination to stymie the New Deal, President Franklin D. Roosevelt floated a plan to increase the size of the Court by one member for each member then serving who was 70 years of age or older. Ostensibly this proposal was intended to aid an overworked Court, but it was seen as a clear attempt on the part of Roosevelt to engineer a Court more conducive to his policies. Though Roosevelt was unsuccessful in securing legislative backing for his Court-packing plan, subsequent Court rulings were much more favorable to New Deal legislation enacted under the auspices of the commerce clause. For example, the Court upheld the National Labor Relations Act, which safeguarded collective bargaining rights for those working in the manufacture of products for interstate commerce, in *NATIONAL LABOR RELATIONS BOARD V. JONES AND LAUGHLIN STEEL CORP.*, 301 U.S. 1 (1937). Further, the Court upheld minimum-wage laws for those engaged in the manufacture of goods destined for interstate commerce in *UNITED STATES V. DARBY LUMBER CO.*, 312 U.S. 100 (1941), overruling *Hammer v. Dagenhart* in the process. And, the Court upheld regulations imposing farm production limits that included not only products intended for interstate commerce but also those intended for home consumption in *WICKARD V. FILBURN*, 317 U.S. 111 (1942).

Later, Congress sought to capitalize on the more expansive view of congressional power under the commerce clause represented by these cases from the end of the New Deal to address diverse social ills. For example, federal regulations requiring DESEGREGATION passed under the auspices of the commerce clause were applied to a small, privately owned recreational club in rural Arkansas in the case of *Daniel v. Paul*, 395 U.S. 298 (1969). The Court validated that application in part because a juke box and the records it played were manufactured out of state, and many of the snack bar items were made with ingredients that came from outside Arkansas. In *HEART OF ATLANTA MOTEL V. UNITED STATES*, 379 U.S. 241 (1964), the Court similarly upheld congressional action under the commerce clause to prohibit public accommodations from discriminating on the basis of race using the CIVIL RIGHTS ACT OF 1964. More recently, however, the Court has invalidated congressional attempts to rely on the commerce clause to prohibit guns in school zones (*UNITED STATES V. LOPEZ*, 514 U.S. 549 [1995]) and to make the federal courts available for civil remedies for crimes involving violence against women (*UNITED STATES V. MORRISON*, 529 U.S. 598 [2000]). In both of these decisions, the Court emphasized the requirement that there be more than an incidental connection to interstate commerce for an activity to be within the reach of congressional authority.

Throughout the Court's history of interpreting the commerce clause, alternatively enhancing and diminishing the scope of congressional authority, the Court has frequently had to balance congressional commerce clause authority against state powers. The Court's initial guidance on this point came in *COOLEY V. BOARD OF WARDENS OF THE PORT OF PHILADELPHIA*, 53 U.S. 299 (1852). The Board of Wardens, created by the state to regulate usage of the port of Philadelphia, required the use of local pilots to enter and leave the port. The owner of two ships challenged this arrangement, arguing that the state, through the Board of Wardens, was impermissibly interfering with interstate commerce by requiring the use of local pilots. In crafting its resolution of this case, the Court developed the doctrine of selective exclusiveness to govern state actions touching on interstate commerce. Under this doctrine, if national uniformity is necessary, then Congress has exclusive authority to regulate such commerce. If, however, the commerce in question is local in nature then the states may engage in regulation, though states may not burden interstate commerce in doing so. In short, while the commerce clause is a positive and explicit grant of authority to Congress, it is simultaneously a restriction on the authority of the states. The states may not burden interstate commerce in the regulation of intrastate commerce.

This principle is often referred to as the negative, or dormant, commerce clause.

In addition to granting Congress authority over interstate and foreign commerce, the commerce clause explicitly gives Congress authority over foreign commerce and commerce with Native American tribes. Early in the nation's history, Congress invoked its authority to regulate commerce with Native American tribes under the commerce clause, primarily to control trade between Indians and non-Indians. Later, Congress attempted to use the commerce clause to legislate regarding criminal activity on Indian reservations in the Major Crimes Act of 1885. Though the Court declined to invalidate the Major Crimes Act, it rejected the idea that the commerce clause granted Congress the authority to regulate the adjudication of internal criminal matters on reservations in *United States v. Kagama,* 118 U.S. 375 (1886). More recently, however, Congress has relied on the commerce clause as a broad grant of authority for regulating the Indian Nations. For example, Congress invoked, in part, the commerce clause as its authority for passing the Indian Child Welfare Act.

For more information: Cooke, Frederick H. *The Commerce Clause of the Federal Constitution.* Littleton, Colo.: F. B. Rothman, 1987; Frankfurter, Felix. *The Commerce Clause under Marshall, Taney and Waite.* New York: Quadrangle Books, 1964; Vermeule, Adrian. "Three Commerce Clauses? No Problem." *Arkansas Law Review* 55 (2003): 1,175–1,183.

—Wendy L. Martinek

commercial speech

Commercial speech refers to forms of communication that often include product or service advertising. This type of speech, while historically not protected by the FIRST AMENDMENT, has been given more constitutional protection in the last 30 years.

Advertising became a part of the national media during the colonial period; however, the extension of First Amendment protection to advertising and commercial speech took many years. Commercial speech is still a controversial and contentious area, with many Supreme Court decisions weaving between full protection and very limited protection.

In the early part of the 20th century, the Court did not allow any protection for commercial speech. In *Valentine v. Chrestensen,* 316 U.S. 52 (1942), a unanimous Court ruled that "purely commercial advertising" did not enjoy protection by the First Amendment. By the 1950s and 1960s, several courts began to chip away at the *Valentine* decision. In *Bigelow v. Virginia,* 421 U.S. 809 (1975), a case that involved the interstate advertising of ABORTION services, the Supreme Court ruled that while commercial speech did not warrant full First Amendment protection, truthful advertising conveying facts and information "of potential interest and value" did merit significant protection. The following year, in *VIRGINIA STATE BOARD OF PHARMACY V. VIRGINIA CITIZENS CONSUMER COUNCIL,* 425 U.S. 748 (1976), the Court ruled that state and federal agencies could police false and misleading advertising but expanded protection of advertising prescription drug prices. The Court ruled that prices were important information for consumers to have.

ATTORNEY ADVERTISING has always been controversial and was forbidden by most state bar associations until *Bates v. State Bar of Arizona,* 433 U.S. 350 (1977). That decision permitted attorney advertising as long is it was not deceptive or illegal and did not contain "misstatements . . . quite inappropriate in legal advertising." Numerous cases since then have strengthened the claims of First Amendment protection for legal advertising, although the Court upheld a Florida state regulation that prohibited lawyers from contacting hurricane victims for 30 days *(Florida Bar v. Went for It, Inc.* 515 U.S. 618 (1995).

In 1980, the Supreme Court established a test for commercial speech in the case *Central Hudson Gas and Electric v. Public Service Commission,* 447 U.S. 557. The Central Hudson test consists of four parts: 1) The message must be truthful, 2) the government interest in constraining the message must be legitimate or substantial, 3) the regulation must directly advance the government interest, and 4) there must be a "reasonable fit" between the restriction and means chosen to achieve the goal.

In recent years, the Court has applied the Central Hudson test to variety of different commercial messages including the advertising of alcohol prices (*44 Liquormart v. Rhode Island,* 517 U.S. 484 [1996]) and casino gambling (*Greater New Orleans Broadcasting Association v. United States,* 527 U.S. 173 [1999]). In both of these cases, the Court struck down laws that restricted advertising. In the *Liquormart* case, the Court ruled that the state interest (promoting temperance) was legitimate, but the means (prohibiting the advertising of prices) was too broad. In the *Greater New Orleans* case, the Court said the federal law that prohibited the advertising of private casinos was so riddled with exceptions that it no longer advanced the government's interest.

While the Supreme Court has expanded protection for truthful advertising, many regulations on advertising still exist. Five federal agencies regulate advertising in one form or another. The Federal Trade Commission (FTC) is generally responsible for false advertising claims. The FTC can use means from publicity to cease-and-desist orders to stop false advertising. The Food and Drug Administration polices product labeling. The Federal Communications Commission regulates compliance with the Public Health Cigarette Smoking Act of 1969, which prohibits cigarette advertising on radio or TV. The Securities and Exchange Commission enforces regulations on advertising stocks and bonds. Finally, the U.S. Postal Service polices false advertisement sent through the mail.

The governmental agencies at the state and local level can enact laws that regulate advertising. Cities have passed ordinances on what kinds of advertising can be placed on billboards close to schools or parks, and state gaming commissions can regulate the advertising that takes place in casinos.

False advertising is generally determined by two standards: specific dishonest claims and deceptive advertising. Dishonest claims are simply false statements about prices, quality, or conditions of products. Deception is more difficult to prove. The FTC uses guidelines that assume the consumer is a "reasonable person" who would probably be deceived in a material way by the advertisement taken as a whole.

For more information: Tedford, Thomas, and Dale Herbeck. *Freedom of Speech in the United States.* State College, Pa.: Strata Publishing, 2005; Sunstein, Cass R. *Democracy and the Problem of Free Speech.* New York: Free Press, 1995.

—Charles Howard

common law and the Constitution

Common law and the Constitution refers to whether there are general rules of federal common law that can be applied by the federal courts. While for nearly 100 years the U.S. Supreme Court ruled that such rules existed, that legal doctrine is no longer accepted.

The common law refers to unwritten rules of tradition and law that affect business and personal life; for example, many of the rules of contract and property law, as well as tort and personal injury law, are rooted in the common law. Common law is a feature of English law dating back to the Middle Ages. When the British colonized North America, they brought the common law to it. English common law was regularly enforced in colonial courts and, eventually, in the state courts after American independence in 1776. The question, however, was whether status should be given to the common law in the federal courts.

Under Section 1 of Article III of the U.S. Constitution, the Supreme Court and federal courts were given diversity jurisdiction to hear suits brought by citizens of one state against citizens in another. Yet, in hearing these cases, Article 34 of the Judiciary Act of 1789 declared, "the laws of the several states, except where the constitution, treaties or statutes of the United States shall otherwise recognize or provide, shall be regarded as rules of decision in trials at common law, in the courts of the United States." Thus, according to this act, the law of the states, including state common law, was to be applied in diversity suits in federal court. The question, though, in a diversity case, was which state's rules or common law to apply. The Court answered that in *Swift v. Tyson,* 41 U.S. 1 (1842).

At issue in *Swift* was what rules of common law to apply in a diversity case involving a contract law dispute. Justice JOSEPH STORY, writing for the Court, rejected the argument that state common law should always be applied in federal court. Instead, he ruled that the Constitution, specifically, Article III, Section 2, allowed the Supreme Court to apply general rules of common law when adjudicating disputes arising out of state courts. In effect, the Constitution recognized or allowed for the courts to discover and apply general federal rules of common law when particular local common law was not applicable or appropriate to use. Under this doctrine recognized in *Swift,* diversity suits in federal court would apply substantive federal common law to resolve cases while also applying or following state rules of civil procedure to determine, for example, what evidence the courts would be permitted to hear.

The *Swift* decision was applied for nearly 100 years. During that time period, it generated significant criticism as a result of its difficulty to apply. One problem was determining the line between local versus uniform rules, or when one should apply which. Another criticism was that the *Swift* doctrine led to the federal courts ignoring state courts or law. In other cases, it enabled situations where individuals who did not like a specific state law moved out of state and filed a diversity suit in order to challenge it. Overall, by the early 20th century, efforts to apply federal common law in diversity suits grew increasingly problematic.

Eventually, in *Erie Railroad v. Tompkins,* 304 U.S. 64 (1938), the Supreme Court overturned the *Swift* decision. Writing for the Court, Justice Louis Brandeis held: "There is no federal general common law. Congress has no power to declare substantive rules of common law applicable in a state whether they be local in their nature or 'general,' be they commercial law or a part of the law of torts. And no clause in the Constitution purports to confer such a power upon the federal courts." Because the *Swift* doctrine had proved to be unworkable and, more important, because there appeared to be no specific language in the Constitution granting a power to declare federal common law, the federal courts would no longer apply it when hearing diversity jurisdiction cases.

Erie Railroad v. Tompkins was a major decision. First, it is important for the proposition that the U.S. Constitution does not contain general rules of common law that can be applied by the federal courts. Second, it is important because it stated that in diversity suits, state law, including state common law, would be the substantive law that would be applied when cases were held in federal court. Finally, as a result of *Erie Railroad v. Tompkins,* the procedural rules of the federal courts in the *Federal Rules of Civil Procedure* would be applied in diversity suits.

For more information: Cantor, Norman F. *Imagining the Law: Common Law and the Foundations of the American Legal System.* New York: HarperCollins, 1997; Friedman, Lawrence M. *A History of American Law: Third Edition.* New York: Touchstone, 2005; Hazard, Geoffrey C., and Michael Taruffo. *American Civil Procedure: An Introduction.* New Haven, Conn.: Yale University Press, 1995.

—David Schultz

Communications Decency Act (1996)

The Communications Decency Act (CDA) was an initiative designed to protect minors from being exposed to obscene and indecent material on the Internet. Specifically, the act made it a crime to knowingly distribute sexually explicit content online that was patently offensive or indecent and not shielded from children who were under 18 years of age. As part of the Telecommunications Act of 1996, the CDA was passed by Congress on February 1, 1996, and signed into law by President Bill Clinton on February 8, 1996. In *Reno v. American Civil Liberties Union,* 521 U.S. 844 (1997), the Supreme Court ruled that the CDA was unconstitutional and had a chilling effect on free speech.

When passed, the Telecommunications Act of 1996 had seven titles. Six of these were a result of committee hearings. Title V—the Communications Decency Act—was authored by Senators Slade Gorton (Republican from Washington) and James Exon (Democrat from Nebraska) and was included in the Telecommunications Act as a result of amendments during floor debates and in executive committee after committee hearings had ceased. A prominent example includes a provision made by Representatives Christopher Cox (Republican from California) and Ron Wyden (Democrat from Oregon), referred to as Section 230, that held Internet service providers legally liable for the content posted online by individuals who use their Internet portals.

The CDA was perceived by some observers as a threat to free speech and FIRST AMENDMENT rights as guaranteed by the U.S. Constitution. Promptly after the act was signed into law, the AMERICAN CIVIL LIBERTIES UNION along with 19 other entities filed a lawsuit challenging its constitutionality. The plaintiffs argued that the CDA was too encompassing and would prohibit the free exchange of ideas among adults on the Internet.

Despite the government's claim of similarity, the Supreme Court noted differences between the need to regulate the content of terrestrial broadcasting versus the content of the Internet. When comparing the Internet with terrestrial broadcasting, the Supreme Court ruled that there was an important difference. Terrestrial broadcasting uses space on the electromagnetic spectrum, which justifies only limited First Amendment protection. In *Reno v. American Civil Liberties Union,* the Court determined that the Internet did not use a scarce spectrum. Unlike with terrestrial broadcasting, the Court reasoned that if parents did not want their children to have access to the Internet, then they were not required to subscribe to an Internet service provider.

The Federal Communications Commission regulates indecent and offensive speech on terrestrial broadcasting and limits material to safe harbor hours when children are not likely to be exposed to the material. In *Reno v. American Civil Liberties Union,* Justice JOHN PAUL STEVENS, writing for the Court majority, distinguished the Internet from terrestrial broadcasting by noting it can "be used to transmit text; [it] can transmit sound, pictures, and moving video images. Taken together, these tools constitute a unique medium—known to its users as 'cyberspace'—located in no particular geographical location but available to anyone, anywhere in the world, with access to the Internet." Furthermore, Justice Stevens noted that unlike "communications received by radio or television, 'the receipt of information on the Internet requires a series of affirmative steps more deliberate and directed than merely turning a dial. A child requires some sophistication and some ability to read and retrieve material and thereby to use the Internet unattended."

Although the Court protected the ability to transmit indecent and patently offensive material via the Internet, the Court did not protect the distribution of obscene material via the Internet. Obscene material is not protected by the First Amendment and may not be distributed via any mass medium. Justice Stevens wrote for the Court: "We are persuaded that the CDA lacks the precision that First Amendment requires when a statute regulates the content of speech. In order to deny minors access to potentially harmful speech, the CDA effectively suppresses a large amount of speech that adults have a constitutional right to receive and to address one another." In sum, the Court ruled that the CDA was overbroad. Justice Stevens asserted the "interest in encouraging freedom of expression in a democratic society outweighs any theoretical but unproven benefit of censorship."

For more information: Aufderheide, Patricia. *Communications Policy and the Public Interest: The Telecommunications Act of 1996.* New York: Guilford Press, 1999.

—John Allen Hendricks

compelling governmental interest

Compelling governmental interest refers to a test or set of objectives the government must offer in order to limit a fundamental right or to justify classifying individuals into suspect classifications. While there is no universal definition or catalog of what compelling interests are, the Supreme Court has articulated many of them over time.

As a rule, the Constitution and the BILL OF RIGHTS have created numerous rights and protections that the Supreme Court has found to be fundamental: The RIGHT TO VOTE, free speech, the free exercise of religion, and the right to HABEAS CORPUS are all deemed to be FUNDAMENTAL RIGHTS that generally cannot be ignored or denied to individuals. However, none of these rights is absolute, and instead, the Court has stated that there may be situations when it would be necessary to limit these rights in some way. For example, the right to habeas corpus may be limited in times of rebellion according to Section 9, Clause 2 of ARTICLE I OF THE U.S. CONSTITUTION.

In cases where there is a need to limit a fundamental right or use a suspect classification, the government must first assert the compelling governmental interest that it wishes to secure. It must then show that the policy or program it is using is the least restrictive means to securing its objective and that, finally, there is no other way of securing that objective except by the action it is taking. Overall, the compelling governmental interest test is very tough to meet, making it very difficult for the government to use suspect classifications, such as race, or limiting fundamental rights, such as the rights to free speech.

In *REGENTS OF THE UNIVERSITY OF CALIFORNIA V. BAKKE*, 438 U.S. 265 (1978), however, the Supreme Court held that the use of race for remedial purposes in AFFIRMATIVE ACTION was permissible in order to promote the compelling governmental interest of promoting educational diversity. Similarly, in *BUCKLEY V. VALEO*, 424 U.S. 1 (1976), the Court said that the compelling governmental interest of addressing political corruption or its appearance permitted the limiting of campaign contributions, even though the latter raised or implicated FIRST AMENDMENT concerns. Overall, the compelling governmental interest test is an important tool for weighing and protecting basic constitutional protections.

For more information: Gottlieb, Stephen E. *Public Values in Constitutional Law.* Ann Arbor: University of Michigan Press, 1994; Schwartz, Bernard. *A History of the Supreme Court.* New York: Oxford University Press, 1993.

—Stephen E. Gottlieb, Albany Law School.

Complete Auto Transit, Inc. v. Brady 430 U.S. 274 (1977)

In *Complete Auto Transit, Inc. v. Brady*, the Supreme Court laid out rules for how states may tax businesses that operate within their borders while also doing business in other communities. The problem the Court was trying to address in this case was what the Constitution permits when taxing businesses that operate in many states.

Complete Auto Transit, Inc., a motor carrier corporation based in Michigan, was transporting cars for General Motors to car dealerships within the state of Mississippi. Mississippi assessed a transportation tax on Complete Auto Transit, Inc., for a sum of $122,160.59. Complete Auto Transit claimed this violated the COMMERCE CLAUSE of Section 8 in ARTICLE I OF THE U.S. CONSTITUTION, which according to *Black's Law Dictionary*, "gives Congress the exclusive power to regulate commerce among the states, with foreign nations and with Indian tribes." The question before the Court: Did Mississippi violate the commerce clause by assessing a transportation tax on Complete Auto Transit, thereby placing an undue burden on the company, which, in turn, affected INTERSTATE COMMERCE?

The Court, in a unanimous decision delivered by Justice Harry Blackmun, concluded the tax did not violate the commerce clause of the Constitution; therefore, the tax was a valid tax. This case set four criteria as prerequisites that need to be met in order to determine whether a state tax is valid and does not cause an undue burden on interstate commerce. The criteria are as follows: The tax must be connected with some activity taking place within the state; the tax must be fair and apportioned based on intrastate, not interstate, commerce; it must be nondiscriminatory; and finally, the tax must be related to services provided by the state. Since Complete Auto Transit had benefit of services in the state (police protection, roads, etc.), the tax was related to services provided by the state. This decision affirmed the ruling of the Mississippi Supreme Court. The aforementioned criteria, according to the U.S. Supreme Court, are valid only if Congress has not instituted any law or regulation affecting such action. Therefore, the Court acknowledged that the state of Mississippi had a right to impose the tax, yet the supremacy of the national government to override such a tax was still a possibility and within the purview of the Constitution.

For more information: Farber, Daniel A., William N. Eskridge, Jr., and Philip P. Frickey. *Cases and Materials on Constitutional Law: Themes for the Constitution's Third Century.* St. Paul, Minn.: West Publishing, 1993.

—Dan Krejci

confrontation clause

The confrontation clause of the SIXTH AMENDMENT to the U.S. Constitution protects the right of criminal defendants to question personally the witnesses against them at trial in order to challenge the reliability of their testimony.

The Sixth Amendment states: "In all criminal prosecutions, the accused shall enjoy the right . . . to be confronted with the witnesses against him." This right ensures that criminal defendants can test, through rigorous questioning, the personal credibility of witnesses and the reliability of their testimony. This right plays an important role in the justice system's truth-seeking process by discouraging perjury and promoting truthful testimony.

The criminal justice system is an adversarial process in which the government has the burden of proving the defendant's guilt of the charged offense beyond a reasonable doubt. To that end, the government's prosecutor presents witnesses and introduces evidence in support of the government's case. The system is characterized as adversarial because the defendant has a right to question each witness and scrutinize each piece of evidence. The confrontation clause entitles the defendant to cross-examine witnesses in order to challenge their truthfulness and the trustworthiness of their testimony. Thus, the defendant's cross-examination may include challenges to the accuracy of the witness's perception, the reliability of his or her recollection, or his or her personal honesty. If a criminal defendant is not afforded an opportunity to challenge the testimony of his accusers and the witnesses against him, the testimony is not admissible at the defendant's trial.

Historically, the confrontation clause was designed to prevent the conviction of a criminal defendant based on written statements or depositions instead of live in-court testimony. Under English common law, written statements, affidavits, and depositions taken out of court were routinely used against criminal defendants at trial. The prosecutor was allowed to rely on such statements at trial even if the witness had an obvious reason to lie, such as the case of a witness who gave a statement in exchange for leniency regarding his own criminal charges. This practice was soundly criticized because it permitted convictions to be rendered based on statements from witnesses who were not subjected to any questions concerning their credibility or reliability. The out-of-court statements were allowed to stand as challenges to the defendant's own in-court protestations of innocence. The injustice of that situation inspired the framers of the U.S. Constitution to include the confrontation clause in the Sixth Amendment.

Generally, the confrontation clause applies only to statements that are testimonial in nature. Testimonial statements are solemn statements given affirmatively to establish a fact, and they are usually given during a formal, structured interview or a legal proceeding. For example, all of the following statements are testimonial: statements while a defendant is entering a guilty plea, affidavits and depositions given under oath, custodial interrogations by police officers, transcripts of prior in-court testimony, and out-of-court statements made in anticipation of use in a trial. Such statements, and those like them, are not admissible in a defendant's criminal trial unless the defendant had the opportunity to question the witness at the time of the statement and the witness is not available to testify at the defendant's trial. On the other hand, the confrontation clause does not prohibit admission of statements that are not testimonial. These statements are given in a casual setting and are not intended to prove a fact, such as casual comments or spontaneous exclamations. These statements lack the formality and structured context to be considered testimonial.

The U.S. Supreme Court has on many occasions decided cases that tested the parameters of the confrontation clause. Most notably, the Sixth Amendment was originally applicable only to criminal cases prosecuted by the federal government; however, in *Pointer v. Texas,* 380 U.S. 400 (1965), the Court held that it was applicable to the states through the DUE PROCESS clause of the FOURTEENTH AMENDMENT. Many other cases have addressed the scope of the protection afforded by the clause. In *Crawford v. Washington,* 541 U.S. 36 (2004), the Court held that the confrontation clause precludes from evidence the out-of-court testimonial statements of witnesses unless the witness is not available to testify at the trial and the defendant had a prior opportunity to cross-examine the witness, regardless of whether the circumstances of the statement make it appear to be reliable. In *Crawford,* the Court ruled inadmissible the out-of-court statement of the defendant's wife concerning the defendant's involvement in an altercation with the victim. That result was compelled by the confrontation clause because the defendant was deprived of the opportunity to cross-examine his wife.

In *Davis v. Washington,* 126 S.Ct. 2266 (2006), the Court examined the admissibility of the recording of a witness's telephone conversation with a 911 operator and the written statement of a domestic violence victim to an investigating police officer. The 911 recording was ruled admissible under the confrontation clause because it was not testimony but was made for the purpose of summoning emergency assistance to an ongoing crisis. The victim's statement to police was ruled inadmissible under the confrontation clause because it was given during a formal, structured interview and was intended to establish the facts of the assault being investigated; therefore, it was testimonial and inadmissible.

In a series of cases, the Supreme Court has recognized that the confrontation clause does not preclude admission in evidence of a statement made while the witness was in contemplation of death, known as a "dying declaration." Nor is the right to confrontation violated by the introduction of the prior sworn testimony of a witness from a proceeding during which the defendant had an opportunity for cross-examination. Another notable exception to the requirement of a face-to-face in-court confrontation was recognized by the Court in its decision in *Maryland v. Craig,* 497 U.S. 836 (1990). In that case, the Court approved a procedure that allowed a child witness, who accused the defendant of abuse, to testify by closed-circuit television from a room outside the courtroom. The confrontation clause was not violated because the procedure ensured the reliability of the testimony by requiring the child to testify under oath, allowing the defendant to cross-examine the child, and permitting the jury to see the child's demeanor. Finally, the Supreme Court has noted that a criminal defendant cannot use the confrontation clause as a shield to subvert the prosecution by causing a witness to be unavailable. Under those circumstances, the unavailable witness's out-of-court statement will be admissible against the defendant under the "forfeiture by wrong-doing" exception to the confrontation clause.

For more information: Garcia, Alfredo. *The Sixth Amendment in Modern American Jurisprudence.* New York: Greenwood Press, 1992; Heller, Francis. *The Sixth Amendment to the Constitution of the United States.* New York: Greenwood Press, 1969.

—Mark A. Fulks

Congress and foreign policy

Directly and indirectly, Section 8 of ARTICLE I OF THE U.S. CONSTITUTION gives or allows Congress a range of foreign-policy powers. These include the power to approve or reject nominations of ambassadors and other officials involved in foreign policy, to ratify or reject treaties with other countries, to regulate trade and commerce, to authorize and appropriate funds to maintain the armed forces, to declare war, to hold committee and subcommittee meetings on foreign-policy issues, to acquire additional territory, to approve foreign military sales, and to pass resolutions stating its foreign-policy position or in support of the president's. In the modern and contemporary constitutional history of the U.S. presidential system, congressional foreign-policy activity has generally been reactive to presidential initiative. Since the Spanish-American War (1898), Congress has rarely set the U.S. foreign-policy agenda.

Limitations on congressional foreign-policy-making began early. The Constitution of 1787 reinforced the political power of the slaveholding southern states in several ways. Legislative foreign-policy-making was restricted. Specifically, Congress was prevented from declaring the international slave trade illegal before 1808 (Article I, Section 9, Clause 1). Moreover, that clause was even shielded from amendment (Article V). At the same time, levying taxes of up to $10 per slave on transoceanic human cargoes was permitted (Article I).

Despite its constitutional power "to declare war" (Article I, Section 8, Clause 11), Congress is disadvantaged in shaping military foreign policy. First, the president is "COMMANDER IN CHIEF of the Army and Navy of the United States" (Article II, Section 2, Clause 1). Second, unlike countries such as the Philippines where senators are elected at-large, U.S. presidents are elected separately if indirectly by a far broader national constituency than any member of the national legislature. Third, Congress implicitly conflates declaring that a state of war exists with the executive decision to commit military forces to combat and thereby places an obstacle in the way of its opening up a formal discussion of whether a state of war should be declared. Fourth, while U.S. presidents have initiated military intervention abroad almost 200 times, Congress has simply let its constitutional power to declare war slip into disuse. It has not done so since June 1942, missing subsequent opportunities to lead national discussions of war and peace. And fifth, Congress has otherwise turned aside from opportunities to clarify its role. During 1916–35, more than a dozen bills and a proposed amendment requiring a plebiscite before declaring war failed to receive sufficient congressional support.

Late in the Vietnam War, discussions leading to passage of the WAR POWERS ACT (1973) raised expectations of a proactive Congress. Supporters of this legislation hoped that it would bridge the gap between congressional and presidential war-making powers by limiting unilateral war made by the chief executive. However, the final draft of the War Powers Act has not seriously limited presidential war-making. Replete with drafting errors, it fails to define *national emergency*. It does not state who is to decide when a presidential report on military intervention is required. Meanwhile, by referring to three different kinds of reports, only one of which involves a 60-day time limit, the War Powers Act allows the president to choose the type that suits his needs. Despite mandating consultation with Congress, the act does not say who in Congress must be consulted. And to stop presidential war-making, the act unluckily designated the "concurrent" resolution. Since concurrent resolutions cannot be vetoed, they were ruled unconstitutional in *INS v. Chadha* (1983).

Treaties are one way to formalize agreement in foreign affairs. Two-thirds of senators present and voting may give the president their "advice and consent" and "concur" in "treaties" proposed by the executive branch (Article II, Section 2, Clause 2). But since "all treaties" are also "the supreme law of the land" (Article VI, Clause 2), treaties share characteristics of statutes (a legislative product). Thus, treaties can become an understandable focus of contention between executive and legislative branches. President Woodrow Wilson's failure to elicit SENATE ratification for U.S. membership in the League of Nations resulted from such a clash, partly because of his unwillingness to elicit the "advice and consent" of key senators in early discussions of the proposed TREATY. Later, during the cold war, senators opposing two 1977 Panama Canal treaties signed by President Jimmy Carter tried but failed a year later to attach limitations on the treaties. But in a changed international climate shortly thereafter, Senate hostility to Carter's proposed SALT II Treaty with the Soviet Union led to suspension of ratification efforts.

U.S. foreign policy since the Civil War has been marked by presidential preference for international executive agreements. By the late 1920s, that preference was cumulatively overwhelming. Reliance on these paraconstitutional instruments extricates the executive branch from having to haggle for votes in the Senate. And the U.S. Supreme Court rejected a challenge to international executive agreements in *United States v. Curtiss-Wright Export Corp.* (1936). Yet congressional dissatisfaction on that point continued to grow during and after the presidency of President Franklin D. Roosevelt. Even so, several proposed constitutional amendments by Senator John Bricker in the late 1940s and early 1950s failed. In a different representative democracy, limitations in the *Konstitusyon* of the republic of the Philippines on the use of international executive agreements contributed to President Corazon Aquino's inability to push through the Military Bases Agreement with the United States in 1991.

Individual members of Congress challenged President Carter's withdrawal of U.S. diplomatic recognition from the Republic of China (Taiwan) in favor of the People's Republic of China with an ineffective court challenge in *Goldwater v. Carter* (1979). Rebounding with unusual unity, veto-proof majorities in Congress rebuked Carter by passing a Taiwan Relations Act stronger than the one he preferred.

The Senate also may approve or reject presidential appointments of the secretaries of state and defense, the national security advisor, ambassadors, and other officials involved in the formulation or implementation of foreign policy. Increasingly, members of the Senate have insisted on being consulted about nominations before they are submitted. And instead of voting to approve or reject a nominee, senators may also resort to filibusters and other delaying tactics in response to a politically objectionable appointment in the hope of causing it to be withdrawn. Even that may not be sufficient. A nominee whose approval has been delayed may be appointed on an interim basis during congressional recesses (Article II, Section 2, Clause 3). In the end, however, the Senate approves most foreign-policy-related nominees.

Although Congress is institutionally ineffective as an independent force in foreign policy, its individual members derive political benefit from targeting specific foreign-policy issues in committee hearings. There they investigate, criticize, and propose alternatives. Amending essential foreign-policy-related legislation—for example, requiring reports on human rights in specific countries—is another way to draw attention to issues. Also, with speeches reported by C-Span or other media, representatives and senators can pressure the president to clarify, defend, and occasionally modify foreign-policy initiatives. Thus, the administration of Ronald Reagan felt compelled to dialogue with noncommunist opponents of the dictator Ferdinand E. Marcos in the Philippines after the 1983 assassination of opposition leader Benigno S. Aquino, Jr.

Congress exercises the power "to regulate commerce with foreign nations . . . and with the Indian tribes" (Article I, Section 8, Clause 3). But if LABOR UNIONS anticipate that their members may lose jobs as a result of proposed trade legislation, then the legislative process can be contentious. The North American Free Trade Agreement would have failed without strenuous efforts by President Bill Clinton. On the other hand, congressional opposition weighed in President George W. Bush's choice not to support Russia's accession to the World Trade Organization in 2006.

Members of Congress have become president, usually first by being elected VICE PRESIDENT. Four of these former legislators are Harry S. Truman, John F. Kennedy, Lyndon B. Johnson, and RICHARD NIXON. However, the separation of powers in the U.S. presidential system prevents members of Congress from simultaneously holding cabinet positions, foreign-policy-related or otherwise. In contradistinction, the parliamentary systems of other representative democracies routinely allow members of national legislatures to serve in cabinet foreign-policy positions.

Separation of powers is incomplete, and the sharing of powers can create unexpected outcomes affecting foreign policy. When the ELECTORAL COLLEGE failed to produce a winner in 1824, Congress elected John Quincy Adams as president early in 1825 (TWELFTH AMENDMENT). Meanwhile, the vice president presides over the Senate and can cast tie-breaking votes on foreign-policy-related and other legislation (Article I, Section 3, Clause 4). And in 1969, for example, the Senate approved the Anti-Ballistic Missile system by a 51-50 vote. Conversely, in the Vietnam War, congressional approval of Representative Gerald R. Ford's nomination as vice president in 1973 indirectly affected foreign policy after President Nixon's forced resignation eight months later.

When public opinion opposes presidential foreign policy, Congress has additional opportunities to react, even if belatedly. For example, the Vietnam War left the United States divided more sharply than at any time since the Civil War. At the time, 18- to 20-year-old males were being drafted to fight in Vietnam. Eventually, in 1971, Congress proposed lowering the voting age in federal elections to eighteen (TWENTY-SIXTH AMENDMENT) while continuing to fund the war. And in the fourth year of the Iraq War, a divided Supreme Court rebuked the Bush administration for its treatment of prisoners detained at Guantánamo Bay in *Hamdan v. Rumsfeld, Secretary of Defense, et al.* (2006), leaving it to a Republican Congress to devise JUDICIAL REVIEW procedures consistent with "Common Article 3" of the four Geneva Conventions ratified by the Senate in 1949.

With the expansion of the RIGHT TO VOTE since 1787, individual representatives and senators in Congress remain susceptible to organized constituent influence on specific foreign-policy issues.

For more information: Currie, David P. *The Constitution in Congress: Democrats and Whigs, 1829–1861.* Chicago: University of Chicago Press, 2005; Dahl, Robert A. *Congress and Foreign Policy.* 1st ed. New York: Harcourt, Brace & Co, 1950; Fleming, Denna Frank. *The Treaty Veto of the American Senate.* New York: AMS Press, 1973; Hallett, Brien. *The Lost Art of Declaring War.* Urbana: University of Illinois Press, 1998; Henkin, Louis. *Foreign Affairs and the United States Constitution.* 2d ed. Oxford and New York: Clarendon Press/Oxford University Press, 1996; Holt, Pat M. *The War Powers Resolution: The Role of Congress in U.S. Armed Intervention.* Washington, D.C.: American Enterprise Institute for Public Policy Research, 1978.

—Vincent Kelly Pollard

Connecticut Compromise (1787)

The Connecticut Compromise, refers to the agreement reached at the U.S. CONSTITUTIONAL CONVENTION between large and small states resulting in the new constitutional "FEDERALISM." The primary author of the Connecticut Compromise was ROGER SHERMAN of Connecticut.

Sherman led a complex negotiation effort through summer 1787 at the Philadelphia Constitutional Convention, where delegates had been gridlocked between the large state plan, or the VIRGINIA PLAN, as proposed by Edmund Randolph of Virginia, and the small state plan, or NEW JERSEY PLAN, as proposed by William Paterson of New Jersey. The Connecticut Compromise combined elements of the Virginia and New Jersey Plans. States would receive two delegates each in the U.S. SENATE, and the number of members of each state in the U.S. HOUSE OF REPRESENTATIVES would be apportioned by population, the states thus being represented in the Senate and the people of the states represented in the House. In addition to these central structural features incorporated into the Constitution, the Connecticut Compromise included provisions for spending bills originating in the House and for the Three-fifths Compromise allowing for the counting of slaves in the apportionment of House seats.

The Connecticut Compromise enabled the Philadelphia convention to move forward and provided the crucial foundation of U.S. federalism.

For more information: Diamond, Martin. "What the Framers Meant by Federalism." In *A Nation of States.* Chicago: Rand McNally, 1974;

Rossiter, Clinton, ed. *The Federalist Papers.* New York: Penguin, 1961.

—Michael W. Hail

Constitutional Convention (1787)

The Constitutional Convention refers to the 1787 meetings called to revise the Articles of Confederation that ultimately resulted in the creation of a new constitution.

By the mid-1780s, many people in the United States recognized that the Articles of Confederation as written were not leading the country in a good direction. Some thought it lacked enough central authority to regulate commerce or foreign affairs, for example, or that it was to slow to respond to pressing issues. Because of these concerns, a convention was called to take place in Philadelphia to amend the articles. Each state was asked to send delegates to this gathering.

The convention was supposed to start in the middle of May, but it was not until May 25 that there were enough delegates (29) present to constitute a quorum. Eventually, 55 made it to the convention, with 29 becoming full timers. The voting on each issue was by state as was the practice in Congress. Until late July, when New Hampshire's delegation arrived, there were just 11 states represented. Rhode Island's legislature was controlled by those opposed to a stronger national government, thus, it did not send any delegates. One of the first issues to come before the delegates was the selection of a chair, and George Washington was unanimously selected to preside over the convention.

Pierce Butler from South Carolina proposed keeping the proceedings of the convention secret, and the delegates voted to do so until the convention was concluded. The idea was readily adopted and rigidly observed by the framers and was generally accepted by the press and public. JAMES MADISON thought the Constitution would never have been adopted if the debates had been public, and his sometime nemesis during the summer of 1787, George Mason, also believed this a necessary precaution to prevent misrepresentations of mistakes.

Madison spent months preparing for the convention, reading all he could find on the history of governments and related topics. While the Virginia delegation waited in Philadelphia for a quorum to congregate, they met and discussed Madison's plan in great detail. They decided that Virginia's governor, Edmund Randolph, would present the plan to the convention, as he had more stature with the rest of the delegates than Madison did. The plan, known as the VIRGINIA PLAN, eliminated the Articles of Confederation and established in its place a strong national government based on popular will.

The plan, also known as the large state plan, removed the state legislatures both structurally and in terms of power from any place in the new government. It established a national legislature consisting of two houses. The people of each state would elect the members of the first house, with representation based on the population of each state. The second house of the legislature would then be elected by the first. The national legislature would have the power to legislate in all cases to which the separate states could not and could nullify all laws passed by a state that contradicted the national legislature. This legislature would also elect a national executive, as well as create and select a national judiciary. This new plan for government would be ratified by the people through assemblies of delegates chosen by the people.

During the debate about the Virginia Plan, Madison and another avowed nationalist, James Wilson of Pennsylvania, almost drove the other delegates too hard in pushing uncompromisingly for this plan. Early debate on the plan favoring the large states focused on how the national legislature would be elected, the length of terms, and how the national executive would be able to negate legislation passed by the national body.

After the Virginia Plan was introduced, William Paterson of New Jersey, who recognized the weaknesses of the current national government under the Articles of Confederation, asked for an adjournment to consider it. On June 14 and 15, 1787, a caucus of small state delegates met to develop a response to the large state plan. Under the Articles of Confederation, each state was

We the People of the United States, in Order to form a more perfect Union, establish Justice, insure domestic Tranquility, provide for the common defence, promote the general Welfare, and secure the Blessings of Liberty to ourselves and our Posterity, do ordain and establish this Constitution for the United States of America.

Article. I.

Section. 1. All legislative Powers herein granted shall be vested in a Congress of the United States, which shall consist of a Senate and House of Representatives.

Section. 2. The House of Representatives shall be composed of Members chosen every second Year by the People of the several States, and the Electors in each State shall have the Qualifications requisite for Electors of the most numerous Branch of the State Legislature.

No Person shall be a Representative who shall not have attained to the Age of twenty five Years, and been seven Years a Citizen of the United States, and who shall not, when elected, be an Inhabitant of that State in which he shall be chosen.

Representatives and direct Taxes shall be apportioned among the several States which may be included within this Union, according to their respective Numbers, which shall be determined by adding to the whole Number of free Persons, including those bound to Service for a Term of Years, and excluding Indians not taxed, three fifths of all other Persons. The actual Enumeration shall be made within three Years after the first Meeting of the Congress of the United States, and within every subsequent Term of ten Years, in such Manner as they shall by Law direct. The Number of Representatives shall not exceed one for every thirty Thousand, but each State shall have at Least one Representative; and until such enumeration shall be made, the State of New Hampshire shall be entitled to chuse three, Massachusetts eight, Rhode Island and Providence Plantations one, Connecticut five, New York six, New Jersey four, Pennsylvania eight, Delaware one, Maryland six, Virginia ten, North Carolina five, South Carolina five, and Georgia three.

When vacancies happen in the Representation from any State, the Executive Authority thereof shall issue Writs of Election to fill such Vacancies.

The House of Representatives shall chuse their Speaker and other Officers; and shall have the sole Power of Impeachment.

Section. 3. The Senate of the United States shall be composed of two Senators from each State, chosen by the Legislature thereof for six Years; and each Senator shall have one Vote.

Immediately after they shall be assembled in Consequence of the first Election, they shall be divided as equally as may be into three Classes. The Seats of the Senators of the first Class shall be vacated at the Expiration of the second Year, of the second Class at the Expiration of the fourth Year, and of the third Class at the Expiration of the sixth Year, so that one third may be chosen every second Year; and if Vacancies happen by Resignation, or otherwise, during the Recess of the Legislature of any State, the Executive thereof may make temporary Appointments until the next Meeting of the Legislature, which shall then fill such Vacancies.

No Person shall be a Senator who shall not have attained to the Age of thirty Years, and been nine Years a Citizen of the United States, and who shall not, when elected, be an Inhabitant of that State for which he shall be chosen.

The Vice President of the United States shall be President of the Senate, but shall have no Vote, unless they be equally divided.

The Senate shall chuse their other Officers, and also a President pro tempore, in the Absence of the Vice President, or when he shall exercise the Office of President of the United States.

The Senate shall have the sole Power to try all Impeachments. When sitting for that Purpose, they shall be on Oath or Affirmation. When the President of the United States is tried, the Chief Justice shall preside: And no Person shall be convicted without the Concurrence of two thirds of the Members present.

Judgment in Cases of Impeachment shall not extend further than to removal from Office, and disqualification to hold and enjoy any Office of honor, Trust or Profit under the United States: but the Party convicted shall nevertheless be liable and subject to Indictment, Trial, Judgment and Punishment, according to Law.

Section. 4. The Times, Places and Manner of holding Elections for Senators and Representatives, shall be prescribed in each State by the Legislature thereof; but the Congress may at any time by Law make or alter such Regulations, except as to the Places of chusing Senators.

The Congress shall assemble at least once in every Year, and such Meeting shall be on the first Monday in December, unless they shall by Law appoint a different Day.

Section. 5. Each House shall be the Judge of the Elections, Returns and Qualifications of its own Members, and a Majority of each shall constitute a Quorum to do Business; but a smaller Number may adjourn from day to day, and may be authorized to compel the Attendance of absent Members, in such Manner, and under such Penalties as each House may provide.

Each House may determine the Rules of its Proceedings, punish its Members for disorderly Behaviour, and, with the Concurrence of two thirds, expel a Member.

Each House shall keep a Journal of its Proceedings, and from time to time publish the same, excepting such Parts as may in their Judgment require Secrecy; and the Yeas and Nays of the Members of either House on any question shall, at the Desire of one fifth of those Present, be entered on the Journal.

Neither House, during the Session of Congress, shall, without the Consent of the other, adjourn for more than three days, nor to any other Place than that in which the two Houses shall be sitting.

Section. 6. The Senators and Representatives shall receive a Compensation for their Services, to be ascertained by Law, and paid out of the Treasury of the United States. They shall in all Cases, except Treason, Felony and Breach of the Peace, be privileged from Arrest during their Attendance at the Session of their respective Houses, and in going to and returning from the same; and for any Speech or Debate in either House, they shall not be questioned in any other Place.

No Senator or Representative shall, during the Time for which he was elected, be appointed to any civil Office under the Authority of the United States, which shall have been created, or the Emoluments whereof shall have been encreased during such time; and no Person holding any Office under the United States, shall be a Member of either House during his Continuance in Office.

Section. 7. All Bills for raising Revenue shall originate in the House of Representatives; but the Senate may propose or concur with Amendments as on other Bills.

Every Bill which shall have passed the House of Representatives and the Senate, shall, before it become a Law, be presented to the President of the

Signed copy of the Constitution of the United States *(National Archives)*

equal, with each having one vote on all matters in Congress. In the Virginia Plan, everything was proportionate to population. New Jersey, New Hampshire, Maryland, Delaware, Connecticut, and even New York had grave concerns that Madison's plan would take equality out of the national legislature. Also weighing on some minds, particularly among the New Yorkers, was the belief that some southern states would soon be approximate in size to large states such as Pennsylvania.

The plan the small states presented to the convention on June 15 became known as the NEW JERSEY PLAN and was essentially a refutation of the Virginia Plan. It was, in fact, more along the lines of what the delegates were originally sent to Philadelphia to do, that is, draft amendments to the Articles of Confederation to ensure that government and country functioned properly. It expanded national power without totally eliminating the current system, and most important, it ensured one state, one vote.

The small state plan called for new powers for the existing congress, including the laying and collecting of taxes, a national executive who would serve one term and be subject to a recall based on the request of state governors, a national judiciary, and the idea that laws passed by the national legislature would take precedence over those passed by the states. On June 19, the New Jersey Plan was defeated 7-3, with one state delegation divided. Prior to the introduction of the New Jersey Plan on June 11, the delegates had overwhelmingly agreed that the lower house should be based on population and elected by the people.

By a 6-5 vote, the delegates had already rejected a proposal by ROGER SHERMAN supporting popular representation in the lower house and equal representation for the state in the upper house. Once the New Jersey Plan was defeated, the convention spent the rest of June on the compromise proposal regarding the makeup of the BICAMERAL LEGISLATURE. At the end of the month, Oliver Ellsworth of Connecticut reintroduced Sherman's motion. On July 2, that motion was defeated on a tie vote 5-5-1, and a committee, with one delegate from each state, was created to develop a compromise on this issue. The committee, led by Elbridge Gerry of Massachusetts, adopted Sherman's original proposal with the stipulation that money bills would originate in the lower house and could not be amended in the upper house. This compromise was vital to winning delegates such as George Mason of Virginia, Gerry, and Randolph to whom the new stipulation corresponded to the principle of no taxation without popular representation. On July 16, the convention voted in favor of the Gerry Committee Plan, also known as the CONNECTICUT COMPROMISE.

Once it was agreed that representation in the lower house would be based on population, the next question was whether slaves should be counted in the population of the southern states. Most northerners thought because the slaves were property, they should not be counted for representation. Wilson proposed what has become known as the Three-fifths Compromise. It provided that all free persons would be counted as well as three-fifths of "all other persons." The other part of this compromise was that this formula would also be used in fixing the amount of money to be raised in each state by any direct tax levied by Congress.

On July 26, the convention adjourned for 10 days so a committee of five could put into some form the resolutions that had been approved in the previous month. On August 6, when the Committee on Detail presented its product, familiar names and phrases that are in the Constitution started to appear. It was this committee who coined the titles *president* and *speaker* as well as the phrases *We the People*, PRIVILEGES AND IMMUNITIES, and *necessary and proper*. Substantively, the most important contributions of this committee were the enumerating of the powers of Congress for the first time and its dealing with a series of problems on state governments.

At the end of August, the delegates turned their attention to the Committee on Detail's proposal on the presidency and defeated four different methods of electing the president. Eventually, the delegates selected members to form a committee to settle outstanding issues. This Committee on Postponed Matters recommended to the convention the adoption of an ELECTORAL COLLEGE in which both the people and the states take part in the election of the president. The second most significant matter settled by this committee was the idea that the president must seek the "advice and consent" of the Senate when selecting members of the executive departments and the judiciary.

During the last days of the convention, the Committee on Style took the 23 articles that had been adopted by the convention and reduced them to seven. The most important single contribution of this committee was the PREAMBLE TO THE CONSTITUTION as it exists today, which is significantly different from the one written by the Committee on Detail.

There was no bill of rights in this document because the delegates never considered it their business to write a bill of rights for the whole nation. Furthermore, they thought there were sufficient protections for personal liberty throughout the text of the document. More practically, adopting a bill of rights would have added weeks to the convention.

When the convention convened for its final day, September 17, 41 of the 55 delegates were in attendance with 38 of them signing the finished document. Mason, Randolph, and Gerry refused to endorse the document with their signatures.

Article VII of the Constitution called for the document to go into effect once the conventions of nine states had ratified it. New Hampshire became the ninth state to ratify the Constitution in June 1788, with Virginia and New York following suit in the next five weeks. In September 1788, the Congress of the Confederation chose New York City as the temporary capital, and the new congress convened early in 1789, with Washington taking the oath of office of president in April 1789.

For more information: Bowen, Catherine Drinker. *Miracle at Philadelphia.* Boston: Little, Brown, & Co., 1966; Madison, James. *Notes of Debates in the Federal Convention of 1787.* Athens: Ohio University Press, 1966; Rossiter, Clinton. *1787: The Grand Convention.* New York: Macmillan, 1966.

—Mark Alcorn

constitutional interpretation

The power of JUDICIAL REVIEW raises the question of how courts should interpret the Constitution.

In his famous lecture on NEUTRAL PRINCIPLES, Professor Herbert Wechsler argued that in order to justify the exercise of judicial review, judges must distinguish themselves from political actors by applying neutral principles to cases. Drawing from Wechsler, some legal scholars and judges, such as Justices ANTONIN GREGORY SCALIA and CLARENCE THOMAS, have argued that the only legitimate method of interpreting the Constitution is to examine its text and history, which, in their view, best reflects the Constitution's original meaning.

Others, such as Professor Ronald Dworkin, contend that courts should interpret the Constitution in light of the fundamental principles underlying it, particularly when text and history are silent or equivocal as to a provision's meaning. According to Dworkin in his 1979 book, *Taking Rights Seriously,* it is up to each generation to determine meaning of the general concepts provided in the Constitution. Whatever one's preferred interpretive methodology, however, there is almost universal agreement, according to constitutional scholar Philip Bobbitt, that there are six methods (or modalities) of constitutional interpretation: text, history, structure, doctrine, ethos, and prudence.

The first method of interpreting the Constitution, and the most obvious given that it is a written document, is to examine the text. A textual approach to interpretation considers what the language of the Constitution means to "a person on the street." This "plain meaning" approach asks, What is the common usage of a particular term or phrase in a particular context? A textualist does not consider what the framers intended by their use of a particular term or phrase, nor does a textualist consider whether the common meaning of a term or phrase is wise or prudent. Prior decisions (precedent) interpreting a term or phrase are immaterial to the inquiry. A textualist may acknowledge that the common meaning of a term has changed over time, but the historical antecedents of a phrase do not control the inquiry, though they may inform it. In short, the present-day, plain reading of the text is paramount under this approach. The opinions of Justice HUGO BLACK embody this approach in cases such as *YOUNGSTOWN SHEET & TUBE V. SAWYER,* 343 U.S. 579 (1952), and *Adamson v. People of State of California,* 332 U.S. 46 (1947).

History provides a second method of constitutional interpretation. The historical method focuses on the original understanding of a constitutional provision as reflected in speeches or writings surrounding the provision's adoption. The difficulty with this approach to constitutional interpretation is that in the absence of a clearer record of what the framers of the Constitution or persons voting to adopt it believed, it is difficult to interpret authoritatively the Constitution based on history alone. For this reason, courts often rely on history to supplement or refute a particular reading of the Constitution derived at through other modes of interpretation.

Structural arguments are a third method of constitutional interpretation. Structuralists derive constitutional meaning from the structure of the text and the relationship between particular textual provisions. The theories of separation of powers, which concerns the allocation of power among the three branches of the federal government, and FEDERALISM, which concerns the allocation of power between federal and state governments—neither of which is expressly mentioned in the text of the Constitution—have been derived through structural arguments. Professor Charles Black, Jr., a renowned professor of constitutional law, was one of structuralism's greatest champions. Two criticisms of structuralism are, first, the process of inferring structural rules to be applied in particular cases is unprincipled, and second, structuralism cannot provide a firm basis for construing personal rights but rather is better suited for construing intergovernmental relationships.

Doctrinalism is the fourth method of constitutional interpretation. Over time, courts hear constitutional cases involving similar factual patterns. In adjudicating these cases, courts develop doctrines—rules, principles, and standards—that govern future decisions pursuant to stare decisis, or precedent (on how the court decided similar cases in the past). Doctrinal arguments are most prevalent in areas of constitutional law where there is no strong textual foundation. In SUBSTANTIVE DUE PROCESS cases, for example, the Court resolves controversies primarily by considering precedent, as in cases like *EISENSTADT V. BAIRD,* 405 U.S. 438, 453 (1972). The principal criticism of the doctrinal modality is that because the constitutional text is itself authoritative, the Constitution does not authorize courts to convert the text into judicial doctrines. Nevertheless, because the Constitution speaks in broad terms, many think that in order to apply the Constitution in a consistent and transparent manner, courts must create doctrines that govern future cases.

Prudentialism is the fifth method. Under this modality, courts consider policy consequences in interpreting the Constitution. Prudentialism is based on the premise that the Constitution is a practical document, not merely an expression of political philosophy. Justice Robert H. Jackson best expressed this premise in *TERMINIELLO V. CITY OF CHICAGO,* 337 U.S. 1, 37 (1949), when he claimed that the Constitution is not "a suicide pact." Accordingly, courts must consider the costs and benefits of their constitutional decisions. Prudentialism often gives rise to a highly pragmatic and economic approach to constitutional interpretation, such as the one endorsed by Judge Richard Posner. While many worry about the broad discretion courts exercise in weighing costs and benefits, prudentialism is nonetheless an oft-applied modality that has long been part of constitutional interpretation.

Ethics is the final modality. Courts interpret the Constitution under this modality by consulting the cultural values expressed in the Constitution. The most fundamental constitutional value is the notion that that the government has limited powers and that ultimate authority therefore resides in the individual. Ethical arguments are thus most common when interpreting the Tenth Amendment, which guarantees states' rights, and the FOURTEENTH AMENDMENT'S DUE PROCESS clause, which guarantees substantive individual liberties. Because ethical arguments are based on inferences from open-textured language, it is similar to the structural approach to constitutional interpretation. A significant difference between these modalities is that structural arguments infer rules from powers granted to governments, and ethical arguments infer rules from powers denied to governments. Ethical arguments are not to be confused with moral arguments, which simply reflect the moral or political values of the interpreter rather than those expressed in the Constitution itself.

In considering these methods of constitutional interpretation, it is important to remember that the methods themselves do not necessarily determine the content of a legitimate constitutional argument. Ultimately, where one falls on this issue is inextricably entangled with the recurring theme in constitutional law of how one conceives of the relationship between constitutional law and politics.

For more information: Breyer, Steven. *Active Liberty: Interpreting Our Democratic Constitution.* New York: Vintage Books, 2005; Tribe, Laurence H., and Michael C. Dorf. *On Reading the Constitution.* Cambridge, Mass.: Harvard University Press, 1991.

—Jesse R. Merriam and Andre Mura

Constitution in exile

Constitution in exile is a phrase employed by legal academics in a lively debate over the nature and legitimacy of constitutional jurisprudence pertaining to economic regulations—pre– and post–New Deal. The circumstances surrounding these debates are somewhat reminiscent of Winston Churchill's description of Russia as "a riddle wrapped in a mystery inside an enigma."

The basic puzzle pertains to the term, itself. Although agreement exists that it was coined by federal judge Douglas H. Ginsburg in a book review he wrote for *Regulation,* the libertarian Cato Institute's review of business and government, most parties to the debate who more or less agree with Ginsburg's policy views disavow the term. Ginsburg specified several doctrines that, in his view, the New Deal–era Supreme Court had ostracized so that they exist "only as part of the Constitution-in-exile." "The memory of these ancient exiles," Ginsburg continued, "banished for standing in opposition to unlimited government, is kept alive by a few scholars who labor on in the hope of a restoration, a second coming of the Constitution of liberty—even if perhaps not in their own lifetimes."

Is the "Constitution in exile" a movement, a straw man, or a red herring? The answer to these questions is consequential, hence contentious. Whether the Constitution in exile is portentous or an academic tempest in a teapot is hotly debated. Some like Cass Sunstein contend that the Constitution in exile is a rallying cry for law professors and judges who seek to restore what Sunstein refers to as "Hoover's Court," "the Constitution as it existed in 1932, before President Franklin Delano Roosevelt's New Deal . . . when the powers of the national government were sharply limited." Not so, reply others, such as David Bernstein and Orin Kerr. While there are law professors (and Supreme Court justices, among them ANTONIN GREGORY SCALIA and CLARENCE THOMAS) who lament the so-called Roosevelt revolution, individual misgivings do not make a movement. As Kerr suggests, Sunstein "is cherry-picking a few comments and imagining that these professors have real influence in order to create the impression of a major movement afoot."

Whether the Constitution in exile is a political agenda or is tantamount to Chicken Little's warning, long-standing, fundamental differences divide American opinion leaders and policymakers over legitimate relations between government and the economy under the Constitution. Judge Ginsburg identified this list of "exiled" constitutional doctrines and clauses: "the nondelegation doctrine . . . along with the doctrines of enumerated powers, unconstitutional conditions, and SUBSTANTIVE DUE PROCESS, and their textual cousins, the Necessary and Proper, Contracts, Takings, and Commerce Clauses." Taken together, these constitute what Edward S. Corwin called, in a seminal 1950 article, a "Constitution of Rights" (what Ginsburg called the "Constitution of liberty") versus a "Constitution of Power." The New Deal Court supplanted the former with the latter with the result that, in Corwin's words, "the Federal System has shifted base in the direction of consolidated national power."

For more information: Bernstein, David E. "Lochner Era Revisionism Revised: *Lochner* and the Origins of Fundamental Rights Constitutionalism." *Georgetown Law Journal* 92 (November 2003): 1; Corwin, Edward S. "The Passing of Dual Federalism." *Virginia Law Review* 36 (1950): 1; Ginsburg, Douglas H. "Delegation Running Riot." *Regulation* 18, no. 1 (1984): 83–87; "Special Symposium Issue: The Constitution in Exile." *Duke Law Journal* 51 (October 2001): 1; Sunstein, Cass R. "Hoover's Court Rides Again." *Washington Monthly* (September 2004), 35–36.

—James C. Foster

contempt of Congress

Although the Constitution does not explicitly grant Congress the power to punish contempt, broadly defined as actions that obstruct the legislative process, this power has been exercised by the Congress since 1795, with the approval of the judiciary in numerous cases. The power is recognized as an inherent power of any legislative body deriving from the practices of the British Parliament and the colonial and state legislatures and necessary for the ability of Congress to perform its work. In addition to its inherent authority to punish contempt, Congress has also passed civil and criminal statutes authorizing the courts to deal with contempt of Congress.

While several early cases of contempt of Congress sought to deal with attempts to bribe congressmen, most of the cases have involved efforts of congressional committees to compel testimony or the production of documents to further an investigation. The only serious limitation placed by the courts on the inherent power of Congress to punish contempt is the requirement that the matter must be within the sphere of Congress's constitutional responsibility, that is, the information being sought is the subject of possible legislation or oversight investigations. In *Kilbourn v. Thompson*, 103 U.S. 168 (1881), the Supreme Court disallowed what it saw as a probe into Kilbourn's personal finances, a rare instance of judicial interference with Congress's contempt power. When the courts are asked to punish contempt of Congress, they will apply individual rights as in any other criminal manner.

Congress has traditionally exercised its inherent authority to punish contempt by passing a citation for contempt and ordering the arrest of the offending party by the sergeant-at-arms, compelling his or her appearance at the bar of either the HOUSE OF REPRESENTATIVES or the SENATE where the individual faces trial by that body. In the trial, the accused has basic DUE PROCESS rights, including RIGHT TO COUNSEL and to confront witnesses. If found in contempt, he or she may be imprisoned for the duration of the congressional session. This procedure was found to be time consuming and unwieldy, and the last person actually imprisoned by Congress for contempt was William MacCracken, an attorney who allowed his client to destroy subpoenaed documents, in 1934.

In 1857, Congress passed a statute making contempt of Congress a crime, drawing the courts into the process of compelling testimony. The current version of the statute makes contempt of Congress a misdemeanor punishable by a fine of up to $1,000 and imprisonment for up to one year (2 U.S.C. Sections 192 and 194). Under the statute, Congress refers the matter to the attorney general to take before a grand jury. It is clear from the legislative history and subsequent practice that the statutory criminal process was meant as an alternative to trial in the House or Senate. When the courts are asked to punish contempt of Congress, they will apply individual rights as in any other criminal matter.

Prosecution for contempt of Congress becomes more problematic when a member of the executive branch is involved. In 1982, Environmental Protection Agency administrator Ann Gorsuch refused a subpoena for documents related to an investigation of the superfund under orders from the president. A contempt citation was passed by the House, but the Justice Department declined to pursue the case. As usually happens, a compromise was eventually reached, whereby the documents were provided to the investigating committee.

For the Senate a third alternative, a civil process, has been adopted, in which the Senate Legal Counsel is directed to seek a court order compelling compliance with the Senate's process. If the individual refuses, he or she may be punished for contempt of court, rather than of Congress (2 U.S.C. Section 288 and 28 U.S.C. Section 1364).

For more information: Fisher, Louis. *The Politics of Executive Privilege.* Durham, N.C.: Academic Press, 2004; Grabow, John C. *Congressional Investigation: Law and Practice.* Upper Saddle River, N.J.: Prentice Hall Law & Business, 1988; Rosenberg, Morton, and Todd B. Tatelman. *Congress's Contempt Power: Law, History, Practice and Procedure.* Washington, D.C.: Congressional Research Service (July 24, 2007).

—James R. Fox

contraceptives

A contraceptive is a device or method for preventing pregnancy. The conscious effort of individuals to control conception, regardless of its legality or social acceptability, is a constant in human history. Laws prohibiting the distribution of contraception or the distribution of information about it were a common feature of late 19th-century U.S. law. Anticontraception laws were of a piece with a range of American laws that regulated sexual behavior, personal relationships, and family life: Many states, for example, criminalized fornication, adultery, ABORTION, and homosexual acts.

Contraceptives did not become a subject of American constitutional law until the 1960s, when the laws of two states still prohibiting contraceptives (Connecticut and Massachusetts) were challenged. Two resulting Supreme Court decisions—*GRISWOLD V. CONNECTICUT,* 381 U.S. 479 (1965), and *EISENSTADT V. BAIRD,* 405 U.S. 438 (1972)—struck down Connecticut's and Massachusetts's anticontraception statutes, respectively, on the ground that they violated a constitutional right of PRIVACY. *Griswold* and *Eisenstadt* were the foundation for the Supreme Court's later holding in *ROE V. WADE,* 410 U.S. 113 (1973), that women have a fundamental constitutional right to abortion. More broadly, the Court's decisions on contraceptives influenced later Court decisions regarding personal and sexual relationships (for example, *LAWRENCE V. TEXAS,* 539 U.S. 558 [2003]).

In 1961, the Supreme Court dismissed an early case involving contraceptive legislation, *POE V. ULLMAN,* 367 U.S. 497 (1961), on procedural grounds. Two dissenting opinions, however, written by Justices JOHN MARSHALL HARLAN and WILLIAM O. DOUGLAS, argued that the Connecticut law at issue was unconstitutional. Four years later, the state's law was again before the Court, in *Griswold v. Connecticut,* and this time, it was struck down. Connecticut's law was particularly vulnerable to constitutional challenge: Connecticut criminalized the use of contraceptives. Any attempt by Connecticut to investigate violations of the law promised to be particularly intrusive and embarrassing.

Writing for the Court in *Griswold,* Justice Douglas determined that a constitutional right to privacy existed and encompassed the use of contraceptives. The Court's opinion featured Douglas's inventive and distinct argument that the right of privacy, while not explicit in the Constitution's text, exists implicitly, because privacy from government intrusion is a necessary condition for the existence and exercise of several of the BILL OF RIGHTS' guarantees. (In later right of privacy cases, the Court ignored this aspect of *Griswold*'s analysis, grounding the right of privacy in the FOURTEENTH AMENDMENT'S DUE PROCESS clause.) Justice Douglas's majority opinion in *Griswold* also contained broad language regarding marital privacy, including the suggestion that rights relating to marriage, like a type of NATURAL LAW, precede and transcend the Constitution.

While *Griswold*'s analysis of the existence of the right of privacy was quite broad, the right's application was quite narrow. Read closely, *Griswold* established only a right of privacy from government investigation and prosecution of the use of contraceptives by married couples.

The Massachusetts law challenged in *Eisenstadt v. Baird* was different from Connecticut's law in two important ways. First, the Massachusetts' law banned the distribution of all contraceptives except to married couples by a physician or pharmacist. Because the law did not prohibit contraceptive use, its enforcement did not necessitate the same degree of intrusiveness into the marital bedroom as Connecticut's law. Second, the law only prohibited the distribution of contraceptives to unmarried individuals.

The Court's majority opinion in *Eisenstadt*, written by Justice WILLIAM J. BRENNAN, JR., dramatically expanded *Griswold's* applicability. *Griswold*, as interpreted by Justice Brennan, was less about a right of privacy from government intrusion into the use of contraceptives and more about a right of autonomy in decision making about family planning. Furthermore, according to Justice Brennan, the constitutional right of *Griswold* was not a product of the marital relationship but was an individual right. As a result, the Court held that a state could not criminalize the distribution of contraceptives to unmarried individuals without violating the EQUAL PROTECTION clause of the Fourteenth Amendment.

In taking *Griswold's* right of privacy beyond its narrow factual foundation, *Eisenstadt* served as a bridge for linking rights regarding contraceptives to a constitutional right to abortion. In addition, *Eisenstadt* contained a sentence that suggested that the choice to have an abortion was a part of the constitutional right of "privacy" established in *Griswold*: "If the right of privacy means anything, it is the right of the individual, married or single, to be free from unwarranted governmental intrusion into matters so fundamentally affecting a person as the decision whether to bear or beget a child."

Note, however, that the Supreme Court worked on the *Eisenstadt* case during the time it was deciding *Roe v. Wade* (the Court decided *Roe* over two Court terms). *Eisenstadt* was written after a majority of justices, working on *Roe*, had determined that a constitutional right to abortion existed. In short, *Eisenstadt* did not influence the justices' decision making regarding abortion rights but rather served as additional justification for it.

In conclusion, the contraceptive decision *Griswold v. Connecticut* did not just impact constitutional doctrine but American politics generally. The decision inspired lawyers and abortion law reform activists to take a judicial path to victory, challenging state anti-abortion laws on constitutional grounds. In addition to waging state-by-state legislative battles, abortion law reformers, after *Griswold*, sought a more permanent, national victory grounded in a constitutional right of privacy/autonomy. Less than a decade later, in *Roe v. Wade*, they achieved it.

For more information: Garrow, David J. *Liberty and Sexuality: The Right to Privacy and the Making of* Roe v. Wade. Berkeley: University of California Press, 1994; Gordon, Linda. *The Moral Property of Women: A History of Birth Control Politics in America*. Urbana: University of Illinois Press, 2002; Johnson, John W. Griswold v. Connecticut: *Birth Control and the Constitutional Right of Privacy*. Lawrence: University Press of Kansas, 2005; Tone, Andrea. *Devices and Desires: A History of Contraceptives in America*. New York: Hill & Wang, 2001.

—James Daniel Fisher

contract clause

The contract clause of the Constitution was an important source of litigation in the 19th century, serving as a limit on the power of state and federal governments. Today, the contract clause appears to have very little effect on what state and local governments do.

In its original design, the contract clause was a supplement to Section 10 of ARTICLE I OF THE U.S. CONSTITUTION's prohibition of state-issued paper money as well as the protection of private contracts against state interference. In the early years of the republic, the Supreme Court took the contract clause to a different level, one that encompassed public contracts. In *FLETCHER V. PECK*, 6 Cranch 87 (1810), the Court had to decide whether a Georgia law annulling the previous legislature's act, which was a result of fraud and authorized the sale of state-owned lands, was a violation of the contract clause. Speaking for a unanimous Court, Chief Justice JOHN MARSHALL found that regardless of whether fraud was involved, in the original land grant law, the law annulling the original act violated the contract clause and was therefore unconstitutional.

The case not only represented a victory for the contract clause but also one for the federal judiciary: This was one of the earliest cases in which the Court declared a state law unconstitutional. *Fletcher v. Peck* laid the foundation for the Court's decision in *Trustees of Dartmouth Colleges v. Woodward*, 17 U.S. 518 (1819). The trustees of Dartmouth brought suit against the state for violating its charter by converting the school from a private institution to a public one. The Court agreed with the trustees by finding that the original charter was an "inviolable" contract, an actual property right, and any attempt on the part of the state to interfere with that contract was "repugnant" to the Constitution.

In the 1830s, the Court began to relax its stance on the contract clause. In 1785, the Charles River Bridge Company had been granted a charter by Massachusetts to operate a bridge. In 1828, the state granted another company, Warren Bridge, a charter to operate a bridge on the same waters free of charge. The Charles River Bridge Company sued on the grounds that per the original contract, it had a monopoly in the area and that Warren Bridge had impaired the obligation of the contract between Charles River Bridge and the state. In *Charles River Bridge v. Warren Bridge*, 36 U.S. 420 (1837), the Court, led by Chief Justice ROGER TANEY, disagreed and found that there was nothing in the original contract that gave Charles River Bridge a monopoly over the waters; therefore, the charter granting the building of a public bridge operated by Warren Bridge did not violate the contract clause.

Furthermore, Taney argued, since there was ambiguity in the contract as to whether a monopoly really existed, the Court should err on the side of promoting the public welfare. In this case, the community had a stake in the promotion of safe and cheap transportation. Taney also feared that advances in technology would be impeded if companies claimed that original (and old) contracts allowed them to stay in business. In a strongly worded dissent, Justice JOSEPH STORY found that the original contract granting Charles River Bridge a charter to operate the bridge (at cost) was clear in its scope and intent. He scolded the Court for ignoring years of precedent establishing the sanctity of the contract clause.

Politically, the decision was a victory for states' rights, and it marked the beginning of a trend for the Court—the idea that the state had the authority to exercise its POLICE POWER to protect the welfare of the community even if it meant that property rights (embodied in existing contracts) were voided. Although the decision in *Warren Bridge* was in favor of the states, Justice Story's dissent was just as much of a pitch for the contract clause as it was a pitch for the Court to hear cases arising from state courts. Story invoked the 25th section of the JUDICIARY ACT OF 1789, which provided for review of state supreme court decisions by the U.S. Supreme Court in cases where a federal law or the Constitution was involved. The states bitterly opposed Section 25 and repeatedly clashed with the Supreme Court over its implementation.

The contract clause as it applied to the taxation of state banks led to some of the most divisive battles over Section 25 of the Judiciary Act. On February 24, 1845, the Ohio General Assembly enacted a law to incorporate the Bank of Ohio. Section 60 of the act required the bank to submit 6 percent of its dividends to the state in lieu of taxes. On March 21, 1851, the General Assembly passed an act imposing a tax on all state banks. The Piqua branch of the bank argued that the tax was a violation of the original contract provided in the 60th section, an argument that was rejected by the Ohio Supreme Court. *Piqua Branch of the State Bank of Ohio v. Jacob Knoup*, 16 Howard (57 U.S.) 369 (1850), was brought before the U.S. Supreme Court by a writ of error issued under Section 25.

The U.S. Supreme Court reversed the decision of the Ohio court on the grounds that Section 60 was a binding contract. Speaking for the Court, Justice John McClean rejected the contention that the Court was bound to respect the construction of a statute by the highest tribunal of a state. McClean argued the Court had the right to review the statute and the state court's construction of the contract clause. Accordingly, if the construction of the contract impairs its obligation (as was the case), the Court was bound to reverse the judgment and protect the Constitution. In *Sandusky v. Wilbor,* 7 Ohio St. 481 (1857), and *Skelly v. Jefferson Bank Branch of Ohio,* 9 Ohio St. 606 (1859), the Ohio Supreme Court argued that Section 60 was not a contract under the U.S. Constitution and rejected the contention that state courts were subordinate to the federal judiciary. In response, the U.S. Supreme Court, in *Jefferson Branch Bank v. Skelly,* 66 U.S. 436 (1861), reiterated the contractual nature of the 60th section, as well as its authority to review and reverse the decisions of state courts.

Although the Supreme Court continued to clash with the Ohio Supreme Court over the contractual nature of the bank taxes, it became clear that the main issue at hand was not whether these taxes violated the contract clause. Rather, it had more to do with whether the state supreme courts had the final word over the construction of the contract clause and, by implication, the Constitution.

In the 20th century, the economic crisis brought on by the Great Depression forced the Court to revisit the contract clause and its relation to the state's police power. In 1933, Minnesota passed an emergency law under its police power temporarily allowing for extensions in protecting homeowners from foreclosures. The loan company argued that the law impaired the obligation of contracts set forth in the Constitution. In *HOME BUILDING AND LOAN ASSOCIATION V. BLAISDELL,* 290 U.S. 398 (1934), Chief Justice Charles Hughes suggested otherwise. He argued that the contract clause was not to be applied with "literal exactness, like a mathematical formula." Rather, it was to be construed broadly and in conjunction with the reserved power of the states to protect the vital interests of the community, especially in an emergency. He also argued that "great clauses" in the Constitution were not to be narrowly construed so as not to adapt to changing circumstances. Hughes cited one of John Marshall's famous phrases: "[W]e must never forget that it is a *constitution* we are expounding . . . a constitution intended to endure for ages to come, and, consequently, to be adapted to the various crises of human affairs" (*MCCULLOCH V. MARYLAND,* 4 Wheaton 316 [1819]). The decision of the Court, in effect, marked the demise of the contract clause.

For more information: Cushman, Barry. *Rethinking the New Deal Court: The Structure of a Constitutional Revolution.* New York: Oxford University Press, 1998; Magrath, C. Peter. *Yazoo: Law and Politics in the New Republic.* Providence, R.I.: Brown University Press, 1966.

—Randa Issa

Cooley, Thomas (1824–1898) *legal scholar*
Thomas Cooley, a renowned legal scholar, argued that the U.S. Constitution contained not only direct limitations on the power of the states but also implied limitations that could be deduced from the political theory underlying the Constitution.

Born near Attica, New York, Cooley completed his legal studies in Adrian, Michigan, and settled in the state. The Michigan senate chose Cooley to compile the state statutes in 1857. The post proved to be a stepping-stone to official reporter of the state supreme court. In 1865, Cooley was elected on the Republican ticket as a justice of the Michigan Supreme Court. He remained on this bench until 1885. During his tenure, the Michigan court became one of the most influential in the country.

Meanwhile, Cooley had joined the newly formed law department at the University of Michigan in 1859 and remained a member of the law faculty until 1884. In 1887, Cooley agreed to serve on the INTERSTATE COMMERCE COMMISSION and became chair. Ill health forced his retirement from public life in 1891. Cooley died in Ann Arbor, Michigan.

Despite his distinguished public service and teaching, Cooley is best known for his writing. His *A Treatise on the Constitutional Limitations Which Rest upon the Legislative Power of the States* (1868) appeared in eight editions, with the last in 1927. The book, for many years, was the best available reference work on state constitutional law and brought order out of the confusion inherent in having a large number of separate, although basically similar, constitutional systems. Cooley emphasized limitations upon power rather than power itself, a popular view in the second half of the 19th century. The courts in this era were generally inclined to accept the principles that restricted legislative power rather than those that sustained it.

Among the principles that owe part of their development to Cooley is LIBERTY OF CONTRACT. In the 1884 edition of the *Limitations,* Cooley listed the right to make contracts among the five natural rights. To date, the doctrine has yet to receive unqualified judicial approval. Cooley also attacked class legislation as a violation of the DUE PROCESS guarantee in passages that were widely quoted. He wrote that a legislature which provides that persons following a lawful trade or employment do not have the capacity to make contracts thereby deprives these people of liberty that is of primary importance to their right to the pursuit of happiness.

Cooley's most notable contribution came with his emphasis on due process as a substantive limitation upon legislative powers. His work played a highly influential role in the early interpretation of the due process clause of the FOURTEENTH AMENDMENT to the Constitution as a support for laissez-faire principles.

For more information: Jacobs, Clyde E. *Law Writers and the Courts: The Influence of Thomas M. Cooley, Christopher G. Tiedeman, and John F. Dillon Upon American Constitutional Law.* Berkeley: University of California Press, 1954.

—Caryn E. Neumann

Cooley v. Board of Wardens of the Port of Philadelphia 53 U.S. 299 (1851)

In *Cooley v. Board of Wardens of the Port of Philadelphia,* the Supreme Court laid out some important rules of FEDERALISM that gave states the authority to regulate local affairs and local issues. In reaching this decision, the Court appeared to place some limits on the COMMERCE CLAUSE authority of the national government.

Pennsylvania passed a law in 1803 that mandated ships entering or leaving Philadelphia's port to retain a local pilot to guide the ship through and out of the harbor. If a ship did not comply, a penalty would be assessed, and the proceeds would be placed in a fund to be used for retired pilots and their dependents. However, a ship leaving (or entering) the harbor would appear to be in INTERSTATE COMMERCE, which Section 8 of ARTICLE I OF THE U.S. CONSTITUTION states is a power of Congress: "The Congress shall have the power . . . To regulate commerce . . . among the several States."

This would seem to suggest that Philadelphia's board was in violation of the commerce clause, but another act of Congress, passed in 1789, stated: ". . . all pilots in the bays, inlets, rivers, harbors, and ports in the United States shall continue to be regulated in conformity with the existing laws of the states . . . until further legislative provision shall be made by Congress." Cooley was a shipowner who refused to hire a local pilot and refused to pay the fine. He argued that the board's policies violated the commerce clause. The Supreme Court defined the question in this case as ". . . whether the grant of the commercial power to Congress did *per se* deprive the States of all power to regulate pilots."

With Justices John McLean and James Moore Wayne in dissent and Justice Daniel concurring in the result but disagreeing with the logic, the majority held that the Pennsylvania law was constitutional. Justice Benjamin Curtis delivered the majority opinion.

The heart of his opinion is the "local-national" distinction. Curtis's words speak clearly to this distinction:

> Whatever subjects of this power [from the commerce clause] are in their nature national, or admit of only one uniform system, or plan of regulation, may justly be said to be of such a nature as to require exclusive legislation by Congress. That this cannot be affirmed of laws for the regulation of pilots and pilotage is plain. The act of 1789 contains a clear and authoritative declaration by the first Congress, that the nature of this subject is such, that until Congress should find it necessary to exert its powers, it should be left to the legislation of the States; that it is local and not national.

The key point of the decision was that Congress can allow the states to handle the purely local aspects of interstate commerce until that body explicitly exercises its power under the commerce clause. According to some legal scholars, the case offers two possible ways to read the commerce clause: The congressional commerce clause power is exclusive and that states lacked all authority to regulate commerce, or in the absence of congressional legislation, the commerce clause imposed no limits on the states.

Cooley is important because it advances the argument that the commerce clause is not an "all or none" principle; that is, there is some role for state regulation of commerce if the subject is local and if Congress has not assumed jurisdiction over the subject (in this instance, pilots). At the same time, it affirms that the commerce clause provides great leverage for Congress on such matters. Some suggest that this is a harbinger of later "balancing tests" in Supreme Court decision making.

For more information: Gunther, Gerald. *Constitutional Law.* 12th ed. New York: Foundation Press, 1991.

—Steven A. Peterson

Cooper v. Aaron 38 U.S. 1 (1958)

In *Cooper v. Aaron,* the Supreme Court ruled that state officials must obey court orders resting on the Supreme Court's authority to interpret the Constitution. This case is important because the Court rejected a serious challenge to its authority and reaffirmed its commitment to integration.

In 1957, Governor Orval Faubus of Arkansas encouraged disobedience to court orders to integrate schools by calling out the state's National Guard to prevent African-American children from entering Central High School in Little Rock. As a result of his actions, President Dwight Eisenhower sent in army troops to enforce the order and protect the children. Due to these troubles, the Little Rock School Board asked the courts for a two-and-a-half-year delay in desegregating their schools. The district court agreed but the Eighth Circuit reversed. The Supreme Court, in an unusual move, expedited hearings by holding oral arguments three days after granting review and issued a decision the very next day ordering the school board to integrate.

To underscore their unanimity, all justices signed the opinion rejecting the claim that states have a right, equal to the courts, to interpret the Constitution and reaffirming the order to desegregate schools. While the Court admitted that Little Rock had had problems resulting from DESEGREGATION, the trouble resulted directly from the actions of state officials. This was contrary to the FOURTEENTH AMENDMENT, which states that no "State" shall deny to any person EQUAL PROTECTION of the laws. The state of Arkansas, by resisting desegregation, was doing that and had to stop.

In response to Governor Faubus's claim that Arkansas is not bound by the Court, the Court reminded Faubus that Article VI of the Constitution declares the Constitution the "supreme Law of the Land" and that, as Chief Justice JOHN MARSHALL had said in *MARBURY V. MADISON,* 1 Cr. 137 (1803), "It is emphatically the province and duty of the Supreme Court to say what the law is." This principle had been respected by the Court and country ever since and is fundamental to the constitutional system. Further, the Court pointed out that state officials take an oath to support the Constitution and any official who refuses to obey a court order violates that oath. Finally, the Court pointed out that even with the addition of three new justices since *BROWN V. BOARD OF EDUCATION*

OF TOPEKA, 349 U.S. 483 (1954), the Court is still unanimous in its view that *Brown* was correctly decided.

In a concurring opinion, Justice Felix Frankfurter chastised his former law students from Harvard who were leading members of the bar in the South for opposing the Court. He reminded them that rejecting the rule of law leads to anarchy.

Overall, this case marked the end of the Court's patience in waiting on southern states to accept *Brown* and begin to desegregate. In a series of cases over the next 20 years, the Court began the implementation of integration through busing, rearranging school zones, and other measures.

For more information: Freyer, Tony. *The Little Rock Crisis.* Westport, Conn.: Greenwood Press, 1984; Klarman, Michael. *From Jim Crow to Civil Rights.* Oxford and New York: Oxford University Press, 2004; Patterson, James T. Brown v. Board of Education: *A Civil Rights Milestone and Its Troubled Legacy.* Oxford and New York: Oxford University Press, 2002.

—Sean Evans

Coppage v. Kansas 236 U.S. 1 (1915)

In *Coppage v. Kansas,* the Supreme Court found the state of Kansas had acted unconstitutionally in passing a law banning "yellow dog" contracts. The law in question prevented employers from requiring employees to sign an agreement stating they would not join a union.

T. B. Coppage was convicted of violating the Kansas law and appealed to the Supreme Court on grounds that the statute violated freedom of contract protected by the DUE PROCESS clause of the FOURTEENTH AMENDMENT. The Court stated that legitimate exercises of the state POLICE POWER could restrict freedom of contract, but there was no relationship in this case between the statute's purpose and the state's police-power goal.

According to the facts described in the majority opinion, an individual named Hedges was employed as a switchman by the St. Louis & San Francisco Railway Company in July 1911. Hedges was also a member of a labor organization called the Switchmen's Union of North America. The plaintiff, Coppage, was employed by the railway company as superintendent, and as such, he requested Hedges to sign an agreement stating he would withdraw from the Switchmen's Union. If Hedges refused to sign the agreement, he was told, he could no longer remain an employee of the company. Hedges refused to sign the agreement or withdraw from the labor organization and was thus fired by Superintendent Coppage.

The majority opinion, written by Justice Mahlon Pitney, approached the constitutional questions of *Coppage* from the precedent of *Adair v. United States,* 208 U.S. 191 (1908). In *Adair,* Justice JOHN MARSHALL HARLAN argued that it is important to preserve the balance of freedoms that exists between employers and employees: "The right of a person to sell his labor upon such terms as he deems proper is . . . the same as the right of the purchaser of labor to prescribe the conditions upon which he will accept such." In other words, the law violated the liberties of both employers and employees as it compelled them to accept certain conditions in the purchasing and selling of labor. Following the logic of *Adair,* Justice Pitney wrote: "if it be unconstitutional for Congress to deprive an employer of liberty or property for threatening an employee with loss of employment, or discriminating against him because of his membership in a labor organization, it is unconstitutional for a state to similarly punish an employer." The judgment of the lower court was thus reversed.

In addition to the majority, Justice OLIVER WENDELL HOLMES, JR., and Justice William R. Day, along with Justice Charles Evans Hughes, issued separate dissenting opinions. Justice Holmes argued that the Constitution does not explicitly prohibit the Kansas law and that *Adair* and *LOCHNER V. NEW YORK,* 198 U.S. 45 (1905), should be overturned, while Justices Day and Hughes commented that they believed the law did not go beyond a legitimate exercise of the police power.

For more information: Schwartz, Bernard. *A History of the Supreme Court.* Oxford and New York: Oxford University Press, 1993.

—Erika N. Cornelius

Corfield v. Coryell 4 Wash. (C.C. 3d) 6 Fed. Cas. 546, No. 3,230 C.C.E.D.Pa. (1823)

Corfield v. Coryell is an important lower court case explaining what *PRIVILEGES AND IMMUNITIES* means in Article IV, Section 2 of the Constitution.

Corfield v. Coryell upheld a New Jersey statute that prohibited nonresidents from harvesting oysters and established terms of forfeiture for vessels so employed. The owner of a vessel accordingly seized contended that the act violated Congress's power to "regulate Commerce . . . among the several States" (Article I, Section 8), the "Privileges and Immunities" clause (Article IV, Section 2), and the Constitution's grant of admiralty and maritime jurisdiction to "the judicial Power" of the United States (Article III, Section 2). Sitting as circuit justice, Bushrod Washington articulated without reference to the BILL OF RIGHTS a broad and substantive interpretation of the privileges and immunities clause, which, nonetheless, did not include the right to harvest oysters.

Addressing the first claim, Washington relied on *GIBBONS V. OGDEN*, 9 Wheat. 22 U.S. 1 (1824), to distinguish between Congress's sole authority to legislate INTERSTATE COMMERCE (Article I, Section 8) and the right retained by states to legislate on subjects within the states, even if such legislation "may indirectly and remotely affect commerce" (4 Wash. [C.C. 3d], 502 [1823]). The act limited oyster harvesting but did not interfere with the free use of the waters for commercial intercourse or trade and thus did not constitute a regulation of interstate commerce.

Washington rejected also the claim that the act violated Article III, Section 2, which, in extending the federal judicial power to cases of admiralty and maritime jurisdiction, removes such cases from the jurisdiction of state courts. The states' power to regulate their fisheries was exclusive when the Constitution was adopted and had not been surrendered to the federal government by Article III, Section 2.

The critical importance of *Corfield v. Coryell*, however, lies in its interpretation of the Constitution's guarantee that "The Citizens of each State shall be entitled to all Privileges and Immunities of Citizens in the several States" (Article IV, Section 2). Addressing for the first time what those privileges and immunities were, Washington identified them as those "which are, in their nature, fundamental; which belong, of right, to the citizens of all free governments; and which have, at all times, been enjoyed by the citizens of the several states which compose this Union" (4 Wash. [C.C. 3d], 503 [1823]). Observing that "what these fundamental principles are, it would perhaps be more tedious than difficult to enumerate," he nevertheless provided a general overview: "Protection by the government; the enjoyment of life and liberty, with the right to acquire and possess property of every kind, and to pursue and obtain happiness and safety; subject nevertheless to such restraints as the government may justly prescribe for the general good of the whole" (4 Wash. [C.C. 3d], 503 [1823]). Deriving from these principles were rights, including that of interstate travel and relocation, the benefit of HABEAS CORPUS, access to state courts, nonpunitive taxation, the franchise as regulated by state law, and "many others." Washington flatly denied, however, that the clause guaranteed to nonresidents all the privileges enjoyed by residents, holding that New Jersey could regulate its common property in a manner discriminatory to nonresidents.

Washington's central holding, that citizens possess FUNDAMENTAL RIGHTS not enumerated in the Bill of Rights but that states may not abridge, would resurface repeatedly in the debates surrounding the FOURTEENTH AMENDMENT, the Civil Rights Act of 1866, and INCORPORATION.

In addition to *Corfield v. Coryell*, two other cases have offered interpretations of the privileges and immunities clause of the Constitution or the privileges or immunities clause of Section 1 of the Fourteenth Amendment. In the *BUTCHER'S BENEVOLENT ASSOCIATION V. CRESCENT CITY LIVE-STOCK LANDING AND SLAUGHTER-HOUSE CO.* (The *Slaughterhouse Cases*), 83 U.S. (16 Wall.) 36 (1873), the Supreme Court rejected claims that the Fourteenth Amendment protected independent butchers from a law that required all animal slaughters to take place in one facility. In dissent, Justice Stephen J. Field contended that the privileges or immunities clause of the Fourteenth Amendment protected the right of butchers to pursue their occupation. Finally, in *Saenz v. Roe*, 526 U.S. 489 (1999), the Supreme Court found that the right of interstate travel is one of the rights protected by the privileges or immunities clause.

For more information: Bogen, David S. *Privileges and Immunities: A Reference Guide to the United States Constitution*. Westport, Conn.: Praeger/Greenwood, 2003; Harrison, John. "Reconstructing the Privileges and Immunities Clause." *Yale Law Journal* 101, no. 7 (1992): 1,385–1,474; Meyers, W. J. "The Privileges and Immunities of Citizens in the Several States." *Michigan Law Review* 1, no. 4 (1903): 286–315; Simson, Gary J. "Discrimination Against Nonresidents and the Privileges and Immunities Clause of Article IV." *University of Pennsylvania Law Review* 28, no. 2 (1979): 379–401.

—Lorna M. Dawson

countermajoritarianism

Countermajoritarianism in the Supreme Court occurs when the Court decides to overturn legislation passed by Congress or a state or local legislative body. The act of declaring legislation unconstitutional through JUDICIAL REVIEW is countermajoritarian because it effectively negates the will of the majority. Pieces of legislation, far more than judicial decrees, represent the policy choices of the majority because they are drafted by elected officials rather than appointed, lifetime-tenured justices. The "countermajoritarian difficulty" posed by judicial review, as ALEXANDER MORDECAI BICKEL describes in *The Least Dangerous Branch* (1962), requires us to balance democratic values against the Court's legacy of preserving the Constitution.

While some argue that the countermajoritarianism of the Supreme Court is a result of its efforts to protect minority rights from being abused by the majority, this countermajoritarian conundrum has sparked what Barry Friedman refers to as an "academic obsession." Scholars question whether the Court is truly countermajoritarian. Robert Dahl argues in *Decision-Making in a Democracy* (1962) that judicial review does not truly present a countermajoritarian threat. Dahl looks at instances where the Supreme Court overturns federal legislation within four years of enactment and finds that in very few instances did the Court rule federal legislation unconstitutional. The Court appeared to behave in a countermajoritarian fashion during political transitions where the judiciary served as the keeper of the prior regime's policy preferences. Court appointments, argues Dahl, permit presidents to quickly realign the Court to reflect current majority concerns.

Conversely, Jonathon Casper argues that by limiting his analysis to federal legislation and judicial review, Dahl misses a significant percentage of the Court's countermajoritarian actions. For instance, when the Court is called upon to interpret rather than constitutionally review statutes, the Court may undermine the majority's legislative intent. The Court is also asked to determine the meaning and/or constitutionality of state legislation. When the Court issues a decision that invalidates a state statute, the effect may be felt nationally. For example, the Court's SCHOOL PRAYER decisions invalidating state and local school prayer practices could be considered prime examples of countermajoritarian behavior.

Scholars also examine the relationship between Court decisions and public opinion when searching for signs of countermajoritarian tendencies. William Mishler and Reginald Sheehan look at how and to what degree the Court responds to trends in public opinion. They suspect that Supreme Court justices gradually modify their decisions to reflect majoritarian concerns over the long run. Specifically, they find that the Court requires approximately five years to bring their decisions in sync with public attitudes.

Finally, Mark Graber argues that judicial review may be considered nonmajoritarian. In many instances, the Court is asked by a divisive majority to resolve controversial issues. In this sense, then, judicial review involves the reversal of policies for which there is no majority consensus.

For more information: Adamany, David W., and Joel B. Grossman. "Support for the Supreme

Court as a National Policymaker." *Law and Policy Quarterly* 5 (1983): 405–437; Bickel, Alexander. *The Least Dangerous Branch: The Supreme Court at the Bar of Politics.* New Haven, Conn.: Yale University Press, 1986; Casper, Jonathon. "The Supreme Court and National Policymaking." *APSR* 70 (1976): 5,066; Dahl, Robert. *Decision-Making in a Democracy: The Supreme Court as a National Policy-Maker.* New York: Irvington Publishers, 1993; Friedman, Barry. "The Birth of an Academic Obsession: The History of the Countermajoritarian Difficulty, Part Five." *Yale Law Journal* 153 (2002): 112; Funston, Richard. "The Supreme Court and Critical Elections." *American Political Science Review* 69 (1975): 795–811; Graber, Mark A. "The Nonmajoritarian Difficulty: Legislative Deference to the Judiciary." *Studies in American Political Development* 7 (1993): 35–73; Mishler, William, and Reginald Sheehan. "The Supreme Court as Countermajoritarian Institution? The Impact of Public Opinion on Supreme Court Decisions." *APSR* 87 (1997): 87–101; Peretti, Terri Jennings. *In Defense of a Political Court.* Princeton, N.J.: Princeton University Press, 1999.

—Alison Gash

County of Allegheny v. ACLU 492 U.S. 573 (1989)

In *County of Allegheny v. ACLU,* the Supreme Court ruled on the constitutionality of RELIGIOUS DISPLAYS ON PUBLIC PROPERTY. In this decision, the Court ruled on two different types of displays, helping to clarify what the ESTABLISHMENT CLAUSE permits.

Starting in 1981, a Roman Catholic group in Pittsburgh had sponsored a crèche displayed on the grand staircase of the Allegheny County Courthouse at Christmastime. In 1982, a Jewish group began sponsoring a menorah displayed outside the City-County Building around the time of Hanukkah. In a deeply divided decision, the Supreme Court held that the crèche violated the FIRST AMENDMENT's establishment clause while the menorah did not violate the establishment clause.

In *LYNCH V. DONNELLY,* 465 U.S. 668 (1984), the Supreme Court had ruled that a crèche could be displayed as a component of a larger holiday display. This reasoning resulted from *LEMON V. KURTZMAN,* 403 U.S. 602 (1971), in which the Supreme Court had used the "principal or primacy effect" to decide whether a statute advances or inhibits religion. The application of this measure to a religious symbol was used in *Lynch* to determine whether a symbol was the primary feature of a display that advances or inhibits religion. The constitutional difficulties with the crèche in *County of Allegheny v. ACLU* arose from the fact that it was displayed without the "sanitizing" effect of other seasonal decorations. According to the logic from *Lynch,* other religious symbols and secular decorations remove the centrality of a religiously based display thereby removing the overtly religious message. The crèche in *Allegheny* was displayed singularly with the words *Gloria in Excelsis Deo* (Glory to God in the highest), accompanied by an angel on the crest above the manger. According to the Supreme Court majority opinion, the crèche being the single object of recognition in the display was tantamount to government endorsement of religion and was therefore in violation of the establishment clause. This decision upheld the finding of the U.S. Court of Appeals for the Third Circuit as it pertained to the crèche.

Regarding the menorah's display at the City-County Building, the Supreme Court, with a majority different from the one ruling about the crèche, found that the display did not violate the establishment clause and stayed true to *Lynch* because the menorah was on display with a 45-foot Christmas tree, accompanied by a sign reading "During this holiday season, the city of Pittsburgh salutes liberty. Let these festive lights remind us that we are the keepers of the flame of liberty and our legacy of freedom." This effectively made the menorah part of a larger display thereby removing the menorah's centrality in the display. The decision on the menorah overruled the finding of the U.S. Court of Appeals for the Third Circuit.

The decision was fragmented and contained a strong minority of justices lining up behind the idea that the crèche did not violate the establishment clause. Associate Justice ANTHONY M. KENNEDY, writing for the minority, stated: "ACCOMMODATION, acknowledgement, and support for religion are an accepted part of our political and cultural heritage, and the Establishment Clause permits government some latitude in recognizing the central role of religion in society." More recent cases such as *McCREARY COUNTY, KENTUCKY V. AMERICAN CIVIL LIBERTIES UNION*, 545 U.S. 844 (2005), in which the Supreme Court rejected a TEN COMMANDMENTS display, and *VAN ORDEN V. PERRY*, 545 U.S. 677 (2005), in which the Supreme Court accepted a display, point to the continued controversy and fragmented decisions of the Court in this area of jurisprudence.

For more information: Choper, Jesse H.; Richard H. Fallon, Jr.; Yale Kamisar; and Steven H. Shiffrin. *Constitutional Law: Cases and Comments*. 10th ed. New York: West Publishing, 2006.

—William Lester

Coyle v. Smith 221 U.S. 559 (1911)

In *Coyle v. Smith*, the Supreme Court declared that the newly admitted state of Oklahoma had the right to move its state capital despite restrictions to the contrary in its enabling act. This case is significant in the development of American FEDERALISM, because the Court ruled that new states enter the Union on "equal footing" with existing states and therefore have the same authority as the "original" states to alter their state governments.

Article IV, Section 3 of the U.S. Constitution provides: "new states may be admitted by the Congress into this Union." In 1906, Congress passed an enabling act authorizing the admission of Oklahoma into the Union. Among its many provisions, the enabling legislation stipulated that Oklahoma's new state capital should be located in the city of Guthrie and could not be moved until after 1913. The voters of Oklahoma subsequently approved the act and the new constitution, and Oklahoma became the 46th state on November 16, 1907.

In 1910, the Oklahoma state legislature, bowing to political and economic pressures, authorized the relocation of the state capital to Oklahoma City. W. H. Coyle, a businessperson from Guthrie, filed suit against Thomas Smith, Oklahoma secretary of state, to enjoin the state from moving its capital. The Oklahoma Supreme Court upheld the 1910 law, and Coyle appealed to the U.S. Supreme Court. The sole question before the Court was "whether the provision of the enabling act was a valid limitation upon the power of the State after its admission, which overrides any subsequent state legislation repugnant thereto."

Justice Horace Lurton delivered the 7-2 majority opinion. Lurton recognized that Congress has constitutional authority to impose conditions of statehood, but once a state enters the Union, it enters on "equal footing" with the other states. According to Lurton, "When a new State is admitted into the Union, it is so admitted with all the powers of sovereignty and jurisdiction which pertain to the original States, and . . . such powers may not be constitutionally diminished, impaired or shorn away by any conditions, compacts or stipulations embraced in the act under which the new State came into the Union." Joining Lurton were Justices William R. Day, JOHN MARSHALL HARLAN, Charles Evans Hughes, Joseph R. Lamar, Willis Van Devanter, and Edward D. White. Justices OLIVER WENDELL HOLMES, JR., and Joseph McKenna dissented without a written opinion.

For more information: Gibson, Arrell Morgan. *History of Oklahoma*. Norman: University of Oklahoma Press, 1984; Graves, W. Brooke. *American Intergovernmental Relations: Their Origins, Historical Development, and Current Status*. New York: Scribner, 1964.

—Richard J. Hardy

Craig v. Boren 429 U.S. 190 (1976)

In *Craig v. Boren*, the Supreme Court created the intermediate scrutiny standard to apply to cases involving gender-based discrimination. The significance of this case is that the Court makes gender a quasi-suspect class and ensures that laws that discriminate against women will be given greater scrutiny than normal legislation.

Curtis Craig, a male between 18 and 21 years old, sought injunctive relief against the enforcement of an Oklahoma law that forbade the sale of low-alcohol-content beer (3.2 beer) to males, but not females, under the age of 21. Craig argued that the law invidiously discriminates against males between the ages of 18 and 21 and violates the FOURTEENTH AMENDMENT's EQUAL PROTECTION clause. A three-judge district court denied relief, and the Supreme Court, in a 7-2 decision, reversed, holding the law violated the equal protection clause.

Writing for the majority, Justice WILLIAM J. BRENNAN, JR., held that laws that discriminate on the basis of gender must serve "important governmental objectives and must be substantially related to achievement of those objectives." While Oklahoma has an important state interest in traffic safety, the law does not relate to that objective for three reasons, according to Brennan. First, statistical evidence shows little relation between 18–20-year-old maleness and drunk driving. Second, Oklahoma considers 3.2 beer nonintoxicating and thus unlikely to promote drunk driving. Third, Oklahoma allows males to drink 3.2 beer but not buy it, which is inconsistent with the purpose of the law.

In his dissent, Justice WILLIAM HUBBS REHNQUIST objected to the decision for two reasons. First, there is no history of discrimination against males to justify a higher standard of review for laws that discriminate against them. Second, the Court creates a new standard without any citation to its source. Moreover, the Court provides no guidance for determining what objectives are important and how to determine whether a law is substantially related to such objective. Justice Rehnquist then attacked the activist majority, claiming that this new standard is simply a justification to strike down laws a majority of the Court opposes. Rather than create a new standard, he would uphold the law because Oklahoma has a rational basis for this distinction.

This case is important because it finally resolved the question of what level of scrutiny should be applied to laws that discriminate on the basis of gender. While the more liberal members of the Court wanted to make gender, like race, a suspect class subject to STRICT SCRUTINY because it is an immutable characteristic, they were unable to command a fifth vote for this position in *Frontiero v. Richardson,* 411 U.S. 677 (1973). In that case, Justice LEWIS FRANKLIN POWELL, JR., noted that women had greater success in the political process and that the Courts should not preempt the political branches as they were debating the Equal Rights Amendment. Realizing that women were more successful than racial groups in the political process but still subject to impermissible stereotypes, the Court eventually determined that gender-based classifications deserved greater scrutiny than normal, although not as much as race deserved.

For more information: Cushman, Clare. *Supreme Court Decisions and Women's Rights.* Washington, D.C.: CQ Press, 2000; Schwarzenbach, Sybil, and Patricia Smith. *Women and the Constitution.* New York: Columbia University Press, 2004.

—Sean Evans

cross burning

Cross burning is an act historically associated with the Klu Klux Klan. Klan cross burning is meant to symbolize racial superiority for whites and hatred toward African Americans. Depending on the content and circumstances of the act of cross burning, it may or may not receive constitutional protection as free speech under the FIRST AMENDMENT.

In *BRANDENBURG V. OHIO,* 395 U.S. 444 (1969), Clarence Brandenburg was convicted of violating a law making it illegal to advocate racial strife by attending a cross-burning ceremony during a Klan rally. The Supreme Court overturned his conviction, stating that unless his actions advocated imminent harm that is likely to occur, then any acts or statements are protected speech under the First Amendment. While in this case cross burning was not directly an issue, its presence was critical to Brandenburg's original conviction because of the historical association with racial violence.

Robert Shelton, imperial wizard of the Ku Klux Klan, stands before a burning cross in Hemingway, South Carolina, 1965. *(Library of Congress)*

Cross burnings have been the subject of legislation attempting to regulate HATE SPEECH. In *R.A.V. v. St. Paul*, 505 U.S. 377 (1992), at issue was a St. Paul, Minnesota, ordinance that made it illegal to burn crosses when one knows that the act will arouse anger or alarm and is carried out on the basis of race, color, creed, religion, or gender. Here Robert A. Viktora (R.A.V.) and others burned a cross across the street from a house where an African-American family was staying. Justice ANTONIN GREGORY SCALIA, writing for the Supreme Court, declared the law unconstitutional as a form of content-based and viewpoint discrimination that was contrary to the First Amendment. In concurrence, Chief Justice WILLIAM HUBBS REHNQUIST saw the law as overbroad, potentially punishing types of speech that deserve protection. Finally, while Justice Harry A. Blackmun and others on the Court agreed that the St. Paul law was unconstitutional, they also sought ways to make it possible to punish HATE CRIMES. Instead of arguing that the law was void as a content-based restriction, they argued that it was unconstitutional because it involved a class of words that are beyond the protection of the First Amendment. Here, they drew upon *CHAPLINSKY V. NEW HAMPSHIRE*, 315 U.S. 568 (1942), arguing that cross burning was like "fighting words" and that the Court had ruled that these types of words are not protected by the First Amendment.

Chaplinsky and *R.A.V.* formed the basis of a third decision involving cross burning that the Court has examined. In *Virginia v. Black*, 538 U.S. 343 (2003), the Supreme Court held that cross burning with intent to intimidate is not a protected act under the First Amendment and thus is similar to fighting words. Writing for the Court, Justice SANDRA DAY O'CONNOR drew upon *Chaplinsky* and *R.A.V.* and argued that the cross burning in this case (which made it illegal to burn a cross with the intent to intimidate another or a group) was both like fighting words and a "true threat" and not mere advocacy of a viewpoint as was the case in *Brandenburg*. However, the burden of proof for the prosecution of acts such as cross burning is to prove that there was direct intent to intimidate through the act, and thus the intent related to the act cannot be inferred from the act of cross burning itself. It must therefore be separately proven as a matter of law to the sufficiency of the court on a case-by-case basis considering the totality of the circumstances.

Overall, it appears that while cross burning in and of itself may be a form of protected speech, if it is done with the intent to intimidate others such that it is a real threat and not a mere symbol or statement of opinions or beliefs, then it is not entitled to First Amendment protection.

For more information: Kalven, Harvey. *A Worthy Tradition: Freedom of Speech in America.*

New York: Harper & Row, 1988; Langran, Robert W. *The Supreme Court: A Concise History.* New York: Peter Lang, 2004.

—Ernest Gomez and David Schultz

cruel and unusual punishment

The Eighth Amendment to the U.S. Constitution bans "cruel and unusual punishment." However, clarification regarding types of punishment has been a source of controversy. More often than not, the death penalty has been the major source of debate concerning whether its use is cruel and unusual, yet other types of punishment, including lengths of sentences, also are examined under the Eighth Amendment.

Historically, at the time of the framing of the Constitution and the writing of the Eighth Amendment, there were literally dozens of crimes that were punishable by death, including murder, some forms of robbery, rape, and other types of sex crimes. Other types of punishment, such as torture, flogging, and a variety of acts of public humiliation, were also used. Gradually, during the 19th and 20th centuries, many of these punishments were eliminated, and the number of crimes in the category meriting death was decreased. These changes in punishment influenced the Supreme Court, in *Trop v. Dulles,* 356 U.S. 86 (1958), in determining if a punishment violated the Eighth Amendment: "[T]he words of the Amendment are not precise, and that their scope is not static. The Amendment must draw its meaning from the evolving standards of decency that mark the progress of a maturing society." In *Trop,* the Court invalidated expatriation as punishment for wartime desertion. The evolving standards of decency have continued to be of great importance in death penalty cases and other evaluations of punishment since 1958.

In terms of the death penalty, the Court has declared four other types of capital punishments to be forms of cruel and unusual punishment. In *COKER V. GEORGIA,* 433 U.S. 584 (1977), the Court found the use of the death penalty to punish someone who had raped an adult woman to be cruel and unusual punishment. In *Eberheart v. Georgia,* 433 U.S. 917 (1977), it was invalidated for kidnapping. In *Roper v. Simmons,* 543 U.S. 551 (2005), the death penalty for individuals under the age of 18 was found to be cruel and unusual, and in *ATKINS V. VIRGINIA,* 536 U.S. 304 (2002), the Court found that executing the mentally retarded was also a violation of the Eighth Amendment.

However, while the Supreme Court in *FURMAN V. GEORGIA,* 408 U.S. 238 (1972), invalidated a Georgia death penalty law, along with those in several other states, the justices did so mostly on DUE PROCESS grounds. Only two justices, Thurgood Marshall and WILLIAM J. BRENNAN, JR., used the *Trop* standard to invalidate as a cruel and unusual punishment. As a result, once the Court was convinced that the due process problems had been addressed, it upheld the punishment in *GREGG V. GEORGIA,* 428 U.S. 153 (1976), a few years later. Even in cases where the actual innocence of the defendant is being asserted as a defense, as in *Herrera v. Collins,* 506 U.S. 390 (1993), a majority of justices have been unwilling to rule that the use of death as a punishment is inherently cruel and unusual. In that case, however, Justices Harry A. Blackmun, JOHN PAUL STEVENS, and DAVID H. SOUTER would have found executing the innocent to be cruel and unusual, and eventually Blackmun would join Marshall and Brennan in arguing that all forms of death as punishment violate the Eighth Amendment. Even though the Supreme Court continues to overturn death penalty convictions, it does so mostly along due process grounds.

Another way the court has addressed the meaning of cruel and unusual punishment is by looking at the proportionality of sentences in relation to the crime committed. For example, in *Weems v. United States,* 217 U.S. 349, (1910), the issue was whether a Philippine law calling for a fine and imprisonment ranging from 12 to 20 years in cases where a public official falsified a public document was cruel and unusual punishment. At the time that the defendant, Paul A. Weems, was indicted and convicted, the Philippines was part of the United States, and it had its Bill of Rights modeled upon the U.S. Bill of Rights including a "cruel and unusual punishment clause." Weems was convicted of falsifying payroll information and given a sentence of 15 years of prison with hard labor and a fine of 4,000 pesetas. Weems's sentence was subsequently upheld by Philippine courts, but the U.S. Supreme Court reversed, finding it disproportionate to the crime committed.

In other cases, such as *Robinson v. California*, 370 U.S. 660 (1962), the Court drew limits as to what the state could punish (in this case, addiction to drugs) and incorporated the proportionality requirement to state offenses. Yet in *Rummel v. Estelle*, 445 U.S. 263, 266 (1980), the defendant, William James Rummel, was convicted in 1973 for obtaining $120.75 under false pretenses. This conviction came after a 1964 conviction for $80 in credit card fraud and a 1969 conviction for forging a check worth $28. Upon his third conviction, Rummel was sentenced to life under a Texas statute that provided for life imprisonment for anyone convicted of three felonies. Rummel appealed his sentence, claiming that life for these crimes was cruel and unusual punishment and a disproportionate sentence to the three crimes, which resulted in his stealing less than $240 in total.

In rejecting Rummel's claims, the Supreme Court first disposed of his arguments that recent cases striking down death as a disproportionate penalty were applicable to his case because death was a unique type of penalty that had attached to it special proportionality issues. Second, the Supreme Court distinguished Rummel's claims from those found in *Weems*, arguing that in the latter case, it was not merely the length of the incarceration that was at issue. Instead, the hard labor and other terms of confinement were also important to the Court's finding the sentence to be cruel and unusual and disproportionate. Third, the Supreme Court argued that objective and not merely subjective factors were required to determine what constituted disproportionality. Appealing merely to judges' personal preferences was an inappropriate way to determine what is cruel and unusual or disproportionate. Once death is no longer an issue, according to the Supreme Court, determinations to what constitutes an appropriate sentence are subjective and best left up to local legislatures to decide.

In *Hutto v. Davis*, 454 U.S. 370 (1982), the Supreme Court again deferred to local legislature determination of what was an appropriate punishment for a crime. The issue here was two concurrent 20-year sentences and a $20,000 fine for the possession of nine ounces of marijuana. In overturning HABEAS CORPUS based on proportionality and the cruel and unusual punishment clause, the Supreme Court indicated that its *Rummel* decision stood for the proposition that SENTENCING GUIDELINES are generally policy issues for the legislatures and not the courts. However, in *Solem v. Helm*, 463 U.S. 277 (1983), the Court reversed itself and invalidated a life sentence imposed on a defendant under a South Dakota statute for issuing a bad check in the amount of $100. Writing for the majority, Justice LEWIS FRANKLIN POWELL, JR., first indicated that proportionality was deeply rooted in English and American law and that it applies to all types of sentences, including felonies, even where death is not a penalty. Rejecting *Rummel*'s claim that death is different in terms of assessment of proportionality, the Supreme Court indicated that it saw no reason to draw a "distinction with cases of imprisonment" versus death. Powell stated:

> In sum, we hold as a matter of principle that a criminal sentence must be proportionate to the crime for which the defendant has been convicted. Reviewing courts, of course, should grant substantial deference to the broad authority that legislatures necessarily possess in determining the types and limits of punishments for crimes, as well as to the discretion that trial courts possess in sentencing convicted criminals. But no penalty is per se constitutional. As the Court noted in *Robinson v. California*, a single day in prison may be unconstitutional in some circumstances.

Yet, in *Harmelin v. Michigan*, 501 U.S. 957 (1991), the Court returned to its *Rummel* standards and appeared to read proportionality out of the Eighth Amendment, again stating that sentencing decisions are legislative determinations. In *Ewing v. California*, 538 U.S. 11 (2003), in upholding

California's three strikes law, the Court seemed to concur in that sentiment.

Overall, the Supreme Court continues to look to the evolving *Trop* standards of decency to help determine what cruel and unusual punishment is. However, except for a few narrow death penalty issues, the Court appears to give wide latitude to legislatures to decide what punishments are appropriate.

For more information: Amar, Akhil Reed. *The Constitution and Criminal Procedure.* New Haven, Conn.: Yale University Press, 1997; LaFave, Wayne R., Jerold H. Israel, and Nancy J. King. *Criminal Procedure.* St. Paul, Minn.: Thomson/West, 2004.

—Ernest Gomez and David Schultz

Cruzan v. Director, Missouri Department of Health 497 U.S. 261 (1990)

Cruzan v. Director, Missouri Department of Health is a significant decision in the area of PRIVACY and health care. The Supreme Court held that clear and convincing evidence must exist that demonstrates an individual's desire to refuse life-sustaining medical care that perpetuates one's existence in an irreversible vegetative condition.

Nancy Cruzan was seriously injured in a car accident, suffering irreversible brain damage that left her in a persistent vegetative state. Cruzan's parents insisted that their adult daughter would not wish to live in such a condition and requested that the hospital withdraw food and liquids, hastening her death. Since the patient was incompetent, explicit expression of her will was obviously not possible. The hospital therefore refused to withdraw life-sustaining care without a court order. The parents petitioned state courts to compel the hospital's compliance with their request. The courts concluded that since she could not communicate, substituting Cruzan's expression of her own wish with a determination as to what her decision would have been was reasonable. In making such a determination, the state supreme court required Cruzan's parents to provide "clear and convincing evidence" that their daughter would not wish to live in a persistent vegetative state. Since the Cruzan family was unable to document Nancy's alleged wish to the court's satisfaction, their request was denied. Cruzan's parents filed suit on their daughter's behalf, arguing that an adult may refuse life-sustaining medical treatment under the DUE PROCESS clause of the FOURTEENTH AMENDMENT.

Writing for the Court, Chief Justice WILLIAM HUBBS REHNQUIST upheld the state court's decision requiring clear and convincing evidence as to Nancy Cruzan's wishes before terminating life-sustaining medical care. Federal case law has long recognized that a competent adult may refuse medical treatment, including that which is life sustaining. This right, however, is not absolute. It must be balanced against the state's interest in preserving life. In so doing, the state court's imposition of the clear and convincing evidence threshold reasonably safeguards the state's interest while preserving the individual's liberty interest. Specifically, in a situation such as this—where the person whose life is at issue cannot speak—the state may require a heightened level of evidence demonstrating the patient's wishes in order to assure that the family is truly advocating their loved one's best interest and not their own preferences.

Thus, the clear and convincing evidence requirement is a reasonable standard that states may impose to protect invalid adults against those who might seek to exploit such a circumstance. This standard balances the state's interest with the individual's liberty interest to refuse medical care; where the state's requirement is satisfied, life-sustaining medical care for an invalid adult may be withdrawn. Conversely, where insufficient evidence as to the individual's will exists, the state's interest in preserving life prevails. Therefore, the state's requirement does not impermissibly frustrate the liberty interest guaranteed by the due process clause of the Fourteenth Amendment.

For more information: Glick, Henry R. *The Right to Die.* New York: Columbia University Press, 1994.

—Melanie K. Morris

DaimlerChrysler v. Cuno 126 S. Ct. 1854 (2006)

In *DaimlerChrysler v. Cuno,* the Supreme Court rejected a challenge to Ohio's tax laws under the DORMANT COMMERCE CLAUSE because the plaintiffs lacked proper STANDING to bring their case in federal court.

DaimlerChrysler arose when 18 Ohio taxpayers filed suit to challenge a development agreement between DaimlerChrysler and the city of Toledo. Under the agreement, DaimlerChrysler received a 10-year exemption from local property taxes and a credit against the state corporate franchise tax in exchange for building a new assembly plant near its existing facilities in Toledo. The district court dismissed the plaintiffs' claims that Ohio's tax laws violated the dormant commerce clause because the property tax exemption and franchise tax credit did not function as protective tariffs or discriminatory proportional taxes.

The U.S. Court of Appeals for the Sixth Circuit affirmed the trial court ruling with regard to the property tax exemption but reversed on the franchise tax credit, concluding that it had a coercive effect and violated the COMMERCE CLAUSE. Both the district court and the court of appeals employed the four-part commerce clause analysis articulated in *COMPLETE AUTO TRANSIT, INC. V. BRADY,* 430 U.S. 274 (1977), which held that a tax provision will survive a commerce clause challenge when it "is applied to an activity with a substantial nexus to the taxing State, is fairly apportioned, does not discriminate against INTERSTATE COMMERCE, and is fairly related to the services provided by the State."

On appeal, the Supreme Court examined whether the plaintiffs had standing to sue under ARTICLE III OF THE U.S. CONSTITUTION and whether this was an appropriate "case or controversy" for the Court to decide. Chief Justice JOHN G. ROBERTS, JR., writing for an eight-member majority, noted that standing requires the plaintiff to show a "concrete and particularized" injury and "redressability" through judicial action.

The injury in this case was "conjectural or hypothetical" because the plaintiffs could not prove that the property tax exemption or the franchise tax credit caused the plaintiffs to suffer heavier tax burdens. Likewise, the issue of "redressability" was speculative because there was no evidence that eliminating the property tax exemption or franchise tax credit would cause the state legislature to reduce the plaintiffs' tax burdens. Chief Justice Roberts rejected the plaintiffs' claim of standing as state taxpayers because the limited scope of federal taxpayer standing under *VALLEY FORGE CHRISTIAN COLLEGE V. AMERICANS UNITED FOR SEPARATION OF CHURCH AND STATE, INC.,* 454 U.S. 464 (1982), "applies with undiminished force to state taxpayers." The Court ruled that the municipal taxpayer standing doctrine of *Massachusetts v. Mellon,* 262 U.S. 447 (1923), could not support a challenge to the state franchise tax credit. The Court also declined to expand the limited exception to the taxpayer standing doctrine established in *FLAST V. COHEN,* 392 U.S. 83 (1968), to permit commerce clause challenges. Justice Ruth Bader Ginsburg, in a separate opinion, concurred with her colleagues in the result but noted her disapproval of the Court's broader precedents on Article III standing limits. The decision in *DaimlerChrysler* demonstrates the Supreme Court's commitment to the principle of limited federal court jurisdiction and the importance of the Article III standing inquiry for plaintiffs.

For more information: *Georgetown Journal of Law & Public Policy* 1, no. 4 (Winter 2006) (symposium issue on *Daimler Chrysler v. Cuno* before the Supreme Court ruling); Mank, Bradford C. "Prudential Standing and the Dormant Commerce Clause: Why the 'Zone of Interests' Test Should Not Apply to Constitutional Cases." *Arizona Law Review* 23, no. 48 (2006): 23–65.

—Joshua A. Kimsey

Dames & Moore v. Regan 453 U.S. 654 (1981)

The *Dames & Moore v. Regan* case grew out of a presidential executive order that blocked access to Iranian assets following the taking of American hostages in Iran in 1979. The Supreme Court ruling upheld the agreements that had settled the hostage crisis.

In 1979 when Americans were taken hostage at the U.S. Embassy in Tehran, Iran, President Jimmy Carter declared a national emergency on November 14. Pursuant to the International Emergency Economic Powers Act (IEEPA), President Carter issued Executive Order 12170, which blocked Iranian assets. Because Iranian assets were frozen, Dames & Moore Corporation filed suit against several Iranian governmental agencies, alleging that services rendered for the Atomic Energy Organization of Iran had not been paid. A federal district court issued orders of attachment that seized the property belonging to some Iranian banks in an effort to secure payment in any judgment that would be entered against the Iranians.

On January 19, 1981, the American hostages were released under terms agreed to by both governments. One of the terms of the agreement was that the U.S. government would drop all legal proceedings of U.S. nationals against Iran and nullify all attachments and judgments via those pending proceedings. President Ronald Reagan then issued Executive Order 12294, reasserting EO 12170 and requiring that banks holding Iranian assets transfer them to the Federal Reserve Bank of New York to be held or dispersed as the secretary of the treasury directed. Dames & Moore, seething from the presidential rebuke, filed action against Secretary of the Treasury Donald Regan, alleging that both EXECUTIVE ORDERS exceeded statutory and constitutional boundaries.

The Supreme Court opinion stated that IEEPA empowered the president to take the actions blocking the transfer of any property of Iran, or any foreign country, within the jurisdiction of the United States. These blocking orders enable the president to have another tool available in negotiations with a hostile country.

Perhaps the key element to the Court's decision was the use Justice Robert Jackson's concurrence in *YOUNGSTOWN SHEET & TUBE V. SAWYER* (1952). Although Jackson was not writing for the Court, his template for when the Supreme Court would support actions undertaken by the president has become the most influential opinion of the case. Jackson argued that the Supreme Court would be most likely to rule in the president's favor when "the President acts pursuant to an express or implied authorization of Congress, [as] his authority is at its maximum, for it includes all that he possesses in his own right plus all that Congress may delegate." Jackson's opinion was cited in the Court's *Dames & Moore* opinion, which was written by former Jackson clerk Justice WILLIAM HUBBS REHNQUIST. Rehnquist stated in the opinion of the Court that from "the inferences to be drawn from the character of the legislation Congress has enacted in the area, such as the IEEPA and the Hostage Act, and from the history of acquiescence in executive claims settlement—we conclude that the President was authorized to suspend pending claims pursuant to Executive Order No. 12294."

Overall, the Supreme Court in its opinion for *Dames & Moore v. Regan* recognized that the president's power is at its maximum when Congress has lent its support and that executive orders are a key instrument in that power.

For more information: Galub, Arthur L. "*Dames and Moore v. Regan.*" In *The Burger Court: 1968–1984.* Danbury, Conn.: Grolier Educational, 1995.

—Tobias T. Gibson

Dartmouth College v. Woodward 17 U.S. (4 Wheat.) 518, 4 L. Ed. 629 (1819)

In *Dartmouth College v. Woodward,* the Supreme Court ruled that Dartmouth College's charter was protected by the U.S. Constitution and the New Hampshire legislature could not constitutionally interfere with the charter. Dartmouth College was privately funded, and the state of New Hampshire did not have the authority to make the school a state institution. The case is important because of its protection of property rights through the CONTRACT CLAUSE of the Constitution.

Dartmouth College was a private institution, and strides were being made by the New Hampshire legislature to turn it into a public institution. In 1816, the New Hampshire legislature attempted to convert the privately funded Dartmouth into a public college. Through the use of three 1816 legislative acts, the New Hampshire legislature amended the college's original charter by adding additional trustees and placing the appointment of future trustees in the hands of the governor. The trustees at the time challenged the New Hampshire legislature. They retained the services of Daniel Webster, an 1801 graduate of Dartmouth College, to represent them against William Woodward, who was newly appointed by the state as Dartmouth's treasurer. The trustees based their claim on the charter that was granted in 1769 to Dartmouth College by King George III. On November 6, 1816, the New Hampshire Superior Court of Judicature ruled on the side of Woodward and the new governing body. The U.S. Supreme Court later reversed the lower court's decision.

Chief Justice JOHN MARSHALL wrote the opinion for the five-person majority. In it, Marshall considered two main points: first, whether the contract was protected by the U.S. Constitution and second, whether the contract is impaired by the 1816 acts. The majority opinion held that the contract is indeed protected by the U.S. Constitution. The majority opinion also held that the 1816 acts of the New Hampshire legislature were not in agreement with the U.S. Constitution.

Justices JOSEPH STORY and Bushrod Washington issued separate concurring opinions. Justice William Johnson concurred for the reasons stated by Chief Justice Marshall. Justice Henry Brockholst Livingston concurred for the reasons stated by the Chief Justice and Justices Washington and Story. Justice Thomas Todd did not participate in this decision, and Justice Gabriel Duvall dissented without issuing an opinion.

The importance of this decision was not immediately recognized. However, in 1885, Sir Henry Maine described the decision by the MARSHALL COURT as "the bulwark of American individualism against democratic impatience and socialistic fantasy."

For more information: Harrison, Maureen, and Steve Gilbert, eds. *Landmark Decisions of the United States Supreme Court VI.* San Diego, Calif.: Excellent Books, 1999; Mason, Alpheus Thomas, and Donald Grier Stephenson, Jr., eds. *American Constitutional Law: Introductory Essays and Selected Cases.* 12th ed. Upper Saddle River, N.J.: Prentice Hall, 1999.

—Jacqueline M. Loubet

deadly force

Deadly force is a legal concept generally understood to be any violent action that is reasonably understood to cause or be the proximate cause of substantial bodily harm or, ultimately, death through the causation of the action. According to the Supreme Court in *Tennessee v. Garner,* 471 U.S. 1 (1985), the use of deadly force by police and law-enforcement officials is examined under the FOURTH AMENDMENT.

In some situations, law-enforcement officials must use deadly force to apprehend or stop an individual. To determine when such force may be used, the Court stated in *Garner* that a balancing of interests test must be used to determine police liability. One must balance the nature of the intrusion on the individual's Fourth Amendment right against the government interests to justify the intrusion. For the citizen, the interest is substantial—not to die.

To overcome this citizen interest, the police must show that the officer believes that the suspect poses a threat of immediate and serious physical harm to the officer or others. For there to be a serious threat the person must be armed. In determining whether the threat is serious, merely being armed or having recently used a weapon is not enough to justify the use of deadly force. Factors to be weighed include asking how proximate to the past crime was force used and does the suspect have a history of past or previous use of the weapon. If law-enforcement officials correctly use deadly force there is no Fourth Amendment violation.

If excessive use of deadly force is determined to be unwarranted, it is an illegal search and seizure under 42 U.S. Code, SECTION 1983, for a violation of civil or other protected rights.

For more information: Kappeler, Victor. *Critical Issues in Police Civil Liability.* Long Grove, Ill.: Waveland Press, 2006.

—Ernest Gomez and David Schultz

Declaration of Independence (1776)

The Declaration of Independence is the founding document of the American nation. Issued by the Continental Congress on July 4, 1776, the declaration announces America's philosophy of government and dedicates the United States of America to the "self-evident truths" that "all men are created equal, that they are endowed by their Creator with certain unalienable Rights, that among these are Life, Liberty and the pursuit of Happiness."

THOMAS JEFFERSON, junior member of the Virginia delegation to the Continental Congress, was the principal author of the Declaration of Independence. Jefferson was chosen to draft the declaration chiefly because of his "masterly pen." The "peculiar felicity" with which the declaration was written plays no small part in the power of its message.

Jefferson drew on other documents in writing the Declaration of Independence, including JOHN LOCKE's *Second Treatise of Civil Government* (1690), Jefferson's own *Summary View of the Rights of British America* (1774), the VIRGINIA DECLARATION OF RIGHTS (1776), and the preamble to the Virginia Constitution (1776). The declaration was informed by the major political theories of the day, but the document is primarily a statement of the Lockean liberal theory of government: The principal purpose of government is to secure individual rights. "To secure these rights," the declaration proclaims, "Governments are instituted among Men."

The Declaration of Independence has been invoked throughout the course of U.S. history to address a host of landmark questions of public policy. ABRAHAM LINCOLN, universally regarded as among the greatest of American presidents, turned to the declaration to help abolish slavery and save the Union, while CLARENCE THOMAS, the nation's highest-ranking African-American jurist, has relied on the declaration when considering questions of CIVIL RIGHTS enforcement. The principles of the declaration also were at the heart of the classic orations of three other giants of African-American history: Frederick Douglass's "What to the Slave Is the Fourth of July?" speech (July 5, 1852); Martin Luther King, Jr.'s "I Have a Dream" address (August 28, 1963); and Malcolm X's speech on "Black Revolution" (April 8, 1964).

The declaration, likewise, has been crucial to the women's rights movement. From 1776 to the present, the principles of the declaration have moved generations of women to demand equality. Abigail Adams echoed the declaration in her letters to her husband, JOHN ADAMS, one of the leading figures of America's founding period as well as the second president of the United States. The most famous document in the history of the women's rights movement—the Declaration of Sentiments (1848)—was modeled directly on the U.S. Declaration of Independence. Carrie Chapman Catt's famous address to the U.S. Congress in 1917 was replete with references to the declaration, too. And the monumental, albeit unsuccessful, Equal Rights Amendment of 1972 sought to guarantee "equal justice under law" to all citizens, regardless of gender.

The Declaration of Independence has similarly inspired peoples around the world in their quest for freedom and equality. The cultural possibilities offered by different languages and the choices

IN CONGRESS, JULY 4, 1776.

The unanimous Declaration of the thirteen united States of America,

When in the Course of human events, it becomes necessary for one people to dissolve the political bands which have connected them with another, and to assume among the powers of the earth, the separate and equal station to which the Laws of Nature and of Nature's God entitle them, a decent respect to the opinions of mankind requires that they should declare the causes which impel them to the separation. —— We hold these truths to be self-evident, that all men are created equal, that they are endowed by their Creator with certain unalienable Rights, that among these are Life, Liberty and the pursuit of Happiness. — That to secure these rights, Governments are instituted among Men, deriving their just powers from the consent of the governed, — That whenever any Form of Government becomes destructive of these ends, it is the Right of the People to alter or to abolish it, and to institute new Government, laying its foundation on such principles and organizing its powers in such form, as to them shall seem most likely to effect their Safety and Happiness. Prudence, indeed, will dictate that Governments long established should not be changed for light and transient causes; and accordingly all experience hath shewn, that mankind are more disposed to suffer, while evils are sufferable, than to right themselves by abolishing the forms to which they are accustomed. But when a long train of abuses and usurpations, pursuing invariably the same Object evinces a design to reduce them under absolute Despotism, it is their right, it is their duty, to throw off such Government, and to provide new Guards for their future security. — Such has been the patient sufferance of these Colonies; and such is now the necessity which constrains them to alter their former Systems of Government. The history of the present King of Great Britain is a history of repeated injuries and usurpations, all having in direct object the establishment of an absolute Tyranny over these States. To prove this, let Facts be submitted to a candid world. —— He has refused his Assent to Laws, the most wholesome and necessary for the public good. —— He has forbidden his Governors to pass Laws of immediate and pressing importance, unless suspended in their operation till his Assent should be obtained; and when so suspended, he has utterly neglected to attend to them. —— He has refused to pass other Laws for the accommodation of large districts of people, unless those people would relinquish the right of Representation in the Legislature, a right inestimable to them and formidable to tyrants only. —— He has called together legislative bodies at places unusual, uncomfortable, and distant from the depository of their public Records, for the sole purpose of fatiguing them into compliance with his measures. —— He has dissolved Representative Houses repeatedly, for opposing with manly firmness his invasions on the rights of the people. —— He has refused for a long time, after such dissolutions, to cause others to be elected; whereby the Legislative powers, incapable of Annihilation, have returned to the People at large for their exercise; the State remaining in the mean time exposed to all the dangers of invasion from without, and convulsions within. —— He has endeavoured to prevent the population of these States; for that purpose obstructing the Laws for Naturalization of Foreigners; refusing to pass others to encourage their migrations hither, and raising the conditions of new Appropriations of Lands. —— He has obstructed the Administration of Justice, by refusing his Assent to Laws for establishing Judiciary powers. —— He has made Judges dependent on his Will alone, for the tenure of their offices, and the amount and payment of their salaries. —— He has erected a multitude of New Offices, and sent hither swarms of Officers to harrass our people, and eat out their substance. —— He has kept among us, in times of peace, Standing Armies without the Consent of our legislatures. —— He has affected to render the Military independent of and superior to the Civil power. —— He has combined with others to subject us to a jurisdiction foreign to our constitution, and unacknowledged by our laws; giving his Assent to their Acts of pretended Legislation: — For Quartering large bodies of armed troops among us: — For protecting them, by a mock Trial, from punishment for any Murders which they should commit on the Inhabitants of these States: — For cutting off our Trade with all parts of the world: — For imposing Taxes on us without our Consent: — For depriving us in many cases, of the benefits of Trial by Jury: — For transporting us beyond Seas to be tried for pretended offences: — For abolishing the free System of English Laws in a neighbouring Province, establishing therein an Arbitrary government, and enlarging its Boundaries so as to render it at once an example and fit instrument for introducing the same absolute rule into these Colonies: — For taking away our Charters, abolishing our most valuable Laws, and altering fundamentally the Forms of our Governments: — For suspending our own Legislatures, and declaring themselves invested with power to legislate for us in all cases whatsoever. — He has abdicated Government here, by declaring us out of his Protection and waging War against us. — He has plundered our seas, ravaged our Coasts, burnt our towns, and destroyed the lives of our people. — He is at this time transporting large Armies of foreign Mercenaries to compleat the works of death, desolation and tyranny, already begun with circumstances of Cruelty & perfidy scarcely paralleled in the most barbarous ages, and totally unworthy the Head of a civilized nation. —— He has constrained our fellow Citizens taken Captive on the high Seas to bear Arms against their Country, to become the executioners of their friends and Brethren, or to fall themselves by their Hands. —— He has excited domestic insurrections amongst us, and has endeavoured to bring on the inhabitants of our frontiers, the merciless Indian Savages, whose known rule of warfare, is an undistinguished destruction of all ages, sexes and conditions. In every stage of these Oppressions We have Petitioned for Redress in the most humble terms: Our repeated Petitions have been answered only by repeated injury. A Prince, whose character is thus marked by every act which may define a Tyrant, is unfit to be the ruler of a free people. Nor have We been wanting in attentions to our British brethren. We have warned them from time to time of attempts by their legislature to extend an unwarrantable jurisdiction over us. We have reminded them of the circumstances of our emigration and settlement here. We have appealed to their native justice and magnanimity, and we have conjured them by the ties of our common kindred to disavow these usurpations, which, would inevitably interrupt our connections and correspondence. They too have been deaf to the voice of justice and of consanguinity. We must, therefore, acquiesce in the necessity, which denounces our Separation, and hold them, as we hold the rest of mankind, Enemies in War, in Peace Friends. ——

We, therefore, the Representatives of the united States of America, in General Congress, Assembled, appealing to the Supreme Judge of the world for the rectitude of our intentions, do, in the Name, and by Authority of the good People of these Colonies, solemnly publish and declare, That these United Colonies are, and of Right ought to be Free and Independent States; that they are Absolved from all Allegiance to the British Crown, and that all political connection between them and the State of Great Britain, is and ought to be totally dissolved; and that as Free and Independent States, they have full Power to levy War, conclude Peace, contract Alliances, establish Commerce, and to do all other Acts and Things which Independent States may of right do. —— And for the support of this Declaration, with a firm reliance on the protection of divine Providence, we mutually pledge to each other our Lives, our Fortunes and our sacred Honor.

John Hancock

Button Gwinnett
Lyman Hall
Geo Walton.

Wm Hooper
Joseph Hewes,
John Penn

Edward Rutledge 1.

Thos Heyward Junr.
Thomas Lynch Junr.
Arthur Middleton

Samuel Chase
Wm. Paca
Thos. Stone
Charles Carroll of Carrollton

George Wythe
Richard Henry Lee
Th Jefferson
Benj. Harrison
Thos Nelson jr.
Francis Lightfoot Lee
Carter Braxton

Robt Morris
Benjamin Rush
Benj. Franklin
John Morton
Geo Clymer
Jas. Smith
Geo. Taylor
James Wilson
Geo. Ross
Caesar Rodney
Geo Read
Thos M:Kean

Wm Floyd
Phil. Livingston
Frans. Lewis
Lewis Morris
Richd. Stockton
Jno Witherspoon
Fras. Hopkinson
John Hart
Abra Clark

Josiah Bartlett
Wm Whipple
Saml Adams
John Adams
Robt Treat Paine
Elbridge Gerry
Step. Hopkins
William Ellery
Roger Sherman
Saml Huntington
Wm Williams
Oliver Wolcott
Matthew Thornton

The Declaration of Independence *(Wikimedia Commons)*

made by individual translators have shaped the reception of the Declaration of Independence in different languages.

Perhaps most important of all, the Declaration of Independence has influenced the political architecture and institutions of the U.S. regime. The declaration was closely linked to the Articles of Confederation, the first constitution of the United States. The two documents formed a completed constitutional covenant offering a set of formative principles and reflecting shared commitments on which America as a nation (a people) and as a state (a government) was founded. The Constitution of 1787, which replaced the Articles of Confederation, and the BILL OF RIGHTS that followed also are grounded in the principles of the Declaration of Independence. What some might regard as merely technical, institutional matters—FEDERALISM, the rule of law, the content of public policy, and the separation of powers—all have proved to be integral to how the Constitution secures individual rights. An analysis of the constitutions of the states, the federal enabling acts defining the terms upon which new states were admitted to the Union, and the congressional statutes and presidential proclamations acknowledging admission demonstrate how closely the states identify with—or, in the case of the Southern states following the Civil War, were forced to identify with—the principles of the declaration.

Members of Congress and American presidents have appealed to the Declaration of Independence throughout the course of U.S. history. They have participated within—and, therefore, have been influenced by—a political context and tradition whose framework and principles were first articulated in the declaration. U.S. Supreme Court justices also have referred to the Declaration of Independence in written opinions in two identifiable, and occasionally interrelated, ways: 1) to determine a formal marker of the independence of the United States of America and 2) to cast light upon the founders' views or the principles underlying the Constitution.

The Declaration of Independence is one of the most valued and sacred political documents in history. It articulates the origins, purposes, and ideals of the U.S. regime, and it has inspired the American people as well as peoples around the world to seek constitutional change to conform to its principles.

For more information: Becker, Carl L. *The Declaration of Independence: A Study in the History of Political Ideas.* Rev. ed. New York: Vintage Books, 1958; Gerber, Scott Douglas. *To Secure These Rights: The Declaration of Independence and Constitutional Interpretation.* New York: New York University Press, 1995; Gerber, Scott Douglas, ed. *The Declaration of Independence: Origins and Impact.* New York: CQ Press, 2002; Maier, Pauline. *American Scripture: Making the Declaration of Independence.* New York: Knopf, 1997.

—Scott D. Gerber

defamation

Defamation is one form of speech that generally does not receive constitutional protection under the FIRST AMENDMENT. However, the Supreme Court has been willing, in the name of the First Amendment, to give broad deference to individuals and the media who wish to criticize public officials, even if there are some factual inaccuracies in the comments being made.

Defamation is one of the oldest torts, or civil wrongdoings, dating back to precolonial English law. Defamation consists of a false statement that is communicated to third persons and causes harm to the reputation of the person who was the subject of the communication. Similar to most torts, defamation generally is governed by state law. While the rules differ from state to state, there are many similarities in defamation law in nearly all jurisdictions of the United States.

Defamation consists of two forms: libel and slander. Libel is a defamatory communication that is in writing or other permanent form, including drawings, broadcasts, and electronic communications. Slander is defamation that occurs orally or in transitory form and not memorialized in some form of documentation.

Harm to reputation may be established by proving a diminution in the regard that others held for the subject of the defamation or that others have shunned or refused to associate with the subject. For individuals, this usually means proving that people actually have had a lower regard for the person because of the defamatory communication. While businesses also may be the subject of defamation, known as "trade libel," a business claimant usually must show that there has been a diminution in income or revenue.

Constitutionally, the Supreme Court drew some limits in *NEW YORK TIMES V. SULLIVAN*, 376 U.S. 254 (1964), when it came to the defamation of public officials. In that case, the Court ruled that the First Amendment requires public officials to show that someone acted with actual malice or reckless disregard of the truth in printing or distributing information about them. The high burden here of showing defamation was to preclude individuals from being chilled or intimidated from exercising their First Amendment rights of free speech or press. In cases subsequent to *Sullivan*, the Court has also extended significant constitutional protection against defamation when speech is directed at public figures. Finally, the courts have generally been unwilling to allow candidates for political office to sue for defamation when they are criticized by their opponents or other individuals or groups. In the interest of promoting robust political debate, the courts have applied the principles of *New York Times v. Sullivan* to protect campaign speech.

For more information: O'Neil, Robert M. *The First Amendment and Civil Liability*. Bloomington: Indiana University Press, 2001; Schwartz, Bernard. *A History of the Supreme Court*. New York: Oxford University Press, 1993.

—Marshall Tanick

Democracy and Distrust (1980)

Democracy and Distrust: A Theory of Judicial Review is a book by John Hart Ely, a law professor, in which Ely argues that judges should interpret constitutional provisions to reinforce representative democracy. Ely's book presents one of the most influential theories of JUDICIAL REVIEW.

In his book, Ely explains why neither of the two predominant alternative theories for interpreting the Constitution are adequate to address many of the most controversial issues. First, he describes what he calls "interpretivism," the view that judges should "confine themselves to enforcing norms that are stated or clearly implicit in the written Constitution." Ely finds this view inadequate because the Constitution contains several vague and ambiguous terms, as well as terms that expressly require judges to apply values or principles outside the Constitution itself.

Ely then dismisses "noninterpretetivism," which is the view that judges should apply norms and values that cannot be discovered within the text of the Constitution. One view among noninterpretivists is that judges should invoke their own personal values when they interpret the Constitution and should invalidate laws that are inconsistent with those values. Ely finds noninterpretivism as equally inadequate as interpretivism in that noninterpretivism does not constrain the judge's discretion and is contrary to many of the democratic theories upon which the Constitution is based.

As an alternative to these two views, Ely proposes his own theory of judicial review. Ely finds inspiration both in the history of the Constitution itself and in the work of the WARREN COURT. The Constitution, in Ely's view, is primarily concerned, not with protecting certain substantive values, but rather with procedural issues. Similarly, although many of the Warren Court's decisions dealt with issues of criminal procedure, which Ely describes as process "in the most ordinary sense," many of the Warren Court's decisions also addressed issues such as free speech and voting rights, which Ely describes as "process in the broader sense—the process by which the laws that govern society are made." In Ely's view, the Warren Court's decisions dealing with the EQUAL PROTECTION clause of the FOURTEENTH AMENDMENT also relied on two procedural principles: "clearing the channels of political change" and "correcting certain kinds of discrimination against minorities."

Judges applying Ely's theory of judicial review would invalidate laws that hamper the opportunity to participate in the political process. For example, the FIRST AMENDMENT's text, which only addresses Congress specifically, does not prohibit the president, the judiciary, or the states from banning speech. A judge applying Ely's theory, however, would hold that the free speech clause should apply equally to all branches of the federal government and to the states as well because free speech rights are "critical to the functioning of an open and effective democratic process." In cases dealing with the equal protection clause, judges applying Ely's theory would invalidate laws that threaten the ability of minorities to participate in and be represented in the political process.

For more information: Dworkin, Ronald. *Freedom's Law: The Moral Reading of the American Constitution.* Cambridge, Mass.: Harvard University Press, 1996; Tribe, Laurence. "The Puzzling Persistence of Process-Based Constitutional Theories." *Yale Law Journal* 89, no. 1,063 (1980).

—Winston E. Calvert

desegregation

Desegregation refers to the ending of racial segregation in, for example, public places, transport, or institutions. It is a term that has been commonly used with reference to the United States, desegregation of the military, and more especially, the U.S. CIVIL RIGHTS movement since the Supreme Court's landmark decision in *BROWN V. BOARD OF EDUCATION OF TOPEKA*, 347 U.S. 483 (1954), forcing the desegregation of schools.

Historically, racial segregation has a long and varied past in the United States. This is not to say that integrationist ideas are a new or 20th-century phenomenon, as the inclusion of the RIGHT TO VOTE for free blacks contained in the original Tennessee state constitution of 1796 illustrates. Unfortunately, such sentiments were not long lasting at the time, and in many cases, reversed (the Tennessee constitution was replaced with a subsequent one in 1834 that did not adopt the same voting rights for free blacks). In the United States, two specific areas of the racial desegregation movement merit particular attention: desegregation in the military and desegregation of the school system.

The U.S. military remained in segregated units based on racial lines until just shortly after World War II. It was with Executive Order 9981 by President Harry S. Truman that racial integration of the armed forces became an issue. Up until this point, blacks and other minorities were segregated into separate units during combat. President Truman chose to use an EXECUTIVE ORDER rather than going through Congress to have legislation passed, as he felt there would be too much opposition within Congress, especially from representatives of the southern states. However, during this same period (1948), Congress debated the Selective Services bill. An amendment to the Selective Services bill, attached in May 1948 by Senator Richard B. Russell, proposed enabling draftees and new inductees in the military to decide whether they wanted to serve in segregated units or not. The attachment was defeated twice. It was with the onset of the Korean War in 1948 and the huge casualties among the segregated units and the need to fill those units with able-bodied soldiers that army commanders accepted for the first time black recruits into white units, thus integrating army units. The practice of integrating units throughout the Korean War demonstrated that integrated combat units could perform adequately, gaining the notice of army high command, who formally announced plans to desegregate in 1951, three years after Executive Order 9981 was issued by President Truman.

It is perhaps the move toward desegregating the school system, however, that the desegregation movement is most associated with. Beginning with the abolitionist movement, the first steps toward desegregation occurred: the abolition of slavery with the THIRTEENTH AMENDMENT to the U.S. Constitution and the granting of citizenship and voting rights under the FOURTEENTH and FIFTEENTH AMENDMENTS immediately following the end of the Civil War. During the Reconstruction era (1865–80), there were more blacks elected to political office than before or since.

Despite these steps toward racial integration during the mid- to late 1800s, racial desegregation took a step backward with the assistance of the U.S. Supreme Court in 1896, with its decision in *Plessy v. Ferguson,* 163 U.S. 537. The Court's decision, which was based on an earlier state supreme court ruling (*Roberts v. City of Boston,* 59 Mass. 198–210 [5 Cush.] [1850]), found segregated schools were permissible under the state's constitution. With *Plessy,* the U.S. Supreme Court ruled that the Fourteenth Amendment did not require racially integrated facilities as long as the facilities were equal, justifying the creation of "Jim Crow" laws and providing legal and constitutional support for the "separate but equal" concept. The *Plessy* ruling had a lasting impact on racial relations in the United States until the 1950s and the U.S. Supreme Court's consideration of *Brown v. Board of Education of Topeka.*

Brown was a landmark case, as the U.S. Supreme Court in a unanimous decision, overturned its previous decision from *Plessy,* stating that the notion of separate but equal was inadequate, as it was found that racially separate facilities were "inherently unequal," even if the facilities of all schools were equally good. Although the *Brown* case declared that separate schools along racial lines were unequal, the Court found it difficult to decide how best to implement its racial desegregation strategy. While the intention was there, the actual desegregating of schools across the country was slow, moving the Supreme Court in its *Brown v. Board of Education II,* 349 U.S. 294 (1955), ruling to order the lower federal courts to require the desegregation of schools with "all deliberate speed." In fact, it was following *Brown II,* in 1957, that the Supreme Court's desegregation strategy would be enforced by President Eisenhower, who sent troops to Little Rock, Arkansas, when the governor, having mobilized the Arkansas National Guard, resisted integration efforts, refusing to allow black students to attend a previously all-white high school. A year later, with states still resisting desegregation orders, the Court ruled that fear of reprisal and social unrest were no excuse for state governments' lack of compliance with the *Brown* ruling (*Cooper v. Aaron,* 368 U.S. 1 [1958]).

Nearly two decades following the 1954 *Brown* decision, the Court still found many obstacles toward desegregation efforts and the means to enforce them. Other significant desegregation incidents the Court dealt with following *Cooper* included its order to Prince Edward County, Virginia, to reopen its schools on a desegregated basis in 1964, after the county had closed the public schools rather than integrate them in 1959, leaving white students to attend private academies and black students unable to attend school until the Ford Foundation funded the creation of private black schools in 1963.

It was not until the adoption of the Civil Rights Act of 1964 that the federal government gained authority to file school desegregation cases and prohibit discrimination in any program, activity, or school that received federal funding. Following the passage of the Civil Rights Act, the Court established "rules" for judging whether school systems were complying with the desegregation mandate in its ruling of *Green v. County School Board of New Kent County, Virginia,* 391 U.S. 430 (1968). The *Green* ruling outlines specific factors for consideration in gauging compliance. These factors include facilities, staff, faculty, extracurricular activities, and transportation. Following this ruling, the Court approved the use of magnet schools, busing, and other "tools" as necessary remedies for overcoming the challenge of residential segregation that impacts and perpetuates school segregation (*Swann v. Charlotte-Mecklenberg Board of Education,* 402 U.S. 1 [1971]). It was not until 1973 that the Supreme Court went further, declaring that while state-sponsored racially segregated schools were unconstitutional, segregation that was a result of private choices was not unconstitutional.

The issue of school desegregation and the means of achieving this end continued to play a large role in American society. In 1986, however, a federal court, for the first time, allowed a school district to be released from desegregation controls after meeting the *Green* factors and allowed the school to return to local control (*Riddick v. School Board of the City of Norfolk, Virginia,* 784 F 2d 521 [4th Circuit] [1986]). Following this precedent, the Supreme Court made it easier for formerly segregated schools to fulfill desegregation orders, thereby releasing them from further constraints (*Board of Education of Oklahoma City v. Dowell,* 498 U.S. 237 [1991]). This ruling illustrated the Supreme Court's changing perspective of desegregation, that the Court felt its desegregation strategies of the 1950s were never meant to be permanent but were intended as remedies that were "limited in time and intent," and that school systems would eventually be returned to local control (*MISSOURI V. JENKINS,* 515 U.S. 70 [1995]).

One would assume that more than 50 years since the landmark *Brown* case was decided by the Supreme Court in 1954, the desegregation rulings and mandates would have proven successful in overcoming segregation in schools. However, despite the progress and forced remedies for countering racial segregation in U.S. schools, a recent study by Harvard's Civil Rights Project has found that schools were in fact more segregated in 2000 than they were in 1970 when busing and other methods were used for desegregating schools.

For more information: Campbell, Duncan. "U.S. Schools Returning to Segregation." *Guardian* (August 10, 2002). Available online. URL: http://www.guardian.co.uk/bush/story/-0,7369,772315,00.html. Accessed June 2, 2008; D'Amato, Anthony A., Rosemary Metrailer, and Stephen L. Wasby. *Desegregation from* Brown *to* Alexander: *An Exploration of Supreme Court Strategies.* Carbondale: Southern Illinois University Press, 1977; Doyle, Mary C. "From Desegregation to Resegregation: Public Schools in Norfolk, Virginia, 1954–2002." *Journal of African American History* 90 (Winter/Spring 2005): 64–83; Raffel, Jeffrey A. *Historical Dictionary of School Segregation and Desegregation: The American Experience.* Westport, Conn.: Greenwood Press, 1998; Wolters, Raymond. "From *Brown* to *Green* and Back: The Changing Meaning of Desegregation," *Journal of Southern History* 70 (May 2004): 317.

—Dale Mineshima-Lowe

DeShaney v. Winnebago County Department of Social Services 489 U.S. 189 (1989)

In *DeShaney v. Winnebago County Department of Social Services,* the Supreme Court ruled that the FOURTEENTH AMENDMENT does not give the government a specific duty to protect an individual from violence committed by another private person.

This case involved a boy, Joshua DeShaney, who suffered several beatings by his father, Randy DeShaney. These beatings took place from 1982 to 1984. In 1982, Randy DeShaney's second wife complained to police that the boy's father had hit the boy in such a manner as to cause marks consistent with child abuse. The Winnebago County Department of Social Services (DSS) conducted an investigation, yet the father denied the charges, and DSS did not pursue the matter further.

During the following year, Joshua was admitted to the hospital with marks and bruises indicative of child abuse. The attending physician notified DSS that Joshua was a possible victim of child abuse. Winnebago County convened a team consisting of a physician, psychologists, a police detective, the county's lawyer, some DSS caseworkers, and hospital staff. This team decided that there was not enough evidence to support an accusation of child abuse; however, the team recommended the father be provided with counseling services, the boy be enrolled in a preschool program, and that the father's girlfriend move out of the home. The boy was returned to the custody of his father. A month later, the hospital contacted DSS and reported that Joshua had returned to the hospital for treatment of suspicious injuries. The caseworker who was assigned to the case did not see any basis for action on the part of DSS. Eventually, in 1984, Joshua was beaten so severely that he suffered brain damage and faced spending his remaining years in an institution for the mentally challenged.

Joshua and his mother brought action against the respondents, Winnebago DSS. The complaint alleged that the DSS had deprived the petitioner of his liberty without DUE PROCESS of law, a violation of his rights under the Fourteenth Amendment. In particular, the DSS had failed to intervene on Joshua's behalf in order to protect him from abuse by his father and that they knew or should have known that the abuse was taking place and that the DSS should have taken steps to provide for Joshua's safety.

The lower courts found in favor of DSS. The case moved to the Supreme Court, and in a 6-3 decision, Chief Justice WILLIAM HUBBS REHNQUIST delivered the opinion, joined by Byron White, JOHN PAUL STEVENS, SANDRA DAY O'CONNOR, ANTONIN GREGORY SCALIA, and ANTHONY M. KENNEDY. The Court found that

> nothing in the language of the Due Process Clause itself requires the State to protect life, liberty, or property of its citizens against invasion by private actors. The Clause is phrased as a limitation on the State's power to act, not as a guarantee of certain minimal levels of safety and security. It forbids the State itself to deprive individuals of life, liberty, or property without "due process of law," but its language cannot fairly be extended to impose affirmative obligation to the State to ensure that those interests do not come to harm through other means.

A state does not incur a duty to protect individuals from violence perpetrated by another private person, especially if a state did not create those problems.

In *Castle Rock v. Gonzales*, 545 U.S. 748 (2005), the Supreme Court ruled that a town and its police could not be sued for the failure to enforce a restraining order that resulted in the murder of a woman. This decision along with *DeShaney v. Winnebago* demonstrate that absent a specific duty to victims, along with some other factors that are under the control of the government, it is hard to demonstrate that public officials have a specific duty to protect individuals from harm.

For more information: Brom, Marne E. "Civil Rights and Civil Rights Acts: An Affirmative Duty to Protect Individuals Who Are Not in the State's Custody from Harm by Private Actors Is Not Imposed on the State by the Fourteenth Amendment's Due Process Clause (Case Note)." *Drake Law Review* 39, no. 4 (Summer 1990): 911–919; Patterson, J. Randall. "Intimate Injuries: Are There Constitutional Law Protections from Family Violence." *Campbell Law Review* 15, no. 1 (Winter 1992): 1–27.

—Dan Krejci

Dickerson v. United States 530 U.S. 428 (2000)

In *Dickerson v. United States*, the Supreme Court held by a 7-2 vote that Miranda rights were a constitutional requirement and therefore could not be superseded by a law passed by Congress. These specific rights were announced in *MIRANDA V. ARIZONA*, 384 U.S. 436 (1966), in which the Supreme Court held that a defendant's statements made while in custodial interrogation could not be used against him or her unless the defendant had been told 1) he/she had the RIGHT TO REMAIN SILENT, 2) anything he/she said could be used against him/her, 3) he/she had the right to an attorney, and 4) if he/she could not afford an attorney, one would be provided.

As a reaction to the ruling in *Miranda v. Arizona*, which required police to read defendants their rights when taken into custodial interrogation, Congress enacted 18 U.S.C. Section 3501, a law allowing admission as evidence statements made by the accused as long as the statements were made voluntarily. According to this law, absence of a Miranda right did not by necessity make such a statement inadmissible.

This law was challenged in *Dickerson*. Charles Dickerson was charged with bank robbery and other crimes. During interrogation, he made a statement to the FBI he later wished to suppress, claiming he had not received his Miranda warnings. The trial court granted his motion. The court of appeals reversed, saying *Miranda* did not enunciate a constitutional rule, so the law enacted by

Congress controlled. Since his statement was voluntary, it was admissible. Thus, the issue became whether the rule from *Miranda* was constitutional in nature or whether it was the Court using its discretion to regulate the admissibility of evidence. If it were the latter, it could be superseded by such an act of Congress.

The Supreme Court agreed with Dickerson. Chief Justice WILLIAM HUBBS REHNQUIST's majority opinion stated that despite prior cases referring to the Miranda warnings as "prophylactic" and "not themselves rights protected by the Constitution" and despite previously carving several exceptions to the requirement, *Miranda* was a constitutional decision. First, the language in *Miranda* and in its progeny often spoke of the warnings being constitutionally required. The exceptions, he argued, "illustrate the principle—not that *Miranda* is not a constitutional rule—but that no constitutional rule is immutable." More important, in *Miranda* and two of its companion cases, the Court applied the requirements to state court decisions. Only if it were a constitutional decision would the Court have had the authority to overrule such state court decisions.

To uphold Section 3501, the opinion states, the Court would have to overrule *Miranda*, and it declined to do so. First, the voluntariness test used before *Miranda* and required by Section 3501 was more difficult for law-enforcement officers to conform to than the *Miranda* requirement. More important, overruling *Miranda* would disregard the principles of stare decisis. Stare decisis is the generally accepted rule that courts should decide similar cases in the same way they ruled in previous decisions. "*Miranda* has become embedded in routine police practice to the point where the warnings have become part of our national culture," the opinion states. It further supported this argument by quoting a preexisting dissent given by Justice ANTONIN GREGORY SCALIA, in which he said: "wide acceptance in the legal culture [is] adequate reason not to overrule [it]." Therefore, the Court stated, though they would not necessarily rule the same way on *Miranda* if it were before the Court now, they refused to overrule it.

Justice Scalia found his own words inapplicable to the present case. He began his dissent by noting the Court may overturn acts of Congress only when the law violates the Constitution. *Miranda*, he says, "however implausibly," was decided on such constitutional grounds; however, he noted, the Court failed to make such a direct statement that it was a constitutional decision, one "surely simple enough to make," because a majority of the present Court (the dissenters Justices CLARENCE THOMAS and Scalia in this case and three of the justices in the current majority in previous cases) had written or joined opinions stating violations of *Miranda* were not perforce constitutional violations. In upholding the rules announced in *Miranda*, the Court assumed a new, "immense and frightening antidemocratic power." Heretofore, the Supreme Court could only overrule a statute when it violated the Constitution. Now, it can also do so when it violates an "announced Constitutional rule."

Justice Scalia criticized the rationale in *Miranda*, stating the idea that a violation of Miranda rules is necessarily a violation of the Constitution has no basis in "history, precedent, or common sense." He also criticized the *Dickerson* opinion and its application of *Miranda*, particularly its reliance on stare decisis, saying it was inapposite since it is no longer reconcilable with existing judicial doctrine.

His solution was to overrule *Miranda* and let the act of Congress control. Doing so, according to Scalia, would allow "the people the wonderful reality that they govern themselves—which means that 'the powers not delegated to the United States by the Constitution' that the people adopted, 'nor prohibited . . . to the States' by that Constitution, 'are reserved to the States respectively, or to the people.'"

Miranda rights, at least at present, are not reserved to the people. However plausible or implausible the rationale may be, they are constitutional in nature since the Supreme Court says they are. There are exceptions, such as statements made to routine booking questions and statements made when there are concerns regarding public safety, but as demonstrated by

Dickerson, substitutes for the rules will not be recognized.

For more information: LaFave, Wayne R., Jerold H. Israel, and Nancy J. King. *Criminal Procedure.* 4th ed. New York: West Publishing, 2004; Weaver, Russell L., Leslie W. Abramson, John M. Burkoff, and Catherine Hancock. *Principles of Criminal Procedure.* New York: West Publishing, 2004.

—Rob DeWees

diplomatic immunity

Diplomatic immunity is a principle of international law that provides foreign diplomats with protection from legal action in the host country. The Vienna Convention on Diplomatic Relations of 1961 and the Vienna Convention on Consular Relations of 1963 codified most modern diplomatic and consular practices, including diplomatic immunity. More than 160 nations are parties to these treaties. The Vienna Convention provides for specific measures that can be taken by both the home and host countries in cases of misuse or abuse of diplomatic PRIVILEGES AND IMMUNITIES. Diplomatic immunity, while not a constitutional issue, is nonetheless an important concept that affects the types of cases the federal courts may hear.

Diplomatic privileges and immunities have served as efficient tools facilitating relations between states. No member state of the United Nations has so far proposed rescinding the convention or rewriting its provisions. The conventions provide immunity to persons according to their rank in a diplomatic mission or consular post and according to the need for immunity in performing their duties. For example, diplomatic agents and members of their immediate families are immune from all criminal prosecution and most civil lawsuits.

Administrative and technical staff members of embassies have a lower level of immunity. Consular officers serving in consulates have an even lower level of immunity. Members of an embassy's service staff and consular employees are immune only for acts performed as part of their official duties.

Modern diplomatic immunity evolved parallel to the development of modern diplomacy. In the 17th century, European diplomats realized that protection from prosecution was essential to doing their jobs, and a set of rules evolved guaranteeing the rights of diplomats. In the 19th century, the Congress of Vienna system reasserted the rights of diplomats and has been ratified by almost every country. In modern times, diplomatic immunity continues to provide a means to safeguard diplomatic personnel from any animosity that might arise between nations. In the United States, if a person with immunity is alleged to have committed a crime or is faced with civil lawsuit, the Department of State alerts the government for which the diplomat works. The Department of State also asks the home country to waive immunity of the alleged offender so that the complaint can be moved to the courts. If immunity is not waived, prosecution cannot be undertaken. However, the U.S. Department of State can ask the diplomat to cease his or her duties in the United States (persona non grata) and leave the nation; the diplomat's visas may be canceled, and the diplomat and his or her family may be barred from returning to the United States. Crimes committed by members of a diplomat's family can also result in this process. On some occasions, diplomatic immunity leads to some unfortunate results: Protected diplomats have violated laws (including those which would be violations at home as well) of the host country. Although the diplomat's nation is responsible for carrying out eventual criminal and civil procedures against him or her, this is often neglected.

Abuse of diplomatic immunity was made more visible by media coverage in the 1990s, ranging from parking violations and child custody law violations to more serious criminal behavior such as domestic abuse and even murder. World headquarters, such as New York City, London, and Paris, have a large number of diplomatic and consular offices. The large number of diplomats often leads to a greater number of legal violations. Historically, the problem of large debts by diplomats has caused problems between host and home country. In some cases, violations have included espionage and smuggling of small high-value items. One of the cases involving espionage took place in 2000, when a Cuban diplomat, expelled by the United States on spying charges, was ordered to give up his diplomatic immunity and was taken into custody by the Federal Bureau of Investigation (FBI).

For more information: Corbett, Percy E. *Law in Diplomacy.* Princeton, N.J.: Princeton University Press, 1967; Frey, Linda, and Marsha Frey. *The History of Diplomatic Immunity.* Columbus: Ohio State University Press, 1999; Nussbaum, Arthur. *A Concise History of the Law of Nations.* New York: Macmillan, 1954; Ogdon, Montell. *Juridical Bases of Diplomatic Immunity: A Study in the Origin, Growth and Purpose of the Law.* Washington, D.C.: J. Byrne & Co., 1936.

—Anna Feygina

discrete and insular minorities

The phrase *discrete and insular minorities* appears in a footnote to *U.S. v. Carolene Products,* 304 U.S. 144 (1938). By itself, that 6-1 Supreme Court decision receives little attention. The footnote, however, is quite a different story. In fact, FOOTNOTE FOUR contained in Justice Harlan Fiske Stone's opinion is generally viewed as the most famous footnote in Supreme Court history, suggesting a rationale for much greater judicial scrutiny of legislation that affects personal liberties and minorities than the rational-basis test applied to laws that involve economic regulation.

Stone's opinion (upholding the Filled Milk Act passed by Congress in 1923 that prohibited milk blended with nondairy fats from entering INTERSTATE COMMERCE) expressed the Court's deference to the legislature in economic matters. After all, in the democratic process, governmental decision making should essentially rest with those who make the law. The presumption that legislative decisions are constitutional, however, is not without limits, precisely the point where footnote four enters the picture.

As originally circulated within the Court, Stone's footnote (shaped by his law clerk Louis Lusky) consisted of two paragraphs, both of which went beyond anything actually required for deciding the case. The first asks whether legislation that serves to limit the operation of the democratic political process should be subject to increased "judicial scrutiny." The second raises the question as to "whether prejudice against discrete and insular minorities may be a special condition, which tends seriously to curtail the operation of those political processes ordinarily to be relied upon to protect minorities, and which may call for a correspondingly more searching judicial inquiry." In other words, when prejudice and discrimination against identifiable and socially isolated groups keeps legislatures from responding to grievances, the standard presumption of constitutionality for legislative acts falls by the wayside.

In response to a point raised by Chief Justice Charles Evans Hughes, Stone added a third paragraph at the beginning of the footnote. That paragraph suggested similar judicial scrutiny when legislation, on its face, appears to violate protections offered by the BILL OF RIGHTS, including those applied to the states through the FOURTEENTH AMENDMENT. Footnote four thus proposes that certain freedoms occupy a preferred position in the constitutional structure and that the courts have a special responsibility to protect those preferred rights in a manner that goes well beyond deference to the political branches. In this sense, it provides a path on which personal liberty and minority rights travel in a constitutional lane quite separate from that of the economic regulation exercised by Congress and state legislatures.

Six years after the *Carolene Products* decision, the Supreme Court, in *KOREMATSU V. UNITED STATES,* 323 U.S. 214 (1944), formally adopted the tentative call found in footnote four regarding a more searching and exacting standard for the judicial scrutiny of laws involving "discrete and insular" racial minorities. And that call continues to resonate in constitutional law, although the doctrinal debate over its validity has not abated.

For more information: Lusky, Louis. *By What Right?* Charlottesville, Va.: Michie Co., 1975;

Mason, Alpheus Thomas. *Harlan Fiske Stone: Pillar of the Law.* New York: Viking Press, 1956.

—Norman Provizer

disparate impact

The disparate impact theory, first articulated by the Supreme Court in the seminal decision *GRIGGS V. DUKE POWER CO.*, 401 U.S. 424 (1971), allows facially neutral employment practices to be deemed illegal under federal equal employment opportunity statutes without evidence of the employer's intent to discriminate. The theory stands in stark contrast to legal standards under the EQUAL PROTECTION clause, which requires proof of INTENTIONAL DISCRIMINATION to establish a constitutional violation.

The *Griggs* case involved a company that had intentionally segregated its workforce prior to the passage of Title VII of the CIVIL RIGHTS ACT OF 1964. African Americans were limited to the low-paying and undesirable positions within the labor department; furthermore, in 1955, the company imposed a high school diploma requirement for hire into any department other than labor. After the passage of Title VII, the company also instituted a two-part written examination procedure for all individuals seeking employment or departmental transfer. The effect of the diploma and testing requirements was to preserve the segregated job lines and to exclude a majority of African Americans from hire or transfer.

In spite of the employer's long history of racial segregation, the Supreme Court did not see the case as one of intentional discrimination, due primarily to the employer's laudatory goal of improving the educational credentials of its workforce and its apparent willingness to pay the educational costs of employees who sought to complete high school. However, recognizing what an obstacle to eradicating EMPLOYMENT DISCRIMINATION such hiring standards could be, the Court held that plaintiffs may establish a prima facie case of discrimination by showing that a facially neutral policy has an adverse impact on a class protected under Title VII. (To this end, the Court gave a nod to the Equal Employment Opportunity Commission's "four-fifths" rule, which states that a minority group's passage rate of less than 80 percent of the dominant group's rate demonstrates adverse impact.) This holding did not preclude the use of such testing or qualification mechanisms but rather required that the employer show that the neutral policies or practices were job related and justified by business necessity to avoid a finding of discrimination. In the *Griggs* ruling, the Court emphasized that "absence of discriminatory intent does not redeem [such] employment procedures" and that "Congress has forbidden . . . giving these devices and mechanisms controlling force unless they are demonstrably a measure of job performance."

Although the Court held that such neutral practices should not be permitted to constitute "built-in headwinds" for minorities and women, the Court declined to extend the disparate impact theory to analogous constitutional claims five years after *Griggs*. In *WASHINGTON V. DAVIS*, 426 U.S. 229 (1976), plaintiffs challenged a written test administered by the DISTRICT OF COLUMBIA police department, which African Americans failed at a rate approximately four times that of whites. Because the lawsuit had been filed in 1970, two years before the applicability of Title VII to public employers, the testing procedures were challenged on equal protection, rather than statutory, grounds. However, although the tests were comparable to those challenged in *Griggs*, the Court not only emphasized that proof of discriminatory intent was necessary for a constitutional violation but expressly rejected the effects-based reasoning of its previous decision, holding, "We have difficulty understanding how a law establishing a racially neutral qualification for employment is nevertheless racially discriminatory . . . simply because a greater proportion of Negroes fail to qualify than members of other racial or ethnic groups."

Following *Davis*, the Court continued to restrict the applicability of the disparate impact theory almost exclusively to Title VII litigation, declining to extend it to claims under the Section 1981 Civil Rights Statute, to FIFTEENTH AMENDMENT voting rights, or to a lawsuit over a road closing. And while the Court allowed application of the theory to a Title VI claim, involving the regulations requiring recipients of governmental funding to comply with nondiscrimination requirements, the complex holding also stated that the statute itself only prohibited intentional discrimination.

In the Title VII arena, however, the development of disparate impact theory continued to ebb and flow. A few years after the *Griggs* decision, the Court elucidated in *Albemarle Paper Co. v. Moody,* 422 U.S. 405 (1975), the requirements for validating written tests and showing job relatedness and business necessity. In 1988, the Court resolved the issue of whether disparate impact theory could be applied in cases in which subjective employment practices (in this case, making promotions based purely on supervisory recommendations) have allegedly led to an adverse impact on minorities. In *Watson v. Fort Worth Bank & Trust,* 487 U.S. 977 (1988), the Court was "persuaded that [its] decisions in *Griggs* and succeeding cases could largely be nullified if disparate impact analysis were applied only to standardized selection practices."

The Court appeared to contract the reach of disparate impact analysis when it made it easier for employers to demonstrate business necessity in *Ward's Cove Packing Co. v. Atonio,* 490 U.S. 642 (1989), holding that "there is no requirement that the challenged practice be 'essential' or 'indispensable' to the employer's business to pass muster." However, Congress legislatively overruled the Court when the 1991 Civil Rights Act restored the definition of business necessity to its pre–*Ward's Cove* standard (42 U.S.C.A. Section 2000e-[2][k]).

In 2005, the Court resolved an issue long in dispute in the federal circuits, namely, the applicability of disparate impact analysis to claims under the Age Discrimination in Employment Act (ADEA). In *Smith v. City of Jackson,* 544 U.S. 228 (2005), the Court held that such claims may be raised under the ADEA but that the scope of disparate impact theory is more limited than under Title VII due to two textual differences between the two statutes.

For more information: Chandler, Ralph Clark, and William A. Ritchie, eds. *The American Constitution at the End of the Twentieth Century.* Kalamazoo: Western Michigan University, 1996.

—Virginia Mellema

District of Columbia

The District of Columbia (D.C.) is the location of the capital of the United States, and the governance of this area is entrusted to Congress under the Constitution.

Congress selected a permanent site for the capital district in 1790. Land in Maryland and Virginia bordering the Potomac River was purchased. Until 1800, residents continued to vote in elections held in those states. In 1801, Congress assumed the exclusive legislative power granted to it over its seat of government by the 1787 Constitution (Article I, Section 8, Clause 17). At that point, nonslave residents lost their equal rights. For the next 160 years, residents of what later was named the District of Columbia were disenfranchised in presidential elections.

In the 1920s, the Voteless League of Women Voters and, in the 1930s, the District Suffrage League championed voting rights and home rule in the District of Columbia. Fearing that the Soviet Union would criticize the United States for D.C. voters' exclusion from presidential elections, the Eisenhower administration and the Department of State supported the TWENTY-THIRD AMENDMENT. So, too, did the modern CIVIL RIGHTS movement, but responding to the District of Columbia's growing African-American population (53.9 percent by 1960), segregationists in Congress insisted on a weakened version. It passed on June 16, 1960. In the second-fastest ratification ever, it was approved by three-fourths of state legislatures in less than nine months. The compromise limited the District of Columbia to "no . . . more [electoral votes] than the least populous state." At the time, the District of Columbia was more populous than several states and would have been allotted more than three electoral votes.

In 1970, Congress restored the nonvoting delegate position that had been tried during 1871–74.

And under the 1973 District of Columbia Home Rule Act, Congress delegated legislative powers to the Council of the District of Columbia while retaining ultimate authority not only in the National Capitol Service Area but also over the entire district. However, substantive reforms advanced no further. Residents of national capital regions in Japan, South Korea, the Philippines, Mexico, Canada and many other representative democracies are not similarly disenfranchised. And despite congressional approval of the D.C. Voting Rights Constitutional Amendment in 1978 to give voting representation in Congress to the District of Columbia, less than half the required number of state legislatures ratified it before the deadline expired in 1985.

Twenty-four years after a statehood movement began, the HOUSE OF REPRESENTATIVES rejected the proposal in 1993. Pro-statehood sentiment has persisted. According to one public opinion poll in 2002, nearly 60 percent of D.C. citizens supported statehood. Also in 1993, the U.S. House of Representatives gave the delegate from the District of Columbia a nondecisive vote on the floor of the House on those occasions when it met as a Committee of the Whole. Previously, the D.C. delegate only voted in committee meetings. Yet, even this modest gesture was withdrawn two months after the Republican landslide in the November 1994 congressional elections.

Barbara Lett-Simmons, democratic elector from the District of Columbia, withheld her vote from Al Gore to protest the District of Columbia's "colonial status" in 2000. Along with felons and ex-felons in most states, D.C. residents have not yet won rights to self-government enjoyed by most of their fellow citizens.

For more information: Richards, Mark David. "The Debates over Retrocession of the District of Columbia, 1801–2004." *Washington History* 16, no. 1 (Spring/Summer 2004): 55–82; Richards, Mark David. "Taxation Without Representation." *Public Perspective* 14, no. 1 (January/February 2003): 11–15.

—Vincent Kelly Pollard

District of Columbia v. Heller, ___ U.S. ___, 128 S.Ct. 2783 (2008)

In *District of Columbia v. Heller,* the U.S. Supreme Court declared unconstitutional on SECOND AMENDMENT grounds a District of Columbia law that banned the possession of handguns, including in one's own home. *Heller* was the first case where a law was found unconstitutional on Second Amendment grounds. The decision also was the first to declare that the Second Amendment protected a personal right of individuals to possess firearms.

While the Second Amendment refers to a right to bear arms, a critical historical and constitutional question has been over whether the right is collective or individual. Specifically, the phrasing of the text of the amendment makes it unclear whether the right to bear arms should be read within the context of the first part of the amendment, which refers to the militia, and, therefore, it only protects a collective right, or whether the language should be read to protect an individual right.

From 1791, when it was adopted as part of the BILL OF RIGHTS, until 2008, the U.S. Supreme Court offered little assistance in interpreting the Second Amendment. In *United States v. Cruikshank*, 92 U.S. 542 (1875), and in *Presser v. Illinois*, 116 U.S. 252 (1886), the Court refused requests to incorporate the amendment as a limit upon states. In *United States v. Miller,* 307 U.S. 174 (1939), the Court implied that the right to bear arms protected more of a collective than an individual right.

District of Columbia v. Heller arose in the context of a District of Columbia law that banned handgun possession. It made it a crime to carry an unregistered firearm, prohibited the registration of handguns, and required residents in their homes to keep lawfully owned firearms unloaded and dissembled or bound by a trigger lock or similar device. The law did allow for some special permits to carry guns. Richard Heller sought to register a handgun for his home, but he was refused a permit. He challenged the law, contending that it violated his Second Amendment rights. A District of Columbia district court dismissed his suit, the court of appeals reversed, agreeing that the Second Amendment protected his individual right to possess a gun in his home for self-defense.

In a 5-4 opinion, Justice ANTONIN SCALIA upheld the court of appeals and ruled in favor of Heller, holding that the Second Amendment does confer an individual right to bear arms. In reaching this decision, the majority drew upon both a textual and historical reading of the Second Amendment. First, it argued that the prefatory language of the amendment—"A well regulated Militia, being necessary to the security of a free State"—while defining its purposes, does not limit the right to bear arms. Second, the Court then undertook a historical analysis of English history, similar state constitutional clauses in place when the Second Amendment was written, and scholarly articles. The Court concluded that these three sources all supported an individual right to possess arms.

The majority also ruled that while the Second Amendment did protect an individual right to bear arms, that did not mean that all efforts to limit or regulate guns or weapons would be found unconstitutional. Justice Scalia noted first that many historical laws preventing felons, for example, from possessing guns would not be affected by this ruling. He also stated that the Second Amendment, like all other amendments, was not absolute, and, therefore, some limits on gun ownership would be permissible.

Writing for the dissent, Justice JOHN PAUL STEVENS argued that the debate over the Second Amendment was not whether it protected an individual or collective right but, instead, over the scope of the right to bear arms. He contended that while the Second Amendment may protect a right to use weapons to hunt and for self-defense, it did not extend to using guns to rob a bank. His argument was that nothing in text, history, or past precedents of the Second Amendment precludes the government from regulating the civilian use of the weapons. He accused the majority of reaching a political decision, one not supported by any new scholarship.

District of Columbia v. Heller was a controversial decision that left many unanswered questions. Scalia's opinion did not offer much guidance regarding what regulations on guns the Second Amendment did permit. Moreover, given that the *Heller* opinion addressed a District of Columbia law, it also did not address the question of whether the Second Amendment was incorporated to apply to the states. Both of these issues will be the basis of future litigation on the amendment.

For more information: Carlson, Andrew. *The Antiquated Right.* New York: Peter Lang, 2002; Cornell, Saul, ed. *Whose Right to Bear Arms Did the Second Amendment Protect?* New York: St. Martin's Press, 2000; Cottrol, Robert J., ed. *Gun Control and the Constitution: Sources and Explorations on the Second Amendment.* New York: Garland Publishing, 1994.

—David Schultz

diversity jurisdiction

Diversity jurisdiction is federal court jurisdiction over lawsuits between citizens of different states. Section 2 of ARTICLE III OF THE U.S. CONSTITUTION provides that the "judicial Power shall extend to all Cases in Law and Equity . . . between Citizens of different States." The statute authorizing diversity jurisdiction provides: "The district courts shall have ORIGINAL JURISDICTION of all civil actions where the matter in controversy exceeds the sum or value of $75,000 . . . and is between Citizens of different states" (28 U.S.C. Section 1332 [a][1]).

The idea behind providing a federal forum for disputes between citizens of different states is to protect out-of-state litigants from potential favoritism (or the perception of favoritism) by state court judges toward their own citizens. In response to criticism of this premise, Chief Justice JOHN MARSHALL once stated: "[h]owever true the fact may be, that the tribunals of the states will administer justice as impartially as those of the nation . . . it is not less true that the constitution itself . . . entertains apprehensions on this subject" (*Bank of*

United States v. Deveaux, 9 U.S. 61, 87 [1809]). Today a lively debate continues over the modern-day need for diversity jurisdiction.

Because the federal courts are courts of limited jurisdiction, Congress and the Supreme Court have worked to limit the reach of diversity jurisdiction. The first major limitation is the statutory requirement that litigants in diversity suits be fighting over at least a minimum amount of money or value to keep trivial cases out of federal court (28 U.S.C. Section 1332[a][1]). The JUDICIARY ACT OF 1789 initially set the amount in controversy at $500. In 1958, Congress increased it to $10,000, then to $50,000 in 1988, and to the current amount of $75,000 in 1996 (Erwin Chemerinski, Federal Jurisdiction 304 [Aspen 2003]). The amount in controversy is judged from the perspective of the plaintiff. All a plaintiff must do is claim more than the $75,000 required by the statute, and federal court jurisdiction exists unless it appears "to a legal certainty that the claim is really for less than the jurisdictional amount" (*Saint Paul Mercy Indemnity Co. v. Red Cab Co.*, 303 U.S. 283, 288 [1938]).

The second major limitation on the federal courts' diversity jurisdiction is judicially created. In *Strawbridge v. Curtiss*, 7 U.S. 267 (1806), the Supreme Court held that the federal courts only had diversity jurisdiction if "complete diversity" existed, that is, only if every defendant is a citizen of a different state from every plaintiff. A party's citizenship is determined by his or her domicile. *Domicile* is defined as the place where an individual has his or her true home, where he or she is physically present and intends to remain (*Mississippi Band of Choctaw Indians v. Holyfield*, 490 U.S. 30, 48 [1989]). If one defendant has his or her domicile in the same state as one plaintiff, diversity is destroyed, and the case must be sent to state court. Despite these limitations, however, diversity jurisdiction remains an important doorway into the federal courts, and so-called diversity cases account for a significant portion of the cases tried in federal court.

For more information: Rowe, Thomas D. "Abolishing Diversity Jurisdiction: Positive Side Effects and Potential for Further Reforms." *Harvard Law Review* 92 (1979): 963–1,012.

—Alaina Fotiu-Wojtowicz

Dolan v. City of Tigard 512 U.S. 374 (1994)

In *Dolan v. City of Tigard*, the Supreme Court ruled that a requirement that an owner dedicate part of her property to a public way in return for obtaining a building permit was an unconstitutional taking of private property without JUST COMPENSATION.

Dolan is among several U.S. Supreme Court opinions, tracing back to 1897, that address the TAKINGS CLAUSE of the Fifth Amendment. *Dolan* also represents a contemporary round in the long-standing debate over the appropriate constitutional relationship between property rights and POLICE POWERS. Furthermore, *Dolan* itself has been the focal point of disputes over whether the decision's "REGULATORY TAKINGS" analysis resurrects a pre–New Deal jurisprudence derived from the controversial *LOCHNER V. NEW YORK*, 198 U.S. 45 (1905).

Acting under its Community Development Code and its Master Drainage Plan, the city of Tigard attached several conditions to a redevelopment permit for which Florence Dolan, owner of A-Boy Plumbing & Electrical, had applied. The conditions required Dolan to cede part of her property for storm drainage system improvements and an additional portion as a pedestrian/bicycle pathway. Dolan's unsuccessful pursuit of variances through a series of administrative and judicial appeals in Oregon venues culminated when the Oregon Supreme Court rejected her petition. The Oregon court's decision turned on its interpretation that a 1987 U.S. Supreme Court decision (*Nollan v. California Coastal Commission*, 483 U.S. 825) held that so long as permit conditions were "reasonably related" to the permit requested, such conditions raised no takings problem.

Speaking through Chief Justice WILLIAM HUBBS REHNQUIST, a 5-4 U.S. Supreme Court reversed. Notably, the Court tacitly disagreed with the Oregon Supreme Court's reading of the *Nollan* test. Repackaging and toughening *Nollan*'s "essential nexus" test, Rehnquist elaborated on the controlling "federal constitutional norm." "We think a term such as 'rough proportionality' best encapsulates what we hold to be the requirement of the Fifth Amendment," he wrote. "No precise mathematical calculation is required, but the city must make some sort of individualized determination that the required dedication is related both in nature and extent to the impact of the proposed development."

Justice JOHN PAUL STEVENS, writing for himself and two other dissenters, took issue with this restated *Nollan* standard. "The correct inquiry," Stevens argued, "should . . . concentrate on whether the required nexus is present and venture beyond considerations of a condition's nature or germaneness only if the developer establishes that a concededly germane condition is so grossly disproportionate to the proposed development's adverse effects that it manifests motives other than land use regulation on the part of the city." The Court's reading of *Nollan* is mischievous twice over, Stevens continued, because "[t]he Court . . . made a serious error by abandoning the traditional presumption of constitutionality and imposing a novel burden of proof on a city implementing an admittedly valid comprehensive land use plan." In addition, the Court "resurrect[ed] . . . a species of SUBSTANTIVE DUE PROCESS analysis that it firmly rejected decades ago." "One can only hope," Stevens added, "that the Court's . . . disavowal of the term 'rational basis' to describe its new standard of review do[es] not signify a reassertion of the kind of superlegislative power the Court exercised during the *Lochner* era."

It remains to be seen if Justice Stevens's hopes will be realized or dashed. Three subsequent takings decisions—*Palazzolo v. Rhode Island*, 533 U.S. 606 (2001); *Tahoe-Sierra Preservation Council v. Tahoe Regional Planning Agency*, 535 U.S. 302 (2002); and *KELO V. CITY OF NEW LONDON*, 545 U.S. 469 (2005)—have muddied, rather than clarified, the situation.

For more information: Crane, Daniel A. "Comment: A Poor Relation? Regulatory Takings after *Dolan v. City of Tigard*." *University of Chicago Law Review* 63 (Winter 1996): 199; Sullivan, Edward J. "Substantive Due Process Resurrected through the Takings Clause: *Nollan, Dolan,* and *Ehrlich*." *Environmental Law* 25 (Winter 1995): 155.

—James C. Foster

dormant commerce clause

The dormant commerce clause refers to a theory of constitutional law that places limits on state regulation of interstate trade, even in the absence of explicit congressional action. This theory of how to interpret the COMMERCE CLAUSE has a long and often controversial history.

The commerce clause of the Constitution gives the federal government power "[t]o regulate Commerce . . . among the several States." The Constitution does not expressly restrict state regulation of interstate trade; however, it is accepted that the grant to the federal government of authority over INTERSTATE COMMERCE implies some limits on the states' authority in that area. The founders called for the CONSTITUTIONAL CONVENTION of 1787 in large part because of divisive trade disputes among the states, which threatened the peace and economic viability of the new nation. The delegates to the Constitutional Convention gave the federal government power to regulate interstate commerce in order to prevent those disputes.

According to JAMES MADISON, the commerce clause was not expected to result in federal regulation of trade. Madison expected that Congress would be unable to pass commerce-related regulations because of the states' conflicting economic interests. Instead, he expected the commerce clause to act mainly "as a negative and preventive provision against injustice among the States themselves." What Madison referred to as the "negative" aspect of the commerce clause is often called the "dormant" commerce clause.

The operation of the so-called dormant commerce clause must not be confused with that of the commerce clause. The dormant commerce clause does not come into play when Congress has passed a law regulating commerce. In that case (unless the regulation is unconstitutional under the commerce clause), the federal law preempts any inconsistent state laws, as all federal regulations do under the SUPREMACY CLAUSE. The dormant commerce clause becomes relevant only when a state law is challenged that regulates a trade-related matter with which Congress has not dealt. In that case, the challenged state law is unconstitutional if the commerce clause implicitly denies the states' power to pass the challenged law.

The dormant commerce clause denies the states power to pass three kinds of laws. First, state laws that overtly discriminate against out-of-state commercial interests for the purpose of protecting the state's own economic interests are unconstitutional. For example, in *Welton v. Missouri,* 1 Otto (91 U.S.) 275 (1876), the Court struck down a Missouri law that required peddlers of goods "not the growth, produce, or manufacture of [Missouri]" to be licensed but did not require peddlers of Missouri goods to be licensed. In *PHILADELPHIA V. NEW JERSEY,* 437 U.S. 617 (1978), the Court struck down a New Jersey law that banned the importation of garbage from sources outside the state. The Court also has struck down ordinances passed by local governments that discriminate against nonlocal interests. In *Dean Milk Co. v. Madison,* the Court struck down a Madison, Wisconsin, ordinance that prohibited the sale of milk processed at plants located outside a five-mile radius of Madison.

In most cases, the state's purpose is not evident on the face of the statute. In such cases, the Court has not hesitated to look beyond the text of the statute for evidence of a protectionist purpose. For example, in *Baldwin v. Seelig,* 294 U.S. 511 (1935), the Court struck down a New York law that banned the sale of milk purchased from milk producers at prices below minimum levels. The law was challenged by a milk dealer who was prohibited by the law from selling milk in New York that he had purchased below the New York minimum price in Vermont. The Court found that the law's purpose was to protect the economic interests of New York milk producers.

In *Bacchus Imports v. Dias,* 468 U.S. 263 (1984), the Court struck down another protectionist law, a Hawaii law that exempted brandy distilled from a root native to the state from the state liquor tax. The Court has sometimes relied on a challenged law's effect as evidence of a protectionist purpose. For example, in *Hunt v. Washington State Apple Advertising Comm'n,* 432 U.S. 333 (1977), the Court struck down a North Carolina law that banned apples graded according to any quality standard other than the U.S. Department of Agriculture standard. In effect, the law excluded apples from the state of Washington, which required its apples to be graded according to higher-quality standards. The Court has upheld state regulations of intrastate commerce that only "incidentally" affect interstate commerce.

In *Milk Control Board v. Eisenberg Farm Products Co.,* 306 U.S. 346 (1939), a law setting minimum prices for Pennsylvania milk was challenged by a New York milk dealer. The Court upheld the law because "[o]nly a small fraction of the milk produced by farmers in Pennsylvania is shipped out of [Pennsylvania]" and "[t]he purpose of the [law] obviously is to reach a domestic situation in the interests of the welfare of the producers and consumers of milk in Pennsylvania." In *H. P. HOOD & SONS V. DU MOND,* 336 U.S. 525 (1949), however, the Court struck down another New York law setting minimum prices for milk, finding that the law's purpose was not to deal with a domestic concern but rather to protect New York milk producers.

Finally, the Court has struck down state laws that do not facially discriminate against out-of-state interests or have an impermissible protectionist purpose but that nevertheless "unduly burden" interstate commerce. In such cases, the Court has applied a balancing test set forth in *Pike v. Bruce Church,* 397 U.S. 137 (1970): "Where the statute regulates evenhandedly to effectuate a legitimate local public interest, and its effects on interstate commerce are only incidental, it will be upheld unless the burden imposed on such commerce is clearly excessive in relation to the putative local benefits." For example, in *SOUTHERN PACIFIC COMPANY V. ARIZONA,* 325 U.S. 781 (1945), the Court struck down a law that prohibited trains of more than 14 passenger cars or 70 freight cars from running on railroads in Arizona. The Court found that the law placed a serious burden on interstate commerce and that that burden was not outweighed by Arizona's interest in train safety. In *Kassel v. Consolidated Freightways,* 450 U.S. 662 (1981), the Court struck down, under the same balancing test, an Iowa law that prohibited most trucks over 55 feet in length from traveling on that state's highways.

For more information: Benson, Paul R. *The Supreme Court and the Commerce Clause, 1937–1970.* New York: Dunellan Publishing, 1970; Schwartz, Bernard. *A History of the Supreme Court.* New York: Oxford University Press, 1993.

—Nathan M. Ingebretson

double jeopardy

Double jeopardy is standing trial for the same offense more than once. It is a procedural defense and understood to be the citizen's right to be protected from prosecution, for the same offense, for a second time after being convicted or acquitted of the offense. The right arises from the Fifth Amendment to the Constitution, where it is delineated that "nor shall any person be subject for the same offense to be twice put in jeopardy of life or limb." Here, the Constitution places limitations on the legal system and specifically the government to limit potential abuse.

Tracing the roots of the concept of double jeopardy leads back to the ancient Athenians and Romans, who had codified the concept. The ban on double jeopardy also has its roots in English common law, and the framers of the Constitution read the writings of British legal thinkers such as Sir WILLIAM BLACKSTONE's *Commentaries on the Laws of England* (1769) and used his writings as a basis for argument.

The concept of double jeopardy can be understood as further defined in three distinct areas, which are protection from retrial after conviction, protection from being tried again for a crime once an acquittal has been rendered within the court, and protection from multiple trials and punishments for the same offense by the same jurisdiction. An example of such a restriction of whether someone can be brought to trial for the same offense is found in the Supreme Court decision in *Fong Foo v. United States,* 369 U.S. 141 (1962), where the Court ruled that it was double jeopardy to bring someone to trial again when he had been acquitted for that offense. The Supreme Court ruled in *Benton v. Maryland,* 39 U.S. 784 (1969), that double jeopardy is incorporated to the states through the DUE PROCESS clause of the FOURTEENTH AMENDMENT to the Constitution.

There are some exceptions to double jeopardy; for example, this Fifth Amendment prohibition applies only to criminal prosecution. Thus, after O. J. Simpson was acquitted in 1995 for the murder of his ex-wife and Ronald Goldman, he was not placed in double jeopardy (according to the Constitution) when he was found responsible for their deaths in a civil trial in 1997. Additionally, the Court has ruled in *Heath v. Alabama,* 474 U.S. 82 (1985), that double jeopardy does not attach when one is prosecuted by separate jurisdictions. Thus, if one faces trial at the state level and is acquitted, double jeopardy does not attach if one is then prosecuted by the federal government. During the 1960s, it was a common practice of the Justice Department to prosecute CIVIL RIGHTS cases in federal court after state acquittals. Double jeopardy does not apply if one is found guilty and then an appellate court reserves the conviction.

Finally, determining exactly when double jeopardy attaches is not always easy to ascertain. While it comes into play once a verdict has been reached in a case, it is not always applicable when one has been acquitted under one statute and then charged under another. Here, the courts say that double jeopardy attaches when one is being prosecuted for the same underlying facts.

The right against double jeopardy is an important constitutional protection. It prevents the government from repeatedly harassing individuals with prosecutions until some court finally convicts or the those charged with crimes give up.

For more information: LaFave, Wayne R., Jerold H. Israel, and Nancy J. King. *Criminal Procedure.* St. Paul, Minn.: Thomson/West, 2004;

Thomas, George C. III. *Double Jeopardy: The History, the Law.* New York: New York University Press, 1998.

—Ernest Gomez and David Schultz

Douglas, William O. (1898–1980) *Supreme Court justice*

William O. Douglas was the longest-serving Supreme Court justice in U.S. history. He was nominated and confirmed in 1939; a debilitating stroke finally forced his retirement in 1975. Throughout his life, Douglas was a relentless champion of individual rights, CIVIL LIBERTIES, and the environment. While on the bench, Douglas was a workhorse, participating in more than 1,200 decisions and drafting nearly 800 dissents. This penchant for dissent earned Douglas the nicknames "the Great Dissenter" and "the Lone Ranger."

Douglas, the second of three children, was born in Maine, Minnesota, on October 16, 1898. When he was very young the Douglas family moved west, finally settling in Washington State. Douglas's early life was quite challenging: Douglas fell ill, nearly dying from a high fever before his second birthday; his father, a Presbyterian minister, died when Douglas was six; and the family struggled with poverty. Douglas overcame this adversity to graduate as valedictorian of his high school class. He received a partial scholarship to attend Whitman College, where, in 1920, he graduated Phi Beta Kappa with a B.A. in English and economics.

After spending a few years as a high school teacher, Douglas decided to attend Columbia Law School. Upon graduation, he practiced law for a brief time before taking a teaching position at Columbia Law School and then at Yale Law School. In 1936, President Franklin D. Roosevelt appointed Douglas to the Securities and Exchange Commission, and in 1937, Roosevelt elevated him to serve as the commission's chairman.

On February 13, 1939, Justice Louis Brandeis retired from the Supreme Court. In March, President Roosevelt summoned Douglas to the White House for "an important meeting." Douglas feared that he was being appointed chair of the Federal Communications Commission, but instead, Roosevelt informed Douglas that he was being nominated to replace Brandeis. Douglas was quickly confirmed by a 62-4 vote in the SENATE and was sworn in on April 17, 1939. Douglas, only 40 at the time, became the second youngest person ever to serve on the Court.

Douglas, along with longtime ally and friend Justice HUGO BLACK, argued for a literalist interpretation of the FIRST AMENDMENT. They believed that the First Amendment's command that "no law" shall restrict freedom of speech should be interpreted literally. Douglas even went further, believing that conduct could also be protected by the First Amendment. He voted to prohibit the punishment of students who wore an armband in protest of the Vietnam War in *TINKER V. DES MOINES INDEPENDENT COMMUNITY SCHOOL DISTRICT,* 393 U.S. 503 (1969). In *COHEN V. CALIFORNIA,* 403 U.S. 15 (1971), he voted to protect the wearing of a jacket with a four-letter expletive in a courthouse as protected speech. And he filed a concurrence in *New York Times Co. v. United States,* 403 U.S. 713 (1971), a plurality opinion that allowed the *New York Times* and the *Washington Post* to publish the classified Pentagon Papers without fearing government censure.

Arguably Douglas's most important and controversial opinion was delivered in *GRISWOLD V. CONNECTICUT,* 381 U.S. 479 (1965). In striking a state prohibition on aiding and abetting or counseling the use of contraception, Douglas articulated a broad constitutional right to PRIVACY. He found that the "specific guarantees in the Bill of Rights have penumbras, formed by emanations from those guarantees that help give them life and substance." Douglas argued that these various guarantees, such as the Fifth Amendment's self-incrimination clause, "create zones of privacy." This notion of privacy, first articulated in *Griswold,* has since been expanded to protect a woman's right to ABORTION, the RIGHT TO DIE, and the rights of sexual intimacy for homosexuals.

In his waning years on the Court, Douglas became frustrated and felt isolated. Though he had been a champion of liberal causes for almost 15 years before Chief Justice Earl Warren and Justice WILLIAM J. BRENNAN, JR. joined the Court, the couple received the credit for leading the liberal bloc. And after the retirement of Justice Black, Douglas never had another close relationship on the bench. Douglas, however, was a true survivor: He survived a heart attack in 1968, three divorces, and multiple IMPEACHMENT attempts. On December 31, 1974, Douglas suffered a serious stroke that left him partially paralyzed and confined to a wheelchair. Though he never recovered, Douglas attempted to continue on the Court. For 11 months he was wheeled into oral arguments and, after usually falling asleep at the bench, carried away by Court personnel. On November 12, 1975, he finally succumbed to the immense pressure on him and announced his retirement.

Douglas died at Walter Reed Army Medical Center in Bethesda, Maryland, on January 19, 1980. He lies buried at Arlington National Cemetery near the graves of Justices Brennan, OLIVER WENDELL HOLMES, JR., Thurgood Marshall, and Potter Stewart. In personal reflection, Douglas had often said that one of his most shameful moments was his vote to uphold President Roosevelt's relocation of Japanese Americans in *KOREMATSU V. UNITED STATES,* 323 U.S. 214 (1944), and one of his proudest moments was his vote to disallow President RICHARD NIXON to use executive privilege to keep the Watergate tapes from Congress in *UNITED STATES V. NIXON,* 418 U.S. 683 (1974).

For more information: Douglas, William O. *The Court Years 1939–1975: The Autobiography of William O. Douglas.* New York: Random House, 1980; Douglas, William O. *Go East Young Man: The Early Years.* New York: Random House, 1974; Murphy, Bruce Allen. *Wild Bill: The Legend and Life of William O. Douglas.* New York: Random House, 2003; Simon, James F. *Independent Journey: The Life of William O. Douglas.* New York: Harper & Row, 1980.

—Raymond V. Carman, Jr.

draft card burning

Draft card burning refers to the destruction of papers inducting one into the military as a means to protest a war or some other government policy. While such an act is clearly political in nature, the Supreme Court has ruled that this is not protected expression under the FIRST AMENDMENT.

The U.S. government issued Selective Service Registration Certificates, or draft cards, to notify young men to report for military duty. When Vietnam War protesters began burning their draft cards, Congress amended the 1948 Universal Military Training and Service Act, also referred to as the Selective Service Act, in 1965, to make the knowing destruction or mutilation of a draft card a felony. Some antiwar protesters, however, continued to burn their cards.

On March 31, 1966, David O'Brien and three of his friends set their draft cards on fire in front of a Boston courthouse as a form of protest to the Vietnam War. After being trampled by angry onlookers, O'Brien and his party were detained and later arrested by FBI agents. O'Brien was convicted of violating the Selective Service Act and sentenced to six years in prison. He appealed his conviction on the grounds that burning his draft card was SYMBOLIC SPEECH. He further claimed that the Selective Service Act had been hastily amended for the purpose of suppressing antiwar dissent.

The U.S. court of appeals agreed that Congress's intent in amending the law violated the First Amendment, yet the court upheld O'Brien's conviction on the grounds of "non-possession" of his draft card, despite the fact that he had not been charged with this offense prior to the appeals ruling. Both O'Brien and the U.S. government, represented by Solicitor General Erwin Griswold, appealed this ruling and the U.S. Supreme Court granted review. In oral argument, Griswold conceded that burning drafts cards may constitute symbolic speech, but he argued that Congress has the power to criminalize O'Brien's conduct, as he fails to report for military duty. When O'Brien burned his draft card, in other words, he impeded the government's communication with the men who are obligated to serve in the military. This case was timely given the heightened controversy relating to antiwar protest.

In *UNITED STATES V. O'BRIEN,* 391 U.S. 367 (1968), all but one of the justices agreed with the government. Writing for the majority, Chief Justice Earl Warren ruled that O'Brien's act of burning his draft card was not protected expression under the First Amendment but a violation of the 1965 amendment to the Selective Service Act. In response to O'Brien's defense that the card in question did not truly provide notification, Warren explained the card's use went beyond simply notification and served an administrative purpose that benefited both the government and the registrant.

In times of war, the courts have questioned whether the acts of protesters are protected under the First Amendment or hinder the functions of government. In this case, Chief Justice Warren broke the precedent of *Stromberg v. California* 283 U.S. 359 (1931) and found that draft card burning was not protected speech under the Constitution. Warren also established that "non-speech" conduct may be regulated by the government if the interest is sufficient to "justify incidental limitations on the First Amendment freedoms."

For more information: Epstein, Lee, and Thomas Walker. *Constitutional Law for a Changing America.* 5th ed. Washington, D.C.: CQ Press, 2004.

—April Willeford

Dred Scott v. Sandford 60 U.S. 393 (1856)

In *Dred Scott v. Sandford* (sic), (the plaintiff's name is actually spelled "Sanford," but was misspelled by a court clerk) the Supreme Court defined the status of African Americans and upheld the constitutionality of slavery as an institution. The decision stated that a black man had "no rights that a white man was bound to respect," and the Court ruled that Congress had no authority to ban slavery in the western territories of the United States. This ruling overturned the MISSOURI COMPROMISE of 1820, a plan that allowed Missouri to enter the Union as a slave state while other northern territories remained free of slavery, thus giving legal sanction to slavery in the United States.

Dred Scott *(Library of Congress)*

The case originated with Dred Scott, a slave born in Virginia whose master moved him to the slave state of Missouri and later transferred him into the free state of Illinois for more than two years and then into the Wisconsin territory, where slavery was prohibited. Dred Scott was finally brought back into Missouri. According to Missouri law, any slave became emancipated once his or her owner took them into a state or territory where slavery was prohibited. (This law had been upheld in the 1836 case *Rachel v. Walker.*) In seeking to challenge the legality of slavery, a lawsuit was filed seeking to obtain the freedom of Dred Scott and his wife based on the fact that he had lived in a free state and the legal status of slavery could not apply to him in the state of Illinois and the Wisconsin territory.

The Missouri Supreme Court ruled in 1852 that a doctrine of "conflict of laws" meant that the laws of the state or territory could not trump the laws of the state that made Dred Scott a slave in the first place. This doctrine became a central part of the appeal to the U.S. Supreme Court, in which the major question to be resolved was, Does residence in a free state invalidate the legal concept of slavery?

The Supreme Court in a 7-2 decision found that the move to a free state did not invalidate the institution of slavery and in fact that the regulations of the expansion of slavery by Congress were unconstitutional. Chief Justice ROGER TANEY wrote the majority opinion for the case and went further than the basic question of the legality of slavery by addressing the legal status of the plaintiff, Dred Scott. Chief Justice Taney wrote that African Americans "were not regarded as a portion of the people or citizens of the Government then formed." Therefore, Dred Scott, as a slave, was not a citizen and therefore had no STANDING to file a lawsuit. Justice Taney also offered that slavery served a beneficial role for those not capable of surviving on their own. He further argued for the inferiority of blacks as a race, stating:

> They were at that time considered as a subordinate and inferior class of beings, who had been subjugated by the dominant race, and, whether emancipated or not, yet remained subject to their authority, and had no rights or privileges but such as those who held the power and the government might choose to grant them.

The question of whether Congress had the right to regulate the expansion of slavery was addressed in the decision when Justice Taney wrote that the power of the government over territories was limited to the expressed powers granted to Congress and that the right of private property (including the right to own slaves) could not be abridged without DUE PROCESS of law. Until these territories came under the express rule of the United States (by joining the Union) and individuals directly violated the laws of the country, any restriction of the ownership of slaves was void. The act of moving across state lines or crossing over into territories did not invalidate state laws; therefore, Dred Scott was not free.

Justice John McLean in his dissenting opinion argued that the power to govern is inherent in the right to acquire territory, thus the laws of Congress (including the Missouri Compromise prohibiting slavery) do apply in this case. He also pointed out that if a slave escapes, that is a breach of a legal arrangement and the slave can be legally reclaimed, yet if a master takes the slave into an area that prohibits slavery, Can the slave be coerced into service without the authority of local law but in fact expressly violating local provisions? This question of local authority as opposed to national power at the root of this case became a bigger political problem and ultimately led to the political upheaval that culminated in the Civil War.

Dred Scott is considered one of the most infamous and disliked Court decisions in American history. It was overturned by Congress with the passage of the FOURTEENTH AMENDMENT.

For more information: Fehrenbacher, Don. *The Dred Scott Case: Its Significance in American Law and Politics.* New York: Oxford University Press, 1978; Higginbotham, A. Leon. *Shades of Freedom: Racial Politics and Presumptions of the American Legal Process.* New York: Oxford University Press, 1996.

—Kevin Anderson

due process

The command that government not deprive anyone of "life, liberty, or property" without "due process of law" is found in the Fifth Amendment (applicable to the federal government) and in the FOURTEENTH AMENDMENT (applicable to state governments). The concept is fundamental in the Anglo-American legal tradition, traceable at least as far back as Chapter 39 of the MAGNA CARTA in 1215.

Taken literally, the language requires government to follow certain procedures before subjecting anyone to such severe penalties as deprivation of life, liberty, or property. But the phrase has also been interpreted as including protection of certain substantive rights, making some deprivations of liberty or property unconstitutional no matter what procedures the government follows. These two components are usually described (arguably redundantly) as "procedural due process" and (arguably oxymoronically) as "SUBSTANTIVE DUE PROCESS." Procedural due process is the older of the two, while substantive due process first appeared in U.S. constitutional law in the decades following the Civil War—growing out of the Supreme Court's interpretations of the Fourteenth Amendment—though the concept can be seen in a few very early Supreme Court decisions and can be traced beyond Magna Carta to the ancient Stoics and their understandings of NATURAL LAW.

The Constitution's fair procedure guarantees serve at least two purposes: helping ensure fair decision making and respecting the fundamental human dignity of persons threatened with adverse governmental action. With respect to the first, consider the criminal trial process. Police may be certain they have their perpetrator, but our system presumes innocence until guilt is proven (a procedural protection not specifically listed in the Constitution but considered fundamental in our legal tradition) in a process where both prosecution and defense can present their case and then allow a jury of the accused's peers make the final determination. Regarding the second, giving people the right to be heard when facing adverse governmental action is a sign of respect for them as human beings.

Not all governmental deprivations are of equal magnitude, and consequently, the question of exactly what process is due becomes crucial. A student facing a three-day suspension from school does not need a full-blown trial by jury; the cost of such a procedure would simply be prohibitive. Yet, on the other hand, someone charged with a capital offense deserves the full panoply of procedural protections accorded by our legal tradition generally and the BILL OF RIGHTS specifically—in particular, the Fourth through Eighth Amendments, concerned primarily with the rights of the accused. It is fair to say that procedural guarantees are at their zenith in criminal cases.

Most criminal trials take place in state courts, just as most criminal offenses are defined by state, not federal, laws. Federal criminal procedures, since 1791, have been held to the standards of the Fourth through Eighth Amendments. However, Supreme Court interpretations of these amendments had little impact nationwide since the Bill of Rights applied only to the national government, not states, though many of the guarantees in the Bill of Rights found counterparts in state constitutions and procedural statutes.

Dramatic changes occurred during the 1960s when the WARREN COURT (1953–69) began applying federal constitutional standards to state criminal processes in a development that has been described as "the nationalization of the Bill of Rights" or "the INCORPORATION of the Bill of Rights into the Fourteenth Amendment." The process began in 1925 when the Court held that freedom of speech was among the liberties protected by the due process clause of the Fourteenth Amendment against state infringement. Shortly thereafter, FREEDOM OF THE PRESS was "incorporated" into the amendment, and by the late 1940s, all of the basic freedoms found in the FIRST AMENDMENT had been applied to the states.

The Warren Court accelerated the process, applying many of the safeguards of the Fourth through Eighth Amendments to the states. Richard H. Fallon, Jr., identifies three lines of criminal procedure cases that constitute the essential legacy of the Warren Court in this respect: 1) the RIGHT TO COUNSEL (SIXTH AMENDMENT), including appointment of a lawyer for criminal defendants who cannot afford to hire one; 2) the RIGHT AGAINST SELF-INCRIMINATION, including the requirement that police provide certain warnings before custodial questioning of criminal suspects; and 3) applying the so-called EXCLUSIONARY RULE to state criminal proceedings (the rule that evidence seized in violation of a suspect's constitutional rights would be excluded from the trial).

Earl Warren was succeeded as chief justice by WARREN E. BURGER, and the Burger Court (1969–86)—and its successor REHNQUIST COURT (1986–2005)—cut back on many of the criminal procedure rulings of the Warren Court. None of the landmark cases were explicitly overruled; rather, these successor courts created a variety of exceptions to the Warren Court rules and in general handed down decisions more favorable to prosecutors than to criminal defendants.

Many of the procedural guarantees found in the Bill of Rights apply only to criminal cases, but the Supreme Court has consistently held that procedural guarantees are essential in civil cases as well. Prominent among the requirements of due process in civil cases are the right to an impartial judge, the right to fair notice of scheduled proceedings, and the right to both present and challenge evidence.

There are other instances beyond the trial setting where the government may take actions against people that may deprive them of liberty or property. Municipal health inspectors may find health code violations and order a restaurant closed until they are corrected. Customs agents may seize contraband that a person purchased abroad and seeks to bring into the country. A public school principal may have reason to place a student in detention or require that student to stay home for several days of suspension. What procedures must governmental agents follow to guide their decision making in such instances?

The traditional approach relied on a distinction between "rights" and "privileges." Government had to respect the due process clause in proceedings involving rights to liberty or property, but not with respect to benefits (privileges) voluntarily conferred on people by the government. What the government voluntarily gave the government could freely take away.

In *GOLDBERG V. KELLY*, 397 U.S. 254 (1970), the Court rejected this distinction and held that a person could not be taken off the welfare rolls without advance notice and the opportunity for a hearing on the facts. The Court assumed that welfare benefits were a form of property. The Court stressed that due process is a flexible concept whose requirements might vary depending on context. The Court elaborated on the appropriate analytical method in *Mathews v. Eldridge*, 424 U.S. 319 (1976), arguing for a balancing approach that addressed three factors: 1) the importance of the interest to the individual (more important interests will require more procedural safeguards), 2) the likelihood that additional procedures will increase the accuracy of the fact-finding process (the higher the likelihood, the greater the procedural requirements), and 3) the burden placed on the government by requiring additional procedures, burden being understood as additional expense.

In U.S. constitutional law, the philosophy undergirding substantive due process can be traced back at least to 1798 and the case of *CALDER V. BULL*, 3 U.S. 386. Supreme Court justice Samuel Chase wrote an opinion in which he argued that the power of American governments is subject not only to specific, written constitutional provisions but also higher principles, such as those found in natural law, which dictate that government must be limited in any attempts to interfere with rights vested in the people by the law of nature. Chase's opinion was rejected by a majority of his colleagues in *Calder* and by an overwhelming majority of judges ever since.

The great era of substantive due process began in the last few decades of the 19th century. By then, the rapid industrialization that followed the Civil War gave rise not only to great prosperity but to serious social problems: CHILD LABOR, sweatshops, unsafe workplaces, excessive working hours, and payment of the lowest wages the market would allow. Many states, as well as occasionally the federal government, sought to pass laws to regulate some of these harmful conditions. The economic interests that found themselves subject to such regulation turned to the due process clause of the Fourteenth Amendment and began to argue that these laws interfered with fundamental liberties protected by natural law and that such interference with basic rights was itself a violation of due process, however legitimate the procedures used to enact the laws.

This approach, seen in the dissenting opinions in the *Slaughterhouse Cases*, 83 U.S. 36 (1872)—the first occasion the Supreme Court had to interpret the newly enacted Fourteenth Amendment—had by the beginnings of the 20th century commanded a majority of the justices, as reflected in the case that gave its name to the *Lochner* era (1905–37). In *LOCHNER V. NEW YORK*, 198 U.S. 45 (1905), the Court overturned a New York law limiting the weekly work hours of bakers. The Court found a "liberty to contract" between an employer and employee (a liberty nowhere spelled out in the Constitution) protected by the Fourteenth Amendment. The New York law was an unreasonable infringement on "the freedom of master and employee to contract with each other in relation to their employment."

Justice OLIVER WENDELL HOLMES, JR., in what is perhaps his most famous dissent, accused the majority of writing into the ambiguous language of the amendment their own laissez-faire philosophy as to the proper relationship between the individual and the state. He argued that a legislature could reasonably conclude that excessive working hours in a trade as dangerous as baking were inimical to the health of the employee and thus harmful to society. As Holmes caustically noted, the "Fourteenth Amendment does not enact Mr. Herbert Spencer's Social Statics."

The *Lochner* era ended in 1937, when a Court dominated by Franklin Roosevelt's appointees and reflecting the New Deal's philosophy of increased governmental regulation reversed course and began to uphold laws addressing a variety of social and economic ills. As the Court noted in *WEST COAST HOTEL V. PARRISH*, 300 U.S. 379 (1937), "[t]he Constitution does not speak of freedom of contract. It speaks of liberty and prohibits the deprivation of liberty without due process of law."

For more information: Abraham, Henry J., and Barbara A. Perrey. *Freedom and the Court.* 8th ed. Lawrence: University Press of Kansas, 2003; Chemerinsky, Erwin. *Constitutional Law: Principles and Policies.* 3d ed. New York: Aspen Publishers, 2006; Fallon, Richard H., Jr. *The Dynamic Constitution.* New York: Cambridge University Press, 2004.

—Philip A. Dynia

Duncan v. Louisiana 391 U.C. 145 (1968)

In *Duncan v. Louisiana,* the Supreme Court held that under the FOURTEENTH AMENDMENT to the U.S. Constitution, a defendant charged with a serious crime in state court has a RIGHT TO TRIAL BY JURY. Gary Duncan had been tried without a jury and convicted in state court for simple battery, a crime punishable under state law with a maximum of two years' imprisonment and a $300 fine. On appeal to the U.S. Supreme Court, Duncan argued that he was entitled to a jury trial for this criminal charge.

The jury trial right is included in the SIXTH AMENDMENT of the BILL OF RIGHTS, which was added to the Constitution a few years after its ratification, but in the leading case of *BARRON V. MAYOR AND CITY COUNCIL OF BALTIMORE,* 7 Pet. 243 (1833), the Court ruled that the rights established in the Bill of Rights applied only to the federal government, not state governments. The Fourteenth Amendment (which was added to the Constitution during Reconstruction) prohibited the states from depriving a citizen of his life, liberty, and property without DUE PROCESS, but that amendment is silent on whether the array of other rights in the Bill of Rights, such as the right to a jury trial, apply to the states. Beginning in the late 19th century, the Court began to address this issue in a series of cases that would continue well into the 20th century. In some cases, the Court held that a particular right found in the Bill of Rights was fundamental in the context of American criminal justice systems and, therefore, was incorporated into the concept of due process applicable to the states under the Fourteenth Amendment. *Duncan v. Louisiana* is an important case in this series.

In concluding that the right to a jury trial was fundamental, the Court noted that the right, which developed as a protection against unchecked governmental power, has deep roots in both English and American law. Jury trials play a central role in every American jurisdiction (both state and federal). The Court also noted that other Sixth Amendment rights, such as the RIGHT TO COUNSEL (*GIDEON V. WAINRIGHT,* 372 U.S. 335 [1963]) and the right to a speedy trial (*Klopfer v. North Carolina,* 386 U.S. 213 [1967]), had already been incorporated into the Fourteenth Amendment.

Although the Court held that the jury trial right is incorporated into the Fourteenth Amendment, it was not willing to extend the right to every criminal case in state courts. Based on Anglo-American legal tradition and the original understanding of the Sixth Amendment's jury trial provision, the Court limited the right to serious offenses, which raised the issue of distinguishing between petty and serious offenses. Rejecting Louisiana's contention that the actual punishment imposed on the defendant should be the basis for classifying the offense, the Court suggested that the length of possible incarceration authorized by the legislature as the penalty for a particular crime is a more useful gauge of its seriousness. After considering both a six-month and a one-year rule, the Court deferred this question to a future case and concluded that because the crime for which Duncan was charged was punishable by two years in prison, it was a serious, not a petty, offense, and therefore, Duncan had a right to a jury trial.

For more information: LaFave, Wayne R., Jerold H. Israel, and Nancy J. King. *Criminal Procedure.* 4th ed. St. Paul, Minn.: Thomson/West, 2004.

—Steven B. Dow

economic protectionism and the states

Economic protection refers to a practice undertaken by states to protect their own businesses and industries at the expense of those located in other states. This practice is a violation of the COMMERCE CLAUSE of the Constitution.

The U.S. Constitution distributes economic and political powers among the federal government and the states. One of the areas in which the Constitution apportions the respective roles and powers of the federal government and the states is INTERSTATE COMMERCE (among states) and international or foreign trade (with other countries).

Clause 3 in Section 8 of ARTICLE I OF THE U.S. CONSTITUTION, known as the commerce clause, grants the U.S. Congress the powers "to regulate Commerce with foreign Nations, and among the several States, and with the Indian Tribes." These powers are sometimes classified into three component parts: foreign commerce clause, the interstate commerce clause, and the Indian commerce clause, which deal with foreign trade, interstate trade, and economic transactions with sovereign tribal governments, respectively.

Whereas the commerce clause grants the federal government the power to regulate interstate commerce, a more expansive doctrinal interpretation has emerged out of the jurisprudence of the Supreme Court and other courts of lower jurisdictions. This doctrine is called the DORMANT COMMERCE CLAUSE, which maintains that states cannot pass laws that restrict interstate commerce. It is a preemptive doctrine in that it prohibits a priori any future state legislation that imposes restrictions on interstate commerce.

The commerce clause, particularly the dormant commerce clause, has been the subject of various and conflicting interpretations within the Supreme Court and among legal scholars. In simple terms, two overriding judicial perspectives or doctrines dominate the debate among Supreme Court jurists and legal scholars concerning the reach of the commerce clause. The first perspective, a minimalist doctrine that is often associated with the conservative wing of the Court, holds that the commerce clause does not grant the federal government exclusive powers over the regulation of interstate commerce, let alone preempt any future law that states could pass to regulate interstate trade. ANTONIN GREGORY SCALIA and CLARENCE THOMAS, the conservative justices of the Court, subscribe to this doctrine that explicitly rejects the dormant commerce clause as unconstitutional.

Proponents of the minimalist interpretation of the commerce clause generally concur, however, that the Constitution grants Congress and the federal government the power to regulate commerce among states and internationally, but this power is neither exclusive nor universal in the sense that states retain some regulatory and legislative mandate over certain aspects and types of interstate commerce. Furthermore, the mandate of the federal government is not unlimited as it may not apply to interstate matters that are only partially or tangentially related to commerce. A slightly different version of the minimalist view maintains that the commerce clause grants both Congress and states "concurrent" powers to regulate interstate commerce. In this view, state regulation of commerce is unconstitutional or invalid only if

Congress passes specific statutes that restrict or remove the economic powers of states.

The second perspective represents a more maximalist doctrinal principle in that it strips the states of all powers to regulate commerce through protectionist measures such as tariffs and vests in the Congress exclusive mandate over most aspects of interstate commerce. Proponents of the second perspective believe that the commerce clause was designed to prevent interstate conflict over commerce, a situation that could result if the states had an exclusive mandate over interstate commerce.

These competing judicial doctrines have produced a vast body of jurisprudence on the subject of economic protectionism, an area of continued conflict between the prerogatives of states as autonomous economic units and the mandate of the federal government. This important state-federal relationship has evolved over time through a series of amendments and precedents, with the Supreme Court and lower courts playing a vital role since the 19th century. The long and established jurisprudence of the Supreme Court and other lower courts on the commerce clause affirms federal authority over interstate commerce. However, recent decisions of the Court seem to give credence to the conservative minimalist doctrine that some state regulation is allowable under the commerce clause.

For more information: Cho, Sungjoon. "Toward a New Economic Constitution: Judicial Disciplines on Trade Politics." *Wake Forest Law Review* 42 (2007): 167–197; Moorman, John W. "Conflicting Commerce Clauses: How Raich and American Trucking Dishonor Their Doctrines." *William & Mary Bill of Rights Journal* 15 (2006) 687–710.

—Daniel G. Ogbaharya

education and the Constitution

The Constitution, the Bill of Rights, and subsequent amendments do not mention education anywhere. Yet, the FIRST AMENDMENT's religion, speech, and press clauses; the FOURTH AMENDMENT's unreasonable searches clause; the Eighth Amendment's CRUEL AND UNUSUAL PUNISHMENT clause; the FOURTEENTH AMENDMENT's DUE PROCESS and EQUAL PROTECTION clauses; and Congress's spending power in Section 8 of ARTICLE I OF THE U.S. CONSTITUTION have all been interpreted by the U.S. Supreme Court in ways that have a major impact on education.

Nothing in the U.S. Constitution requires a state to have a public elementary and secondary school system or a public higher education system. In *SAN ANTONIO V. RODRIGUEZ,* 411 U.S. 1 (1973), the Supreme Court rejected the argument that a free public education was a fundamental right under the Fourteenth Amendment due process or equal protection clauses. However, every state constitution requires that residents be provided a free public education, or in some states a free and "adequate" public education.

While educational plans and policies have historically been viewed as the province of the states, the federal government in the last 40 years has played a major role in setting national education standards and providing aid to promote access to education programs for lower-income populations. Beginning in 1965, with passage of the Elementary and Secondary Education Act (ESEA), through to 2001, with passage of the No Child Left Behind Act, Congress has used its "spending" power under Article I, Section 8 to set national education policy as a condition to federal grants to states. Congress has also passed antidiscrimination laws under the same spending clause authority, including Title VI of the CIVIL RIGHTS ACT OF 1964, which prohibits discrimination based on race or national origin in programs receiving federal funds, and Title IX of the Education Amendments of 1972, which prohibits discrimination based on gender in education programs receiving federal funds.

The Supreme Court has also found that other parts of the Constitution have a significant impact on education. In the case of *TINKER V. DES MOINES INDEPENDENT COMMUNITY SCHOOL DISTRICT,* 393 U.S. 503 (1969), the Supreme Court said that students retain the First Amendment right to freedom of speech in school. In the ruling, the highwater mark for recognition of STUDENT RIGHTS, the Court stated: "It can hardly be argued that either students or teachers shed their constitutional rights to freedom of speech or expression at the schoolhouse gate." In *Tinker,* the Court ruled that students who wore black armbands to school to call for a truce in the Vietnam War should not have been punished because there was no evidence that their conduct threatened to disrupt school activities.

In subsequent First Amendment rulings, however, the Court limited freedom of speech and press rights, finding that schools may prohibit speech that is lewd or profane (*Bethel School District v. Fraser,* 478 U.S. 675 [1986]) and that officials may censor speech or publications that bear the imprimatur of the school, as long as officials have a legitimate pedagogical reason (*HAZELWOOD SCHOOL DISTRICT V. KUHLMEIER,* 484 U.S. 260 [1988]).

Hazelwood involved a school newspaper, but it has been applied to restrict yearbooks, school plays, and a range of other speech. Courts have generally protected students' right to criticize school officials or policies on personal Web pages created outside school. However, in *MORSE V. FREDERICK,* ___ U.S. ___ (2007), the Supreme Court ruled that a student display of a banner at a school event appearing to advocate the use of illegal drugs was not protected by the First Amendment. This decision seemed to significantly retract on many of the expressive rights that the Court had supported since *Tinker.*

Courts have also generally ruled that schools have some control but cannot engage in viewpoint discrimination when students wear T-shirts with messages on them. However, while the Supreme Court has not addressed the issue, lower courts have upheld school restrictions on hair length, hats, and clothing. Dress codes have been widely affirmed by courts, finding neither a free expression problem nor any issue of PRIVACY under the due process clause of the Fourteenth Amendment.

The high court has handled dozens of cases applying the religion clauses to public education. The Court has ruled that the ESTABLISHMENT CLAUSE prohibits formal, organized SCHOOL PRAYER, whether in the classroom (*ENGEL V. VITALE,* 370 U.S. 421 [1962]), at graduation (*LEE V. WEISMAN,* 505 U.S. 577 [1992]), or at a varsity football game (*Santa Fe Independent School District v. Doe,* 530 U.S. 290 [2000]). Other activities are prohibited, too, when they are designed to promote religion, including the teaching of creationism (*EDWARDS V. AGUILLARD,* 482 U.S. 578 [1987]) and other religiously motivated attempts to undermine the teaching of evolution.

At the same time, students have both a free speech right and a free exercise clause right to pray at school, as long as it is not organized by or promoted by school officials. And schools should be able to teach courses about the history of religion or comparative religion, as long as the curriculum does not promote religion. School officials may not discriminate against religious organizations; when schools allow clubs to meet after school, religious clubs cannot be excluded simply because their focus is religious (*GOOD NEWS CLUB V. MILFORD CENTRAL SCHOOL,* 533 U.S. 98 [2001]).

In numerous cases, the Supreme Court has read the establishment clause to impose some limits on when federal aid can go to private religious schools or to support religious education. The Court placed strict limits for many years (*LEMON V. KURTZMAN,* 403 U.S. 602 [1971]), but more recently, the Court has said tax dollars may flow to religious schools if they are part of a general aid program that does not engage in religious indoctrination (*Agostini v. Felton,* 521 U.S. 203 [1997]). The Court has also upheld SCHOOL VOUCHERS, where parents use tax dollars to pay for private schools, including religious schools (*ZELMAN V. SIMMONS-HARRIS,* 536 U.S. 639 [2002]).

In the area of privacy and security, the Supreme Court has ruled that students have a reduced expectation of privacy in school and may be subjected to searches under the Fourth Amendment based on the reasonableness of the circumstances (*NEW JERSEY V. T.L.O.,* 469 U.S. 325 [1985]). The Court has also upheld drug testing without any individual suspicion for students participating in extracurricular activities (*BOARD OF EDUCATION POTTAWATOMIE COUNTY V. EARLS,* 536 U.S. 822 [2002]).

Lower courts have found no Fourth Amendment problem with metal detectors at school entrances or with most locker searches.

The Supreme Court dealt with the Eighth Amendment's cruel and unusual punishment clause in the context of corporal punishment in school. In *Ingraham v. Wright*, 430 U.S. 651 (1977), the Court ruled that imposition of corporal punishment did not trigger the Eighth Amendment because it was not punishment for a crime.

Ingraham also involved the due process guarantee of the Fourteenth Amendment. The Court ruled that students did not have a right to notice, a hearing, or other procedural safeguards prior to corporal punishment. In other contexts, particularly punishment in the form of suspension or expulsion from school, the Supreme Court said students facing suspension of 10 days or less do have due process rights, including a right to notice, details of evidence and charges, and a right to give their version of events (*Goss v. Lopez*, 419 U.S. 565 [1975]).

The equal protection clause of the Fourteenth Amendment has been another source of Court rulings and interplay between education and the Constitution. In *BROWN V. BOARD OF EDUCATION OF TOPEKA*, 347 U.S. 483 (1954), the Supreme Court ruled that segregated public schools violated the equal protection guarantee of the Fourteenth Amendment and, over the next 40 years, presided over efforts to desegregate public schools, first in southern states, and then throughout the nation. In *Freeman v. Pitts*, 503 U.S. 467 (1992), the Supreme Court suggested that federal courts should relinquish control of school systems that had met their obligation to eliminate segregation.

As emphasis on eliminating formal segregation began to wane, a new focus developed on the use of race in admissions to promote diversity in the classroom. In a narrow ruling in *REGENTS OF THE UNIVERSITY OF CALIFORNIA V. BAKKE*, 438 U.S. 265 (1978), the Supreme Court kept the door open to the use of race as one factor in admissions for higher education programs in order to promote diversity. Returning to this form of AFFIRMATIVE ACTION 25 years later, the Supreme Court ruled in *GRUTTER V. BOLLINGER*, 539 U.S. 306 (2003), that race could be considered among numerous other values to achieve a diverse law school classroom at the University of Michigan. However, in *GRATZ V. BOLLINGER*, 539 U.S. 244 (2003), the Court ruled that Michigan's use of race as a fixed point value in the undergraduate admissions process was too much like a rigid quota and violated the Fourteenth Amendment.

Finally, in *Parents Involved in Community Schools v. Seattle School District No. 1*, ___ U.S. ___ (2007), and its companion case, the Court ruled that race may not be used as a factor in determining assignment plans for schools. Whether this case means that the use of race as a factor in education has ended remains to be seen.

For more information: Imber, Michael, and Tyll Van Geel. *A Teacher's Guide to Education Law.* 3d ed. Mahwah, N.J.: Lawrence Erlbaum, 2005; Raskin, Jamin B. *We the Students: Supreme Court Cases for and about Students.* 2d ed. Washington, D.C.: CQ Press, 2003; Russo, Charles J. *Reutter's The Law of Public Education.* 6th ed. New York: Foundation Press, 2006.

—Stephen Wermiel

Edwards v. Aguillard 482 U.S. 578 (1987)

In *Edwards v. Aguillard*, the Supreme Court reviewed Louisiana's Balanced Treatment for Creation Science and Evolution Science in Public School Instruction Act and declared it unconstitutional. This case is the foundation for the contemporary movement supporting inclusion of INTELLIGENT DESIGN theory in public education.

The Louisiana law, though not requiring any theory on life's origins be taught, required that creation theory must be included if evolution theory was taught, or vice versa. Because the law did not forbid the teaching of evolution, it did not run afoul of the precedent established in *Epperson v. Arkansas*, 393 U.S. 97 (1968); however, it did face problems with the precedent established in *LEMON V. KURTZMAN*, 403 U.S. 602 (1971).

Parents, teachers, and religious leaders challenged the state law as an unconstitutional violation of the First Amendment's ESTABLISHMENT

CLAUSE. The state attorney general argued that the objective of the law was to ensure that "academic freedom" was provided for teachers who desired to teach alternative theories to evolution. Unfortunately for the state, the bill's author's remarks in the legislative record belied this argument. Senator Keith stated: "My preference would be that neither [creationism nor evolution] be taught." Consequently, the Court noted, "Such a ban on teaching does not promote—indeed, it undermines—the provision of a comprehensive scientific education."

Justice WILLIAM J. BRENNAN, JR., delivered the 7-2 majority opinion, stating the law violated the first prong of the Lemon test (a test for determining whether there is a violation of the establishment clause) since it lacked a secular legislative purpose. Justice ANTONIN GREGORY SCALIA's dissent challenged that the majority's conclusion was hasty because the appellate court's decision to grant summary judgment never allowed evidence to be introduced on legislative intent. Yet, Justice Brennan noted:

> the Act evinces a discriminatory preference . . . requiring curriculum guides be developed and resource services supplied for teaching creationism but not for teaching evolution, limiting membership on the resource services panel to "creation scientists," and forbidding school boards from discriminating against "creation scientists," and teaching creation science, while failing to protect teachers of other theories or those refusing to teach creation science.

Brennan's statement made Justice Scalia's remarks disingenuous. Also, Scalia argued for abandoning *Lemon*'s purpose test altogether, stating this prong serves as "a test which exacerbates the tension between the Free Exercise and Establishment Clauses."

The Lemon test's second prong presented problems for the law, too. The Court noted: "The Act is designed either to promote the theory of creation science . . . or to prohibit the teaching of a scientific theory disfavored by certain religious sects." The legislative record details the view that "a creator [was] responsible for the universe and everything in it." Furthermore, the legislative history clearly indicates "creation science" embodies a religious belief that a supernatural creator was responsible for the creation of humankind.

Third, the law entangled the interests of church and state by seeking "the symbolic and financial support of government to achieve a religious purpose." Because Louisiana proposed to develop special curricula and provide teaching resources for the clear purpose of advancing creation theory but none for evolution theory, this excessively involved the state and education authorities in advancing a theistic viewpoint in violation of *Lemon* and the First Amendment's establishment clause.

For more information: Forrest, Barbara, and Paul R. Gross. *Creationism's Trojan Horse: The Wedge of Intelligent Design.* New York: Oxford University Press, 2004; Numbers, R. L. *The Creationists: The Evolution of Scientific Creationism.* Berkeley: University of California Press, 1993.

—Christy Woodward Kaupert

Edwards v. California 314 U.S. 160 (1941)

In *Edwards v. California,* the Supreme Court held that the COMMERCE CLAUSE (in Section 8 of ARTICLE I OF THE U.S. CONSTITUTION) bars states from restricting interstate travel.

The decade of the 1930s witnessed the Great Depression, in which scores of businesses went bankrupt and millions of Americans became unemployed. People in the southwestern states were additionally impacted by farm foreclosures caused by poor agricultural methods, oppressive heat, severe droughts, and dirt storms. Among the hardest-hit states in the so-called Dust Bowl were Arkansas, Kansas, Oklahoma, and Texas. Thousands of farmers and laborers from the Dust Bowl were forced to pack their belongings and seek employment in other states. California was one of the states that offered hope for these displaced Americans.

The mass migration of Americans was not without controversy. This sudden influx of newcomers strained state budgets and limited resources. As a result, more than 20 states enacted laws restricting the movement of indigents into their borders. The Welfare and Institutions Code of California was emblematic of efforts to stem the tide of migration from the Dust Bowl. Section 2615 of that act provided: "Every person, firm or corporation . . . that brings or assists in bringing into the State any indigent person who is not a resident of the State, knowing him to be an indigent person, is guilty of a misdemeanor."

In December 1939, Fred F. Edwards, a resident of Marysville, California, drove his automobile to the home of his wife's brother, Frank Duncan, in Spur, Texas. Duncan was unemployed and Edwards agreed to help his brother-in-law in finding work in California. Together, the two men returned to California with just $20 between them. After arriving in California, Duncan lived with Edwards's family for 10 days, until he could receive federal governmental assistance. Edwards was convicted of violating Section 2615 and sentenced to six months in county jail. The California Supreme Court affirmed the conviction, and Edwards appealed.

The U.S. Supreme Court reversed Edwards's conviction. Writing for the Court, Justice James F. Byrnes noted that California had exceeded its Tenth Amendment POLICE POWER by unduly restricting the freedom of travel. While the Court recognized a state's legitimate interests in prohibiting criminals from entering its borders, Byrnes made it clear that poverty and immorality are not synonymous and that Section 2615 violated the commerce clause. Joining Byrnes were Justices Felix Frankfurter, Stanley Reed, Harlan Fiske Stone, and Owen Roberts. Justice WILLIAM O. DOUGLAS, supported by Justices HUGO BLACK and Frank Murphy, offered a concurring opinion in which he asserted that the right of Americans to INTERSTATE COMMERCE is a fundamental right that states cannot restrict. A second concurring opinion, written by Justice Robert Jackson, asserted that property qualifications and travel restrictions on U.S. citizens violate the PRIVILEGES AND IMMUNITIES clause of the FOURTEENTH AMENDMENT.

This case is important in federal-state relations because it broadened the application of the commerce clause and clarified rights of citizens to move freely and seek housing and employment in other states. Jackson's opinion in this case also provided the groundwork for *Saenz v. California* (1999), where the Supreme Court struck down residency requirements for state welfare benefits on grounds of privileges and immunities.

For more information: Gregory, James N. *American Exodus: The Dust Bowl Migration and Okie Culture in California*. New York: Oxford University Press, 1998; Lange, Dorthea, and Paul S. Taylor. *An American Exodus: A Record of Human Erosion in the Thirties*. New Haven, Conn.: Oakland Museum/Yale University Press, 1969.

—Richard J. Hardy

Eighteenth Amendment (1919)

The Eighteenth Amendment to the Constitution, which was ratified in 1919, banned the manufacturing and the sale of alcohol for consumption in the United States. It was subsequently repealed with the TWENTY-FIRST AMENDMENT in 1933.

The Eighteenth Amendment is commonly dismissed as a disaster, an inappropriate police regulation in the Constitution that met with deserved failure. It was asserted from the time of its passage that the Prohibition amendment had been slipped by the American people while they were at war and many, presumably hard-drinking, soldiers were abroad. The amendment, however, was ratified by all but two state legislatures, and in only a few of those states was the victory close. No prior amendment was enacted with such near unanimity.

Some have asserted that the amendment was sumptuary legislation, but many of its supporters were careful to note that they opposed the sale of intoxicating liquor because of the social costs that came with it. It was the sale, not drinking, of intoxicating liquors that was prohibited. Sales in general and saloon drinking in particular could not be considered as private acts beyond the legitimate legislative jurisdiction of the state. It was asserted, most famously by H. L. Mencken, that Prohibition was foisted on to the American people by rural evangelicals, ("Christian Moronia," as he called rural America), attempting to impose a Puritan sensibility, a hatred of pleasure, on the United States, and doing so because of their mean-spirited resentment that others were having a good time.

Yet Prohibition was also supported by Robert Woods, Lillian Wald, Jane Addams, and other stalwarts of the Progressive movement. They believed in using law for uplift and thought that their program was supported by the best scientific data and expertise. The American Medical Association had declared against intoxicating beverages. Empirical verification supposedly confirmed the threat that alcoholic beverages posed to the human germ plasm, as it was called, and intoxicating liquor's role in stimulating criminal activity. There was indeed widespread disgust with the excesses of public drinking occurring in the saloon and fear of the threat to public order posed by what social historians now term homosocial inebriation. Wartime centralization of powers and regimentation eased the way to further regulatory control from Washington.

Even most southern members of Congress, peculiarly concerned with the preservation of states' rights, voted for Prohibition, or more precisely, as some of them argued, voted to let the states decide whether to enact a prohibitory amendment. The amendment may not have been passed without wartime concern for protecting the food supply, hostility to German-American brewers, and increasingly centralized regimentation, but that does not make it illegitimate. The fact that the details of the actual amendment, in particular the language granting concurrent authority to the states and federal government to enforce it, do not seem to have been subject to much thought, sug-

Law officials raid a cellar during Prohibition. *(Library of Congress)*

gests that it was perhaps drafted and evaluated in haste, although the Anti-Saloon League insisted that there had been 70 years of deliberate experimentation with less drastic restrictions.

For all that support for Prohibition was widespread, except in large cities, it was also somewhat thin and not always carefully considered. Few people seem to understand that, in theory, national Prohibition would be more comprehensive than had been state prohibition. Although two-thirds of the U.S. population was subject to state prohibition in 1917, few states were bone dry. Sale for beverage purposes was prohibited within the state, but alcoholic beverages could still be imported, for instance. While only manufacture, sale, and transportation of intoxicating liquors for beverage purposes were prohibited by the Eighteenth Amendment, a national ban posed the first serious threat to all access to alcoholic beverages.

The focus of Prohibition rhetoric was the saloon. The Anti-Saloon League, the most effective instrument in engineering passage of the amendment, was the prototype of a single-issue lobbying organization. Its general counsel, Wayne Wheeler, drafted the language of the Eighteenth Amendment and then, as the "dry boss," as he happily called himself, was the chief strategist of its enforcement until his death in 1927. The Anti-Saloon League refused to include in the amendment any prohibition of drinking. Whether this was because they thought that the American people in general would not approve of such direct regulation of personal behavior or that rich and powerful Americans who could stockpile intoxicating beverages would cease supporting Prohibition for their employees, or whether they simply focused only on stimulated public sale of alcoholic beverages or some combination of these, is unclear.

As contemporary observers noted, national Prohibition was simply another variation in a long line of regulatory strategies. Only the manufacture, sale, and transportation of intoxicating liquors were prohibited and only for beverage purposes. Such liquors, with restrictions, were still available for medicinal and sacramental purposes, exceptions which led to widespread evasion. Cider was not banned, perhaps because it would be impossible to prevent natural fermentation. This led to allegations that the Volstead Act, the congressional act enforcing Prohibition, permitted the farmer his drink of choice, but it deprived the urban worker of his beer. The prohibition of sale but not consumption focused on commerce in alcoholic beverages but invited charges that the rich were permitted to stockpile while the poor were deprived. Any flexibility was criticized, perhaps unfairly, as discriminatory.

Enforcement of Prohibition was also criticized. First of all, it was pursued on the cheap, whether because the Anti-Saloon League wanted to avoid taxpayer resistance or because its supporters really expected resistance to cease once the amendment was enacted. States quickly abandoned any enforcement efforts. The federal government fell into a pattern of periodic sweeps accompanied by over-sanguine predictions that enforcement, once reorganized, would turn a corner and become effective. The corner was never reached. Enforcement was probably not helped by Wheeler's refusal to allow enforcement officers to be under civil service protection. He thought this would permit the selection of true believers and thus more effective enforcement (or perhaps, he just thought this would facilitate his personal authority). The result was a thriving patronage system. As Charles Merz observed, Congress responded to evasion not by funding more effective enforcement but by passing more punitive and unenforced laws. This only highlighted the perceived gap between law and practice and spurred a national lamentation about American disobedience.

To call Prohibition a failure, however, is an overstatement. Historians now conclude that increased price and decreased availability did tend to reduce access to alcoholic beverages, to the poor in particular. At the margin, abuse was reduced. Visits to speakeasies were an item for conspicuous consumption by the wealthy, whether male or female, ending the homosociability of public alcoholic beverage consumption. Urban defiance of Prohibition, publicized by the press, which featured glimpses of celebrity culture, led to an impression that the law was being flouted everywhere.

What ended Prohibition was the Great Depression. No longer was there apparent empirical verification of its economic benefits. Regaining lost tax revenues looked increasingly attractive. Finally, many Americans tired of the continuous controversy over alcoholic beverages. They had hoped and expected that with Prohibition, the country could cease the intense national debate over alcoholic beverage regulation that was distracting attention from other important issues. This had not occurred. The hope grew that greater harmony and a less liquor-obsessed politics would be achieved by repeal.

For more information: Clark, Norman. *Deliver Us from Evil: An Interpretation of American Prohibition.* New York: W.W. Norton, 1976; Pegram, Thomas. *Battling Demon Rum: The Struggle for Dry America, 1800–1933.* Chicago: Ivan R. Dee, 1998.

—Steve Diamond

Eisenstadt v. Baird 405 U.S. 438 (1972)

In *Eisenstadt v. Baird,* the U.S. Supreme Court expanded the implied constitutional right to PRIVACY, ruling that single men and women were entitled to the same access to birth control that was provided to married couples.

Massachusetts and numerous other states made it a crime to prescribe CONTRACEPTIVES until 1965 when the Supreme Court, in *GRISWOLD V. CONNECTICUT,* 381 U.S. 479 (1965), ruled that the right to privacy implicit in the Bill of Rights protected the right of married couples to use birth control devices in their homes. The next year, the Massachusetts legislature amended state law to permit doctors to prescribe contraception to married couples.

The *Eisenstadt* case arose in 1967 when Bill Baird, a New York birth control and ABORTION rights advocate, delivered a lecture on contraception to some 2,000 students at a Boston University auditorium. After the lecture, he offered the audience the chance to come up to the stage to pick up packages of contraceptive foam. One student did, and Boston police arrested Baird for violating the law that prohibited exhibition and distribution of contraceptives to unmarried persons.

Baird was convicted in state court of exhibiting and distributing contraceptives; the Massachusetts Supreme Court upheld only the distributing conviction, ruling that the ban on exhibiting birth control violated the FIRST AMENDMENT. Baird challenged his conviction in federal court after serving a three-month jail sentence. A federal district court upheld his conviction, but the U.S. Court of Appeals for the First Circuit overturned it. Thomas Eisenstadt, the sheriff of Suffolk County, which includes Boston, appealed to the U.S. Supreme Court.

By a 6-1 vote, the Supreme Court ruled that the Massachusetts law violated the EQUAL PROTECTION clause of the Fourteenth Amendment, because it discriminated against unmarried individuals. Although the *Griswold* decision had relied heavily on the concept of marital privacy, Justice WILLIAM J. BRENNAN, JR., wrote in *Eisenstadt* that marriage is just a relationship of two individuals and that the privacy interests involved belong to the individuals.

In the most oft-cited portion of the opinion, Brennan is widely credited with planting a strong statement that would bolster the Court's ability to find a constitutional right to abortion in a case that was pending at the same time, *ROE V. WADE,* 410 U.S. 113 (1973). "If the right of privacy means anything, it is the right of the individual, married or single, to be free from unwarranted governmental intrusion into matters so fundamentally affecting a person as the decision whether to bear or beget a child," Brennan wrote in *Eisenstadt.* The statement was quoted in *Roe* a year later.

Brennan said that the Massachusetts law was marked by contradictions that made it difficult to find any reasonable justification for it. The law, he said, permitted access to contraceptives to prevent disease but not to prevent pregnancy and permitted married persons access to contraceptives even for extramarital sexual activity. All of these contradictions undermined any justifications for the law offered by the state, the Court said. Chief Justice WARREN E. BURGER dissented, saying the Court was interfering with areas of legitimate state regulation without any constitutional justification. Justices LEWIS FRANKLIN POWELL, JR., and WILLIAM HUBBS REHNQUIST joined the Court after the case was argued and so did not take part in the decision. The Supreme Court decision invalidated similar laws in at least two dozen other states.

For more information: Garrow, David J. *Liberty and Sexuality: The Right to Privacy and the Making of* Roe v. Wade. New York: Macmillan, 1993; Lucas, Roy. "New Historical Insights on the Curious Case of *Baird v. Eisenstadt*." *Roger Williams University Law Review* 9, no. 9 (2003): 9–55.

—Stephen Wermiel

electoral college

The electoral college is a mechanism established in the Constitution as part of the process for choosing the president and vice president of the United States.

The CONSTITUTIONAL CONVENTION in 1787 had difficulty reaching closure on how to choose the president. After rejecting a variety of methods ranging from popular vote to selection by Congress, the delegates finally determined that the president should be chosen by a group of electors. This decision is often explained in terms of the limited political knowledge of the average citizen of 1787. A more plausible motivation was the need to win support of the small states for the Constitution. The creation of a SENATE with equal representation of states, an early small state victory, became the foundation for an electoral college that gives the small states a numerical advantage.

The term *electoral college* does not appear in the Constitution, but its original description is found in Section 1 of ARTICLE II OF THE U.S. CONSTITUTION. (The word *college* here means a group of people with a common purpose.) Each state was to choose a number of electors equal to the number of that state's U.S. representatives and senators. Since each state is constitutionally granted one representative and two senators, regardless of size, the smallest number of electoral votes a state can have is three.

Meeting in the state capital, each elector would cast votes for two candidates, at least one of whom was from a different state than the elector's. The results would be tallied by Congress. The top vote-getter would become president if he received a majority (based on the number of electors, not of total votes cast), and the runner-up would be vice president. If two tied, both receiving a majority, the HOUSE OF REPRESENTATIVES would choose between them. If no one received a majority, the House would choose from among the top five, with each state delegation casting only one vote. If two people tied for second place, the Senate would choose between them.

After a tie occurred in 1800, the TWELFTH AMENDMENT was added to the Constitution, in 1804, requiring electors to indicate separate choices for president and vice president. If there is no majority for president, the House, still voting by states, chooses from the top three. If no one wins a majority of votes for vice president, the Senate chooses from the top two. In 1961, the TWENTY-THIRD AMENDMENT gave the DISTRICT OF COLUMBIA three electoral votes. Thus, with the House of Representatives currently set at 435, and a Senate of 100, the electoral college consists of 538 electors.

Other than the addition of these amendments, the electoral college technically functions as conceived by the framers. However, in actuality, it was transformed early in its history by the emergence of political parties, the decision by states to choose electors by popular vote, the appearance of partisan lists of electors pledged to a particular candidate, and the appearance of the "winner-take-all" rule (currently used in all states except Maine and Nebraska) in which the candidate winning the popular vote in a state receives all of that state's electoral votes.

The electoral college is capable of producing various anomalies. One is the potential for "faithless electors," those who make their own choice rather than voting for the candidate to whom they are pledged. (This has rarely happened and never affected the outcome of an election.) Another is a president who wins an overwhelming majority of electoral votes but a bare majority or mere plurality of the popular vote, as was the case in 1980 when Ronald Reagan won 489 of 538 electoral votes but only 51 percent of the popular vote. Yet another is a candidate who wins the popular vote while losing the electoral vote, as happened in 2000 when Al Gore won 48.38 percent of the popular vote and George W. Bush 47.87 percent, but Bush won the election with 273 electoral votes to Gore's 266. (The Green Party candidate, Ralph Nader, won 2.74 percent.)

Mathematically, the electoral college contains a small state bias because of the inclusion of the two votes per state based on Senate seats. In 2000, Bush carried 30 states to Gore's 20 plus the District of Columbia. Of Bush's 30 states, 21 had electoral votes in the single digits, and only three had 21 or more votes, while only 10 Gore states had fewer than 10 electoral votes and four had more than 21.

The terms *red states* (Republican states) and *blue states* (Democratic states), featured prominently in the media after the 2000 election, were based on winners of states' electoral votes. They illustrate the potential of electoral vote counts to make the partisan divide appear more skewed than it actually is. The term *purple state* was subsequently coined for closely divided states to correct this misimpression.

Under the winner-take-all rule, the largest states may also have a particular advantage. A candidate can secure the presidency by winning the 11 most populous states for a narrow victory of 271 to 268 electoral votes, regardless of the size of the popular vote in those top 11 or in the rest of the country. The argument is often made that large states are also favored because candidates spend more time campaigning in them; however, there is no reason to think they would spend less time in the large population centers in a popular vote system.

The 2000 election was unusual in that the winner was ultimately decided by the U.S. Supreme Court in a 5-4 opinion in *Bush v. Gore*, 531 U.S. 98 (2000). This scenario developed out of the desperate need of both major candidates, after all other states' results had been tallied, to win Florida's 25 electoral votes. The case resulted from challenges to a host of voting irregularities in Florida. Had the Court awarded the votes to Gore, he could have claimed a decisive victory with both the popular vote and 291 electoral votes, while Bush's victory was won with a bare margin in the electoral college and despite trailing Gore in the popular vote.

Opponents of the electoral college noted that in a popular vote, winner-take-all election the country could have escaped this travail. The rejoinder by electoral college supporters was that direct election would not eliminate corruption at the polls, and a national recount could be more costly, time-consuming, and polarizing than even the Florida debacle.

Many proposals have been offered to abolish or reform the electoral college. Public opinion polls show a strong preference for direct popular vote. Reform proposals include abolishing electors but keeping the electoral vote so that state popular vote outcomes would be converted to electoral votes without risk of "faithless electors"; choosing electors by congressional districts with the two votes representing the Senate seats going to the statewide popular vote winner, as currently done in Maine and Nebraska; dropping the winner-take-all rule and dividing each state's electoral vote among the candidates proportional to their share of the popular vote (usually without actual electors, thus allowing fractions); and dropping the two votes based on a state's Senate seats and having an electoral college based only on the number of representatives in each state. None of the proposed solutions is without its own problems.

Arguments against change include an assertion that the system has worked so far, that it is an ingredient of FEDERALISM, and that change in one part of the Constitution may lead to pressure to change other parts. Nationwide change would require either a constitutional amendment or agreement among states to make changes within their constitutional power (such as changing the winner-take-all rule). Either method would likely be difficult to achieve because of the vested interest of small states in the current system and because neither major political party shows much interest in change.

For more information: Best, Judith A. *The Choice of the People? Debating the Electoral College.* Lanham, Md.: Rowman & Littlefield Publishers, 1996; Longley, Lawrence D., and Neal R. Peirce. *The Electoral College Primer 2000.* New Haven, Conn.: Yale University Press, 1999; Rainey, Glenn W., Jr., and Jane G. Rainey. "The Electoral College: Political Advantage, the Small States, and Implications for Reform." In *Counting Votes: Lessons from the 2000 Presidential Election in Florida.* Gainesville: University Press of Florida, 2004.

—Jane G. Rainey

Eleventh Amendment (1795)

The Eleventh Amendment prohibits suits in federal court by citizens of one state against a state different from their own. This amendment was adopted in order to protect the sovereign immunity of states against lawsuits. Throughout U.S. history, the Eleventh Amendment has been invoked to insulate state governments against a host of different types of lawsuits. Under the REHNQUIST COURT, this amendment was often invoked, along with the Tenth Amendment, to protect state power.

Sovereign immunity is an ancient legal concept that comes to the United States from English common law. According to this concept, the king or the government generally cannot be sued without its consent. In writing the Constitution, the framers appeared to have overlooked or undervalued state sovereign immunity, permitting citizens of one state to sue a state different from their own under Section 2 of ARTICLE III OF THE U.S. CONSTITUTION.

The Eleventh Amendment was ratified in 1795 to overturn the Supreme Court decision of *CHISOLM V. GEORGIA,* 2 U.S. 419 (1793), where the Court ruled it had jurisdiction to hear a suit as a matter of ORIGINAL JURISDICTION involving a dispute between an individual's estate (in South Carolina) and the state of Georgia for debts, specifically nonpayment of military supplies. The fear was that without the Eleventh Amendment protection of sovereign immunity, states would be bankrupted by suits arising from the Revolutionary War.

Since its adoption, the Eleventh Amendment has had an unusual history. In *Hans v. Louisiana,* 134 U.S. 1 (1890), the Court stated that the Eleventh Amendment is a general blanket of sovereign immunity that protects states from lawsuits brought by its own citizens or those of another state. There are some exceptions. In *EX PARTE YOUNG,* 209 U.S. 123 (1908), one exception was that state officials could be sued individually if they sought to enforce unconstitutional laws. Another exception, as developed in *Welch v. Texas Department of Highways,* 483 U.S. 468 (1987), was that Congress, in some circumstances, could abrogate, or break, sovereign immunity as long as it clearly intended to do that. Initially, in *Pennsylvania v. Union Gas Company,* 491 U.S. 1 (1989), the Court ruled that Congress could use its COMMERCE CLAUSE power to abrogate sovereign immunity but, subsequently, in *Seminole Tribe of Florida v. Florida,* 517 U.S. 44 (1996), decided that the federal government can only abrogate state sovereign immunity via the FOURTEENTH AMENDMENT because the commerce clause is limited by the Eleventh Amendment.

Under the Rehnquist Court, the Eleventh Amendment was employed to limit lawsuits by individuals against states. In limiting these suits, the Court often linked the Eleventh to the Tenth Amendment as a constitutional means to limit federal power. For example, in *ALDEN V. MAINE,* 527 U.S. 706 (1999), the Court held that state sovereign immunity bars state employees from suing a state to comply with the federal Fair Labor Standards Act. In *Board of Trustees of the University of Alabama v. Garrett,* 531 U.S. 356 (2001), the Court held that state sovereignty prohibited the state employees from being able to sue under Title I of the Americans with Disability Act (ADA). In *FEDERAL MARITIME COMMISSION V. SOUTH CAROLINA STATE PORTS AUTHORITY,* 535 U.S. 743 (2002), the Court ruled that sovereign immunity barred suits against states before federal administrative law bodies. However, in *TENNESSEE V. LANE,* 541 U.S. 509 (2004), the Supreme Court ruled that states may be sued if they denied disabled individuals access to the courts. This decision appeared to limit some of the more far-ranging applications of sovereign immunity and the Eleventh Amendment.

For more information: Orth, John V. *The Judicial Power of the United States: The Eleventh Amendment in American History.* New York: Oxford University Press, 1987.

—David Schultz

Ellsworth Court (1796–1800)

The Ellsworth Court refers to the Supreme Court under Chief Justice Oliver Ellsworth. During his term, the Ellsworth Court began the process of giving life to the Supreme Court as a real institution and not simply a description found in ARTICLE III OF THE U.S. CONSTITUTION.

Oliver Ellsworth was a Founding Father of great distinction. Ellsworth was a leader of the Federalist Party and served in several key leadership roles during the revolutionary and founding era, including representing Connecticut at the CONSTITUTIONAL CONVENTION, service to Connecticut in Congress, and his work in the construction of the JUDICIARY ACT OF 1789. Ellsworth also served as the third U.S. Supreme Court chief justice.

Ellsworth was born in Windsor, Connecticut, on April 29, 1745, and raised there. He pursued his collegiate studies at Yale College, later transferring to and graduating from the College of New Jersey (Princeton University) in 1766. Ellsworth initially began his studies in theology but later changed his focus to law and was admitted to the bar in 1771. As an active member of the Federalist Party, Ellsworth quickly turned to politics and served as a member of the state general assembly from 1773 to 1776. His involvement in the political arena did not end there, as he served as a member of the Continental Congress and Governor's Council, as well as a delegate at the Constitutional Convention. Additionally, Ellsworth served as a judge for the Connecticut Superior Court. Ellsworth was later elected to office as a U.S. senator, serving from 1789 to 1796. Ellsworth was nominated by President George Washington to serve as chief justice in the early spring of 1796. Though Ellsworth's tenure as chief justice lasted only three years, there were several significant cases, ranging from Congress's power to tax to ratification of constitutional amendments, as well as issues of jurisdiction. There were many cases argued before the Ellsworth Court that settled a variety of issues pertaining to what many view today as common practice within the governmental system.

The first case that was heard under the Ellsworth Court was *HYLTON V. UNITED STATES*, 3 U.S. 171 (1796). The *Hylton* case dealt with a law enacted by Congress that imposed a tax on carriages owned by individuals or businesses. The plaintiff argued that the carriage tax was not apportioned and was a direct tax. Subsequently, the plaintiff contended that Congress violated its TAXING AND SPENDING POWERS as outlined by the Constitution. The Court struck down the plaintiff's argument and held that the tax imposed by Congress was constitutional, as it was an indirect tax. In the *Hylton* case, the Court defined a direct tax as one that could not be apportioned and reasoned that the carriage tax at issue was properly apportioned.

In 1798, the Ellsworth Court was faced with another issue involving the constitutionality of an act of Congress. In *Hollingsworth v. Virginia*, 3 U.S. 378 (1798), the Court heard arguments that involved the constitutionality of the president's involvement in the ratification of constitutional amendments. In *Hollingsworth,* the Ellsworth Court affirmed that no presidential signature was required for Congress to propose an amendment to the Constitution. While the *Hollingsworth* decision was narrowly tailored to the particular facts in contention, it was clear in the Court's early years that it was committed to protecting the integrity of the newly ratified Constitution.

Late in Chief Justice Ellsworth's tenure, the Court exercised for the first time its ORIGINAL JURISDICTION as enumerated in Article III, Section 2, of the Constitution. In *New York v. Connecticut,* 4 U.S. 3 (1799), the Court exercised its ability to hear a case in a dispute to which a state is a party. In the *New York* case, there was a dispute between two states over the right to a tract of land, the "Connecticut gore." The Court held that New York was not a party to the ejectment action and had no interest at stake. The case was significant because it was the first time the Supreme Court used original jurisdiction to hear a case.

In 1800, after three and a half years of service as chief justice, Ellsworth announced his resignation. The Ellsworth Court made great advancements in the Supreme Court's young history to protect and uphold the newly established Constitution. The Ellsworth Court's jurisprudence followed the conservative judicial restraint of prior Federalist courts and strengthened national institutions and FEDERALISM.

For more information: Buchanan, James M. "Oliver Ellsworth, Third Chief Justice." In *Journal of Supreme Court History*. Washington, D.C.: Supreme Court Historical Society, 1991; Marbach, Joseph R., Ellis Katz, and Troy E. Smith, eds. *Federalism in America*. Westport, Conn.: Greenwood Publishing, 2005.

—Michael W. Hail and Sarah E. Wilson

Embargo Act of 1807

The Embargo Acts were a series of laws passed between 1806 and 1808 during THOMAS JEFFERSON's second term as president of the United States. The aim was to punish Great Britain for its operations against U.S. ships.

The British were experiencing a shortage of sailors, mainly because of the harsh conditions on board English ships and because many British sailors preferred working on American ships, where conditions were better. The Royal Navy consequently started stopping U.S. vessels and impressing those sailors they suspected were British deserters. Americans understood impressments as an incursion on their independence. The peak of this conflict was the boarding of the USS *Chesapeake* by the sailors of the HMS *Leopard* off the coast of Maryland on June 21, 1807. The British announced to the USS *Chesapeake* that they would board the American vessel on the grounds that they were looking for deserters. When the Americans refused, the HMS *Leopard* discharged its cannons against the USS *Chesapeake*, leaving 18 Americans wounded and three dead. The British finally boarded the ship and took away four deserters.

One of Jefferson's first measures was to issue a proclamation by which British ships were not allowed to navigate U.S. waters. Among other actions such as the Non-Importation Act of December 1807, the Jeffersonian government began issuing a series of Embargo Acts. The first one was passed on December 22, 1807. It prohibited American ships from sailing foreign waters unless specifically allowed by the president himself, it did not allow exports from the United States by sea or land, and it did not authorize certain British products to enter the United States. This Embargo Act struck a terrible blow to foreign trade, which was one of the most important American activities at the time. After the outbreak of war in Europe in 1783, the United States had dominated overseas trade. Most ships with tropical products such as coffee, sugar, tea, and pepper sailed first into the United States, and their cargoes were reshipped in order not to be intercepted. The European war was also highly beneficial for grain and cotton growers. The economy of the young United States was based on its capacity to remain neutral. After the acts were passed, however, American exports dropped by 80 percent.

In January 1808, Jefferson passed a second Embargo Act by which all American ships had to pay a fee of twice the value of the vessel and its cargo. Since many merchants did not follow the Embargo Acts regulations, a third one was passed in March 1808 prohibiting the exportation of any goods by sea or land and punishing violators of such rule with fines up to $10,000. The third act also endowed the president with the authority to reject, implement, or grant exceptions to this embargo.

The fourth Embargo Act (also known as the Enforcement Act) passed in April 1808 and enabled port authorities to bring to trial any merchant they believed had violated the embargo. The act also established that it was the president's right and duty to use the army and the navy to administer the Embargo Acts.

Three days before Jefferson left office, Congress repealed the Embargo Acts. Congress decided to pass the Non-Intercourse Act on March 1, 1809, which repealed all the acts except those that affected Great Britain and France. Since the Non-Intercourse Act was also ineffective, it was substituted in 1810 by Macon's Bill Number 2 that lifted the rest of the embargoes.

For more information: Cray, R. E. "Remembering the USS *Chesapeake*: The Politics of Maritime Death and Impressment." *Journal of the Early Republic* 25, no. 3 (2005): 445–474; Frankel, J. A. "The 1807–1809 Embargo Against Great Britain." *Journal of Economic History* 42, no. 2 (1982): 291–308; Kaplan, Lawrence S. "Jefferson, the Napoleonic Wars, and the Balance of Power." *William and Mary Quarterly* 14, no. 2 (1957): 196–217; Scofield, M. E. "The Fatigues of His Table: The Politics of Presidential Dining During the Jefferson Administration." *Journal of the Early Republic* 26, no. 3 (2006): 449–469.

—Laura Gimeno-Pahissa

eminent domain

Eminent domain is the power of the government to take private property for a public use as long as JUST COMPENSATION is paid. While this power is considered an inherent attribute of state governments and sovereign power, the Fifth Amendment to the Constitution defines the eminent domain power of the federal government. While in *BARRON V. MAYOR AND CITY COUNCIL OF BALTIMORE*, 32 U.S. 243 (1833), the Supreme Court had ruled that the eminent domain provisions of the Fifth Amendment did not apply to the states, starting with *Chicago, Burlington & Quincy Railroad Company v. Chicago*, 166 U.S. 226 (1897), the Court declared that the just compensation requirement applied to the states through the DUE PROCESS clause of the FOURTEENTH AMENDMENT. Today, all of the provisions of the Fifth Amendment are incorporated as limits upon state power.

The power of eminent domain is one of the basic powers of government, along with taxation and the regulation of commerce at the federal level and the POLICE POWER with the states. The power of eminent domain traces back to English common law, under which individuals owned or used land subject to the superior need and ability of the monarchy to acquire property for its uses. Traditionally, the superior right of the crown to take property from individuals resided in the need of the government to further some public projects, such as to build roads or bridges. When this power was passed on to the American colonies and then on to the original thirteen states, these requirements generally limited their ability to use eminent domain; however, there was no requirement to pay just compensation. But, starting with the Vermont Constitution after the Revolutionary War, eminent domain and just compensation provisions were codified in state laws.

Interpretations of the Fifth Amendment's eminent domain provisions generally center on three questions: 1) What is a taking? 2) What is a public use? and 3) What constitutes just compensation? All three of these issues have been the subject of intense and often heated CONSTITUTIONAL INTERPRETATION by the Supreme Court.

Generally, the Supreme Court has stated that a taking occurs when there is either a direct or physical taking or invasion of property or when a regulation is so extensive that it has effected a taking. In *LORETTO V. TELEPROMPTER MANHATTAN CATV CORP.*, 458 U.S. 419 (1982), the Supreme Court stated that any type of physical invasion or trespass of private property would constitute a taking. This could be when the government formally takes the property to build a highway, bridge, or a school or when it uses the property for some purpose, such as water runoff or drainage.

In addition, in *Pennsylvania Coal Company v. Mahon*, 260 U.S. 393 (1922), Justice OLIVER WENDELL HOLMES, JR., argued that while some government regulation of private property is permitted, especially if one is using property in a way that constitutes a nuisance, if the regulation goes too far it could constitute a taking, necessitating the payment of compensation to the owner. In this case, the courts have called this action a REGULATORY TAKING. A taking, according to the Court in *First Evangelical Church of Glendale v. County of Los Angeles,* 482 U.S. 304 (1987), can occur whether the government assumes permanent or even temporary control of property.

A second issue in eminent domain surrounds what constitutes a valid public use. Traditional public uses limited the taking of private property to building roads, highways, jails, schools, bridges, and other facilities used by the public. This type of use of eminent domain narrowly construed the power to the taking of real property (land and buildings) for a finite type of project associated with usual government projects. However, over time, this narrow reading of public use has been greatly expanded to where public use no longer means used by the public. Instead, a valid public use is any taking that would secure the public benefit, good, or welfare.

For example, in *WEST RIVER BRIDGE V. DIX,* 47 U.S. 507 (1848), the Court held that all types of property—including contracts and franchises—could be acquired by eminent domain. In *Berman v. Parker,* 348 U.S. 26 (1956), the Court ruled it was a valid public use to take unblighted property for the purpose of slum clearance. In *HAWAII HOUSING AUTHORITY V. MIDKIFF,* 467 U.S. 229 (1984), the Court upheld the use of eminent domain in order to break up land monopolies or large estates and sell smaller units to tenants. Justice SANDRA DAY O'CONNOR, writing for the Court, declared that the meaning of public use was equal to that of the scope of a state's police power. In effect, states had broad authority to take private property for all types of public uses including not just building bridges or highways but also for slum clearance, building cemeteries, sports stadiums, public housing, and other purposes. In *KELO V. CITY OF NEW LONDON,* 545 U.S. 469 (2005), many argued that the U.S. Supreme Court pushed the public use provision too far, upholding the taking of private property for economic development purposes as constituting a valid public use. The *Kelo* decision was seen by many as a significant erosion of property rights, and it resulted in many state and local governments restricting the power of eminent domain.

The third issue in eminent domain litigation is that once a taking has occurred, the owner must be paid just compensation for the property that has been taken. Just compensation, according to the Court, means that the owner must be paid fair market value for the property. Fair market value is determined by asking what a reasonable buyer would give the owner in a private sale. To determine this, the courts often use one of three methods to value property. First, they would look to what price was paid for similar properties. Second, they would look at what it would cost to replace or rebuild the property. Third, they look to the income of investment value of the property, seeking to determine its worth in terms of its income stream. Courts are often required to use all three of these valuation techniques when seeking to ascertain what constitutes just compensation for property.

Overall, eminent domain is a powerful and necessary tool of the federal and state governments, and it is subject to numerous restrictions under the Fifth Amendment. Yet, many defenders of property rights worry that the eminent domain had been abused and that more restrictions need to be imposed on it.

For more information: Schultz, David. *Property, Power, and American Democracy.* New Brunswick, N.J.: Transaction, 1992; Schultz, David. "What's Yours Can Be Mine: Are There Any Private Takings after *City of New London v. Kelo*?" *UCLA Journal of Environmental Law and Policy* 24, no. 195 (2006).

—David Schultz

employment discrimination

Employment discrimination refers to making illegal employment decisions based on an employee's race, color, age, creed, religion, national origin, gender, or disability. While the Constitution has been interpreted to ban INTENTIONAL DISCRIMINATION on the basis of race and other factors through the EQUAL PROTECTION clause of both the FOURTEENTH AMENDMENT and the Fifth Amendment, most of the law regarding employment discrimination is found in legislation adopted by Congress.

All employment practices, including application procedures; interviewing; testing; selecting and hiring; layoff and seniority policies; evaluation procedures; the distribution of organizational rewards such as pay, leave, training, and promotions; and disciplining and firing; may be subject to discrimination claims. Numerous federal antidiscrimination laws are in place to reduce discrimination and harassment in the workplace; these include Title VII of the CIVIL RIGHTS ACT OF 1964 and, as amended in 1991, the Age Discrimination in Employment Act (ADEA) of 1967, the Pregnancy Discrimination Act of 1978, and the Americans with Disabilities Act (ADA) of 1990. In addition, the federal government and many states and municipalities forbid discrimination based on sexual orientation, political affiliation, and marital status. Some states give additional antidiscrimination protections to workers and groups who are not covered by federal law.

The U.S. Supreme Court *in McDonnell Douglas Corporation v. Green*, 411 U.S. 792 (1973), describes how to build a prima facie showing of hiring discrimination. A prima facie case (or a case that is valid at first glance) could be created by demonstrating that 1) applicants or employees belonged to a protected group, 2) they applied for and were qualified for the position, 3) they were rejected despite meeting the job qualifications, and 4) employers continued, after rejection, to seek employees with the same qualifications.

To prove illegal employment discrimination, an applicant or employee must show disparate treatment or DISPARATE IMPACT. Disparate treatment claims demonstrate that an employer treated a particular group differently from another group. For example, racial prejudice resulted in one group, say white employees, getting hired or promoted over black employees. Under disparate treatment, plaintiffs must show that employers intentionally discriminated against them.

In contrast, disparate impact claims involve employment practices that appear neutral on the surface and, therefore, not deliberately discriminatory in nature. Although the practice makes no reference to race, color, sex, religion, or national origin, it may in practice have an adverse effect on a protected group and no effect on groups who are not in the protected category. For example, if a correctional facility requires all prospective prison guards to stand at least five feet, four inches tall, the height requirement could have a disparate impact on women, who are often shorter than men. The correctional facility may be sued for disparate impact discrimination unless it can show a job-related need for the height requirement. Employers cannot excuse discriminatory treatment by saying they did not intend to discriminate. If a plaintiff makes an initial showing of discrimination, the employer must provide a legitimate, nondiscriminatory reason for an adverse employment practice or decision.

The Civil Rights Act of 1964 became the centerpiece of antidiscrimination law and spawned other major employee protection legislation. Title VII of the Civil Rights Act of 1964 put fair employment practices in the spotlight. Title VII forbids employers from discriminating against employees in hiring, termination, classification, and compensation and on terms, conditions, or privileges of employment based on race, color, religion, gender, or national origin. Because every worker has a race, a color, a gender, a religion (or no religious beliefs), and a national origin, persons with any of these characteristics are protected against discrimination. Thus, men and women are protected from gender discrimination such as sexual harassment. European Americans and African Americans are protected against race, color, and nationality discrimination. Protestants, Catholics, Jews, and Muslims are protected against religious discrimination. Congress passed the law first and foremost to protect African Americans and women from discriminatory practices, but, in practice, the law is quite broad and extends protections to many more groups.

As women entered the workforce after World War II in record numbers, many employers discriminated against married women by refusing to hire them for fear that their work productivity would be interrupted by pregnancy. Often women were fired or asked to resign once they became pregnant. To address this, Congress passed the Pregnancy Discrimination Act, which requires employers to treat pregnant women the same as other job applicants or employees. Employment practices that discriminate against an employee due to pregnancy, childbirth, or medical conditions associated with pregnancy are encompassed under Title VII and are a form of gender discrimination.

Age discrimination spurred additional legislation. Under the Age Discrimination in Employment Act, it is illegal to make discriminatory employment decisions against those who are 40 years of age or older if the employer regularly employs 20 or more employees. The ADEA does not protect employees younger than 40 who were denied a job because they were too young. If age is an important component of one's job and is related to one's ability to perform the job, such as being an effective firefighter, certain employees may not be covered by the ADEA. Most ADEA suits are based on disparate treatment, claiming that the age discrimination was intentional.

To combat discrimination against qualified disabled applicants and employees, Congress passed the Americans with Disabilities Act, prohibiting physical or mental disability discrimination and requiring employers to make reasonable accommodations for the disabled. The ADA provides three definitions of disability: 1) being substantially impaired and thus unable to perform a major life activity, such as being blind, 2) being on the record as having a disability and being fired because of this medical history, and 3) being regarded as having a disability such as being overweight and being perceived as unable to perform required job duties. To accommodate the disabled, employers should ensure that work facilities are accessible to the qualified disabled applicants or employees. This could become expensive, and consequently, the courts have held that such accommodations cannot impose an "undue hardship" on employers by requiring significant expense given the agency's size and financial resources. The ADA applies to all public employees and private employers who employ 15 or more employees.

Disabled demonstrators rally in Los Angeles, California, to protest the decision of the state of California to challenge in the Supreme Court the Americans with Disabilities Act of 1990. *(McNew/Newsmakers)*

With increased workplace diversity and with approximately 47 million U.S. residents age five or older speaking a language other than English, national origin discrimination claims are on the rise. National origin discrimination refers to employment decisions that are linked to a person's birthplace or culture. One controversy associated with this area of discrimination law occurred when some employers implemented "English-only" policies at work. Numerous workers have challenged these policies as a form of national origin discrimination. Employers with English-only policies justified them on grounds of safety, business necessity, and workplace efficiency; however, courts have ruled that employers may not require employees to speak in English at all times on the job. Employees have freedom to express themselves in situations where they are not required to perform work-related duties, such as their lunch breaks. Blanket English-only policies have been challenged and generally are not upheld unless they are clearly related to a legitimate agency or business concern.

To improve Title VII's effectiveness, Congress passed the Equal Employment Act of 1972. With this legislation, the Equal Employment Opportunity Commission (EEOC) became the primary enforcer of federal laws prohibiting job discrimination. It uses Title VII to protect employees who file discrimination claims or aid in investigations from retaliation. Title VII antidiscrimination provisions apply to private employers, state and local governments, and educational institutions that have 15 or more employees. The federal government, LABOR UNIONS, and employment agencies must also comply with Title VII. Employment discrimination law is constantly changing as new groups assert their rights and demand equal protection.

One major exception to most federal employment discrimination laws concerns churches and other religious organizations. These entities are permitted both by way of exemption and because of the free exercise clause of the FIRST AMENDMENT to discriminate in hiring for religious reasons. Thus, Catholic churches are permitted to restrict the hiring of priests to males who meet the specific requirements of that faith.

For more information: Allred, Stephen. *Employment Law: A Guide for North Carolina Public Employers.* Chapel Hill: Institute of Government, University of North Carolina at Chapel Hill, 1999; Center for Education and Employment Law. *Desktop Encyclopedia of Public Employment Law.* 15th ed. Malvern, Pa.: Center for Education and Employment Law, 2005; Conway, M. Margaret, David W. Ahern, and Gertrude A. Steuernagel. *Women and Public Policy: A Revolution in Progress.* 3d ed. Washington, D.C.: CQ Press, 2005; Gold, Michael Evan. *An Introduction to the Law of Employment Discrimination.* Ithaca, N.Y.: Cornell University Press, 2001; Jasper, Margaret C. *You've Been Fired: Your Rights and Remedies.* Oxford and New York: Oceana Publications, 2005; Twomey, David P. *Employment Discrimination Law: A Manager's Guide: Text and Case.* Mason, Ohio: Thomson, West Legal Studies in Business, 2005.

—Ruth Ann Strickland

Employment Division v. Smith 494 U.S. 872 (1990)

By a vote of 6-3, the U.S. Supreme Court, in *Employment Division v. Smith,* reversed Oregon's highest court and held that, despite guarantees of the First and Fourteenth Amendments, a state law aimed at preventing drug abuse may punish Native Americans for using peyote in a religious exercise. Associate Justice ANTONIN GREGORY SCALIA's majority opinion, joined by Chief Justice WILLIAM HUBBS REHNQUIST and Associate Justices Byron White, JOHN PAUL STEVENS, SANDRA DAY O'CONNOR, and ANTHONY M. KENNEDY, argued that Oregon's law was valid since it did not target religion directly but interfered with it only incidentally.

The case arose when a private drug counseling organization fired Alfred Smith and Galen Black for ingesting a proscribed hallucinogen and the Division of Employment Security subsequently refused to pay them unemployment benefits because their employer discharged them for work-related misconduct. Although Oregon did not pay the men any benefits, neither did it prosecute them for drug use.

Scalia distinguished between *Smith,* which involved a criminal act, and two previous cases where the government was ordered to pay unemployment benefits. A Seventh-Day Adventist fired for refusing to work on Saturday (*Sherbert v. Verner,* 374 U.S. 398 [1963]) and a Jehovah's Witness who quit his job when he was transferred to making military equipment (*Thomas v. Review Bd. of Indiana Employment Security Div.,* 450 U.S. 707 [1981]) were both guaranteed payments on the basis of religious freedom.

Further, Scalia maintained that the Constitution guarantees the right to religious belief and profession of faith but not necessarily the right to engage in physical acts such as ingesting peyote. In some hybrid cases where FREEDOM OF RELIGION combines with other liberties, such as free speech, the Court has prohibited government interference. But Scalia refused to employ what he called a balancing test, or what the minority referred to as STRICT SCRUTINY, to weigh the harm of granting or not granting a religious exception to a generally applicable criminal statute. Instead, he argued that a neutral law of general applicability did not conflict with the right to exercise religion freely.

Justice Harry A. Blackmun filed a dissenting opinion in which Justices WILLIAM J. BRENNAN, JR., and Thurgood Marshall joined. He maintained that the majority departed from well-settled FIRST AMENDMENT jurisprudence of strict scrutiny, where government allows a religious exemption to a general law unless there is a compelling interest that cannot be served by less restrictive means. For example, the Court allowed an exemption to compulsory school attendance for Amish children on the basis of their religious beliefs. It decided that a few children leaving school at age 16 did not damage the educational system (*WISCONSIN V. YODER*, 406 U.S. 205 [1972]). Blackmun pointed out that nearly half the states and the national government provide an exception for bona fide members of the Native American Church to use peyote in religious exercises. In other words, a state or the nation may grant a religious exception to a law, but the Constitution does not require it.

Two previous decisions also failed to use strict scrutiny in considering free exercise of religion. In 1986, Chief Justice WARREN E. BURGER ruled the government was justified in not paying welfare benefits to a Native American family that refused to obtain a Social Security number for their daughter on grounds that it would take away the purity of the girl's spirit and violate her Native American religious beliefs. Burger claimed a number was facially neutral in religious terms and that "[t]he free exercise clause simply cannot be understood to require the Government to conduct its own internal affairs in ways that comport with the religious beliefs of particular citizens" (*Bowen v. Roy*, 476 U.S. 693 [1986]).

Two years later, Justice O'Connor spoke for the Court in allowing the U.S. Forest Service to build a road in a national forest as an internal governmental matter despite the fact that it desecrated sacred Indian land (*Lyng v. Northwest Indian Cemetery Protective Assn.*, 485 U.S. 439 [1988]).

In 1993, using its authority under Section 5 of the FOURTEENTH AMENDMENT, Congress passed the RELIGIOUS FREEDOM RESTORATION ACT (PL 103-141) in an attempt to enforce the amendment by requiring the Court to use strict scrutiny in cases of FUNDAMENTAL RIGHTS. But in *Boerne v. Flores*, 521 U.S. 507 (1997), the Court declared the measure void as a violation of separation of powers. Then, in 2000, Congress passed the Religious Land Use and Institutionalized Persons Act to apply strict scrutiny in certain cases. It was upheld in part by *Cutter v. Wilkinson*, 544 U.S. 709 (2005).

For more information: Emenhiser, JeDon. "The G-O Road Controversy: American Indian Religion and Public Land." Available online. URL: http://www.humboldt.edu/~jae1/emenLyng.html. Accessed May 7, 2008; *Employment Div. v. Smith*. Available online. URL: http://caselaw.lp.findlaw.com/scripts/get-case.pl?navby=case&court=us&vol= 494&page=872. Accessed May 7, 2008; Epps, Garrett. *To an Unknown God: Religious Freedom on Trial*. New York: St. Martin's Press, 2001; Long, Carolyn. *Religious Freedom and Indian Rights: The Case of* Oregon v. Smith. Lawrence: University of Kansas Press, 2000.

—JeDon Emenhiser

Engel v. Vitale 370 U.S. 421 (1962)

Engel v. Vitale was the first Supreme Court case to address government-sponsored prayer in public schools. In this case, with two justices not participating, the Court ruled 6-1 that a prayer composed by a government violated the ESTABLISHMENT CLAUSE of the FIRST AMENDMENT.

The case, brought by Jewish and Unitarian parents, challenged the constitutionality of a prayer composed by New York's Board of Regents, a state body, and required to be recited daily in their children's school: "Almighty God, we acknowledge our dependence upon Thee, and we beg Thy blessings upon us, our parents, our teachers, and our Country." Although the prayer was intended as nondenominational, they argued that it was contrary to their beliefs.

Justice HUGO BLACK, writing for the majority, stated that it is not the business of government to compose prayers. He reviewed the history of the established church and religious persecution in England, including the role of Parliament in imposing the Book of Common Prayer as the only acceptable form of worship. He then summarized the colonial history of establishment and persecution by the same groups who had left England to seek religious freedom. All this history, he said, was well known to the founders and shaped their thinking as they crafted the establishment clause.

He portrayed the Founding Fathers as "men of faith in the power of prayer" who did not want the content of their prayers to be determined by elected or hereditary leaders. He depicted the establishment clause as a protection not just for religious minorities but as an expression of belief by the founders that "religion is too personal, too sacred, too holy to permit its 'unhallowed perversion' by a civil magistrate."

He contributed to the Court's working interpretation of the First Amendment by stating that coercion need not be present for the establishment clause to be violated. Indirect coercion, such as that a child might experience when given the choice of leaving the classroom during the prayer, was also an inappropriate use of government authority.

In a footnote, he offered reassurances that *Engle* would not signal the end of public patriotic observances that incidentally touched on religion, such as singing patriotic songs invoking God or reciting the DECLARATION OF INDEPENDENCE.

Justice WILLIAM O. DOUGLAS, however, wrote a concurring opinion in which he suggested that everything from the Court crier to the community Christmas tree might be in violation of the establishment clause. He defined the issue in monetary terms and said government should not fund religious exercises regardless of how small the cost involved. He expressed his view that the Court had erred in its decision in *EVERSON V. BOARD OF EDUCATION*, 330 U.S. 1 (1947), in which he had been a part of the majority, and endorsed the *Everson* dissent of Justice Wiley Rutledge.

The lone dissenter, Justice Potter Stewart, insisted that in the absence of coercion, there was no establishment clause violation. He played on the "tradition" theme, declared the history of the Book of Common Prayer irrelevant, and quoted the entire third verse of the "Star-Spangled Banner," as an example of government recognition of the role of religion in the United States. The justification for upholding New York, he asserted, had been summed up 10 years earlier in the assertion, "We are a religious people whose institutions presuppose a Supreme Being" (the words, ironically, of Justice Douglas in *ZORACH V. CLAUSON*, 343 U.S. 306, 1952).

The Court's decision in *Engel* prompted widespread public and governmental condemnation of the ruling including congressional hearings and calls for a constitutional amendment.

For more information: Fisher, Louis. *Religious Liberty in America: Political Safeguards.* Lawrence: University Press of Kansas, 2002; Fraser, James W. *Between Church and State: Religion and Public Education in a Multicultural America.* New York: St. Martin's Griffin, 1999.

—Jane G. Rainey

English Bill of Rights (1689)

The English Bill of Rights of 1689 is one of the basic documents of the English constitution and a precursor of the American BILL OF RIGHTS. It is also a supporting document for Scottish, Irish, New Zealand, and other Commonwealth statements of rights and for the United Nations Declaration of Human Rights, as well.

Adopted by the Parliament of England (1 Will & Mar. sess. 2 c. 2), the full name of the English Bill of Rights (1689) is An Act Declaring the Rights and Liberties of the Subject and Settling the Succession of the Crown. It was adopted, like the American Bill of Rights, as a legal device for controlling the government.

The adoption of the English Bill of Rights came at the end of decades of struggle between the Stuart dynasty and the English establishment. The English monarchy had been restored, following the beheading of Charles I and Oliver Cromwell's rule during the English Protectorate, with the accession in 1660 of Charles II (1630–85). When Charles II suddenly died, it opened the way for his brother James to become king. James II was a dedicated Roman Catholic in a very Protestant England. He was married to Mary of Modena, who, along with James, sought ways to restore Roman Catholicism as the controlling religion in England.

On April 16, 1687, James II issued a declaration of indulgence that allowed Roman Catholics and Protestant dissenters to worship publicly. He also abrogated the Test Act, which mandated a religious test of conformity to Anglicanism. Most people in England suspected that James's expressions of religious tolerance were a sham. His hidden agenda was believed to be the regaining of control by Roman Catholics. James's veiled attempt to Romanize the English army after the failed revolt of the duke of Monmouth inflamed public suspicions even further.

On June 10, 1688, a son, Prince James Francis Edward, was born to James II and Queen Mary. The threat of a Roman Catholic heir to the English throne moved prominent English leaders to seek to replace James with his Protestant daughter Mary, who was married to Prince William, the stadtholder of the United Provinces of Holland. On November 5, 1688, Prince William landed with an armada of 15,000 men at Torbay on the southwest coast of England. The date was significant because it was the same date as the Gunpowder Plot of 1605, an attempt by Roman Catholics to blow up Parliament. Opposition collapsed, and James II was permitted to escape to France on December 23, 1688.

A convention of Parliament drafted the Declaration of Right, which was accepted by William and Mary on February 13, 1689, at Whitehall. Having given their assent to the Declaration of Right, subsequently they were offered the throne and were crowned on December 16, 1689. Their royal assent effectively ended rule by the divine right of kings and instituted instead a constitutional parliamentary sovereignty. Parliament adopted the Declaration of Right on December 16, 1689, as the English "Bill of Rights."

The Bill of Rights banned accession to the English throne by Roman Catholics. It also indicted King James II with attempting to extirpate the Protestant religion, the laws of the kingdom, and the liberties enjoyed by people in the kingdom. The specific charges included the unlawful exercise of power, abuse of power in matters of religion, taxation without the permission of Parliament, high-handed prosecutions, and abuse of the members of Parliament. He was also accused of abusing the judicial system by using corrupt jurors, levying excessive fines, imposing cruel punishments, and using the proceeds of judicial convictions as rewards for supporters. These abuses by the monarchy violated the rights of Parliament, of religious liberty, and of citizens. When William and Mary agreed to the Declaration of Right, they agreed to parliamentary sovereignty. They were also agreeing to a broadening of CIVIL LIBERTIES that would eventually spread religious liberty and other rights around the globe.

The English Bill of Rights, along with the MAGNA CARTA of 1215, were of significant influence on the U.S. Constitution and Bill of Rights. First, the necessity of a bill of rights was central to the debates surrounding the RATIFICATION OF THE CONSTITUTION in 1787. Anti-Federalists who opposed the Constitution criticized it for its lack of a bill of rights, such as the one found in England. Federalists such as ALEXANDER HAMILTON, who supported the Constitution, denied the need for a bill of rights because many of the provisions found in documents such as the English Bill of Rights were already placed in the new proposed Constitution. The English Bill of Rights was also influential in terms of its content, which, among other protections, secured many religious liberties and granted individuals the right to petition the monarch to address grievances. These provisions later would appear in the U.S. Constitution's FIRST AMENDMENT.

For more information: Hill, Christopher. *The Century of Revolution, 1603–1714*. London:

Thomas Nelson, 1961; Pocock, J. G. A. *Three British Revolutions, 1641, 1688, 1776.* Princeton, N.J.: Princeton University Press, 1980; Straka, Gerald M. *The Revolution of 1688 and the Birth of the English Political Nation.* Lexington, Mass.: Heath, 1973; Swisher, Clarice, ed. *England.* San Diego, Calif.: Greenhaven Press, 2003; Trevelyan, George Macaulay. *England Under the Stuarts.* New York: Barnes & Noble, 1965.

—Andrew J. Waskey

environmental regulation

The power of the U.S. Congress to regulate environmental problems is based on Section 8's COMMERCE CLAUSE under ARTICLE I OF THE U.S. CONSTITUTION, which provides that "Congress shall have the power . . . to regulate commerce with foreign nations, and among the several states." Because Congress has no general POLICE POWER, it may only regulate those environmental issues that fall within its commerce clause power, and the scope of this power is rapidly changing.

Under the commerce clause, Congress may regulate three main categories of activity: 1) the use of the channels of INTERSTATE COMMERCE; 2) the instrumentalities of interstate commerce, or persons or things in interstate commerce; and 3) activities having a substantial relation to interstate commerce (*UNITED STATES V. LOPEZ,* 514 U.S. 549, 558–59 [1995]). With the Supreme Court's decisions in *United States v. Lopez* and *UNITED STATES V. MORRISON,* limitations have been placed on Congress's power to regulate under the commerce clause, and significant questions have been raised regarding the constitutionality of the major federal environmental statutes.

In the Clean Water Act (CWA), Congress sought to limit the discharge of pollutants into "navigable waters," which the act defined to be "the waters of the United States." Because navigable waters are channels of interstate commerce and have a substantial effect on interstate commerce, it is constitutional for Congress to regulate them under its commerce clause power. In the past, however, the agencies charged with carrying out regulation under the CWA have interpreted it expansively, taking the position that they could regulate both navigable lakes and rivers that cross state lines as well as smaller streams, ditches, culverts, and wetlands that are adjacent to navigable waters or have a hydrological connection to navigable waters. This issue was first addressed by the Supreme Court in *United States v. Riverside Bayview Homes, Inc.,* 474 U.S. 121 (1985). There, the Court held that the CWA could cover wetlands that are located directly adjacent to traditional navigable waters. The Court reasoned that "the transition from water to solid ground is not necessarily or even typically an abrupt one" and that the federal government was acting properly within its commerce clause power when it interpreted the act to include these wetlands.

However, in *Solid Waste Agency of N. Cook County v. United States,* 531 U.S. 159 (2001), the Supreme Court held that the government had gone too far in its interpretation of the Clean Water Act. In that case, the government sought to regulate an isolated gravel pit that filled with water seasonally. The application of the CWA to this pit was based on a theory that migratory birds used it as a habitat and that the industries surrounding migratory birds, such as birdwatching and tourism, had a substantial effect on interstate commerce, bringing this regulation within Congress's commerce clause power. The Court struck down this regulation, holding that where the only tie between the regulated water and interstate commerce was the presence of migratory birds, its regulation under the commerce clause power raised serious constitutional questions. In 2006, the Supreme Court spoke to this issue again in *Rapanos v. United States,* 126 S. Ct. 2208. There, the Court struck down regulation of wetlands that were connected to navigable waters by human-made drains and ditches with an only intermittent flow of water. As in *Solid Waste Agency of N. Cook County,* the Court noted that the government's interpretation of the act to cover these wetlands stretched the outer limit of Congress's commerce clause power and raised difficult constitutional questions. Undoubtedly, the question of how far the federal government may go in its regulation of water pollution will continue to pose difficult constitutional questions.

The commerce clause is also the source of Congress's power to protect endangered species under the Endangered Species Act (ESA). Litigants have argued that the federal government lacks the power to prohibit the harming of species that live entirely within a single state because this type of regulation goes beyond its limited power to regulate interstate commerce. To date, the Supreme Court has declined to consider cases raising the constitutionality of these types of regulations, but the courts of appeals have addressed the issue in light of the Supreme Court's recent jurisprudence in other areas of commerce clause litigation. In *National Association of Home Builders v. Babbitt*, 130 F.3d 1041 (DC Cir.) (1997), the U.S. Court of Appeals for the District of Columbia Circuit upheld the application of the ESA to the Delhi sands flower-loving fly, a species of fly found only in two counties in California.

The court held that the application of the ESA to this species was appropriate as a regulation of the use of the channels of interstate commerce, reasoning that this regulation was justified as an aid to the ESA's prohibitions against transporting and selling endangered species in interstate commerce. The court also held that this application of the ESA was constitutional because the extinction of species, if allowed, would have a substantial effect on interstate commerce. The court noted that such regulation was needed to prevent destructive interstate competition, a regulatory objective that has long been held to be constitutional under the commerce clause. Several years later, in *Rancho Viejo v. Norton*, 323 F.3d 1062 (DC Cir.) (2003), the D.C. circuit court again upheld the application of the ESA in the case of the arroyo southwestern toad, a rare species living in California, finding that case to be indistinguishable from *National Association of Home Builders*. The U.S. Supreme Court declined to hear both cases. A three-judge panel of the U.S. Court of Appeals for the Fifth Circuit reached a similar holding in *GDF Realty v. Norton*, 326 F.3d 622 (5th Cir.) (2003), and despite an extensive dissent from other judges in the circuit, the Supreme Court also declined to hear that case. Thus, significant questions remain as to the constitutionality of many applications of the ESA.

Questions regarding the constitutionality of federal environmental regulation will undoubtedly continue to occupy the courts as they refine and interpret the Supreme Court's landmark commerce clause decisions in *United States v. Lopez* and *United States v. Morrison*.

For more information: Broderick, Gregory T. "From Migratory Birds to Migratory Molecules: The Continuing Battle over the Scope of Federal Jurisdiction Under the Clean Water Act." *Columbia Journal of Environmental Law* 30 (2005): 473–523; Klein, Christine A. "The Environmental Commerce Clause." *Harvard Environmental Law Review* 27 (2003): 1–68; Mank, Bradford C. "Can Congress Regulate Intrastate Endangered Species Under the Commerce Clause? The Split in the Circuits over Whether the Regulated Activity Is Private Commercial Development or the Taking of Protected Species." *Brooklyn Law Review* 69 (2004): 923–1,001.

—Johanna Hickman

equal protection

The Fourteenth Amendment, ratified in 1868, provides that "No State shall . . . deny to any person within its jurisdiction the equal protection of the laws." The amendment's primary concern was to protect certain legal rights of the newly freed slaves. Contemporary understandings of the equal protection clause see it as a guarantee that all persons similarly situated receive equal treatment before the law. The government must not make arbitrary, capricious, and unreasonable distinctions among individuals; for example, a rule that people with red hair may not be granted a driver's license even though they meet all other legal qualifications would be a violation of the equal protection clause (at least absent some compelling evidence regarding the driving proclivities of redheads).

The Fourteenth Amendment is directed at state governments, but the federal government is also held to equal protection standards identical to those applied to the states. In the case of *Bolling v. Sharpe*, 347 U.S. 497 (1954), the Supreme Court held that the DUE PROCESS clause of the Fifth Amendment, applicable to the national government, should be understood as containing implicitly an equal protection component. The equal protection tests and analytic approaches detailed below are identical for Fourteenth Amendment challenges to state action or Fifth Amendment challenges to federal action.

Not all governmental classifications raise equal protection problems. Granting driving licenses or the vote to 18-year-olds but not 12-year-olds is a reasonable (or at least not unreasonable) classification, even if there are some 12-year-olds who would qualify for Daytona and can recite the Constitution forward and backward.

Modern equal protection doctrine recognizes a variety of situations that may raise equal protection problems and reviews government classifications using several levels of judicial scrutiny ranging from very deferential review that makes it easy for legislation to pass constitutional muster to a level of scrutiny so strict that very few classifications subject to its intensity can survive constitutional challenge.

The lowest level of Supreme Court review is known as "rational basis review." In addressing the central equal protection question of when people are sufficiently similar in relevant respects that they must be treated equally, the Court using rational basis review applies a test of means-ends rationality to the governmental classification. In short, the Court inquires whether the classification is rationally related to a legitimate governmental objective. Thus, if the government's objective is to have safe drivers on the road, a requirement of good vision for a driver's license and thus denial of a license to blind persons do not constitute a violation of the constitutional rights of the blind. With respect to a right to drive, the blind and the sighted are not similarly situated.

At the other end of the analytic spectrum is a type of review known as "STRICT SCRUTINY." A classification subjected to this level of scrutiny must serve some "overriding" or "compelling" governmental interest, and the means chosen to achieve the government's goal must be very carefully and narrowly crafted to achieve that objective. There are basically two types of classifications that trigger such intense scrutiny: those that involve what the Court has described as "suspect classifications" and those that impinge on FUNDAMENTAL RIGHTS. Suspect classifications are those that are extremely likely to involve a governmental effort to harm some minority, so likely that the Court will immediately be suspicious when the law contains such a classification. Fundamental rights, at least for equal protection purposes, are relatively limited, including, most prominently, the RIGHT TO VOTE, the right to access to the judicial process, the right to travel both interstate and abroad, and certain aspects of the right to PRIVACY.

The quintessential example of a suspect classification is race. Given the origins of the Fourteenth Amendment, as well as U.S. history of discrimination against African Americans, it is not surprising that the contemporary Court views racial classifications with such extreme disfavor. But this was not always the case.

While the framers of the Fourteenth Amendment wanted to protect certain CIVIL RIGHTS of African Americans (for example, guaranteeing to them equal ability with whites to enter into contracts, purchase property, or serve on juries), they were not necessarily eager to protect what they considered political or social rights, such as the right to vote (political) or the right to equal access to a variety of public accommodations (social). This distinction was at the heart of the Court's decision in the infamous case of *Plessy v. Ferguson*, 163 U.S. 537 (1896), in which the Court upheld a Louisiana law requiring separate railroad cars for whites and all other races. Faced with an equal protection challenge to the law, the Court held that as long as the separate facilities were equal, there was no constitutional violation. The Court said that the commingling of the races in public was a matter of social relationships and that the state's decision to prevent such interaction was a reasonable one. Thus was born the notion of "separate but equal" as the Court in effect gave its imprimatur to a wave of state laws requiring segregation in a variety of public facilities, including public schools. The lone dissenter in *Plessy*, Justice JOHN MARSHALL HARLAN, wrote that the "equality" Louisiana provided was a thin disguise for serious inequality. As he understood the Constitution, "there is in this country no superior, dominant, ruling class of citizens. . . . Our constitution is color-blind."

Plessy was reflective of prevalent racial attitudes (racism) in America, both in the North and South. These attitudes would not begin to change until the middle of the 20th century and even then (as now) very slowly. The origin of the notion of suspect classifications is *KOREMATSU V. UNITED STATES*, 323 U.S. 214 (1944). In that case, the Court upheld the federal government's program of excluding from their homes on the West Coast persons of Japanese ancestry, accepting the military's (specious) arguments that they constituted a threat to U.S. war efforts against Japan. The opinion by Justice HUGO BLACK did, nonetheless, assert that racial classifications are suspect, that they must be subjected to intense judicial scrutiny, and that they are justifiable only if serving an exceedingly important governmental interest as in this case—victory against Japan.

Post–World War II United States was a very different nation from post–Civil War United States. The African-American soldiers who had fought the racist regime of the Nazis returned to an America where they continued to be second-class citizens according to the laws of many states. About the same time, the National Association for the Advancement of Colored People (NAACP) stepped up its program of legal challenges to the doctrine of separate but equal, scoring some important successes in the field of graduate and legal education by pointing out the dramatic inequalities of the separate facilities.

By the 1950s, the NAACP was ready for a head-on challenge to separate but equal. In *BROWN V. BOARD OF EDUCATION OF TOPEKA*, 347 U.S. 483 (1954), the Supreme Court held that, at least in the field of public elementary and secondary education, separate educational facilities were inherently unequal and thus a violation of the Fourteenth Amendment. Subsequent decisions called for the elimination of governmentally mandated segregation in a variety of public facilities, from courtrooms to restrooms. At the same time, an invigorated CIVIL RIGHTS movement began pressing Congress for new laws that would prevent discrimination by private actors, culminating in such landmark laws as the CIVIL RIGHTS ACT OF 1964 and the Federal Open Housing Act of 1968.

The 1970s saw an extension of equal protection principles to a classification—gender—that the Fourteenth Amendment's framers would probably never have foreseen. With the rise of the women's movement, challenges to gender-based classifications were inevitable. Over several decades, the Court developed for gender classifications what came to be known as an "intermediate" level of judicial scrutiny, tougher than rational basis review but not as strict as strict scrutiny. Intermediate scrutiny was consistent with the view that discriminations based on outmoded stereotypes about the "proper" role of women must be struck down but that certain "real" differences between the sexes must be acknowledged. In *CRAIG V. BOREN*, 429 U.S. 190 (1976), the Court held that gender-based discriminations must "serve important governmental interests" and be "substantially related to the achievement of those objectives." In *United States v. Virginia*, 518 U.S. 515 (1996), Justice Ruth Bader Ginsburg moved the Court a little closer to strict scrutiny review in holding that gender classifications can only be upheld on the basis of "an exceedingly persuasive justification." The fact remains that a majority of the justices have refused to consider gender-based discriminations suspect in all circumstances.

It is unlikely that most of the framers of the Fourteenth Amendment expected the equal protection clause to outlaw many of the forms of racial discrimination that later courts did. Nor is it likely that they expected the clause to be used to defeat governmental programs designed to protect rather than harm racial minorities; the Congress that proposed the amendment also enacted a variety of such programs to aid former slaves (for example, the Freedmen's Bureau). The issue of AFFIRMATIVE ACTION (race-based governmental programs designed to benefit racial minorities) became a matter of increasing controversy in the 1970s. The Supreme Court's tortuous decisional route culminated in *ADARAND CONSTRUCTORS, INC. v. PEÑA*, 515 U.S. 200 (1995), where a majority of the REHNQUIST COURT justices held that even benign racial classifications must be held to the standard of strict scrutiny.

The barrier to affirmative action programs created by strict scrutiny is formidable but not insurmountable, as the Court showed in *GRUTTER V. BOLLINGER*, 539 U.S. 306 (2003). By a 5-4 vote, the Court upheld a law school admission program that took race into account as one of many factors that could contribute to a diverse student body, a governmental objective deemed sufficiently compelling to survive strict scrutiny. The crucial fifth vote was provided by Justice SANDRA DAY O'CONNOR, who retired from the Court in 2006.

For more information: Fallon, Richard H., Jr. *The Dynamic Constitution.* New York: Cambridge University Press, 2004; Nowak, John E., and Ronald D. Rotunda. *Principles of Constitutional Law.* St. Paul, Minn.: Thomson/West, 2005; Seidman, Louis Michael. *Constitutional Law: Equal Protection of the Laws.* New York: Foundation Press, 2003.

—Philip A. Dynia

Escobedo v. Illinois 378 U.S. 478 (1964)

In *Escobedo v. Illinois,* the Supreme Court ruled that the SIXTH AMENDMENT guarantees that a person being held in police custody has a RIGHT TO REMAIN SILENT and a right to speak to an attorney.

In this case, the police denied the defendant his right to visit with counsel during investigations into an 11-day-old murder. The defendant had been arrested for the murder but, at that time, had made no statement and with his lawyer's efforts was able to get a writ of HABEAS CORPUS. During interrogation, Danny Escobedo made several requests to see and meet with his counsel. The lawyer was within the building but was repeatedly denied his right to visit with his client. The 22-year-old defendant, Escobedo, later made damaging statements to a government attorney and confessed to the murder of his brother-in-law for which he was being held after the police had denied him opportunity to discuss strategy or rights with his counsel. The defense counsel argued that Escobedo was denied his rights as they related to remaining silent and that the police did not inform him of those rights.

The Supreme Court determined that Escobedo had been denied his RIGHT TO COUNSEL and highlighted the individual right to remain silent from discussion. Justice Goldburg wrote for the majority, and in his opinion, he offered that the Sixth Amendment retained within the spirit of the Constitution a set of absolute rights, and it was through this lens, coupled with other cases of the time, that the now-famous Miranda Warning Card statement was created and must be read to all arrestees.

The conviction that Escobedo had received at the state level and was affirmed by the state supreme court was overturned because the U.S. Supreme Court recognized that protections within both the Fourteenth and Sixth Amendments and their aggregate rights implications had been denied to the defendant. For example, without counsel and under the pressure he faced through interrogations and interviews, Escobedo had been denied the RIGHT AGAINST SELF-INCRIMINATION. The Court believed that when a custodial interrogation becomes more than just questioning or general inquiry, anyone in this space under the suspicion of law enforcement is due a higher care level. This landmark case became part of the operational procedures within all law enforcement when dealing with subjects under scrutiny. The Court, furthermore, extended the EXCLUSIONARY RULE within this case, establishing that coerced confessions without the aid of counsel were excluded from being evidence for further law-enforcement prosecutions. The holding in this case has helped to protect the individual rights of those being detained or in the custody of the police. It has encouraged more procedural issues now recognized to be retained in the Fifth Amendment.

For more information: Schwartz, Bernard. *A History of the Supreme Court.* New York: Oxford University Press, 1993.

—Ernest Gomez

establishment clause

The establishment clause of the FIRST AMENDMENT is one of the two clauses meant to address the role of religion in U.S. society. Interpreting what this clause mandates has been a source of controversy on the Supreme Court.

The establishment clause is the portion of the First Amendment that states: "Congress shall make no law respecting an establishment of religion." Together with the free exercise clause (the following six words of the amendment), ". . . nor prohibiting the free exercise thereof," the establishment clause is intended to insure the religious liberty of the American people. Though seemingly simple and straightforward, the clause is far from unambiguous in its meaning and implementation, and its history may be best understood as a quest by courts, lawmakers, scholars, and the public to agree on how to define and apply it. The difficulty of this task has stemmed both from inability to reach consensus about the establishment clause itself and from inherent tensions between the establishment clause and the free exercise clause.

There is general agreement that the establishment clause prohibits the creation of an official church by the federal government, but beyond that, conflicts have emerged over the level of government affected, the meaning of "establishment of religion," and even the word *respecting.*

Initially, the establishment clause was assumed to apply only to the federal government. Most colonies had established churches but disestablished them in the 1780s and 1790s. Massachusetts, in 1833, was the last to do so. Issues concerning separation of church and state arose from time to time in the 19th century, but it was not until the 1940s that the Supreme Court, using the FOURTEENTH AMENDMENT, specifically "incorporated" both religion clauses (the establishment and free exercise clauses) to apply to the states. When this action was taken on behalf of the establishment clause, in *EVERSON V. BOARD OF EDUCATION,* 330 U.S. 1 (1947), the door was clearly open for legal challenges that continue to the present.

In *Everson,* the Court set forth an expansive view of the establishment clause that in varying degrees continues to influence jurisprudence in this area. In a powerful and sweeping statement, Justice HUGO BLACK began with the idea that neither the state nor federal government can set up a church or "pass laws which aid one religion, aid all religions, or prefer one religion over another." He detailed other forbidden activities, such as levying taxes to support religion, and concluded: "In the words of [THOMAS] JEFFERSON, the clause against establishment of religion by law was intended to erect a 'wall of separation' between Church and State." Critics of this interpretation of the establishment clause like to point out that, as Black noted, the Constitution does not speak of a "wall of separation" between church and state, and indeed, this metaphor may have led to as much conflict as the establishment clause itself has as to what role religion should play in public life.

In 1971, the Court in *LEMON V. KURTZMAN,* 403 U.S. 602 (1971), addressed the word *respecting,* (meaning in this context "regarding" or "with respect to"), explaining that a law did not have to set up a state religion to be "respecting" an establishment of religion. Indeed, it might be merely a "step that could lead to such establishment and hence offend the First Amendment."

Alternative interpretations of the establishment clause have been offered by justices, lawmakers, and others either from their own ideological perspectives or as advocates of "original intent," the idea that the Court's task is to interpret the Constitution as its creators would have done. This is complicated, because a review of proposed wordings of the establishment clause by the first Congress in 1789 indicates that not all drafters of the First Amendment thought alike on this matter. However, some clearly wanted to do more than simply forbid an established church, and most drafts that were considered used broader terms than *church, sect,* or *denomination.*

Another recurring issue is the relation between the establishment clause and the free exercise

A prayer opened the first session of the Continental Congress, illustrating the complex relationship of religion and government in the United States. *(Billy Graham Museum)*

clause. Some have argued that a strict "neutrality" interpretation of the establishment clause runs the risk of violating the free exercise clause, particularly as it applies to individuals in public positions who wish to express religious views. And, what does it mean to be neutral? Must all references to God be deleted from public life? (The word *public* in this sense refers to matters pertaining to government property and personnel, not to activities in public view but on private property such as a Nativity scene on a church lawn.) Some have argued also that forbidding government-sponsored religious activities in public schools and other government-owned facilities violates the free exercise rights of students; however, the Court stated that the free exercise clause "never meant that a majority could use the machinery of the State to practice its beliefs" (*Abington Township v. Schempp*, 374 U.S. 203 [1963]). Finally, some have argued that the Court was violating the establishment clause when it used the free exercise clause to allow minority religious groups to engage in behavior not legal to the citizenry at large, such as allowing Amish children to leave school after the eighth grade in contradiction to compulsory education laws.

Establishment clause cases generally fall into two categories: those primarily involving financial outlays by government in support of religion and those primarily involving symbolic support in public schools and other public places. Early financial cases addressed the desire of parochial schools to obtain state aid on the basis that by educating children, they were taking a burden off the state. In the landmark *Everson* case, the Court, despite its expansive definition of the establishment clause, upheld money for bus transportation to Catholic schools by reasoning that the money benefited children directly. The Court later did the same for the loan by the state of textbooks to children. After that, the Court began to draw the line, disallowing such items as instructional materials or teacher salary supplements that benefited the school more directly. The tide began to turn, however, in *Agostini v. Felton,* 114 U.S. 2481 (1997), in which the Court, in a 5-4 decision, overruled its position in *Aguilar v. Felton,* 105 U.S. 3232 (1985), and allowed government-provided teachers to offer remedial education in parochial schools. Meanwhile, the issue of vouchers to help families who chose to educate their children in parochial schools became a rallying cry not just for Catholic schools but for conservative Protestant schools. In *ZELMAN V. SIMMONS-HARRIS,* 536 U.S. 639 (2002), the Court upheld by a 5-4 vote a voucher program for children in substandard schools. To the four dissenters, this case in essence overturned *Everson.*

A recent financially related but non-school-related establishment clause issue about which the constitutionality has yet to be resolved by the courts is President George W. Bush's "faith-based initiatives." Under this, for the first time, money is available to religious organizations to use in providing social services without requiring those organizations to maintain strict separation between their social service activities and their religious mission.

While financial considerations have not been absent from public school establishment clause rulings, these cases have focused more often on the use of state power via public school authorities to endorse, support, and promote religion through such activities as teacher-led prayer recitations and the use of the government to promote the religion of the majority, generally Protestant Christianity. Major Supreme Court public school cases have addressed released time for religious instruction during the school day, various forms of officially led or government-endorsed prayers in public schools, restrictions on the teaching of evolution and the required teaching of the biblical creation story or some disguised variant of it, and posting of the TEN COMMANDMENTS. Lower courts have dealt with an even wider assortment of variations on these issues. With the exception of allowing religious instruction outside the school building but during the school day, the Court, although often very divided, has taken a consistently separationist position in its application of the establishment clause to public schools. In cases involving religious symbolism in public places, the Court has been more sympathetic to the accommodationist position, allowing, for example, prayers in state legislatures or government-sponsored displays of Nativity scenes, menorahs, or Ten Commandments monuments, but only in situations in which they can make a convincing argument that tradition or context has the overall effect of secularizing what would otherwise be considered religious.

The Court articulated in *Lemon v. Kurtzman* a three-part test for establishment clause violations. In essence, a government action must have a secular purpose and a primary effect that is secular, and it may not become entangled with religion or promote religious divisiveness. The purpose and effect prongs were drawn from *Abington Township v. Schempp,* while the entanglement prong came from *Walz v. Tax Commissioner,* 397 U.S. 664 (1970), in which the Court upheld the right of governments to grant property tax exemptions to churches under a concept of "benevolent neutrality."

Far from foolproof, the Lemon test soon proved itself open to manipulation and criticism. In some cases, both the majority and the dissent used the Lemon test to try to prove their points. In others, the Court just ignored it. Some justices began to openly deride it in their opinions. Most colorfully, Justice ANTONIN GREGORY SCALIA described it as "like some ghoul in a late-night horror movie" (*LAMB'S CHAPEL V. CENTER MORICHES UNION FREE SCHOOL DISTRICT,* 508 U.S. 384 [1993]). While the Lemon test has not been totally disavowed by the Court, some justices have begun sending up trial balloons with alternative tests, allowing for a more accommodationist application of the establishment clause.

At the start of the 21st century, and with a decidedly more conservative membership, the Court appeared to be gradually reshaping its standards for judging establishment clause cases. It is too soon to predict how dramatic any changes might be; however, as America becomes more religiously diverse, interpreting and applying the establishment clause will probably continue to be a challenge for government.

For more information: Davis, Derek. "Separation, Integration, and Accommodation: Religion and State in America in a Nutshell." *Journal of Church and State* 43, no. 1 (Winter 2001): 5–17; Formicola, Jo Renee, et al. *Faith Based Initiatives and the Bush Administration: The Good, the Bad, and the Ugly.* Lanham, Md.: Rowman & Littlefield Publishers, 2003; Morgan, Richard E. *The Supreme Court and Religion.* New York: Free Press, 1972; Witte, John, Jr. *Religion and the American Constitutional Experiment.* Boulder, Colo.: Westview Press, 2000.

—Jane G. Rainey

Everson v. Board of Education 330 U.S. 1 (1947)

In *Everson v. Board of Education,* the Supreme Court held that the government could reimburse parents for the cost of sending their children to Catholic schools on public buses.

The case arose from a New Jersey law that allowed local school districts to provide transportation to and from public, private, and religious schools. One local school district authorized a transportation subsidy for parents who sent their children to a religious school via public buses. A local taxpayer sued, claiming that this practice violated the ESTABLISHMENT CLAUSE of the FIRST AMENDMENT.

In an opinion by Justice HUGO BLACK, the Supreme Court held that the establishment clause means, at a minimum, that neither a state nor the federal government can set up a church. Furthermore, government cannot pass laws that aid religion, force a person to go to or not to go to a church against their will, or force a person to profess belief or disbelief in any religion. Adopting THOMAS JEFFERSON's metaphor, Justice Black explained that the establishment clause erects a wall of separation between church and state, which must be "high and impregnable." Even the slightest breach of that wall of separation would be unconstitutional.

Justice Black explained, however, that the establishment clause does not prohibit a state from spending tax-raised funds to pay for transportation of students at religious schools if it is part of a general program under which it pays for the transportation of students attending public and other private schools. This subsidy was similar to providing ordinary government services such as fire and police protection, which could not be denied to schools simply because of their religious nature. The Court held that the First Amendment merely required a state to be neutral toward religion, not to be against it. Here, New Jersey did not contribute any money or in any way support Catholic schools; it simply provided a transportation program to help children get to their schools. The law was therefore constitutional.

Justice Wiley B. Rutledge dissented, arguing that the subsidy supported religion via use of the taxing power. In Justice Rutledge's view, the objective of the establishment clause was to create "a complete and permanent separation of the spheres of religious activity and civil authority by comprehensively forbidding every form of public aid or support for religion." Government aid to religion had no less destructive force than state interference with religious practice: "Establishment" and "free exercise" are similar ideas and represented merely different facets of the single great and fundamental freedom.

For more information: Hunt, Thomas. *Religion and Schooling in Contemporary America.* New York: Garland Publishing, 1997.

—Winston E. Calvert

Ewing v. California 538 U.S. 11 (2003)

A companion case with *Lockyer v. Andrade,* 538 U.S. 63 (2003), *Ewing v. California* upheld

California's three strikes law against an Eighth Amendment CRUEL AND UNUSUAL PUNISHMENT challenge. The California law required defendants with two or more "serious" or "violent" felony convictions be sentenced to life imprisonment. Though the Supreme Court was split, five justices found that California's legislature was within its constitutional boundaries when deciding that "three strikes and you're out" was a constitutional way of dealing with the problem of recidivism.

The litigation commenced when Gary Ewing, while out on parole from a nine-year prison term, stole three golf clubs from a pro shop. He was charged with and convicted of grand theft, a felony. Under California law, trial courts have discretion in reducing some felonies to misdemeanors so as to escape the three strikes sentence. Therefore, Ewing, having four previous felony convictions, asked the trial court to reduce his conviction to a misdemeanor. The judge refused, and Ewing was sentenced to 25 years to life in prison. The California court of appeal affirmed the trial judge's decision, and the California Supreme Court denied review. The U.S. Supreme Court then granted Ewing's petition for certiorari.

In announcing the judgment of the Court and writing a plurality opinion that also included Chief Justice WILLIAM HUBBS REHNQUIST and Justice ANTHONY M. KENNEDY, Justice SANDRA DAY O'CONNOR declared California's three strikes law did not violate the Eighth Amendment's proportionality principle. In other words, the California legislature was within its discretion in deciding that lengthy prison sentences for criminals who commit numerous violent felonies fit the severity of the crime. Furthermore, Justice O'Connor wrote, the state law "reflects a rational legislative judgment, entitled to deference, that offenders who have committed serious or violent felonies and who continue to commit felonies must be incapacitated."

Both Justice ANTONIN GREGORY SCALIA and Justice CLARENCE THOMAS wrote concurring opinions. Justice Scalia agreed that the three strikes law did not violate the Eighth Amendment, but he chastised the plurality for applying the concept of proportionality to prison sentences, since, in his view, the proportionality requirement only applied to retributive punishments such as executions. Justice Thomas wrote to express his view that the Eighth Amendment does not include a proportionality requirement and that the Court's attempt to decipher one has been a failure.

Justices JOHN PAUL STEVENS, DAVID H. SOUTER, Ruth Bader Ginsburg, and STEVEN G. BREYER dissented. Writing the principal dissent, Justice Breyer concluded that Ewing's sentence was "grossly disproportionate" and, therefore, violative of the Eighth Amendment's prohibition on cruel and unusual punishments. Particularly troublesome to the dissenters was that between 1945 and 1994, when the three strikes law was enacted, "*no one* like Ewing could have served more than *10* years in prison." Recidivists served shorter terms than Ewing's 25 years, and the 25 years to life in prison sentence has traditionally been reserved for criminals "convicted of crimes far worse than Ewing's."

Ewing v. California might be best understood as another example of the REHNQUIST COURT's conservative tilt on law and order issues. Unlike the more liberal WARREN COURT, the Rehnquist Court has been more willing to allow states to fashion unique remedies to the problems of crime.

For more information: Delaney, Blake J. "A Cruel and Unusual Application of the Proportionality Principle in Eighth Amendment Analysis: *Ewing v. California* (2003)." *Florida Law Review* 56 (2004): 459–469.

—Kyle L. Kreider

exclusionary rule

The exclusionary rule provides that evidence obtained by police officers in violation of the FOURTH AMENDMENT prohibition of unreasonable searches and seizures is not admissible in a criminal trial to prove guilt. The rule was applied by the U.S. Supreme Court to the states in *Mapp v. Ohio*, 367 U.S. 642 (1961). The primary purpose of the exclusionary rule is to deter police misconduct. While some proponents argue that the rule emanates from the Constitution, the

Supreme Court has indicated it is merely a judicially created remedy for violations of the Fourth Amendment.

Application of the exclusionary rule may lead to the exclusion of important evidence and the acquittal of persons who are factually, if not legally, guilty. Consequently, the rule has been the subject of intense debate. Proponents argue it is the only effective means of protecting individual rights from police misconduct, while critics decry the exclusion from trial of relevant evidence. Despite calls for its abolition and shifts in the composition of the Supreme Court, the exclusionary rule remains entrenched in American jurisprudence. But while the rule has survived, it has not gone unscathed. Supreme Court decisions have limited the scope of the rule and created several exceptions.

In *WEEKS V. UNITED STATES*, 232 U.S. 383 (1914), the Supreme Court held that evidence illegally obtained by federal law-enforcement officers was not admissible in a federal criminal trial. At the time, the Fourth Amendment did not apply to the states. Because the *Weeks* decision applied only to the federal government, state law-enforcement officers were still free to seize evidence illegally without fear of exclusion in state criminal proceedings. Additionally, evidence seized illegally by state police could be turned over to federal law-enforcement officers for use in federal prosecutions as long as federal officers were not directly involved in the illegal seizure. This was known as the "silver platter doctrine."

In *WOLF V. COLORADO*, 338 U.S. 25 (1949), the Supreme Court applied the Fourth Amendment to the states, incorporating it into the DUE PROCESS clause of the FOURTEENTH AMENDMENT; however, the Court refused to mandate the remedy of the exclusionary rule. Just three years later, the Court modified its position somewhat, holding in *Rochin v. California*, 342 U.S. 165 (1952), that evidence seized in a manner that "shocked the conscience" must be excluded as violative of due process under the Fourteenth Amendment. Exactly what type of conduct shocked the conscience was left to be determined on a case-by-case basis. The exclusionary rule thus became applicable to state criminal proceedings, but its application was uneven.

Finally, in 1961, in *Mapp v. Ohio*, 367 U.S. 643 (1961), the Court took the step it failed to take in *Wolf* and explicitly applied the remedy of the exclusionary rule to the states. The Court did so because it acknowledged that the states had failed to provide an adequate alternative remedy for violations of the Fourth Amendment.

The Supreme Court, in *Mapp*, stated that the exclusionary rule serves at least two purposes: the deterrence of police misconduct and the protection of judicial integrity. In recent years, however, the Court has focused almost entirely upon the deterrence of police misconduct, leading to the creation of several exceptions to the rule. Additionally, the Court has held that the exclusionary rule does not apply to a variety of proceedings other than the criminal trial.

In *Massachusetts v. Sheppard*, 468 U.S. 981 (1984), the Supreme Court held that evidence obtained by the police acting in good faith on a search warrant issued by a neutral and detached magistrate, that is ultimately found to be invalid, may nonetheless be admitted at trial. The Court stressed that the primary rationale for the exclusionary rule—deterrence of police misconduct—did not warrant exclusion of evidence obtained by police who act reasonably and in good faith reliance upon the actions of a judge. By "good faith," the Court meant the police were unaware that the warrant was invalid.

The Court emphasized that the GOOD FAITH EXCEPTION did not apply to errors made by the police, even if the errors were entirely inadvertent. The exception applies only to situations where the police relied on others who, it later turns out, made a mistake. Subsequent cases reiterated this point. In *Illinois v. Krull*, 480 U.S. 340 (1987), the Court extended the good faith exception to instances where the police act in reliance on a statute that is later declared unconstitutional. In *Arizona v. Evans*, 514 U.S. 1 (1995), the Court refused to apply the exclusionary rule to evidence seized by a police officer who acted on reliance of a computer entry, made by a court clerk, that was later found to be in error.

The Court has also established the "inevitable discovery" exception to the exclusionary rule. This exception, developed in *Nix v. Williams,* 467 U.S. 431 (1984), permits the use at trial of evidence illegally obtained by the police if they can demonstrate that they would have discovered the evidence anyway by legal means. The burden is on the police to prove they would in fact have discovered the evidence lawfully even if they had not acted illegally.

The Supreme Court has been reluctant to extend the reach of the exclusionary rule to proceedings other than the criminal trial. The Court has consistently refused to apply the exclusionary rule to evidence seized by private parties if they are not acting in concert with or at the behest of the police. The rule does not apply to evidence presented to the grand jury. An unlawful arrest does not bar prosecution of the arrestee, as the exclusionary rule is an evidentiary rule rather than a rule of jurisdictional limitation. The rule is inapplicable in both civil tax assessment proceedings and civil deportation proceedings. The exclusionary rule does not apply to parole revocation hearings.

The Court has also been reluctant to apply the exclusionary rule to aspects of the criminal trial that are not directly related to the determination of guilt. Thus, illegally obtained evidence may be used to impeach a defendant's testimony or to determine the appropriate sentence for a convicted defendant.

The exclusionary rule has aroused much debate since its application to the states some 40 years ago. The rule remains in place, although its application has been limited and exceptions created. Nonetheless, the rule still has a major and continuing impact on police practices, acting as the primary constraint on unlawful searches and seizures. No other remedies have proven effective at deterring police misconduct.

The Supreme Court has refused numerous opportunities to discard the rule, so as long as the exclusionary rule exists, it will serve, to some extent, as a limitation on police overreaching. It will also continue to result in the freeing of some "guilty" people. It is both the reward and the price we pay for living under a government of limited powers.

For more information: Amar, Akhil Reed. *The Constitution and Criminal Procedure.* New Haven, Conn.: Yale University Press, 1997; del Carmen, Rolando V. *Criminal Procedure: Law and Practice.* 7th ed. Belmont, Calif.: Wadsworth/Thomson, 2006; Hemmens, Craig, John Worrall, and Alan Thompson. *Criminal Justice Case Briefs: Significant Cases in Criminal Procedure.* Los Angeles: Roxbury, 2004.

—Craig Hemmens

executive orders

Executive orders are documents that the president of the United States issues unilaterally that have the force of law. They are one of some two dozen types of unilateral presidential directives, another of which is proclamations, that are legally identical to executive orders and often used interchangeably (*Wolsey v. Chapman,* 101 U.S. 755 [1879]). Executive orders are an important tool of the presidential office and have figured in many interesting moments in American political history.

There is no official definition of executive orders; there is no law, nor even an executive order, that defines what an executive order is. They are written documents that the president designates as such and that direct the actions of government officials or bodies. Executive orders help the chief executive manage the enormous executive branch of the federal government. Many executive orders are for minor administrative matters, but others have a dramatic impact on government and society. Since executive orders give presidents the means to enact binding public policies by a mere stroke of the pen, presidents have often used them to circumvent Congress and the rigors of the normal policy-making process.

Just as there is no strict definition of executive orders, there is also some ambiguity with regard to their formatting, numbering, and cataloging. Several executive orders have proscribed the format for future executive orders, but these norms are routinely ignored, and in practice, executive orders vary greatly in terms of form and style. The U.S. government's cataloging of executive orders is spotty, as hundreds or even thousands of early executive orders have been lost forever. Indeed, the government's official sequential numbering of executive orders starts only with one of ABRAHAM LINCOLN's directives, ignoring all earlier orders and even some subsequent ones. In 1935, the hundreds of executive orders issued by Franklin Roosevelt made the government's poor accounting of executive orders acutely problematic, so Congress required that all future executive orders and proclamations be published in the *Federal Register*. Today, executive orders from 1933 to the present—at least those that are not secret and classified—can be found online via the National Archives.

Executive orders are not mentioned in the Constitution, but they may be justified in terms of the broad grant of executive power and other ambiguous phrases that can be construed to confer power on the president in ARTICLE II OF THE U.S. CONSTITUTION. Courts have held that executive orders cannot contradict a clear constitutional provision or the expressed will of Congress (a law). However, there is a great deal of leeway between those two limits, and presidents have issued executive orders for a host of purposes that are politically and constitutionally controversial. Executive orders can be justified in terms of the president's constitutional authority or can be authorized by legislation calling for some particular presidential action or determination, but many executive orders do not invoke any specific justification. The legislative and judicial branches can overturn executive orders, but they seldom do so. The Supreme Court's decision to strike down Harry Truman's executive order seizing the nation's steel industry (*YOUNGSTOWN SHEET & TUBE v. SAWYER*, 343 U.S. 579 [1952]) is an exception to the rule that the other branches generally do not resist presidential lawmaking by executive order. Future presidents can issue executive orders to overturn their predecessors' executive orders, and they often do so.

Virtually every president has issued executive orders or similar directives. Early examples include George Washington's Neutrality Proclamation and Abraham Lincoln's Emancipation Proclamation; however, executive orders were generally used infrequently before the 20th century. There was a large increase in their use under Theodore Roosevelt, who utilized them for land conservation and various other matters. The number of executive orders issued continued to climb through the presidency of Franklin Roosevelt, who used them to fight the depression and to prosecute World War II, including ordering the internment of some 120,000 Americans of Japanese descent in 1942. There has been a drop-off in the number of executive orders issued from the postwar era to the present, from a couple hundred a year to just a couple dozen. Nevertheless, presidents since the mid-20th century have issued executive orders for many important purposes, including to desegregate the military, to establish the Peace Corps and AFFIRMATIVE ACTION, to prohibit the United States from assassinating foreign political leaders, to limit or alter governmental regulations, to create new executive agencies, to establish national monuments, and to advance certain positions about ABORTION, organized labor, and environmental protection. Despite periodic outcries over particular executive orders, they continue to be an important and powerful presidential tool in the 21st century.

For more information: Cooper, Phillip J. *By Order of the President: The Use and Abuse of Executive Direct Action*. Lawrence: University Press of Kansas, 2002; Dodds, Graham G. "Executive Orders Since Nixon." In *Executing the Constitution*. New York: State University of New York, 2006; Mayer, Kenneth R. *With the Stroke of a Pen*. Princeton, N.J.: Princeton University Press, 2001; U.S. House Committee on Governmental Operations. "Executive Orders and Proclamations: A Study of a Use of Presidential Powers, 1945–1956." December 1957.

—Graham G. Dodds

Ex parte Grossman 267 U.S. 87 (1925)

In *Ex parte Grossman*, the Supreme Court ruled that the pardoning power of the president of the

United States extended to include the pardoning of an individual who had been held in contempt of court. The case is significant because it helped define the constitutional breadth of the power of the president to pardon individuals.

Ex parte Grossman involved Philip Grossman, an individual who was charged in November 1920 with the offense of maintaining a nuisance at his business by selling alcoholic beverages in violation of the National Prohibition Act (better known as the Volstead Act) and the EIGHTEENTH AMENDMENT. The district court judge issued a restraining order, yet two days after the order, Grossman was charged with selling liquor to people on the premises of his business. He was arrested, tried, and convicted of contempt of court for ignoring the restraining order. He was sentenced to one-year imprisonment, to be served in the Chicago House of Corrections, and ordered to pay court costs and a fine of $1,000 to the United States. The circuit court of appeals affirmed the lower court decision.

In December 1923, President Calvin Coolidge issued Grossman a presidential pardon (commutation) under the condition that Grossman pay the $1,000 fine. Grossman accepted the pardon and its conditions. In May of the following year, the district court, ignoring the presidential pardon, ordered Grossman imprisoned in the Chicago House of Corrections. The case was appealed to the Supreme Court.

The question before the Court in this situation was, Did the president have constitutional powers to commute Grossman's sentence for contempt of court? According to Section 2, Clause 1 of ARTICLE II OF THE U.S. CONSTITUTION, "The President . . . shall have power to grant Reprieves and Pardons for Offences against the United States, except in Cases of Impeachment." The Court concluded, in a unanimous decision, the pardon for criminal contempt of court was in the purview of the powers granted to the president by the Constitution.

For more information: Schwartz, Bernard. *A History of the Supreme Court.* New York: Oxford University Press, 1993.

—Dan Krejci

Ex parte McCardle 74 U.S. 506 (1869)

In *Ex parte McCardle,* the Supreme Court ruled that it lacked the jurisdiction to hear a HABEAS CORPUS petition by an individual even though it had already heard oral arguments in his case. *McCardle* is considered important because it affirms the broad power of Congress to affect or change the APPELLATE JURISDICTION of the Supreme Court.

After the Civil War, over President Andrew Johnson's VETO, Congress adopted the Reconstruction Acts imposing military rule in the South. Military rule would be lifted only if new constitutions were adopted, elections were held, and the Southern states accepted both the THIRTEENTH AMENDMENT and FOURTEENTH AMENDMENT, abolishing slavery and guaranteeing rights to former slaves, respectively. Constitutional conventions required approval in elections in which a majority of eligible voters cast ballots, and some Southern whites attempted to block new conventions by refusing to vote.

William McCardle, the editor of the *Vickburg* (Mississippi) *Times,* wrote fiery editorials urging whites to boycott the voting and, some believed, threatening harm to whites who did vote. McCardle was charged before a military commission with impeding Reconstruction. He sought a writ of HABEAS CORPUS in federal court under an 1867 law that had been passed to assure court proceedings to free the families of slaves who had enlisted in the Union Army. The lower court denied a writ of habeas corpus, and McCardle appealed to the Supreme Court.

The Supreme Court heard arguments in the first week of March 1868. Fearful that the Court would strike down military reconstruction in the South, Congress passed a law, over the veto of President Johnson, that took away the Supreme Court's habeas corpus jurisdiction under the 1867 law. On April 6, the Court adjourned without deciding the *McCardle* case. Justices Robert Cooper Grier and Stephen Johnson Field stated that the Court should have reached a decision.

More than a year later, the Court heard arguments about whether the repeal of its habeas corpus jurisdiction could affect a case it had already heard. On April 12, 1869, the Court announced that the congressional repeal of jurisdiction had deprived the Court of its authority. ARTICLE III OF THE U.S. CONSTITUTION allows Congress to "make exceptions to the appellate jurisdiction" of the Supreme Court, and Congress had done so. In *Ex parte McCardle*, Chief Justice Salmon P. Chase declared for a unanimous Court that the justices would not look into the motives of Congress. It was enough that Congress had exercised its constitutional authority. "Jurisdiction is the power to declare the law," the chief justice said, "and when it ceases to exist, the only function remaining to the court is that of announcing the fact and dismissing the cause." Within weeks, in a private letter, the chief justice disclosed his view that if the Court had decided the *McCardle* case, it "would doubtless have held that his [McCardle's] imprisonment for trial before a military commission was illegal."

The Court was careful in *McCardle* not to concede that Congress could deprive it completely of all habeas corpus jurisdiction. Instead, Chief Justice Chase warned that the 1868 congressional action took away only the Court's habeas corpus jurisdiction granted in the 1867 law, but "it does not affect the jurisdiction [over habeas corpus] that was previously exercised [by the Court]."

In later cases, including *Ex parte Yerger*, 75 U.S. 85 (1869), and *Felker v. Turpin*, 518 U.S. 651 (1996), the Court avoided a confrontation with Congress over the underlying issue in *McCardle*—whether Congress can deprive the Court entirely of jurisdiction in certain kinds of cases—by finding that the Court retained jurisdiction under other existing laws.

For more information: Fairman, Charles. *History of the Supreme Court of the United States*. Vol. 6: *Reconstruction and Reunion, 1868–88*. New York: Macmillan: 1971.

—David Adamany

Ex parte Milligan 71 U.S. 4 Wall. 2 (1866)

In *Ex parte Milligan*, the Supreme Court ruled that an American citizen could not be tried by military commission when the civil federal courts were open and operational. The significance of the *Milligan* decision was that it limited the ability of the president to try American citizens without all the constitutionally protected guarantees when accused of a crime.

In March 1863, Congress passed an act authorizing the suspension of the writ of HABEAS CORPUS by the president during the ongoing rebellion. The following September, ABRAHAM LINCOLN suspended the writ of habeas corpus for cases concerning prisoners of war, spies, and those aiding and abetting the enemy, as well as for members of the armed services accused of being in violation of the laws of war. Lamdin P. Milligan was a resident of Indiana, a citizen of the United States, and a civilian. He was arrested on October 5, 1864, at his home and was tried by military commission. Milligan and four other conspirators were accused of planning to liberate prisoners of war in a Union prison and were charged with conspiracy against the United States, inciting insurrection, and violating the laws of war. Milligan was found guilty of all charges and was sentenced to death by hanging.

Justice David Davis wrote the majority opinion for the Supreme Court and was joined by Justices Nathan Clifford, Stephen Johnson Field, Robert Cooper Grier, and Samuel Nelson. The Court reversed the ruling of the military commission, arguing that a civilian could not be denied a civilian trial when the civil federal courts are operational. Furthermore, Davis held that military commissions could not be organized in a state that had not been invaded and had not been engaged in the rebellion. The Court held that military commissions could not be used to try a citizen that was not a resident of a rebellious state nor a prisoner of war and had no affiliation to the military of the United States. Furthermore, Congress could not grant such power to the executive to create the commissions in question.

Chief Justice Salmon P. Chase wrote a dissent, joined by Justices James Moore Wayne, Noah Haynes Swayne, and Samuel Freeman Miller, believing that military commissions were indeed allowed to be set up by Congress. Chase reiterated that the Constitution grants Congress the authority to make rules concerning the government of the army and navy, as well as the authority to set up courts inferior to the Supreme Court. One such court that can be set up is a military commission if the conditions of war require it. Chase placed emphasis on the power of Congress, not the courts, to decide whether the conditions of war require such action.

Overall, *Milligan* appears to be an important statement by the Court, protecting individual rights as well as limiting the power of the executive in times of war. However, since this time, the federal courts have decided cases more in line with Chase's dissent rather than the Court opinion, stating that if Congress authorizes the commissions, they stand up to judicial scrutiny (as in *Ex parte Quirin,* 317 U.S. 1 [1942], and *Eisentrager v. Johnson,* 339 U.S. 763 [1950]). Even *Hamdan v. Rumsfeld,* 548 U.S. 557 (2006), in which the Court stated that the military commissions of the George W. Bush administration were not constitutionally authorized, could have stood up to judicial scrutiny had Congress given more explicit authorization for their establishment.

For more information: Fisher, Louis. *Presidential War Power.* Lawrence: University Press of Kansas, 2004; Henkin, Louis. *Constitutionalism, Democracy, and Foreign Affairs.* New York: Columbia University Press, 1990; Henkin, Louis. *Foreign Affairs and the United States Constitution.* Oxford: Clarendon Press, 1996.

—Amanda DiPaolo

Ex parte Young 209 U.S. 123 (1908)

In *Ex parte Young,* the Supreme Court held that the ELEVENTH AMENDMENT does not prevent suits against state officials for prospective injunctive relief, even if that injunctive relief would enjoin an official state policy.

Around the turn of the 20th century, Minnesota passed a law limiting railroad rates. The railroads believed these regulations were unconstitutional and sought to prevent their enforcement, but getting the case to court was problematic. Although ordinarily someone could have violated the law and challenged its validity when arrested, Minnesota had an inordinately large fine of $2,500 for each violation and imprisonment for as long as five years. Because of this, the railroads were unlikely to find anyone willing to test the validity of the law. Instead, the shareholders of the railroads brought a lawsuit in federal court seeking an INJUNCTION against the attorney general of Minnesota, Edward Young, individually, to prevent him from enforcing the state law. Young claimed that granting the injunction would be a violation of the Eleventh Amendment and Minnesota's sovereign immunity.

A full understanding of the importance of *Ex parte Young* requires a basic understanding of the Supreme Court's reading of the Eleventh Amendment. The text of the Eleventh Amendment reads: "The Judicial power of the United States shall not be construed to extend to any suit in law or equity, commenced or prosecuted against one of the United States by Citizens of another State." Despite the plain language of the amendment, in *Hans v. Louisiana,* 134 U.S. 1 (1890), the Supreme Court held that the Eleventh Amendment expressed a broader concept of sovereign immunity. This principle protects states from suits in federal court not only by citizens of other states but also from suits by a state's own citizens.

Unwilling to completely trust the states to uphold the Constitution and the CIVIL RIGHTS of its citizens (as was the case of Jim Crow laws), the Supreme Court has devised limited exceptions to this broad concept of sovereign immunity. The most important of these exceptions was announced in *Ex parte Young.* The Supreme Court held that neither the Eleventh Amendment nor the principle of sovereign immunity barred suits for prospective injunctive relief against state officers. In so holding, the Court created a legal fiction. Because a state can give no officer the power to act contrary to the Constitution, when a state officer does act contrary to the Constitution, he is stripped of state power and can no longer hide behind the state's immunity from suit in federal court. The Supreme Court, speaking through Justice Rufus Wheeler Peckham, held: "The act to be enforced is alleged to be unconstitutional, and if it be so, the use of the name of the State to enforce an unconstitutional act to the injury of complainants is a proceeding without the authority of and one which does not affect the State in its sovereign or governmental capacity." It is through this important exception that individuals are able to hold states accountable for at least some violations of their constitutional rights in federal court.

For more information: Currie, David P. "Sovereign Immunity and Suits Against Government Officers." *Supreme Court Review* 162 (1984) 149–168; Davis, Kenneth Culp. "Suing the Government by Falsely Pretending to Sue an Officer." *University of Chicago Law Review* 29 (1962) 435–459.

—Alaina Fotiu-Wojtowicz

ex post facto clause

The ex post facto clause is located in Section 9, Clause 3 and Section 10, Clause 1 of ARTICLE I OF THE U.S. CONSTITUTION. It describes one of the rights individuals have in the United States: protection from the government's punishing individuals retroactively for acts that were not illegal at the time they were committed. Of the two ex post facto provisions in Article I, Section 9 places the prohibition on the federal government, and Section 10 places the prohibition on state government.

In *CALDER V. BULL*, 3 Dall. 386 (1798), Justice Samuel Chase expanded upon this basic understanding of the clause to provide three other circumstances that will trigger an ex post facto violation. These categories, announced more than 200 years ago, are still considered good law today.

One of these violations occurs when government "aggravates" a crime, or changes the crime's definition to make the offense greater than it used to be. In *Stogner v. California*, 539 U.S. 607 (2003), a slim 5-4 majority of the U.S. Supreme Court held that a state was precluded from lengthening the statute of limitations for certain sex offenders. Justice STEPHEN G. BREYER ruled that once the statute of limitations has expired on an individual, the state may not put that person back in jeopardy of being arrested and punished by increasing its length. The Court decision only reached those individuals whose statute of limitations had run out; it did not foreclose the possibility of extending the statute of limitations on those who were still prosecutable. Justice ANTHONY M. KENNEDY dissented, holding that simply extending the statute of limitations for an offense did not aggravate a crime and that the statute was reasonable because children often take considerable time—sometimes years—in reporting sexual abuse.

Another way, identified in *Calder*, to violate the ex post facto clause occurs when government retroactively increases the punishment for a crime. Once a person has been sentenced, is currently incarcerated, or has already served his or her sentence, the person is no longer subject to further punitive sanctions for that infraction. The state is free to stiffen the penalties for a criminal offense, but it can only do so against new offenders. This understanding of the ex post facto clause does not restrict a judge from using a person's prior convictions to increase the severity of the sentence for a current infraction. Shortening the sentences of incarcerated individuals also does not implicate the clause. This includes commuting the sentence of those sitting on death row to life imprisonment (even though some individuals might regard this as a worse punishment).

The courts have determined that a person must experience a punishment in order to claim a violation; therefore, civil actions are not covered by the clause if they are only restrictive or regulatory in nature. A factory that contaminated the environment before criminal antipollution laws were enacted could still be found liable for monetary damages if it could be shown that their actions caused harm to other individuals. But attempting to prosecute the company's officers for criminal culpability would be barred as a retroactive sanction.

Because civil confinements are considered treatment and not punishment, the Supreme Court held in *Kansas v. Hendricks*, 386 U.S. 605 (1997), that the clause does not bar the state from forcibly transferring individuals to custodial medical facilities once they have finished serving their prison terms. This is becoming a more common, though controversial, disposition for pedophiles and other sex offenders. Also, requiring sex offenders to report their whereabouts or register with the local police after serving their sentence does not fall under the ex post facto clause. In SMITH V. DOE, 538 U.S. 84 (2003), the Supreme Court upheld Alaska's Sex Offender Registration Act because it deemed the law to have a regulatory and not a punitive effect.

Finally, the *Calder* decision held that changing the rules of evidence to make it easier to prosecute individuals is another form of retroactive punishment prohibited by the clause. For example, a statutory defense that a suspect had available to him at the time the state commenced its prosecution cannot be retroactively eliminated by passing a new law.

The rationale behind ex post facto protections is not that an individual should necessarily escape a punishment he or she deserves, but that eyewitnesses become untrustworthy over time and evidence grows stale. Nor should an individual have to indefinitely preserve potentially exculpatory evidence against a prosecution in the distant future in order to prove his or her innocence.

For more information: Elster, Jon. *Retribution and Reparation in the Transition to Democracy.* New York: Cambridge University Press, 2005; Teitel, Ruti G. *Transitional Justice.* New York: Oxford University Press, 2000.

—Tim Gordinier

fairness doctrine

From 1949 to 1987, the Federal Communications Commission (FCC) enforced the so-called fairness doctrine in order to ensure that the American public could see and hear a variety of viewpoints when they tuned in to the nation's radio and television stations.

The idea was simple. Because frequencies on the broadcast spectrum are limited, only a very few people will ever receive a broadcast license. Since far more people wanted to be on the air, and get their messages out, than there were frequencies available, the FCC created regulations to promote FIRST AMENDMENT freedoms and a broadcasting system that would operate in the "public interest." This idea has its foundation in the Federal Radio Act (later changed to the Federal Communications Act), which stated that those operating a federally licensed broadcast station must do so for the "public convenience, interest and necessity."

The fairness doctrine had two primary parts. The first part required that broadcasters air programming that dealt with controversial matters of importance to the community. The second part required giving those with alternative views on those issues a chance to respond on the air for free if a paid sponsor was unavailable to do the job. Members of Congress, the FCC, and the courts believed that broadcasting could be regulated in ways that the print media could not due to the scarcity of broadcasting signals and the relative ease with which a newspaper could be printed.

In 1959, Congress passed legislation that appeared to codify the fairness doctrine. Lawmakers changed Section 315 of the Federal Communications Act to say that nothing in the act would relieve broadcasters of their "obligation under this chapter to operate in the public interest and to afford reasonable opportunity for the discussion of conflicting views on issues of public importance." Years later, the courts found that the language used by Congress was merely suggestive and was not, in fact, a codification of the doctrine.

But in 1969, the U.S. Supreme Court upheld the fairness doctrine in *Red Lion Broadcasting v. Federal Communications Commission,* 395 U.S. 367. The plaintiff broadcasters in the case criticized the fairness doctrine on the grounds that it impinged on their ability to use their frequency in the same way a newspaper publisher could. The broadcasters argued that a publisher could say whatever he or she wished, within the scope of the First Amendment, in the pages of the newspaper and was not required to provide space for an opponent of that view, while a broadcaster did not enjoy the same freedom. The Court ultimately rejected the argument. Justice Byron White said that because broadcasters are required to operate in the public interest, they have "a duty to discuss both sides of controversial public issues." Furthermore, "It is the right of the viewers and listeners, not the right of the broadcasters which is paramount." Justice White added: "It is the purpose of the First Amendment to preserve an uninhibited marketplace of ideas . . . rather than to countenance monopolization of that market, whether it be by the Government itself or by a private licensee."

Eventually, however, broadcasters convinced the FCC, the courts, and Congress of their right to unfettered speech. The convergence of the ever-expanding choices for programming through cable and satellite television and an increasing acceptance of deregulation during the presidency of Ronald Reagan led to the demise of the fairness doctrine. In 1987, the FCC repealed the fairness doctrine on constitutional grounds. The U.S. Court of Appeals for the Third Circuit upheld that decision in *Syracuse Peace Council v. FCC,* 867 F. 2d 654 (1989), although not on the same constitutional basis as the FCC. Judge Stephen Williams said simply that the FCC had the power to make the determination, and a decision that "the fairness doctrine no longer serves the public interest is a policy judgment." The court relied on the commission's findings that the media landscape had become sufficiently varied to ensure that controversial issues would get coverage and that the media outlets would represent the various positions on those issues. Also, the court supported the commission's view that government involvement in the editorial process, by telling broadcasters they were required to address controversial issues, was "offensive." Judge Kenneth Starr in his concurring opinion addressed the FCC's constitutional arguments and agreed with them. Congress passed a fairness in broadcasting law after the decision was handed down, but President Reagan vetoed it.

Although the fairness doctrine has been defunct for some time, debate continues as to whether it should be resurrected. For instance, the controversy surrounding the anti–John Kerry documentary "Stolen Honor: Wounds That Never Heal" during the 2004 election intensified the debate. The Sinclair Broadcasting Group, a company with connections to conservative causes and politicians, planned to air the documentary on its 62 televisions station during primetime, just prior to the election. Pro-Kerry and pro–fairness doctrine forces argued that this was an inappropriate use of the public airwaves. Although Sinclair ultimately aired only portions of the film in a format more akin to a news program, the discussion of whether to revive the fairness doctrine was not, and is not, settled.

For more information: Simmons, Steven J. *The Fairness Doctrine and the Media.* Berkeley: University of California Press, 1978.

—Jim Jacobson

fair trial–free press

The term *fair trial–free press* refers to the difficult balance in U.S. law between assuring the SIXTH AMENDMENT right of criminal defendants to a fair and impartial trial and the FIRST AMENDMENT right of the media and the public to access to information.

These rights are often in tension and have led to U.S. Supreme Court decisions, substantial commentary and debate, and to suggested fair trial–free press guidelines. One side of the conflict presents lawyers in a criminal case, especially the defense lawyer, who must make sure the defendant receives a fair trial in which the jury is unbiased, particularly by pre-trial publicity and media coverage during the trial. On the other side is the media's interest in aggressively seeking information about a crime, including matters that may be inadmissible at trial and details of evidence introduced at trial.

The Supreme Court said in *NEBRASKA PRESS ASSOCIATION. V. STUART,* 427 U.S. 539 (1976), that the framers of the Constitution allowed the tension to exist:

> The problems presented by this case are almost as old as the Republic. Neither in the Constitution nor in contemporaneous writings do we find that the conflict between these two important rights was anticipated, yet it is inconceivable that the authors of the Constitution were unaware of the potential conflicts between the right to an unbiased jury and the guarantee of FREEDOM OF THE PRESS.

Moreover, the Court also noted in *Nebraska Press*, in an opinion written by Chief Justice WARREN E. BURGER, that the BILL OF RIGHTS did not prioritize between the First and Sixth Amendment interests:

> The authors of the Bill of Rights did not undertake to assign priorities as between First Amendment and Sixth Amendment rights, ranking one as superior to the other . . . if the authors of these guarantees, fully aware of the potential conflicts between them, were unwilling or unable to

> resolve the issue by assigning to one priority over the other, it is not for us to rewrite the Constitution by undertaking what they declined to do.

A variety of rules and approaches have been tried to achieve a balance between the competing interests. Often it falls to trial judges to decide, especially in high-profile cases, whether there are steps that can be taken prior to or during a trial to maintain the defendant's right to a fair trial. But the Supreme Court, interpreting the First Amendment, has limited the tools available to judges. In *Richmond Newspapers, Inc. v. Virginia,* 448 U.S. 555 (1980), the Supreme Court ruled that there is a First Amendment right of the press and the public to have access to criminal trial, so closing trials to the public is generally not an option. This right, the Court said, exists even if the defendant wants a closed trial out of public view. A defendant would likely have to show that a public proceeding would actually prejudice his or her ability to get a fair trial.

The Court has also said that judges seeking to protect the fair trial interests of defendants must have a very high justification before they may restrict what the media may publish. In *Nebraska Press,* where a trial judge had barred the press from publishing details of confessions, the Supreme Court said that such prior restraints on publication are heavily disfavored under the First Amendment and should be a rarely used last resort to preserve the atmosphere for a fair trial. In many jurisdictions, judges must first deal with pretrial publicity by questioning the jurors carefully about their knowledge of the case, by sequestering the jury, or by moving the trial to another location in order to find a jury pool that has not been exposed to too much media coverage.

While the Court has read the First Amendment to allow relatively few limits on the media, the justices have found more leeway in efforts to restrict what lawyers may say about pending cases. This is because the speech and conduct of lawyers is subject to regulation by state bars and state supreme courts. In *Gentile v. State Bar of Nevada,* 501 U.S. 1030 (1991), the Supreme Court upheld the restriction adopted by most states, that lawyers may be prohibited from making statements that pose a "substantial likelihood of material prejudice" to a defendant's fair trial interests.

One widespread approach to the problem is the adoption of fair trial–free press guidelines. Since 1968, the American Bar Association (ABA) has proposed and updated guidelines designed to achieve a balance between the interests of the media and those of defendants facing trial. The most recent version was approved by the ABA in 1991; the guidelines are very influential on state bar ethical rules and on state legislatures.

For more information: Dienes, C. Thomas, Lee Levine, and Robert C. Lind. *Newsgathering and the Law.* 2d ed. Charlottesville, Va.: Lexis Law Publishing, 1999; Smolla, Rodney A. *Smolla and Nimmer on Freedom of Speech.* New York: Clark, Boardman, Callaghan, 1996.

—Stephen Wermiel

Fay v. Noia 372 U.S. 391 (1963)

In *Fay v. Noia,* the U.S. Supreme Court decided that a criminal defendant's failure to appeal a state court conviction, which rested solely upon the defendant's coerced confession, did not result in a forfeiture of HABEAS CORPUS review in federal court.

In a more general sense, the Court, in *Fay,* was confronted with a question of FEDERALISM. Although the state conceded that Noia's confession was coerced, the state argued that the judgments of its courts were entitled to deference in the federal courts because Noia had not appealed his conviction and intervention by the federal courts would disturb the balance of power between the state and federal governments. Historically, the authority of federal courts to review state court convictions had been confined by the doctrine of comity. (The rule on comity means that one court should support decisions made by another court). However, the extraordinary circumstances presented by Noia's case inspired a reaffirmation of the supremacy of the federal government.

Noia and two codefendants were charged with felony murder. At trial, the only evidence against them was their confessions. They were convicted as charged and sentenced to life in prison. Noia did not appeal his conviction; however, after his codefendants won their release because their confessions had been coerced, Noia sought relief through a postconviction proceeding. His confession also had been coerced; nevertheless, he was denied relief. A state procedural rule required an appeal as a prerequisite to postconviction review. Under that rule, his claim was considered forfeited because he had not appealed.

After being denied relief in state court, Noia filed an application for writ of habeas corpus in federal court. At that time, the doctrine of comity generally insulated the decisions of state courts from federal oversight for two reasons. First, federal courts would not review any issues that were decided by the state courts based on state law rather than federal law. Under these circumstances, the state court decision was said to rest on "independent and adequate state law" grounds. Second, federal courts would not review any issues that had not been raised in the state courts. This rule was referred to as the requirement of "exhaustion," and a failure to exhaust a claim resulted in a "procedural default." In Noia's case, the U.S. district court denied relief, applying both of these rules even though the state conceded that Noia's confession had been coerced; however, the U.S. court of appeals reversed that decision, concluding that the doctrine of comity was overcome by the extraordinary circumstances of the case.

After accepting the case for review, the U.S. Supreme Court concluded that the writ of habeas corpus existed to provide a remedy for "criminal proceedings so fundamentally defective as to make imprisonment pursuant to them constitutionally intolerable." In accordance with that principle, the Court held that Noia's imprisonment for a conviction tainted by a coerced confession could not be permitted. Concerning the issue of federalism, the Court noted that the statutory authority of federal courts to release state prisoners by issuing a writ of habeas corpus was directly linked to post–Civil War efforts to deal with the former Confederate states.

Accordingly, the federal courts were found to be superior to the states when it came to unconstitutional imprisonment. The Court concluded that the doctrine of comity was a guide for the exercise of power, rather than a restraint. The Court also noted that the doctrine of comity was a procedural rule rather than a "rule distributing power as between the state and federal courts." Therefore, in the relationship between the national government and the state governments, the authority of the federal courts takes precedence over state law. According to the Court, that result was inherent in the federal system established by the U.S. Constitution.

For more information: Harriger, Katy J. "The Federalism Debate in the Transformation of Federal Habeas Corpus Law." *Publius: The Journal of Federalism* 27, no. 3 (Summer 1997): 1–22.

—Mark A. Fulks

Federal Baseball Club of Baltimore, Inc. v. National League of Professional Baseball Clubs 259 U.S. 200 (1922)

In a unanimous 1922 decision, the Supreme Court held in *Federal Baseball Club of Baltimore, Inc. v. National League of Professional Baseball Clubs* that a national professional baseball league did not constitute an illegal monopoly. Monopolies were prohibited under the Sherman Antitrust Act, which was passed by Congress and signed into law by President Benjamin Harrison in 1890. The Sherman Antitrust Act made illegal all contracts that resulted in the restraint of trade or commerce among or between states or foreign nations.

In the early 1900s, the organization of professional baseball had yet to reach the form that we know today. In 1913, eight baseball clubs formed the Federal League of Professional Baseball Clubs, which had teams in Baltimore, Brooklyn, Buffalo, Chicago, Indianapolis, Kansas City, Pittsburgh, and St. Louis. At the same time, there existed what was called the major league clubs, which consisted of the familiar National and American Leagues, with 16 teams in 11 major cities.

The major leagues and Federal League competed until 1915, when they entered into what was called a peace agreement that resulted in the dissolution of all Federal League teams except the Baltimore baseball club. The Baltimore club filed a lawsuit alleging that the peace agreement created a restriction on its ability to field a team of competent baseball players, thereby causing significant monetary damages.

The trial court agreed with this argument and ruled in favor of the Baltimore club. The National League appealed the decision to the District of Columbia court of appeals. The D.C. court of appeals reversed the decision of the trial court. In its opinion, the court of appeals first argued that the concept of trade, as commonly defined, required the transfer of something, whether it be persons, commodities, or intelligence, from one place or person to another (*National League v. Federal Baseball Club*, 269 F. 681, 684 [1920]).

Under this definition, the court of appeals went on to argue that the business of baseball did not constitute trade: The game of baseball is not susceptible to being transferred. The players, it is true, travel from place to place in INTERSTATE COMMERCE, but they are not the game: "The exertions of skill and agility which [the fans] witness may excite in them pleasurable emotions, but the game effects no exchange of things according to the meaning of 'trade and commerce' as defined above."

Consistent with this reasoning, the court of appeals held that the contracts of the major leagues were directly related to the major league goal of retaining baseball players for their teams and did not "directly affect the movement of the [Baltimore club] on interstate commerce. Whatever effect, if any, they had, was incidental, and therefore did not offend against the statute."

The Baltimore club appealed this decision to the U.S. Supreme Court, which granted review. In a short unanimous opinion, Justice OLIVER WENDELL HOLMES, JR., largely endorsed the opinion of the D.C. court of appeals. Justice Holmes noted personal effort, not related to production, is not a subject of commerce. "That which in its consummation is not commerce does not become commerce among the States because the transportation [of the personal effort] takes place." To this day professional baseball retains its exemption from the Sherman Antitrust Act.

For more information: Mack, Connie, and Richard M. Blau. "The Need for Fair Play: Repealing the Federal Baseball Antitrust Exemption." *Florida Law Review* 45 (1993): 201–220.

—Ryan C. Black

Federal Communications Commission v. Pacifica Foundation 438 U.S. 726 (1978)

In *Federal Communications Commission v. Pacifica Foundation*, the U.S. Supreme Court ruled that the Federal Communications Commission (FCC) could regulate indecent speech on the nation's airwaves and punish broadcasters for programming that, while not obscene, as that term had been defined by the Court, was still well outside the mainstream. The case was significant because the Court said that while indecent speech aired on broadcast stations was protected by the FIRST AMENDMENT, it only enjoyed limited protection.

The case stemmed from Pacifica's airing of a recording of George Carlin's comedy routine about certain "dirty" words. The recording was part of a discussion about language and was used to show that, at least in Carlin's opinion, some people had silly attitudes about language. The FCC received a complaint from a man who heard the broadcast with his young son when it aired in the middle of the afternoon. The commissioners ruled that Pacifica would receive a note in its broadcast license renewal file because federal law forbids the use of "any obscene, indecent, or profane language by means of radio communications." The FCC found that it could take this action because, although the speech was not obscene, it was patently offensive and because unlike other forms of communication, broadcasting has special qualities that lend itself to this type of regulation. Among these special qualities are that, first, unsupervised children have access to radios, and second, radios are generally found in places, such as the home, where people's PRIVACY interests are entitled to extra deference. The U.S. court of appeals overturned the commission's decision, but the Supreme Court agreed with the FCC.

In its 1978 decision, in which the plurality opinion was written by Justice JOHN PAUL STEVENS, the Court held that the FCC's action did not constitute censorship because it took place after the broadcast aired. Had the commission taken its action prior to the airing of Carlin's monologue, then it would have been censorship. Furthermore, Stevens wrote that despite an earlier Supreme Court ruling that found a law similar to the one invoked by the FCC in which indecency and OBSCENITY were essentially equivalent, in this instance the law was clear that indecent speech and obscene speech are different. The Court stated that it was not prohibiting indecent material entirely, but stations could air it only when children were not likely to be listening. Also, because broadcasting "invades" people's homes where they have the right to be left alone, "To say that one may avoid further offense by turning off the radio when he hears indecent language is like saying that the remedy for assault is to run away after the first blow." Justice LEWIS FRANKLIN POWELL, JR., wrote a separate opinion that agreed with the Court's overall decision but questioned whether the Court should determine the relative merits of various types of speech and degree of protection each deserves.

The dissenting members of the Court wrote that a minority of parents who think that monologues such as Carlin's might be desirable for their children to hear should have the right to hear that material. They also noted that as the Court had ruled in analogous situations that whatever discomfort an offended listener might suffer when hearing indecent speech, he or she can always "flick the off button." Moreover, they said that the Court's ruling showed that the majority failed to appreciate the fact that there are many people who think and act differently from the members of the Court and "do not share their fragile sensibilities."

The *Pacifica* case has served as an important foundation on which censorship advocates have fought broadcasters in the decades that followed.

For more information: Heins, Marjorie. *Not in Front of the Children: Indecency, Censorship and the Innocence of Youth.* New York: Hill & Wang, 2001.

—Jim Jacobson

Federal Election Commission v. Beaumont et al. 539 U.S. 146 (2003)

In *Federal Election Commission v. Beaumont et al.*, the Supreme Court ruled that the prohibition barring contribution or expenditure from certain federal elections that applies to corporations also applies to nonprofit advocacy corporations and is consistent with the FIRST AMENDMENT. This decision extends the ban on corporate direct investment to candidates to include nonprofit advocacy corporations.

North Carolina Right to Life, Inc. (NCRL), a nonprofit advocacy corporation, filed suit against the Federal Election Commission (FEC), challenging the constitutionality of 2 U.S.C. Section 441(b). Section 441(b) bans direct corporate investment but allows corporate investment in a political action committee (PAC) to carry out the political purposes sought. NCRL had funded state electoral candidates directly but funded federal electoral candidates through a PAC. NCRL sought to provide direct contributions to a particular candidate rather than take the extra step of locating (or creating) a PAC for that purpose.

The district court granted summary judgment in favor of NCRL, finding Section 441(b) unconstitutional with respect to direct contributions and indirect expenditures. A divided U.S. Court of Appeals for the Fourth Circuit affirmed the judgment, relying on *Federal Election Commission v. Massachusetts Citizens for Life, Inc.*, 479 U.S. 238, 253-254 (1986), which found it unconstitutional to ban independent expenditures by Massachusetts Citizens for Life. However, a conflict existed with respect to a Sixth Circuit decision on direct contributions (*Kentucky Right to Life v. Terry*, 108 F. 3d 637, 645-646 [1997]). The Supreme Court took up the issue with respect to direct contributions to answer this conflict.

Justice DAVID H. SOUTER delivered the opinion of the majority of the Court that found a long history of protection of the political process from potential abuses of corporations. There is concern that the state (and federal) laws that allow corporations to amass wealth for the economic benefit of corporate shareholders would be used instead to provide an unfair advantage in the political sphere. Similarly, there is just as much concern that the capital accumulated or donated for an economic purpose from or for the benefit of an individual would be used by the corporation to support a political candidate the individual did not support or want to support. These concerns make a strong case for the regulation of direct corporate funding.

The majority then distinguished *Massachusetts Citizens for Life, Inc.* and *Federal Election Commission v. National Right to Work Commission*, 459 U.S. 197 (1982), reasoning that "restrictions on contributions require less compelling justification than restrictions on independent spending." The concern over independent direct support for a candidate in a federal election justified the need for a broad "prophylactic" rule such as Section 441(b).

Finally, the majority rejected NCRL's argument to use STRICT SCRUTINY in reviewing Section 441(b) under the First Amendment. The standard of review for political financial restrictions depends on the importance of the "political activity at issue" to the speaker or actor. Historically, the activity at issue, political contributions, is seen as merely marginal in importance and requires a modest standard of review. The majority reversed the court of appeals decision because a nonprofit advocacy corporation shares the same advantages as a corporation and the issue of abuse and advantage are equally of concern for both corporations. Therefore, it is not a violation of the First Amendment to restrict the use of direct corporate funding toward a candidate in a federal election.

Justice ANTHONY M. KENNEDY concurred in the judgment of the Court only because the decision was limited to direct corporate funding and did not seek to review the distinction between contributions and expenditures for all CAMPAIGN FINANCE regulations. Justices CLARENCE THOMAS and ANTONIN GREGORY SCALIA dissented from the opinion because they felt strict scrutiny should be applied to cases of finance reform that restrict political speech in a broad prophylactic way. If such a standard was applied, Justice Thomas argued, Section 441(b) would not survive that higher standard and would therefore be unconstitutional.

For more information: Hasen, Richard L. *The Supreme Court and Election Law.* New York: New York University Press, 2003.

—Julian M. Davis

Federal Election Commission v. Colorado Republican Federal Campaign Committee 518 U.S. 604 (1996)

In *Federal Election Commission v. Colorado Republican Federal Campaign Committee*, the Supreme Court decided the government could not limit the ability of political parties to engage in expenditures that are made "independent" of the party's candidates.

The 1974 Federal Election Campaign Act (FECA) established an amount that a political party could spend "in coordination" with the party's candidate for office. In April 1986, before the Colorado Republican Party (CRP) had selected its candidate for the U.S. SENATE, the CRP aired a radio advertisement attacking the Democratic Party's candidate for the U.S. Senate.

Because the CRP gave its ability to spend "coordinated" money to another political party committee, the Democratic Party filed a complaint with the Federal Election Commission (FEC). The complaint alleged that by spending money on the radio ad, the CRP had violated the "coordinated expenditure" limit. The FEC agreed and filed a complaint in federal court against the CRP. After working its way through the appeals process, the case wound up before the U.S. Supreme Court.

The Supreme Court reviewed the factual evidence in the case, which revealed that the CRP's officers and staff decided to air the radio advertisement about the Democratic candidate without communicating with either of the Republican candidates for the party's nomination. The Supreme Court, in issuing its decision in favor of the CRP, reviewed the underlying rationale for the regulation of CAMPAIGN FINANCE—preventing corruption or the appearance of corruption. The Court explained that its prior rulings essentially concluded that individuals, candidates, and political committees that were not political parties could engage in unlimited independent expenditures. This protection for "independent" speech, the Supreme Court explained, was because the independent nature of such "speech" makes independent ads less valuable to the candidate and will not result in "improper commitments" from the candidate.

The Supreme Court ultimately concluded that the government could not deny political parties the ability to engage in independent speech. This case has had a significant influence on political campaigns in the United States since the decision was issued, although unsuccessful attempts have been made to limit the impact of the Supreme Court's 1996 ruling.

In 2002, the U.S. Congress passed the Bi-Partisan Campaign Reform Act (BCRA). The BCRA made a number of changes to the FECA and included a provision that forced political parties to choose between making "independent expenditures" and making "coordinated expenditures." This provision, among others, was the subject of lawsuits that were ultimately decided by the Supreme Court in *MCCONNELL V. FEC*, 540 U.S. 93 (2003). The Supreme Court concluded that it was unconstitutional to force political parties to make this selection and ruled that political parties could engage in both independent and coordinated speech.

In the 2004 election, the Republican and Democratic Parties each spent $62,215,195 in "coordinated expenditures" on behalf of their candidates for president. In addition, the Republican Party spent $88,032,382 and the Democratic Party spent $176,491,696 in "independent expenditures" on behalf of their candidates for president.

For more information: Bauer, B. *More Soft Money Hard Law.* 2d ed. Washington, D.C.: Perkins Coie, 2004; Malbin, M. J., ed. *The Election After Reform: Money, Politics, and Bipartisan Campaign Reform Act.* Lanham, Md.: Rowman & Littlefield, 2006.

—Jason Torchinsky

Federal Election Commission v. Wisconsin Right to Life, Inc. ___ U.S. ___ (2007)

In *Federal Election Commission v. Wisconsin Right to Life, Inc.*, the U.S. Supreme Court ruled that Section 203 of the Bipartisan Campaign Reform Act (BCRA) of 2002 was an unconstitutional violation of the FIRST AMENDMENT as applied to certain forms of political speech.

The protection of political speech is at the core of what is covered by the First Amendment. However, both Congress and the courts have also recognized that political activities and speech by certain actors, such as LABOR UNIONS and corporations, may receive less protection than offered to individuals because of the potential of the former two to corrupt the political process. Starting in 1907, with the passage of the Tillman Act, and then in 1947, with the Taft-Hartley Act, it has been illegal for corporations and labor unions to undertake activities that seek directly to influence federal elections. Among other things, the Tillman and Taft-Hartley Acts made it illegal for corporations and unions to run political advertisements that seek to influence the election or defeat of a candidate for federal office. However, it is often difficult to decide if statements or advertisements made by these actors violate these two laws.

In *BUCKLEY V. VALEO*, 424 U.S. 1 (1976), the Supreme Court sought to clarify what speech was protected by the First Amendment versus that which could be regulated or prohibited. In footnote 52 and the accompanying text, the Court distinguished express advocacy from issue advocacy. In arguing that express advocacy included appeals that used what has come to be known as the "magic words"—*vote for, elect, support*—the Court sought to distinguish electoral speech that would receive First Amendment protection from that which would not, especially when it came to particular speakers such as labor unions or corporations. The Tillman and Taft-Hartley Acts barred corporations and unions from directly seeking to influence federal elections. The express versus issue advocacy distinction supposedly maintained the bar on speech directly affecting federal elections by these and other actors, such as nonprofits, but preserved their First Amendment rights to comment on matters of public concern.

The express versus issue advocacy distinction became the loophole. Unions, corporations, and nonprofits all exploited it to influence federal elections by simply running ads that did everything an express advocacy ad did except say "vote for" or "support." Instead, these ads often asked viewers to call a senator or representative and ask him or her why he or she opposed a given issue or piece of legislation.

Section 203 of BCRA, or the McCain-Feingold law, tried to fill in the loophole. It defined "electioneering communication" to be any political speech depicting or referring to an identifiable federal candidate within 30 days of a primary or 60 days of a general election to be presumed to be directed at influencing a federal election, and therefore, if the ad were made by a corporation or union, it would be illegal. In *McConnell v. FEC*, 540 U.S. 93 (2003), the Supreme Court upheld Section 203 against a facial charge of unconstitutionality but left open claims that it might violate the First Amendment in an applied challenge.

In the *Wisconsin Right to Life* case, at issue was a challenge by an ideological nonprofit corporation that wanted to run ads urging viewers to contact their senators to oppose efforts to filibuster federal judicial nominations. These ads would run within 30 days of a Wisconsin primary, the state where the ads would air. Wisconsin Right to Life sought a declaratory judgment against the FEC, claiming that section 203 was unconstitutional. Initially, a three-judge panel denied the request for an INJUNCTION, and the Supreme Court vacated and remanded the decision. A federal district court then agreed with Wisconsin Right to Life, and the Supreme Court upheld the decision.

Writing for the Court, Chief Justice JOHN G. ROBERTS, JR., ruled that the ad or speech was not functionally equivalent to express advocacy and therefore deserved First Amendment protection. Because this or similar ads were not clearly directed toward federal candidates, the general justification to regulate political contributions or corporate or union speech to address corruption was not present. In addition, Chief Justice Roberts stated that, as applied, Section 203 was overbroad in banning the type of speech that was protected by the First Amendment. In his concurrence, Justice ANTONIN GREGORY SCALIA argued that the Court had effectively overturned its *McConnell* decision, while in dissent Justices DAVID H. SOUTER, JOHN PAUL STEVENS, Ruth Bader Ginsburg, and STEPHEN G. BREYER would have upheld Section 203.

The *Wisconsin Right to Life* decision effectively restores the express advocacy–issue advocacy rule to status quo prior to BCRA. The importance of the decision is that it leaves open also the possibility of a return to the types of political ads and speech that BCRA sought to regulate and control. For advocates of CAMPAIGN FINANCE reform, this is a step backward, while for many First Amendment supporters, it is a protection of core free speech rights.

For more information: Schultz, David. "*Buckley v. Valeo, Randall v. Sorrell,* and the Future of Campaign Financing on the Roberts Court." *Nexus* 12 (2007): 153–176.

—David Schultz

federalism

Federalism involves the division of authority, power, and function between a national government and state governments. In federalism, the national government's sovereignty is limited by the partially retained autonomy of the states. This makes federalism a hybrid between unitary government and confederation. Federalism began in the United States with the signing of the U.S. Constitution in 1787, which replaced the Articles of Confederation under which the budding nation had united in pressing for independence from Great Britain. The concept of federalism is rooted structurally in the Constitution, most prominently in the Tenth Amendment.

Federalism is an institutional design feature evident throughout the U.S. Constitution. As explained by JAMES MADISON and ALEXANDER HAMILTON in the *FEDERALIST PAPERS*, federalism's potential benefits are many. Federalism lends itself to CHECKS AND BALANCES, a reduction in the monopolistic potential of factions, and the heightening of national security through an enlargement of governable territory. Federalism enriches policy choices at the state level, amplifies representation through the abundance of electoral offices, and stimulates a nation's economic engine as commercial interests benefit from wider market opportunities.

The attractions of federalism remain impressive. In *GREGORY V. ASHCROFT*, 501 U.S. 452 (1991), U.S. Supreme Court justice SANDRA DAY O'CONNOR delivered the opinion of the Court majority, writing that the "federalist structure" of the Constitution "assures a decentralized government that will be more sensitive to the diverse needs of a heterogenous society." Continuing, O'Connor declared that federalism allows for "more innovation and experimentation in government" while making "government more responsive by putting the States in competition for a mobile citizenry." These considerations and others have been expounded philosophically and studied empirically by political scientists specializing in federalism and publishing academic work in serials such as *Publius: The Journal of Federalism.* Notably, scholars such as Samuel Beer, Martin Diamond, Daniel Elazar, Donald Lutz, and Vincent Ostrom have provided comprehensive theories and topical histories that describe the American experience with federalism from germination to its full blossom in the modern bureaucratic state. Other political scientists including Thomas Dye, John Kincaid, David Walker, and Deil Wright have supplemented that work with empirical research, statistical findings, and erudite analysis.

The high court's work continues to be animated by the complexities of competitive sovereignty. As Justice O'Connor stated when writing for a united court in *Tafflin v. Levitt*, 493 U.S. 455 (1990), "We begin with the axiom that, under our federal system, the States possess sovereignty concurrent with that of the Federal Government, subject only to limitations imposed by the SUPREMACY CLAUSE." But just a year later, the Court was again ruffled by disagreement about federalism. In *Coleman v. Thompson*, 501 U.S. 722 (1991), Justice Harry A. Blackmun wrote a dissenting opinion for three justices, claiming that the six justice majority was mistaken in thinking the case to be about federalism. Blackmun stated that federalism "has no inherent normative value." He then asserted an earlier claim by Justice WILLIAM J. BRENNAN, JR., that federalism "is a device for realizing the concepts of decency and fairness which are among the fundamental principles of liberty."

While the philosophy of federalism is subject to debate, a de facto description of federalism appears in the Tenth Amendment of the BILL OF RIGHTS, effective 1791. Reflecting the sentiments of the new nation's first Congress and the apprehensions of reluctant signers of the Constitution (the so-called Anti-Federalists), the Tenth makes this sweeping declaration: "The powers not delegated to the United States by the Constitution, nor prohibited by it to the States, are reserved to the States respectively, or to the people." The structure of the Constitution shows a multifaceted and sometimes concurrent sharing of authority, creating, in the words of Madison, "a certain degree of obscurity" in the document. This vagueness existed, Madison declared in *Federalist* 37, because the convention was faced with an "arduous task" in trying to balance the authority of the general government with that of the state governments, an observation echoed by Justice ANTHONY M. KENNEDY two centuries later in *UNITED STATES V. LOPEZ*, 514 U.S. 549 (1995).

The U.S. Constitution was but a proposed foundation of government until ratified by nine of the 13 original American states, the states employing conventions of delegates "chosen by the People thereof" as instructed by the CONSTITUTIONAL CONVENTION in September 1787. The phrase *the people* reflects back to the first sentence in the Constitution, namely, "We the People of the United States, in Order to form a more perfect Union . . . do ordain and establish this Constitution." In this meaningful construction, the emphasis is on a people in their union existence. Still, the constitutional formula is for state-governed elections for Congress. Hence, a conceptual duality exists: The Tenth Amendment and its associated features in the Constitution planted alongside centralizing elements in the original document.

The first milestone in the evolution of federalism was laid when the U.S. Supreme Court established precedence for JUDICIAL REVIEW in *MARBURY V. MADISON*, 5 U.S. 137 (1803). The particulars of the case aside, the high court dramatically expanded its role in determining the division of authority between the respective states and the national government. Once the Court's reach was extended, a series of cases presented themselves, allowing the Court to elevate the role of jurisprudence in settling power struggles. In the landmark case *MCCULLOCH V. MARYLAND*, 17 U.S. 316 (1819), the Court held that Congress had the power to create a bank of the United States without reliance upon an enumerated constitutional power. This decision began the process of hemming in the Tenth Amendment's reach in protecting state powers.

The *McCulloch* decision clarified the supremacy of the national government, as did many cases that followed. In *GIBBONS V. OGDEN*, 22 U.S. 1 (1824), the power of the Congress was asserted by the high court, reducing the ability of the states to regulate commerce. Likewise, in *Worchester v. Georgia*, 31 U.S. 515 (1832), the Court held that the Cherokee Nation within the state of Georgia was a self-governing and distinct community, its legal compunctions being to the U.S. government, not the state of Georgia. This decision moved the fulcrum supporting the seesaw of federalism in favor of the national government, if only incrementally.

In *Prigg v. Pennsylvania*, 41 U.S. 539 (1842), the Supreme Court struck down laws that northern states devised to protect fugitive slaves, the Court viewing such laws as interdicted by Congress's 1793 Fugitive Slave Act. As the nation lurched toward Civil War, Congress passed the Fugitive Slave Act of 1850. The act was rebuffed when the Wisconsin Supreme Court declared it unconstitutional in 1854. The national high court soon reversed the state court but to little avail once the Wisconsin legislature claimed JOHN C. CALHOUN's nullification doctrine. This particular conflict over the shape of evolving federalism climaxed judicially with the U.S. Supreme Court's declaration of the constitutionality of the Fugitive Slave Act in *DRED SCOTT V. SANDFORD*, 60 U.S. (19 How.) 393 (1857). However, the fight over federalism would continue to build after Civil War guns fell silent.

The U.S. Supreme Court's jurisprudence on federalism vacillated in the decades following the Civil War. In *Wabash v. Illinois*, 118 U.S. 557 (1886), a six-justice majority circumscribed the ability of states to regulate railroad rates within their own jurisdictions on rail traffic passing through. But in *Muller v. Oregon*, 208 U.S. 412 (1908), the Court upheld the state of Oregon's right to regulate labor laws in conjunction with the state's interest in women's health. *UNITED STATES V. DARBY LUMBER CO.*, 312 U.S. 100 (1941), came to reflect the high court's emerging understanding of federalism: The Court overturned the precedence of *HAMMER V. DAGENHART*, 247 U.S. 251 (1918), which used the Tenth Amendment as a barricade to the national government's interference in matters of commerce deemed to be local. In the unanimous *Darby* decision, the Court maintained that the Tenth Amendment did not give the states any more power than they possessed by reason of what was given or reserved to them elsewhere in the Constitution, the Tenth thus being clarified as a mere "truism" to "allay fears" of Anti-Federalists. The Court majority would continue to be enamored by this line of reasoning in the decades that followed, a change becoming evident in *New York v. United States*, 488 U.S. 1041 (1992), and affirmed in *PRINTZ V. UNITED STATES*, 521 U.S. 898 (1997). In both instances, the nation's highest court endeavored to argue that the Tenth Amendment does contain principles of federalism and is not a mere encapsulation of federalist sentiment.

It was only a few years earlier, in *GARCIA V. SAN ANTONIO METROPOLITAN TRANSIT AUTHORITY*, 469 U.S. 528 (1985), that the five justice majority in a sharply divided court argued for a political process definition of federalism. This is the argument that the balance of power in federalism is contingent on the electorate's choosing congressional representatives who uphold state interests (hence, "representational federalism" in the parlance of political scientists). In a dissent joined by Justices WILLIAM HUBBS REHNQUIST and O'Connor, Justice LEWIS FRANKLIN POWELL, JR., stated that the "States' role in our system of government is a matter of constitutional law, not of legislative grace" and that "an unelected majority of five justices . . . rejects almost 200 years of the understanding of the constitutional status of federalism." In a separate dissent, Justice O'Connor argued that federalism was nearing irrelevance as the set of activities beyond the reach of the commerce power became "negligible."

Earlier in the Court's jurisprudential evolution, the struggle to define federalism took a turn with the ratification of the FOURTEENTH AMENDMENT in 1868, the amendment providing "DUE PROCESS" and "EQUAL PROTECTION" clauses as ammunition for the national government in managing the wayward ambitions of the states. For a time, the Court used the due process clause in an activist sense to curtail worker protections arising from progressive-era reforms at the state and national level. In so doing, the Court cast a shadow on its credibility, most notably in *LOCHNER V. NEW YORK,* 198 U.S. 45 (1905). Eventually, the nation's preeminent court adjusted its jurisprudence and began using the due process clause to advance the long repressed CIVIL RIGHTS of African Americans, ruling in *BROWN V. BOARD OF EDUCATION OF TOPEKA,* 347 U.S. 483 (1954), that separate is not equal in racially segregated education. *Brown* was a landmark ruling because it undid the Court's earlier work in *PLESSY V. FERGUSON,* 163 U.S. 537 (1896), in which separate facilities in railroad cars were not deemed unconstitutional even with the Fourteenth Amendment in place. Thus, the *Brown* decision came to suggest what is now widely assumed by court observers, namely, that high-profile decisions by the U.S. Supreme Court are affected by cultural constraints and the political environment.

While the U.S. Constitution remains the world's seminal document of full-fledged federalism, more than two dozen nations have adopted federal political arrangements, notably Australia, Canada, Germany, India, and Russia, among others. With the spread of federalism, the scholarly study of its applications is on the increase, a visible proponent being the International Association of Centers for Federal Studies (IACFS). In spite of the fact that federalism is increasingly viewed as a "best practices" design for representative democracy, a complex global situation may produce centrifugal forces that federal nations attempt to manage by concentrating domestic powers in national or global bureaucracies. The threat of terrorism, the complications of global warming, the complexities of multinational commerce, and the realities of educational and economic insufficiency for millions of Americans may produce increasingly consequential incursions of federal power into areas formerly under state control. Ultimately, the American electorate will share a role alongside the U.S. federal court system in determining the future role of constitutional federalism in American governance.

For more information: Beer, Samuel H. *To Make a Nation: The Rediscovery of American Federalism.* Cambridge, Mass.: Belknap Press of Harvard University Press, 1993; Dye, Thomas. *American Federalism: Competition Among Governments.* Lexington, Mass.: Lexington Books, 1990; Epstein, Lee, and Thomas G. Walker. *Constitutional Law for a Changing America: Institutional Powers and Constraints.* 5th ed. Washington, D.C.: CQ Press, 2004.

—Timothy J. Barnett

Federalist Papers (1787–1788)

The *Federalist Papers,* or *The Federalist,* a series of articles composed by ALEXANDER HAMILTON, JAMES MADISON, and JOHN JAY in order to push for the ratification of the newly written Constitution, were first published as a set in 1788. Many articles within the set are viewed as highly influential and classic republican and democratic treatises, offering readers an excellent resource to better interpret, understand, and support the Constitution today and at the time of ratification.

Following the closure of the CONSTITUTIONAL CONVENTION and the signing of the final document in Philadelphia in 1787, the Constitution was sent to all of the states for ratification. Once it was released to the public, it suffered virulent attacks throughout the young nation.

Separation between those who were in favor of the Constitution and those who were against it led to the creation of the country's first de facto political parties, known as the Federalists and the Anti-Federalists. The Anti-Federalists opposed the new Constitution because they believed that it overcentralized power in the young nation at the expense of the state governments. They began publishing articles in newspapers throughout the country but particularly in New York. The first Anti-Federalist authors used such surnames as *Cato* and *Brutus*, and their articles appeared as soon as late September 1787.

In response, Hamilton organized a powerful and persuasive team of writers in defense of the Constitution. He considered many of the delegates at the Constitutional Convention, as well as other prominent members of the political society. Ultimately, he collaborated mostly with Madison, author and father of the Constitution. Others included Jay, who was suffering from an illness that hampered his productivity, and William Duer, who had some of his compositions rejected and disputed by Hamilton. Interestingly, Hamilton also contacted Gouverneur Morris to collaborate with him on the project, but Morris rejected Hamilton's proposal. Nevertheless, Hamilton assembled a primarily three-person team well capable of fulfilling his goal of defending the Constitution to better explain the new form of government and to convince citizens to ratify it.

Following in the footsteps of the Anti-Federalists, Hamilton, Madison, and Jay chose to write under a shared Roman surname. They selected the name *Publius* because they believed that it was a stronger representation of their character, especially compared to the names of *Caesar, Brutus*, and *Cato*. *Publius*, a derivative of another name the authors used, *Publicola*, means "friend of the people" in Latin. Notably, it was not the first time Hamilton had selected this name, having used it to author three letters attacking Maryland Continental Congress delegate Samuel Chase in 1778.

The articles that came to be the *Federalist Papers* began appearing in three New York publications, the *Daily Advertiser*, the *Independent Journal*, and the *New York Packet*, starting in late October 27, 1787. Although primarily concentrated in New York in the beginning, Hamilton actively promoted their publication in other states. Initially, the articles were published rather frequently; often, three or four new articles appeared every week. In all, 85 articles were published, and actual authorship of most of the articles has been determined, while scholars have used various types of statistical analysis to rediscover for certain who wrote one of the roughly 12 contested articles. Hamilton was the most prolific writer in the project, authoring roughly three-fourths of all of the articles, while Madison came in second, with a sickly Jay authoring the fewest.

Federalist 1, the first to appear, as they were numbered chronologically, written by Hamilton, introduced and outlined the goals and subjects of the following articles. The six subjects were 1) the utility of the Union, 2) the insufficiency of the present confederation, 3) the necessity of a stronger government, 4) the conformity of the proposed Constitution to republican government, 5) the relationship between federal and state government, and 6) the additional securities of the new government. The subjects were covered somewhat chronologically as well; the first subject was covered by *Federalists* 2–14; the second, by 15–22; the third, by 23–36; the fourth, by 27–84; and the fifth and sixth, by 85. Interestingly, as the writing and publishing occurred, the subjects were not covered equally, as Hamilton, Madison, and Jay were interested themselves in some of the topics more than the others. Hamilton's proposed fifth and sixth subjects were, as a result of these different interests and developments of opinion, covered only rather briefly in *Federalist* 85.

Not only did the *Federalist Papers* adamantly support the Constitution, they also went on the offensive against the proposed amendments, known today as the BILL OF RIGHTS. *Federalist* 84 particularly attacks the Bill of Rights. This opposition came directly from a controversy that developed at the end of the Constitutional Convention, as some feared that the new document did not list or specify the rights of the people to be protected by the new government. Hamilton himself disliked the proposed Bill of Rights because he feared that if the rights were listed, the rights that were inherent and not listed would not be respected later by individuals or by the government.

Among Hamilton, Madison, and Jay, none of them shared the same views on the Bill of Rights. For many citizens and ultimately for many states, the Constitution could not be ratified without a Bill of Rights. For those who feared an empowered central government developing into a tyrannical regime, the Bill of Rights restrained the new government from doing so. In the end, the Bill of Rights played an important role in allaying the fears of those who were ultimately to vote in favor the Constitution with the understanding that the list of rights amended to the document would not be interpreted by the government, courts, or public as exhaustive, as Hamilton had feared.

The *Federalist Papers* became very popular not just among scholars and politicians but also among the general public who were interested in the new government. As a result, they were frequently republished together even after the ratification debate. They were first republished together in 1788 and went on to be republished internationally. Besides offering scholars an incredible insight into the Constitution and the debate around it during the time of ratification, the papers are often consulted by U.S. judges, but their use as a citation is controversial due to the articles' lack of legal status.

For more information: Founding Fathers Online. "The *Federalist Papers* E-Text." Available online. URL: http://www.foundingfathers.info/federalistpapers/. Accessed May 12, 2008; Hamilton, Alexander, James Madison, and John Jay. *The Federalist Papers*. New York: Bantam Classics, 1982; Ketcham, Ralph. *The Anti-Federalist Papers and Constitutional Convention Debates*. New York: Signet Classics, 2003.

—Arthur Holst

Federal Maritime Commission v. South Carolina State Ports Authority 535 U.S. 743 (2002)

In *Federal Maritime Commission v. South Carolina State Ports Authority*, the Supreme Court ruled that state sovereign immunity precluded independent administrative agencies from adjudicating private claims against nonconsenting states. Justice CLARENCE THOMAS, writing for the 5-4 majority, affirmed the lower court's decision, extending the protection that the ELEVENTH AMENDMENT provides to nonconsenting states in federal courts to administrative proceedings that appear similar to judicial processes. Before this case, the Eleventh Amendment applied only to exercises of "judicial power of the United States."

A cruise ship operator filed a private complaint with the Federal Maritime Commission (FMC) after the South Carolina State Ports Authority (SPSCA) continued to deny its ships berth in one of its port facilities. The operator's ships contained gambling facilities and believed the denials by the SPSCA were discriminatory and thus were a violation of the Shipping Act of 1984. The operator filed for injunctive relief and reparations. The FMC referred the matter to an administrative law judge (ALJ). The ALJ determined that the SCSPA was entitled to sovereign immunity because it was an arm of the state and dismissed the complaint. The cruise ship operator decided not to appeal the case.

The FMC nevertheless decided to review the ALJ's ruling and reversed the ALJ's decision on the grounds that Congress had given it the authority to adjudicate such complaints. SCSPA then filed an appeal with the U.S. Court of Appeals for the Fourth Circuit, which reversed the FMC's decision. The court found that the FMC's procedure for resolving private complaints "walks, talks, and squawks very much like a lawsuit" and that state sovereign immunity precludes lawsuits against nonconsenting states in federal court. The FMC was therefore barred from adjudicating the operator's complaint.

Writing for the majority, Justice Thomas found that since private parties could not sue nonconsenting states in federal court pursuant to the Eleventh Amendment, they are not permitted to do so in this case. He further stated: ". . . if the framers thought it an impermissible affront to a State's dignity to be required to answer the complaints of private parties in federal courts, we cannot imagine that they would have found it acceptable to compel a State to do exactly the same thing before the administrative tribunal of an agency such as the FMC."

Justice JOHN PAUL STEVENS wrote a separate dissent finding the majority opinion not reflective of the legislative history of the Eleventh Amendment. Justices Stevens, DAVID H. SOUTER, and Ruth Bader Ginsburg joined Justice STEPHEN G. BREYER's dissent wherein he vigorously challenged the majority opinion. He argued that there was no textual basis for the majority's decision in the Constitution. He reasoned that Congress gave the FMC the authority to hold adjudicatory proceedings when it formed the FMC as an independent administrative agency. He reminded the majority that administrative agencies are a part of the executive branch, not the judicial branch, because they execute the law, which includes making rules and "adjudicating matters in dispute." Thus, the Eleventh Amendment was not applicable in the dissent's view.

For more information: Bladuell, Hector G. "Twins or Triplets? Protecting the 11th Amendment Through a Three Prong Arm-of-the-State Test." *Michigan Law Review* 105 (2007): 837–865; Brennan, Patrick McKinley. "Against Actual Sovereignty: A Cautionary Note on the Normative Power of the Actual." *Notre Dame Law Review* 82 (2006): 181–224; Chemerinsky, Erwin. "Looking Backward, Looking Forward: The Legacy of Chief Justice Rehnquist and Justice O'Connor, the Assumption of Federalism." *San Diego Law Review* 58 (2006): 1,763–1,791; Sullivan, Kathleen M. "From States' Rights Blues to Blue States' Rights: Federalism After the Rehnquist Court." *Fordham Law Review* 75 (2006): 799–813.

—Cleveland Ferguson III

Feiner v. New York 340 U.S. 315 (1951)

The case of *Feiner v. New York* raises the issue of the "heckler's VETO," the ability of an angry crowd to disrupt an otherwise protected speech. Here, the Supreme Court ruled that a sidewalk speaker had crossed the line by inciting the crowd and that the police were therefore justified in restricting his speech. This case is significant because the Court attempts to draw the constitutional line between free speech and public safety.

On the evening of March 8, 1949, college student Irving Feiner delivered a fiery speech on the sidewalk in a predominately black shopping area in Syracuse, New York. The purpose of his speech was to spark interest in an upcoming rally sponsored by the Young Progressives of America. A crowd of about 80 people gathered as Feiner stood on a wooden box shouting through a loud speaker attached to his car. Among other things, Feiner shouted: "President Truman is a Bum," "Mayor Costello is a champagne-sipping bum; he does not speak for the Negro people," and "The Negroes don't have equal rights, they should rise up in arms and fight for their rights." The crowd began to spill into the streets when two police officers arrived. The crowd grew "restless," and one bystander shouted to police, "If you don't get that son of a bitch off, I will go over and get him off there myself." Sensing danger, the officers asked Feiner to stop speaking. He refused. After ignoring repeated warnings, Feiner was arrested, charged, and found guilty of disorderly conduct and sentenced to 30 days in county jail. The conviction was affirmed by the New York Court of Appeals, and Feiner appealed to the U.S. Supreme Court arguing that police action violated his right to free speech under the FIRST and FOURTEENTH AMENDMENTS.

On certiorari, the U.S. Supreme Court upheld the conviction. Speaking for a six-member majority, Chief Justice Fred M. Vinson noted that Feiner was arrested not for the content of his speech but for his threat to public order and safety. Vinson wrote:

> We are well aware that the ordinary murmurings and objections of a hostile audience cannot be allowed to silence a speaker, and are also mindful of the possible danger of giving overzealous police officials complete discretion to break up otherwise lawful meetings. . . . But we are not faced here with such a situation. It is one thing to say that the police cannot be used as an instrument for the suppression of unpopular views, and yet another to say that, when, as here, the speaker passes the bounds of argument or persuasion and undertakes incitement to riot, they are powerless to prevent a breach of the peace.

Joining Vinson were Justices Stanley Reed, Felix Frankfurter, Robert Jackson, Harold Burton, and Tom C. Clark.

In a strong dissent, Justice WILLIAM O. DOUGLAS argued that Feiner was acting within his First Amendment free speech rights, and the police officers had an affirmative duty to protect him from angry onlookers. According to Douglas,

> Public assemblies and public speech occupy an important role in American life. One high function of the police is to protect these lawful gatherings so that the speakers may exercise their constitutional rights. When unpopular causes are sponsored from the public platform, there will commonly be mutterings and unrest and heckling from the crowd. When a speaker mounts a platform it is not unusual to find him resorting to exaggeration, to vilification of ideas and men, to the making of false charges. But those extravagances . . . do not justify penalizing the speaker by depriving him of the platform or by punishing him for disorderly conduct.

Justices HUGO BLACK and Sherman Minton also signed their names to the dissent.

Thus, the demarcation between allowing unpopular speech and breaking up an assembly because it may be harmful to public safety appears fuzzy at best.

For more information: Greenawalt, Kent. *Fighting Words: Individuals, Communities, and Liberties of Speech.* Princeton, N.J.: Princeton University Press, 1996; Stone, Geoffrey R. *Perilous Times: Free Speech in Wartime from the Sedition Act of 1798 to the War on Terrorism.* New York: W. W. Norton & Co., 2004; Walker, Samuel. *Hate Speech: The History of an American Controversy.* Lincoln: University of Nebraska Press, 1994.

—Richard J. Hardy

Ferguson v. Skrupa 372 U.S. 726 (1963)

Ferguson v. Skrupa is notable primarily because, in a unanimous decision, the U.S. Supreme Court rejected decisively—if not necessarily definitively—a pre–New Deal DUE PROCESS jurisprudence epitomized by the controversial *LOCHNER V. NEW YORK*, 198 U.S. 45 (1905). That jurisprudence, known as economic SUBSTANTIVE DUE PROCESS, is skeptical of exercises of the POLICE POWERS that regulate privately ordered market relations.

Frank C. Skrupa ran a debt-adjusting business in Kansas. His firm violated a Kansas statute that made "it a misdemeanor for any person to engage 'in the business of debt adjusting' except as an incident to 'the lawful practice of law in this state.'" The statute defined *debt adjusting* as "making . . . a contract, express, or implied with a particular debtor whereby the debtor agrees to pay a certain amount of money periodically to the person engaged in the debt adjusting business who shall for a consideration distribute the same among certain specified creditors in accordance with a plan agreed upon." Acting on Skrupa's challenge to the law, a divided three-judge panel of the U.S. District Court for the District of Kansas enjoined its enforcement, holding that the regulation violated the due process clause of the FOURTEENTH AMENDMENT. The district court's reasoning resembled that in *Adams v. Tanner,* 244 U.S. 590 (1917), a U.S. Supreme Court decision that distinguished between "useful" businesses, which states could not prohibit under the Fourteenth Amendment, and businesses "inherently immoral or dangerous to public welfare," which states could prohibit.

Speaking through Justice HUGO BLACK, the U.S. Supreme Court reaffirmed that it had abandoned the *Adams* analysis and its underlying conception of due process. "There was a time," Black wrote, "when the Due Process Clause was used by this Court to strike down laws which were thought unreasonable, that is, unwise or incompatible with some particular economic or social philosophy." No longer, Black explained: "We have returned to the original constitutional proposition that courts do not substitute their social and economic beliefs for the judgment of legislative bodies, who are elected to pass laws."

Economic substantive due process has been buried, exhumed, and reburied so many times it resembles a doctrinal Lazarus. Was it *WEST COAST HOTEL V. PARRISH,* 300 U.S. 379 (1937)—the so-called Switch in Time That Saved Nine—that signaled the end of the *Lochner* era? Or did *Williamson v. Lee Optical of Oklahoma, Inc.*, 348 U.S. 483 (1955), sound its death knell? Was *Ferguson* the tipping point? Actually, processes of constitutional change being open textured as they are, no single case can mark the conclusive end, or the beginning. Justice WILLIAM O. DOUGLAS's assertion in *Williamson* that "[t]he day is gone when this Court uses the Due Process Clause of the Fourteenth Amendment to strike down state laws, regulatory of business and industrial conditions, because they may be unwise, improvident, or out of harmony with a particular school of thought," may be formally accurate, but it misjudges the elasticity of doctrine.

For more information: McCloskey, Robert G. "Economic Due Process and the Supreme Court: An Exhumation and Reburial." *Supreme Court Review.* (1962): 34–62; McUsic, Molly S. "The Ghost of *Lochner:* Modern Takings Doctrine and Its Impact on Economic Legislation." *Boston University Law Review* 76 (October 1996): 650; Sanders, Anthony B. "Comment: Exhumation Through Burial: How Challenging Casket Regulations Helped Unearth Economic Substantive Due Process in *Craigmiles v. Giles.*" *Minnesota Law Review* 88 (February 2004): 668.

—James C. Foster

Field, Stephen J. (1816–1899) *Supreme Court justice*

Stephen J. Field was a U.S. Supreme Court justice from May 20, 1863, until December 1, 1897. Known primarily for his steadfast defense of individuals' prerogative to control their property free from government regulation, Field also played a volatile role in California history. One California episode led to a landmark Supreme Court decision.

Born in Connecticut on November 4, 1816, the entrepreneurial Field migrated to California shortly after gold was discovered there in 1849. Reestablishing his law practice in Marysville, Field immediately became immersed in local politics. Within three days of arriving in Marysville, on January 15, 1850, he was elected *alcade* (the Spanish term for chief magistrate). That same year saw feisty Field cross swords with two local judges, William Turner and William T. Barbour. The latter challenged Field (abortively) to a duel. In 1857, Field was appointed to the new California Supreme Court as a free-soil, antislavery Democrat. He became chief justice in 1859 following David S. Terry's retirement. Field and Terry later met in a fateful 1889 encounter where Terry was shot to death by Field's bodyguard, Federal Marshal David Neagle. Terry had threatened Field's life due to a decision adverse to Terry that Field had rendered in his capacity as a judge on the U.S. Circuit Court for the Northern District of California. Neagle was arrested and charged with murder under California law. The U.S. Supreme Court ordered the marshal released in *IN RE NEAGLE,* 135 U.S. 1 (1890). (Field did not participate.)

Civil War–era politics led ABRAHAM LINCOLN to appoint Field to the Supreme Court. To dilute possible judicial opposition to Lincoln's controversial wartime policies and to give Lincoln another appointment, Congress had expanded the Court's membership to 10 in March 1863. Field joined the Court at a tumultuous time in American history, and fear of chaos formed his jurisprudence. The stormy 1876 presidential election, which had to be decided by an electoral commission on which Field served, convinced him that social dissolution was never a remote prospect and that property—

held by individuals and protected by a strong judiciary—was the essential fortification. As the vehicle for his constitutional defense of property, Justice Field found fertile ground in the DUE PROCESS clause of the FOURTEENTH AMENDMENT.

In three pivotal dissenting opinions, Field laid the doctrinal foundations for what conventionally is termed economic SUBSTANTIVE DUE PROCESS. Economic substantive due process holds that property rights intrinsically limit government's ability to regulate. In the *Slaughterhouse Cases,* 16 Wallace 36 (1873), and in *MUNN V. ILLINOIS,* 94 U.S. 113 (1877), he chided his colleagues for not drawing a line between regulation and confiscation. In the *Legal Tender Cases,* 12 Wallace 457 (1870), Field opined: "The legislature . . . cannot change innocence into guilt, or punish innocence as a crime, or violate the rights of an antecedent lawful private contract, or the right of private property." Field's dissenting view of due process became the majority position six years after his 1899 death in *LOCHNER V. NEW YORK,* 198 U.S. 45 (1905).

For more information: Bergen, Philip, J., Owen M. Fiss, and Charles W. McCurdy. *The Fields and the Law: Essays.* New York: Federal Bar Council, 1986; Kens, Paul. *Justice Stephen Field: Shaping Liberty from the Gold Rush to the Gilded Age.* Lawrence: University Press of Kansas, 1997; Tocklin, Adrian, M. "*Pennoyer v. Neff:* The Hidden Agenda of Stephen J. Field." *Seton Hall Law Review* 28 (1997): 75.

—James C. Foster

Fifteenth Amendment (1870)

The Fifteenth Amendment, added to the Constitution in 1870, prohibited discrimination against voters on the basis of race or previous condition of servitude. It was intended to ensure that black men were able to vote in federal and state elections (women were not guaranteed the vote until passage of the NINETEENTH AMENDMENT in 1920.) Despite the amendment's clear language, however, many states successfully prevented black citizens from voting for nearly another century. The Fifteenth Amendment was not fully implemented until Congress passed the VOTING RIGHTS ACT OF 1965.

The Fifteenth Amendment was enacted for two main reasons. Southern states had been required to extend the vote to black men as a condition of reentry into the Union after the Civil War, but 16 of the Northern states continued to limit voting to white men. Some members of Congress supported the Fifteenth Amendment to address this problem. Others had more partisan motives. They believed that the Fifteenth Amendment would help Republicans keep control over Congress and many state legislatures, because black citizens strongly favored the Republican Party, viewing it as the party of abolition.

African Americans flocked to the polls once they were given the ballot. During Reconstruction (1865–76), hundreds of thousands registered to vote. More than 1,500 black men were elected to political office in the former Confederate states. But many whites fiercely opposed the Fifteenth Amendment. The Ku Klux Klan, the Knights of the White Camillia, and others waged a war of intimidation, beating and even killing blacks who tried to vote. When Democrats regained control of Southern legislatures at the end of Reconstruction, they began passing laws that were technically color blind but clearly designed to keep blacks from voting. Such laws included poll taxes, literacy tests, requirements that all voters show vouchers proving their "good character," and property ownership qualifications. Other laws made it very complicated to even register to vote. Because such laws also threatened to prevent many whites from voting, many states also enacted grandfather clauses, which waived the voting restrictions for any man whose grandfather had been entitled to vote; a requirement black men obviously could not meet. Southern states were able to do this because under the U.S. Constitution, states are free to determine what qualifications citizens need to be eligible to vote. (Many Northern states also had voter qualification laws, but these laws were rarely passed specifically to keep blacks from voting.)

The combination of new laws and voter intimidation effectively stripped blacks of their RIGHT TO VOTE, despite the Fifteenth Amendment.

One of several commemorative prints marking the enactment on March 30, 1870, of the Fifteenth Amendment and showing the parade celebrating it, which was held in Baltimore, Maryland, on May 19 of the same year *(Library of Congress)*

Many decades would pass before black citizens fully regained this right. In 1915, the Supreme Court struck down grandfather clauses (*Guinn v. United States*, 238 U.S. 347). It struck down "white primary" laws in 1944 (SMITH V. ALLWRIGHT, 321 U.S. 649). Such laws allowed political parties to exclude blacks from membership, which then prevented them from voting in primary elections. And in 1960, the Court ruled that states could not gerrymander their legislative districts to minimize black voting power (GOMILLION ET AL. V. LIGHTFOOT, MAYOR OF TUSKEGEE, ET AL. 364 U.S. 339).

Congress took several small steps to enforce the Fifteenth Amendment in the late 1950s and early 1960s, but massive CIVIL RIGHTS demonstrations, combined with the 1964 murder of white activists attempting to register black voters in Mississippi, convinced it to pass a comprehensive law guaranteeing black citizens the right to vote. The 1965 Voting Rights Act outlawed literacy tests and other Jim Crow laws designed to prevent blacks from voting and gave federal examiners the power to monitor voting laws and register black citizens to vote. Its effects were immediate: 250,000 southern black voters registered to vote within a year.

For more information: Finkelman, Paul. *African Americans and the Right to Vote.* New York: Garland, 1992; Vallely, Richard M. *The Two Reconstructions: The Struggle for Black Enfranchisement.* Chicago: University of Chicago Press, 2004.

—Ellen Ann Andersen

First Amendment (1791)

The First Amendment to the U.S. Constitution prohibits Congress from interfering with the expressive freedoms of individuals and persons such as corporations, LABOR UNIONS, and political parties. It prohibits the government from abridging or limiting freedom of speech, press, assembly, religion, or the RIGHT TO PETITION THE GOVERNMENT. In addition, it also prohibits the government from establishing religion. The First Amendment is one of the original 10 BILL OF RIGHTS that amended the Constitution in 1791 and was proposed by JAMES MADISON. While originally this amendment did not apply to the states, it has been incorporated via the DUE PROCESS clause of the FOURTEENTH AMENDMENT. Now all of its clauses also restrict state and local governments.

Many legal philosophers consider the First Amendment to be the most important of all the provisions of the Bill of Rights, yet there was significant debate over whether it or any of the Bill of Rights was necessary. Anti-Federalists criticized the proposed new constitution of 1787 as giving too much power to the national government and as defective because it lacked a bill of rights. ALEXANDER HAMILTON, writing in *Federalist* 85, said that no bill of rights was necessary because, among other things, nothing in the proposed Constitution gave the national government the power to limit FREEDOM OF THE PRESS. Thus, a bill of rights was unnecessary since it would seek to limit a power Congress did not possess. Few were impressed by this argument, and eventually Madison agreed to introduce a bill of rights in Congress in 1787. When he did that, the rights that eventually worked their way into the present First Amendment were at the top of the list of items to be addressed.

The First Amendment contains six restrictions: The government cannot 1) establish a religion, 2) prohibit the free exercise of religion, 3) abridge freedom of speech, 4) abridge freedom of the press, 5) abridge the right to peaceful assembly, or 6) deny the right to petition the government. Many of the prohibitions here directly relate back to grievances the founders had against King George III and which they described in the DECLARATION OF INDEPENDENCE.

Efforts to interpret the six prohibitions in the First Amendment have resulted in literally thousands of U.S. Supreme, lower federal, and state court cases. At the core of these cases are questions about what exactly the First Amendment is prohibiting. For example, What does it mean to establish a religion? What is speech? What constitutes a peaceful assembly? While some would contend that a literal or formal reading of the Constitution produces clear answers to these questions, most are not persuaded. Instead, efforts either to interpret what the framers intended or to ascertain what the basic goals of the different clauses or prohibitions are, or even efforts to apply a 200-year-old document to new technologies such as the World Wide Web and YouTube (which the framers could not have foreseen), have resulted in many questions about what the First Amendment means.

The first two prohibitions of this amendment address religion. When one reads the First Amendment one notices that there are two distinct INJUNCTIONS regarding religion, stating that "Congress shall make no law respecting an establishment of religion, or prohibiting the free exercise thereof." These two clauses, referring to establishment of religion (ESTABLISHMENT CLAUSE) and free exercise (free exercise clause) raise important questions in addition to the ones noted above. Particularly, what is a religion? Do religious beliefs include simply ideas or beliefs about a god, or do they include particular practices, such as a religious service, animal sacrifice, or baptisms? Does the idea of religion only refer to a belief in a god, or could not other firmly held beliefs be considered a form of religion? Is devil worship a religion?

The free exercise and establishment clauses independently serve different purposes but can also be in conflict. Generally, one can look at the free exercise and establishment clauses separately, but on occasion they can conflict. For example, in dissent in *ABINGTON TOWNSHIP V. SCHEMPP*, 374 U.S. 203 (1963), Justice Potter Stewart indicated a paradox:

> [T]he fact is that while in many contexts the Establishment Clause and the Free Exercise Clause fully complement each other, there are areas in which a doctrinaire reading of the Establishment Clause leads to irreconcilable conflict with the Free Exercise Clause. A single obvious example should suffice to make the point. Spending federal funds to employ chaplains for the armed forces might be said to violate the Establishment Clause. Yet a lonely soldier stationed at some far-away outpost could surely complain that a government which did not provide him the opportunity for pastoral guidance was affirmatively prohibiting the free exercise of his religion. And such examples could readily be multiplied.

As Justice Stewart noted, both the free exercise and establishment clauses stipulate distinct constitutional requirements, yet the difficult part is defining what both of the clauses require and how to sort out conflicts between them. Performing both of these tasks is not the product of scientific deduction but involves difficult political and social choices that do not easily yield a correct answer.

In the 1940 case *Cantwell v. Connecticut,* 310 U.S. 296, the Supreme Court declared that the free exercise of religion was a fundamental right that could only be limited with a compelling state interest. But what is religion, and what are religious beliefs? Do they include all beliefs and practices or only some? In *United States v. Seeger,* 380 U.S. 163 (1965), the Supreme Court attempted to answer this question when it sought to determine what type of beliefs constitute a religion, in this case, granting one an exemption from military service as a conscientious objector:

> Does the term "Supreme Being" as used in s 6(j) mean the orthodox God or the broader concept of a power or being, or a faith, "to which all else is subordinate or upon which all else is ultimately dependent"? . . . Some believe in a purely personal God, some in a supernatural deity; others think of religion as a way of life envisioning as its ultimate goal the day when all men can live together in perfect understanding and peace. There are those who think of God as the depth of our being; others, such as the Buddhists, strive for a state of lasting rest through self-denial and inner purification; in Hindu philosophy, the Supreme Being is the transcendental reality which is truth, knowledge and bliss . . . The essence of religion is belief in a relation to God involving duties superior to those arising from any human relation.

In *Seeger,* the Court argued that religious belief is some type of sincere commitment to a set of principles. But could a set of philosophical beliefs constitute a religious belief? In *Wisconsin v. Yoder,* 406 U.S. 205 (1972), a case involving the refusal of the Amish to send their children to school beyond eighth grade, the Court claimed no:

> A way of life, however virtuous and admirable, may not be interposed as a barrier to reasonable state regulation of education if it is based on purely secular considerations; to have the protection of the Religion Clauses, the claims must be rooted in religious belief. Although a determination of what is a "religious" belief or practice entitled to constitutional protection may present a most delicate question, the very concept of ordered liberty precludes allowing every person to make his own standards on matters of conduct in which society as a whole has important interests.

Here, the Court seeks to distinguish secular or philosophical beliefs from religious ones. But that is not an easy task. What if one's religious beliefs are quite unorthodox, involving the belief that the supreme being is some ultimate cosmic force that created the universe in a big bang billions of years ago. Is this a secular or spiritual belief? The comments in *Yoder* seem to imply that society, and not the individual, must at some point make a determination as to what is a religious belief.

Another question growing out of efforts to define religion involves identifying what features or facets are important to religion. Besides identifying beliefs, most religions also have important practices and traditions that are crucial to their faith. Many religions have communions, religious services, prayers, or other practices that are performed as part of a religious ceremony. May the state or government regulate these practices, or does the free exercise of religion give one a right to do whatever one wants as long as it is part of a religious ceremony? Could one engage in polygamy? Use of illegal drugs? Animal sacrifice? Human sacrifice?

In *United States v. Seeger*, the Supreme Court sought to determine how far free exercise protects religiously motivated behavior. The Court stated that "[t]here are clear limits here, and religion must conform to secularized rules regarding behavior. Thus, 'belief' can not be regulated, but practices can." Despite the fact that certain practices are very much linked to and define a religion, the courts have distinguished religious belief from practice, claiming the former cannot be regulated while the latter may.

In *Employment Division v. Smith*, 494 U.S. 872 (1990), the Court again sought to define the limits of free exercise and government regulation. Here, the majority of the Supreme Court held that it was permissible to deny unemployment benefits to individuals who had been fired from their job because they tested positive for the use of peyote (a drug). The peyote was used during a Native American religious ceremony that took place outside work. Here again, the Court invoked the belief versus practice distinction and also argued that because the use of peyote was illegal it could be banned in the interest of regulating the use of drugs in society. Despite the fact that the Court has argued in *Cantwell* and *Barnette* that free exercise of religion is a fundamental right that may not be subject to the "vicissitudes of political controversy," Justice Antonin Gregory Scalia and a majority of the Court seem willing to permit elections and majoritarian politics to determine the scope of protection that free exercise of religion is entitled to.

In contrast to free exercise, the establishment clause imposes a different duty on the government: not to proscribe religion or religious beliefs. The question arises, What does it mean to establish a religion? Is it adopting an official national religion? Does it mean no reference to religion or God at all, including Christmas, Easter, or Hanukkah displays? Does it ban prayer in public school, including silent prayer? These are all good questions, and it is not easy to decide what the establishment clause means.

To understand this clause, legal scholars and judges often adopt either a "high wall" or "accommodationist" stance. The high-wall position can trace its roots to a January 1, 1802, speech by Thomas Jefferson in which he argued that the establishment clause meant the building of a "wall of separation between Church and State." The reason for the wall is both to prevent churches from using the government to oppress others and to prevent the state from regulating or interfering with any religion. Conversely, the accommodationist position reminds us that we are a religious nation with a long history of church and state interaction. This interaction occurs in the form of public proclamations, Thanksgiving, and in respecting the free exercise of individuals to practice their religions. For the accommodationist, maintaining a high wall of separation might move the state beyond simply being neutral toward religion and instead actually oppressing religious liberty. Determining which of these understandings of the establishment clause is correct is difficult, and the Supreme Court itself has often changed its mind and adopted conflicting views of what this clause prohibits.

The Supreme Court has sought to create a rule to determine when the establishment clause has been violated. The Supreme Court formulated this rule in *Lemon v. Kurtzman*, 403 U.S. 602 (1971). In this case, Rhode Island and Pennsylvania sought to expend state funds either to reimburse private schools for the cost of teachers' salaries, textbooks, and instructional materials in secular materials or to supplement directly these teacher's salaries. The Court answered no in both cases. This case sets down a three-part test to clarify the establishment question:

> Every analysis in this area must begin with consideration of the cumulative criteria developed by the Court over many years. Three such tests

> may be gleaned from our cases. First, the statute must have a secular legislative purpose; second, its principal or primary effect must be one that neither advances nor inhibits religion, finally, the statute must not foster "an excessive government entanglement with religion."

The Lemon test, as this three-part test has come to be known, requires a statute to satisfy all three prongs of the test before it will be upheld and deemed not a violation of the establishment clause. Thus, a statute must have a secular purpose, neither advance nor inhibit religion, nor foster excessive entanglements with religion. While the Lemon test may sound simple, since its formulation in 1971, the debate to determine the meaning of the establishment clause has continued.

While the Lemon test has recently been used to help clarify establishment clause violations, many cases in the 1950s and 1960s were important in formulating the current law on the establishment clause. In these cases, the Supreme Court struck down either Bible readings, posting of the Ten Commandments, or recitation of a teacher-led prayer to start the public school day. For example, in *Engel v. Vitale,* 370 U.S. 421 (1962), the issue was whether the New Hyde Board of Education could, upon the recommendation of the New York State Board of Regents, begin each public school day by having a "nonsectarian" prayer read in class? Additionally, in *Abington v. Schempp,* the question was whether the state of Pennsylvania may require 10 verses of the Bible to be read at the start of every school day and allow any child who objected to be exempt from the reading upon written parental request? In both cases, the Court reached the same conclusion, that these activities were clearly violations of the establishment clause.

The particular concern of permitting prayer in school involves the question of coercion. Specifically, even though many of the programs for prayer allowed students not to participate, some on the Court felt that it would be very hard for children to go against their teacher or peers and not pray. In effect, they would feel forced to pray or take part in religious activities that they might not support.

When decided, *Engel v. Vitale* and these other cases were quite controversial, and they remain so today. Many people view these decisions as "taking God out of the schools," as hostility to religion, or as the cause of the undermining of school discipline or the loss of morality in society. Hence, there remains significant demand in some school districts to reinstate prayer or some type of religious education into public schools. Two controversial decisions worth noting are *Wallace v. Jaffree,* 472 U.S. 38 (1985), and *Lee v. Weisman,* 505 U.S. 577 (1992). In both cases, not only was the Court asked to revisit its earlier decisions on SCHOOL PRAYER, but it was also asked to rethink the Lemon test.

At issue in the first case was an Alabama law that started each day with a one-minute moment of silence. This moment could be used for prayer, silent meditation, or whatever the students preferred. For some, this moment of silence lacked the coerciveness of a read prayer that required active participation. During this meditation minute, no one would know if one was praying or doing something else. Despite this claim, a divided Supreme Court struck down the prayer. Important to the reasoning of the majority was reference to the records of the Alabama legislature indicating that the sponsor of this law authorizing the moment of silence saw this bill as a first step toward returning prayer to public schools.

In citing this legislative intent and history, the Court argued that the law failed the Lemon test. First, the law clearly was not secular in its intent but had a religious purpose. Second, the law was not neutral and instead its aim was to support religion.

Conversely, Justice WILLIAM HUBBS REHNQUIST in dissent saw this silent moment as lacking the coerciveness of the prayers struck down in *Engel v. Vitale.* Rehnquist also used the occasion to argue that past establishment clause rulings were erratic, that the application of the Lemon test was inconsistent, and that many of these rulings supported some type of state-church interaction in the schools.

In *Lee v. Weisman,* the issue was the delivery of a state-written nondenominational prayer at public junior and high school graduation ceremonies. More specifically, a rabbi opened up the ceremony with an invocation that referred to God. There was also a benediction delivered by the rabbi that referred to God. This case tested the applicability of school prayer cases to school activities that take place outside of the normal school day. Moreover, given what appeared to be a more conservative Court that seemed sympathetic to religion, there was hope that a majority of the justices would seek to change or abandon the Lemon test.

However, the Court struck down the prayer, although the justices were badly divided. Justice ANTHONY M. KENNEDY, who had previously criticized the Lemon test, wrote for the majority and argued that students really were not free to excuse themselves from their graduation ceremony and that they were in fact being forced to listen to the prayer. Additionally, the fact that the school had helped compose the prayer was also upsetting to him and the majority. He noted that this type of state composition of a religious message is what the establishment clause was meant to ban. Finally, Justice Kennedy rejected a rethinking of the Lemon test, stating that there was no need to review it at this time.

In dissent, four justices argued that the benediction and invocation were part of a long-standing practice in American history and that they had in many ways lost their religious nature. Instead, they were part of the rites of passage for graduation. Moreover, Justices Scalia, Rehnquist, Byron White, and CLARENCE THOMAS argued that the Lemon test had problems and that it needed to be rethought or rejected.

Both *Wallace* and *Lee* appear to indicate that almost all types of prayer are banned from school. However, with a divided Court, a change in a few justices might change some things. Moreover, these opinions do not indicate whether at baccalaureate ceremonies prayers are unconstitutional. Would student-composed and -recited prayers at graduation be permitted? Would prayers by players before a football game be unconstitutional? Perhaps yes, but where is the element of coercion here? Are students really required to play football, attend sporting events, or assist in writing a prayer? Additionally, the Court in *Marsh v. Chambers,* 463 U.S. 783 (1983), itself has upheld prayer before the start of Congress each day and has ruled that this was not coercive and unconstitutional. What is the difference between allowing that prayer and what might be a moment of silence during graduation or before a sports event?

Another area of concern for the establishment clause is with public display of holiday or religious symbols. In *LYNCH V. DONNELLY,* 465 U.S. 668 (1984), the question was whether the city of Pawtucket, Rhode Island, in cooperation with its downtown merchants, could erect a Christmas display in a privately owned park adjacent to City Hall when that display included, among other things, a Santa Claus and a crèche or Nativity scene that was owned by the city. Writing for a majority of the Court, Chief Justice WARREN E. BURGER held that this display was permissible and that it was not a violation of the establishment clause. Burger rejected the high wall theory of the establishment clause and argued instead that there was a long history of governmental accommodation with religion in America. After indicating that neither U.S. history nor the intent of the Founding Fathers seemed hostile to some church-state interaction, Burger proceeded to use the Lemon test to indicate that the establishment clause would not preclude the type of display found in Pawtucket.

In applying the three-part Lemon test, Chief Justice Burger failed to find an excessive entanglement. He observed that the cost of the crèche and its maintenance were small and that the crèche was displayed next to other items, such as reindeer, which were not religious but more symbolic of the secular holiday mood of goodwill and cheer. Because of this context of several different symbols, Burger concluded for the Court: "We are satisfied that the City has a secular purpose for including the crèche, that the City has not impermissibly advanced religion, and that including the crèche does not create excessive entanglement between religion and government."

In dissent, Justice WILLIAM J. BRENNAN, JR., and the minority argued that in fact an excessive entanglement had occurred and that both the first and third prongs of the Lemon test had been violated. Brennan's argument was that while perhaps up to this point there was no excessive entanglement between Pawtucket or other cities and churches, this decision would potentially lead to conflicts in the future. This is exactly what happened in Pittsburgh, Pennsylvania, a few years later in *Allegheny v. ACLU,* 492 U.S. 573 (1989).

The city of Pittsburgh sought to erect a Christmas crèche on the grand staircase of the Allegheny County courthouse and place a menorah outside the city-county building, next to a Christmas tree and a sign saluting Lady Liberty. Four justices, Kennedy, White, Rehnquist, and JOHN PAUL STEVENS would have upheld both displays as constitutional; three justices, Thurgood Marshall, Stevens, and Brennan, would have struck down both; Justices SANDRA DAY O'CONNOR and Harry A. Blackmun struck down the first display but permitted the menorah. The result was that the display of the crèche, even though it was next to other displays including a Santa Claus, was found to violate the establishment clause because it was a state endorsement of religion. However, the display of the menorah was found to be constitutional because, for the Court, the "menorah's message is not exclusively religious. The menorah is the primary visual symbol for a holiday that, like Christmas, has both religious and secular dimensions." Hence, while the crèche in Pawtucket was not religious, in Pittsburgh it was, despite the fact that the display of the menorah was not. In reaching all three of these holdings, the Court sought to use the same Lemon test to interpret the same establishment clause. Despite what would appear to be an easy task, nine justices could not agree on the correct result dictated by past rulings and the Constitution, and it is not easy to determine who, if any, of the justices was correct.

A final establishment clause issue occurs where particular religious views might endorse a specific set of laws or public policies. For example, religious views on the sabbath were once influential in the passage of "blue laws." Blue laws prevented certain types of businesses from being open on Sunday. In two cases, *Gallagher v. Crown Kosher Super Market,* 366 U.S. 616 (1961), and *Braunfeld v. Brown,* 366 U.S. 599 (1961), Orthodox Jewish merchants objected to these laws. The basis of their objection was that since they were already closed on Saturday, the Jewish sabbath, the Sunday closing law forced them to close an additional day, and it hurt their businesses. The Supreme Court rejected their claims, indicating that there was an independent secular rule for the Sunday closings despite the religious origin of these laws and the impact they had on Orthodox Jews.

The prohibition on the abridgment of free speech raises the most questions. For example, does it prevent the government from passing any laws regulating or prohibiting speech? A literal or absolutist reading of the text of the First Amendment would seem to suggest that. However, there are numerous exceptions the courts have made to this. On one level, criminal laws making extortion or blackmail illegal regulate speech but nonetheless have been upheld because they are not the kind of speech the First Amendment was meant to protect.

There are competing philosophies regarding what the free speech clause is supposed to protect. One school of thought, as articulated by Alexander Meiklejohn, argues that the First Amendment's core purpose is to protect the political speech of individuals. Steve Shiffrin believes that it is to protect the right to criticize, while Thomas Emerson sees its purpose as to promote self-expression. Lee Bollinger argues that the First Amendment seeks to help promote toleration. These competing perspectives on the free speech clause are more than academic; they affect what types of speech or communications will receive protection. In effect, they will decide what counts as speech for the purposes of the First Amendment.

Over time, the Supreme Court has examined numerous types of communication and found them to be speech. These include flag burning (*TEXAS V. JOHNSON,* 491 U.S. 397 [1987]), CROSS BURNING (*R.A.V. V. ST. PAUL,* 505 U.S. 377 [1992]), the use of offensive language in a court (*COHEN V. CALIFORNIA,* 283 U.S. 359 [1971]), and sexually explicit materials (*Miller v. California*, 413 U.S. 15 [1973]). Conversely, the Court has stated that libel is not speech (*New York Times v. Sullivan*, 376 U.S. 254 [1964]) and that obscene materials (*Miller v. California*) are also exempt from First Amendment protection. There is then a category of communications that may be speech but nonetheless either entitled to some or very little First Amendment protection. For example, nude but nonobscene dancing is expressive, but it does not receive much constitutional protection (*Barnes v. Glen Theatre*, 501 U.S. 560 [1991]), and money is not speech, but it may receive some First Amendment protections in the context of political contributions and expenditures (*Buckley v. Valeo*, 424 U.S. 1 [1976]).

The test for when something is or is not protected by the First Amendment has evolved over time. Initially, William Blackstone in his book *Commentaries on the Laws of England*, which was influential in early American law, argued that seditious libel (criticism of the government) was the goal of free speech. The 1735 New York acquittal of publisher Peter Zenger in colonial America on charges of seditious libel against the British government reaffirmed this notion of what free speech protected.

Modern notions regarding the scope of the protections of the First Amendment free speech clause begin in *Schenck v. United States*, 249 U.S. 47 (1919). Here, in upholding the conviction of two individuals accused of violating the 1917 Espionage Act during World War I by seeking to disrupt military recruitment, Justice Oliver Wendell Holmes, Jr., stated that speech was no longer protected under the First Amendment when it posed a "clear and present danger" that it would bring about the evils Congress intended to prevent.

In *Masses Publishing Co. v. Patten*, 244 Fed. 535 (D.NY) (1917), Judge Learned Hand adopted the "incitement" test to decide on the scope of free speech, arguing that if the speech stops just short of inciting or urging others to break the law, it is protected under the First Amendment. The incitement and clear and present danger tests became encapsulated into the "imminent lawless" test in *Brandenburg v. Ohio*, 395 U.S 444 (1969), when the Court stated that speech is protected until such time as it advocates imminent lawlessness or violence that is actually imminent. In effect, mere advocacy of ideas or beliefs is protected by the First Amendment, regardless, it appears, of what those ideas advocate.

Another issue affecting interpretations of the free speech clause is whom and what it protects. Historically, the First Amendment only protected individual speech. However, the Supreme Court has also extended free speech protections to, for example, corporations, labor unions, and political parties, in some cases ruling that commercial speech or advertising is entitled to some First Amendment protection. Finally, in interpreting the First Amendment, the Supreme Court has had to address issues of how to regulate speech on public property, when it involves government employees, when speech and nonspeech activity are intertwined, and in the context of new technologies such as the World Wide Web and the Internet. In all these areas, complex rules have been fashioned to interpret what the First Amendment prohibits.

Freedom of the press is a fourth protection found in the First Amendment. The trial of Peter Zenger seemed to establish a broad right to use the press to criticize the government. In fact, during the Revolutionary War, pamphlets and the presses were routinely used to criticize the British, and the battle over ratification of the 1787 Constitution was fought in part in the newspapers. Three cases define the current framework for freedom of press under the First Amendment. In *Near v. Minnesota*, 283 U.S. 697 (1931), the Supreme Court struck down as unconstitutional a Minnesota law that made it illegal to publish "obscene, lewd, and lascivious" or "malicious" materials. The law gave a judge the power to shut down a paper that violated or attempted to violate this law. The Court ruled that this law constituted prior restraint, which was prohibited under the First Amendment.

In *New York Times v. Sullivan*, the Court voided an Alabama law and verdict that found a newspaper had committed libel in publishing material that contained some inaccuracies in its criticism of a public official. The Court ruled that unless one demonstrated actual malice, the criticism of a public official would not be found to be libelous. *New York Times* was heralded as a monumental defense of freedom of press, vindicating constitutionally what the trial of Zenger had begun. Finally, in *New York Times v. United States*, 403 U.S. 713 (1971), the Supreme Court upheld the decision of a paper to publish the Pentagon Papers, classified information critical of the United States's involvement in Vietnam. As in *Near*, the Court ruled against censorship.

Freedom of the press addresses other issues, too. For example, are reporters required to divulge sources in their stories when subpoenaed? In *Branzburg v. Hayes*, 408 U.S. 665 (1972), the Supreme Court rejected claims that the First Amendment contained a shield law protecting reporters. However, many states do have shield laws, and the federal government has debated enacting one. In addition, the First Amendment seems to treat print, radio, television, and the Internet differently. Because the public owns the television and radio airwaves, the Court has been more willing to allow some regulation of speech, especially to prevent minors from viewing sexually explicit materials, in particular during prime and day time and on the major networks. Different rules have been allowed for cable. However, the Court has given more protection for print materials, and increasingly it seems to be rejecting content regulation on the Internet.

The right to a peaceful assembly is a fifth protection found in the First Amendment. In *NAACP v. Alabama*, 357 U.S. 449 (1959), a unanimous Supreme Court ruled that Alabama's request of a CIVIL RIGHTS group to make its membership list public infringed on its right of freedom of association. In *Roberts v. United States Jaycees*, 468 U.S. 609 (1984), the Court rejected freedom of association claims on the part of the Jaycees to refuse to admit women to their organization as members. However, in *BOY SCOUTS V. DALE*, 530 U.S. 640 (2000), and in *HURLEY V. IRISH-AMERICAN GAY, LESBIAN & BISEXUAL GROUP OF BOSTON*, 515 U.S. 557 (1995), the Court upheld exclusion of homosexuals from membership in the Boy Scouts or from marching in a St. Patrick's Day parade. In both cases, the Court ruled that freedom of association also entailed the right not to associate with others. In other contexts, the right of freedom of association has been invoked by political parties to restrict who can participate in their primaries.

Finally, the right to petition the government is often ignored in litigation and has often been examined under the right of assembly and association decisions as in *BUCKLEY V. AMERICAN CONSTITUTIONAL LAW FOUNDATION*, 525 U.S. 182 (1999), where the Court struck down some requirements a state had imposed on individuals hired to gather signatures for ballot propositions. The right to petition the government also includes the right of individuals and groups to hire lobbyists to advocate on their behalf.

Overall, the First Amendment contains numerous protections for expressive freedoms that are critical both to self-identity and to the functioning of a democracy. The amendment touches issues ranging from music and art censorship to prayer in school and political demonstrations. Given this breadth, it is not surprising that there are perhaps more controversy and litigation surrounding it than any other amendment.

For more information: Bollinger, Lee C. *The Tolerant Society: Freedom of Speech and Extremist Speech in America.* New York: Oxford University Press, 1986; Emerson, Thomas I. *Toward a General Theory of the First Amendment.* New York: Random House, 1966; Harry Kalven, Jr. *A Worthy Tradition: Freedom of Speech in America.* New York: Harper & Row, 1988; Meiklejohn, Alexander. *Free Speech and its Relation to Self-Government.* New York: Harper & Row, 1948; Shiffrin, Steven. *The First Amendment, Democracy, and Romance.* Cambridge, Mass.: Harvard University Press, 1990.

—David Schultz

flag burning amendment

The flag burning amendment refers to efforts to overturn a Supreme Court decision that made the act of burning the American flag a protected FIRST AMENDMENT expression.

In June 1989, the U.S. Supreme Court issued a controversial decision in the case *TEXAS V. JOHNSON*, 491 U.S. 397. In that decision, it held a man convicted under a Texas law for burning an American flag at the 1984 Republican Convention was engaged in protected speech and reversed his conviction. The decision set off a firestorm of protest from many quarters and led several groups and politicians to call for an amendment to the Constitution to protect the flag from desecration.

Immediately after the decision was handed down by the Supreme Court, individuals began to call for a constitutional amendment to protect the flag. Senator George Mitchell said: "I do not believe that Americans have to see the flag, that symbolizes their freedom to speak, devalued and cheapened in the cause of preserving that freedom." On June 20, 1989, President George H. W. Bush also called for a constitutional amendment to protect the flag, stating, "But before we accept dishonor to our flag, we must ask ourselves how many have died, following the order to 'Save the Colors!'"

The HOUSE OF REPRESENTATIVES held hearings on the flag amendment in July. During the hearings, the committee heard from veterans on both sides of the question. Pro-amendment speakers emphasized the patriotic appeal of the flag as a symbol of national pride and honor. Anti-amendment speakers emphasized the flag as a symbol of freedom and argued that the amendment would undermine constitutional guarantees of freedom of speech.

In September 1989, the SENATE subcommittee voted to recommend a statute protecting the flag but rejected a constitutional amendment.

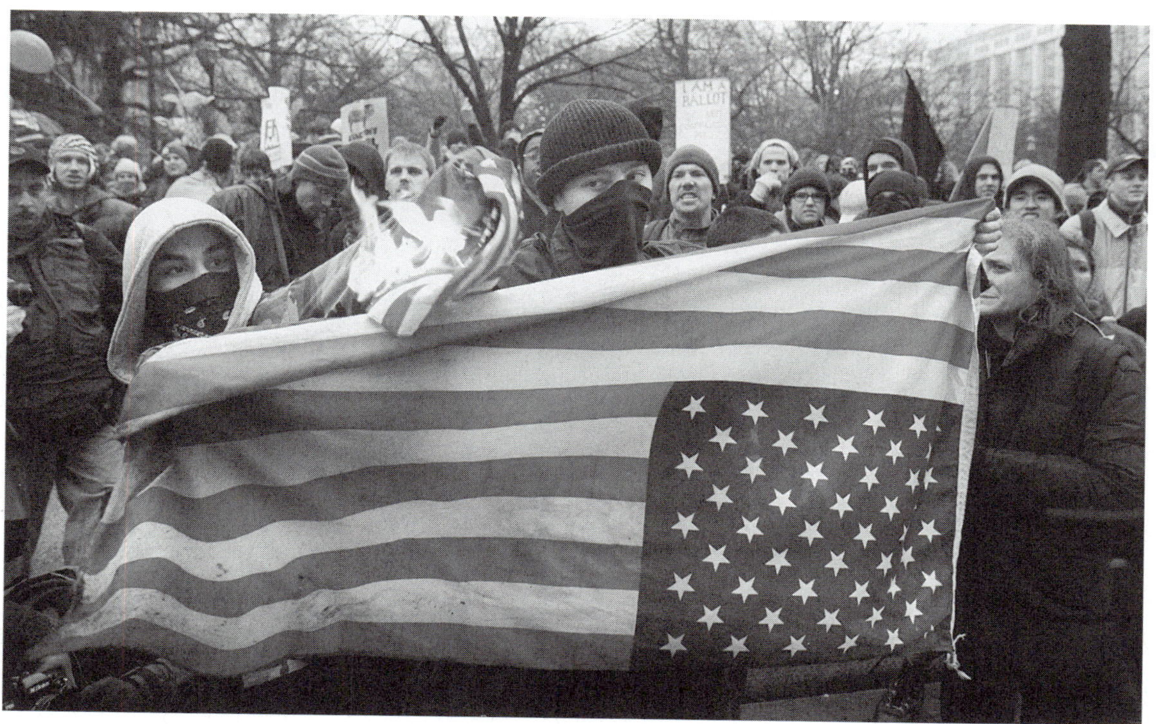

Protesters burn an American flag in Washington, D.C., at the inauguration of President George W. Bush. *(Levine/Getty Images)*

The House of Representatives supported a statute later that month by a wide margin. In October, the Senate rejected a constitutional amendment by a 51-48 vote.

In June 1990, the Supreme Court struck down the statute that had been enacted in a case styled *United States v. Eichman,* 496 U.S. 310. That month a poll revealed that 59 percent of Americans supported a constitutional amendment to protect the flag. Once again, however, the flag amendment was defeated. Pro-amendment speakers spent much of their time on the defensive arguing that the amendment would not be a threat to freedom of speech and was consistent with the national commitment to the Constitution. Anti-amendment speakers focused on the strengths of the constitutional system and supported broad First Amendment interpretations. Anti-amendment forces also relied heavily on individuals with military service to bolster their case that the proposed amendment was not needed to honor veterans.

Since 1990, there have been various attempts to resurrect the flag amendment with little success. The attempts have generally been pushed by some veterans groups and occasionally used to embarrass political opponents. However, since the wave of flag burnings predicted by the pro-amendment side has never materialized, there has been less and less public passion about the issue.

For more information: Goldstein, Robert Justin. *Flag Burning and Free Speech: The Case of* Texas v. Johnson. Lawrence: University Press of Kansas, 2000; Howard, Charles. *A Lonely Place of Honor: A Rhetorical Analysis of the Movement to Amend the Constitution to Prevent Flag Burning.* Dissertation. University of Kansas, 1992.

—Charles Howard

Flast v. Cohen 392 U.S. 83 (1968)

In *Flast v. Cohen,* the Supreme Court ruled that taxpayers had STANDING to challenge in federal court the constitutionality of how the federal government spent money.

Florance Flast and a number of other taxpayers challenged the constitutionality of the Elementary and Secondary Education Act of 1965, which called for federal monies to be spent on instructional materials for use in religious schools. Flast et al, challenged the act on the grounds that spending money in this way would violate the FIRST AMENDMENT's prohibition on the establishment of religion and its guarantee of free exercise of religion.

The Court held, by an 8-1 vote, that Flast et al. did have standing to challenge the constitutionality of taxpayer monies that would be spent under the law's provisions. In Chief Justice Earl Warren's majority opinion, he first distinguished this case from the Court's ruling in *Frothingham v. Mellon,* 262 U.S. 447 (1923). In *Frothingham,* the Court held that, in the main, most taxpayer suits challenging how the federal government exercised its taxing and spending power would fail to allege the type of direct injury necessary to gain standing in federal court.

Was the general rule in *Frothingham* applicable in *Flast*? According to the Court majority, the answer was no. First, Warren stated that the *Frothingham* ruling was not necessarily a constitutional requirement, that it was rooted in a policy concern that the federal courts not get bogged down with frivolous taxpayer lawsuits. Instead, Warren announced a two-part test to guide federal courts in deciding whether taxpayers had standing to sue over how federal monies were spent. Part one of the test was whether a taxpayer had established "a logical link between that status and the type of legislative enactment attacked." This meant that a taxpayer could show standing only if the expenditure was an exercise of congressional taxing and spending power, and not just an incidental expenditure per a regulatory scheme. Part two of the test was that taxpayers had to show how a specific constitutional limitation had bearing on Congress's taxing and spending power (such as the First Amendment).

As applied to these case facts, the monies being spent under the act were done so per Congress's taxing and spending authority (thus, satisfying the first part of the test). Additionally, as Flast et al, were alleging a specific constitutional infringement, that is, violation of the First Amendment's

ESTABLISHMENT CLAUSE, Flast satisfied the second part of the test and had standing to sue.

There were a number of concurring opinions, highlighted by Justice WILLIAM O. DOUGLAS's, that would have explicitly overturned the *Frothingham* decision and allowed broader taxpayer standing to sue in federal courts than even Warren's majority opinion granted. The lone dissent was authored by Justice JOHN MARSHALL HARLAN, who acknowledged the *Frothingham* decision went too far in restricting taxpayer standing but who was apprehensive about the majority ruling's dramatically increasing the caseloads of the federal courts.

Some observers commented that the *Flast* decision was characteristic of the WARREN COURT's effort to increase the public's access to the federal courts to protect constitutional rights. Though Warren, in his majority opinion in *Flast,* refused to predict whether the ruling would lead to a slew of lawsuits challenging how the federal government spent taxpayer dollars, later Supreme Courts strictly maintained the two-part Flast test, refusing to grant standing unless the federal courts could redress specific constitutional errors related to how Congress spent tax dollars.

Despite the decision in this case, taxpayer standing has not been extended to other issues beyond establishment clause challenges. In fact, in *Hein v. Freedom from Religious Foundation,* U.S. ___ (2007), the Supreme Court ruled that taxpayers did not have standing to challenge President George W. Bush's faith-based initiatives program. In reaching this conclusion, several justices suggested that *Flast* should be overturned.

For more information: Schwartz, Bernard. *A History of the Supreme Court.* New York: Oxford University Press, 1993.

—John M. Aughenbaugh

Fletcher v. Peck 10 U.S. (6 Cranch) 87 (1810)

Fletcher v. Peck was the first case in which the Supreme Court found a piece of state legislation unconstitutional and therefore overturned the state action.

This case stemmed from Georgia, in which a preliminary bill of sale of 35 million acres of land, which came to be the Mississippi Territory, was authorized by the Georgia legislature to the Georgia Mississippi Company. The bill itself was controversial because only one of the legislators who had voted to authorize the bill had not been bribed. The Georgia Mississippi Company subsequently sold 11 million acres of the original parcel to the New England Mississippi Land Company. On the same day as the sale, the succeeding Georgia state legislature voted to repeal the original sale.

The land speculators attempted to get Congress to allow the sale, but due to a change in the party in power, the attempt failed. Eventually, the conflict found its way to the Supreme Court and proved to be an exceptionally interesting case. In what is largely seen as a collusive suit, New England Mississippi Land Company shareholder Robert Fletcher filed suit against coshareholder John Peck, in which Fletcher alleged a breach of covenant in a fabricated deed of a part of the company's land in the Mississippi Territory.

The case was granted a writ of error, sought by Fletcher, by the U.S. Supreme Court, after the original decision in a circuit court decision found for Peck. At the Supreme Court, Peck was represented by future Supreme Court justice JOSEPH STORY and another attorney, while Fletcher was represented by Luther Martin, a reputed drunkard. In oral arguments, the Peck attorneys offered an excellent case for their client, while Fletcher's attorney offered a weak case by failing to address two major disputes of the case.

Chief Justice JOHN MARSHALL announced the decision on March 16, 1810, and found all of the original details of the covenant legitimate. In other words, the original sale by the Georgia legislature established an obligation of sale. The subsequent repeal of the sale was unconstitutional, because Article I, Section 10 of the U.S. Constitution says that no state may pass legislation that impairs the obligation of contract. This decision was significant, in part, because the justices originally were not sure they should hear the case based on its collusive nature.

The decision in the case was made possible by several contributing factors, this despite there being no specific constitutional provision that allows the Supreme Court to invalidate state laws. First, the Court had already decided *MARBURY V. MADISON* (1803), which provided for JUDICIAL REVIEW. Second, due to the collusive nature of the case, the parties themselves would not object to outcome; indeed, that was the desired outcome of the case. Moreover, the political trend leading up to the decision was that the national courts had allowed the Jefferson administration to build the powers of the presidency and Congress; meanwhile, the political institutions had allowed the Courts to nationalize power.

For more information: Lynch, Joseph M. "*Fletcher v. Peck:* The Nature of the Contract Clause." *Seton Hall Law Review* 13 (1982): 1–20; Robertson, Lindsay G. "'A Mere Feigned Case': Rethinking the *Fletcher v. Peck* Conspiracy and Early Republican Legal Culture." *Utah Law Review* (2000): 249–265.

—Tobias T. Gibson

Florida Prepaid Postsecondary Education Expense Board v. College Savings Bank 527 U.S. 627 U.S. (1999) and *College Savings Bank v. Florida Prepaid Postsecondary Education Expense Board* 527 U.S. 666 (1999)

Florida Prepaid Postsecondary Education Expense Board v. College Savings Bank and *College Savings Bank v. Florida Prepaid Postsecondary Education Expense Board* were two related decisions arising out of the same sets of facts, in which the Supreme Court limited Congress's authority to compel states to respond to private suits for false advertising and patent infringement. By expanding state sovereignty, these cases represented another opportunity for the Court to alter the balance of power between the states and the federal government.

In 1987, the College Savings Bank, chartered in Princeton, New Jersey, created a program that permitted parents to invest in certificates of deposit for their children's future college expenses; the bank owned the patent on the methods of administering the accounts. Shortly thereafter, the Florida Prepaid Postsecondary Education Expense Board, a state agency, established a similar tuition savings program for Florida residents. A few years later, the bank sued the state for patent infringement, claiming the state had violated the Patent Remedy Act (PRA) of 1992, a federal law that allowed private individuals to sue states for patent infringement.

Citing the Supreme Court's rulings on state immunity from lawsuits, the state claimed it could not be sued. The bank argued that the PRA was a proper exercise of congressional authority under the FOURTEENTH AMENDMENT to enforce the DUE PROCESS clause of the Fourteenth Amendment. The lower courts held that Congress had clearly indicated its intent to allow states to be sued for patent infringement and that it had authority under the Fourteenth Amendment to prohibit states from depriving patent holders of their property rights without due process.

In *Florida Prepaid Postsecondary Education Expense Board v. College Savings Bank*, the U.S. Supreme Court reversed, dismissing the claim against the state agency. In his opinion for a five-justice majority, Chief Justice WILLIAM HUBBS REHNQUIST found that Congress had exceeded its authority in enacting the PRA. The Court concluded that Congress did not have the power to enact a law holding states accountable under the PRA.

The bank also filed a separate lawsuit against the state for misrepresentation under the Trademark Remedy Clarification Act (TRCA) of 1992, a law declaring that states engaging in interstate marketing are subject to private suit under the 1946 Trademark Act (the Lanham Act). The state argued it was immune on this charge as well, and the lower courts agreed.

In *College Savings Bank v. Florida Prepaid Postsecondary Education Expense Board*, the Supreme Court affirmed, declaring that the state was immune from suit. Speaking for the same majority, Justice ANTONIN GREGORY SCALIA reiterated that Congress's power to revoke the state's immunity was limited to its authority to enforce the guarantees of the due process clause of the Fourteenth Amendment. The bank argued that Congress had the proper authority to enforce the due process clause, but the Court held that because there were no property rights involved, the due process clause was not implicated, and Congress therefore lacked the power to revoke the state's immunity.

In denying Congress the power to authorize individuals to sue states for violations of federal law, the Court helped change the balance of power of the U.S. federal system.

For more information: Mezey, Susan Gluck. "The U.S. Supreme Court's Federalism Jurisprudence: *Alden v. Maine* and the Enhancement of State Sovereignty." *Publius: The Journal of Federalism* 30 (2000): 21–38; Samardzija, Michael R. "Philosophical and Doctrinal Foundations: Federal Trademark Infringement and State Sovereign Immunity: A Case Note." *Journal of Contemporary Legal Issues* 12 (2001): 9–15.

—Susan Gluck Mezey

Florida v. J.L. 529 U.S. 266 (2000)

In *Florida v. J.L.*, the U.S. Supreme Court held that an anonymous telephone tip saying that someone was carrying a concealed weapon did not provide the necessary reasonable suspicion that would justify a police officer stopping a trio of individuals and subjecting them to a protective patdown search for weapons.

A police department received an anonymous telephone tip that a young black male, standing at a specific bus stop and wearing a plaid shirt, was carrying a concealed gun. When officers arrived at the bus stop, they saw three young black males, one of whom was wearing a plaid shirt. Other than the information from the tip, there was no reason to suspect that any of the three was engaging in illegal conduct. An officer approached the male wearing the plaid shirt (referred to in the Court's opinion as "J.L."), frisked him, and seized a gun from his pocket. J.L., who was a minor, was charged with the unlicensed possession of a concealed firearm. After the state's high court ruled that the search was unconstitutional, the state appealed to the U.S. Supreme Court.

The Court began the analysis by citing TERRY V. OHIO, 392 U.S. 1 (1968), which held that a police officer may 1) stop and briefly detain a person if the officer has reasonable suspicion that he or she was engaging or about to engage in criminal activity and 2) conduct a protective patdown search of the suspect for weapons if the officer has reasonable suspicion that he or she is armed and dangerous. The question in *Florida v. J.L.* was whether an anonymous telephone tip, without additional information, provided the reasonable suspicion necessary to justify the STOP AND FRISK of J.L.

The Court observed that unlike a tip from a known informant whose reliability can be assessed, an anonymous tip typically lacks "sufficient indicia" of reliability to provide reasonable suspicion. In some cases, the Court has found that an anonymous tip with detailed prediction of a suspect's future movements, coupled with police observation that those predictions were accurate, provided reasonable suspicion. In this case, however, the Court found that the tip completely lacked any indicia of reliability; that is, there was no way to assess the informant's reputation for truthfulness and accuracy, no way to assess the basis of the informant's knowledge, and no way to hold them responsible if the allegations are false. The tip also lacked the predictive information that might have allowed the police to assess the information's reliability. The fact that the officer discovered a gun in J.L.'s pocket was not relevant because, under the rule in *Terry*, the officer must have reasonable suspicion before stopping a suspect and subjecting the person to a patdown. In light of the foregoing, the Court concluded that the telephone tip did not provide the officers with reasonable suspicion. As a result, the patdown search was unconstitutional, and the gun was, therefore, inadmissible under the EXCLUSIONARY RULE.

For more information: Drummond, Rob. "*Florida v. J.L.*: Phone Calls, Guns, and Searches." *American Journal of Criminal Law* 27 (2000):

415–420; LaFave, Wayne R, Jerold H. Israel, and Nancy J. King. *Criminal Procedure.* 4th ed. St. Paul, Minn.: Thomson/West, 2004.

—Steven B. Dow

footnote four

Footnote four is the most famous and influential footnote in American constitutional law because it provides the framework for analysis of constitutional questions by distinguishing between laws deserving strict judicial scrutiny and those entitled to only minimal scrutiny.

When Justice Harlan Fiske Stone wrote the opinion in *U.S. v. Caroline Products Co.*, 304 U.S. 144 (1938), and its footnote four, the Supreme Court had abandoned an agenda that had actively protected economic interests and property rights from state and national government regulation. His *Caroline Products* decision confirmed the Court's altered agenda when it rejected a DUE PROCESS claim that a federal statute forbidding interstate shipment of adulterated milk was unconstitutional. In the past, he supported the regulation because the congressional record provided a rational basis for the statute. Then in footnote four, Justice Stone suggested a new agenda for the Court by identifying three circumstances in which greater judicial scrutiny of state and national laws might be appropriate: first, if the laws restricted the exercise of the Bill of Rights protections and their application to the states by the FOURTEENTH AMENDMENT; second, if the laws restricted the democratic political process, including the right to participate, organize, express political views, assemble, and vote; and third, if the laws affected "DISCRETE AND INSULAR MINORITIES" (religious, racial, and national minority groups who are hated and feared by the majority and who are unable to use the political process to protect themselves).

Justice Stone's *Caroline Products* opinion and footnote four are a defining constitutional legal moment. His opinion confirmed that the Court would continue to presume that laws addressing economic subjects were constitutional and to lower the level of its scrutiny of these laws by using rational basis analysis. His footnote suggested that the Court should not presume that laws concerning CIVIL LIBERTIES and CIVIL RIGHTS were constitutional and should heighten the level of its examination of these laws by using STRICT SCRUTINY analysis.

The Supreme Court responded to Justice Stone's *Caroline Products* opinion and footnote four by creating a two-track system to structure its analysis of constitutional questions. When the Court now considers laws that are claimed to infringe a fundamental right, such as the freedom to speak, practice a religion, or vote, or laws that create a suspect classification based on race, ethnicity, or nationality, it will doubt their constitutionality, use Track One analysis, and be likely to strike down these laws unless they are narrowly tailored to serve a COMPELLING GOVERNMENTAL INTEREST. When, however, the Court considers laws that involve economic regulations, it will presume their constitutionality, use Track Two, and be likely to uphold these laws if they employ a rational means to advance a legitimate government interest. To these two tracks, the Court has added an Intermediate Track, which it uses to examine quasi-suspect laws that may discriminate on the basis of gender or illegitimacy and to uphold these laws only if they are substantially related to the achievement of an important governmental objective.

For more information: Miller, Geoffroy. "The True Story of Carolina Products." In *Supreme Court Review 1987* edited by Philip B. Kurland, Gerhard Casper, and J. Hutchison, 397–428. Chicago: University of Chicago Press Journals, 1988; Tribe, Laurence. *American Constitutional Law.* 3d ed. New York: Foundation Press, 2000.

—William Crawford Green

foreign affairs and the Constitution

The realm of foreign affairs has often presented unique and complex legal and constitutional questions in the United States, because the Constitution divides foreign relations authority between the legislative and executive branches of government, with a significant sharing of these responsibilities. For example, the power to engage in a military operation is authorized in both Article I—granting Congress the authority to declare war and to raise and establish the military—and Article II—authorizing the president to lead the military as COMMANDER IN CHIEF. Similarly, the authority to negotiate agreements internationally is given to the president initially, with the advice and consent of the SENATE. Thus, the overlapping of authority creates an "invitation to struggle" whereby the separate branches of government diligently pursue additional powers. Since the Constitution does not explicitly distinguish between domestic and foreign affairs, the judiciary often is involved in settling questions of foreign policy powers.

Historically, the courts were fundamental participants in the formulation of U.S. foreign policy because of particular CONSTITUTIONAL INTERPRETATIONS. During the early 19th century, the judiciary adjudicated several disputes between the legislative and executive branch over the boundaries of foreign affairs decision making. In *Bas v. Tingy*, 4 U.S. 37 (1800), the Supreme Court ruled that only Congress is able to declare either an "imperfect" (limited) war or a "perfect" (general) war. In *Talbot v. Seeman*, 5 U.S. 1 (1801), the Court determined that all powers of war are constitutionally vested in Congress. In *Little v. Barreme*, 6 U.S. 170 (1804), Chief Justice John Marshall held that President Adams's instructions to seize hostile ships were in conflict with Congress and therefore illegal. Finally, in the *Prize Cases*, 67 U.S. 635 (1863), the Supreme Court ruled that the president, in his capacity as commander in chief, possesses the power to repel sudden attacks against the United States. These early cases demonstrated the judiciary's assertiveness in defining constitutional parameters within which the political branches of government operated.

While the courts were active participants in foreign affairs during the early 19th century, the next century witnessed an exercise of judicial restraint in these disputes. Consequently, the president successfully expanded his constitutional authority, although not without some legal controversy. The two most prominent foreign affairs decisions in the 19th century proscribe somewhat contradictory rules for presidential authority. The first case, *UNITED STATES v. CURTISS-WRIGHT EXPORT CORP.*, 299 U.S. 304 (1936), involves the question of whether the president can place embargoes on arms and munitions exports to specific countries in order to promote peace. Writing on behalf of the Court, Justice George Sutherland relied on a quote from JOHN MARSHALL (later Chief Justice of the Supreme Court) in 1800, "The President is the sole organ of the nation in its external relations, and its sole representative with foreign nations." Based on these words, Justice Sutherland concluded that the president had vast authority when conducting the nation's foreign affairs.

In contrast to the rule established in *Curtiss-Wright* is the Court's decision in *YOUNGSTOWN SHEET & TUBE COMPANY v. SAWYER*, 343 U.S. 579 (1952). In this case, President Truman issued an executive order directing Secretary of Commerce Sawyer to seize control of most of the steel mills in the United States. Truman believed this action was necessary in order to avoid a potential strike by the steelworkers that might adversely affect the military involved in the Korean War. While the majority opinion ultimately declared the president's actions unconstitutional, this case is most noteworthy because of a concurring opinion written by Justice Robert H. Jackson. In the concurrence, Justice Jackson outlined three zones of authority for presidents in the realm of foreign affairs.

The first zone occurs when the president acts in accordance with congressional authorization. Here, the president is most powerful because he can rely on his constitutional authority under Article II and on Congress's constitutional authority in Article I. In contrast, the last zone occurs when the president acts in direct opposition to Congress. Here, presidential authority is weakest because he must subtract Congress's Article I authority away from his powers under Article II. Finally, Justice Jackson describes the second zone of authority as the "zone of twilight." This occurs when the president acts and Congress is silent, and it is unclear whether these situations are constitutional. While the rulings in these two cases contradict each other, it is clear that the courts are important in determining the constitutional authority to conduct foreign affairs. Therefore, what most individuals take for granted regarding foreign relations is the product of a long historical development in which the courts played a vital role.

Part of the reason for the growing deference toward executive power in foreign affairs involves an increased use of certain threshold issues, such as the political question doctrine and the act of state doctrine, to limit judicial resolution of foreign policy disputes. The political question doctrine developed from concerns surrounding separation of powers and the Constitution. It holds that some questions, although important to the general public, may not be appropriate for resolution by the courts; rather, they are best left to the political branches of government. In the case *BAKER V. CARR*, 369 U.S. 186 (1962), Justice WILLIAM J. BRENNAN, JR., indicated that questions surrounding foreign affairs potentially presented political questions that were best resolved by either the legislative or executive branch. Since this decision, federal courts have often invoked the political question doctrine to avoid deciding foreign policy issues. For example, a recent appeal to the D.C. Circuit Court of Appeals asked the appellate judges to overturn a federal district court decision prohibiting a lawsuit against the United States and former National Security Advisor Henry Kissinger by the survivors of a murdered Chilean general. In issuing the majority opinion in the case *Schneider v. Kissinger,* 412 F. 3d 190 (2005), Circuit Judge Sentelle stated that "there could still be no doubt that decision-making in the fields of foreign policy and national security is textually committed to the political branches of government" (at 194).

In a similar fashion, the act of state doctrine evolved from Supreme Court decisions involving the actions of another sovereign state. In the case *Underhill v. Hernandez,* 168 U.S. 250 (1897), Chief Justice Fuller announced that "every sovereign State is bound to respect the independence of every other sovereign State, and the courts of one country will not sit in judgment on the acts of the government of another done within its own territory" (at 252).

For the next 60 years, U.S. federal courts adhered to this rationale, and in 1964 the Supreme Court officially labeled this precedent the "act of state doctrine" in the case of *Banco Nacional de Cuba v. Sabbatino,* 376 U.S. 378 (1964). Since this decision, there has been an ongoing legal debate between the judiciary and Congress about the appropriateness of the act of state doctrine. In 1988, Congress passed the Hickenlooper Amendment, 22 U.S.C. Section 2370 (e)(2), which states that no U.S. court shall invoke the act of state doctrine to decline to rule on a case involving international law and property rights. Following this amendment, several lower federal courts issued rulings which limited its effect (for example, see *FOGADE v. ENB Revocable Trust,* 263 F. 3d 1274 [2001]) and reasserted the act of state principle announced in *Sabbatino.*

Despite the development of the political question and act of state doctrines, which call for judicial deference in foreign affairs, courts consistently receive cases involving foreign policy concerns. In many instances, these concerns also involve CIVIL LIBERTIES, which consequently create a legal dilemma for judges since they are traditionally viewed as protectors of individual rights. Judge Cummings of the Seventh Circuit Court of Appeals captures this judicial balancing role when he states:

> While the courts will scrutinize executive and legislative action in several substantive areas touching on foreign relations, the standard of review in those cases is nonetheless a very deferential one. For example, an area concerning foreign affairs that has been uniformly found appropriate for JUDICIAL REVIEW is the protection of individual or constitutional rights from government action (*Flynn v. Schultz,* 748 F. 2d. 1186 [1984]).

It is therefore apparent that judges presiding in the federal courts view their responsibilities in a similar fashion. The opinions consistently stress an initial deference to the policymaking branches of government, especially in foreign affairs, while at the same time monitoring potential infringements of constitutional liberties. However, as the cases above illustrate, maintaining an appropriate balance between foreign affairs and the Constitution is not an easy task.

For more information: Adler, David Gray, and Larry N. George. *The Constitution and the Conduct of American Foreign Policy*. Lawrence: University of Kansas Press, 1996; Charney, Jonathan I. "Judicial Deference in Foreign Relations." *American Journal of International Law* 83 (1989): 805–814; Fisher, Louis. *Constitutional Conflicts Between Congress and the President*. 4th ed. Lawrence: University of Kansas Press, 1997; Franck, Thomas M. *Political Questions/Judicial Answers: Does the Rule of Law Apply to Foreign Affairs?* Princeton, N.J.: Princeton University Press, 1992; Fry, Earl H., Stan A. Taylor, and Robert S. Wood. *America the Vincible: U.S. Foreign Policy for the Twenty-First Century*. Englewood Cliffs, N.J.: Prentice Hall, 1994; Genovese, Michael A. *The Power of the American Presidency, 1789–2000*. New York: Oxford University Press, 2001; Peterson, Paul E. "The President's Dominance in Foreign Policy Making." *Political Science Quarterly* 109 (Summer 1994): 215–234; Rosati, Jerel A. *The Politics of United States Foreign Policy*. 2d ed. Fort Worth, Tex.: Harcourt Brace, 1999.

—Kirk A. Randazzo

Foreign Intelligence Surveillance Act of 1978

The Foreign Intelligence Surveillance Act of 1978 (FISA) defines what intelligence-gathering activities in the United States are permitted and how they are to be conducted. Since 1978, FISA has been amended repeatedly, including revisions made by the PATRIOT ACT in 2001 and by the Protect America Act of 2007. It is codified at 50 U.S.C. Section 1801 et seq.

FISA, passed in the wake of revelations of abuses by the intelligence community in spying on Americans, prohibits the electronic surveillance of "U.S. persons" without a warrant and establishes the Foreign Intelligence Surveillance Court, which issues warrants to allow surveillance of people involved in espionage or terrorism or acting as agents of a foreign power. In some situations warrants may be issued retroactively. A U.S. person is defined as an American citizen or corporation or a legal permanent resident.

The enactment of FISA came after a series of published reports and congressional investigations in the mid-1970s revealed that a number of government agencies, including the FBI, CIA, and NSA had harassed and spied on Americans engaged in lawful activities, particularly critics of the Vietnam War and CIVIL RIGHTS activists. The law was intended to prevent future abuses while allowing legitimate intelligence-gathering activities to continue.

FISA has been criticized as both a toothless law that places few practical limits on government surveillance and as a cumbersome limitation on intelligence gathering that is ill-suited to the realities of international terrorism. The Bush administration has also suggested that it is an unconstitutional infringement on the president's power as COMMANDER IN CHIEF under ARTICLE II OF THE U.S. CONSTITUTION.

In 2002, the Foreign Intelligence Surveillance Court denied a request by the Justice Department seeking to give prosecutors routine access to intelligence information, ruling that the Justice Department and FBI had misled the court on at least 75 occasions in order to obtain FISA warrants. This ruling was ultimately overturned in the first-ever session of the Foreign Intelligence Surveillance Court of Review, an appellate court set up by FISA.

Warrant requests are rarely denied under FISA. According to annual reports filed with Congress, through 2005, the FISA court had denied just four requests out of 20,806 it received. All four of those denials came in 2003.

In December 2005, a Pulitzer Prize-winning series of stories by the *New York Times* revealed that since 2002 a program administered by the National Security Agency had engaged in eavesdropping in the United States without warrants, an apparent violation of FISA's requirements. President Bush confirmed that he had authorized the program but he and other administration officials insisted that it was a necessary and legal response to the threat on international terrorism.

Defending the program, they argued that the *Times* had acted irresponsibly in revealing its existence, that Congress had implicitly authorized it in 2001 by passing the Authorization for Use of Military Force and the PATRIOT Act, and that in any case the president already possessed the power to authorize such a program under Article II of the U.S. Constitution. In response to concerns regarding whether the president had the authority to order this surveillance, Congress passed the Protect America Act in 2007, which authorizes him to order warrantless WIRETAPPING of intelligence targets located outside the United States. While some have argued that these searches violate the FOURTH AMENDMENT, the courts have thus far not allowed suits contesting this issue to proceed.

For more information: Bazan, Elizabeth B. *The Foreign Intelligence Surveillance Act: An Overview of the Statutory Framework and Recent Judicial Decisions.* Washington: Congressional Research Service, 2004; Perritt, Henry H., Jr. *Law and the Information Superhighway.* 2nd ed. New York: Aspen Law and Business, 2001; Risen, James, and Eric Lichtblau. "Bush Lets U.S. Spy on Callers Without Courts: Secret Order to Widen Domestic Monitoring," *New York Times,* 16 December 2005.

—Thomas C. Ellington

44 Liquormart v. Rhode Island 517 U.S. 484 (1996)

In *44 Liquormart v. Rhode Island,* the Supreme Court struck down a Rhode Island law that prohibited the advertising of liquor prices. Although it was a nominally unanimous verdict, the opinions were complex and included a number of concurrences. The Court could not agree on a basic reasoning even after coming to the same conclusion about the law's constitutionality. The importance of this case lies in the Court's defense of commercial free speech rights.

The law in question was enacted in 1956 and banned Rhode Island liquor stores from advertising within the state by any means other than signs or tags within the store. The law was challenged and struck down by a district court, and that decision was reversed by the First Circuit Court of Appeals before the case was taken to the Supreme Court. The district court ruled that the ad ban was more extensive than necessary and used studies from the Federal Trade Commission to dispute the allegation that advertising would increase alcohol consumption. The Court of Appeals reversed and found "inherent merit" in the state's assumption that competitive advertising would lower prices and increase consumption.

Justice JOHN PAUL STEVENS, writing for a majority of justices, declared that Rhode Island did not meet a heavy burden of proof for banning all advertisements. He said, "However, when a State entirely prohibits the dissemination of truthful, nonmisleading commercial messages for reasons unrelated to the preservation of a fair bargaining process, there is far less reason to depart from the rigorous review that the FIRST AMENDMENT generally demands." Stevens's opinion also goes a long way to rejecting a previous COMMERCIAL SPEECH case, *POSADAS DE PUERTO RICO ASSOCIATES V. TOURISM CO. OF P. R.*, 478 U.S. 328 (1986). In that case, the Court had given the legislature a great deal of latitude in regulating commercial speech but Stevens rejects much of the *Posadas* reasoning and states, "We decline to give force to its highly deferential approach." The state of Rhode Island argued that they had a state interest in promoting temperance and that banning liquor ads was a way of achieving that. Stevens employed the Central Hudson test in determining that the legislation at issue was broader than necessary to meet the state's compelling interest in the restricting advertising.

Justice CLARENCE THOMAS, in a concurring opinion, rejected the Central Hudson test entirely. According to Thomas, "I do not see a philosophical or historical basis for asserting that 'commercial' speech is of 'lower value' than 'noncommercial' speech." Another concurrence, written by Justice SANDRA DAY O'CONNOR, agreed that the Rhode Island law failed the Central Hudson test, but interpreted the test more narrowly than did Stevens's opinion. Those who joined in this concurrence (including Chief Justice WILLIAM HUBBS REHNQUIST, the author of the *Posadas* decision) called for narrower protection of advertising but still regarded the Rhode Island law as failing the Central Hudson test.

The lack of agreement about the reasoning in *44 Liquormart* illustrates the complexity with which the Court has dealt with the issue of commercial speech. In many cases, the Court has refused to give full protection to advertising and other forms of commercial speech. Yet in case after case, the Court has established differing boundaries and justifications for some restrictions as opposed to others.

For more information: Smith, Craig R. "44 Liquormart: Unanimity without Consensus." *Free Speech Yearbook* 26 (1998): 1–14.

—Charles C. Howard

Fourteenth Amendment

The Fourteenth Amendment is one of three constitutional amendments adopted by Congress after the Civil War during Reconstruction that was meant to protect the rights and liberties of recently freed slaves. However, the Fourteenth Amendment has become one of the most important constitutional amendments ever, with various provisions of it used to address discrimination, the rights of individuals facing government hearings, economic regulation, and the application of the Bill of Rights to state governments.

The Fourteenth Amendment was originally proposed in Congress by Representative John Bingham of Ohio on June 13, 1866, and ratified on July 28, 1868. The reasons for the amendment were to offer constitutional protection to the rights of the recently freed slaves and to overturn earlier Supreme Court decisions that the Reconstruction Republicans in Congress did not like. For example, following the Civil War, many southern states adopted Black Codes and other legal provisions which limited the rights of African Americans. While Congress had adopted in April, 1866, the Civil Rights Act of 1866, which sought to guarantee the rights of these individuals by overriding the Black Codes, there were questions whether this law was constitutional. Moreover, also because of the unpopular Supreme Court decision in *DRED SCOTT V. SANDFORD*, 60 U.S. 393 (1857), which had declared that African Americans could never be citizens, there was additional concern that any effort to protect the rights of the freed slaves would be found unconstitutional.

The Fourteenth Amendment is composed of five sections. The first section is perhaps the most important. It overturns *Dred Scott* by declaring that all persons "born or naturalized in the United States" are citizens of both the country and the state where they reside. Section 1 also guarantees to all citizens that no state shall deprive any person of their "privileges or immunities." This first section of the Fourteenth Amendment declares that no one shall be deprived of their life, liberty, or property without DUE PROCESS of law, and it prevents states from denying individuals EQUAL PROTECTION of the law.

Sections 2 and 3 appear aimed at punishing southern states that continued to deny freed slaves their rights. Section 2 sanctions states by reducing the size of the congressional delegation or the number of electoral votes they have for president if they deny any males of their state age 21 or over the RIGHT TO VOTE. It does provide for one exception: States may deny individuals the right to vote if they have participated in a rebellion or a crime. This exception was cited by the Supreme Court in a controversial decision, *Richardson v. Ramirez,* 418 U.S. 24, (1974), where the Supreme Court upheld felon disenfranchisement laws that took away the voting rights of individuals, either temporarily or permanently, of those who had committed felony crimes. In this decision, Justices WILLIAM HUBBS REHNQUIST, WILLIAM J. BRENNAN, JR., and Thurgood Marshall engaged in a heated debate over the historical meaning of Section 2.

Section 3 prevented previous members of Congress from holding office if they engaged in rebellion against the United States. Effectively, this provision meant that former members of Congress who then supported the South during the Civil

War could not again be elected to Congress unless a two-thirds vote of both houses permitted this.

Section 4 of the Fourteenth Amendment appears to sanction the ability of Congress to provide for pensions for individuals who were veterans of the Civil War. Finally, Section 5 was a general provision that granted Congress the power to enforce the provisions of the entire amendment.

The most significant litigation and impact surrounding the Fourteenth Amendment is found in Section 1. There, three clauses—the privileges or immunities, due process, and equal protection—have had important and wide ranging histories with major constitutional importance.

PRIVILEGES AND IMMUNITIES are referred to in two sections of the Constitution. Article IV, Section 2 of the Constitution stipulates that the citizens of each state "shall be entitled to all the Privileges and Immunities of the Citizens in the several States." Section 1 of the Fourteenth Amendment declares that no state can "abridge the privileges or immunities of citizens of the United States." Notwithstanding the slight change in phrasing in the two different clauses, what exactly are the privileges or immunities that are referenced in the Fourteenth Amendment? In *CORFIELD V. CORYELL,* 6 F. Cas. 546 (1823), Supreme Court Justice Bushrod Washington, while riding circuit court, stated that the privileges and immunities of Article IV included:

> Protection by the government; the enjoyment of life and liberty, with the right to acquire and possess property of every kind, and to pursue and obtain happiness and safety; subject nevertheless to such restraints as the government may justly prescribe for the general good of the whole. The right of a citizen of one state to pass through, or to reside in any other state, for purposes of trade, agriculture, professional pursuits, or otherwise; to claim the benefit of the writ of HABEAS CORPUS; to institute and maintain actions of any kind in the courts of the state; to take, hold and dispose of property, either real or personal; and an exemption from higher taxes or impositions than are paid by the other citizens of the state; may be mentioned as some of the particular privileges and immunities of citizens, which are clearly embraced by the general description of privileges deemed to be fundamental: to which may be added, the elective franchise, as regulated and established by the laws or constitution of the state in which it is to be exercised.

It is these rights, referred to in *Corfield,* and which were again mentioned in statute in the Civil Rights Act of 1866, that seem to be the privileges or immunities protected by the Fourteenth Amendment. However, in the *Slaughterhouse Cases,* 83 U.S. 36 (1873), the Supreme Court narrowed the scope of the privileges or immunities clause so much that most scholars had declared it dead. This was true until *SAENZ V. ROE,* 536 U.S. 489 (1999), when the Court struck down as unconstitutional a state law limiting welfare benefits in cases involving recent immigrants to the state. The Court used the privileges or immunities clause in ruling that the right to interstate travel was one of the rights protected by it.

The due process clause of Section 1 has also been an important source of litigation and constitutional law. First, due process has taken on two different types of meanings—substantive and procedural. SUBSTANTIVE DUE PROCESS was an important legal concept developed by the Supreme Court beginning in the 1870s and lasting until the New Deal. In cases such as *LOCHNER V. NEW YORK,* 198 U.S. 45 (1905), and *ADKINS V. CHILDREN'S HOSPITAL,* 261 U.S. 525 (1923), the Court used substantive due process as a legal doctrine to place limits on state regulation of the economy. Substantive due process, also known as LIBERTY OF CONTRACT or economic due process, was also employed to protect property rights. In both cases, substantive due process employed STRICT SCRUTINY when the Court examined legislation affecting the economy or property rights. It was not until 1938 in *United States v. Carolene Products,* 304 U.S. 144 (1938), that the Court seemed to officially bring a close to substantive due process.

Procedural due process generally refers to the rights of individuals to have hearings or be informed about government procedures when they are facing a challenge or threat to their personal or property rights. In cases such as *Goldberg v. Kelly*, 397 U.S. 254 (1970), and *Mathews v. Elbridge*, 424 U.S. 19 (1976), the Court has used procedural due process to determine if and what types of hearings are due to individuals facing the potential loss of government employment or benefits.

The due process clause has also been important in incorporating or applying numerous provisions of the Bill of Rights to the states. In *BARRON V. MAYOR AND CITY COUNCIL OF BALTIMORE*, 32 U.S. 243 (1833), the Supreme Court had ruled that the various provisions of the Bill of Rights did not place limits on states. However, starting with *Chicago, Burlington & Quincy Railroad Company v. Chicago*, 166 U.S. 226 (1897), the Court declared that the TAKINGS CLAUSE of the Fifth Amendment applied to the states through the due process clause of the Fourteenth Amendment. After that, in *GITLOW V. NEW YORK*, 268 U.S. 652 (1925), the Court applied the FIRST AMENDMENT free expression clauses to the states via the due process. Gradually, through what has become known as selective INCORPORATION, almost all of the Bill of Rights, with the notable exception of the Second and THIRD AMENDMENTs, has been applied to the states through the due process clause.

Finally, the equal protection clause of the Fourteenth Amendment has been the subject of significant and varied interpretation. Originally, the clause was meant to ensure that states treat all persons as legally the same. However, in *MINOR V. HAPPERSETT*, 88 U.S. 162 (1875), the Court rejected claims that the equal protection clause granted women the right to vote. In addition, in *SANTA CLARA COUNTY V. SOUTHERN PACIFIC RAILROAD*, 118 U.S. 394 (1886), the Court declared business corporations to be persons under the Fourteenth Amendment, but in *PLESSY V. FERGUSON*, 163 U.S. 537 (1896), the Court rejected claims that the equal protection clause barred laws that racially segregated African Americans from whites. During the first half of the 20th century, the equal protection clause was an ineffective tool in challenging discrimination until *BROWN V. BOARD OF EDUCATION*, 347 U.S. 43 (1954), declared school segregation unconstitutional under that clause. In *BOLLING V. SHARPE*, 347 U.S. 497 (1954), a companion case to *Brown*, the Court performed a reverse incorporation, applying the equal protection clause to the federal government.

Since *Brown*, the equal protection clause has been used to challenge numerous discrimination laws as they affect race, gender, age, and national origin. When the government classifies individuals by one of these categories, such as race, the Court will generally subject the law to either strict or some other form of heightened scrutiny, demanding of the government some COMPELLING GOVERNMENTAL INTEREST before it will allow such a classification. When a suspect or SEMI-SUSPECT classification is not employed, the equal protection clause will require that the government have a rational basis for its distinction. In this case, it is generally easy for the government to prevail.

The equal protection clause has been invoked to justify or attack numerous government activities since the 1970s. The clause has been important in challenging laws that discriminate against women, such as *Frontiero v. Richardson*, 411 U.S. 677 (1973). The clause has been at the center of disputes involving AFFIRMATIVE ACTION and reapportionment in cases such as *GRUTTER V. BOLLINGER*, 539 U.S. 306 (2003), and *SHAW V. RENO*, 509 U.S. 630 (1993), where the Court struggled with the permissibility of using race in college admissions or in the drawing of legislative and congressional district lines. In *BUSH V. GORE*, 531 U.S. 98 (2000), and *REYNOLDS V. SIMS*, 377 U.S. 533 (1964), the equal protection clause was invoked in matters affecting the right to vote. Finally, some are increasingly arguing that the equal protection clause should be used to invalidate laws that discriminate against gays and lesbians.

Overall, some scholars such as Bruce Ackerman have argued that the adoption of the Fourteenth Amendment should be seen as effecting a major constitutional restructuring in the United States. It did that by rearranging state and federal power, giving the national government more power over the former than it had before the Civil War to protect individual rights.

For more information: Kelly, Alfred, Winfred Harbinson, and Herman Belz. *The American*

Constitution: Its Origins and Development. New York: W.W. Norton & Company, 1991; Schwartz, Bernard. *A History of the Supreme Court.* New York: Oxford University Press, 1993.

—David Schultz

Fourth Amendment

The Fourth Amendment protects individuals against unreasonable searches and seizures and generally requires the government to obtain a warrant, issued by a judge, upon showing of reasonableness, before one's person, home, or property can be searched. The Fourth Amendment is one of the original ten, the Bill of Rights that amended the Constitution in 1791, which was proposed by JAMES MADISON. While originally this amendment did not apply to the states, it has been incorporated via the DUE PROCESS clause of the FOURTEENTH AMENDMENT to apply to the states.

The Fourth Amendment, along with the Fifth, Sixth, Seventh, and Eighth, were adopted to provide for the protection of those accused of crimes. In the case of the Fourth Amendment, its adoption can be traced to the experiences of the American colonies under British rule. The authorization of the use of general warrants by the British government to search persons and properties in the colonies was one of the abuses alluded to when the 1776 DECLARATION OF INDEPENDENCE provided a bill of particulars regarding why the United States sought its independence from Britain.

In interpreting the Fourth Amendment, several issues arise. These include when does the Fourth Amendment apply, what constitutes a search and seizure, the requirements necessary to obtain a warrant, when a warrant is required, and what to do with evidence that has been illegally obtained.

In *OLMSTEAD V. UNITED STATES,* 277 U.S. 438 (1928), the Supreme Court originally rejected the application of the Fourth Amendment to electronic eavesdropping or surveillance. The Court ruled that only physical things could be searched and seized. However, in *Katz v. United States,* 389 U.S. 37 (1967), the Court rejected this argument, instead contending that the Fourth Amendment applied to protect expectations of PRIVACY. Specifically, the Court stated that the Fourth Amendment would apply when an individual had an expectation of privacy that was respected or endorsed by society. In *Katz,* the Court stated that individuals had expectations of privacy in making telephone calls from public phone booths. However, the Court has ruled that there is no expectation of privacy in placing one's trash out on public property for pickup. There is also no expectation of privacy in most public places or in one's automobile. However, there is generally a very high expectation of privacy in one's home or apartment, and as the Court stated in *KYLLO V. UNITED STATES,* 533 U.S. 27 (2001), the presumption is that a warrant is almost always needed when searches here occur.

The Fourth Amendment bans unreasonable searches and seizures. This phrase has been interpreted by the Supreme Court in *Boyd v. United States,* 116 U.S. 616 (1886), to require that the search be reasonable. Reasonable has been interpreted to require that there is particular or specific suspicion that an individual is suspected of a crime or that some location contains illegal goods. The reasonableness requirement demands that the police produce individualized and not general suspicion. Merely believing one is a member of a large group of individuals whom the police may think are involved in criminal activity is not enough to justify the search as reasonable.

Thus, in order to obtain a search warrant the government must do three things. First, they must have reasonable suspicion or probable cause that one has done something illegal. Second, they must then state with particularity whom they wish to arrest or search, or what items they wish to inspect. Third, the police or other law enforcement officials must obtain a search warrant validly issued by a neutral magistrate or judge.

The Fourth Amendment applies only when a search and seizure has occurred. The Court has developed a complex body of law to determine when one or a thing has been searched and seized. In *United States v. Mendenhall,* 446 U.S. 544 (1980), the Supreme Court decided that one was seized when a person was not free to leave. In

Florida v. Bostick, 501 U.S. 429 (1991), the Court ruled that searches of passengers on buses and other public places were not necessarily unreasonable or involved a seizure because one might be free to leave. In terms of a search, drug sniffs by dogs in public places do not constitute a search, nor does a flight by an airplane over a property. However, a search would include the use of a thermal heat detector directed at a house to detect the use of lamps to grow marijuana.

The Court has created a general presumption that search warrants are required to search homes or individuals. Yet it has also carved out numerous exceptions to this presumption. A search warrant is not required if one consents to a search (*Schneckloth v. Bustamonte,* 412 U.S. 218 [1972]; if the search is incident to an arrest (*CHIMEL V. CALIFORNIA,* 395 U.S. 752 [1969]; if the search is limited to looking for weapons (*TERRY V. OHIO,* 392 U.S. 1, 19 [1968] [STOP AND FRISK]); if necessary due to exigent circumstances (*United States v. Watson,* 423 U.S. 411 [1976]) or due to a public safety (*New York v. Quarles,* 467 U.S. 649 [1984]); if there is a risk of evidence's being destroyed (*U.S. v. MacDonald,* 335 U.S. 451 [1948]); or if the police are in hot pursuit of a suspect (*Warden v. Hayden,* 387 U.S. 294 [1967]).

In addition, no warrant is required if items are in plain view of the police (*Arizona v. Hicks,* 480 U.S. 321 [1987]) or if the items will inevitably be discovered (*Nix v. Williams,* 467 U.S. 431 [1984]). Finally, warrants are not required for searches of automobiles (*Carroll v. United States,* 267 U.S. 132 [1925]), border searches (*Almeida-Sanchez v. United States,* 413 U.S. 266 [1973]), or for administrative inventory searches (*Camera v. Municipal Court,* 387 U.S. 523 [1967]).

In some situations, the government or law enforcement officials may secure evidence or materials in violation of the Fourth Amendment. In *WEEKS V. UNITED STATES,* 232 U.S. 383 (1914), the Court held that the Fourth Amendment barred the prosecution from introducing evidence seized by federal officials during illegal searches. This rule is commonly called the EXCLUSIONARY RULE. Based on the *Weeks* decision, the exclusionary rule applied only to federal cases. The Court later extended the exclusionary rule to state cases in *Mapp v. Ohio,* 367 U.S. 643 (1961). However, in *New York v. Harris,* 495 U.S. 14 (1990) the Court ruled that the exclusionary rule does not bar the introduction of illegally obtained evidence for the purposes of impeaching a witness. Such evidence may also be introduced at grand jury proceedings. Generally, third parties cannot object to exclusionary rule violations; only those who have been subject to the illegal search and seizure can.

The exclusionary rule and warrant requirements of the Fourth Amendment are often viewed by some as an impediment to police apprehending criminals. There is little evidence that the two hamstring law enforcement activity. Moreover, since 9/11, the PATRIOT ACT has eased the requirements for obtaining the search warrants in national security matters. President George Bush was criticized for authorizing electronic surveillance of telephone and internet messages in apparent violation of the FOREIGN INTELLIGENCE SURVEILLANCE ACT OF 1978, which outlined procedures to obtain warrants from a special court in cases like this. While the ACLU and other groups sought to challenge these warrantless searches, the courts have not been receptive to hearing these cases.

Overall, the Fourth Amendment represents an important constitutional protection of individual rights that places several requirements upon the government when it seeks to search individuals, property, or places.

For more information: LaFave, Wayne R., Jerold H. Israel, and Nancy J. King. *Criminal Procedure.* St. Paul, Minn.: Thomson West, 2004.

—David Schultz

Franklin, Benjamin (1706–1790) *publisher, scientist, inventor, diplomat, statesman*

Benjamin Franklin was an inventor, publisher, and diplomat and one of the most prominent figures of the American Revolution. He was born on January 17, 1706, in Boston, Massachusetts. He is best known as a major Revolutionary War figure and as one of the Constitution's Founding Fathers.

Benjamin Franklin. Portrait by Charles Willson Peale *(Library of Congress)*

During his youth, Franklin learned how to print and to publish from his older brother who worked in Boston. Once he learned what he believed was necessary to be successful in printing, Franklin left Boston alone and on his own will, establishing himself in the bustling city of Philadelphia.

In Philadelphia, Franklin became one of the most prominent American statesmen. He set up a printing business, selling almanacs and newspapers. He gained notoriety as the publisher of *Poor Richard's Almanack* and *The Pennsylvania Gazette*. He expanded into the merchant sector, accruing significant wealth, which he used to finance numerous projects in Philadelphia and throughout the colonies and later the young nation. In Philadelphia, particularly, he established the first public library and the first volunteer fire department in America, as well as setting up the predecessor of the University of Pennsylvania. His personal interests varied as well; he made significant advances in science and technology, specifically in electricity and eyesight.

Franklin was a prominent member of the Pennsylvania Assembly, but lost his seat in the Paxton Boys Affairs. This setback, however, allowed him to return to England as a diplomat from Pennsylvania to petition the King on colonial self-rule in 1764. Soon after, he became more of a voice for many colonies, while arguing against the Stamp Act and the Townshend Acts, leading to his rise as one of the most famous and popular pro-American radicals.

He traveled around Britain, Ireland, and France and met with King Louis XV. Everywhere, Franklin's exploits in electrical research, publishing, and diplomacy preceded him. In 1775, as tensions worsened, Franklin's pro-American activities forced him to leave England. When he reached America, open war had already begun, and he was selected as a delegate to the Second Continental Congress from Pennsylvania. In 1776, he was a member of the drafting team for the DECLARATION OF INDEPENDENCE, which he signed soon after.

During the war, Franklin was America's diplomat to France, where he was well received. He successfully negotiated a critical military alliance and ultimately the Treaty of Paris in 1783, granting independence to the United States. He finally returned home in 1785, as turmoil from the failing Articles of Confederation was increasing. He soon after freed his two slaves, becoming an ardent abolitionist.

Although aged and in retirement, Franklin agreed to join the CONSTITUTIONAL CONVENTION in Philadelphia as a delegate in 1787. As the Convention seemed to be degenerating, Franklin acted as a calming force and power. On the last day of the Convention, Franklin, who was 81, wrote a speech that he was too weak and gout-ridden to deliver, which is generally judged to be one of the masterpieces of the Convention. On September 17, 1787, fellow Pennsylvanian delegate James Wilson read it aloud. In it, he appealed for unity behind the new government even though he and others had certain minor qualms with the final proposal. He argued that although it had faults, in his opinion, it could get no better. Soon after, he signed the new Constitution, becoming the only man to sign all three of America's most crucial and formative documents: the Declaration of Independence, the Treaty of Paris, and the Constitution.

For more information: "Ben Franklin on the Federal Constitution." Available online. URL: http://lexrex.com/enlightened/writings/franklin_on_const.htm. Accessed May 12, 2008; Brands, H. W. *The First American: The Life and Times of Benjamin Franklin.* New York: Anchor Publishing, 2002; Collier, Christopher. *Decision in Philadelphia: The Constitutional Convention of 1787.* New York: Ballantine Books, 1987.

—Arthur Holst

freedom of religion

Freedom of religion is a distinguishing attribute of the American ethos. It is also a feature of the U.S. Constitution as amended in the congressionally formulated Bill of Rights. The FIRST AMENDMENT begins famously, "Congress shall make no law respecting an establishment of religion, or prohibiting the free exercise thereof." The 13 states that ratified the constitution had varying ways of defining religion and defending religious liberties. Recognizing the differences, the first Congress chose broad terms. According to constitutional scholar John Witte, the terminology summarizes a range of principles such as liberty of conscience, religious equality, religious pluralism, and separation of church and state. The federal government was thus restrained by declaration from a legal power to privilege any religious sect or interfere with any state's decisions regarding the religious liberties of sects or individuals.

During the American colonial era, religious liberty tended to be communitarian, moralistic, and exclusive. Most immigrants who migrated to America in search of religious freedom did not seek an environment of religious pluralism but a context liberated from the control of European ecclesiastical institutions. While the religious pluralism of Roger William's Providence Plantation was a harbinger of religious toleration that would spread, most Pilgrims, Puritans, and religionists saw no philosophical contradiction in setting up community-based religious establishments in America. From this point of view, palatable religious liberty developed more from competitive circumstances, experimental learning, and the advent of FEDERALISM than from purposeful design.

The nature of religious liberty began to change when the 13 original American states turned away from the Articles of Confederation and formulated a federal constitution. Under the Articles, the union was merely a league of friendship—power at the center being diminutive. In this context, there was no need of a shared understanding of private or public religion, although a good deal of commonality existed. Each state's constitution created its own unique place for religion. Some states had moved to religious pluralism, some had partial establishments, and a few still held to full establishments. The challenge for the 1787 CONSTITUTIONAL CONVENTION was to satisfy those who felt the convention best served states' interests by remaining silent on religious liberty as well as others who wanted a positive declaration that all powers pertaining to religion remained with the states. The convention chose to leave it up to the new U.S. Congress regarding how best to deal with the issue.

In 1789 the first session of Congress began their work on a bill of rights. Many members of this Congress, including JAMES MADISON, had been delegates to the Constitutional Convention, so there was little loss of continuity. The Congress and its committees worked their way through 20 proposals and drafts on religious freedom before agreeing upon wording that proved to be brilliant for the times. The final construction of the religion clauses in the Bill of Rights effectively prevented the federal government from meddling in the religious affairs of the states prior to the nation's cultural readiness for such incursions. Such readiness was a long way off as evidenced over a half century later in *Permoli v. First Municipality of New Orleans,* 44 U.S. (3 How.) 589 (1844) when the Court ruled unanimously that citizens' religious liberties were not protected by the Constitution but only by the laws of the respective states.

In formulating the religion clauses, the Congress dropped the popular House-sponsored phrase "nor shall the rights of conscience be infringed"—religious conscience potentially broadening the nature of actions defendable as religious expression. A question illustrating the connection of conscience to action appeared in the landmark case *Reynolds v. United States,* 98 U.S. 145 (1879). In *Reynolds,* a unanimous Court ruled against religiously justified polygamy, the Court stating that human action could be regulated even if beliefs could not. The same jurisprudential latitude remained evident a century later when the REHNQUIST COURT held that freedom of religion did not give individuals, including Native Americans, the right to smoke the sacramental hallucinogenic peyote when use of the drug was prohibited by neutral and rational state law (*EMPLOYMENT DIVISION V. SMITH,* 494 U.S. 872 [1990]). The flexibility of this jurisprudence is rooted in the decision of the Founders not to federally define religion in the Constitution.

In present times, not all of what is constitutionally guaranteed in the First Amendment's religion clauses is clear, leading to a "tangled jurisprudence" according to Kenneth Wald and many political scientists. Some legal theorists follow a "thick reading" of the religious clauses while others advocate a "thin reading." The thick reading mines inferences and clues from the first Congress's work, concluding that the democratic majority had specific intent that is knowable today. By contrast, the thin reading suggests an intentional vagueness so that later generations could make the constitutional guarantees secure a framework of religious freedoms pertinent to the times. Not surprisingly, jurisprudence has drifted toward the politicization of the clauses as the only means of surmounting interpretative impasses. Still, this situation has not stopped the search for universal principles.

The Court's search for principles to replace federalism in the religion clauses gained traction with the DUE PROCESS and EQUAL PROTECTION clauses of the FOURTEENTH AMENDMENT. In *PIERCE V. SOCIETY OF SISTERS,* 268 U.S. 510 (1925), the Supreme Court ruled against an Oregon law aimed at undermining Catholic schools as alternative venues of education. The Court claimed a "fundamental theory of liberty," clarifying this idea a few years later in *Cantwell v. Connecticut,* 310 U.S. 296 (1940). In *Cantwell,* the Court decided that the Fourteenth Amendment had "rendered the legislatures of the states as incompetent as Congress" to enact laws that work to deprive people "of their liberty without due process of law." In this instance, Jehovah's Witnesses were affirmed in their liberty to proselytize in a Connecticut city without a solicitation license, while the city's apparent effort to protect the community's religious tendencies failed the high court's emerging standard. *Cantwell* thus incorporated the Fourteenth Amendment against the First Amendment's free exercise clause. But it would take another seven years before the Court would duplicate the new jurisprudence in regard to the no ESTABLISHMENT CLAUSE.

When the Court decided *EVERSON V. BOARD OF EDUCATION,* 330 U.S. 1 (1947), it formalized on a national level a judicial philosophy of disestablishment that many of the states had significantly moved toward in their constitutions—mostly on a piecemeal basis. Full-scale sectarian establishment at the state level failed much earlier because religious liberties achieved through religious pluralism within states had stronger appeal than did religious freedom accomplished through federalism between states. Nevertheless, fragmentary establishment continued in some states—state majorities wishing to discourage unpopular sects from populating, proselytizing, or creating disruptive influences in their communities. In these matters, it would take a long series of U.S. Supreme Court decisions to build a metaphorical wall of separation between church and state.

As the passage of time demonstrated, the high court found that a wall of separation did not always facilitate fundamental religious freedoms, these liberties better protected in some instances by policies of ACCOMMODATION. Consequently, the Court followed an accommodating line of church and state jurisprudence in about half of its important religious cases from 1943 to 2003. The difficulty is that the nationalization of religious liberties has put the establishment clause in frequent disjunction with the free exercise clause.

The U.S. Supreme Court faces a large challenge in finding neutral ground when one person's free exercise of religion conflicts with another person's religious belief against that exercise, or some group's free exercise seems like a public establishment of religion to an opposing group. Prior to the INCORPORATION of the Fourteenth Amendment against the First, the choice of which freedom to protect was merely an expression of federalism, each state having its own formula. But in the modern era, federalism in religion has become mostly unconstitutional, opening the way for religiously interested groups to litigate for public policy wins in a national context. Many of these contests have involved religious speech and displays, religious schooling, Bible reading and prayer in public schools, and the teaching of evolution. Major precedent-setting cases involving public education include *ENGEL V. VITALE,* 370 U.S. 421 (1962), *Epperson v. Arkansas,* 393 U.S. 97 (1968), and *LEMON V. KURTZMAN,* 403 U.S. 602 (1971). In cases involving issues of licensing, labor laws, government grants and benefits, tax exemptions, civil powers, equal access, and medical care, *McGowan v. Maryland,* 366 U.S. 420 (1961), and *Sherbert v. Verner,* 374 U.S. 398 (1963) stand as landmark decisions, both addressing Sabbath Day issues.

Some leading scholars who observe problems in the evolving jurisprudence are at the same time sanguine about the outcomes, the Court showing finesse in balancing its decisions between accommodation and separatism. Many astute observers conclude that the Court's nuanced approach is stimulative of the continuing vitality of religion in America. With the expansion of religious diversity and the development of the commercial state, the breakdown of religious federalism was inevitable, requiring a national level intervention by the high Court. In spite of some uncertainties as to where the Court's jurisprudence will lead, polls show that most Americans believe the U.S. Constitution continues to be the world's gold standard for protecting freedom of religion.

For more information: Wald, Kenneth D. *Religion, and Politics in the United States.* 4th ed. Lanham, Md.: Rowman & Littlefield Publishers, 2003; Witte, John, Jr. *Religion and the American Constitutional Experiment.* 2nd ed. Boulder, Colo.: Westview Press, 2005.

—Timothy J. Barnett

freedom of the press

Freedom of the press refers to one of the expressive freedoms found in the FIRST AMENDMENT. THOMAS JEFFERSON once said that "our liberty depends on the freedom of the press, and that cannot be limited without being lost." The framers of the U.S. Constitution ensured that Jefferson's sentiment would live on by including a clause in the First Amendment of the Bill of Rights that protects freedom of the press: "Congress shall make no law . . . abridging the freedom of speech, or of the press." Although the press in the United States does not operate free of all restrictions, the U.S. Supreme Court has given reporters, editors, and publishers a great deal of latitude in terms of what they can say in their pages, on the airwaves, and now in cyberspace.

But long before Jefferson wrote those words or the colonists fought the Revolutionary War or the founding fathers drafted the Constitution, the trial of a New York printer demonstrated the importance Americans placed on maintaining a free press. John Peter Zenger was the printer and editor of the *New York Weekly Journal,* which published articles critical of New York's colonial governor. In November 1734, the governor had Zenger arrested and jailed for 10 months on the charge of SEDITIOUS LIBEL. Philadelphia Attorney Andrew Hamilton, who defended Zenger, admitted to the jury that Zenger published the offending stories but argued that if the information in the articles were true, then he should not be found guilty for his criticism of the government. Zenger was acquitted despite the judge's instructions that he be convicted.

If the Zenger trial marked the beginning of American jurisprudence regarding freedom of the press in the United States, then the next 200-plus years have been spent determining the boundaries of that freedom. Generally, it is accepted that the press is entitled to no more freedom than the public. However, the U.S. Supreme Court has issued numerous rulings that have dealt directly with the press's ability to gather information and publish that information.

One of the central tenets of press freedom in the United States is the near total prohibition on prior restraint. This means that if the government wants to stop a newspaper or other media outlet from presenting material to the public, it better have a very compelling reason for doing so. *Near v. Minnesota*, 283 U.S. 697 (1931), crystallized that notion when it struck down a Minnesota law that allowed government officials to prevent the publication of "malicious, scandalous and defamatory" periodicals.

Furthermore, if a publisher had been stopped from publishing such a periodical, the publisher had to receive government approval before resuming operations. Although the *Near* Court found the law unconstitutional, it was not ready to say that the government had no recourse at all in preventing the publication of certain information. Chief Justice Charles Evans Hughes wrote that the publication of troop movements could be prevented prior to publication. He added that "the primary requirements of decency may be enforced against obscene publications. The security of the community life may be protected against incitements to acts of violence and the overthrow by force of orderly government." Despite these apparent loopholes that allowed the government to engage in prior restraint, the Supreme Court continued to set the bar quite high when it came to the notion of prior restraint.

In the famous Pentagon Papers case the Court ruled against the Nixon Administration, which claimed that national security required the Court to enjoin the *New York Times* and the *Washington Post* from publishing classified documents about the country's conduct of the Vietnam War. In an extremely brief decision, the Court wrote that the government failed to meet its "heavy burden" to stop the publication of the Pentagon Papers.

Furthermore, the government cannot use the back door to stifle the press when it can not get in the front. *Grosjean v. American Press*, 297 U.S. 233(1936), dealt with a state tax on ads in publications that had a circulation of more than 20,000 copies a week. The Court found the law violated the First Amendment. The Court said that the press could be treated as the government would treat any other business, but it could not create laws that would single out the media and lead to prior restraint or limit circulation. Justice George Sutherland, writing for the Court, said that when the framers wrote the First Amendment, it "was meant to preclude the national government, and, by the Fourteenth Amendment, to preclude the states, from adopting any form of previous restraint upon printed publications, or their circulation, including that which had theretofore been effected by . . . well known and odious methods," such as the English tradition of taxing the press.

Sutherland added, "The form in which the tax is imposed is, in itself, suspicious. It is not measured or limited by the volume of advertisements. It is measured alone by the extent of the circulation of the publication in which the advertisements are carried, with the plain purpose of penalizing the publishers and curtailing the circulation of a selected group of newspapers." Just as the government cannot curtail publishing under the First Amendment's free speech clause, it cannot compel it either. In *Miami Herald Publishing Co. v. Tornillo*, 418 U.S. 241 (1974), the U.S. Supreme Court struck down a Florida statute that required newspapers to give access to candidates when they ran political editorials critical of the candidates.

But the cases interpreting freedom of the press have addressed more than just prior restraint. For example, the Supreme Court has issued a ruling establishing how much the press can say about someone, even if what the media outlet says hurts that person's reputation. The ultimate defense to a libel claim is, of course, the truth. Until 1964, however, state common law governed these cases. In that year, the U.S. Supreme Court applied the First Amendment to the question of libel and gave the press a defense beyond simply the truth. The case that gave rise to this enhanced defense resulted from an advertisement related to the Civil Rights movement that ran in the *New York Times*. The ad criticized the Montgomery, Alabama, police department and contained some facts that were incorrect. Although he was not mentioned by name, L. B. Sullivan, Montgomery's police commissioner, sued the *Times* for libel and won. The newspaper appealed. The Supreme Court ruled in NEW YORK TIMES V. SULLIVAN, 376 U.S. 254 (1964), that the government cannot, under the First and Fourteenth Amendments, award damages to a public official for a defamatory falsehood relating to his or her official conduct unless the official proves "actual malice." Also, the Court determined that a public official could be libeled only if the press published the statement with knowledge of its falsity or with reckless disregard of whether it was true or false. The Court made its determination in order to promote the nation's "commitment to the principle that debate on public issues should be uninhibited, robust and wide-open, and that it may well include vehement, caustic and sometimes unpleasantly sharp attacks on government and public officials." Although *Sullivan* dealt with statements about public officials, over time, other cases have applied the principles developed in *Sullivan* to public figures as well.

Beyond protecting the press's ability to publish news and giving reporters and editors some leeway to make mistakes, the First Amendment also protects the news-gathering function of the media. Justice Byron White said in BRANZBURG V. HAYES, 408 U.S. 665 (1972), that although reporters do not have a First Amendment privilege to refuse to answer grand jury questions directly related to criminal conduct the journalists witnessed, his opinion did not "suggest that news gathering does not qualify for First Amendment protection." He added that "without some protection for seeking out the news, freedom of the press could be eviscerated."

The reporters in the case had argued that without being able to keep information and sources confidential they would have a difficult time convincing people to talk to them and give them the information necessary to keep the public informed. Despite the Court's rejection of their argument, White's opinion also noted that grand juries were prevented from using their powers to drive a wedge between journalists and their sources. "Official harassment of the press undertaken not for the purposes of law enforcement but to disrupt a reporter's relationship with his news sources would have no justification." Although the First Amendment may not provide all the protection that journalists would like, many states have adopted so-called "shield laws" that permit reporters to protect their sources when subpoenaed to testify in court.

Meanwhile, the Supreme Court has often sided with journalists when it comes to gaining access to court proceedings. For the most part, the question of the ability of the press to attend criminal trials has been settled since the Supreme Court ruled in *Richmond Newspapers, Inc. v. Virginia,* 448 U.S. 555 (1980). Chief Justice WARREN EARL BURGER wrote that the right to attend trials is implied in the First Amendment. He opined that "people in an open society do not demand infallibility from their institutions but it is difficult for them to accept what they are prohibited from observing." The press stands in for those people unable to attend important trials. Again, as with so many rights guaranteed by the First Amendment, the right to attend trials is not absolute. *Globe Newspaper Co. v. Superior Court,* 457 U.S. 596 (1982), clarified the *Richmond* opinion by explaining that "where the State attempts to deny the right of access in order to inhibit the disclosure of sensitive information [in a trial], it must be shown that the denial is necessitated by a COMPELLING GOVERNMENTAL INTEREST and is narrowly tailored to serve that interest." In other words, under some circumstances, trials may be closed.

Today, as the press migrates from traditional media, like newspapers and television, to new forms of news-gathering and dissemination on the Internet, questions about the application of the First Amendment's guarantees of press freedom to these new technologies continue to arise. Already the Supreme Court has ruled that the strictest level of scrutiny must be applied when evaluating a government regulation that implicates First Amendment freedoms as it relates to the Internet (for example, in *Reno v. ACLU, 521* U.S. 844 [1997]). And a court in New York ruled in 2001 that an online news organization had the same rights as a traditional media outlet when it came to questions of libel. The opinion of the court, citing the *New York Times v. Sullivan* case, said that the Web site in question is entitled to heightened protection under the First Amendment.

For more information: Harrison, Maureen, and Steve Gilbert. *Freedom of Press Decisions of the United States Supreme Court.* San Diego, Calif.: Excellent Books, 1996; Reves, Richard. *What the People Know: Freedom and the Press.* Cambridge, Mass.: Harvard University Press, 1998.

—Jim Jacobson

Fuller Court

Chief Justice Melville W. Fuller presided over the Supreme Court during a pivotal era of American history, from 1888 to 1910. The Fuller Court confronted a variety of issues emanating from the sweeping economic and social changes that transformed American society at the end of the 19th century.

The Court under Fuller's leadership fashioned a constitutional jurisprudence grounded on principles of limited national government, state autonomy, and high regard for the rights of property owners. Adhering to the views of the framers of the Constitution, members of the Fuller Court believed that liberty and property were indissolubly linked. Liberty, defined largely in economic terms, was the guiding spirit of the Fuller Court. Protection of private property and contractual freedom was deemed necessary to restrain the reach of government and thus safeguard individual liberty.

Although the Court under Fuller gave heightened protection to the rights of property owners, it is important to keep the work of the Court in historical perspective. Rather than making a sharp break with the past, the Fuller Court built upon time-honored constitutional themes. Moreover, the Court functioned broadly within the contours of public opinion. Fuller and his colleagues spoke for the conservative political coalition that dominated American public life at the end of the 19th century. Lastly, for all its dedication to property rights, the Fuller Court upheld most economic regulations and allowed room for moderate reform.

In its efforts to vindicate property rights, the Fuller Court rendered a number of important decisions and embraced a broad reading of constitutional guarantees. For example, the Fuller Court construed the DUE PROCESS clause of the FOURTEENTH AMENDMENT as a check on state legislative authority. The Court struck down regulations found to constitute an unreasonable or arbitrary interference with property rights as a violation of due process. In a line of decisions, Fuller and his colleagues limited the power of the states to impose rates on railroads and turnpikes, asserting a judicial role to inquire into the reasonableness of charges set by states. This trend culminated in *Smyth v. Ames,* 169 U.S. 466 (1898), in which the Fuller Court insisted that railroads were constitutionally entitled to a "fair return" upon the "fair value" of their property. Designed to protect investors and regulated industries against unreasonably low or confiscatory rates, the *Smyth* rule made federal courts the final arbiter of the reasonableness of imposed rates.

In addition, the Fuller Court interpreted the liberty component of the due process clause to encompass freedom of contract. The Court in *Allgeyer v. Louisiana,* 165 U.S. 578 (1997), defined liberty as more than just freedom from physical restraint and as embracing the right to pursue any lawful calling and to enter contracts for that purpose. To be sure, the Fuller Court never took the position that contractual freedom was absolute. Still, the justices treated contractual freedom as a constitutional baseline and expected states to demonstrate a good reason, such as safeguarding public health, safety, or morals, for laws that limited this right. In *Holden v. Hardy,* 169 U.S. 366 (1898), for instance, the Fuller Court sustained a state law that restricted the hours of work in underground mines as a health measure. On the other hand, in the famous case of *LOCHNER V. NEW YORK,* 198 U.S. 45 (1905), the Court, by a 5-4 vote, struck down a New York law limiting hours of work in bakeries as an abridgment of the LIBERTY OF CONTRACT. The majority was not persuaded that the baking trade was unhealthy and could find no direct relationship between hours of work and the health of bakers. In the same vein, the Fuller Court in *Adair v. United States,* 208 U.S. 161 (1908), struck down a congressional statute that outlawed so-called yellow dog contracts in the rail industry. It reasoned that the measure was an arbitrary interference with the right of employers and employees to bargain over the terms of employment.

The Fuller Court, however, was prepared to sustain workplace regulations to safeguard persons seen as vulnerable in the workplace. In *Muller v. Oregon,* 208 U.S. 412 (1908), the justices upheld a state law restricting working hours for women in factories and laundries to 10 hours a day. Emphasizing the health needs and maternal function of women, they found that the statute was a reasonable exercise of POLICE POWER, which trumped the freedom of contract. In *Muller,* the Fuller Court mirrored prevailing societal attitudes about the appropriate function of women.

Besides a broad reading of the due process norm, Fuller and his colleagues did much to strengthen the TAKINGS CLAUSE of the Fifth Amendment as a shield for individual property rights. In *Monongahela Navigation Co. v. United States,* 148 U.S. 312 (1893), the Fuller Court insisted that the determination of JUST COMPENSATION when private property was appropriated by government was a judicial function. The Court defined just compensation in terms of market value. Moreover, in *Chicago, Burlington, and Quincy Railroad Co. v. Chicago,* 166 U.S. 226 (1897), the Court ruled that payment of just compensation when private property was taken for public use was an essential element of due process guaranteed by the Fourteenth Amendment against state abridgment. This decision marked the first acceptance by the Supreme Court of the view that the due process clause made certain fundamental provisions of the Bill of Rights applicable to the states. Fuller and his colleagues even grappled with the question of whether a regulation could so reduce the value of land as to be tantamount to a taking.

Despite these steps to fashion a muscular takings jurisprudence, the Fuller Court allowed the states latitude in exercising the power of EMINENT DOMAIN and imposing land use regulations. The Court repeatedly insisted that private property could be taken by eminent domain only for a public use and not for the private benefit of another. Yet the Fuller Court frequently deferred to state legislative declarations of what amounted to public use, recognizing that there was a wide variety of local conditions across the nation. In addition, the Court allowed localities to impose some land use regulations. For example, in *Welch v. Swasey,* 214 U.S. 91 (1909), the Court upheld a restriction on the height of buildings in sections of Boston as a valid exercise of the police power to protect public safety against fire.

The Fuller Court's respect for private property and the role of the states in the federal union also found forceful expression in *POLLOCK V. FARMERS' LOAN AND TRUST COMPANY,* 157 U.S. 429, 158 U.S. 601 (1895). At issue was the constitutionality of the 1894 income tax, the first peacetime levy on incomes. In two opinions, the Court invalidated the levy as a "direct tax" which, according to the Constitution, had to be apportioned among the states according to population. The Court pictured the direct tax clauses as provisions crafted to protect both state autonomy and owners of property by curtailing congressional taxing power. It bears emphasis that the Fuller Court made no systematic attempt to prevent the taxation of wealth. The Court upheld both federal and state inheritance taxes, as well as the authority of states to tax business corporations.

Fuller and his colleagues steadfastly championed free trade among the states. They vigorously wielded the dormant commerce power to eliminate state-imposed barriers to the flow of goods in the national market. Thus, the Fuller Court repeatedly held that states could not bar interstate shipments of liquor despite local prohibition laws, nor impede the import of food products from other jurisdictions.

Still, the Fuller Court sought to preserve a role for the states in governing the economy. This was made clear by *United States v. E.C. Knight Company,* 156 U.S. 1 (1895), in which the Court limited the reach of the Sherman Anti-Trust Act and distinguished between commerce and manufacturing.

Congress was confined to regulating trade among the states. Fuller and his colleagues were concerned that permitting congressional power over INTERSTATE COMMERCE to encompass all economic activity would be inconsistent with the basic idea of a national government of enumerated powers. On the other hand, the Fuller Court enforced the anti-trust laws where the authority of Congress was clear, such as interstate railroading.

By and large, the line between production and commerce articulated in *E.C. Knight* governed COMMERCE CLAUSE jurisprudence until the New Deal era. The Fuller Court, however, was surprisingly receptive to the use of the commerce clause by Congress to indirectly control public health and morals, matters traditionally reserved for the states. In *Champion v. Ames,* 188 U.S. 321 (1903), the Court determined that Congress could ban the transportation of lottery tickets from state to state. The practical effect of this decision was to sanction a federal police power based on the claim of regulating interstate commerce.

The Fuller Court was not supportive of the fledging movement to organize LABOR UNIONS. The Court affirmed the growing use of INJUNCTIONS against strikes in the case of *IN RE DEBS,* 158 U.S. 564 (1895). Upholding the contempt conviction of union leader Eugene V. Debs for violating an injunction to cease interfering with trains in interstate commerce, Fuller and his colleagues broadly invoked federal authority to remove any obstructions to interstate commerce and the movement of mail. Similarly, in *Loewe v. Lawlor,* 208 U.S. 274 (1908), the Fuller Court applied the Sherman Anti-Trust Act to labor union activities. This decision raised the specter that secondary boycotts or other union actions could be seen as combinations in restraint of trade and thus render unions liable for damages. Unions would not gain greater legal protection until enactment of New Deal labor legislations in the 1930s.

In contrast to its activist record championing the rights of property owners, the Fuller Court demonstrated little interest in the claims of racial minorities, criminal defendants, and persons who breached accepted codes of moral behavior. The Court consistently maintained that the guarantees of the Bill of Rights, aside from the just compensation requirement, did not apply to the states. Hence, Fuller and his colleagues generally deferred to state governance of race relations, criminal justice, and public morals.

The Fuller Court put its seal of approval on the emerging system of racial segregation in the southern states. In *PLESSY V. FERGUSON,* 163 U.S. 537 (1896), the justices brushed aside challenges to a Louisiana law requiring railroads to assign white and black passengers to separate cars. Even more striking was *Berea College v. Kentucky,* 211 U.S. 45 (1908), in which the Court ruled that Kentucky could make it illegal for a private school to teach white and black students together. Nor did the Fuller Court resist the movement to disenfranchise blacks and exclude blacks from jury service in the South. Although the Fuller Court's record on CIVIL RIGHTS was bleak by modern standards, in fairness it should be noted that the Court reflected the racial attitudes of the age.

Likewise, the Fuller Court allowed the states wide autonomy over the administration of criminal justice. In *TWINING V. NEW JERSEY,* 211 U.S. 78 (1908), for example, the Court held that the Fifth Amendment's privilege against self-incrimination was not an essential element of liberty embedded in the notion of due process and effective against the states. Yet the decision also suggested that some rights guaranteed by the Bill of Rights might be safeguarded against state action because denial of them would violate due process. The implications of this suggestion would not be realized until long after the end of Fuller's tenure. Unlike its hands-off approach to state criminal proceedings, the Fuller Courts generously construed the Bill of Rights in federal prosecutions. In *Hale v. Henkel,* 201 U.S. 43 (1906), the Court ruled that business corporations were protected under the FOURTH AMENDMENT against unreasonable searches and seizures, but that such entities were not entitled to Fifth Amendment guarantees.

The acquisition of overseas territories by the United States following the Spanish-American War of 1898 raised contentious political and legal issues. In a cluster of decisions known as the *Insular Cases* (1901–04), the Fuller Court grappled with the constitutional status of these territories. Thus, in the leading case of *Downes v. Bidwell,* 182 U.S. 244 (1901), the Court concluded that the Constitution did not automatically extend to the overseas possessions and that the inhabitants were subject to control by Congress. The upshot of the *Insular Cases* was judicial support for the policy of overseas expansion.

The triumph of the New Deal and liberal statism in the 1930s eclipsed much of the work of the Fuller Court for decades. Only in recent years has the Supreme Court again been receptive to curtailing congressional power over economic life and to defending the rights of individual property owners. This development has triggered renewed interest in the jurisprudence of the Fuller Court.

For more information: Ely, James W., Jr. *The Chief Justiceship of Melville W. Fuller, 1888–1910.* Columbia, S.C.: University of South Carolina Press, 1995; Ely, James W., Jr. "The Fuller Court and Takings Jurisprudence." *Journal of Supreme Court History* 2, no. 120 (1996); Fiss, Owen M. *Troubled Beginnings of the Modern State, 1888–1910.* New York: Macmillan Publishing, 1993; Gillman, Howard. "More on the Origins of the Fuller Court's Jurisprudence: Reexamining the Scope of Federal Power over Commerce and Manufacturing in Nineteenth-century Constitutional Law." *Political Science Quarterly* 49, no. 2 (1996): 415–437.

—James W. Ely, Jr.

Fullilove v. Klutznick 448 U.S. 448 (1980)

In *Fullilove v. Klutznick,* the Supreme Court extended its confused jurisprudence on the question of what constitutional standard should apply to remedial race-based governmental action. Fifteen years before *ADARAND CONSTRUCTORS, INC. V. PEÑA* established that all governmentally imposed racial classifications should be analyzed under a STRICT SCRUTINY standard, the Court in *Fullilove* held that a minority business enterprise set-aside was constitutional, but the plurality decision failed to conclusively establish the proper level of constitutional analysis.

Petitioners in *Fullilove* included associations of construction contractors and subcontractors who sought to enjoin enforcement of the minority business enterprise (MBE) provision of the Public Works Employment Act of 1977. The provision required that, absent an administrative waiver, at least 10 percent of federal funds granted for local public works projects had to be used by the state or local grantees to procure services or supplies from businesses owned by U.S. citizens who were "Negroes, Spanish-speaking, Orientals, Indians, Eskimos, [or] Aleuts." Thus, contracts were awarded to MBEs even when they were not the lowest bidders. Both the district court and the Second Circuit upheld the validity of the program.

Chief Justice WARREN BURGER, writing an opinion in which Justices LEWIS FRANKLIN POWELL, JR., and Byron White joined, held that the objectives of the MBE provision were to ensure, without hard and fast quotas, that grantees would not employ procurement practices that Congress had concluded might result in perpetuation of the effects of prior discrimination which had limited or foreclosed access by minority businesses to public contracting opportunities. The objectives of the MBE program were well within Congress's spending power, and in fact, could have been justified under the COMMERCE CLAUSE or the FOURTEENTH AMENDMENT as well. Furthermore, the MBE program was not constitutionally defective merely because of the disappointed expectations of nonminority firms who had not themselves engaged in discrimination; when effectuating a limited and properly tailored remedy to cure the effects of prior discrimination, a "sharing of the burden" by innocent parties was not impermissible. The program was not under inclusive (in that the benefit was limited to specific minority groups) because there was no evidence that Congress had inadvertently excluded an identifiable disadvantaged group, nor was the program over inclusive (in that some minority businesses might unjustly benefit). The administrative program specifically provided a waiver and exemption procedure to identify and eliminate from participation MBEs who were not bona fide or attempted to exploit the remedial aspects of the program by charging unreasonable prices not attributable to the present effects of past discrimination. In addition, the pilot program nature of the MBE provision meant that its limited extent and duration, as well as Congressional reassessment prior to any extension, provided additional safeguards.

Justices Thurgood Marshall, WILLIAM J. BRENNAN, JR., and Harry Blackmun concurred in the judgment but asserted more definitively that the proper inquiry for determining the constitutionality of racial classifications that provide benefits to minorities for the purposes of remedying the present effects of past racial discrimination should be whether the classifications serve *important governmental objectives* and are *substantially related* to the achievement of those objectives. Hence, where the race-based governmental action was remedial in nature, the level of constitutional inquiry should be more than the RATIONAL BASIS TEST but less than a strict scrutiny analysis used for non-remedial racial classifications.

Justices Potter Stewart and WILLIAM HUBBS REHNQUIST dissented, asserting that all governmental racial distinctions were equally invidious and that "the rule cannot be any different when the persons injured by a racially biased law are not members of a racial minority." Justice JOHN PAUL STEVENS also dissented, going so far as to suggest that the regulation was "slapdash" and imprecise and that if the government was going to make "a serious effort to define racial classes by criteria that can be administered objectively," it should consult the laws from the Nazi regime.

The emotionally charged rhetoric and constitutional confusion over AFFIRMATIVE ACTION which had begun with *REGENTS OF THE UNIVERSITY OF CALIFORNIA V. BAKKE* would continue over the next decade and a half. However, the Court in 1995 finally eschewed any intermediate level of scrutiny for remedial race-based governmental classifications and affirmed that all such racial distinctions would be evaluated under strict scrutiny. Thus, *Fullilove* was relegated to the position of a jurisprudential stepping-stone on the path to racial fungibility.

For more information: Spann, Girardeau. *The Law of Affirmative Action: Twenty-Five Years of Supreme Court Decisions on Race and Remedies.* New York: New York University Press, 2000.

—Virginia Mellema

fundamental rights

Fundamental rights are those rights that are explicitly or implicitly protected by the United States Constitution and Bill of Rights and given their importance, are accorded special status by the judiciary. These rights include the right to PRIVACY, to vote, to procreate, free speech, and FREEDOM OF RELIGION.

Historically, fundamental rights coincide with the natural rights assigned to every human being and with those rights listed in the U.S. Bill of Rights. They prescribe the limits of intervention and interference of the central government in citizens' lives and can only be partially and transitorily restricted under a state of exception; for instance, in case of national emergencies like a war, a spate of terrorist attacks, or civil unrest, when security concerns prevail over certain CIVIL LIBERTIES and personal entitlements. However, even a partial suspension or infringement of these rights must be strictly scrutinized by the Supreme Court.

The origin of the concept of fundamental rights grows out of a series of eugenics laws that were first adopted in the early part of the 20th century. By 1914, marriage restriction laws targeting "feebleminded" citizens had been enacted in more than half the states, and by 1917, 15 states had passed sterilization laws. But "only" a few thousand sterilizations had been actually performed, mainly because nearly half of such laws had been struck down on the ground that they violated DUE PROCESS, freedom from CRUEL AND UNUSUAL PUNISHMENT, and the EQUAL PROTECTION clause. A second wave of eugenics laws coincided with the Immigration Restriction Act (1924) and Virginia's Act to Preserve Racial Integrity (1924). In 1924, Virginia also passed a law authorizing the involuntary sterilization of alleged mental defectives. This law was upheld 8–1 by the Supreme Court in *Buck v. Bell,* 274 U.S. 200 (1927). Justice Oliver Wendell Holmes, Jr., who was joined by Louis D. Brandeis and William Howard Taft, influenced by a crude scientific naturalism, a pessimistic anthropology, and a corrosive skepticism, wrote in the now infamous opinion for the Court that "the principle that sustains compulsory vaccination is broad enough to cover cutting the Fallopian tubes. . . . Three generations of imbeciles are enough."

As a result of this decision, nearly half the U.S. states passed eugenics laws authorizing compulsory and nonvoluntary sterilization. Sterilization rates dramatically increased, especially during the Depression, when few families were prepared to put up with the social protection of what was perceived to be a disproportionate number of dependent people and did not protest against the systematic infringement of their fundamental rights. *Buck v. Bell* was effectively overturned by the Supreme Court in *Skinner v. Oklahoma,* 316 U.S. 535 (1942), which defined procreation "one of the basic civil rights of man" and sterilization an invasion of fundamental interests which, according to Justice William O. Douglas, "in evil or reckless hands" could have genocidal consequences.

In *Palko v. Connecticut,* 302 U.S. 319 (1937), Justice Benjamin Cardozo described fundamental rights as those "implicit in the concept of ordered liberty" and which represent "fundamental principles of liberty and justice which lie at the base of all our civil and political institutions." While Cardozo articulated the concept of fundamental rights to determine which Bill of Rights protections are incorporated through the Fourteenth Amendment to apply to the states, his concept of fundamental rights was applied in *Skinner v. Oklahoma* when it came to the right to procreate, and it has also come to be applied to most if not all Bill of Rights protections. It also applies to the right to vote, to marry, and to privacy. Through the early 1970s, the Supreme Court seemed willing to find new fundamental rights in the Constitution. Except for the right to die in *Cruzan v. Missouri,* 497 U.S. 261 (1990), the Court of late seems unwilling to add or create more fundamental rights.

In order for the government to restrict a fundamental right it must demonstrate and pass a compelling governmental interest test. Such a test poses a high burden and it is thus not easy to restrict a fundamental right.

For more information: Morone, James A. *Hellfire Nation: The Politics of Sin in American History.* New Haven, Conn.: Yale University Press, 2003; Nieman, Donald G., ed. *The Constitution, Law, and American Life: Critical Aspects of the Nineteenth-Century Experience.* Athens: The University of Georgia Press, 1992; Reilly, Philip R. *The Surgical Solution. A History of Involuntary Sterilization in the United States.* Baltimore, Md.: Johns Hopkins University Press, 1991.

—Stefano Fait and David Schultz

Furman v. Georgia 408 U.S. 238 (1972)

In *Furman v. Georgia,* the United States Supreme Court determined that the then current procedures in place for implementation of the death penalty violated the cruel and unusual clauses of the Eighth and Fourteenth Amendments of the Constitution. The Court issued its decision in *Furman v. Georgia* per curiam, meaning that the decision itself was issued in the name of the Court rather than in the name of one justice. The decision was 5–4 that "the imposition and carrying out of the death penalty in these cases constitute cruel and unusual punishment in violation of the Eighth and Fourteenth Amendments." The cases were remanded to the lower courts for further proceedings. Although the decision was issued per curiam, all of the justices in the majority chose to file separate concurring opinions. The fact that all five of the justices chose to file separate opinions is an indication of the significance of the case.

Although the decision was named for the *Furman* case, the Court addressed three different cases in its decision. In each of these cases, the death penalty was imposed: in one case for murder and in two cases for rape. Only two of the justices (William J. Brennan, Jr., and Thurgood Marshall) believed that the death penalty was unconstitutional in all situations. The remaining three justices in the majority focused on the constitutionality of the death penalty with regard to its implementation. The concurring opinions expressed concern with regard to the arbitrary nature of the implementation of the death penalty, the frequency of its imposition, and its imposition with regard to a select group of minorities as opposed to the population as a whole.

In his concurring opinion, Justice WILLIAM O. DOUGLAS stated that it was unconstitutional to implement a penalty that society would not apply to the general population but only to a specific group. Justices Potter Stewart and Byron White wrote that the sentences were cruel in the sense that they went beyond what the state legislatures had determined to be the appropriate punishment for the crime and were unusual in that the death penalty is not usually imposed for murder and rarely imposed for rape. In all of the concurring opinions, the justices refer to how often the death penalty is imposed. It was apparent that one of the considerations the Court was concerned with was the standard by which society judges a punishment.

The decision in *Furman v. Georgia* did not conclude that the death penalty itself was unconstitutional. Rather, the Court determined that the current procedures in place for implementation of the death penalty violated the cruel and unusual clauses of the Eighth and Fourteenth Amendments of the Constitution. This decision made it possible for the states to rewrite their laws in order to reinstate the death penalty. A case *(GREGG V. GEORGIA)* would come before the Court in 1976 that successfully rewrote the procedures allowing the reinstatement of the death penalty in those states that had previously had it. *Furman* is significant because it was the first time the Supreme Court held that the death penalty was unconstitutional. This holding applied only to how the penalty was carried out, however, and did not mean there were not circumstances in which the death penalty was appropriate.

For more information: *Furman v. Georgia*, 408 U.S. 238 (1972); Jolly, Robert W., Jr., and Edward Sagarin. "The First Eight After Furman: Who Was Executed With The Return of The Death Penalty?" *Crime and Delinquency* 30, no. 4 (1984): 610–629; Keil, Thomas J., and Vito, Gennaro F. "The Effects of the Furman and Gregg Decisions on Black-White Execution Ratios in the South." *Journal of Criminal Justice* 20, no. 3 (1992): 217–245; Wells, Diane. "Federal Habeas Corpus and the Death Penalty: A Need for a Return to the Principles of Furman." *Journal of Criminal Law and Criminology* 80, no. 2 (1989): 427–484.

—Valerie Bell

Garcia v. San Antonio Metropolitan Transit Authority 469 U.S. 528, 105 S.Ct. 1005 (1985)

In *Garcia v. San Antonio Metropolitan Transit Authority*, the Supreme Court held that the Tenth Amendment to the Constitution that recognizes powers reserved to the states places no limitations on Congress's INTERSTATE COMMERCE powers and, consequently, Congress does have the authority to apply the Fair Labor Standards Act (first enacted in 1938 and amended in 1974) to states and municipalities.

The Court's decision in *Garcia* overturned its holding of less than a decade earlier in *NATIONAL LEAGUE OF CITIES V. USERY*, 426 U.S. 833 (1976), in which it had argued that essential state functions are beyond the authority of Congress to regulate. The Court reasoned in *Garcia* that there was no clear line to be drawn between "essential" and "nonessential" state functions and, thus, its previous decision in *National League of Cities* had established an unworkable standard that should be abandoned. Further, the Court argued that courts should not be the ones to determine what functions should be or should not be performed by the states; that is, what is or is not an essential function. That question, the Court argues here, should be left to the people through their representatives. In the *Garcia* doctrine, the Court reasons that the appropriate arena for deciding what functions the states should perform is the democratic process and not the courts because, absent a clear constitutional standard to measure what is and is not an essential state function, court line-drawing would amount to an unprincipled supplanting of the policy judgment of elected bodies for that of unelected courts. The Court argues that because the people in the states and, thus, the states themselves also influence congressional action, the democratic process can limit over-reaching by Congress in its exercise of its interstate commerce powers. Or put differently, the appropriate check on Congress's power is the people exercising the electoral franchise, not the courts exercising policy preferences.

Garcia overturned the 1976 decision in *National League of Cities* with the same narrow 5-4 majority. Justice Harry Blackmun was in the majority in both cases, reversing course and providing the necessary fifth vote, making a new majority in *Garcia* and returning interstate COMMERCE CLAUSE doctrine to that which had been established in 1937 that recognized a broad authority of Congress to use its own judgment in the regulation of interstate commerce. *National League of Cities* had broken with past doctrine to limit Congress's authority under the interstate commerce clause in favor of strengthening the states' authority under the Tenth Amendment. These two cases bracket alternative views of the principle of FEDERALISM that undergirds the American constitutional order. Federalism is the principle that both the national and state governments derive their authority directly from the people and each retains powers not given to the other and as well exercises overlapping and shared powers.

The *National League of Cities* Court understands federalism as state sovereignty with reserved powers that operate as limits on the national government. In this view, the national power is understood as that remaining after carving out authority for the states. Conversely, the *Garcia* Court understands federalism as the national government's having supreme power in all areas where the Constitution gives it authority. Under *Garcia,* the states' power is residual to national power, not the reverse. Although the Supreme Court continues to vacillate between these opposing views, the judgment handed down in *Garcia* favoring the national power over that of the states remains current doctrine.

For more information: Kahn, Ronald, and Kenneth Ira Kersch. *The Supreme Court and American Political Development.* Lawrence: University Press of Kansas, 2006; Tushnet, Mark V. *A Court Divided: The Rehnquist Court and the Future of Constitutional Law.* New York: W.W. Norton Co., 2005.

—Julian M. Davis and Phyllis Farley Rippey

gay and lesbian rights

The Supreme Court's serious attention to, and support for, gay and lesbian rights has been a relatively recent development. Before the 1990s, the Court's approach was one of either complete lack of concern or outright hostility. Even when giving these rights its fullest consideration, the Court has declined to apply the same level of protection for sexuality as for race and gender.

One of the Court's earliest gay and lesbian rights cases, *ONE v. Olesen,* 355 U.S. 772 (1958), helped to create the modern gay rights movement in the United States by applying FIRST AMENDMENT-protective OBSCENITY standards, as stated in *ROTH v. U.S.,* 354 U.S. 476 (1957), to gay and lesbian periodicals. This lessened censorship and allowed the mail system to be a mechanism for social and political organizing. At the same time, however, the Court let stand the federal government's classification of sexual minorities as possessing "psychopathic" personalities for immigration purposes (*Boutilier v. INS,* 387 U.S. 118 [1967]). Most of the justices did nothing to challenge the anti-gay climate of the 1950s and 1960s and likely exacerbated the situation by utilizing morally condemnatory language typical of the times. Not all legal elites viewed gay and lesbian rights in the same manner, however. In 1955, The American Law Institute recommended, as a part of its Model Penal Code, the decriminalization of consensual sex acts between persons of the same gender.

The decades of the 1970s and 1980s saw little movement in a positive direction for gay and lesbian rights from the Supreme Court. Indeed, U.S. courts were generally unsympathetic to gay rights claims even after the start of the gay rights political movement after the Stonewall Riots in 1969. Legal calls for SAME-SEX MARRIAGE in the early 1970s were quickly rejected by state courts (*Singer v. Hara,* 522 P. 2d 1187 [Wash. 1974]). The Supreme Court rebuffed a sodomy law challenge in *Doe v. Commonwealth's Attorney,* 425 U.S. 901 (1976).

The high point for Supreme Court resistance to gay and lesbian rights claims was the case of *BOWERS v. HARDWICK,* 578 U.S. 186 (1986). In that case, a narrow 5–4 majority upheld Georgia's anti-sodomy law. The Court refused to apply evolving PRIVACY standards, because, the majority reasoned, homosexuality had long been disfavored by society and the law. In a concurring opinion, Chief Justice WARREN BURGER described homosexuality by quoting WILLIAM BLACKSTONE in describing sodomy as a "malignity worse than rape." In a vigorous dissent, Justice Harry Blackmun saw this issue as one of privacy rights and would have invalidated the Georgia law. The case was almost decided the other way, with Justice LEWIS FRANKLIN POWELL, JR., changing his vote, originally asserting in conference discussions that the anti-sodomy law violated the Eighth Amendment's ban on "cruel and unusual" punishment, particularly for its status as a felony. The decision was a blow to the gay and lesbian rights movement and shifted the litigation focus of the movement away from federal courts to state courts. Many state courts invalidated sodomy laws under state constitutional jurisprudence and some readdressed and validated arguments for same-sex marriage and relationship equality. However, the continued constitutionality of sodomy laws continued to be an obstacle for the movement, because, while seldom enforced, they were often cited to deny rights, such as employment, child custody and visitation, and military service for gays and lesbians.

The Court significantly shifted its approach to gay and lesbian rights in *ROMER v. EVANS,* 517

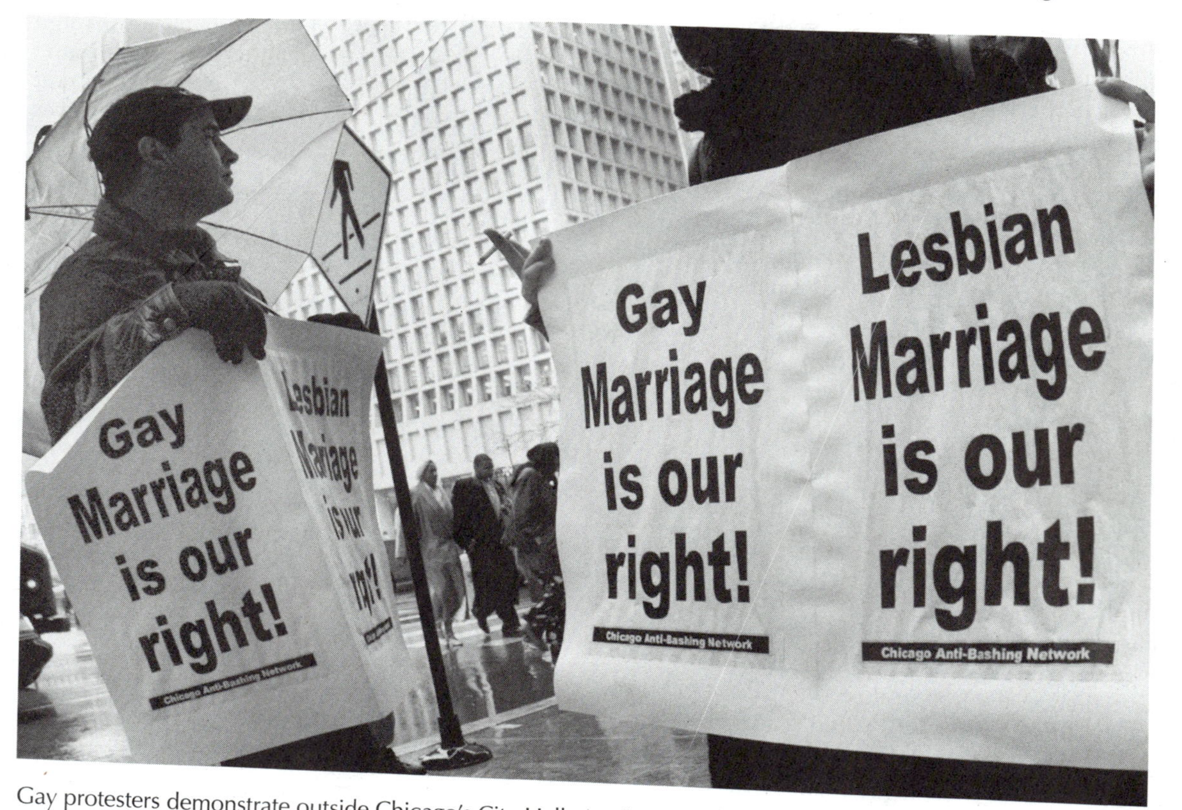

Gay protesters demonstrate outside Chicago's City Hall to call attention to the issue of gay marriage. *(Tim Boyle/ Getty Images)*

U.S. 620 (1996). Here the Court struck down Colorado's Amendment 2, which invalidated all local laws outlawing sexual orientation discrimination. Justice ANTHONY M. KENNEDY did not break new constitutional ground with his decision, in that he did not claim that sexuality was similar to race or gender under the EQUAL PROTECTION clause, but he applied a vigorous RATIONAL BASIS TEST to conclude that the Colorado amendment was without any legitimate purpose other than animus toward gays and lesbians. Justice ANTONIN GREGORY SCALIA vigorously dissented, arguing that the Colorado enactment was a legitimate exercise of the moral sentiments of the citizens of the state and that the majority had "mistaken a Kulturkampf for a fit of spite."

Despite this seeming turn for the Court, gays and lesbians did not fare well when groups wished to exclude them from participation in activities and organizations. Generally, freedom of speech and association were seen to trump equality concerns. In *HURLEY V. IRISH-AMERICAN GAY, LESBIAN, AND BISEXUAL GROUP OF BOSTON*, the Court unanimously decided that organizers of South Boston's St. Patrick's Day parade could exclude gays, despite the presence of a sexual orientation-inclusive anti-discrimination law in Massachusetts. The parade was "expressive association." A divided Court allowed the exclusion of gays from the Boy Scouts in *BOY SCOUTS OF AMERICA V. DALE*, 530 U.S. 640 (2000) on similar grounds.

Perhaps the biggest advance for gay and lesbian rights came in *LAWRENCE V. TEXAS*, 539 U.S. 55[illegible] (2003). In this 6-3 decision, the Court overrule[illegible] *Bowers* and held that sodomy laws violated the rig[illegible] to PRIVACY, thereby applying privacy jurispruden[illegible] to same-sex sexuality. Indeed, Justice Kennedy's opinion was a sweeping repudiation of *Bowers*. "*Bowers* was not correct when it was decided, and it is not correct today," Kennedy asserted. Largely relying on the arguments of gay rights and history scholars who submitted amicus curiae briefs, Kennedy rejected the notion that homosexuality was so historically disfavored that it could not be included in the right to privacy. The decision also included potentially sweeping language that was quite affirmative of gays and lesbians and their relationships. As in *Romer,* this triggered a strong dissent from Justice Scalia, who claimed that the decision had broader implications than the issue of sodomy laws. In particular, he argued that the opinion appeared to open the door to the eventual sanction of same-sex marriage by the Court.

The issue of same-sex marriage was certainly implicated by the *Lawrence* decision, but most change on the issue has come from state courts invoking state constitutional provisions concerning equal protection and DUE PROCESS/privacy (*Goodridge v. Dept. of Public Health,* 798 N.E. 941 [Mass. 2003]). For gay and lesbian rights to ...lude same-sex marriage nationally, the Supreme ...rt would likely need to invalidate the Defense ...arriage Act (1 U.S.C. § 7, 28 U.S.C. § 1738[c]), ...h prohibits the recognition of same-sex mar... for federal purposes.

...ore information: Gerstmann, Evan. *The ...utional Underclass: Gays, Lesbians, and ...ure of Class-Based Equal Protection.* Chi... ...iversity of Chicago Press, 1999; Murdoch, ...d Deb Price. *Courting Justice: Gays and ...v. the Supreme Court.* New York: Basic ...01; Pierceson, Jason. *Courts, Liberal... ...ights: Gay Law and Politics in the U.S.* ... Philadelphia, Pa.: Temple University

—Jason Pierceson

...gden 22 U.S. 1 (1824)

...Ogden, the Supreme Court ruled ... government's power to regulate ...MMERCE involved not only the buying and selling of goods between states, but also the navigation involved in delivering them. The court's broad interpretation of the COMMERCE CLAUSE expanded the federal government's power in this area and was a significant factor in the development of FEDERALISM in the United States.

In 1808, the state legislature of New York awarded Robert Fulton and Robert Livingston a steamboat monopoly that included commerce on interstate waterways. Aaron Ogden was given a sub-license under this agreement for all ferry business on the waterways between Elizabethtown, New Jersey, and New York City, New York. Ogden was frustrated to find Thomas Gibbons operating steamboat ferries on the same waters—waters he believed to be exclusively licensed to him through the state of New York. Gibbons refused to cease operation of his steamboats, declaring he held a federal coasting license granted to him by the U.S. Congress in February of 1793.

Ogden's lawyers took issue with Gibbons's federal license. While Congress had the ability to regulate sales of goods between states, Ogden's lawyers claimed it did not have the ability to regulate issues regarding navigation, in effect, maintaining a narrow definition of commerce. Navigation, they contended, is regulated by states, not the federal government. Therefore, the New York monopoly was constitutional and Gibbons's federal coasting license was not. Gibbons lost his case in the New York state court and eventually appealed to the U.S. Supreme Court.

At issue in *Gibbons v. Ogden* was not just the definition of commerce but the power of the federal government over state affairs. By 1824, it was still somewhat unclear where the state governments' powers ended and where the federal government's powers began. The Tenth Amendment to the U.S. Constitution states that all powers not specifically stated in the Constitution as belonging to the federal government or denied to the states are reserved for the states or to the people. *Gibbons v. Ogden* was essentially a disagreement over how the Tenth Amendment and the nature of federalism in the United States should be interpreted. This general issue of commerce was simply an element of that debate.

In 1824, Chief Justice JOHN MARSHALL delivered the court's opinion. In it he writes, "Few things were better known, than the immediate causes which led to the adoption of the present constitution. . . . the prevailing motive was to regulate commerce; to rescue it from the embarrassing and destructive consequences, resulting from the legislation of so many different States, and to place it under the protection of a uniform law." Using a broad interpretation of the term "commerce," Marshall noted that it is the interstate commerce clause in Article 1, Section 8 of the Constitution as well as the SUPREMACY CLAUSE that gives the federal government the greater power in this matter, regardless of what is being transported or how it is being carried.

The MARSHALL COURT not only confirmed the validity of Gibbons's federal coasting license, but also, in defining a broad role for the federal government in the regulation of interstate commerce, extended the reach of the federal government's power further into state affairs. This decision laid the groundwork for expanding federal powers into a variety of commercial areas, far beyond the simple sale of hard goods across state borders.

It is worth noting, however, that more recent Supreme Court decisions have exhibited more skepticism toward congressional power in this area. In particular, the REHNQUIST COURT's 1995 decision in *UNITED STATES V. LOPEZ* set broad limits to what can realistically be defined as a commerce-related activity. While generally supporting the spirit of the *Ogden* decision, modern courts have been cautious not to allow the commerce clause to become a near-universal justification for the expansion of federal power.

For more information: Schwartz, Bernard. *A History of the Supreme Court.* New York: Oxford University Press, 1993.

—Mark C. Milewicz

Gideon v. Wainwright 372 U.S. 335 (1963)
In this case, the Supreme Court ruled that the SIXTH AMENDMENT requires the state to provide counsel for the defendants in criminal matters so as to assure their ability to receive a fair trial with proper representation.

In this case, the state failed to provide counsel for the defendant. There was a judicial question of whether or not Gideon received a fair trial, thereby violating the dual rights ascribed within the DUE PROCESS clause as protected by the Sixth and FOURTEENTH AMENDMENTS. The ability of the indigent to retain counsel at all trials became a modern practice irrespective of the absence of specific language within the Sixth Amendment. With the Gideon case, it became clear that the right to a fair trial should not be a function of income or standing in the community. Gideon had committed a break-in and entering of the premises of a pool hall with the intent to complete a theft and subsequently appeared in court with an appearance of being too poor to afford a lawyer. When Justice HUGO BLACK delivered the opinion of the court, it was clearly understood that the defendant could not afford counsel for his breaking and entering felony arrest. The defendant could not afford counsel and the courts refused to grant him counsel in the lower level case.

In addition, the defendant defended himself and was believed to have done remarkably well but was convicted anyway. The complete decision by the high Court affirmed that the *BETTS V. BRADY* precedence was no longer good law and that the Sixth Amendment does provide for assistance to counsel unless the refusal of counsel is done by a reasonable and mentally unimpaired person who would otherwise need counsel. Twenty-two states filed amicus curiae briefs suggesting that the Betts case should be removed and that the Gideon case should be the corrective case which would reverse the law on the subject. The Florida courts detailed that only a capital offense in the state of Florida could be assigned counsel, which was how the previous interpretations of the RIGHT TO COUNSEL had been viewed by some states. The belief by the state of Florida that the responsibility for the lower levels of justice was in the hands of a smooth working system was quickly dissipating, as the amount of crime and criminal cases for misdemeanor offenses increased rapidly during the time period of the case discussion and decision.

Ultimately, the need to have counsel to assist the person in a criminal trial became commonplace in all states at every level, whether capital or minor in offense.

For more information: *Gideon v. Wainwright,* 372 U.S. 335 (1963); Graham, Fred P. *The Due Process Revolution: The Warren Court's Impact on Criminal Law.* Rochelle Park, N.J.: Hayden Book Co., 1971; Lewis, Anthony. *Gideon's Trumpet.* New York: Random House/Vintage, 1966; Kamisar, Yale, Fred Edward Inbau, Thurman Wesley Arnold, and A. E. Dick Howard. *Criminal Justice in Our Time.* Charlottesville: Published for the Magna Carta Commission of Virginia [by] the University Press of Virginia, 1965.

—Ernest Gomez

Gitlow v. People of the State of New York 268 U.S. 652 (1925)

In *Gitlow v. New York,* the United States Supreme Court ruled that the FIRST AMENDMENT applied to states by way of the DUE PROCESS clause of the FOURTEENTH AMENDMENT. By incorporating that amendment, the Supreme Court in this case protected those rights from infringement by state governments. The case is also an important continuation of the debate on the Court between those who advocated the bad tendency test in free speech cases and those who preferred the CLEAR AND PRESENT DANGER TEST.

In November 1919, Benjamin Gitlow, a well-known leader of the left wing of the Socialist Party and a member of the New York State Legislature, was arrested. His arrest was part of the Red scare that occurred following the Russian revolution. Gitlow's crime was the publication and distribution of 16 thousand copies of a pamphlet, The Left Wing Manifesto. This document, modeled on the Communist Manifesto, called for an immediate and violent uprising of the proletariat to overthrow the system of capitalism and the government in the United States.

New York prosecuted Gitlow under its criminal anarchy law, which prohibited advocating the violent overthrow of the government. Gitlow and his attorney, Clarence Darrow, argued that the New York statute was an unconstitutional infringement on free speech. Despite the fact that the manifesto itself produced no revolution or any other unlawful action, Gitlow was convicted by a jury and sentenced the maximum term of five to 10 years in prison.

Gitlow, with the assistance of the AMERICAN CIVIL LIBERTIES UNION, appealed to the Supreme Court. The question before the Court was whether the New York law was a constitutional exercise of power or whether it unconstitutionally infringed on free speech rights. The decision was a 7-2 majority, with the Court upholding Gitlow's conviction. The majority, utilizing the bad tendency test, argued that incitement to violence was not protected speech. Justice Edward T. Sanford wrote that "a single revolutionary spark may kindle a fire" and that "every presumption is to be indulged in favor of the validity of the statute." The majority believed that no explicit danger need exist before government may limit speech.

Justices OLIVER WENDELL HOLMES, JR., and Louis D. Brandeis dissented and advocated for the clear and present danger test. Under that test, Gitlow had done nothing that produced a danger sufficiently real to warrant his rights to free speech being infringed. These justices challenged the majority's notion that speech can be regulated because of possible, intangible negative effects. In their view, the danger posed by Gitlow's pamphlet was simply too insubstantial to warrant government action. Holmes argued, "Every idea is an inducement to someone."

Ultimately, Benjamin Gitlow served less than two years of his sentence. He was eventually pardoned by New York Governor Alfred Smith, and he spent the remainder of his life active in the American Communist movement.

The most lasting outcome of this case was the incorporation of the First Amendment into the Fourteenth Amendment. In the majority opinion, the Court wrote that "freedom of speech and of the press—which are protected by the First Amendment—are among the fundamental personal rights and 'liberties' protected by the Fourteenth Amendment from impairment by the states." Thus, while the Court had allowed the law in New York to remain in effect, it had prohibited states from infringing on freedom of speech or of the press. It would, however, take future cases to fully define the limits of that right.

For more information: Gitlow, Benjamin. *'I Confess': The Truth about American Communism.* Freeport, N.Y., Books for Libraries Press, 1972; Irons, Peter. *A People's History of the Supreme Court.* New York: Penguin, 1999.

—David A. May

Goldberg v. Kelly 397 U.S. 254 (1970)

In *Goldberg v. Kelly* the Supreme Court extended the protection of the DUE PROCESS clause of the FOURTEENTH AMENDMENT to welfare recipients whose payments may be terminated. Prior to cessation of aid, the Court held, the state agency must provide advance notice and must also conduct an evidentiary hearing allowing the recipients to submit evidence regarding their continuing eligibility for the program. Essentially, *Goldberg* prohibits the arbitrary termination of welfare benefits.

New York State residents receiving public assistance from the Aid to Families with Dependent Children program (state-administered aid partially funded by the federal government) filed suit because their benefits were terminated without advance notice and without an opportunity to demonstrate their continuing eligibility for the program. The recipients argued that this practice offended the due process clause of the Fourteenth Amendment.

Writing for the Court, Justice WILLIAM J. BRENNAN, JR., agreed with the welfare recipients. Brennan concluded that although some government benefits may be terminated without holding an evidentiary hearing, welfare benefits of the kind at issue here are of an essential nature. These benefits assist low-income individuals in meeting basic food, clothing, and shelter needs. Termination of such assistance abruptly and arbitrarily undermines the subsistence of individuals with very limited resources. Further, arbitrary termination of assistance might deprive eligible individuals of the only means by which to provide for their basic subsistence needs. Therefore, the Court concluded, recipients must be afforded advance notification of proposed termination. Additionally, a quasi-judicial administrative hearing on the recipient's continuing eligibility for the program must be held prior to cessation of payments.

Despite administrative concerns as to the expense mandatory pre-termination evidentiary hearings may generate (in terms of resources required to administer this process, as well as the cost of paying welfare benefits to individuals no longer eligible for the program), administrative efficiency and fiscal stewardship cannot outweigh the due process interest of welfare recipients. Termination of benefits designed to meet basic subsistence needs of the poor constitutes a potentially serious governmental action. Therefore, individuals must be afforded the opportunity to challenge the government's evidence and to present documentation verifying their continuing eligibility prior to cessation of welfare benefits.

In fact, the Court opinion noted that affording welfare recipients an evidentiary hearing advanced the government's interest as well. Public assistance, Justice Brennan surmised, is not charity; rather, it promotes the general welfare of America's citizens and its careful administration must be safeguarded. The due process protections required here achieve this end.

For more information: Miller, Arthur S. *Politics, Democracy, and the Supreme Court: Essays on the Frontier of Constitutional Theory.* Westport, Conn.: Greenwood Press, 1985.

—Melanie K. Morris

Goldwater v. Carter 444 U.S. 996 (1979)

In *Goldwater v. Carter,* 444 U.S. 996 (1979), the Supreme Court rejected a challenge to the president's authority to unilaterally terminate a United States TREATY, but a split majority provided no clear rationale for the Court's ruling. Four members of the Court felt the case presented a nonjusticiable "political question." Another justice argued for dismissal because the case was not ripe for JUDICIAL REVIEW, while yet another member of the Court favored dismissal without explaining his reasoning.

President Jimmy Carter gave notice of termination of the Mutual Defense Treaty with Taiwan in December 1978, as part of the process of normalizing relations with the government of China. Following President Carter's action, several members of Congress (including Senator Barry Goldwater of Arizona) filed suit claiming injury to their "legislative right to be consulted and to vote on the termination of the 1954 Mutual Defense Treaty." The District Court for the DISTRICT OF COLUMBIA ruled that because the Mutual Defense Treaty was part of the "law of the land" under the SUPREMACY CLAUSE of the Constitution, termination required ratification by two-thirds of the SENATE or a majority of both chambers of Congress. A split panel of the Court of Appeals for the District of Columbia Circuit reversed that decision, ruling that President Carter did not exceed his authority by taking action to withdraw from the treaty.

The Supreme Court reversed the Court of Appeals' decision and remanded the case with instructions to dismiss the complaint. Justice WILLIAM HUBBS REHNQUIST's plurality opinion argued the case presented a nonjusticiable "political question" because it involved the interaction between the president's power over foreign relations and Congress's power to negate presidential action. Notably, while favoring dismissal based on the political question doctrine, Justice Rehnquist did not refer to the leading case of *BAKER V. CARR*, 369 U.S. 186 (1962). Justice LEWIS FRANKLIN POWELL, JR., concurred in the judgment but viewed the case as not ripe for judicial review because Congress and the president had not yet reached a "constitutional impasse."

Powell noted that the political question doctrine, as set forth in *Baker*, involved three questions: 1) whether the issue involved "resolution of questions committed by the text of the Constitution to a coordinate branch of Government," 2) whether resolution of the case required the Court to "move beyond areas of judicial expertise," and 3) whether "prudential considerations counsel against judicial intervention." After reviewing these factors, Powell concluded that if the case had been ripe for review, it would not present a political question but rather a basic issue of CONSTITUTIONAL INTERPRETATION. Justices Harry Blackmun and Byron White argued the case should be given full briefing and oral argument on the issues, rather than dismissing on JUSTICIABILITY grounds. Justice WILLIAM J. BRENNAN, JR., writing in dissent, was the only member of the Court to reach the underlying question and concluded that the President had the power to unilaterally terminate the treaty arising from his authority to recognize and withdraw recognition of foreign governments. The outcome of *Goldwater* effectively recognized broad executive power over foreign affairs but created additional confusion regarding the Court's application of the political question doctrine.

For more information: O'Donnell, Joshua P. "The Anti-Ballistic Missile Treaty Debate: Time for Some Clarification of the President's Authority to Terminate a Treaty." *Vanderbilt Journal of Transnational Law* 35 (2002): 1,601–1,636; Restatement (Third) of the Foreign Relations Law of the United States § 339.

—Joshua A. Kimsey

Gomillion et al. v. Lightfoot, Mayor of Tuskegee, et al. 364 U.S. 339 (1960)

In *Gomillion v. Lightfoot,* the Supreme Court ruled that the broad powers of a state to fix the political boundaries of its municipalities is limited by the FIFTEENTH AMENDMENT since it forbids states from depriving any citizen of the RIGHT TO VOTE on account of their race. So a state statute which had the effect of depriving African Americans of their right to vote in Tuskegee, Alabama, because of their race was not immune to attack simply because the mechanism employed by the legislature was a "political" redefinition of municipal boundaries.

In 1957, the Alabama state legislature passed an act to redefine the political boundaries of the city of Tuskegee, replacing what had been a region with a square shape covering the entire urban area with a 28-sided figure. In so doing, the legislature excluded all but four or five black voters from the city limits of Tuskegee and placed them in a district with no whites. Consequently, the legislative act deprived blacks of their right to vote in Tuskegee elections on account of their race. The so-called Act No. 140 transformed the city from one whose municipal limits formed a square to one which Justice Frankfurter described as "uncouth and strangely irregular."

The petitioners in *Gomillion v. Lightfoot* were all African Americans who once were the 400 black residents of the city of Tuskegee before the legislative redistricting. Unencumbered by the *Colegrove v. Green* (1946) ruling presuming the court's unwillingness to "enter the political thicket," C. G. Gomillion and other disenfranchised black citizens of Tuskegee filed an injunctive action against the enforcement of the Alabama statute at the Federal District Court in Alabama. They sought a declaratory judgment to set aside the state action that created the boundaries as an unconstitutional violation of the Fifteenth Amendment, denying their right to vote on account of race. More specifically, they argued that (a) the act altered the shape of Tuskegee from a square to an irregular 28-sided figure; (b) that it would eliminate from the city all but four or five of its 400 black voters without eliminating any white voter; and (c) that the effect of the law was to deprive blacks of their right to vote in Tuskegee elections on account of their race. The district court responded by dismissing the complaint for lack of judicial authority to declare the act invalid and to change boundaries of municipal corporations fixed by a state legislature.

While on appeal the Fifth Circuit upheld that decision, on certiorari the U.S. Supreme Court was confronted with the following questions: 1) whether the Alabama state action (redrawing electoral district boundaries) was reviewable by the courts, and 2) whether the state's action that effectively disenfranchised blacks from the city of Tuskegee trammeled on their constitutional rights in violation of the Fifteenth Amendment of the U.S. Constitution. Reversing the district court in unanimous opinion, Justice Felix Frankfurter observed that the issue was not whether the petitioners could prove that Alabama's Act 140 was meant to disenfranchise the African-American voters but rather whether the act *did* in fact disenfranchise African-American voters of their constitutional rights. Ruling on the review powers of the court to review redistricting questions, the Supreme Court held that while states may be insulated from JUDICIAL REVIEW when they exercise powers wholly within the domain of state interest, such insulation is not carried over when state powers are used as instruments to circumvent federally protected rights.

The Alabama legislature, Justice Frankfurter observed, was unable to identify "any countervailing municipal function" which the act was designed to serve. Although a state's power "to establish, destroy, or reorganize by expansion or contraction of its cities, counties, and other local unities" is a broad power, Justice Frankfurter noted the exercise of that power is nonetheless subject to the restrictions of the Fifteenth Amendment and therefore judicially reviewable. Citing *Hunter v. Pittsburgh* (1907), the Supreme Court held that states' powers over their municipal corporations must abide by the standards set in the U.S. Constitution and may not use their constitutional powers to achieve unconstitutional ends.

Distinguishing further *Gomillion* from COLEGROVE V. GREEN, a case in which the Court ruled that issues of redistricting were political and therefore not reviewable by courts, Justice Frankfurter noted that the decisive facts in this case, taken as proved, are wholly different from the considerations found controlling in *Colegrove.* The *Colegrove* case, he observed, involved a complaint of discriminatory apportionment of congressional districts where appellants complained only of a dilution of the strength of their votes as a result of legislative inaction over a course of many years. However, the petitioners in *Gomillion* in the Court's view complained that an affirmative legislative action deprived them of their votes and the consequent advantages that the ballot affords. Specifically, the court noted, in *Gomillion* the legislature did not merely redraw the Tuskegee city limits with incidental inconvenience to the petitioners, it deprived them of the municipal franchise, a consequent right, and changed the city's boundaries to deny the exercise of their right to vote under the Fifteenth Amendment. While in form this may be a mere act of redefining metes and bounds, according to the Court the inescapable human effect was to despoil colored citizens, and only colored citizens, of their enjoyed voting rights. Therefore, when a legislature singles out a readily isolated segment of a racial minority for special discriminatory treatment, it violates the Fifteenth Amendment.

While ruling that petitioners were entitled to prove their allegations at trial, the Supreme Court held that a constitutional power cannot be used as a means to attain an unconstitutional result—that is, "acts generally lawful may become unlawful when done to accomplish an unlawful end." Concurring with the decision of the Court more generally, Justice Charles Evans Whittaker disagreed with the reasoning. He argued instead that since the petitioners' may still vote, just not in the reformed Tuskegee district, the decision should be based on the EQUAL PROTECTION clause of the FOURTEENTH AMENDMENT rather than the Fifteenth Amendment. To Whittaker, because the equal protection clause of the Fourteenth Amendment prohibits the unlawful segregation of citizens by race, the state action was unconstitutional and must be reversed.

Two aspects of the *Gomillion* decision are noteworthy. First, the relief granted by the Court was not premised upon the petitioner's showing of intent or a malevolent purpose on the part of the state of Alabama. The Court assumed instead that there were no rightful aims in the legislative mind when it so radically altered the boundaries of Tuskegee, one of the few areas in the state where blacks—many of them associated with Tuskegee College and the federal hospital there—were beginning to vote in substantial numbers.

Second, the relief could have been granted without limiting the power of the state to alter or enlarge municipal boundaries for legitimate reasons, since no whites would have lost either their vote or proper power to vote by a court order requiring that Tuskegee retain its original boundaries. While the most important aspect of this case is the ruling that courts would hence correct state efforts to deny blacks the right to vote on account of their race or color, it has proven to be of little precedential value in subsequent gerrymandering or vote-dilution challenges even in cases where the impact on black voting power is at issue.

Judicial commitment to the eradication of discrimination in the electoral process has often faltered when confronted with challenged actions that appear normal but for their effect on the black vote, especially where the relief requested would undermine white voting power. The Court seems to have forgotten that the case was decided under the broad mandate of the Fifteenth Amendment and not under the much more nebulous standard of the Fourteenth Amendment's equal protection clause suggested by Justice Whittaker in his concurring opinion in *Gomillion*. In most voting right cases, the Court has shifted the standard for review from the Fifteenth to the Fourteenth Amendment. In *Whitcomb v. Chivas* (1971), for example, the Court not only used the Fourteenth Amendment as the standard for review, but also cited *Gomillion* as if the case had been decided on Fourteenth Amendment grounds.

In the end, while the shift in the Court's approach makes *Gomillion v. Lightfoot* of little precedential value, it nevertheless represents the first case the Court entered into the "political thicket" of redistricting that opened the flood gates for the Court ruling on apportionment and redistricting as justiciable issues in federal courts (as in *BAKER V. CARR* [1962], *Gray v. Sanders* [1963], *Westbury v. Sanders* [1964], and *REYNOLDS V. SIMS* [1964]).

For more information: Ryden, David K. *The U.S. Supreme Court and the Electoral Process.* Washington, D.C.: Georgetown University Press, 2002.

—Marc G. Pufong

Gonzales, Attorney General v. Carhart

05-380 (2007)

In a 5-4 decision, the Supreme Court upheld the federal Partial Birth Abortion Ban Act of 2003.

Although in 2000 the Court had found an almost identical Nebraska law unconstitutional in *Stenberg v. Carhart,* 530 U.S. 914, seven years later the justices held that the federal act avoided the defects of the Nebraska law. They ruled that it did not impose an undue burden on a woman's right to abortion and that the lack of an exception for the mother's health was not unconstitutional.

Based on rulings in *ROE V. WADE,* 410 U.S. 113 (1973), and *Planned Parenthood of Southeastern Pennsylvania v. Casey,* 505 U.S. 833 (1992), until *Gonzales v. Carhart,* the Court had affirmed three principles: a woman's right to terminate a pregnancy before viability with minimal interference from the government; a state's interest in restricting abortions after viability while allowing exceptions for pregnancies where the mother's life or health was in danger; and that from the outset the state has an interest in both the mother's health and in the life of the fetus "that may become a child."

Justice ANTHONY M. KENNEDY wrote the opinion for the Court in *Gonzales v. Carhart.* It emphasized the government's legitimate interest in preserving and promoting fetal life and argued that the law was only a structural mechanism which did not present a substantial obstacle to a woman's right to terminate her pregnancy. Much of the text of the opinion described the banned procedure, which the medical profession calls intact dilation and evacuation (intact D&E). These details were used as evidence that the law clearly prohibited only one specific method of abortion, that its scope was not vague or overbroad, and that physicians had other alternatives for terminating second-term pregnancies. Kennedy cited disagreements among doctors about whether the procedure was ever necessary as proof of "medical uncertainty" that it might be required to protect a woman's health. For all of those reasons, the Court majority found no need for a health exception.

Kennedy's opinion, in which he was joined by Chief Justice JOHN G. ROBERTS, JR., and Justices ANTONIN GREGORY SCALIA, CLARENCE THOMAS, and SAMUEL ALITO, was controversial for its use of provocative language. It used terms such as "unborn child" and "baby" rather than fetus. It referred to physicians as "abortion doctors," and quoted verbatim congressional testimony from a nurse who described "the baby's little fingers and feet." The opinion also advanced the theory that women would "come to regret their choice to abort the infant life they once created and sustained" and cited ethical and moral, rather than constitutional concerns, as a basis for the law.

Justice Ruth Bader Ginsburg wrote a strong dissent, joined by Justices JOHN PAUL STEVENS, DAVID H. SOUTER, and STEPHEN G. BREYER. The dissenters claimed that the lack of a health exception was a significant departure from the Court's earlier decisions. They noted that a consensus did exist among professional medical associations that the intact D&E procedure was sometimes necessary for some women. Ginsburg's opinion also suggested that allowing ethical and moral concerns "untethered" to any specific government interest to override FUNDAMENTAL RIGHTS set a dangerous precedent. The dissent found the assumptions about women's fragile emotional state an "antiabortion shibboleth." They expressed concern that because the Court was "differently composed," the justices allowed Congress to override their decision in *Stenberg v. Carhart.* Ultimately the dissenters were skeptical that the majority really intended to affirm the essential holdings of *Roe* and *Casey.*

For more information: Reagan, Leslie J. *When Abortion Was a Crime: Women, Medicine, and Law in the United States, 1867–1973.* Berkeley: University of California Press, 1997.

—Mary Welek Atwell

Gonzales v. Oregon 546 U.S. 243 (2006)

Gonzales v. Oregon is a U.S. Supreme Court decision upholding Oregon's Death with Dignity Act (ODWDA). While decided as a matter of statutory interpretation, *Gonzales* also pertains to FEDERALISM. Furthermore, although the Court did not address the question of physician-assisted suicide, *Gonzales* added fuel to the fires of controversy surrounding the practice.

Oregon voters narrowly approved Ballot Measure 16 in 1994. This initiative established specific procedures under which a patient diagnosed as terminally ill could obtain a prescription for a lethal dose of drugs with which they could end their life. The Oregon Legislative Assembly tried to repeal ODWDA by referring Ballot Measure 51 to voters in 1997. This attempt failed by a greater margin than the original initiative had passed. The Bush administration weighed in against ODWDA in 2001. On November 9 of that year, Attorney General John D. Ashcroft issued an interpretative rule under the federal Controlled Substances Act (CSA), the statute regulating use of the drugs physicians prescribed under ODWDA. Ashcroft's interpretative rule declared physician-assisted suicide "not a 'legitimate medical purpose'" under the CSA, saying that "prescribing, dispensing, or administering federally controlled substances to assist suicide violates" the CSA, and that "[s]uch conduct by a physician . . . may 'render his registration . . . inconsistent with the public interest' and therefore subject to possible suspension or revocation."

Speaking through Justice ANTHONY M. KENNEDY, the Supreme Court invalidated this interpretation, 6-3. The Court described Ashcroft's claim of executive authority as "extraordinary," characterizing it as "unrestrained." "If the Attorney General's argument were correct," wrote Kennedy, "his power to deregister necessarily would include the greater power to criminalize even the actions of registered physicians, whenever they engage in conduct he deems illegitimate." "The structure of the CSA," the Court held, "conveys unwillingness to cede medical judgments to an Executive official who lacks medical expertise."

Having disposed of the particular question of the Attorney General's authority, the Court discussed the dispute's significance for federalism. "The structure and operation of the CSA," Kennedy noted, "presume and rely upon a functioning medical profession regulated under the States' POLICE POWERS. . . . Oregon's regime is an example of the state regulation of medical practice that the CSA presupposes." By contrast, Ashcroft's position would "effect a radical shift of authority from the States to the Federal Government to define general standards of medical practice in every locality."

Gonzalez hardly settled the question of physician-assisted suicide. The intensity of disagreement over social issues like ODWDA is suggested in the two dissents. Justice ANTONIN GREGORY SCALIA, arguing that Ashcroft had authority to issue his interpretative rule, observed: "Virtually every relevant source of authoritative meaning confirms that the phrase 'legitimate medical purpose' does not include intentionally assisting suicide." Justice CLARENCE THOMAS chided the majority for inconsistently beating a "hasty retreat" from its own year-old precedent in *GONZALES V. RAICH*, 545 U.S. 1 (2005), where it upheld Congress's authority under the COMMERCE CLAUSE to prohibit the local cultivation and use of marijuana in compliance with California law.

For more information: Behuniak, Susan M., and Arthur G. Svenson. *Physician-Assisted Suicide: The Anatomy of a Constitutional Law Issue.* Lanham, Md.: Rowman & Littlefield, 2003; Datlof, Steven B. "Beyond *Washington v. Glucksberg:* Oregon's Death with Dignity Act Analyzed from Medical and Constitutional Perspectives." *Journal of Law & Health* 14 (1999/2000): 23–44; Young, Ernest A. "Just Blowing Smoke? Politics, Doctrine, and the Federalist Revival after *Gonzales v. Raich.*" *Supreme Court Review* 2005 (2005): 1–50.

—James C. Foster

Gonzales v. Raich 545 U.S. 1 (2005)

In *Gonzales v. Raich*, a six-member majority ruled that Congress's Article I, Section 8 power "[t]o make all Laws which shall be Necessary and Proper" under the COMMERCE CLAUSE included the ability to prohibit the intrastate and non-commercial growing of marijuana for medicinal purposes. Furthermore, the Court ruled Congress had in fact done so in passing the Controlled Substances Act of 1970 when it criminalized the manufacture, sale, and possession of marijuana.

The decision struck down California's 1996 law that exempted from criminal prosecution physicians recommending the medical use of marijuana as well as patients and their caregivers possessing marijuana to be used for medical purposes with a prescription or recommendation from their doctor. While the medical use of marijuana remains controversial, proponents argue it provides relief from nausea, vomiting, seizures, chronic pain, and the lack of appetite caused by a number of diseases and their treatment. Ten other states—Alaska, Colorado, Hawaii, Maine, Maryland, Montana, Nevada, Oregon, Vermont, and Washington—had similar laws in place at the time of the *Raich* decision. To be eligible, most states required that patients register, and all states limited patients and their caregivers to small amounts of the drug. In 2005, enrollment in all states was estimated to be over 100,000.

The decision came as something of a surprise because the Court has handed down a series of FEDERALISM decisions—most importantly *UNITED STATES V. LOPEZ,* 514 U.S. 549 (1995), and *UNITED STATES V. MORRISON,* 529 U.S. 598 (2000)—in the previous decade that limited federal government power to regulate in areas that were traditionally controlled by the states. In a majority opinion written by Justice JOHN PAUL STEVENS, the Court found that Congress can regulate "purely local activities that are part of an economic 'class of activities' that have substantial effect on INTERSTATE COMMERCE" (17), and that the Controlled Substance Act "is squarely within Congress's commerce power" (19). Stevens found that cultivating marijuana, even when not intended for sale, has an impact on the national supply and demand for marijuana. Stevens also expressed sympathy for the plaintiffs and "the troubling facts of this case" (9), and he encouraged other institutions to find a way for medical marijuana use to continue. He noted that "the voices of voters . . . may one day be heard in the halls of Congress" (33). Justices ANTONIN GREGORY SCALIA and ANTHONY M. KENNEDY each sided with the federal government in the medical marijuana case, in contrast to their usual opposition to the expansion of federal government power.

Interestingly, in Justice SANDRA DAY O'CONNOR's dissent, she noted that she opposed the program but believed that there were limits to Congress's power to regulate commerce; if noneconomic activity such as this can be regulated, it "threatens to sweep all of productive human activity into federal regulatory reach" (49). Similarly, Justice CLARENCE THOMAS noted in a separate dissent that "our federalist system, properly understood, allows California and a growing number of other states to decide for themselves how to safeguard the health and welfare of its citizens."

The Court's decision did not end the debate, however. Distribution of medical marijuana continued in several states, even as the federal Drug Enforcement Administration began to pursue violators. Lobbying efforts encouraging Congress to pass legislation that will legalize medical marijuana nationally or at least allow each state to decide for itself are being pursued. The controversy over medical marijuana is only one recent example of the scope of federal government power and the proper role of the nation and the states. ENVIRONMENTAL REGULATIONS and physician-assisted suicide are other examples.

For more information: Young, Ernest A. "Just Blowing Smoke? Politics, Doctrine, and the Federal Revival after *Gonzales v. Raich.*" *Supreme Court Review* 2005 (2005): 1–50.

—William R. Wilkerson

good faith exception

The good faith exception to the EXCLUSIONARY RULE allows courts to admit evidence seized by police in violation of the FOURTH AMENDMENT into trial. The exclusionary rule provides that evidence obtained by police officers in violation of the Fourth Amendment guarantee against unreasonable searches and seizures is generally not admissible in a criminal trial to prove guilt. The rule was applied by the U.S. Supreme Court to the states in *Mapp v. Ohio,* 367 U.S. 642 (1961). The primary purpose of the exclusionary rule is to deter police misconduct (Carmen, 2006).

The exclusionary rule is perhaps the most controversial legal issue in criminal justice. Application of the rule may lead to the exclusion of important evidence and the acquittal of persons who are factually (if not legally) guilty. Proponents of the rule argue it is the only effective means of protecting individuals from illegal police searches, while critics decry the fact that application of the rule leads to the exclusion from trial of relevant evidence, making it harder to convict criminal defendants (Hemmens et al., 2004). Supreme Court decisions over the years have limited the scope of the rule, and created several exceptions.

Perhaps the most well known exception is the good faith exception, created by the Supreme Court in *Massachusetts v. Sheppard,* 468 U.S. 981 (1984). In this case, the Court held that evidence obtained by police officers acting in good faith on a search warrant issued by a neutral and detached magistrate that is ultimately found to be invalid may nonetheless be admitted at trial. The Court stressed that the primary rationale for the exclusionary rule—deterrence of police misconduct—did not warrant exclusion of evidence obtained by police who act reasonably and in good faith reliance upon the actions of a judge. By "good faith" the Court meant the police were unaware that the warrant was invalid.

The Court emphasized that the good faith exception did not apply to errors made by the police, even if the errors were entirely inadvertent. The exception applies only to situations where the police relied on others who, it later turns out, made a mistake. Subsequent cases reiterated this point. In *Illinois v. Krull,* 480 U.S. 340 (1987), the Court extended the good faith exception to instances where the police act in reliance on a statute that is later declared unconstitutional. In *Arizona v. Evans,* 514 U.S. 1 (1995), the Court refused to apply the exclusionary rule to evidence seized by a police officer who acted in reliance on a computer entry made by a court clerk, which was later found to be in error.

The exclusionary rule has aroused much debate since its application to the states some 40 years ago. The rule remains in place, although its application has been limited to exceptions created by the Supreme Court. Nonetheless, the rule still has a major and continuing impact on police practices, acting as the primary constraint on unlawful searches and seizures. So long as the exclusionary rule exists, it will serve, to some extent, as a limitation on police overreaching. It will also continue to result in the freeing of some guilty people. It is both the reward and the price we pay for living under a government of limited powers.

For more information: Carmen, Rolando del. *Criminal Procedure: Law and Practice.* 7th ed. Belmont, Calif.: Wadsworth/Thomson, 2006; Hemmens, Craig, John Worrall, and Alan Thompson. *Criminal Justice Case Briefs: Significant Cases in Criminal Procedure.* Los Angeles: Roxbury, 2004.

—Craig Hemmens

Good News Club v. Milford Central School

533 U.S. 98 (2001)

In *Good News Club v. Milford Central School,* the Supreme Court held that when a government agency opens its property to the public for First Amendment purposes, the free speech clause prevents the school from excluding groups on the basis of their viewpoint—including their religious viewpoint. In other words, religious organizations should be treated neutrally and given access to school grounds on the same basis as other groups. This case upheld the principle established in *Lamb's Chapel v. Center Moriches Union Free School District,* 508 U.S. 384 (1993).

Milford Central School established a policy authorizing residents of the school district to use its building after school for instruction in education or the arts, as well as for social, civic, recreational, and entertainment purposes. In accordance with the school's policy, the Good News Club, a private Christian organization for children, requested permission to hold its weekly meetings on school grounds. The school denied the request because the club's proposed uses, such as singing religious songs, presenting Bible lessons, memorizing scriptures, and praying, amounted to religious worship and were prohibited by the community use policy. The club challenged the school's decision, arguing that the denial of the club's application violated its free speech rights.

The Supreme Court held that the school violated the club's free speech rights by prohibiting it from meeting on school grounds. In his opinion for the Court, Justice CLARENCE THOMAS explained that Milford Central School operated a "limited PUBLIC FORUM." Although a government that operates a limited public forum is not required to allow persons to engage in every type of speech, the power to restrict speech is qualified. Speech restrictions must not discriminate against speech based on viewpoint and must be reasonable in light of the forum's purpose. The school's policy discriminated against the Good News Club on the basis of its religious viewpoint, and there was, in the Court's view, no logical difference between the Good News Club's invocation of Christianity and the invocation of teamwork, loyalty, or patriotism by other associations to provide a foundation for their lessons.

The Court also held that permitting the club to meet on the school's premises would not violate the ESTABLISHMENT CLAUSE of the First Amendment. The club's meetings would be held after school hours, would not be sponsored by the school, and would remain open to any student who obtained parental consent. Moreover, the school made its forum available to other organizations. The Court rejected the school's argument that elementary school children would perceive that the school was endorsing the club's Christian message and would feel coerced to participate in its activities.

Justice DAVID H. SOUTER dissented, in an opinion joined by Justices JOHN PAUL STEVENS and Ruth Bader Ginsburg, arguing that the Court's opinion is ridiculous and "ignores reality." If the Court is serious in its decision, Justice Souter thought, the holding amounts to the "remarkable proposition" that any public school opened for civic meetings must be opened for use as a church, synagogue, or mosque.

For more information: Hitchcock, James. *The Supreme Court and Religion in American Life.* Vol. 1, *The Odyssey of the Religion Clauses.* Princeton, N.J.: Princeton University Press, 2004.

—Winston E. Calvert

Gramm-Rudman-Hollings Act

The Gramm-Rudman-Hollings Act (GRH), also known as the Balanced Budget and Emergency Deficit Control Act of 1985, attempted to legislate a balanced federal budget by 1991. It reflected a conservative political movement that strongly opposed increased government spending. GRH was declared unconstitutional as a violation of separation of powers in *BOWSHER V. SYNAR*, 478 U.S. 714 (1986).

By 1985, budget deficits had created a panic among lawmakers who feared an impending economic collapse for the United States. President Ronald Reagan accused the Democratic-led Congress of being unable to rein spending. Congressional Democrats blamed the ballooning deficit on Reagan's tax cut in 1981 that lowered taxes for those in the highest tax brackets in an attempt to produce a trickle-down effect in the economy. Reagan's defense buildup was also faulted for running up huge bills.

Senator Phil Gramm, a Republican from Texas, a former economics professor at Texas A&M University who had once listed his research project as getting rid of government, had sought a balanced budget since arriving in Congress in 1979. In August 1985, Gramm proposed tacking a mandatory deficit reduction plan onto a debt-ceiling bill. He recruited Warren Rudman (Republican from New Hampshire) and Ernest Hollings (Democrat from South Carolina) as cosponsors. Democrats supported the bill because Reagan would have to scale back defense spending if he wanted a balanced budget. Reagan Republicans backed the bill because they thought that Democrats would be forced to cut social spending. Traditional Republicans voted for GRH because of a belief that Reagan might have to modify his refusal to raise taxes to achieve a balanced budget. With all parties on board, GRH passed.

GRH required automatic spending cuts divided equally between defense and nondefense spending should the president and Congress prove unable to agree upon a budget. Social Security expenditures, interest on the national debt, and some programs targeted at the poor were exempt from the automatic cuts. GRH set a timetable of reduced budget deficits beginning in 1985 and ending in 1991. It contained a clause that suspended action in the event of a recession, resuming spending cuts in the first year of recovery.

Events during the passage of GRH spelled problems for the future of the reform. The law made no distinction between useful and essential government actions and pork-barrel expenditures. Congress protected favored programs, and, due to constitutional problems, the institutional means for enforcing the automatic cuts was weak. In 1986, the Supreme Court ruled that the automatic cuts were unconstitutional. GRH did not have the power to make these cuts since the office of Comptroller of the Currency remained vested with this authority. The 1987 revision of GRH transferred that authority to the president. With the revision, Congress also moved the target date for a balanced budget to 1993. However, the Omnibus Budget Reconciliation Act of 1990 repealed GRH. At this time, the Council of Economic Advisers asserted that GRH had helped reduce the deficit by limiting its growth. Others, including Rudman, categorized GRH as simply a bad law.

For more information: Schier, Steven E. *A Decade of Deficits: Congressional Thought and Fiscal Action.* Albany: State University of New York Press, 1992.

—Caryn E. Neumann

Granholm v. Heald 544 U.S. 60 (2005)

In *Granholm v. Heald* and its companion case, *Swedenburg v. Kelly*, 544 U.S. 60 (2005), the Supreme Court invalidated state liquor laws regulating direct wine shipments by out-of-state wineries to in-state customers as a violation of the COMMERCE CLAUSE.

In *Granholm*, the federal district court upheld a Michigan statute permitting in-state direct shipment by wineries, but requiring out-of-state wineries to use state-licensed wholesalers and retailers. The Sixth Circuit reversed, because this discriminatory treatment violated the commerce clause. In *Swedenburg*, out-of-state wineries challenged a New York statute permitting them to make direct wine shipments, but imposing on them an unequal financial burden. The federal district court granted the wineries summary judgment, but the Second Circuit reversed, because the statute was a valid exercise of the state's TWENTY-FIRST AMENDMENT authority.

Justice ANTHONY M. KENNEDY's opinion for the Court was structured by the commerce clause, which created a national common market and permitted state laws to discriminate against trade in that market only in the narrowest circumstances. The Michigan and New York laws violated the commerce clause by permitting direct shipment by in-state wineries, but forbidding or discouraging direct shipment by out-of-state wineries. State laws which violate the commerce clause can be saved by the Twenty-first Amendment only if they use non-discriminatory means to advance a legitimate government purpose. Justice Kennedy acknowledged that Michigan and New York had a legitimate Twenty-first Amendment interest in protecting minors and collecting taxes. The states had, however, provided little evidence for their claim that these laws were necessary because minors used the Internet to purchase out-of-state wines and out-of-state wineries failed to pay state liquor taxes. The states could, therefore, achieve their legitimate purposes only with evenhanded laws either permitting direct shipment on equal terms or prohibiting all direct shipment.

Justice JOHN PAUL STEVENS, joined by Justice SANDRA DAY O'CONNOR in a brief dissent, argued that the Twenty-first Amendment had placed liquor in a special category, because it was a moral evil. The majority's decision, he argued, had displaced the policy choice made by the framers of the amendment and had treated "alcohol as an ordinary article of commerce, subject to substantially the same market and legal controls as other consumer products."

Justice CLARENCE THOMAS, joined by Chief Justice WILLIAM HUBBS REHNQUIST and Justices Stevens and O'Connor, issued a lengthy dissent which argued that the majority opinion contained three faults. First, it misinterpreted the Webb-Kenyon Act (1913) and the Twenty-first Amendment, which authorize states to discriminate in favor of in-state direct liquor shipments. Second, it was at odds with the Court's early Twenty-first Amendment jurisprudence allowing discrimination against out-of-state liquor producers. Third, it misrepresented the Court's recent Twenty-first Amendment jurisprudence and relied upon *Bacchus Imports v. Diaz* (1986), which should be overruled, because it stood alone as the Court's only decision holding that the amendment does not authorize discrimination against out-of-state liquor.

Granholm v. Heald altered the constitutional regime for alcoholic beverage control. States were not permitted to interpret their Twenty-first Amendment authority so broadly as to provide their wineries with a competitive advantage by discriminating against the direct shipment of wine in the interstate marketplace.

For more information: Millis, Matthew B. "Let History Be Our Guide: Using Historical Analogies to Analyze State Response to a Post-*Granholm* Era." *Indiana Law Journal* 81 (2006): 1,097–1,123.

—William Crawford Green

Gratz v. Bollinger 539 U.S. 244, 123 S.Ct. 2411 (2003)

In *Gratz v. Bollinger,* the Supreme Court struck down the undergraduate admissions policy used by the University of Michigan's College of Literature, Science, and the Arts. The policy admitted prospective students based on a comprehensive 150 point system. African-American, Hispanic, and Native American candidates were automatically granted 20 of the 100 points necessary for guaranteed admission. This point allotment made it so that virtually every student belonging to one of the favored minority groups was granted admission. Two white students who were denied admission brought this suit against the university's president, alleging that the admissions policy violated the EQUAL PROTECTION clause of the FOURTEENTH AMENDMENT, Title VI of the CIVIL RIGHTS ACT OF 1964, and 42 U.S.C. Section 1981.

Chief Justice WILLIAM HUBBS REHNQUIST delivered the opinion of the Court, joined by Justices SANDRA DAY O'CONNOR, ANTONIN GREGORY SCALIA, ANTHONY M. KENNEDY, and CLARENCE THOMAS. In its decision, the Court relied heavily on *REGENTS OF THE UNIVERSITY OF CALIFORNIA V. BAKKE,* 438 U.S. 265 (1978), and *GRUTTER V. BOLLINGER,* 539 U.S. 306 (2003), the companion case to *Gratz* decided the same day. The Court struck down the policy as a violation of the equal protection clause and, necessarily, as a violation of 42 U.S.C. Section 1981.

In order to be constitutional, a race classification must be narrowly tailored to achieve a compelling state interest. The Court ruled that the automatic point allotment was not narrowly tailored because there was no process for individualized review of each applicant's credentials. In this manner, the policy was more like the quota system described in *Bakke* than the nonnumerical weighting system used by the University of Michigan Law School in *Grutter.*

The university offered two main arguments in support of its position. First, it argued that there was a policy in place by which applicants with characteristics deemed important to the composition of the freshman class were separated and flagged for review without regard to the point system. The Court noted, however, that this process was rarely used and only served to undermine the system as a whole, since the university deemed race to be an important characteristic, but it did not flag every application from a student of a preferred minority group for further review.

The university also argued that individual review of each application was not feasible given the vast number of applications received each year. The Court responded by arguing that administrative challenges do not make an otherwise flawed system constitutional. After all, as the Court noted in *Grutter,* the law school individually reviews over 3,500 applications for its incoming class of approximately 350 students, a ratio of 10 applications for each available spot.

After 25 years, the confusion caused by the plurality decision in *Bakke* was put to the test and clarified by a majority of the Court in both *Grutter* and *Gratz.* However, given the variety of programs aimed at correcting racial injustice in education, it is unlikely this issue is permanently settled.

For more information: Greene, Linda S. "The Constitution and Racial Equality After Gratz and Grutter." *Washburn Law Journal* 43 (Winter 2004): 253–283.

—Dylan R. Kytola

Gravel v. United States 408 U.S. 606 (1972)

In *Gravel v. United States,* the Supreme Court, in a 5-4 vote with William J. Brennan, Jr.; William O. Douglas; Thurgood Marshall; and Potter Stewart dissenting, held that the speech and debate clause privilege of the Constitution applies to congressmen and their aides in the performance of their duties but does not extend beyond that.

The Constitution authorizes the Senate and the House of Representatives to discipline its members. However, Article 1, Section 6 of the Constitution, referred to as the speech and debate clause, also provides safeguards for its members against harassment and intimidation. This privilege of membership has its roots in British practice. The English Parliament in its historical struggles with the British Crown asserted that its members were immune from arrest during its sessions, and the English Bill of Rights of 1689 embodies this guarantee. In the American Constitution, without the protection of the speech and debate clause, a U.S. president could order the arrest or otherwise intimidate members of Congress who are in opposition to administration goals and policies. The speech and debate clause provision ensures the integrity of the legislative process through the independence of the individual legislators during the performance of their legislative duties and serves to reinforce the separation of powers among the government's three branches.

Interpretation of the language of Article 1, Section 6 has generally centered on a definition of what is legitimate legislative activity and generated two kinds of constitutional questions: what is protected and who is protected within the speech and debate clause? *Gravel v. United States* addressed both what and who was to be protected.

On June 29, 1971, Senator Mike Gravel, Democrat from Alaska, held a public meeting of the Subcommittee on Buildings and Grounds of which he was the chair. Before the hearing began, Gravel made a statement regarding the Vietnam War and then read portions of a classified government document entitled *History of the United States Decision-Making Process on Vietnam Policy,* now known as the Pentagon Papers, which provided details of U.S. involvement in the war. Senator Gravel proceeded to introduce the document into the committee's record and arranged for possible republication of the document. There were also media reports that a member of Gravel's staff, Dr. Leonard Rodberg, had spoken with a second publisher regarding possible republication of the classified documents. A grand jury was convened to investigate whether or not any criminal violations had occurred concerning the handling of classified materials. Dr. Rodberg was subpoenaed to testify. Senator Gravel moved to quash the subpoena as a violation of the speech and debate clause, because ordering the aide to testify was tantamount to having the senator testify, which according to Senator Gravel would violate the speech and debate clause.

The district court denied the motion by Senator Gravel but limited the questioning of Senator Gravel's aide. The court of appeals affirmed the motion's denial but modified the protective order in ruling that congressional aides and other persons may not be questioned regarding legislative acts and that limiting the questioning was within the scope of the congressional privilege intended by the speech and debate clause, thereby foreclosing further inquiry by the grand jury. The government petitioned for certiorari to the Supreme Court, challenging the ruling of the court of appeals.

The Supreme Court answered the question of what is protected by the speech and debate clause by upholding the right of a grand jury to inquire into the circumstances under which a member obtained classified government documents and arranged for their private republication. The Court reasoned that the speech and debate clause recognizes speech, voting, and other legislative acts to be immune from liability; however, the speech and debate clause does not extend to either senator or aide immunity to violate an otherwise valid criminal law in preparing or implementing legislative acts.

The Supreme Court's decision in the *Gravel* case not only answered what was protected under the speech and debate clause but also explicitly answered who was protected under the speech and debate clause by fully bringing congressional staff as well as congressional members under the speech and debate clause's protection. In recognizing the expanding role of staff, the Court acknowledged that the rapidly changing technology necessary in the performance of legislative duties makes the day-to-day work of congressional aides equivalent to being an alter ego of the congressional member. Not to recognize congressional staff accordingly would significantly diminish the intended effect of the speech and debate clause.

Gravel illustrated that legislative acts are not all-encompassing. The heart of the speech and debate clause is speech or debate in either House. In this case, the private publication arrangements by Senator Gravel were not part and parcel of the legislative process.

For more information: Kalven, Harvey. *A Worthy Tradition: Freedom of Speech in America.* New York: Harper & Row, 1988.

—William W. Riggs

Green v. County School Board of New Kent County, Virginia 391 U.S. 430 (1968)

In *Green v. County School Board of New Kent County, Virginia,* the U.S. Supreme Court displayed its frustration with the slow pace of school DESEGREGATION in the 14 years after *BROWN V. BOARD OF EDUCATION,* 347 U.S. 483 (1954), and ordered school systems to make progress "that promises realistically to work now."

In the landmark *Brown* ruling in 1954, the Supreme Court ruled that operation of separate school systems for black and white children violated the EQUAL PROTECTION clause of the FOURTEENTH AMENDMENT. The following year, in *Brown v. Board of Education (Brown II),* 349 U.S. 294 (1955), the Supreme Court urged school systems to begin dismantling segregation "with all deliberate speed," but did not set any deadlines or impose any penalties for noncompliance.

Response in many southern states ranged from open resistance and defiance to mere noncompliance. In New Kent County, Virginia, a rural area outside of Richmond, the school board did virtually nothing for a decade to try to eliminate the separate white and black schools that state law had required. Then the school board adopted a freedom-of-choice plan, which meant any student could attend any school. A federal district court and the U.S. Court of Appeals for the Fourth Circuit largely upheld the choice plan.

In an unanimous decision written by Justice WILLIAM J. BRENNAN, JR., the Supreme Court said New Kent County had not done nearly enough to eliminate the remnants of a segregated school system. He said the goal was to stop running dual school systems and to begin to operate a "unitary" system.

The Court noted that in three years under the freedom-of-choice plan, not a single white student had changed schools; and although 115 black students had moved to the white school, 85 percent of black children were still attending an all-black school. Instructing federal judges on how to evaluate freedom-of-choice systems, Brennan said, "Of course, the availability to the board of other more promising courses of action may indicate a lack of good faith; and at the least it places a heavy burden upon the board to explain its preference for an apparently less effective method."

A key portion of Brennan's decision observed that segregation traditionally involved racial separation not just for pupil assignment, but also for transportation, staff, teachers, extracurricular activities, and facilities. These came to be known as the "*Green* factors," and for nearly 25 years federal judges took the approach that segregation had to be eliminated in all of these facets of school operation at the same time. However, in *Freeman v. Pitts,* 503 U.S. 467 (1992), the Supreme Court ruled that if a school system eliminated the effects of segregation in one facet, a federal court could release the school system from court supervision as to that factor.

The Court's determination in *Green* to have school systems get on with the task helped show officials that the justices were serious and that delay was no longer acceptable.

In 2001, the formerly white New Kent School and the formerly black George Watkins School were designated national historic landmarks.

For more information: Orfield, Gary, and David Thronson. "Dismantling Desegregation: Uncertain Gains, Unexpected Costs." *Emory Law Journal* 42 (1993): 759–790.

—Stephen Wermiel

Gregg v. Georgia 428 U.S. 153 (1976)

In this case the Supreme Court reestablished the death penalty, subsequently answering the question of whether the imposition of the death penalty sentence was not allowable under the Eighth and FOURTEENTH AMENDMENTS of the Constitution.

The *FURMAN V. GEORGIA,* 408 U.S. 238 (1972), case, which halted the practice of prescribing death as a penalty was overturned by the *Gregg* decision. The focus of the opponents of the death penalty was that the application of such a rule of law is subjecting the defendant to "cruel and unusual" punishment. The deterrent nature of the death penalty was not a rationale the high court used to allow the penalty of death to be again established, but rather the manner in which the decision was reached. The Supreme Court held that under the Constitution, with a majority decision of 7 to 2, a punishment of death did not violate either the Eighth or Fourteenth Amendment in every scenario.

In more recent years, the view of the death penalty and the application of sentences of death have spurred a revamping and reanalysis of whether or not the system retains DUE PROCESS flaws. The commission of heinous crime when someone willfully kills another with the intent to do so in a depraved manner rises to a level of indifference to human life, and these cases have been determined to be acceptable for the application of the death penalty. The subject matter for the case involved the careful application by the state of Georgia and their methodological approach to application of such a penalty within the law through the separation of sentencing and trial. A careful contextual analysis was performed by the judiciary so as to determine whether the application is acceptable based upon similar scenarios and cases.

Gregg had committed a robbery and double murder. The case went to trial, where he was convicted of his crimes and sentenced to death, whereupon he challenged that the application of the death sentence would be CRUEL AND UNUSUAL PUNISHMENT. The jury decided that the behavior where Gregg could be sentenced to death were the convictions that he received for the counts of murder. The jury believed that the murders were completed during the commission of a capital crime and that the murders where intentional and wanton, which in sum rose to the level deemed appropriate for application of the death penalty. The automatic review by the Georgia State Supreme Court believed that no error in law was made, the prescription for the penalty of death had been reached in an unbiased manner, and no arbitrary factors were overlooked, so the conviction should stand.

For more than a few justices, the contradictions of *Gregg* finally proved too much. Of the original seven-vote *Gregg* plurality, two justices—Harry Blackmun and LEWIS FRANKLIN POWELL, JR.—came to publicly regret their endorsement of CAPITAL PUNISHMENT, and another—JOHN PAUL STEVENS—seems on a case-by-case basis to be headed the same way. SANDRA DAY O'CONNOR spent her last years on the Court shutting many of the doors *Gregg* had opened—execution of juveniles and the retarded, for instance—and expressing her grave reservations about capital representation. Justice ANTHONY M. KENNEDY seems to have inherited her unease. Recent attitudes within the high court suggest that the tide may be again turning, as is evidenced by the Supreme Court's decisions to limit the execution of both juveniles and those of challenged intelligence.

For more information: Hemmens, Craig, Katherine Bennett, and Barbara Belbot. *Criminal Justice Case Briefs. Significant Cases in Corrections.* Los Angeles, Calif.: Roxbury Pub. Co., 2004.

—Ernest Gomez

Gregory v. Ashcroft 501 U.S. 452 (1991)

In *Gregory v. Ashcroft*, the Supreme Court ruled that Missouri's constitutional mandatory retirement of state judges at the age of 70 did not violate the Age Discrimination and Employment Act of 1967 (ADEA) and did not violate the EQUAL PROTECTION clause of the FOURTEENTH AMENDMENT. This ruling upheld the states' right to determine the terms of judicial service without a clear indication by Congress to override state sovereignty.

Judges Gregory and Nugent filed suit against Governor Ashcroft, seeking to overturn a Missouri constitutional provision requiring mandatory retirement of state judges at the age of 70. Article V, 26 of the Missouri Constitution states, "All judges other than municipal judges shall retire at the age of seventy years." Gregory and Nugent argued that the ADEA prevents age discrimination against an "employee." The section of the ADEA in controversy defines an employee as "an individual employed by an employer except that the term 'employee' shall not include any person elected to public office in any State or political subdivision of any State by the qualified voters thereof, or any person chosen by such officer to be on such officer's personal staff, or an appointee on the policymaking level or an immediate adviser with respect to the exercise of the constitutional or legal powers of the office" (29 U.S.C. 630[f]). They also argue that the treatment of judges, as separate from other state employees and/or municipal judges, is a violation of the equal protection clause of the Fourteenth Amendment. Gregory and Nugent were appointed to their judicial positions but retain their positions through retention elections, which are at times unopposed.

The United States district court granted Governor Ashcroft's motion to dismiss, ruling that the ADEA did not apply to the judges because they are "appointees on the policymaking level" and because under the equal protection clause test, there is a rational basis for seeking judicial retirement at the age of 70. The U.S. Court of Appeals for the Eighth Circuit affirmed the lower court dismissal. The Supreme Court affirmed the lower courts' ruling and Justice SANDRA DAY O'CONNOR delivered the opinion of the court.

The majority reasoned that the state of Missouri enacted this constitutional provision under the state's sovereignty, requiring a clear statement by the federal Congress to upset that sovereign authority. The court ruled that such a usurpation of authority by the federal government against a state government requires a "clear statement" of that intent. Since no clear statement exists, the Supreme Court felt no such attempt was made.

O'Connor then reasoned that state judges are ambiguous as to whether they are or are not covered by the ADEA exception of employee. She felt a clear statement by Congress to include state judges is warranted in an issue touching on the question of FEDERALISM and sovereignty. It is more likely that state judges would be excluded, in order to avoid difficult questions of federalism, than included. Therefore, the judges fall under the ADEA exception of "appointee on the policymaking level."

Since age is not a "suspect classification" under the equal protection line of cases, and Gregory and Nugent have not claimed a fundamental right to continue to practice as judges, the state need only assert a "rational basis" for its classification under the state constitution. O'Connor offered and evidenced several rational reasons for disparate treatment of state judges and held that the Missouri constitutional provision did not violate the equal protection clause of the U.S. Constitution.

Justices Harry Blackmun and Thurgood Marshall dissented tracing the congressional debate to a discussion regarding only an "elected official's first line advisers" in the exceptions to the ADEA. Similarly, they would have deferred to the EEOC's interpretation of the statute the EEOC must administer and regarded the state judges as covered under the ADEA.

Justices Byron White and JOHN PAUL STEVENS concurred in part and in the judgment but dissented with regard to the use of the plain statement rule as being unworkable and unwise to resolve this and most other disputes.

This case is important because it limits the reach of federal intrusion on state sovereignty but does so without addressing a fundamental problem, federal power under the COMMERCE CLAUSE.

For more information: Peterson, Paul E. *The Price of Federalism.* Washington, D.C.: Brookings Institution, 1995.

—Julian M. Davis

Griggs v. Duke Power Co. 401 U.S. 424 (1971)

In *Griggs v. Duke Power,* the Supreme Court held that Title VII of the CIVIL RIGHTS ACT OF 1964 prohibits employment practices that discriminate against persons based on race, even if the intent behind the practices was benign. The importance of this landmark ruling resided with the Court's interpreting Title VII to prohibit both disparate treatment (behavior) and impact (consequences of seemingly nondiscriminatory practices).

In this case, Duke Power, which had prior to the passage of the 1964 Civil Rights Act separate job classifications depending upon the employee's race, required all applicants for traditionally white classifications to pass two aptitude tests and have a record of completing high school. Griggs and other black employees at the company's generating plant brought suit, claiming that the aptitude tests and high school diploma were not job related and affected a disproportionate number of blacks regarding promotion, transfer, or employment.

Chief Justice WARREN EARL BURGER, writing for a unanimous Court (Justice WILLIAM J. BRENNAN, JR., not participating), stated that Congress's purpose in Title VII of the 1964 Civil Rights Act was to achieve equality in employment opportunities and to remove any barriers that had tended to favor white employees over employees of other races. Moreover, Burger emphasized how Congress was not trying to grant jobs to persons unqualified for positions, but rather, it was attempting to remove those methods that businesses used to maintain segregation or discrimination in the workplace.

After reviewing the purpose of the law, Burger then made clear that the Act not only prohibited overt discrimination, but "also practices fair in form but discriminatory in operation." Unless a business could show that a test, requirement, etc. could be shown to relate to job performance, the practice was not allowed under the Act. Applied to the case facts, the Court said that there was little evidence presented by Duke Power to suggest that the aptitude tests and high school diploma were related to the jobs to which blacks were applying (with the burden of proof falling on the company to show that the practice was not discriminatory). Rather, the company felt that the tests and diploma requirements would improve the overall quality of the workforce. Though the intent of the company was not discriminatory in purpose (improving overall quality), its impact was felt in disproportionate numbers by blacks who were eliminated for employment consideration.

Subsequent case law in this field developed the notion that plaintiffs (those alleging DISPARATE IMPACT) initially had to show that there was statistical evidence that one group was suffering discrimination at the hands of business, but then, the defendant had the burden to prove that its practices were a business necessity. In 1989, however, a more conservative Court held in *Ward's Cove Packing Co. v. Atonio* (1989) that the plaintiff had the burden of proof at all times, making it more difficult for individuals to demonstrate disparate impact. Congress, in the Civil Rights Act of 1991, made it clear that the standard prior to the *Ward's Cove* decision was to be followed in disparate impact cases.

For more information: Roberts, Gary E. "Issues, Challenges, and Changes in Recruitment and Selection." In *Public Personnel Administration: Problems and Prospects.* 4th ed. Upper Saddle River, N.J.: Prentice Hall, 2003.

—John M. Aughenbaugh

Griswold v. Connecticut 381 U.S. 479 (1965)

In the case of *Griswold v. Connecticut,* the United States Supreme Court held that the Constitution holds an implicit right to PRIVACY which is guaranteed to American citizens through the First, Third, Fourth, Fifth, and Ninth Amendments.

The defendants in *Griswold* were an executive director of the Planned Parenthood League of Connecticut and a licensed doctor and Yale Medical School professor who served as the medical director for the New Haven, Connecticut, Planned Parenthood League center. The facts in the case alleged that both defendants gave "information, instruction, and medical advice to married persons as to the means of preventing conception." A Connecticut statute made the use of CONTRACEPTIVES a criminal offense. The defendants were convicted of having violated the statute as accessories to the crime for having disseminated the contraception information. It should be noted that no users of the contraception information, married or single, were ever charged in the case.

Justice WILLIAM O. DOUGLAS begins by using the amendments listed above to illustrate his points on privacy. The FIRST AMENDMENT's right of association stands for the principle that one may associate with whom one wants and it remains a private matter. The THIRD AMENDMENT's prohibition against the quartering of soldiers during peacetime illustrates that American citizens should not have to fear private discussions in their own homes because of having to house a soldier there who might be spying on them. The FOURTH AMENDMENT's protection against unreasonable search and seizure guarantees a citizen's protection from the unreasonable viewing of his or her possessions and actions without a proper determination of probable cause. The Fifth Amendment's protection from self-incrimination means that a citizen may keep private information which would tend to incriminate him in a certain criminal action. The NINTH AMENDMENT's reservation of non-enumerated rights to the people of the United States implies that the right of privacy is not specifically granted to the government, but to the people. These amendments create a "penumbra" or "zone of privacy" under which the right of married people to use contraceptives falls.

The Court ruled that the right of privacy to use birth control within the confines of marriage was a legitimate right and thus concluded that the Connecticut Gen. Stat. § 53-32 (rev. 1958) was unconstitutional, reversing the defendants' convictions.

For more information: Schwartz, Bernard. *A History of the Supreme Court.* New York: Oxford University Press, 1993.

—Kelli Styron

Grutter v. Bollinger 539 U.S. 306 (2003)

In *Grutter v. Bollinger,* a sharply divided Court ruled that using race in a narrowly-tailored admissions policy furthered the state school's compelling interests and did not conflict with the EQUAL PROTECTION clause of the FOURTEENTH AMENDMENT, Title VI of the CIVIL RIGHTS ACT OF 1964, or with 42 U.S.C. Section 1981.

The case arose when Barbara Grutter, a white woman, sued Dean Lee Bollinger when the University of Michigan law school denied her admission under a policy that included an affirmative effort to enroll a critical mass of underrepresented minority students. The university claimed that race was only one of several factors it used to select a diverse student body that would contribute to the school's character and the legal profession. Grutter argued the admissions policy favored minorities over Caucasians.

Justice SANDRA DAY O'CONNOR, who wrote for herself, and Justices JOHN PAUL STEVENS, DAVID H. SOUTER, Ruth Bader Ginsburg, and STEVEN G. BREYER relied heavily on Justice LEWIS FRANKLIN POWELL, JR.'s landmark opinion in *REGENTS OF THE UNIVERSITY OF CALIFORNIA V. BAKKE,* 438 U.S. 265 (1978), where Powell sustained the use of race as one factor in admitting students for the purpose of fostering a robust exchange of ideas within a heterogeneous class environment.

Chief Justice WILLIAM HUBBS REHNQUIST, joined by Justices ANTONIN GREGORY SCALIA, ANTHONY M. KENNEDY, and CLARENCE THOMAS, dissented. Rehnquist maintained that the admissions policy was not narrowly tailored but was a veiled attempt to achieve racial balancing. He concluded that, since the numbers of admissions of various minorities differed from one another and were close to the proportion of minorities in the applicant pool, they must have been based on race and ethnicity rather than upon some notion of critical mass.

In a companion case, GRATZ V. BOLLINGER, involving the undergraduate College of Literature, Science, and the Arts, a 6-3 Court invalidated an admissions procedure that automatically gave a 20-point bonus out of a 100-point total to each African-American, Hispanic, and Native-American applicant. Chief Justice Rehnquist, who wrote for the majority, called the policy a functional equivalent of a quota and said it offended *Bakke*, since it was not narrowly tailored to achieve a compelling interest.

For more information: Devins, Neal. "Explaining *Grutter v. Bollinger.*" *University of Pennsylvania Law Review* 152, no. 1 (2003): 347–383; Guinier, Lani. "Admissions Rituals as Political Acts: Guardians at the Gates of Our Democratic Ideals." *Harvard Law Review* 117, no. 1 (2003): 113–225.

—JeDon Emenhiser

guarantee clause (U.S. Constitution Article IV, Section 4)

The Constitution's guarantee clause directs the federal government to "guarantee to every State in this Union a Republican Form of Government"—not a government run by a particular political party, but a government run by representatives of the people.

The clause represents an important allocation of power within the federal structure, but the text neither defines a "republican" form of government nor clarifies what federal officials should do to effect the guarantee. It was designed in part to reassure states that the new national government would commit to protect each state against attempts to topple its government. Various commentators have since suggested that, absent this sort of insurrection, the clause should be interpreted to protect or forbid different ways in which representatives are elected, representative power is apportioned, or the legislative process is carried out.

There is, however, no definitive interpretation of the scope of the guarantee clause, because the judicial branch—the usual final arbiter of legal meaning—has largely tied its own hands. In the last 150 years, the Supreme Court has generally said that Congress and the president, not the courts, should decide whether a particular practice violates the guarantee. In other words, the Supreme Court has usually said that the rights granted by the clause are "nonjusticiable."

This approach began with LUTHER V. BORDEN, 48 U.S. (7 How.) 1 (1849). By 1841, Rhode Island was the only state where real estate ownership was still required to vote. With support from some of the state's propertied voters, disenfranchised and disaffected citizens established their own constitution and government; the dispute then turned violent, in what became known as Dorr's Rebellion. A state official named Borden arrested one of the rebelling citizens, named Luther, and allegedly damaged his property. When Luther sued, the dispute turned in part on which government was legitimate. The Supreme Court refused to decide the question, saying that under the guarantee clause, Congress alone—and not the courts—had the right to choose between two ostensibly legitimate governments.

Over the next century, this line of reasoning expanded: the political branches alone had the right to decide whether the guarantee of a republican government prohibited a state from legislating by popular initiative (*Pacific States Telephone & Telegraph Co. v. Oregon*, 223 U.S. 118 [1912]); prohibited a legislature from delegating decisions to a probate judge (*Ohio ex rel. Bryant v. Akron Metropolitan Park Dist.*, 281 U.S. 74 [1930]); or prohibited the federal government from demanding that states seek federal approval for certain legislation (*City of Rome v. United States*, 446 U.S. 156 [1980]).

The Supreme Court's refusal to decide cases under the guarantee clause was not absolute. On occasion, it has decided that certain practices do not unduly detract from a state's republican governmental structure. A state still maintains its republican form of government, for example, when a state court and not the legislature changes municipal boundaries (*Forsyth v. Hammond,* 166 U.S. 506 [1897]); when a state commission and not the legislature regulates milk prices, (*Highland Farms Dairy v. Agnew,* 300 U.S. 608 [1937]); and when a federal statute provides monetary incentives for states to act in certain ways (*New York v. United States,* 505 U.S. 144 [1992]).

Thus, when rights under the guarantee clause are asserted, courts sometimes decide not to decide, and sometimes they decide that the practice in question does not deprive the state of a republican form of government. Very few courts to date have decided that a particular policy offends the guarantee clause and must be overturned.

Congress has also exercised that power only in the rarest of cases. After the Civil War, for example, Congress agreed to admit or readmit states into the Union only as they agreed to extend the franchise to African Americans. In several of these instances, Congress declared explicitly that its power to exact these conditions arose under the guarantee clause. As Senator Charles Sumner recognized, this exceedingly rare but exceedingly powerful exercise of authority rendered the clause a "sleeping giant."

Since the 1860s, with few exceptions, neither Congress nor the courts have done much to articulate the contours of the rights guaranteed by the guarantee clause. Yet this does not mean that the clause is entirely a dead letter. In 1992, the Supreme Court signaled that a case might one day again present claims under the guarantee clause that federal courts are competent to resolve. Until then, the clause will likely remain patiently "sleeping."

For more information: Ely, John Hart. *Democracy and Distrust: A Theory of Judicial Review.* Cambridge, Mass.: Harvard University Press, 1980; Merritt, Deborah Jones. "The Guarantee Clause and State Autonomy: Federalism for a Third Century." *Columbia Law Review* 88 (1988): 1–78; Wiecek, William. *The Guarantee Clause of the U.S. Constitution.* Ithaca, N.Y.: Cornell University Press, 1972.

—Justin Levitt

gun control

See RIGHT TO BEAR ARMS; *PRINTZ V. UNITED STATES; UNITED STATES V. LOPEZ*

habeas corpus

Habeas corpus is a legal proceeding in which a prisoner asks a court to evaluate the legality of his or her detention. After the prisoner files a petition with the court, the court orders the governmental official with custody of the prisoner to appear in court, with the prisoner, and explain the legal justification for the detention. If the court determines that the detention is unlawful, the court has the authority to order the prisoner immediately released. For this reason, the writ of habeas corpus, often referred to as the "Great Writ," has always been considered an important means for protecting personal freedom from unlawful and arbitrary government action. The overriding purpose of habeas corpus is to keep the executive departments of government accountable to the judiciary.

The term habeas corpus comes from the Latin phrase *habeas corpus ad subjiciendum,* which means have the body to submit to the authority of the court. The writ of habeas corpus originated in the common law and traces its roots to the Habeas Corpus Act of 1679 enacted by the British Parliament. It was later included in the Constitution of the United States. Article 1, Section 9 states: "The Privilege of the Writ of Habeas Corpus shall not be suspended, unless when in Cases of Rebellion or Invasion the public Safety may require it."

Originally, habeas corpus was a procedure for the federal judiciary to evaluate the legality of the federal government's authority as a purely jurisdictional matter. In other words, it was a proceeding in which the courts sought to answer the question of whether the prisoner's detention was a legitimate exercise of the federal government's authority. In those cases, the government official could justify the legality of the detention of a prisoner by showing the court documents, such as a warrant or a judgment of conviction, which ordered the official to imprison the individual. Over the years, however, both the availability of the Great Writ and the nature of claims that could be considered have been expanded significantly. First, in 1867, the U.S. Congress enacted a habeas corpus statute that extended the writ to include consideration of whether a state prisoner's detention violated of any of the rights protected by the U.S. Constitution. Then, following the ratification of the FOURTEENTH AMENDMENT as the BILL OF RIGHTS was applied to the states, the types of claims that could be asserted against state officials as constitutional violations grew substantially.

By the 1970s, habeas corpus was viewed as a means for asserting any provision of the national constitution as a challenge to the legality of any detention imposed by any government. This included challenges to incarceration following a criminal conviction, detention immediately following arrest, and commitment to a mental institution. It also included challenges to the nature of the detention.

However, it was most often used by state inmates as a means of post-conviction review of their criminal convictions in state court under the U.S. Constitution in federal court. The expansion of the procedure to include allegations of constitutional violations that occurred at trial led to comprehensive review of state court criminal trials in the federal courts. Most notably, state inmates were afforded a forum to allege that they were denied the RIGHT TO COUNSEL under the SIXTH AMENDMENT. Such claims constitute the bulk of the claims reviewed by federal courts in habeas corpus proceedings.

Eventually, the broad review exercised by the federal courts became the subject of great controversy. The federal courts increasingly disliked the remarkable increase in their caseloads caused by habeas corpus petitions filed by state inmates. Meanwhile, the general public began to criticize the federal courts because of the delays caused by habeas corpus litigation and what seemed to be unending abuse of the justice system by inmates. The courts responded by placing limits on the filing of habeas corpus petitions and the claims that could be raised, including: the requirement that claims first be raised at every level of the state courts; the preclusion of claims seeking retroactive application of new rules of constitutional law; the application of a lower standard of the HARMLESS ERROR doctrine; and an absolute preclusion of claims under the FOURTH AMENDMENT's search and seizure clause.

The public backlash against habeas corpus review in federal courts led to the enactment of the Anti-Terrorism and Effective Death Penalty Act of 1996 (AEDPA). This statute created new prerequisites for habeas corpus review, codified some of the judicially created limitations, and created special procedures for death penalty cases. Notably, the AEDPA imposed a one-year time period for seeking habeas corpus review, required all state court procedures to be pursued before seeking habeas corpus review, and prohibited the filing of multiple petitions. More importantly, the AEDPA imposed a requirement that federal courts defer to the judgment of the state courts unless that judgment was unreasonable and placed a substantial limitation on a prisoner's right to an evidentiary hearing in federal court. The unreasonableness standard and the prohibition of hearings substantially limited the availability of habeas corpus relief for state prisoners.

Nevertheless, habeas corpus remains a very important remedy for state prisoners. It is generally referred to as the third tier of review because it follows the two tiers of review available in most state court systems: trial and direct appeal, and post-conviction review. In that context, the writ of habeas corpus remains an important safeguard of individual liberty. It provides a forum in federal court through which violations of rights protected by the U.S. Constitution may be corrected in cases in which the state courts fail to do so.

The controversy surrounding the availability of the writ and the nature of claims that can be raised continues. The question is whether a state prisoner may pursue a claim of innocence as part of a federal habeas corpus proceeding. In the past, claims of innocence have been precluded from habeas corpus review because the determination of guilt has been considered a factual question reserved for the jury to resolve, rather than a legal question to be resolved in federal court. State and federal courts have long recognized that, under the U.S. Constitution, an accused person is entitled to a fair trial, not a perfect trial. Thus, there has been an implicit recognition that even the procedural protections afforded to an accused in the criminal justice system may not preclude the accused from being convicted of a crime he or she did not commit.

However, if the accused received a fundamentally fair trial, the Constitution will not have been violated. Moreover, the procedural rules applied to habeas corpus petitions have precluded claims of innocence except as a means of setting aside the procedural limitations to federal review. But as DNA evidence becomes more sophisticated, questions are being raised concerning the availability of habeas corpus review for claims of innocence that cannot be raised in state courts. The resolution of that question could alter the nature and scope of federal habeas corpus review and open habeas corpus up to jury trials on the prisoner's claim of innocence.

The right of habeas corpus, including to whom it applies and where, was raised in the context of the war on terrorism following the terrorist attacks against the United States on September 11, 2001.

After these attacks, President George W. Bush created a facility at the U.S. Naval Station at Guantánamo Bay, Cuba, to incarcerate individuals who were suspected of being involved in the events of 9/11 or other acts of terrorism. These individuals were declared by the president to be "enemy combatants," not entitled to protections under international law, such as the Geneva Convention Relative to the Treatment of Prisoners of War, and were ordered held without habeas corpus protection. The president contended that since these individuals were either enemy combatants, noncitizens, or were located at a faculty outside of United States' sovereign control, habeas did not apply.

In a series of decisions, the Supreme Court rejected these arguments. In *HAMDI V. RUMSFELD*, 542 U.S. 507 (2004), the Court ruled that a U.S. citizen could not be held indefinitely on U.S. soil without a right to habeas corpus review. In *RASUL V. BUSH*, 545 U.S. 466 (2004), it ruled that aliens being held in confinement at the U.S. military base in Guantánamo Bay, Cuba, were entitled to have a federal court hear challenges to their detention under the federal habeas corpus statute. In *Hamdan v. Rumsfeld*, 548 U.S. , 126 S.Ct. 2749 (2006), the Supreme Court ruled that a Yemeni national held at Guantánamo Bay was entitled to habeas review of his detention and trial before a special military commission. The Court ruled that the Detainee Treatment Act (DTA) of 2005, which sought to deny habeas review to any alien detained at this facility did not apply to persons whose cases were in the courts at the time the act was adopted. Congress then adopted the Military Commissions Act (MCA) of 2006, which sought to preclude courts from having habeas jurisdiction over detained aliens determined to be enemy combatants. Finally, in *BOUMEDIENE V. BUSH*, ___ U.S. ___, 128 S.Ct. 2229 (2008), the Court ruled that the MCA provided inadequate substitution for habeas and that individuals detained at Guantánamo Bay were entitled to have civil courts review their detentions.

Overall, these recent decisions reaffirm the broad scope of the right of habeas corpus to individuals detained by the United States government in areas under its control.

For more information: Freedman, Eric M. *Habeas Corpus: Rethinking the Great Writ of Liberty*. New York: New York University, 2003; Neeley, Mark E., Jr. *The Fate of Liberty: Abraham Lincoln and Civil Liberties*. Oxford: Oxford University Press, 1992; ; Schultz, David. "Democracy on Trial: Terrorism, Crime, and National Security Policy in a Post 9-11 World," *Golden Gate Law Review* 38 (2008): 195–248.

—Mark A. Fulks

Hague v. Committee for Industrial Organizations 307 U.S. 496 (1939)

In *Hague v. CIO*, the Supreme Court voided a municipal ordinance that required a permit for public assembly in streets, parks, and other public spaces. The decision overturned *Davis v. Massachusetts*, 167 U.S. 43 (1897), which had upheld the right of the states to use their POLICE POWERS to broadly regulate assembly in public spaces. The effect of overturning *Davis v. Massachusetts* was to shift the emphasis from state regulation of speech itself to state regulation of the public space. Mitchell (2003, 70) states, "By arguing that the streets, parks, and public spaces constituted a kind of PUBLIC FORUM, the Court found a means of regulating not speech itself but the space in which the speech occurred." This is reflected in the subsequent cases of *Thornhill v. Alabama*, 310 U.S. 88 (1940), and *Carlson v. California*, 310 U.S. 106 (1940), in which the Supreme Court upheld picketing as a form of public assembly.

Members of the Committee for Industrial Organization (CIO) were denied a permit to assemble in a public space on the grounds that their assembly would violate a Jersey City antilittering ordinance. The intention of the CIO members was to hand out flyers purporting the benefits of the National Labor Relations Act of 1935. The true intention of city officials was to prevent the CIO from politically organizing in Jersey City. Mayor Frank Hague believed the CIO's presence would undermine his efforts to attract industrial investment. Some of the CIO members distributed leaflets and pamphlets in public spaces and were subsequently searched, arrested, and transported to New York City. The CIO filed suit, arguing that the ordinance was unconstitutional on the grounds that it violated the privileges or immunities clause of the FOURTEENTH AMENDMENT. The CIO argued that its members should be afforded protection of their right to peaceful assembly, against arbitrary infringement by the state, as citizens of the United States. The District Court and Circuit Court of Appeals ruled in favor of the CIO. The City of Jersey City appealed to the Supreme Court, citing *Davis v. Massachusetts,* in which the Supreme Court had ruled in 1897 that the broad use of police powers by the state for purposes of promoting "the public convenience" was constitutional.

Justice JOHN G. ROBERTS, JR. wrote the plurality opinion with Justice HUGO BLACK and Chief Justice Charles Evans Hughes concurring. Justice Roberts negates the decision made in *Davis v. Massachusetts* that the "City's ownership of streets and parks is as absolute as one's ownership of his home . . . though the city holds the streets in trust for public use, the absolute denial of their use to the respondents is a valid exercise of the police power." Roberts differentiates *Davis v. Massachusetts* from *Hague v. CIO* by noting a difference between measures to promote the public convenience and "the exercise of the right of assembly for the purpose of communicating views entertained by speakers." Justice Roberts then provides a historical antecedent for the protection of the right of assembly in public spaces by arguing that the use of the streets for assembly, from ancient times, has been part of the privileges, immunities, rights, and liberties of citizens.

Hague v. CIO is an important case because it legitimized the use of public space for purposes of peaceful political assembly. The Supreme Court was careful, however, not to refute the power of states to discern their own use of police powers in order to promote order and convenience. The general rule that developed from *Hague v. CIO* was that the use of public space can be regulated through content-neutral, time, manner, and place regulations, but that expression itself can not. Public officials may not act under cover of law to regulate public assembly and expression when the intent is to discriminate against organizations with views or opinions that may be counter to the interests of the government's leadership. The expression of political ideas, promoted via public assembly, is a right protected under the Fourteenth Amendment's privileges or immunities clause. In later cases, for which *Hague v. CIO* set a precedent, there would be a shift from the use of the Fourteenth Amendment's privileges or immunities clause to the Fourteenth Amendment's DUE PROCESS clause.

For more information: Mitchell, Don. *The Right to the City: Social Justice and the Fight for Public Space.* New York: Guilford Press, 2003.

—J. David Granger

Haig v. Agee 453 U.S. 280 (1981)

In a 7-2 decision, the Supreme Court held in *Haig v. Agee* that the secretary of state had acted within his constitutional and statutory authority in revoking the passport of Philip Agee, a former CIA operative who was engaged in a campaign to reveal the identities of American covert intelligence operatives worldwide. The decision established that citizens do not have an absolute right to hold a passport and that one could be denied or revoked on the basis of national security concerns.

Philip Agee was a covert operative for the Central Intelligence Agency from 1957 until 1968. Agee left the agency disenchanted with American foreign policy and abuses by the CIA. In 1974, Agee announced a "campaign to fight the United States CIA wherever it is operating" (283). This campaign primarily involved revealing the identities of CIA operatives and sources, particularly those operating under diplomatic cover. His 1975 book, *Inside the Company,* included a 23-page appendix listing individuals and organizations that had assisted the CIA. In 1978, Agee founded the Covert Action Information Bulletin, best known for its "Naming Names" column, which was dedicated to blowing the cover of intelligence agents. Agee's actions helped inspire the passage of the 1982 Intelligence Identities Protection Act (50 U.S.C. Section 422).

In 1979, the secretary of state revoked Agee's passport on the grounds that Agee's activities were causing significant harm to American national security. Agee filed suit, claiming the revocation amounted to an infringement on his right to travel under the Fifth Amendment, as well as his FIRST AMENDMENT right to criticize the government.

The district court supported Agee's position, as did the Court of Appeals for the District of Columbia. The Supreme Court agreed to hear the case, holding oral arguments on January 14, 1981, and delivering its decision on June 29, 1981.

In addition to his claim that the revocation of his passport violated his constitutional rights, Agee argued that the secretary of state had overstepped his statutory authority, as the 1926 Passport Act (22 U.S.C. Section 211a) made no provision for the revocation of passports. The government's position was that the secretary of state had sufficient authority to revoke Agee's passport and that its revocation was not an infringement on Agee's constitutional rights. The Court agreed and in a 7-2 decision overturned this circuit court's ruling, allowing the revocation of Agee's passport to stand.

Chief Justice Warren Burger wrote for the majority and was joined by Justices Potter Stewart, Byron White, Harry Blackmun, Lewis Franklin Powell, Jr., William Hubbs Rehnquist, and John Paul Stevens. Justice Blackmun also filed a concurring opinion, and Justice William J. Brennan, Jr., filed a dissent, which was joined by Justice Thurgood Marshall.

The Court held that despite the absence of explicit language providing for the revocation of passports under the 1926 Passport Act, the secretary still possessed sufficient authority to revoke Agee's passport. The Court also rejected Agee's First and Fifth Amendment claims, holding that the revocation decision was predicated not on Agee's words per se, but upon actions that caused harm to American national security.

For more information: Agee, Philip. *Inside the Company: CIA Diary.* New York: Stonehill Publishing Co., 1975; Leigh, Monroe. "Judicial Decisions: *Haig v. Agee.* 101 S.Ct. 2766." *The American Journal of International Law* 75 (1981): 962–963.

—Thomas C. Ellington

Hamdi v. Rumsfeld 542 U.S. 507 (2004)

In *Hamdi v. Rumsfeld,* the Supreme Court ruled that an American citizen could not be held indefinitely on American soil without a right to habeas corpus review. The significance of the *Hamdi* decision was that it limited the ability of the president to detain American citizens in the war on terrorism after September 11, 2001, and it reaffirmed the basic right of Americans to have a judge determine whether they have been illegally detained.

On September 11, 2001, Al Qaeda terrorists hijacked four commercial airplanes and used them in several attacks against the United States. Subsequently, Congress authorized the president to use all "necessary and appropriate force" against any persons, organizations, and nations that aided or supported these acts of terrorism. The president then used this authorization to send troops to Afghanistan against al-Qaeda and the Taliban regime that had supported them. Yaser Hamdi, an American citizen, was captured in Afghanistan, and he was classified as an "enemy combatant" because he had supposedly taken up arms against the United States. Hamdi was placed in indefinite detention in a naval brig in South Carolina and denied access to legal counsel. Hamdi's father sought habeas corpus review for his son in federal court, claiming that the incarceration violated the Fifth and Fourteenth Amendments. The district court ruled in favor of Hamdi, ordering him released, and the Fourth Circuit Court of Appeals reversed. The Supreme Court reversed, holding that Hamdi was entitled to a hearing to determine the factual basis for why he was being held.

Justice Sandra Day O'Connor wrote for a four-person plurality that also included Chief Justice William Hubbs Rehnquist and Justices Anthony M. Kennedy and Stephen G. Breyer. In this opinion, O'Connor argues that while Congress had authorized the detention of enemy combatants, Congress could not do so indefinitely. Moreover, even recognizing the power of Congress to fight the war on terrorism and authorize the detention of those considered to be enemy combatants, the basic principles of the federal habeas corpus law grant American citizens—even though captured on foreign soil during combat—being detained on American soil some right to contest the factual basis for why they are being incarcerated.

Justice O'Connor also addressed a second claim that the courts should not second-guess the president when it comes to decisions made regarding military matters. While acknowledging the important separation of powers argument here and the respect that the courts ought to afford the president when it comes to sensitive foreign policy and military matters, O'Connor argued that the interest Hamdi had in the protection of his rights outweighed the interest the government had in detaining him without granting access to the courts. In short, O'Connor and the four-person plurality opinion did not see JUDICIAL REVIEW of Hamdi's detention as posing a major threat or having a "dire impact" upon the government's war-making functions.

In a separate concurrence, Justices DAVID H. SOUTER and Ruth Bader Ginsburg generally agreed with the O'Connor opinion, but they also questioned whether the congressional resolution authorized Hamdi's detention. Specifically, they cited the Non-Detention Act (18 U.S.C. Section 4001[a]), which places limits upon the ability of Congress to authorize the detention of American citizens. This act, passed in response to the internment of Japanese Americans during World War II, required very clear and manifest authority by Congress before the president could detain American citizens. In this case, Souter and Ginsburg did not see that clear authority.

Overall, *Hamdi* was an important statement by the court regarding the protection of individual liberties and on the power of the president in emergencies. In many ways, it stands in refutation to an earlier precedent, *KOREMATSU V. UNITED STATES*, 323 U.S. 214 (1944), which had upheld the forced relocation of over 120,000 Japanese Americans during World War II, without offering any evidence that these individuals were security threats to the country. The *Hamdi* opinion was issued the same day that *RASUL V. BUSH* was decided. In *Rasul*, the U.S. Supreme Court ruled that aliens being held in confinement at the American military base in Guantánamo Bay, Cuba, were entitled to have a federal court hear challenges to their detention under the federal habeas corpus statute. Taken together, the *Hamdi* and *Rasul* opinions will now require the president to justify before a court the detaining of individuals on American soil who are suspected of being terrorists.

For more information: Adler, David Gray, and Robert George, eds. *The Constitution and the Conduct of American Foreign Policy.* Lawrence: University Press of Kansas, 1996; Henkin, Louis. *Constitutionalism, Democracy, and Foreign Affairs.* New York: Columbia University Press, 1990; Henkin, Louis. *Foreign Affairs and the United States Constitution.* Oxford: Clarendon Press, 1996.

—David Schultz

Hamilton, Alexander (ca. 1755–1804) *U.S. Constitution framer, federalist leader, first secretary of the treasury*

Alexander Hamilton, lawyer, statesman, signer of the Constitution, coauthor of *THE FEDERALIST PAPERS*, founder of the Federalist Party, the first Secretary of the Treasury, and arguably the most influential Founder never to become President, was born on January 11, 1755 or 1757, in the British West Indies, and died on July 12, 1804, after being wounded in a duel with Aaron Burr. He came to the American colonies in 1773 and studied at King's College. During the Revolutionary War, he fought in a volunteer company, served as George Washington's aide-de-camp, and represented New York in the Continental Congress. After the war, Hamilton practiced law in New York and defended many British loyalists from vindictive patriots. He was instrumental in establishing the Bank of New York in 1784.

In 1786, spurred by increasingly frequent commercial disputes among the states, delegates from the states—Hamilton among them—gathered at Annapolis, Maryland. The result of the Annapolis Convention was a resolution, drafted by Hamilton, calling for another convention in 1787 to consider amendments to the Articles of Confederation. Hamilton had long found fault with the Articles. A persistent critic of the fractious state governments and a zealous supporter of a strong, cen-

Alexander Hamilton. Engraving *(Library of Congress)*

tralized federal government, he was frustrated by the impotence of the federal authority established under the Articles. In the years immediately following independence, that government had been unable to deal with the former colonies' financial woes, regulate commerce, or respond to alarming episodes of domestic turmoil. Hamilton hoped that the delegates to the convention would do more than merely amend the Articles of Confederation. He envisioned a new constitution and a new government.

Hamilton was appointed by New York to the CONSTITUTIONAL CONVENTION. However, because the two other delegates from New York opposed his ideas, his state and its one vote always sided against him. Consequently, Hamilton's influence at the Convention was limited. He said very little of importance in debate; in his most notable remarks, he apparently argued for the abolition of the state governments and for an elected "monarch" who, once elected, would serve a life term. In addition, at the Convention he was a firm advocate of a powerful president or executive, especially in the areas of foreign policy and defense. The record of the Convention also suggests that Hamilton had serious misgivings about the new constitution, as it took shape. He put aside his doubts once the Convention's work was complete, however. He served on the Committee of Style and Arrangement, which, in a mere four days, crafted the Constitution in its final form. He was the only New York delegate to sign the document.

Hamilton made his greatest contribution to the Constitution, and to constitutional law, after the Convention. From 1787 to 1788, as the states debated ratification, Hamilton, JAMES MADISON, and JOHN JAY defended the new Constitution in a series of 85 essays titled *The Federalist*. Of those 85, Hamilton wrote 51. He authored all the essays on the executive and judicial branches (numbers 67–77 and 78–83, respectively); he also wrote on the SENATE, military affairs, and taxation. Lawyers, judges, and constitutional scholars regard the collected *Federalist* essays as the most authoritative contemporary commentary on the Constitution.

In 1789, Hamilton was appointed by President Washington as the first secretary of the treasury. At Hamilton's urging, the federal government assumed the states' war debts, funded the national debt, imposed a tax on spirits, and, in 1791, created a national bank. The establishment of the national bank raised important constitutional questions. Opponents argued that the federal government lacked the power to create a bank, because that power was not specifically granted by the Constitution. Hamilton, whose more flexible interpretation of the Constitution favored active federal involvement in economic matters, countered with his theory of implied powers. He contended that the Constitution granted Congress additional unenumerated powers related to those that were specified, through the NECESSARY AND PROPER CLAUSE. That clause, he argued, should be interpreted flexibly, "to give a liberal latitude to the exercise of specified powers." In the landmark Supreme Court case *McCulloch v. Maryland*, 17 U.S. (4 Wheat.) 316 (1918), Justice J. MARSHALL adopted Hamilton's reasoning.

Hamilton resigned his position as Treasury Secretary in 1795, after his political foes uncovered the fact that he had been involved in an affair. He did not retire from public life, however. He resumed his legal practice in New York and was a strong force in the Federalist Party, which he had founded in the early 1790s, until the party's collapse in 1800.

For more information: Chernow, Ron. *Alexander Hamilton*. New York: Penguin Press, 2004.

—Nathan M. Ingebretson

Hammer v. Dagenhart 247 U.S. 251 (1918)

In *Hammer v. Dagenhart*, the Supreme Court ruled that Congress does not have the power under the COMMERCE CLAUSE to regulate CHILD LABOR within the individual states. The decision represented a narrow interpretation of congressional power to regulate commerce, and it dealt a temporary blow to national efforts to address the problem of child labor.

During the Industrial Revolution, many business owners and stockholders favored the use of child workers because it resulted in greater profits. By the 1910s, spurred by Progressive reformers, a national consensus had developed in favor of limiting children's work, and many states passed legislation regulating the practice. Despite this consensus, exemptions in southern states and lack of effective enforcement of state laws led to efforts to pass national legislation to curb child labor. The Constitution, however, does not give Congress the enumerated power to regulate hours and working conditions for labor within the states. In an attempt to regulate child labor indirectly, Congress passed the Keating-Owen Act of 1916 under its authority to regulate commerce between the states. The law prohibited producers and manufacturers from shipping in INTERSTATE COMMERCE any product made by children under 14 or merchandise that had been made in factories where children between 14 and 16 had been permitted to work more than eight hours a day, six days a week, or at night. Roland Dagenhart, who worked in a cotton mill in Charlotte, North Carolina, with his two sons, ages 13 and 15, challenged the law with the support of the Executive Committee of Southern Cotton Manufacturers.

Justice William R. Day, writing for the majority, was joined by Chief Justice Edward White and Justices Mahlon Pitney, Willis Van Devanter, and James McReynolds. Justice Day wrote that Congress does not have the authority to regulate commerce of goods manufactured by children and therefore the Keating-Owen Act was unconstitutional. Day distinguished previous cases where the Court upheld federal attempts to control lotteries, prostitution, and liquor, by arguing that the manufacture of cotton was not a moral evil. According to Day, the regulation of child labor within states is purely a state authority. He used the Tenth Amendment to support his argument, although he misquoted the provision with regard to powers delegated to Congress. Day claimed that there is no power vested in Congress to require the states to exercise their POLICE POWER so as to prevent unfair competition. He warned that to allow Congress such authority would end freedom of commerce and the power of the states over local matters and thus "our system of government would be practically destroyed."

In dissent, Justice OLIVER WENDELL HOLMES, JR., joined by Justices Joseph McKenna, Louis D. Brandeis, and John H. Clarke, argued that the law did not preempt state authority to regulate child labor within a state. States have discretion to regulate their internal affairs, but when "they seek to send their products across state lines they are no longer within their rights." Congress can regulate commerce that crosses state lines even though it may have an indirect effect upon the activities of the states. Holmes concluded that the public policy of the United States is shaped to benefit the nation as a whole, and Congress may enforce its policy by all means at its command.

The *Hammer* decision was eventually overturned in *UNITED STATES V. DARBY LUMBER*, 312 U.S. 100 (1941). In *Darby*, the Court upheld the Fair Labor Standards Act using many of the arguments in Holmes's dissent in *Hammer*. Congress now has broad authority to regulate labor, wages, and working conditions under the commerce clause.

For more information: Novkov, Julie. "Our Towering Superstructure Rests on a Rotten Foundation: *Hammer v. Dagenhart* (1918)." In *Creating Constitutional Change: Clashes Over Power and Liberty in the Supreme Court,* edited by Gregg Ivers and Kevin T. McGuire, 119–133. Charlottesville: University of Virginia, 2004.

—John Fliter

Hand, Learned (1872–1961) *federal judge*
Judge Billings Learned Hand (born January 27, 1872, and died August 18, 1961) was arguably the most distinguished American judge to never be appointed to the United States Supreme Court.

Learned Hand, whose seemingly prophetic name is a compilation of family surnames, was born and grew up in Albany, New York. Samuel Hand, Learned's father, was an Albany attorney and judge of some distinction. Samuel Hand passed away when Learned was 14 years old, leaving a deep impression on young Learned. After his father's death, he would continue to be be strongly influenced by his mother, Lydia Coit Learned Hand, a Calvinist Congregationalist. Learned Hand would continue to struggle, however, with religious and self-doubts.

Studying both philosophy and law at Harvard University, Hand studied under several noted philosophers, including George Santayana. He began the private practice of law, first in Albany in 1897, and then in New York City in 1902. At the age of 30, Hand married Bryn Mawr College graduate Frances Fincke. They would go on to have three daughters and a complicated 59-year marriage.

Ascending to his first federal judgeship as judge of the U.S. District Court, Southern District of New York in 1909, he was nominated by President William H. Taft. After his confirmation, he remained in this position until he was appointed to a higher federal court as judge for the U.S. Court of Appeals for the Second Circuit. President Calvin Coolidge made this nomination in 1924, and Judge Learned Hand was confirmed the same year. He was to remain on this court until his death in 1961. During this judgeship he would be chief judge from 1948–51. His remarkable 52-year tenure as a federal judge was the longest one in history in 1961. It was marked by his abiding belief in judicial restraint and largely by a lack of partisanship. Hand said of himself that he was "a conservative among liberals, and a liberal among conservatives."

Judge Hand heard many landmark cases and was particularly noted for his abilities with tort law, contract law, antitrust law, income tax law, federal criminal law, and free-speech issues. He delivered a particularly famous opinion in the case of *Masses Publishing Co. v. Patten,* 244 F. 535 (1917), where Judge Hand urged the use of the "incitement test" which would later be adopted by the U.S. Supreme Court.

Judge Hand was never appointed to the U.S. Supreme Court because of various political reasons. One significant one was his support of Theodore Roosevelt after Roosevelt's split with the Republican Party in 1912. This greatly displeased William H. Taft and the Republicans, guaranteeing that Hand would not get a nomination to the Supreme Court for many years to come. When President Franklin Delano Roosevelt took office, he was encouraged to nominate Judge Hand to the U.S. Supreme Court. He decided that Hand was too old at the age of 70. Of course, Judge Hand remained on the federal bench another 19 years after this, doing some of his finest judicial work.

In perhaps his most famous speech, which was delivered in New York City's Central Park in 1944 at the "I Am an American Day" ceremony, he famously said, "The spirit of liberty is the spirit which is not too sure that it is right." Perhaps this begins to guide us toward the spirit of Hand's career as the notedly impartial jurist who leaves a legacy of important federal decisions spanning more than five decades.

For more information: Gunther, Gerald. *Learned Hand: The Man and the Judge.* New York: Knopf, 1994.

—Maria Collins Warren

Harlan, John (John Marshall Harlan) (1833–1911) *Supreme Court justice*
John Marshall Harlan, in his 34 years on the Supreme Court (1877–1911), was the third most

frequent dissenter in the history of the Court, authoring 376 dissents among his 1,161 opinions. Prior to OLIVER WENDELL HOLMES, JR., he had been the sole consistent dissenter in the economic SUBSTANTIVE DUE PROCESS era. He believed in judicial self-restraint regarding legislative economic-proprietarian enactments.

Harlan was born in Kentucky. He attended Centre College and Transylvania University. His father, a close friend of Henry Clay, had been a member of Congress and state attorney general and secretary of state. Harlan, a slaveowner, became a member of the Know-Nothing Party. He served as a county judge in 1858. Harlan was in the Union army during the Civil War, though he supported the property rights of slave owners and opposed the THIRTEENTH AMENDMENT.

Harlan was Kentucky attorney general from 1863 to 1867. He was an unsuccessful candidate for governor in 1871 and 1875. He was appointed to the Supreme Court by Rutherford Hayes. By that time, Harlan had become a Republican and a moderate on the rights of blacks. He was the only dissenter in the *CIVIL RIGHTS CASES*, 109 U.S. 3 (1883), a decision declaring the Act of 1875 unconstitutional on the grounds that the FOURTEENTH AMENDMENT applied to state action only and not to discrimination by private individuals.

Harlan opposed the Court's tendency to declare governmental regulation of business unconstitutional, for example, in his solitary dissent in the 1895 case of *UNITED STATES V. E. C. KNIGHT CO.*, 156 U.S. 1, where the Court pulled the teeth from the Sherman Antitrust Act, saying it did not apply to manufacturing.

In *LOCHNER V. NEW YORK*, 198 U.S. 45 (1905), he dissented against the majority's declaring a New York State maximum hour law unconstitutional as in violation of the Fourteenth Amendment.

Harlan's most familiar dissent was in *PLESSY V. FERGUSON*, 163 U.S. 537 (1896), where the majority interpreted the Fourteenth Amendment as allowing separate but equal treatment of the races. Harlan disagreed that it was only in the minds of colored people that the statute requiring separate facilities in public ACCOMMODATIONS stamped blacks with a badge of inferiority.

He was the first justice to advocate the total applicability of the federal BILL OF RIGHTS to the states in *Hurtado v. California*, 110 U.S. 516 (1884); *Maxwell v. Dow*, 176 U.S. 581 (1900); and *TWINING V. NEW JERSEY*, 211 U.S. 78 (1908).

For more information: Latham, Frank B. *The Great Dissenter.* New York: Cowles, 1970.

—Martin Gruberg

Harlan, John Marshall (1899–1971) *Supreme Court justice*

John Marshall Harlan was the grandson of the earlier Justice JOHN HARLAN. His father was a reform-minded Chicago mayor. Harlan was born in Chicago and went to Princeton, Oxford (as a Rhodes Scholar), and New York Law School. He was an air force colonel during World War II. He was named by President Eisenhower to the U.S. Court of Appeals (1954) and then to the U.S. Supreme Court (1955–71).

Harlan's opinions were models of judicial craftsmanship. He was a disciple of Felix Frankfurter, arguing that the courts should stay out of the "political thicket." He dissented in *BAKER V. CARR*, 369 U.S. 186 (1962) in a case regarding malapportionment of legislative districts and in *Wesberry v. Sanders*, 376 U.S. 1 (1964), and *REYNOLDS V. SIMS*, 377 U.S. 533 (1964), two other cases involving equitable representation.

Unlike his grandfather, he opposed the nationalization of the Fifth Amendment in *Malloy v. Hogan*, 378 U.S. 1 (1964), and *Pointer v. Texas* 380 U.S. 400 (1965). Harlan opposed "stifling flexibility in the States," in departing from DUE PROCESS standards in the BILL OF RIGHTS. He preferred a case-by-case approach. Harlan dissented from *MIRANDA V. ARIZONA*, 384 U.S. 436 (1966), expanding the rights of defendants in criminal cases. Harlan also followed a case-by-case pattern in cases involving Communist defendants (*SCALES V. UNITED STATES*, 367 U.S. 203 [1961]); *Noto v. United States*, 367 U.S. 290 [1961]) and allegedly obscene literature (*ROTH V. UNITED STATES* and *Alberts v. California*, 354 U.S. 476 [1957]).

With failing health and eyesight, Harlan retired from the Supreme Court in September, 1971, and died two months later.

For more information: Shapiro, David L., ed. *The Evolution of a Judicial Philosophy: Selected Opinions and Papers of Justice John M. Harlan.* Cambridge, Mass.: Harvard University Press, 1969; Yarborough, Tinsley E. *John Marshall Harlan: Great Dissenter of the Warren Court.* New York: Oxford University Press, 1992.

—Martin Gruberg

harmless error

The harmless error doctrine is a principle of constitutional law that is implicated whenever a criminal defendant's constitutional rights are violated. Under the harmless error doctrine, courts are required to evaluate the actual effect of a constitutional error on a defendant's trial before granting a new trial. The question in this evaluation is whether the court can conclude beyond a reasonable doubt that the error did not contribute to the defendant's conviction in light of the nature and extent of the proof of the defendant's guilt.

The harmless error doctrine was first applied by the U.S. Supreme Court to a constitutional error in the landmark case of *Chapman v. California,* 386 U.S. 18 (1967). In *Chapman,* the defendants exercised their rights not to testify under the Fifth Amendment to the U.S. Constitution. In response, the prosecutor exercised his right under the state constitution to draw an inference of guilt from the defendants' silence. After the defendants were convicted, in an unrelated case, the inference of guilt relied upon by the prosecution was found to be a violation of the Fifth Amendment. Thus, in *Chapman,* the issues were whether a constitutional error could be harmless and whether the violation of the defendants' Fifth Amendment rights was harmless or automatically required a new trial. The Supreme Court rejected the automatic-reversal argument and concluded that a constitutional error may be deemed harmless if the reviewing court can conclude that the violation was harmless beyond a reasonable doubt.

Subsequently, in *Arizona v. Fulminante,* 111 S.Ct. 1246 (1991), the Supreme Court explained how the harmless error rule should be applied, drawing a distinction between structural errors and process errors. Structural errors undermine the constitutional framework for criminal prosecutions. For example, structural errors include violations of the RIGHT TO COUNSEL, to a public trial, or to a trial by jury. In contrast, process errors occur within the framework during the presentation of the case to the jury. Process errors include errors in the admission of evidence acquired in violation of the constitution, such as coerced confessions, illegally seized evidence, and tainted witness identifications, erroneous jury instructions, and restrictions on the defendant's right to cross-examine witnesses. The difference between these two types of errors is that the effect of process errors may be evaluated to determine any direct effect on the outcome of the trial. Structural errors, however, affect the intangible benefits of the justice system's core fabric. For that reason, structural errors cannot be evaluated in light of the evidence.

The harmless error doctrine recognizes that, under the facts and circumstances of a particular case, a constitutional error may be so insignificant and inconsequential that it could not have affected the result of the trial. Typically, in a case in which the prosecution's proof of the defendant's guilt is overwhelming, constitutional errors will be considered harmless and the defendant will not be entitled to a new trial. On the other hand, in cases that are more closely contested and the prosecution's proof is barely sufficient, constitutional errors will not be harmless and the defendant will be entitled to a new trial.

For more information: Bentele, Ursula, and Eve Cary. *Appellate Advocacy: Principles and Practice.* Cincinnati: Anderson Publishing, 1998; Traynor, Roger J. *The Riddle of Harmless Error.* Columbus: Ohio State University Press, 1970.

—Mark A. Fulks

Harris v. McRae 448 U.S. 297 (1980)

In *Harris v. McRae,* the Supreme Court held that the government may refuse to provide funds for abortions for poor women.

After ABORTION became legal in 1973, a number of state governments reacted by limiting payments for abortion expenses in their state medical assistance (Medicaid) programs for indigent women. Medicaid is a joint federal-state program administered by the state. Most lower federal courts found these funding regulations illegal. In June 1977, the Supreme Court decided in *Beal v. Doe,* 432 U.S. 438 (1977), and *Maher v. Roe,* 432 U.S. 464 (1977), that states may interpret the Medicaid law to restrict public funding of abortions. *Maher,* the more important of the cases, was challenged on constitutional grounds; the plaintiffs claimed that the Connecticut regulation restricting Medicaid funds violated the EQUAL PROTECTION clause by differentiating among women on the basis of their wealth. Although the Court acknowledged that the regulation made it less likely that women in poverty would be able to obtain abortions, it held that the state had not violated the Constitution because it imposed no restrictions on their access to abortion. The state was not responsible for their inability to obtain abortions; their poverty was responsible.

Congress had entered the debate over federal funding of abortions when it enacted the Hyde Amendment in 1976. Sponsored by Representative Henry Hyde, Republican from Illinois, it prohibited the federal government from funding abortions through the Medicaid program unless the woman's life was threatened by the pregnancy. Over the next several years, there were several versions of the amendment that allowed Medicaid funding for abortions in specified circumstances, such as if the pregnancy resulted from rape or incest or when physical and long lasting health damage would result if the pregnancy were continued.

The first attack on the Hyde Amendment came when New York City's Planned Parenthood filed suit in a New York federal district court. On January 15, 1980, the court held that the Hyde Amendment violated the FIRST and Fifth AMENDMENTS of the United States Constitution.

On appeal, in *Harris v. McRae,* Justice Potter Stewart announced the opinion for the Supreme Court. Relying on *Maher,* he stressed that the Hyde Amendment did not interfere with a woman's constitutionally protected right to an abortion. He explained that although the government cannot restrict the woman's choice to have an abortion, it was not obligated to remove obstacles it did not place there. Because a poor woman's access to abortion is restricted by her indigency, not by any barrier placed there by the federal government, Stewart rejected the argument that Congress was discriminating against poor women by refusing to pay their abortion expenses.

The dissenting justices argued that the Hyde Amendment imposed a moral code on poor women only and denied their ability to exercise their right to PRIVACY just as effectively as the laws had done when it was illegal before 1973. Justice Thurgood Marshall predicted that as a result of this decision, women seeking abortions would be forced to resort to dangerous methods to secure them.

For more information: Dickinson, Thomas. "Limiting Public Funds for Abortions: State Response to Congressional Action." *Suffolk University Law Review* 13 (1979): 923–959; Perry, Michael. "The Abortion Funding Cases: A Comment on the Supreme Court's Role in American Government." *Georgetown Law Journal* 66 (1978): 1,191–1,245; Tolchin, Susan. "The Impact of the Hyde Amendment on Congress: Effects of Single Issue Politics on Legislative Dysfunction, June 1977–June 1978." *Women and Politics* 5 (1985): 91–106.

—Susan Gluck Mezey

Harris v. New York 401 U.S. 222 (1971)

In *Harris v. New York,* the United States Supreme Court held that although a defendant's statements obtained by the police in violation of the rule in *MIRANDA V. ARIZONA,* 384 U.S. 436 (1966), could not be used against the defendant during the prosecutor's case for purposes of proving guilt, they could be used by the prosecutor during the defendant's case for purposes of attacking the defendant's credibility.

The police obtained statements from the defendant without properly warning him of his RIGHT TO COUNSEL as required by the *Miranda* rule. Even though the statements were not coerced or involuntary, the EXCLUSIONARY RULE barred them from the prosecutor's case (referred to as the case in chief). The prosecutor made no use of the statements in his case in chief, but when the defendant testified in his own behalf, the prosecutor introduced the statements (which conflicted with the defendant's testimony) for the purpose of attacking the defendant's credibility (referred to as IMPEACHMENT). After the defendant was convicted and after an unsuccessful appeal to the state's high court, he appealed to the U.S. Supreme Court.

The Court stated that even though the *Miranda* rule prohibits using the statements against the defendant in the prosecutor's case in chief, it does not follow that the statements should be prohibited for all *other* collateral purposes. To the extent that the rule is necessary to deter police misconduct, the majority was satisfied that such conduct would be sufficiently deterred by barring improperly obtained statements from the prosecutor's case in chief. Moreover, the Court suggested that the impeachment process was valuable for the jury in assessing the defendant's credibility and barring the statements from the trial would unnecessarily undermine that process.

Finally, the Court noted that the defendant was not required to testify, but once he chose to do so the protection provided by the *Miranda* rule should not enable the defendant to commit perjury without the risk of being confronted by his prior conflicting statements. The Court concluded that the statements, although obtained in violation of the *Miranda* rule, could be used to impeach the defendant.

During the years since the decision in *Harris v. New York*, the Court has permitted improperly obtained evidence to be used for other collateral purposes, specifically grand jury proceedings (*United States v. Calandra*, 414 U.S. 338 [1974]), parole revocation hearings (*Pennsylvania Board of Pardons and Parole v. Scott*, 524 U.S. 357 [1998]), and immigration deportation hearings (*Immigration and Naturalization Service v. Lopez-Mendoza*, 468 U.S. 1032 [1984]).

For more information: Clymer, Steven D. "Are Police Free to Discard *Miranda*?" *Yale Law Journal* 112 (2002): 447–552; LaFave, Wayne R., Jerold H. Israel, and Nancy J. King. *Criminal Procedure*. 4th ed. St. Paul, Minn.: Thomson/West, 2004.

—Steven B. Dow

Hatch Act of 1939 (amended 1940 & 1993)

The Hatch Act of 1939, amended in 1993, is a federal law designed to prohibit federal employees and other government employees who are paid primarily by federal funds from engaging in partisan political activity. The act was named after Senator Carl Hatch of New Mexico. Its official name is "An Act to Prevent Pernicious Political Activities."

Though access to public employment in return for political favors certainly ante-dates the presidency of Andrew Jackson (1829–37), the "spoils system" became pervasive during Jackson's term of office and continued mostly unchallenged until civil service reformers were able to get the Pendleton Act (1883) passed into law. Fundamentally, the Pendleton Act began to set criteria for public employment that called for qualified individuals to fill government jobs. This was in contravention to the spoils system, whereby government jobs were often given to individuals on the basis of their political allegiance. Implicit in the reform of civil service at the time of the Pendleton Act was the idea of a politically neutral public administration. Under the spoils system, not only was government employment given to individuals for political allegiance but the very jobs they occupied and their associated public organizations were often used to ensure a benefactor's reelection.

With the Pendleton Act as the initial salvo in the attack on patronage, the succeeding years continued to see the rise of civil service reform while patronage slowly declined. In 1938, it was reported that Democratic Party politicians had misused Works Progress Administration (WPA) funds and staff in order to influence the 1938 congressional elections. Upon investigation, it was disclosed that

WPA employees had indeed used their positions to win votes for the Democratic Party. Senator Carl Hatch of New Mexico, a Democrat, sponsored legislation that received widespread support that would deal with future abuses of public employment for partisan advantage. Hence, the Hatch Act was passed on August 2, 1939, with a revision passed on July 19, 1940, that extended the act to state and local employees whose pay included any federal funds.

The Hatch Act restricted political campaign activities by all federal employees below the policymaking level. In fact, the act states that federal employees must not take "any active part" in political campaigns. Further, public officials were forbidden from using promises of jobs, promotion, financial assistance, contracts, or any other benefit in order to force campaign contributions or to get political support.

The Hatch Act was not without its opponents. While the act sought to remove the spoils system by maintaining a politically neutral public administration, those public employees impacted by the act saw it as an infringement upon their FIRST AMENDMENT rights as American citizens. The Supreme Court heard cases challenging the constitutionality of the Hatch Act upon free speech and freedom of association grounds in both 1947 and 1974. In both instances, the Supreme Court upheld the constitutionality of the act. In each case, the Court ruled that the violation of an individual's right to free speech and association was outweighed by the public's need to have a government system free of patronage. Government employment was also reasoned to be a voluntary association that public employees freely choose to pursue. Therefore, the acceptance of limitations is a prerequisite to the acceptance of public employment.

With public employees becoming more numerous and well educated, the pressure to reform the Hatch Act became more intense. On October 6, 1993, President Bill Clinton signed legislation to reform the Hatch Act. Under the new provisions of the act, federal employees gained the right to take an active role in political campaigns. Now federal employees on their own time and with their own private resources may run for elective office where no candidate represents a political party (nonpartisan election), assist in voter registration drives, express opinions about candidates and issues, volunteer in a campaign, contribute to a political campaign, display campaign paraphernalia, and participate (even as candidates) in local or state political parties.

However, federal employees may not be candidates for elective office where any candidate represents a political party (partisan election), raise funds for a partisan political campaign, allow their names to be used in fund-raising for a partisan political campaign, or participate in a telephone bank to raise money for a partisan campaign or to raise money for their union's political action committee from anyone other than union members.

While the Hatch Act has evolved from being very restrictive to federal employees' political involvement to recognizing some off-duty political involvement, the act still restricts federal employees and those state and local employees paid with even some federal funds from being completely free in their political activities even on their own time. The Hatch Act aims to achieve a public bureaucracy that is not touched directly by partisan politics in its day-to-day operation.

For more information: Office of Special Counsel (U.S.). The Hatch Act and Federal Employees: Permitted and Prohibited Activities for Employees Who May Engage in Partisan Activity. 2006.

—William Lester

hate crimes

A hate crime is a crime that is committed because of the victim's characteristics, such as his or her race, gender, ethnicity, religion, sexual orientation, or disability. While one may ask, are not all crimes based on hate, hate here represents hatred of a person's characteristics and the group that he or she identifies with. Hate crimes, while primarily associated with white supremacist groups, can be committed by anyone.

Hate crimes have an effect not only on the individual targeted, but the group targeted as well. For this reason, many regard hate crimes as a greater crime against society. Additionally, psychologists have stated that the fear that resonates in a particular community after a hate crime is very real and measurable. Because this type of crime has additional effects that a regular crime does not, both the federal and state governments have found it appropriate to enact laws imposing additional penalties for this behavior.

For instance, if an individual commits assault because of a person's race, for instance, he or she will face an additional charge and an increased penalty due to the hate crime. All states but one (Wyoming) have some type of hate crime provision in effect. Further, all but three states (Wyoming, Indiana, and South Carolina) have hate crime penalties for bias-motivated violence and intimidation. In addition, numerous states have laws creating increased penalties for hate-based vandalism of religious institutions.

Among the states, however, there is a vast disagreement over what constitutes a characteristic or group for purposes of determining a hate crime. California and the DISTRICT OF COLUMBIA, for example, have laws stating that if a crime is committed because of one's race, religion, ethnicity, sexual orientation, gender, disability, political affiliation, age, or transgender/gender identity it should be classified as a hate crime. These two jurisdictions are of the most inclusive. On the other hand, Montana includes only race, religion, and ethnicity in its definition.

The increased penalty component of state hate crimes laws was challenged in *Wisconsin v. Mitchell,* 508 U.S. 476 (1993). In *Wisconsin v. Mitchell,* the Supreme Court ruled that a defendant's FIRST AMENDMENT rights were not violated because of the increased penalty. A unanimous Supreme Court rejected the idea that a state could not punish an individual based on the defendant's motive. The Court further distinguished a hate crime from HATE SPEECH and hateful thoughts. Yet, even with the Court's ruling, many today believe that hate crime laws violate the First Amendment.

The federal government has also enacted hate crime laws, but in their current form the statutes are limited in their applicability. Currently, federal hate crime penalties can be attached only to actions already illegal under federal law (called the base crime). Over the past few years, however, there has been a push in Congress to expand and pass new federal hate crime legislation. This new legislation would penalize an individual who commits a crime because of the victim's characteristics (as described above), regardless of whether the base crime (e.g., assault or murder) is prohibited under *federal* law.

Those that argue for federal hate crime legislation believe that hate crimes are crimes that know no state borders and that they impact the country as a whole. It is also believed that federal hate crime legislation can be constitutionally rationalized under both the COMMERCE CLAUSE and the THIRTEENTH AMENDMENT. Those that argue against such legislation believe that criminal penalties are best left to the states and that the federal government does not have sufficient ability to legislate under the principles of FEDERALISM.

Cross burning is a unique hate crime, and penalizing such activity was recently addressed by the Supreme Court in *Virginia v. Black,* 538 U.S. 343 (2003). In *Virginia v. Black,* a very fractured Court held that a state can criminalize cross burning only when there is an intent to intimidate and not when the cross burning was done for purely political purposes. The Court clarified its previous holding in *R.A.V. v. City of St. Paul,* 505 U.S. 377 (1992), which struck down a Minnesota CROSS BURNING statute. In sum, the Court has stated that when a statute criminalizes cross burning when done so with an intent to intimidate for any reason, it will pass constitutional scrutiny.

For more information: Abel, Jason. "Americans Under Attack: The Need for Federal Hate Crime Legislation in Light of Post-September 11 Attacks on Arab Americans and Muslims." *Asian Law Journal* 12 (2005): 41–65; Abel, Jason. "Balancing a Burning Cross: The Court and *Virginia v. Black.*" *John Marshall Law Review* 38 (2005): 1,205–1,226.

—Jason Abel

hate speech

Hate speech targets members of social groups on the basis of their identity. While the earliest victims of hate speech were members of racial and religious minorities, the victims of hate speech have also included women, gays and lesbians, and immigrants. Hate speech can take a variety of forms, ranging from one- and two-word slurs to book length attacks, such as the *Protocols of the Elders of Zion,* which claims the world is run by a Jewish conspiracy. The motives of the purveyors of hate speech vary—some appear motivated almost entirely by hatred of their victim, while others use hate speech to attract followers to their cause. Victims of hate speech experience it as disempowering, which has led some critical race theorists to consider hate speech as a restriction on the victim's FIRST AMENDMENT rights.

The rise of the Nazis led several European countries and American states to enact hate speech laws. In *State v. Klapprott,* 22 A.2d 877 (1941), the New Jersey Supreme Court upheld a New Jersey hate speech law. Revulsion at racial policies of the Nazis increased support for hate speech laws. During the 1950s, 1960s, and early 1970s, many European countries strengthened their hate speech laws. Developments in the United States initially followed a similar path, as demonstrated by the Supreme Court in *BEAUHARNAIS V. ILLINOIS,* 343 U.S. 250 (1952), which upheld an Illinois group libel law.

But support for hate speech laws soon evaporated. In part this was a reaction to the excesses of McCarthyism. It also reflected a fear that restrictions of speech would be used against opponents of the Civil Rights movement, a possibility Justices HUGO BLACK and WILLIAM O. DOUGLAS already suggested in their dissenting opinions in *Beauharnais* and which came to fruition in cases such as *NAACP v. Alabama,* 357 U.S. 449 (1958), and *NEW YORK TIMES V. SULLIVAN,* 376 U.S. 254 (1964), both of which pitted the free speech rights of CIVIL RIGHTS protesters against southern segregationists. The Vietnam War era saw a similar pattern—in cases such as *TINKER V. DES MOINES SCHOOL DISTRICT,* 303 U.S. 503 (1969), and *COHEN V. CALIFORNIA,* 403 U.S. 15 (1971), protesters relied on freedom of speech to protect their right to oppose the war.

Meanwhile, the restrictions of speech from the McCarthy era were gradually rolled back. In *BRANDENBURG V. OHIO,* 395 U.S. 444 (1969), the Supreme Court held that restrictions on speech were permissible only to stop direct incitement to immediate lawless action. As a result, during the Skokie controversy, the Seventh Circuit in *Collin v. Smith,* 578 F.2d 1197 (7th Cir, 1978) had little trouble upholding the right of Nazis to march in a community with a large proportion of Holocaust survivors. While many people resigned from the ACLU in protest, the affair was seen by others as an important vindication of freedom of speech.

During the 1980s, the broad opposition to hate speech laws began to crack. Inspired by a new generation of legal scholars—the critical race theorists—colleges and universities enacted speech codes. While some of these codes, including those at the Universities of Michigan and Wisconsin, were found unconstitutional by lower courts, the momentum for restrictions on hate speech laws grew as municipalities passed laws banning hate speech and adding prison time to those convicted of bias-motivated crimes.

In *R.A.V. V. ST. PAUL,* 505 U.S. 377 (1992), the Supreme Court held that a city could not ban only those "fighting words" (a category of speech the Court held in *CHAPLINSKY V. NEW HAMPSHIRE,* 315 U.S. 568 [1942], was undeserving of First Amendment protection) based on racial or religious hatred. *R.A.V.* suggested that those speech codes that singled out specific types of hate speech were unconstitutional. Furthermore, because *R.A.V.* involved a CROSS BURNING, many lower courts concluded that the case made laws banning cross burning unconstitutional.

Two later rulings substantially narrowed the potential scope of *R.A.V.* First, in *Wisconsin v. Mitchell,* 508 U.S. 476 (1993), the Court upheld the constitutionality of sentence enhancement laws. This allowed communities to register their condemnation of bias crimes without running afoul of the First Amendment. A second narrowing came with *Virginia v. Black,* 538 U.S. 343 (2003), where the Court upheld a Virginia law banning cross burning when done with the intent to intimidate. Discussing the history of cross burning and the Ku Klux Klan at great length, the Court held that racial intimidation is a "true threat" which the state has the power to prevent. The impact of the "true threat" language on hate speech laws remains to be seen.

For more information: Delgado, Richard, and Jean Stefancic. *Must We Defend Nazis?: Hate Speech, Pornography, and the New First Amendment.* New York: New York University Press, 1997; Downs, Donald Alexander. *Nazis in Skokie: Freedom, Community, and the First Amendment.* Notre Dame, Ind.: University of Notre Dame Press, 1985; Kahn, Robert A. "Cross-Burning, Holocaust Denial, and the Development of Hate Speech Law in the United States and Germany," *University of Detroit Mercy Law Review* 83 (2006): 163–194; Walker, Samuel. *Hate Speech: The History of an American Controversy.* Lincoln, Nebr.: University of Nebraska Press, 1994.

—Robert A. Kahn

Hawaii Housing Authority v. Midkiff 467 U.S. 229 (1984)

The *Hawaii Housing Authority v. Midkiff* case dealt with creation of state legislation to redistribute land from a small number of private landowners to the larger population. This question about land redistribution in Hawaii came about following extensive hearings held in the mid-1960s, where the state legislature discovered that land was distributed into the hands of a small minority within the state.

From its investigations, the legislature found that the federal and state governments owned nearly 49 percent of the land in Hawaii, but another 47 percent was owned by only 72 private landowners—demonstrating a severe concentration of landownership that the legislature felt needed to be combated for the betterment of all within the State of Hawaii. To this end, the Land Reform Act was passed in 1967 by the Hawaii State Legislature to forward the idea of land redistribution. The act adopted a method of redistribution that would transfer property from lessors (landowners) to lessees. This was done through having the land condemned, so as not to be disadvantageous to landowners with regard to taxes paid for money gained from the sale of land.

However, the act was challenged by a landholder, Frank E. Midkiff. The case presented the question of whether the Land Reform Act of 1967 passed by the Hawaii state legislature violated the public use clause of the Fifth Amendment and was brought eventually to the U.S. Supreme Court for adjudication. The Court's decision contrasted *Midkiff* to a previous landmark case that used EMINENT DOMAIN power to condemn lands for private interest. *Berman v. Parker,* 348 U.S. 26 (1954), was a landmark decision made by the U.S. Supreme Court which refined the public use clause and use of private property with JUST COMPENSATION. The case opened the way for successive cases whereby property could be condemned based on economic considerations that pertain to a public purpose and would therefore be considered constitutional.

Based on this precedent, the Supreme Court concluded in a unanimous decision of 8 to 0 that the Hawaii Land Reform Act of 1967 was constitutional, as it served the public purpose of regulating the current land distribution that was a legacy of the ancient oligopoly of Hawaii. In delivering the opinion of the Court, Justice SANDRA DAY O'CONNOR stated that

> The Fifth Amendment of the United States Constitution provides, in pertinent part, that "private property [shall not] be taken for public use, without just compensation." These cases present the question whether the Public use Clause of the Amendment, made applicable to the States through the FOURTEENTH AMENDMENT, prohibits the State of Hawaii from taking, with just compensation, title in real property from [467 U.S. 229, 232] lessors and transferring it to lessees in order to reduce the concentration of ownership of fees simple in the State. We conclude that it does not.

The Court noted that the Land Reform Act was rationally related to a conceivable public purpose and that the debates relating to the forced redistribution of land should be handled by legislatures rather than the federal courts. The decision favored the State of Hawaii, as it was felt that the act was a classic exercise of the state's POLICE POWERS for correcting a situation within the public interest and that this satisfied the public use doctrine provided for by *Berman v. Parker*. The Court also added that it felt that property taken by eminent domain and transferred to private beneficiaries did not condemn the law (Land Reform Act of 1967) to having a solely private purpose, and therefore it did not contradict the Fifth Amendment's public use clause.

This case is of significance as it highlights the issue of judicial deference to legislative decisions taken in the public's interest. In *Midkiff*, the Court acknowledges that state legislatures are as capable as Congress in determining exercise of power in their specific spheres of authority for making judgments involving public interests and purposes. Therefore this case establishes that if a state or the federal legislature determines that there exist substantial reasons for extension of its authority to serve a public use or interest, then the courts must defer to the legislature's decision, as it can better assess public interests.

For more information: Allen, Tom. *The Right to Property in Commonwealth Constitutions.* Cambridge: Cambridge University Press, 2000; Mercuro, Nicholas, and Warren J. Samuels, eds. *The Fundamental Interrelationships Between Government and Property.* Stamford, Conn.: JAI Press, 1999.

—Dale Mineshima-Lowe

Hazelwood School District v. Kuhlmeier

484 U.S. 260 (1988)

In *Hazelwood School District v. Kuhlmeier*, the U.S. Supreme Court upheld the authority of a public school principal to censor the content of a school newspaper when there is a legitimate educational justification and when the paper is part of the curriculum.

The ruling has broader impact than just school newspapers, applying to yearbooks, school plays, Web sites, and any situation in which student speech may be perceived as bearing the imprimatur of the school. Moreover, the reasoning in *Hazelwood* has been applied by some federal courts to allow college officials to restrict student speech and student publications at public colleges and universities.

The case originated in a school district in St. Louis, Missouri. Editors of the Hazelwood East High School student newspaper, the Spectrum, prepared articles in May, 1983, on teenage pregnancy and on the impact of divorce on students. The pregnancy article recounted the experiences of three students whose names were changed in the story. The high school principal believed the three might still be identified by some readers. The divorce article, as shown to the school principal, used some real names and did not give the parents a chance to respond (apparently the real names were deleted in a version that was not shown to the principal). The principal believed there was no time to change the stories and so killed two pages of the paper, leaving a four-page publication instead of the six that were planned.

The editors sued in federal court, believing the principal's action violated their FIRST AMENDMENT rights. A federal judge ruled against the students, but the U.S. Court of Appeals for the Eighth Circuit reversed and found a First Amendment violation. The appeals court said the articles could not be censored because they posed no risk of "material and substantial" disruption, the legal standard from the leading STUDENT RIGHTS case of *TINKER V. DES MOINES INDEPENDENT COMMUNITY SCHOOL DISTRICT*, 393 U.S. 503 (1969).

In a 5-3 ruling written by Justice Byron R. White, the Supreme Court changed the standard and ruled in favor of school officials. The newspaper was produced by the journalism class, the Court noted. The Court said that *Tinker* dealt with independent student speech which presented different issues than speech that was part of official school activities or the curriculum and that would be perceived as having the imprimatur of the school. The Court said that school officials could control the content of speech that might be seen as the school's message as long as the official action was "reasonably related to legitimate pedagogical concerns." This new standard would make it much easier for officials to control student speech.

Justice WILLIAM J. BRENNAN, JR., wrote a strong dissent that was joined by Justices Thurgood Marshall and Harry Blackmun. The dissent faulted the majority for citing the *Tinker* case, saying the Court "denudes high school students of much of the First Amendment protection that *Tinker* itself prescribed."

For more information: Goodman, Mark. "From Consistency to Confusion: The Legacy of *Hazelwood School District v. Kuhlmeier*." *Communications Lawyer* 10, no. 1 (1993): 1–20; Hafen, Bruce C., and Jonathan O. Hafen. "The Hazelwood Progeny: Autonomy and Student Expression in the 1990's." *St. John's Law Review* 69 (1995): 379–419.

—Stephen Wermiel

Heart of Atlanta Motel v. United States 379 U.S. 241 (1964)

In *Heart of Atlanta Motel v. United States,* the Supreme Court upheld Title II of the CIVIL RIGHTS ACT OF 1964. Title II of the Civil Rights Act of 1964 prohibited racial discrimination in places of public accommodation, such as hotels and motels. The question this case presented was whether the U.S. Congress had exceeded their constitutional powers and violated the COMMERCE CLAUSE by prohibiting businesses from choosing their customers. Ultimately, the decision of the U.S. Supreme Court upheld the Civil Rights Act of 1964.

Before 1964, the United States was a very segregated country, and the major concept that dominated the Supreme Court when it came to race relations was "separate but equal," dating back to *PLESSY V. FERGUSON,* 163 U.S. 537 (1896). This concept was not a reality, and while black people and white people were separate, they were not equal. However, the precedents from the Supreme Court began changing with cases such as *Powell v. Alabama,* 287 U.S. 45 (1932); *Smith v. Allwright,* 321 U.S. 649 (1944); *Sweatt v. Painter,* 339 U.S. 629 (1950); *McLaurin v. Oklahoma State Regent,* 339 U.S. 637 (1950); *BROWN V. BOARD OF EDUCATION OF TOPEKA,* 347 U.S. 483 (1954); *NAACP v. Alabama,* 357 U.S. 449 (1958); and *Boynton v. Virginia,* 364 U.S. 454 (1960).

Despite these precedents from the Court, segregation still prevailed, especially in the South. Congress, relying on constitutional powers granted to them controlling INTERSTATE COMMERCE, acted to ease the plight of blacks in a segregated society by passing the Civil Rights Act on July 2, 1964, which banned racial discrimination in public places.

A large motel in Atlanta, Georgia, called the Heart of Atlanta, refused to rent rooms to black customers even following the Civil Rights Act of 1964. Refusing to comply with the act, the owner, an attorney, filed suit in a federal court with the contention that the Civil Rights Act went beyond the powers granted in the Constitution to Congress to regulate interstate commerce. The owner further argued that the act violated his Fifth Amendment rights because it placed controls over his property without DUE PROCESS of the law and violated his THIRTEENTH AMENDMENT rights by forcing him into the servitude of blacks by forcing him to rent rooms to them. The United States countered these arguments by showing accommodation restrictions on blacks interfered with interstate travel and that the other claims were outside of the scope of the Fifth and Thirteenth Amendments. The federal district court agreed with the United States and the owner appealed to the Supreme Court.

Justice Tom Clark delivered the opinion of the Supreme Court, with Justice Arthur Goldberg, Justice HUGO BLACK, and Justice WILLIAM O. DOUGLAS concurring on December 14, 1964. The Court upheld the Civil Rights Act determining that Congress did act within the jurisdiction granted to them in the interstate commerce clause. Since the hotel received most of its customers from other states, it did participate in interstate commerce. The Court found no merits in the arguments of the violation of the owner's Fifth and Thirteenth Amendment rights. The

Civil Rights Act of 1964, passed by Congress, received the support of the judiciary with this Supreme Court decision.

For more information: Cortner, Richard. *Civil Rights and Public Accommodations: The Heart of Atlanta Motel and McClung Cases.* Lawrence: University Press of Kansas, 2001; Mayer, Robert, ed. *The Civil Rights Act of 1964.* San Diego, Calif.: Greenhaven Press, 2004.

—Carol Walker

high crimes and misdemeanors

High crimes and misdemeanors are the classes of offenses to which Congress's power of IMPEACHMENT extends under Article II, Section 4 of the federal Constitution. From the Constitution's earliest days, this clause's exact meaning has been the chief issue of dispute in virtually every significant impeachment procedure in the HOUSE OF REPRESENTATIVES and trial in the SENATE.

The full language of the constitutional text says, "The President, VICE PRESIDENT, and all civil Officers of the United States shall be removed from Office on Impeachment for, and Conviction of, TREASON, Bribery, or other high Crimes and Misdemeanors." The first impeachment, that of District Judge John Pickering in 1804, established a tradition of misapplying and/or omitting to rely explicitly upon this language. Pickering was either a drunkard, as his opponents held, or insane, as his friends argued, and thus clearly in need of removal from the bench; the problem was whether drunkenness or insanity might be said to constitute a "high crime" or "high misdemeanor."

The Senate removed him without exactly answering the question. As Raoul Berger demonstrated, either of the characterizations of Pickering would have justified the Senate in concluding that he had committed a "high crime" or "high misdemeanor," if the Senate had looked to pre-1788 English precedent for those terms' definitions. Berger argues that here, as in other cases (e.g., of "bribery" in the same clause), the Constitution's authors clearly intended for English usage to determine their words' meaning.

The Senate, however, has not been clear in relying on English precedent. Therefore, not only in the Pickering case, but in those of Justice Samuel Chase, President William Clinton, and numerous others, defendants have argued that the impeachment power extends only to indictable offenses. Although their argument has often been rejected, it has formed a leitmotif for the public political defense that necessarily accompanies impeachments of significant officers (if not of lower-court judges). Most notably, this defense manifested itself in the Clinton matter in the slogan "He only lied about sex."

To say that the Senate has been whipsawed by this argument is not to deny that Congress has occasionally been led in the opposition direction. Thus, in moving the impeachment of Justice WILLIAM O. DOUGLAS in 1970, Representative Gerald Ford argued that high crimes and misdemeanors were whatever the House and Senate agreed them to be at a given moment. In practical terms, as the Pickering precedent shows, he was right—if perhaps a bit too bold for comfort. In another, later case, the Senate removed a judge from the bench for bringing his office "into scandal and disrepute." President Johnson's impeachment centered on his violation of an unconstitutional statute—along with leading congressmen's desire to remake the Constitution along the British model by subordinating the presidency to the Congress. The impeachment power is the mechanism by which Congress can police the behavior of high elected and appointed officers, and its awesomeness has led political actors to favor desuetude to overuse.

For more information: Berger, Raoul. *Impeachment: The Constitutional Problems.* Cambridge, Mass.: Harvard University Press, 1973; McKitrick, Eric. *Andrew Johnson and Reconstruction.* New York: Oxford University Press, 1988.

—Kevin R. C. Gutzman

Hiibel v. Nevada 542 U.S. 177 (2004)

In *Hiibel v. Nevada,* the Supreme Court ruled that individuals stopped by the police can be required to identify themselves. The significance of this decision lies in rejection of arguments that a state law requiring people to identify themselves to the police does not constitute either a FOURTH AMENDMENT unreasonable search and seizure or a violation of the Fifth Amendment's RIGHT AGAINST SELF-INCRIMINATION. Moreover, the *Hiibel* opinion addressed some legal questions about identifying oneself to the police that had not been previously addressed by the Court.

In *TERRY V. OHIO*,, 392 U.S. 1 (1968), the Supreme Court upheld the authority of police officers to briefly stop, question, and frisk individuals whom they had a reasonable suspicion to believe are engaged in criminal activity. *Terry*'s STOP AND FRISK rule is considered to be one of the exceptions to the Fourth Amendment's requirement that a warrant is required to undertake a search. The *Terry* opinion can be considered a pro-police ruling, giving them more leeway to investigate crimes, but it has also been condemned as giving them too much power to randomly stop and harass individuals. Critics of the ruling see *Terry* as granting the police so much power to stop and search people that it has led to, among other things, RACIAL PROFILING.

In the case of Larry Hiibel, he was stopped by Nevada police in the context of a county sheriff's investigating an assault. When asked to identify himself he refused and was then charged with a violation of a state law that required individuals to identify themselves when they are stopped by police and are being questioned about a crime. At his court appearance, Hiibel argued that the state law requiring him to identify himself violated both his Fourth and Fifth Amendment rights. The Court rejected his arguments and convicted him for violating the law. Hiibel appealed his case through to the Nevada Supreme Court, and his arguments were rejected each time. In reviewing the decision of the Nevada Supreme Court, the U.S. Supreme Court also rejected his claims.

Writing for the majority, Justice ANTHONY M. KENNEDY first noted that stop and identify statutes had a long history in American and English law, serving their purpose to prevent vagrancy. However, in cases such as *Brown v. Texas,* 443 U.S. 47 (1979), the Court had struck these general types of law down as a violation of the Fourth Amendment, because they permitted the police to stop people even if they were not suspected of doing anything wrong. However, the Nevada law, unlike the earlier stop and identify or vagrancy laws, did not authorize the police to stop and compel identification except in the context of a reasonable suspicion that the person had committed a crime.

Second, Kennedy noted that *Terry* had authorized the stopping of individuals based upon reasonable suspicion and that as part of routine questioning, asking for identification is a typical police activity. Asking a suspect for identification serves several important governmental functions. For example, it allows the police to determine if they have the right suspect. Thus, asking for identification is a reasonable extension of the *Terry* exception to the Fourth Amendment warrant requirement.

The Court also rejected Hiibel's Fifth Amendment claim. Here they argued that the Fifth Amendment permits one to refuse to provide information that is self-incriminating. Merely providing one's name, according to the Court, was not self-incriminating.

In a lone dissent, Justice JOHN PAUL STEVENS contended that Hiibel's Fifth Amendment rights were violated. He argued that the Fifth Amendment protection against self-incrimination applies outside of a criminal court setting and that this right should require the police to have probable cause and not merely reasonable suspicion before they can require a person to provide identification.

Hiibel thus extended the *Terry* exception to upholding laws that require individuals to identify themselves in certain settings. It did not authorize broad authority of the police simply to randomly stop and ask people to identify themselves. However, in light of concerns about how *Terry v. Ohio* had already allegedly led to the practice of police stopping people based upon their race, critics of *Hiibel* will see this opinion as giving the government even more authority to stop and question individuals.

For more information: Heumann, Milton, and Lance Cassak. *Good Cop, Bad Cop: Racial Profiling and Competing Views of Justice.* New York: Peter Lang Publishing, 2003.

—David Schultz

Hodgson v. Minnesota 497 U.S. 417 (1990)
In *Hodgson v. Minnesota,* the Supreme Court upheld a parental notification law for minors seeking abortions, although in this case a law requiring both parents to consent was declared unconstitutional.

During the 1980s, an increasing number of state legislatures enacted parental involvement laws, requiring parental consent for minors seeking abortions or mandating that doctors notify parents before performing an abortion on a minor. Proponents of such laws argue that parents should be involved in their daughter's decision to have an ABORTION. Opponents claim most pregnant teenagers inform their parents anyway, and it is unrealistic and harmful to assume that parental involvement benefits every teen.

On June 26, 1990, the Supreme Court addressed the issue of a two-parent notification requirement in a Minnesota case. The law was passed in 1981 as an amendment to the Minors' Consent to Health Services Act. Subdivision Two of the amendment required a physician to notify both parents of an unemancipated minor before performing an abortion. Minors living with divorced or separated parents were not exempted from the law, nor were those whose parent deserted the family. The law allowed notification of only one parent if the other one were dead or could not be found after "reasonably diligent effort." There was also an exemption to the notice requirement in cases of emergency, or when both parents consented in writing to the abortion, or if the minor had previously been certified to the authorities as a victim of sexual or physical abuse. Finally, physicians were required to wait 48 hours after the notification before performing the abortion.

Subdivision Six of the law specified that a judicial bypass procedure would take effect if Subdivision Two were declared unconstitutional by a court. The bypass allowed the pregnant minor to attempt to convince a judge that she was sufficiently mature to make the abortion decision herself or that an abortion without notice would be in her best interests.

The lower courts were divided on the constitutionality of the law and, on appeal, five justices found Subdivision Two unconstitutional because it was not reasonably related to a legitimate state interest. A different five-justice majority sustained Subdivision Six; four justices would have found the law constitutional with or without the bypass provision.

Speaking for the Court on Subdivision Two, Justice JOHN PAUL STEVENS echoed the lower court's findings that only about half the minors in Minnesota lived with both biological parents and that the effect of notifying the absent parent was potentially harmful to the teenager. Even with both parents present, Stevens said, criminal reports show there is a realistic danger of violence against the teen. Additionally, he noted that even though most petitions were granted, the bypass procedure was often traumatic for the teenager.

Stevens rejected the state's argument that the two-parent notice furthered its interests in the teenager, the parent, or the family because the state can fulfill its obligation to the minor by notifying one parent and permitting that parent to decide whether to notify the other or whether the notice would be detrimental to the teenager. He dismissed the state's position that the family functions best if both parents are involved in a teenager's abortion decision, saying that the state cannot attempt to mold the family into its idealized image.

Speaking for the new majority of five, Justice SANDRA DAY O'CONNOR agreed that Subdivision Two was unconstitutional. But she concluded that Subdivision Six was constitutional because the danger threatened by the two-parent notification requirement is removed when the teenager can avoid notifying one or both parents by applying to the courts for a bypass.

Thus, the Court upheld Minnesota's two-parent notification law as long as it contained a judicial bypass provision.

For more information: Bowers, James R. *Pro-Choice and Anti-Abortion.* Westport, Conn.: Praeger Publishers, 1994; Mezey, Susan Gluck. *Elusive Equality: Women's Rights, Public Policy, and the Law.* Boulder, Colo.: Lynne Rienner Publishers, 2003.

—Susan Gluck Mezey

Holmes, Oliver Wendell, Jr. (1841–1935)

Supreme Court justice

Oliver Wendell Holmes, Jr., was a distinguished poet, historian, philosopher of law, Massachusetts judge, and an associate justice of the U.S. Supreme Court. He was born March 8, 1841, in Boston, Massachusetts, the eldest child of the famous writer and physician for whom he was named.

Holmes graduated from Harvard in 1861 and was shortly afterward commissioned a first lieutenant in the 20th Massachusetts Regiment of Volunteers. He was seriously wounded in the battles of Ball's Bluff, Antietam, and Chancellorsville.

Holmes was both proud and humble about his war service. At Memorial Day ceremonies he gave addresses ("In Our Youth Our Hearts Were Touched with Fire," and "The Soldiers' Faith," 1895) to fellow veterans that glorified in part the sacrifices of those who had fought and died. In 1864, brevet Colonel Holmes resigned his commission and returned to Boston where he entered Harvard Law School. He did not like the traditional curriculum and was to urge that changes be made. In 1866, he graduated with a law degree and traveled in Europe. Holmes was admitted to the Massachusetts bar in 1867. From 1867 until 1882 he practiced law, was the editor of the *American Law Review* (1870–73), edited the 12th edition of Chancellor JAMES KENT's *Commentaries on American Law* (1873), and lectured at Harvard on law.

In 1881, Holmes' Lowell Institute lectures were published as *The Common Law.* Holmes argued that the common law was the result of human experience, rather than the product of deduction from abstract principles. In December of 1882, Holmes was appointed to the Supreme Judicial Court of the State of Massachusetts. In 1899, he became its chief justice. While on the Massachusetts Court, Holmes wrote over 1,000 opinions. His writings on constitutional issues were to be decisions that had lasting impact.

In 1902, President Theodore Roosevelt appointed Holmes to the U.S. Supreme Court. He remained there 30 years, resigning his seat on January 12, 1932, having served with four chief justices. He died in Washington, D.C., March 6, 1935, and was buried in Arlington Cemetery. Holmes wrote 873 opinions while serving on the Supreme Court. The most prolific justice in the Court's history, he gained a reputation as a progressive and as the "Great Dissenter" in cases such as *LOCHNER V. NEW YORK* (1905) and *ADKINS V. CHILDREN'S HOSPITAL* (1923). Holmes believed that unless a law was egregiously bad, judges should practice "judicial restraint." His dissents gave guidance to attorneys on how to bring and win similar cases.

Holmes believed in freedom of speech. In *Schenk v. United States* (1919), his opinion favored limiting the power of government to regulate speech even in a time of war. He wrote that unless there was a "clear and present danger" that a speech would cause some violent harm, it should not be stopped. To prevent even odious ideas from being expressed was in his view to inhibit the free "marketplace of ideas."

The next year, in *MISSOURI V. HOLLAND* (1920), Holmes upheld the government's right to engage in regulating the hunting of migratory waterfowl. His opinion stated the Court's view of inherent powers of the president and the Congress to make laws in the area of international conservation.

At times, Holmes seemed to side with libertarians. During World War I, Holmes disagreed with the Court's majority when it refused to grant citizenship to a Hungarian, Rosika Schwimmer, because she was a pacifist. In *Frank v. Mangum* (1915), he dissented, and in *Moore v. Dempsey* (1923) he wrote the majority opinion. Holmes confronted the problem of lynching.

One of Holmes's most notorious cases was *BUCK V. BELL* (1927). The case involved a Virginia law requiring the sterilization of epileptics and the mentally ill. Buck was a female with a feeble mind. Holmes agreed with Virginia's decision to compel her sterilization, declaring that three generations of imbeciles was enough. Holmes supported Social Darwinism and pragmatism. He rejected the doctrine of natural rights. He opposed legal formalism and SUBSTANTIVE DUE PROCESS, contributing instead to the development of legal realism.

For more information: Bowen, Catherine Drinker. *Yankee from Olympus: Justice Holmes and His Family.* Boston: Houghton Mifflin Company, 1962; Frankfurter, Felix. *Mr. Justice Holmes and the Supreme Court.* 2nd ed. Cambridge, Mass.: Harvard University Press, 1961; Howe, Mark DeWolfe. *Justice Oliver Wendell Holmes.* Cambridge, Mass.: Harvard University Press, 1957–63; Novick, Sheldon M. *Honorable Justice: The Life of Oliver Wendell Holmes.* Boston: Little, Brown, 1989.

—Andrew J. Waskey

Home Building and Loan Association v. Blaisdell 290 U.S. 398 (1934)

In *Home Building and Loan Association v. Blaisdell,* the Supreme Court upheld Minnesota's moratorium on home foreclosures during the Great Depression. The Court reasoned that the economic emergency justified the alteration of private agreements and that state action violated neither the U.S. Constitution's CONTRACT CLAUSE (Article I, Section 10) nor the FOURTEENTH AMENDMENT's equal protection or due process clauses.

In the throes of the Great Depression, many Minnesotans became unemployed and lost their homes due to the inability to make mortgage payments. In 1933, the Minnesota state legislature declared an emergency and imposed a moratorium on home foreclosures. Chapter 339 of the act permitted qualified debtors to make reasonable monthly payments and prohibited creditors from foreclosing for two years. The law did not wipe out the homebuyers' debts; it merely permitted them to adjust their payment schedules to stave off foreclosures.

In 1928, John and Rosella Blaisdell secured a $4,056.39 loan from the Home Building and Loan Association to purchase a large, two-story, 14-room home in Minneapolis, Minnesota. The couple lived in just three rooms and rented the remaining rooms to help make the monthly mortgage payments. In 1933, the couple fell on hard times and encountered difficulty renting their rooms. Using Chapter 339, the Blaisdells secured a state court judgment to adjust and extend their monthly payments on the remaining balance of their mortgage. The lender filed suit in state court alleging the moratorium violated a) the U.S. Constitution's contract clause, which bans states from "impairing the obligation of contracts," b) the Fourteenth Amendment's ban on states' taking property without DUE PROCESS, and c) the Fourteenth Amendment's mandate that the states grant all citizens, including lenders, EQUAL PROTECTION of the law. The state courts ruled for the Blaisdells, and the Home Building and Loan Association appealed to the U.S. Supreme Court.

Chief Justice Charles E. Hughes delivered the opinion of the Court in which Justices Louis Brandeis, Harlan Fiske Stone, Owen Roberts, and Benjamin Cardozo joined. The central focus of the majority opinion was striking a balance between the contract clause and the state's POLICE POWERS. After tracing the origins and development of the contract clause, Chief Justice Hughes surmised that contracts, while sacred, are not absolute and, that in this instance, the State of Minnesota had legitimately used its police powers under the Tenth Amendment to promote the public good during an actual emergency. Moreover, the Court believed that the law in question did not actually obliterate private contracts, but temporarily modified them to prevent widespread foreclosures and certain economic calamity. Thus, the Court affirmed the lower court decision.

A strong dissent was offered by Justice George Sutherland and supported by Justices Willis Van Devanter, James McReynolds and Pierce Butler. Sutherland believed the majority misinterpreted the framers' intent and that the state moratorium clearly ran afoul of the contract clause. Wrote Sutherland, "If the provisions of the Constitution cannot be upheld when they pinch as well as when they comfort, they may as well be abandoned."

This case is illustrative of the growing rift on the Supreme Court between the conservative and liberal justices during the early days of the New Deal. The conservative block, consisting of Justices Sutherland, McReynolds, Van Devanter, and Butler, believed that the Court should exercise restraint in interpreting the Constitution and frequently voted against ever-increasing government regulation of the free market. The liberal coalition, comprised of Brandeis, Stone, Cardozo, and to varying degrees Hughes and Roberts, frequently supported the government's initiatives to ameliorate the social and economic problems associated with the Great Depression.

For more information: Leuchtenburg, William E. *The Supreme Court Reborn: The Constitutional Revolution in the Age of Roosevelt.* New York: Oxford University Press, 1995; McConnell, Grant. *Private Power and American Democracy.* New York: Knopf, 1966; White, G. Edward. *The Constitution and the New Deal.* Boston: Harvard University Press, 2000.

—Richard J. Hardy

House of Representatives

ARTICLE I OF THE U.S. CONSTITUTION defines the legislative branch of the national government to consist of the U.S. House of Representatives along with the SENATE. Together, the two houses are known as the Congress. Of the two houses of Congress, the U.S. House of Representatives was designed to be the most democratic. At the founding, House seats were the only directly elected federal positions. They were also designed to be closer to the people by serving a shorter term.

Article I of the Constitution details the structure and the power of the House and the Senate. For the House, the article states that it will share legislative power with the Senate, and the two together will have all legislative power for the federal government. Representatives were to be elected every two years, and this was designed to make the House a more responsive body. One must be at least 25 to serve in the House, and one must have been a citizen of the United States for seven years and be a resident of the state one is elected from as well.

House seats are divided among the states by population, with each state being given at least one representative. By statute, the current number of members is capped at 435, but this is not a constitutional requirement. Before the abolition of slavery, the population was considered the whole of all free persons and "three-fifths of all others." Now it is all persons counted by the census. The seats must be apportioned according to the ONE PERSON, ONE VOTE principle that means that each House district must be approximately the same size in terms of population, especially among districts within each state. The office of the speaker of the House is created in Article I, and it is said that the House may select that person and other officers. These other officers have been created over the years and include majority and minority leaders, majority and minority whips, and various other positions such as the clerk of the House, the parliamentarian, and others.

The House has a number of formal powers, laid out in the Constitution. One of the major formal powers of the House is the ability to make laws. Lawmaking is not a simple process, and it may be checked by a number of processes. Both houses of Congress must pass identical legislation, and the president may VETO any piece of legislation that passes both Houses. A veto may be overridden only by a two-thirds majority of each house. Legislation may also fail to pass constitutional muster and be struck down by the court system.

The House has the power to impeach the president or other executive or judicial officials according to Article I, and the Senate may then vote to convict or acquit the subject of the IMPEACHMENT. The House is required to originate any finance bills, including taxation and spending. Such bills still require passage in both houses. There are a number of other powers granted to the House, such as the establishment of the post office, the regulation of commerce (which leads to an important implied power), and the ability to raise armies and declare war. Finally, in the event that no presidential ticket receives enough electoral votes to win, the House selects the president of the United States. They did that twice: once in 1800 when they selected THOMAS JEFFERSON to become president and then in 1824 when they picked John Quincy Adams for that position.

The House also has a number of restrictions placed on it. It is forbidden from granting PATENTS of nobility, for example, from passing bills of attainder (which would convict a person of a crime without a court process), from making ex post facto laws (laws that would take effect retroactively), or from suspension of the writ of HABEAS CORPUS, which demands that the state produce a prisoner and show cause as to why he or she is being held.

The House has a number of implied powers. These are powers not expressly mentioned in the Constitution, but which have been found necessary to support a constitutional function of the House. The classic example of an implied power is the creation of a national bank. In *MCCULLOCH V. MARYLAND,* 17 U.S. (4 Wheat) 316 (1819), the Court ruled that the creation of a bank was appropriate to support the powers of the Congress to appropriate and to maintain an army. A relative to the implied powers of the House is the COMMERCE CLAUSE. The ability of the House to regulate various forms of commerce, and in particular INTERSTATE COMMERCE, has allowed greatly expanded powers for the federal government. This power was confirmed and expanded in *WICKARD V. FILBURN,* 317 U.S. 111 (1942), and in *KATZENBACH V. MCCLUNG,* 379 U.S. 294 (1964). Almost anything that affects any commerce is now considered to affect interstate commerce, and this has allowed for a great deal of expansion in bureaucratic regulation, CIVIL RIGHTS, and other issues (Spaeth and Smith, 1991, 85).

The House of Representatives is an integral part of American government, and is covered extensively in the Constitution. It provides a cornerstone of American democracy by giving the people a voice in the creation of their laws.

For more information: Dodd, Lawrence C., and Bruce Oppenheimer. *Congress Reconsidered.* 8th ed. Washington, D.C.: CQ Press, 2005; Mason, Alpheus Thomas, and Donald Grier Stephenson, Jr. *American Constitutional Law.* 12th ed. Upper Saddle River, N.J.: Prentice Hall, 1999.

—Matthew W. Barber

housing and the Constitution

The U.S. Constitution does not recognize a right to housing. However, the Supreme Court and policymakers have used CONSTITUTIONAL INTERPRETATION to directly and indirectly shape fair housing initiatives.

Housing discrimination on the basis of race, color, religion, sex, handicap, familial status and national origin is currently (and primarily) prohibited by the Fair Housing Act of 1968 and its amendments and Title VI of the CIVIL RIGHTS ACT OF 1964. In early housing discrimination cases, the EQUAL PROTECTION clause had been used primarily to eliminate housing discrimination by government entities. In *BUCHANAN V. WARLEY,* 245 U.S. 60 (1917), the Court argued that racially-based zoning laws constituted DUE PROCESS violations.

In *SHELLEY V. KRAEMER,* 334 U.S. 1 (1948), the Court ruled that racially-biased restrictive covenants, although private, could be considered equal protection violations if state courts enforced them. In this case, a white family received state court support in their efforts to uphold their neighborhood's private agreement to prevent African Americans from purchasing homes in the community. While the private agreement or restrictive covenant, on its own, did not violate the equal protection clause, state court enforcement of the agreement should be considered sufficient government involvement as to constitute an equal protection clause violation. Recent decisions suggest that private individuals may be held in violation of the equal protection clause if they are working in concert with public entities.

The Court has also established a standard of intent for housing cases involving potential equal protection clause violations. In *Village of Arling-*

ton Heights. v. Metropolitan Housing Development Corp., 429 U.S. 252 (1977), the Court stated that plaintiffs are required to demonstrate "proof of racially discriminatory intent or purpose . . . to show a violation of the Equal Protection Clause." The THIRTEENTH AMENDMENT has been cited less frequently in the Court's fair housing doctrine but has played a critical role in legitimating fair housing legislation. For example, in *Jones v. Mayer*, 392 U.S. 409 (1968), the Court argued that the enforcement sections of the Thirteenth Amendment granted Congress the authority to impose restrictions on the sale or rental of private property in order to eliminate barriers preventing racial minorities from procuring properties.

Constitutional rulings in non-housing CIVIL RIGHTS cases have paved the road for fair housing doctrine. In many respects, the Court's ruling in *BROWN V. BOARD OF EDUCATION*, 347 U.S. 483 (1954), which ended the "separate but equal" doctrine established in *PLESSY V. FERGUSON*, 163 U.S. 537 (1896), opened the door for all instances of racial segregation, both public and private, to be considered suspect. Housing advocates have used the Court's decision in *HEART OF ATLANTA V. U.S.*, 379 U.S. 241 (1964), to thwart arguments that housing policies, such as programs requiring landlords to accept tenants with federal vouchers that offset the cost of housing, violate the landlord's constitutionally guaranteed right to freedom of contract. In this case, the Court argued that a business did not have the "right" to establish its own grounds for serving customers, free from government intrusion.

For more information: Massey, Douglas, and Nancy Denton. *American Apartheid: Segregation and the Making of the Underclass.* Cambridge, Mass: Harvard University Press, 1993; National Low-Income Housing Coalition. "Fifty Years Later: *Brown v. Board of Education* and Housing Opportunity" (2004). Available online. URL: www.nlihc.org. Accessed May 12, 2008; Yinger, John. *Closed Doors, Opportunities Lost: The Continuing Costs of Housing Discrimination.* New York: Russell Sage Foundation, 1995.

—Alison Gash

H. P. Hood & Sons, Inc. v. Du Mond 336 U.S. 525 (1949)

Hood & Sons v. Du Mond was a Supreme Court decision striking down New York's decision to deny a license to a Massachusetts-based milk distributor to operate a facility to collect and deliver milk in INTERSTATE COMMERCE. The majority opinion, written by Justice Robert H. Jackson and supported by a bare five-justice majority, articulated a strong presumption in favor of free trade among the states and against state efforts to impede the flow of interstate commerce. Justice HUGO BLACK, joined by Justice Frank Murphy, and Justice Felix Frankfurter, joined by Justice Wiley B. Rutledge, wrote dissenting opinions.

The petitioner, Hood, operated two milk-receiving depots in New York State before the dispute giving rise to this case and supplied milk to Boston. Hood applied for a license to operate a third facility at Greenwich, New York, but the application was rejected by the Commissioner of Agriculture and Markets of New York (Du Mond), citing a reduction in local supply of milk if the application were accepted, an attendant increase in cost to competing dealers, adequate markets for existing producers, and a likelihood of destructive competition. Hood appealed to the state courts, raising an objection under the COMMERCE CLAUSE, but the New York Court of Appeals upheld the state's denial. The U.S. Supreme Court accepted the case under certiorari jurisdiction and reversed the state court in Hood's favor.

The Court's decision struck down the New York regulation denying Hood an extension of his license because the grounds for doing so, protection of within-state economic interests, were inadequate to overcome the commitment to free trade among the states represented in the Constitution by the commerce clause. In the absence of congressional legislation, the majority argued, the Court was responsible for ensuring that states do not restrain trade in interstate commerce in the interest of local economic advantage.

Justice Jackson's opinion does not deny that state interests include protecting citizenry from public health hazards or safety concerns, but that economic protection cannot be the basis for restraining commerce among the states in the absence of congressional support. In support of its position, New York argued that its regulation was consistent with the federal regulatory system for milk, but the Court rejected this contention.

Justice Black, in his dissent, faults the Court for abandoning previous approaches, which sought to balance the interests of commerce with state regulatory concerns so long as the state effect on interstate commerce did not interfere with congressional action. This position represents something of a compromise for Justice Black, who in general disdained balancing approaches in constitutional law but preferred the established judicial efforts to balance national markets with local needs to the majority's position that even non-discriminatory state regulations affecting interstate commerce were presumptively unconstitutional absent congressional approval. Justice Black, who reads congressional inactivity as permission for state regulation, rather than constitutional prohibition of it, wrote that the Court's position in Hood potentially left substantial amounts of economic activity free from all regulation, as Congress could not possibly address all of the local concerns in question and states were now prohibited from doing so.

Justice Frankfurter would have sent the case back to the state court for further proceedings so that the Court could better assess whether extension of Hood's license would genuinely lead to destructive competition. His dissent argues that the Court inappropriately treats a question of balancing competing interests as a question of absolutes.

For more information: Furtado, Manuel L. "Constitutional Law: State Regulation of Interstate Commerce." *California Law Review* 37 (1949): 667–671; Mendelson, Wallace. "Recent Developments in State Power to Regulate and Tax Interstate Commerce." *University of Pennsylvania Law Review* 98 (1949): 57–68; Michel, Jack. "*Hood v. Dumond*: A Study of the Supreme Court and the Ideology of Capitalism." *University of Pennsylvania Law Review* 134 (1986): 657–701.

—Scott E. Graves

Humphrey's Executor v. United States 295 U.S. 602 (1935)

In *Humphrey's Executor v. United States*, the Supreme Court ruled that the president does not have the power to remove commissioners of independent agencies that perform legislative and judicial functions for policy purposes. This case is significant because it guarantees regulatory agencies independence from the president to perform their duties in a non-partisan manner.

In 1931, President Herbert Hoover appointed William Humphrey, a conservative, to serve as a commissioner on the Federal Trade Commission (FTC). According to the Federal Trade Commission Act, a commissioner could be removed by the president only for "inefficiency, neglect of duty, or malfeasance in office." However, in 1933, President Franklin D. Roosevelt asked Humphrey to resign, because he opposed many New Deal programs that the FTC had jurisdiction over. Humphrey refused, and President Roosevelt dismissed him on policy grounds. Even though Humphrey died shortly thereafter, the executor of his estate filed suit to recover his salary. On certificate from the Court of Claims, the Supreme Court ruled for Humphrey's estate, holding that Congress has the power to restrict the removal of certain officials for one or more causes.

Writing for a unanimous court, Justice George Sutherland distinguished between officials performing executive functions and those performing quasi-legislative and/or quasi-judicial functions. In *Myers v. United States*, 272 U.S. 52 (1926), the Court held that the president could remove officials who perform executive functions for any cause. However, the Court claims that Congress created the FTC to perform legislative functions by investigating unfair methods of competition and suggesting remedies and judicial functions by adjudicating unfair trade practices cases. Thus, the FTC is not part of the executive branch, because any executive power it performs, it does so as an agency of the legislative or judicial branch.

Justice Sutherland also points out that the authority of Congress to create these agencies to act independently of the executive is undoubted and incident to this is the power to fix the term of office and condition of removal. Moreover, the legislative language, legislative reports, and general purpose of the legislation demonstrate congressional intent to create a body of experts free from political control.

Finally, the Court ruled that presidential removal violates the separation of powers, because the ability to remove makes the commissioner dependent on the executive. Since the FTC performs legislative and judicial functions, this would mean that the president would exercise legislative and judicial power which the Constitution forbids.

This decision has had a significant impact on the administrative structure of government. The independence granted regulatory agencies insures impartial administration of the law and provides stability, because a change in presidents will not change the policies of the agency. However, many believe this leads to ineffective and inefficient policy, because independent agencies can pursue policies that compete with and are contradictory to policies pursued by other agencies and departments. This is especially troubling since the agencies are not directly accountable to anyone.

For more information: James, Scott. *Presidents, Parties, and the State: A Party System Perspective on Democratic Regulatory Choice, 1884–1936.* Cambridge: Cambridge University Press, 2001; Stone, Alan. *Economic Regulation and the Public Interest: The Federal Trade Commission in Theory and Practice.* Ithaca, N.Y.: Cornell University Press, 1977.

—Sean Evans

Hunt v. Cromartie 532 U.S. 234 (2001)

In *Hunt v. Cromartie,* the U.S. Supreme Court held that the district court made a mistake when it found that the state of North Carolina violated the EQUAL PROTECTION clause in its 1997 redrawing of its 12th Congressional District's 1992 boundaries and that it was based on "erroneous findings."

In *SHAW V. RENO,* 509 U.S. 630 (1993), the U.S. Supreme Court, for the first time, acknowledged a basis for which action could be brought by anyone of any race to dispute redistricting plans. If the plans were drawn unconstitutionally on the "uses of race," then anyone could challenge them. Under the Fourteenth Amendment, race is considered a "suspect category." Therefore, legislative decisions that are based on race are subject to STRICT SCRUTINY.

The *Shaw* case involved a "bizarre"-shaped Congressional district. It was drawn to satisfy Department of Justice demands that the state create another largely African-American district. It was more than 160 miles long and very narrow in width, a "snakelike shape." It connected various, unrelated sections of African-American voting populations (47 percent). The Court found that if a redistricting map is "so bizarre on its face that it is 'unexplainable on the grounds other than race,'" it should be held to "strict scrutiny."

In *Shaw v. Hunt,* 517 U.S. 899 (1996), the Petitioners claimed that the state of North Carolina violated the FOURTEENTH AMENDMENT's equal protection clause. The Court ruled that the redrawing of a North Carolina congressional district to include a majority of African Americans could not be justified because it did violate the equal protection clause of the Fourteenth Amendment to the U.S. Constitution.

Following the Supreme Court's decision, that the district had been unconstitutionally drawn, the state made a new redistricting plan in 1997. After the boundaries had been redrawn, Martin Cromartie again disputed the boundaries of the 12th District, stating that it resulted in racial gerrymandering.

Before there could be any review of the evidence or what action should be taken, the district court granted Cromartie a "summary judgment," stating the Court found that the new boundaries had also been drawn with respect to race. Hunt appealed to the U.S. Supreme Court, which in turn agreed to hear the case, *Hunt v. Cromartie,* 526 U.S. 541 (1999).

The Court found that even though there was strong evidence of racial gerrymandering, the North Carolina General Assembly's real intentions were in question and there should be more of an investigation. Since racial gerrymandering is of constitutional significance there should be a strict evaluation. So the fact that the accusations were so lightly dismissed without a full trial was "erroneous." The Court reviewed the district court's findings only to see if there was error and if the decision was based on accurate evidence. Another reason for the review is that there was no intermediate court review. The U.S. Supreme Court reversed the district court's decision, stating that the evidence was inadequate and "erroneous" to show an unconstitutional race-based objective.

When the case was sent back, the district court again found, after a three-day trial, that the legislature's decisive factor was "race driven" in drawing the 1997 boundaries. The conclusion was based on three factors; the district's shape, the splitting of towns and counties, and its heavily African-American voting population, all of which the Court deemed inappropriate with relation to the "summary judgment." In the appeal, the Court reviewed the district court's findings, and in a 5-4 opinion the Court reversed the district court's conclusion that the state violated the equal protection clause when redrawing the 1997 boundaries. Also, the decision was based on "erroneous findings."

Justice STEPHEN G. BREYER delivered the opinion of the Court, joined by Justice JOHN P. STEVENS, Justice SANDRA DAY O'CONNOR, Justice DAVID H. SOUTER, and Justice Ruth Bader Ginsburg. He wrote for the Court that "the primary evidence upon which the District Court relied for its 'race, not politics,' conclusion is evidence of voting registration, not voting behavior."

In opposition to the ruling were Justice CLARENCE THOMAS, Chief Justice WILLIAM HUBBS REHNQUIST, Justice ANTONIN GREGORY SCALIA, and Justice ANTHONY M. KENNEDY. The opposing justices cited that they did not believe that the district court committed "clear error." The VOTING RIGHTS ACT requires authorities to consider issues of race when drawing district lines. The Shaw case states that one should not make decisions based on race. A governmental entity must consider two different legal requirements when drawing redistricting lines; the Voting Rights Act and the requirements of *Shaw*.

For more information: Ryden, David K. *The U.S. Supreme Court and the Electoral Process*. Washington, D.C.: Georgetown University Press, 2002.

—Thomas Caiazzo

Hurley v. Irish-American Gay, Lesbian & Bisexual Group of Boston 515 U.S. 557 (1995)

In *Hurley v. Irish-American Gay, Lesbian & Bisexual Group of Boston*, the Supreme Court ruled that the sponsor of the annual St. Patrick's Day-Evacuation Day Parade did not have to include members from an Irish gay, lesbian, and bisexual group because to force it to do so would violate its FIRST AMENDMENT rights.

The unanimous ruling by the Court, written by Justice DAVID H. SOUTER, held application of the public accommodations law to require the inclusion of a party the sponsor did not wish to include violated the sponsor's free speech rights. The issues raised in this case include the extent of a public accommodations law, the primacy of the First Amendment's free speech guarantee, and the nature of a parade in the PUBLIC FORUM as a form of expression. The interesting twist in this case is that the group at issue, the group that wished to participate in the parade, was an organization of gay, lesbian, and bisexual descendants of Irish immigrants known as GLIB. The Massachusetts State Court had ordered the parade sponsors to include the GLIB contingent, citing the public accommodations law.

The Court found that the parade was an open recreational event because its sponsors, the South Boston Allied War Veterans Council, had been granted authority to organize and conduct the parade since 1947 through a permit process that has involved no other applicant. The Court agreed with the sponsors that their parade is nonetheless a private event, despite as many as 20,000 marchers and up to 1 million viewers, because of the private sponsorship, irrespective of the size

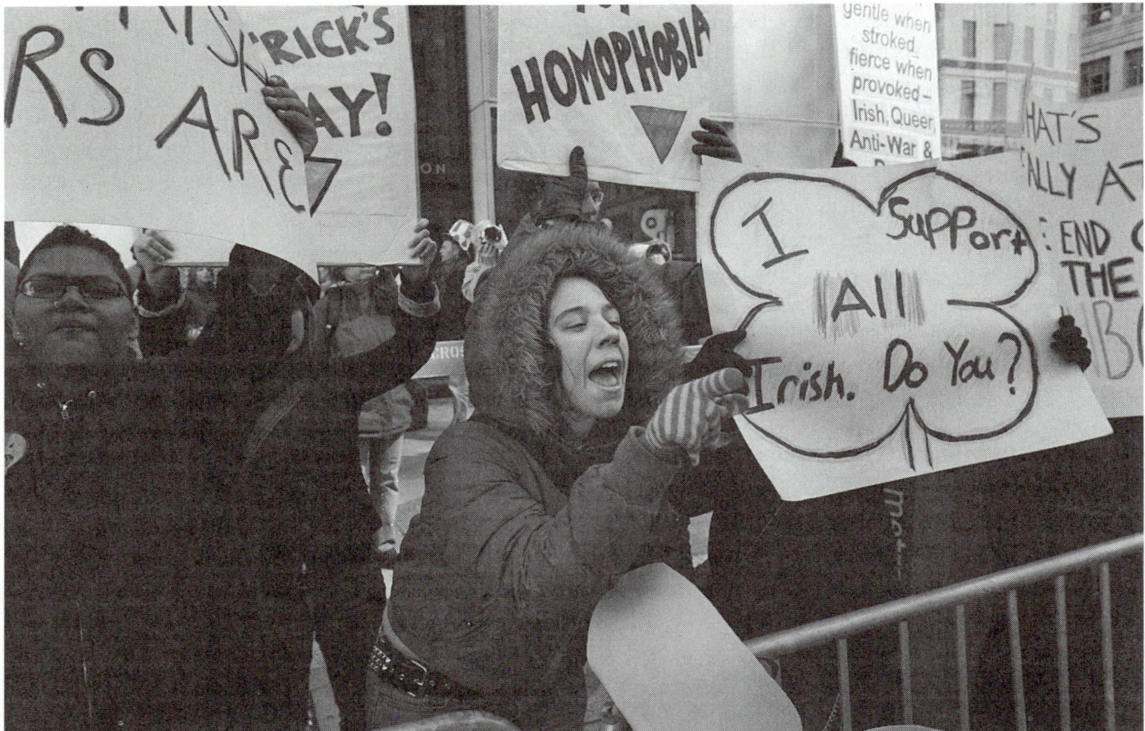

Demonstrators protest the policy of New York's St. Patrick's Day Parade organizers not to allow gay groups to march openly in the procession, as it makes its way up Fifth Avenue on March 17, 2006. *(Michael Nagle/Getty)*

or location of the audience. As regards parade participants, the Court found that although they were not directed to communicate a specific message, the entire parade was organized to impart a collective message with respect to each other and any bystanders along the way, and so was a form of expression. The Court agreed with the sponsors, who maintained that GLIB intended to express its own viewpoint in celebration of its members' sexual identity as gay, lesbian, and bisexual descendants of Irish immigrants and that this particular expression conflicts with the parade organizers.

The issue of whether in fact the two expressions collided was resolved in favor of the sponsor, a private speaker whose First Amendment rights included making this determination, one that is beyond the state's power to control. Each parade participant's expression of whatever viewpoint it wishes is perceived by spectators as part of the overall parade message, so not to allow the parade's sponsors to determine whether this or that message conforms to the overall message would infringe on their free speech rights, which include the right to decide on the content of its own message as well as what it does not wish to have said in its parade.

Massachusetts's public accommodations law was determined not to target speech or discriminate on the basis of content beyond mandating that the state prohibit discrimination against individuals or groups on the basis of proscribed grounds, such as sexual orientation. The parade's sponsors indicated that they would welcome the participation of members of GLIB, just not as a unit marching under its own banner. Hence, regardless of the wisdom of the parade's sponsors in exercising their freedom of association by not including GLIB and not desiring to have a statement made regarding sexual orientation during the parade, they were well within their rights.

For more information: Murdoch, Joyce, and Deb Price. *Courting Justice: Gay Men and Lesbians v. the Supreme Court.* New York: Basic Books, 2001.

—Gordon A. Babst

Hylton v. United States 3 U.S. 171 (1796)

Hylton v. United States is an important case that set the groundwork for JUDICIAL REVIEW in the United States. This 1796 opinion of the Supreme Court explicitly considered the constitutionality of a federal law, thus indirectly addressing the extent to which the Court had the power of judicial review. In the end, the Court did not exercise such review, but the simple fact of considering it is important historically, as it presaged *MARBURY V. MADISON* (1803).

In 1794, the Congress passed a law assessing a tax of 16 dollars on "carriages for the conveyance of persons." Daniel Hylton refused to pay the tax on his carriages. He contended that this tax amounted to a "direct tax," prohibited by the U.S. Constitution. The United States brought suit against Hylton, alleging that he had violated the law and that the law had been properly passed. As Justice Samuel Chase put it, the question in this case is simple: "whether the law of Congress . . . entitled 'An act to lay levies upon carriages, for the conveyance of persons,' is unconstitutional and void?" Thus, he defines this case as explicitly addressing the constitutionality of a federal law.

The decision was rendered by seriatim opinions. Justices Chase, William Paterson, and James Iredell delivered opinions, all agreeing that the law was to be upheld. Justice James Wilson recused himself, since he had expressed a prior opinion on the case in the Circuit Court of Virginia. Justice William Cushing did not take part, since he had been prevented from attending the oral argument. Newly appointed Chief Justice Oliver Ellsworth had been sworn in after argument and declined to take part in the decision.

Chase's opinion explored the extent to which the tax was "direct," and he decided that it was not. He concludes, with a consideration of the power of the Court to declare laws unconstitutional, in these words: "It is unnecessary, at this time, for me to determine, whether this court, constitutionally possesses the power to declare an act of Congress void, on the ground of it being contrary to, and in violation of, the Constitution; but if the court have such power, I am free to declare, that I will never declare it, but in a very clear case."

Paterson likewise concludes that the tax is not direct, as does Justice Iredell. Justice Wilson, as noted, recused himself, but he did allude to the issue of judicial review when he concluded that "I shall now, however, only add, that my sentiments, in favor of the constitutionality of the tax in question, have not been changed." By implication, if he could be in favor of constitutionality, he could also be against it under different circumstances.

This is, then, one of the precursors of *Marbury v. Madison.* Walter Murphy, James Fleming, and Sotirios Barber note the importance of *Hylton v. U.S.*, as well as *Hayburn's Case* (1792) and *Yale Todd's Case* (1794) (presented in *U.S. v. Ferreira*, 54 U.S. 40 [1851]) in raising issues of judicial review, with the last named case actually invalidating provisions of federal law.

For more information: Langran, Robert W. *The Supreme Court: A Concise History.* New York: Peter Lang Publishing, 2004.

—Steven A. Peterson

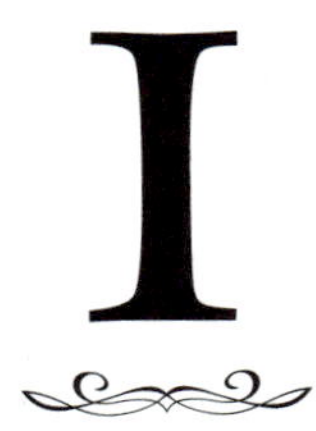

Illinois v. Caballes 543 U.S. 405 (2005)
In *Illinois v. Caballes,* the U.S. Supreme Court ruled that police may use drug dogs during routine traffic stops, even if they lack probable cause or reasonable suspicion that the vehicle contains illegal drugs. This decision gives the police tremendous discretion to search for drugs without any evidence that the person or vehicle being searched actually possesses drugs. The use of canines as a legitimate drug detection tool was established in *United States v. Place,* 462 U.S. 696 (1983). In *Place,* the Court ruled that a canine sniff was reasonable because a sniff reveals only illegal drugs, which are contraband and illegal to possess.

Caballes was stopped for speeding by an Illinois state trooper. After stopping Caballes, the trooper conducted a routine registration and criminal record check. While a warning ticket was being written, the record check came back indicating that Caballes had a prior arrest for marijuana distribution. The trooper sought consent from Caballes to search his vehicle, but Caballes refused. At this point, approximately 10 minutes into the traffic stop, a second trooper arrived with a drug dog, and he ran the dog around Caballes's vehicle. The canine alerted, and a subsequent search of the vehicle revealed a large quantity of marijuana. Caballes was arrested.

Prior to trial, Caballes filled a motion to suppress the evidence, arguing that the use of the drug dog without probable cause or reasonable suspicion of drug possession violated the FOURTH AMENDMENT. Caballes acknowledged that the amount of time it took to conduct a criminal record check and to write the warning ticket was reasonable. The state acknowledged that no reasonable suspicion that there were drugs in Caballes's vehicle existed prior to the canine alert. The suppression motion was denied, and Caballes was convicted. The state trial court held that the length of the traffic stop was not unduly increased by the canine sniff and that the canine was sufficiently reliable to create the probable cause needed by the officers to conduct a search of Caballes's vehicle. The Illinois Supreme Court reversed this decision, holding that the troopers lacked "reasonable suspicion" that Caballes was involved in criminal activity, and that reasonable suspicion was required before a canine could be used during a routine traffic stop.

The U.S. Supreme Court reversed the Illinois Supreme Court and upheld the use of drug dogs during routine traffic stops. First, the Court noted that when a traffic stop is both legitimate and conducted in a reasonable manner, then a canine sniff during the stop is not a search because a sniff of the exterior of a vehicle does not violate a person's legitimate expectation of PRIVACY. Second, the Court determined that since a person does not have a legitimate privacy interest in the possession of illegal drugs, a canine sniff, which only exposes illegal drugs, does not infringe upon a person's legitimate privacy interest. Thus, a canine sniff is not a search for purposes of the Fourth Amendment, and neither "probable cause" nor "reasonable suspicion" are needed to conduct a canine sniff of the exterior of a vehicle.

For more information: Hemmens, Craig, Jennifer Ashley, and Simon Billenge. "Who Let the Dogs Out?: Drug Dogs in Court." *Criminal Justice Studies* 20, no. 3 (2007): 177–196; Hemmens, Craig, John Worrall, and Alan Thompson. *Crimi-*

nal Justice Case Briefs: Significant Cases in Criminal Procedure. Los Angeles: Roxbury Publishing, 2004.

—Jennifer J. Ashley

Illinois v. Gates 462 U.S. 213 (1983)

In *Illinois v. Gates,* the Supreme Court established rules for when an anonymous tip could be used as the basis of a search warrant under the FOURTH AMENDMENT.

Warrants are generally required under the Fourth Amendment. To secure a warrant, law enforcement officials need to establish probable cause before a judge that they will find some illegal contraband such as drugs. However, what do police officers need to produce to establish probable cause? In many cases, informants provide that. But what if the tip they receive is anonymous? In *Aguilar v. Fenton,* 473 U.S. 402 (1985), the Supreme Court stated that it was permissible to use hearsay evidence to establish probable cause but one must show that the informant is credible and reliable.

In *Spinelli v. United States,* 393 U.S. 410 (1969), the Court first tried to clarify the standards that must be met to use an anonymous tip to establish probable cause. At issue was whether there was probable cause to search an individual based upon a tip that a person was involved in gambling, that he was traveling into and out of a particular apartment, that the apartment contained two telephones, and that this individual engaged in luxury, and when that information was verified by FBI observation of that person. The Court said that, here, there was not enough information of the underlying circumstances in the tip to determine how the conclusion could be reached. For a tip to be used it must meet *Aguilar* standards, and it must meet reliability and credibility as independent standards. The Court also stated that there be independent corroboration of the tip.

Gates revisits and revises the *Spinelli* standards. Here, at issue was whether there was probable cause to issue a search warrant of a residence and car based upon an anonymous letter detailing a drug purchase when the major facts of the letter were independently corroborated by a subsequent police investigation. The Supreme Court said yes. In supporting its decision, the Court said that there were two factors associated with using an anonymous tip for the purposes of establishing probable cause: the basis of knowledge and its veracity. Probable cause is established in a totality of circumstances test that a search will uncover wrongdoing instead of following a two-step process as suggested by *Spinelli.*

Gates thus appeared to make it easier to obtain a search warrant based on an anonymous tip. Even with the relaxed standards, though, independent corroboration of such a tip is generally required under the Fourth Amendment.

For more information: LaFave, Wayne R., Jerold H. Israel, and Nancy J. King. *Criminal Procedure.* St. Paul, Minn.: Thomson/West, 2004.

—Ernest Gomez and David Schultz

impeachment

The power to impeach federal officers is one of the greatest powers held by the U.S. Congress, but this power is rarely utilized. This power allows Congress to keep a check on both the executive and judicial branches. The HOUSE OF REPRESENTATIVES can bring up impeachment charges on a federal official, and afterwards the official is brought to trial by the SENATE. They can then choose to convict the official with a two-thirds vote of the Senate and remove him or her from office. Congress has the ability to impeach the president, VICE PRESIDENT, cabinet members, federal judges, and the chief justice and associate justices of the U.S. Supreme Court. Impeachment does not hold any criminal or civil penalties, simply removal from public office and possibly ineligibility for future attempts to run for office.

Impeachment was a major consideration during the CONSTITUTIONAL CONVENTION. The U.S. Constitution provides for the power of impeachment, but rather vaguely. It is unclear as to who qualifies as a civil officer and thus holds a federally impeachable office. We can see this in Article II, Section 4 of the U.S. Constitution, which states

Illustration by T. R. Davis of George T. Brown, sergeant-at-arms, serving a summons on President Johnson, in *Harper's Weekly,* March 28, 1868 *(Library of Congress)*

that "the President, Vice President and all civil Officers of the United States, shall be removed from Office on Impeachment for, and Conviction of, TREASON, Bribery, or other HIGH CRIMES AND MISDEMEANORS." The most frequent target of impeachment is federal judges who hold lifetime appointments.

The impeachment process has its origins in 14th-century England. During this period, the struggling English Parliament utilized the impeachment process to force the officers of the king to be held accountable. The king himself was not impeachable, but the ministers and judges were punishable for criminal activity and abuse of power by use of impeachment. In the early American colonies, the governments made use of this English process of impeachment. They had a system by which the lower legislative house would bring charges and the upper legislative body would issue judgment.

During the Constitutional Convention, the framers wished to keep provisions for impeachment. They did not want severe sanctions as in England such as fines, imprisonment, or even death. In the English system, the House of Commons had the ability to impeach practically anyone for crimes and misdemeanors. However, the framers wished to focus impeachment procedures on specific federal offices rather than on individuals. The idea was to protect the interest of the public rather than punish specific individuals.

The Constitution is clear about the process of impeachment. Article I lays out which chamber is in charge of the different processes involved in the impeachment process. Section 2 sets out that the House of Representatives "shall have the sole power of impeachment" and Section 3 states that the U.S. Senate has "the sole power to try all impeachments." It is also specified in Article II, Section 2 that the president does not have the ability to grant reprieves and pardons in cases of impeachment.

The impeachment process has not been utilized on many occasions. Because of this, there has not been a standard procedure for initiating impeachments. A few ways in which impeachments have been brought about are by a letter from the president, a resolution filed by a member of the House of Representatives to conduct an investigation, and sometimes the House Judiciary Committee issues a resolution.

When an impeachment resolution is passed in the House of Representatives, the House then selects who will serve as prosecutors during the trial in the Senate. The House of Representatives then provides the Senate with the articles of impeachment and notifies them that there is a need to hold a trial. The trial that takes place in front of the Senate is similar to that of a criminal trial where each side has the opportunity to present evidence and call witnesses, and the official that is being tried has the right to have an attorney. Generally, the president pro tempore of the

Senate or the vice president presides over the trial, and the chief justice is usually on hand to rule on evidence and answer questions. During a closed session at the end of the trial, the Senate deliberates the guilt or innocence of the accused person. The Senate votes on each article of impeachment, and if any article receives a two-thirds vote, then they rule to convict the official. Finally, the Senate votes whether or not to remove a guilty official from office and whether or not he or she is eligible to hold a federal office in the future.

Throughout American history, few individuals have been subject to impeachment. In 1804, Federalist Party Supreme Court Justice Samuel Chase was impeached by the Democratic-Republican House over disputes regarding his handling of trials. The Senate, with Vice-President Aaron Burr presiding, acquitted him in 1805. Among presidents, the Republican House impeached Andrew Johnson in 1868 in disputes over the handling of Reconstruction. The Senate acquitted him by one vote. In 1974, the House Judiciary Committee voted on several articles of impeachment against President RICHARD NIXON that included obstruction of justice arising out of Watergate and for engaging in secret bombings of Cambodia. Nixon resigned before the full House voted to impeach. Finally, in 1998, the House voted to impeach President William Clinton on four charges arising out of the special prosecutor's investigation into his affairs with Monica Lewinsky and Paula Jones. The Senate acquitted him on all charges.

For more information: Bacon, Donald C., Roger H. Davidson, and Morton Keller, eds. *The Encyclopedia of the United States Congress*. New York: Simon and Schuster, 1995; Nelson, Michael, ed. *Guide to the Presidency*. 2nd ed. Washington, D.C.: Congressional Quarterly, 1996.

—Jacqueline M. Loubet

imports, taxes on

Tariffs, or taxes on imports, played an integral role in the American push for independence from Great Britain. Accordingly, tariffs assumed a place of central importance in the Constitution. The authority to impose a tariff is allocated to Congress by Article 1, Section 8 of the U.S. Constitution as part of congressional power to lay and collect taxes. Import taxes must be uniform, imposed throughout the United States.

Throughout U.S. history, taxes on imports have been used to raise revenue, to protect American manufacturers from foreign competition, or to retaliate against other nations. The demand for revenue, however, has been the driving force behind tariff policy. The leaders of the new nation recognized that the government needed to create a revenue system to provide for operating expenses while paying down the debt left over from the American Revolution. However, any new level of taxation would compete with numerous state and local revenue streams. Congress realized that federal revenue needed to come from tariffs, since Americans imported a large number of manufactured goods along with raw materials, such as molasses. In 1789, the first tariff act passed under the Constitution after considerable debate. Many of the northern states, interested in developing their own manufacturing industries, demanded high protective tariffs, while the agriculture-based southern states saw low tariffs as being in their best interests. Throughout the 19th century, protection of the iron, cotton manufacturing, wool, hemp, and other domestic industries remained a recurrent theme in tariff bills.

The challenge to free trade posed by the tariff has long been controversial. Robert Walker, secretary of the treasury in the administration of President James K. Polk and a proponent of free trade, engaged in an inclusive reading of Article 1, Section 8. He interpreted the Constitution as requiring Congress to both impose and collect taxes. In reality, Walker's concern proved unwarranted as Congress never laid duties that it could not collect. Merchants, on selecting goods to import, had to pay the congressionally predetermined duty for the given product.

The Supreme Court has occasionally ruled on tariffs. In *POLLOCK V. FARMERS LOAN AND TRUST COMPANY*, 157 U.S. 429 (1895), the Court struck down an income tax provision included in the Wilson-Gorman Tariff Act of 1894 on the grounds that it was a direct tax under the U.S. Constitution. Passage of the SIXTEENTH AMENDMENT in 1913 made the Court decision moot. As other forms of government financing gained popularity, the tariff dimmed in importance. Protectionist sentiment in Congress took precedence to the revenue needs of the government. The Hawley-Smoot Tariff Act of 1930 constituted the peak of U.S. duties. Following the Great Depression, the international community generally acknowledged that tariffs damaged world trade and contributed to slowed economic growth.

For more information: Elliott, Orrin. *The Tariff Controversy in the U.S., 1789-1833.* Palo Alto, Calif.: Stanford University, 1892; Sorenson, Leonard R. *Madison on the "General Welfare" of America: His Consistent Constitutional Vision.* Lanham, Md.: Rowman & Littlefield, 1995.

—Caryn E. Neumann

impoundment

Impoundment refers to the practice of a chief executive to not spend money appropriated by the legislature. Presidents have exercised the impoundment power since the early republic. The impoundment of funds has often been used to respond to changing events, such as entering a war, and to prevent waste by making federal projects more efficient. The Constitution does not expressly allow for the exercise of the power of impoundment, and its authority is derived from legislation. The president does have the power of the VETO, which if used successfully, reduces the need for impoundment.

The question of impoundment raises the larger issue of who has the "power of the purse" to determine budgetary priorities and direct federal funds. Presidents began expanding their control over economic and budgetary matters with the administration of Franklin D. Roosevelt. Until the time that President RICHARD NIXON came into office, impoundments were infrequent and temporary, usually involving small amounts of money, and Congress often supported their use. However, Nixon sought to impound funds at an unprecedented level, claiming that it was an inherent presidential power to refuse to spend appropriated monies for projects he did not support and to control deficit spending by the Democratic-dominated Congress. The City of New York filed a lawsuit challenging Nixon's impoundment of funds, and the Supreme Court ruled that presidents had no constitutional authority to withhold funds allotted by law (*Train v. City of New York*, 420 U.S. 35 [1975]).

Congress also challenged Nixon, claiming he used impoundment as selective law enforcement. To recapture its control of federal funds and stop the perceived presidential encroachment onto its budgetary turf, Congress passed the Congressional Budget and Impoundment Control Act of 1974. A primary purpose of this act was to constrain the use of impoundments by codifying the chief executive's impoundment authority. Two new procedures were established. Under the act, a president may propose to rescind, or cancel, appropriations, although Congress must agree by a majority vote within forty-five days for the rescission to take effect. A president may also recommend to defer spending appropriated funds within a one-year time frame. The act created a Congressional Budget Office and permanent committees in both chambers to provide support to members of Congress in the form of cost estimates and a budget timetable for tracking spending. These reforms added a measure of coherence to the budgetary process, since before this there was no real coordination between the congressional committees that raised revenues and those that spent the monies.

There is general agreement that the passage of the 1974 act has led to a reassertion of the role of Congress in the budgetary process, although room for improvement remains as deadlines for enacting budget resolutions are routinely missed and partisanship on budget matters has increased. Nevertheless, Congress still tends to respond to priorities set by chief executives.

For more information: Cronin, Thomas E., and Michael A. Genovese. *The Paradoxes of the American Presidency.* 2nd ed. New York: Oxford University Press, 2004; Fisher, Louis. *Constitutional*

Conflicts between Congress and the President. 4th ed. Lawrence: University Press of Kansas, 1997.

—Rebecca Wiggins

incorporation

Incorporation refers to the process where the Supreme Court has utilized the Constitution's FOURTEENTH AMENDMENT to require state governments to apply to their citizens the CIVIL LIBERTIES specified in the BILL OF RIGHTS. Even though most of the Bill of Rights has now been incorporated to apply to states, not all of the provisions are binding on them. The process of incorporation has been a gradual one, taking place during most of the 20th century, with the bulk of that occurring after World War II.

Because the national government conceived by the CONSTITUTIONAL CONVENTION would possess only the delegated and enumerated powers, the delegates, especially those who were members of the Federalist Party, such as ALEXANDER HAMILTON, deemed a bill of rights unnecessary. During the battle over RATIFICATION OF THE CONSTITUTION, the omission of a bill of rights attracted criticism from the Anti-Federalists. In September 1789, JAMES MADISON, in the first Congress, proposed 12 amendments, 10 of which, once ratified in December 1791, became the Bill of Rights. Insofar as the Constitution's purpose was to establish the national government, it followed that the amendments were designed to restrict national government actions that would deprive citizens of civil liberties. Accordingly, the first words of the FIRST AMENDMENT are "Congress shall make no law." In proposing the amendments, Congress did not intend to place restrictions on state governments' actions, and, in ratifying them, the state legislatures did not anticipate that such restrictions would be imposed on them. The U.S. Supreme Court affirmed the inapplicability of the Bill of Rights at the state level in its 1833 opinion in the case of *BARRON V. MAYOR AND CITY COUNCIL OF BALTIMORE*, 32 U.S. (7 Pet.) 243 (1833). This circumstance left citizens unprotected, at least as far as the Constitution and the national government were concerned, when state governments mistreated them by refusing to recognize their entitlement to civil liberties.

In the aftermath of the Civil War, Congress and the state legislatures placed three amendments into the Constitution to protect African Americans. The THIRTEENTH AMENDMENT reaffirmed the prohibition against slavery, the Fourteenth Amendment established the right of blacks to enjoy the status of national and state citizenship, and the FIFTEENTH AMENDMENT prohibited denial of the RIGHT TO VOTE based on race. Section 1 of the Fourteenth Amendment states, "All persons born or naturalized in the United States, and subject to the jurisdiction thereof, are citizens of the United States and of the state wherein they reside. No state shall make or enforce any law which shall abridge the privileges or immunities of citizens of the United States; nor shall any state deprive any person of life, liberty, or property, without DUE PROCESS of law; nor deny to any person within its jurisdiction the EQUAL PROTECTION of the laws." This section would take on significance beyond the intention to ensure that African Americans would be recognized as citizens.

Ratification of the Fourteenth Amendment prompted attorneys for criminal defendants and other litigants to appeal adverse decisions of state supreme courts to the U.S. Supreme Court based on the claim that the amendment had established state-level protections of civil liberties. At first, such attorneys invoked the amendment's PRIVILEGES AND IMMUNITIES clause. The U.S. Supreme Court rebuffed such claims, rejecting the suggestion that "privileges and immunities" ought to be interpreted as a reference to specific liberties (*Slaughterhouse Cases,* 83 U.S. [16 Wall.] 36, 74–80 [1873]). Attorneys then directed the Court's attention to the provision of the amendment that prohibited any state government from "depriv[ing] any person of life, liberty, or property, without due process of law." Again, the Court was initially skeptical. For example, in its opinion in the case of *Hurtado v. California,* 110 U.S. 516, 534–535 (1884), the Court offered an argument based on "nonsuperfluousness." In *Hurtado,* when the Court was urged to interpret "due process" as encompassing the right to indictment by a grand jury prior to criminal prosecution, the court observed that in the Fifth Amendment "due process" and the right to "indictment by a grand jury" are delineated separately; it surmised, then, that the right to "indictment by a grand jury" would be a component of "due process" only if the first Congress had indulged in superfluous verbiage. The Court concluded that Congress would not have done so; therefore, "due process" and the right to "indictment by a grand jury" must be separate concepts and one does not imply the other.

While state governments pressed the Supreme Court to interpret "due process" as only a *procedural* protection that a fair hearing or trial would fully satisfy, attorneys for criminal defendants and other parties to litigation called on the Supreme Court to interpret "due process" as being *substantive,* encompassing protection of civil liberties. The latter argument succeeded in 1897 in the case of *Chicago, Burlington & Quincy Railroad Co. v. Chicago*, 166 U.S. 226, 241 (1897), when the Supreme Court interpreted the Fourteenth Amendment's protection against deprivation of life, liberty, and property without due process not only to guarantee a hearing before property is taken by EMINENT DOMAIN but also to require that JUST COMPENSATION be paid.

In its opinion in the case of *GITLOW V. NEW YORK,* 268 U.S. 652, 665-666 (1925), the U.S. Supreme Court linked the First Amendment's protection of freedom of speech and the press to the Fourteenth Amendment's due process clause. In regarding the Fourteenth Amendment's offer of "liberty" to incorporate, by implicit reference, what the Court called "fundamental personal rights and 'liberties'" identified in the First Amendment, the Court thus decreed that citizens' freedom of speech and the press is protected against attempts by state governments to deny it. Since its *Gitlow* decision, the Court has similarly interpreted the Fourteenth Amendment to incorporate by reference numerous other civil liberties listed in the Bill of Rights to make them applicable to the state governments, as shown in the following list.

FIRST AMENDMENT

- religion, establishment: *EVERSON V. BOARD OF EDUCATION of the Township of Ewing*, 330 U.S. 1 (1947); free exercise, *Cantwell v. Connecticut*, 310 U.S. 296 (1940)
- freedom of speech and the press: *Gitlow v. New York*, 268 U.S. 652 (1925); press, specifically: *NEAR V. MINNESOTA*, 283 U.S. 697 (1931)
- assembly: *DeJonge v. Oregon*, 299 U.S. 353 (1937)

FOURTH AMENDMENT

- search and seizure: *WOLF V. COLORADO*, 338 U.S. 25 (1949), EXCLUSIONARY RULE applied in *Mapp v. Ohio*, 367 U.S. 643 (1961)
- issuance of warrant, *Ker v. California*, 374 U.S. 23 (1963)

FIFTH AMENDMENT

- DOUBLE JEOPARDY: *Benton v. Maryland*, 395 U.S. 784 (1969)
- self-incrimination: *Malloy v. Hogan*, 378 U.S. 1 (1964)
- private property (decided without use of the incorporation doctrine): *Chicago, Burlington & Quincy Railroad Co. v. Chicago*, 166 U.S. 226 (1897)

SIXTH AMENDMENT

- speedy trial: *Klopfer v. North Carolina*, 386 U.S. 213 (1967)
- public trial (decided using the due process clause of the Fourteenth Amendment without use of the incorporation doctrine): *In re Oliver*, 333 U.S. 257 (1948)
- trial by jury: *DUNCAN V. LOUISIANA*, 391 U.S. 145 (1968)
- impartial jury: *Parker v. Gladden*, 385 U.S. 363 (1966)
- confront witnesses: *Pointer v. Texas*, 380 U.S. 400 (1965)
- compulsory process for witness testimony (subpoena): *Washington v. Texas*, 388 U.S. 14 (1967)

- counsel, in capital cases: *Powell v. Alabama,* 287 U.S. 45 (1932); in felony cases: *GIDEON V. WAINWRIGHT,* 372 U.S. 335 (1963); in any case in which imprisonment may be a penalty, *Argersinger v. Hamlin,* 407 U.S. 25 (1972)

EIGHTH AMENDMENT

- excessive fines: *Cooper Industries, Inc., v. Leatherman Tool Group, Inc.,* 532 U.S. 424 (2001)
- CRUEL AND UNUSUAL PUNISHMENT: *Robinson v. California,* 370 U.S. 660 (1962)

NINTH AMENDMENT

- "other [rights] retained by the people": *GRISWOLD V. CONNECTICUT,* 381 U.S. 479 (1965), in which the court found the right to PRIVACY to be one such "other" right.

So far, the Court has not ruled that either the Second Amendment (RIGHT TO BEAR ARMS), the THIRD AMENDMENT (quartering of troops), or the SEVENTH AMENDMENT (RIGHT TO TRIAL BY JURY) are incorporated to apply to the states through the Fourteenth Amendment.

For more information: Cortner, Richard C. *The Supreme Court and the Second Bill of Rights: The Fourteenth Amendment and the Nationalization of Civil Liberties.* Madison: University of Wisconsin Press, 1981; Curtis, Michael Kent. *No State Shall Abridge: The Fourteenth Amendment and the Bill of Rights.* Durham, N.C.: Duke University Press, 1986.

—Barry D. Friedman

injunction

An injunction is a remedy awarded by a judge to order a party to stop doing a particular act or activity. It may also order specific action by a party, although this was traditionally known as a Writ of Specific Performance. The significance of injunctions for America today is their widespread usage, from domestic violence injunctions to prevent harassment to prior restraint injunctions against a newspaper or Internet Web site in publishing a story. The wide use of injunctions today is evidence that the traditional remedy available at law—monetary damages—was not sufficiently effective in protecting people, resolving disputes, or solving problems.

Injunctions were an early invention first used by courts of equity, such as the English courts of chancery, to supplement the courts of law, such as the courts of common pleas. Medieval English lawyers created the injunction and many other forms of equitable writs to enjoin parties from violating principles of justice and good conscience, also known as maxims of equity. Until recent decades, lawyers were trained in these hundreds of maxims of equity, which were written in English and based on successful experiences in meting out justice, in administering property and estates, and in the teachings of great people, politicians, philosophers, and figures in history. The purpose of injunctions was not just focused on some past act, but to forbid parties from continuing to commit acts that were unjust, inequitable, injurious to the plaintiff, and so forth in ways that were not adequately protected by the courts of law. Thus, the first maxim of equity: "When the law fails, equity prevails."

ARTICLE III OF THE U.S. CONSTITUTION announced the merger of law with equity in all federal courts. Courts of law were formerly constrained to rather ineffective remedies such as the Writ of Mandamus to obtain a document. With the Article III merger, as well as widespread merger of law and equity in the states, injunctions today are used in the law to obtain broad, sweeping changes of behavior and effect large-scale organizational changes in behavior to conform with the requirements of law.

The practice of injunctions in federal courts has come to focus on prejudgment use, final injunctions, and sanctions for violating injunctions. The preliminary injunction and TEMPORARY RESTRAINING ORDER (TRO) are the most numerous injunctions, designed to preserve the status quo and prevent further harm until further judicial proceedings resolve the dispute. They may be called preliminary injunctions or interlocutory injunctions because they are granted at some early point in a lawsuit and are temporary until a later judicial resolution of the dispute. By contrast, the final injunction is granted after a judicial process has determined the rights of the parties to a dispute and orders permanent changes in activities. Federal judges today often label these as the "final order" in a case. The conventional sanction for violating an injunction is the contempt citation, designed by the judge to include fines, jailtime, or whatever is necessary to bring parties into compliance. To implement injunctions, judges have used special masters, monitors, ombudsmen, receivers, human rights committees, and expert panels who inspect, report, recommend action, and even close down or take over public organizations.

The Supreme Court in *BROWN V. BOARD OF EDUCATION*, 347 U.S. 483 (1954), allowed federal courts to issue injunctions to remedy and end the segregation of public schools. With increasing judicial involvement in the administration of public organizations, the traditional remedies at law were regarded as inappropriate. Monetary damages to individual plaintiffs had little effect on improving constitutional conditions. Judges have increasingly turned instead to the injunction at a structural, institution-wide level to create a more constitutional society. A wide range of remedies is provided for by 42 U.S.C. 1983; once a federal CIVIL RIGHTS violation is established, the violator is liable "in an action at law, suit in equity, or other proper proceeding for redress." Liability at law may result in nominal, compensatory, or punitive monetary damages, while liability in equity focuses on injunctive relief. Following the Supreme Court's lead in *SWANN V. CHARLOTTE-MECKLENBURG BOARD OF EDUCATION*, 402 U.S. 1 (1971), federal district courts have constructed broad and flexible injunctions to redress institution-wide problems in schools, prisons, public housing, and other large-scale public organizations. *MISSOURI V. JENKINS*, 495 U.S. 33 (1990) further expanded equitable power to uphold a "power of the purse" for federal judges to issue injunctions that order local and state governments to levy their own tax increases to pay for court-ordered constitutional changes.

For more information: Chilton, Bradley. *Prisons Under the Gavel: The Federal Court Takeover of Georgia Prisons.* Columbus: Ohio State University Press, 1991; Fiss, Owen. *The Civil Rights Injunction.* Bloomington: Indiana University Press, 1978.

—Bradley Chilton

In re Debs 158 U.S. 564 (1895)

The Supreme Court decided in *In re Debs* that the courts could issue INJUNCTIONs to halt a strike or work stoppage.

The issues arising in *Debs* stem from a depression that left much of the country out of work, and many large companies were cutting wages at an alarming rate. Pullman Palace Car Company in Chicago, Illinois, was an organization that manufactured and loaded Pullman cars, or sleeper cars, for the railroad. On May 11, 1894, workers walked off the job in a massive strike to protest the loss of benefits and wages in the company. The workers had recently organized into the American Railway Union (ARU), led by Eugene V. Debs.

An aggravating factor in this strike was that the Pullman Company had a company town adjacent to the factory, and when the workers went on strike, they essentially forfeited their homes as well as their pay. Many people were out of work and literally homeless in the streets during this struggle, and the strike quickly gained national attention. In June, the ARU boycotted all railroads that carried Pullman cars. Moreover, members of the union began destroying cars and rails, and damaged signals on the rail lines. Workers who remained on the job refused to handle trains with Pullman cars. The strike turned to riot in Chicago.

Meanwhile the railroads requested an injunction from the court preventing any interference with railroad business and arguing that the Pullman cars were essential in INTERSTATE COMMERCE and transporting U.S. mail. At this point, Attorney General Richard Olney created a unit of 5,000 special deputies to dampen the violence in

Chicago and built a case of criminal conspiracy against the unions. The violence grew worse in Chicago, and President Grover Cleveland sent in armed troops to end the rioting.

The federal circuit court granted an injunction that prohibited the union leaders and followers from hindering the activities of the railroad in any way. Eugene V. Debs and many others were first arrested on the criminal conspiracy charge, but one week later they were arrested on violation of the injunction. Debs was sentenced to a term of six months in prison, but he asked for a writ of HABEAS CORPUS because he was denied his right to a trial by jury when he was tried in a court of equity.

Justice David Brewer wrote for a unanimous Supreme Court and struck down the writ of habeas corpus. Brewer argued that the country had the right to full sovereignty within its enumerated powers and that it had every right to prevent any obstruction of the growth of its commerce. Brewer wrote, "We hold it to be an incontrovertible principle, that the government of the United States may, by means of physical force, exercised through its official agents, execute on every foot of American soil the powers and functions that belong to it. This necessarily involves the power to command obedience to its laws, and hence the power to keep the peace to that extent." Brewer asserted that the U.S. mail and commerce are vested in the government. As such, Congress retains the power over these activities and may protect them as is seen to be fit. Brewer praised the use of lawful action by the railroads over the violent action of the strikers and rejected Debs's contention of his RIGHT TO TRIAL BY JURY. Brewer determined that in the case of public nuisance, such as the Debs case, a court of equity may be used to hear grievances brought by the Attorney General. Therefore, Debs was lawfully imprisoned without a jury on matters of contempt of court, as the injunction charged him with for violating its terms and stipulations.

The importance of this case lies in the introduction of court-supported injunctions against labor strikers and their unions. Up until the New Deal era, corporations would use injunctions against unions to break up strikes and return to normal production. This proved to be a strong tool for big corporations and created a weakness in the labor movement.

For more information: Salvatore, Nick. *Eugene V. Debs: Citizen and Socialist.* Champaign: University of Illinois Press, 2007; Schwartz, Bernard. *A History of the Supreme Court.* New York: Oxford University Press, 1993.

—Katherine J. Davis and Tobias T. Gibson

In re Gault 387 U.S. 1 (1967)

The United States Supreme Court, in *In re Gault,* 387 U.S. 1 (1967), held that juveniles were entitled to specific DUE PROCESS rights under the FOURTEENTH AMENDMENT during delinquency proceedings when the possibility of secure confinement exists. Specifically, juveniles had the Fifth Amendment privilege against self-incrimination and the SIXTH AMENDMENT rights of the notice of charges against them, the presence of an attorney, and the ability to confront and cross-examine witnesses.

On June 8, 1964, 15-year-old Gerald Gault was taken into custody for allegedly placing obscene telephone calls to his neighbor, Mrs. Cook. Mrs. Cook notified the police, and Gerald was taken into custody while his parents were at work. Gerald was adjudicated delinquent and sentenced to the state training school until the age of 21. However, Gerald was never formally notified of the charges against him, the complainant Mrs. Cook never appeared in court to testify, Gerald was not represented by an attorney, and no formal transcript of the proceedings was made. Furthermore, the penalty specified for adults who violated the same law was limited to either a $50 fine or no more than two months imprisonment.

Prior to this case and the case of *Kent v. United States* (1966), in which certain due process rights were awarded to juveniles during a transfer hearing, the juvenile justice system was based upon the philosophy of *parens patriae.* This meant that the state was to act in the best interest of the child, and the child was to be treated and rehabilitated in a clinical manner as opposed to a punitive manner.

Instead, as the court observed in the *Kent* case, "The child often receives the worst of both worlds: lack of procedural fairness and substandard treatment" (Whitehead and Lab, 2004: 241).

In *Gault,* the Supreme Court ruled that the due process requirements of the Fourteenth Amendment required that certain rights were to be afforded juveniles during an adjudication hearing in which secure confinement was a possible outcome. First, the Court stated that "sufficient notice must be given in advance of scheduled court proceedings, so that reasonable opportunity to prepare can be afforded" (387 U.S. 1 at 33).

Second, the Court stated that the juvenile and his/her parents must be notified of their right to obtain counsel, or if they cannot afford counsel, their right to appointed counsel to represent the juvenile. The Court reasoned that the juvenile "needs the assistance of counsel to cope with problems of law, to make skilled inquiry into the facts, to insist upon regularity of the proceedings, and to ascertain whether he has a defense and to prepare to submit it."

Third, the Court stated that the privilege against self-incrimination was to be applied to juvenile proceedings to ensure that confessions are voluntary, meaning they are not coerced or suggested or the product of fright or despair. Finally, the Court stated that absent a valid and voluntary confession, a determination of delinquency cannot be made in the absence of sworn testimony and the opportunity to confront and cross-examine witnesses.

For more information: *In Re Gault,* 387 U.S. 1 (1967); *Kent v. United States,* 383 U.S. 541 (1966); Whitehead, J., and S. Lab. *Juvenile Justice: An Introduction.* Cincinnati, Ohio: Anderson Publishing Co., 2004.

—Amanda Freeman

In re Neagle 135 U.S. 1, 10 S. Ct. 658, 34 L. Ed. 55 (1890)

In this case, the Court held that "The Executive Power" included the power to assign a federal marshal to serve as the bodyguard to a Supreme Court justice and insulated the marshal from murder charges stemming from his discharge of that duty. *In re Neagle* expanded the scope of the implied powers of the executive branch through an expansive reading of the president's duty to "take Care that the Laws be faithfully executed" (Article II, Section 3), confirming the existence of inherent executive prerogative power in domestic affairs.

After David S. Terry, a disgruntled litigant, repeatedly and publicly threatened Justice Stephen J. Field, the attorney general of the United States directed the U.S. marshal for the Northern District of California to appoint David Neagle deputy marshal for the district, specifically to protect Field. While Field was riding circuit in California, Terry boarded the train and assaulted him. Neagle identified himself as "an officer" and, when Terry appeared to reach for a weapon, shot and killed him (135 U.S. 1, 53 [1890]). Subsequently charged with murder by California, Neagle successfully sued for a writ of HABEAS CORPUS in the federal circuit court, which discharged him from California's custody. The sheriff appealed to the Supreme Court.

The opinion of the Court, delivered by Justice Samuel Miller, held that Neagle, as an officer of the United States, could not be tried by California, and thus was properly discharged. The crux of the difficulty, however, was that according to federal statute, one petitioning for a writ of habeas corpus was required to show that he was held in custody for actions taken pursuant to "a law of the United States" (135 U.S. 1, 58 [1890]). Although no statute authorized Neagle to serve as Field's bodyguard, the Court held that Field was entitled to the protection necessary for him to discharge his official duties. As Congress had not done so, the Court held that the executive branch properly could authorize such protection due to the president's obligation to "take Care that the Laws be faithfully executed" (Article II, Section 3). This duty is not limited only to laws but extends to "the rights, duties, and obligations growing out of the Constitution itself, our international relations, and all the protection implied by the nature of the government under the Constitution" (135

U.S. 1, 64 [1890]). The Court held finally that Neagle's actions were in fact justified by a positive law, under which federal marshals had in every state the same powers to execute federal laws as did state sheriffs in executing state laws: as a California sheriff could keep the peace and prevent a murder, so could Neagle.

In dissent, Justice Lucius Lamar (and Justice Melville W. Fuller) denied the executive branch possessed implied powers in domestic matters and contended that if Neagle sought to be discharged from custody for actions taken pursuant to a law, there had to be a law. Absent an express statute authorizing Neagle's actions, the federal government could not intervene in California's prosecution.

For more information: Roche, John P. "Executive Power and Domestic Emergency: The Quest for Prerogative." *The Western Political Quarterly* 5, no. 4 (1952): 592–618; Rossiter, Clinton Lawrence, and Richard P. Longaker. *The Supreme Court and the Commander in Chief.* New York: Cornell University Press, 1976; Votaw, Dow. "Judicial Vendetta: California Style." *The Western Political Quarterly* 12, no. 4 (1959): 948–961.

—Lorna M. Dawson

intelligent design

Believers in intelligent design (ID) assert that biological life is too complex to have entirely arisen naturally through evolutionary principles, and so the only plausible alternative explanation is that life was designed by some powerfully intelligent supreme being—in other words, god. In recent years, a few states and many city and county school boards have attempted to have ID taught in public schools alongside evolution, which is the scientific theory that life has evolved by a natural process of small accumulated changes and adaptations to the environment over hundreds of millions of years. The teaching of ID in school raises ESTABLISHMENT CLAUSE issues under the FIRST AMENDMENT.

The idea of ID evolved from the concept of creationism, a religious belief based on a literal reading of the creation account from the Christian Bible, which states that the Earth, including life, was created in six days roughly several thousand years ago. Creationists sought to require creationism be taught alongside evolution in public schools, but the U.S. Supreme Court, in *Epperson v. Arkansas,* 393 U.S. 97 (1968), ruled this to be a violation of the establishment clause in the First Amendment to the U.S. Constitution, which prohibits government from imposing a religious belief or practice on individuals. Because of this decision, and because of the evidence for an old Earth, many creationists adapted by arguing that although the Earth is old, life is too complex for naturally-occurring change to fully account for all of life's evolution. Therefore, some extremely powerful intelligence must have designed and created life and has been guiding evolution throughout Earth's history. In late 2005, a federal court made national headlines when it ruled that the town of Dover, Pennsylvania, could not teach ID in public school biology classes. The court declared that ID was "a religious view, a mere relabeling of creationism" and thus remained a constitutional violation of the First Amendment's establishment clause because it would impose a particular religious belief on all students.

Besides the constitutional issue, there are many problematic issues in teaching ID as an alternative to evolution. First, there is nothing about evolutionary theory or belief in god that necessarily contradict one another. A powerful intelligence could have designed a universe that evolves completely through a process of natural selection. Second, because ID is a religious belief that lacks any way to be tested through repeatable observation, it does not meet the definition of science, so most scientists argue that it is not appropriate to teach in science classes. Third, a current lack of explanation for some of life's complexity does not necessarily mean an intelligent designer was involved, as it might simply be that evolutionary theory has not yet discovered the natural mechanisms involved. Indeed, as evolutionary science progresses, there are increasingly fewer aspects of life that it is unable to explain. Fourth, even if complexity indicates the work of an intelligent designer, it does not necessarily indicate a supreme being, as life on Earth could have been created by other powerful and intelligent beings, such as super technologically advanced space aliens. Fifth, ID contains an internal problem, because according to ID's principle that complexity always indicates a designer, then because god is complex, god must have been designed, which designer must have had a designer, and so on in an infinite regress.

Finally, ID proponents often argue that schools should teach the controversy about evolution and ID and that a failure to do so breeds ignorance by preventing students from being exposed to alternative viewpoints, especially about evolution, because it is not a fact but only a theory. Scientists reply by asserting that the vast majority of scientists believe the evidence overwhelmingly supports evolution as much as any other scientific theory like gravity; and thus there is no actual scientific controversy, only a religious and political controversy. Scientists also argue that if political or religious dissenters are able to require their own non-scientific theories be taught as alternatives, then public school students would have to learn alchemy in chemistry class, astrology in astronomy class, and voodoo in physics class, as well as beliefs that the Earth is flat or that the sun revolves around the Earth. Thus, scientists assert that teaching students "facts" that are not supported by the evidence breeds ignorance. Nevertheless, ID supporters vow to continue to push for political and legal changes that will allow or require ID to be taught in public schools alongside the scientific theory of evolution.

For more information: Brockman, John, ed. *Intelligent Thought: Science versus the Intelligent Design.* New York: Vintage Press, 2006; Shermer, Michael. *Why Darwin Matters: The Case Against Intelligent Design.* New York: Times Books, 2006; Young, Matt, and Taner Edis, eds. *Why Intelligent Design Fails: A Scientific Critique of the New Creationism.* Rutgers, N.J.: Rutgers University Press, 2004.

—Rick A. Swanson

intentional discrimination

Intentional discrimination has been held by the U.S. Supreme Court to violate the EQUAL PROTECTION clause of the FOURTEENTH AMENDMENT to the Constitution. Intentional discrimination, also known as disparate treatment, and neutral conduct are the two major categories of discriminatory behavior. Both forms of discrimination can have an adverse impact on protected groups.

Typically, intentional discrimination is proved circumstantially, through evidence of pretext. A plaintiff persuades the court that an explanation for discriminatory conduct is not believable and is only offered as a pretext to cover discrimination. The plaintiff argues that it is reasonable to infer that the true explanation is intentional discrimination. Pretext can be proved if a defendant provides false information, by evidence of bias, by statistical evidence, and, most commonly, by evidence that similarly situated individuals of a different class were treated differently than the complainant. "Similarly situated" people are those individuals who would be treated in the same manner because of their similar qualifications or situations. In a 1993 decision, *St. Mary's Honor Center v. Hicks,* U.S. 113 S. Ct. 2742, the U.S. Supreme Court held that even if a person claiming discrimination proves that the employer's explanation is a lie, the plaintiff might not win. To establish intentional discrimination, the court must be persuaded that an explanation is a lie constructed specifically to cover discrimination.

Various cases, including *REGENTS OF THE UNIVERSITY OF CALIFORNIA V. BAKKE* in 1979, that have come before the U.S. Supreme Court have hinged on the matter of intentional discrimination with respect to CIVIL RIGHTS.

Title VII of the CIVIL RIGHTS ACT, as the Court has ruled, prohibits only intentional discrimination on the basis of race, color, religion, sex, or national origin. Federal agencies are empowered to enact regulations necessary to enforce the law, and these regulations may have disproportionately adverse effects on particular racial groups, notably whites. In a U.S. Supreme Court decision in the 1970s involving Detroit, the Court made it clear that federal courts could not integrate predominantly black city schools with predominantly white ones unless there was intent to segregate on account of race.

As Justice Ruth Bader Ginsburg declared during her nomination hearing, it is permissible under the Constitution to discriminate or to classify provided there is a rational basis for it. However, courts have ruled that some practices that are ostensibly rational may be an attempt at intentional discrimination. This form of discrimination is known as disparate or adverse impact. Minimum height requirements for jobs may disproportionately screen out women and people of various national origins, such as Asians and Hispanics. Educational requirements, such as requiring employees to possess high school diplomas, have been found by some courts to have an adverse impact on certain protected groups. Tests that measure physical agility can have an adverse impact on women. Requirements that employees be clean shaven have been found to have an adverse effect on African-American men, who are disproportionately affected by a medical condition that is aggravated by shaving. Lastly, cognitive ability tests can have adverse impacts on protected groups. When a charge of intentional discrimination based on race, sex, religion, color, or national origin is made, the practice is typically assessed with statistics. Numbers will be used to compare the rate at which protected group members are excluded by the employer's practice as compared to the rate at which non-group members are excluded. A selection rate for any race, sex, or ethnic group which is less than 80 percent of the rate for the group with the highest rate of selection will generally be regarded as evidence of adverse impact. In a court case, it is the person challenging the practice who must prove that it is intentional discrimination.

If adverse impact is proven, a practice is not automatically banned. A business necessity may permit EMPLOYMENT DISCRIMINATION. A court upheld a fire department's "no beards" rule based on the department's showing that firefighters must be clean shaven in order to wear the respirators needed to breathe in smoke-filled environments. Another court rejected a "no beards" rule that was based on the employer's belief that customers preferred to deal with clean shaven men. An employer must accommodate the religious practices of employees unless doing so causes an undue hardship. Reasonable accommodation can include flexible scheduling and lateral transfer or change of assignment.

For more information: U.S. Equal Employment Opportunity Commission. *Theories of Discrimination: Intentional and Unintentional Employment Discrimination.* Washington, D.C.: U.S. Equal Employment Opportunity Commission, Technical Assistance Program, 1995.

—Caryn E. Neumann

intent of the framers (originalism)

The power of the courts to review laws with a view to deciding on their constitutionality is today understood to be an essential component of the American constitutional system. The legitimacy of JUDICIAL REVIEW is thus no longer even seriously questioned. But how a judge is to interpret the Constitution, and the nature and extent of judicial power to strike down the law as unconstitutional—these are questions that are perpetually debated. Originalism—the broad concept that one must look to the original understanding, the original meaning, or the original intentions of the framers of the Constitution—is one of the important schools of thought in this debate.

The originalist argument, simply put, is this: if the courts, which are not elected, are to have the power to strike down laws passed by a democratically elected government, that power cannot rest on simply the political opinions of judges, or on what judges personally believe to be higher principles of justice or more progressive and enlightened views of law. That power must instead derive from some more objective and authoritative source—what the framers of the Constitution intended when they wrote and agreed on the Constitution. Judges must decide based upon what the Constitution actually means and not what they think it ought to mean. What was originally intended when the law of the Constitution was established?

Answering this question should be the guiding source of any investigation into how a case should be decided.

Within the school of jurisprudence known as originalism, there are different understandings of what originalism means. One school argues that judges must look to the written text of the Constitution and to what was the original public meaning of that text at the time it was framed. Another school of thought argues that we must look to how those who ratified the Constitution understood it. Finally, there are those who contend we must look primarily to the intentions of the framers as embodied not only in the text of the Constitution, but also as elucidated in the debates and writings of the framers at the time of ratification. Most famous among these writings are *THE FEDERALIST PAPERS* and the various debates between the Federalists and Anti-Federalists.

It is important to note that this latter school of thought takes the interpreter beyond the text of the Constitution and to a broader understanding of the principles and ideas that provide the foundation of the Constitution. Understanding the framers' original intent thus looks to documents like the DECLARATION OF INDEPENDENCE and the broader classical liberalism of the Enlightenment that is embodied in the Constitution.

The debate over whether original intent can and should guide judicial interpretation has gone on since 1787 but has become especially prominent in reaction to the progressive, activist jurisprudence of the Supreme Court in the 1960s and '70s. Critics argued that the Court had gone too far in striking down laws as unconstitutional. An ethic of judicial self-restraint no longer seemed operative, and the Supreme Court seemed to its critics to be usurping the powers of the elected legislatures by means of a sort of judicial subjectivism and thus looking to find ways to rationalize results that a majority on the Court held desirable. The interpretation of the law of the Constitution, it was argued, had strayed so far from what the Constitution actually said that the Supreme Court was now simply putting forward its own view of what the Constitution should mean rather than what its framers had originally intended it to mean.

As a general rule, conservatives have argued in favor of the doctrine of original intent jurisprudence, and liberals or progressives have argued against it. Conservatives would like the courts to be more restrained in using their powers to strike down laws as unconstitutional, and they believe that by interpreting the Constitution in the light of the original intent of the framers judges would necessarily be more restrained in their use of judicial power. But it is not clear that there is in fact any necessary connection between the idea of original intent and the practice of judicial restraint. At times the Supreme Court has been activist in striking down laws as unconstitutional while persuasively justifying their decisions on the basis of the original intent of the framers. Chief Justice JOHN MARSHALL did exactly this, first establishing the power of judicial review in the landmark case of *MCCULLOCH V. MARYLAND.*

For more information: Jaffa, Harry V. *Original Intent and the Framers of the Constitution: A Disputed Question.* Washington, D.C.: Regnery Gateway, 1994; O'Neill, Johnathan. *Originalism in American Law and Politics: A Constitutional History.* Baltimore, Md.: Johns Hopkins University Press, 2005; Rakove, Jack N. *Original Meanings: Politics and Ideas in the Making of the Constitution.* New York: Knopf, 1996.

—Patrick Malcolmson

intergovernmental tax immunity

Intergovernmental tax immunity refers to exemption of one government from the taxes of another. The U.S. Constitution does not expressly immunize the federal government from state taxation, nor immunize the states from federal taxation. *MCCULLOCH V. MARYLAND,* 17 U.S. 316 (1819), inferred the federal government's immunity from Article VI, Section 2, the SUPREMACY CLAUSE. *McCullloch* held that Maryland could not impose a tax on notes issued by the Bank of the United States, because a state may not use its taxing power "to retard, impede, burden, or . . . control" the federal government. *McCulloch* did not address the issue of federal taxation of state governments but suggested that states did not enjoy reciprocal immunity.

After *McCulloch,* however, the Court inferred state tax immunity from the Tenth Amendment, crafted the doctrine of intergovernmental tax immunity, and then extended the doctrine to bar taxation of one government's employees by the other government. *Dobbins v. Commissioners,* 41 U.S. 435 (1842), invalidated a state tax on a federal employee; and COLLECTOR V. DAY, 78 U.S. 113 (1871), held that the salaries of state judges were immune from federal taxation. Subsequently, the Court extended state immunity to protect state proprietary activities, to private businesses selling goods to state governments, and to the interest earned on state bonds. The Court also barred state taxation of private businesses selling goods to and leasing land from the federal government, because the economic incidence, or burden to pay the tax, would be passed on to the federal government.

These expansive interpretations deprived federal and state governments of substantial revenues and led the Court to narrow the scope of intergovernmental tax immunities. *James v. Dravo Construction Co.,* 302 U.S. 134 (1937), discarded the economic incidence test, limited federal tax immunity to its legal incidence, or obligation to pay the tax, and upheld a nondiscriminatory state tax on a private business. *Helvering v. Gerhardt,* 304 U.S. 405 (1938), overruled *Day* and permitted the federal government to levy a nondiscriminatory income tax on state civil servants. *Graves v. New York ex rel. O'Keefe,* 306 U.S. 466 (1939), overruled *Dobbins* and permitted non-discriminatory state taxation of federal employees. After *Graves,* the doctrine became even more limited, barring only taxes imposed directly on one government by another and only taxes that discriminated against the employees and private businesses who had dealings with a government.

Today, federal tax immunity exists only when the legal incidence of the tax falls directly upon the federal government, its property, or one of its entities. Federal employees are not immune as long as the tax is non-discriminatory. *United States v. County of Fresno,* 429 U.S. 452 (1977), upheld a state tax on the use by federal employees of housing provided as part of their compensation, because the tax was similar to a state tax. Nor may states impose discriminatory taxes on federal employees. *Davis v. Michigan,* 489 U.S. 803 (1989), rejected a state income tax on federal government employee retirement benefits that exempted state employee retirement benefits from taxation.

Private businesses who use federal property are no longer immune from nondiscriminatory state taxes. *City of Detroit v. Murray Corp.,* 355 U.S. 489 (1958), sustained state taxation of a private company's use of machinery owned by the federal government and leased to the company for use in the business. A companion case, *United States v. City of Detroit,* 355 U.S. 466 (1958), upheld a state tax on the use of tax-exempt federal property, because the state had imposed a similar tax on the owners of nonexempt private property. Since *United States v. New Mexico,* 455 U.S. 720 (1982), the Court has taken a narrow approach to federal tax immunity when it decided that private contractors were not so closely connected that the contractor stood "in the government's shoes."

Since 1937, the Court has limited state tax immunity to the performance of its basic governmental functions. *New York v. United States,* 326 U.S. 572 (1946), rejected the distinction between government and proprietary activities as unworkable in an age of increasingly diverse state governmental activities and articulated a new state immunity principle which permitted a federal nondiscriminatory tax to be applied to the state's bottling and sale of water. The Court further limited the state immunity doctrine in *Massachusetts v. United States,* 435 U.S. 444 (1977), when it sustained a federal annual registration tax on civil aircraft to a state police helicopter, because the tax was based on a fair approximation of the state's use of the national aviation system. Since *Massachusetts,* the federal government may tax even a basic state government activity if the nondiscriminatory tax recoups the cost of benefits received from the federal government.

For more information: McCloskey, Robert G. *The American Supreme Court.* 4th ed. Chicago:

University of Chicago Press, 2004; Sullivan, Kathleen, and Gerald Gunther. *Constitutional Law.* 15th ed. New York: Foundation Press, 2004.

—William Crawford Green

intermediate level scrutiny test

The intermediate level scrutiny test is used by the courts to determine if some semi-suspect classifications, such as gender, are permissible under the EQUAL PROTECTION clause of the Constitution.

The equal protection clause of the FOURTEENTH AMENDMENT provides that "no State shall . . . deny to any person within its jurisdiction the equal protection of the laws." In guaranteeing equality under the law, the Constitution requires states to justify their decisions to treat persons as legally different. Under the equal protection doctrine, states may treat people differently when they base it on relevant differences among the individuals.

The U.S. Supreme Court formulated a two-tier level of scrutiny to determine whether laws were constitutional. The first, applying the strictest standard of review, is used in cases involving laws based on race or national origin. When such a law is challenged as unconstitutional, the government must show it has a "compelling" reason for the law and demonstrate that it is "necessarily" related to the objectives it seeks to achieve. The second, known as minimal scrutiny, is used to judge laws that classify people on the basis of changeable characteristics such as wealth or age. Under minimal scrutiny, the state must simply show it has a "legitimate" reason for the law and demonstrate that the means are "rationally" related to the ends it seeks to achieve.

The level of scrutiny is crucial to the outcome of the case. Statutes reviewed under minimal scrutiny almost always receive the Court's approval; conversely, laws reviewed under STRICT SCRUTINY are almost always struck. In the 1970s, when the federal courts became a forum for the debate over sexual equality, the Supreme Court was asked to determine whether laws that differentiated on the basis of sex were consistent with the equal protection clause.

Reed v. Reed, 404 U.S. 71 (1971), marked the beginning of the Court's new approach to constitutional sex equality doctrine. For the first time, the Court struck a state or federal law on the grounds of sex discrimination. Although it acknowledged that the Idaho law favoring men over women as estate administrators to expedite probate had a legitimate purpose, it held that the classification on the basis of sex was not substantially related to the state's goal.

In *Frontiero v. Richardson,* 411 U.S. 677 (1973), the Court reviewed a law that required women—but not men—to show they provided more than half of their family's support in order to receive benefits. Four justices, WILLIAM J. BRENNAN, JR., Thurgood Marshall, Byron White, and WILLIAM O. DOUGLAS, voted to raise the level of scrutiny for sex-based laws, because they believed that, like race and national origin, sex was unrelated to ability and deserved the same searching scrutiny as these other classifications. However, although a majority voted to strike the law, there was no majority support for changing the level of scrutiny.

In *CRAIG V. BOREN,* 429 U.S. 190 (1976), the Court formally adopted the intermediate (or heightened) scrutiny test for laws based on sex. The case arose as a challenge to an Oklahoma law allowing 18-year-old women—but not men—to buy beer. A lower federal court upheld the law, but the Supreme Court reversed. Speaking for a 5-4 Court, Justice William J. Brennan, Jr. announced that prior cases established that sex-based classifications "must serve important governmental objectives and must be substantially related to achievement of those objectives" (*Craig v. Boren,* 1976, 197). Reviewing earlier cases, Brennan noted that the Court has refused to approve laws based on stereotypical ideas of men's and women's roles. Although the purpose of the Oklahoma law was important, that is, reducing incidents of driving under the influence of alcohol, the Court held that it did not pass the new intermediate scrutiny test because the sex-based classification was not substantially related to this goal.

Writing in dissent, Chief Justice WILLIAM HUBBS REHNQUIST objected that the majority had simply imposed a higher level of scrutiny on laws relating to sex differences without justification on the basis of precedent. He argued that this was particularly inappropriate in cases of men challenging sex-based classifications. Because there was no history of discrimination against men, Rehnquist said he would only apply minimal scrutiny to the Oklahoma law and, in his view, it was constitutional.

In *MISSISSIPPI UNIVERSITY FOR WOMEN V. HOGAN*, 458 U.S. 718 (1982), in a challenge to the university's women-only nursing program, Justice SANDRA DAY O'CONNOR added a new dimension to the intermediate level scrutiny test by explaining that in order to defend a sex-based classification, the state must present an "exceedingly persuasive justification" for it. The Court also held that it will apply the heightened form of scrutiny whenever a sex-based classification is challenged, regardless of which sex raises the issue.

For more information: Cushman, Claire, ed. *Supreme Court Decisions and Women's Rights.* Washington, D.C.: Congressional Quarterly Press, 2001; Mezey, Susan Gluck. *Elusive Equality: Women's Rights, Public Policy, and the Law.* Boulder, Colo.: Lynne Rienner Publishers, 2003.

—Susan Gluck Mezey

international law and the Constitution

Constitutional scholars and prominent justices of the Supreme Court strongly disagree on the proper application of international law in the making of domestic statutes and interpretation of the Constitution.

Originalists like Justice ANTONIN GREGORY SCALIA maintain that international legal documents and traditions have limited role, if any, in constitutional jurisprudence since the potential for deviating from the original intent of the framers is high when judges resort to foreign legal traditions and treaties in interpreting the Constitution.

Constitutional comparativists like Justice ANTHONY M. KENNEDY, on the other hand, uphold the constitutional principle that, as long as foreign laws do not directly contravene democratic values, they can serve as useful precedents to and vital sources of judicial decisions and domestic lawmaking. Also closely identified with those who ascribe to the LIVING CONSTITUTION tradition of judicial interpretation, constitutional comparativists stress the importance of international legal precedents in dealing with modern constitutional dilemmas, such as the treatment of members of transnational terrorist networks captured in the "Global War on Terror," and in formulating international agreements that are crucial to confronting global challenges such as genocide, the illegal use of CHILD LABOR, climate change, PATENTS rights over living organisms, species extinction, illicit (human and narcotic) trafficking, and so on. This comparative constitutional perspective is in keeping with the fact that the writers of the Constitution heavily borrowed from English Common Law and European democratic political theory.

The U.S. Constitution provides at least three different methods in which international treaties and agreements can be directly incorporated into domestic law. First, courts of various tiers and prerogatives may refer to international legal obligations and commitments when interpreting domestic statutes. Second, Congress could refer to international laws in making domestic laws. That is, domestic laws could integrate or incorporate provisions of an international TREATY. Third, although the Constitution grants the president the power to negotiate and sign international treaties in particular and conduct foreign relations in general, the treaty SUPREMACY CLAUSE of the Constitution, Article VI, requires the SENATE to ratify treaties with a majority two-thirds vote. Once a treaty is signed by the president and ratified by the Senate, it becomes the "Supreme Law of the Land."

Given that the constitutional framers drew a great deal from English Common Law in crafting the Constitution, customary international laws—established customs, principles and practices adhered to by a community of nations out of universal respect for human rights and due to obligatory treaties—also strongly influence constitutional jurisprudence. Prohibitions against slavery and genocide, freedom from detention without DUE PROCESS of law, and the rights of prisoners of war to humane treatment are some of the most commonly accepted customary international laws. These fundamental human rights are enshrined in such landmark international treaties as the International Convention on Civil and Political Rights and the Third Geneva Convention on the conduct of war and the treatment of prisoners of war. Given that the United States has signed and ratified both conventions, the prolonged detention in Guantánamo, Cuba, of "enemy combatants" captured in the "War on Terror" in Afghanistan and other parts of the world is widely believed to be a violation of U.S. obligations under customary international law. Human rights organizations including Amnesty International, Human Rights Watch, and AMERICAN CIVIL LIBERTIES UNION (ACLU) have repeatedly criticized the Bush administration's treatment of "enemy combatants" as clear violations of the aforementioned human rights conventions.

The Bush administration responds to these criticisms by insisting that the prisoners held at Guantánamo, Cuba, are "enemy combatants" who do not enjoy the same rights as conventional prisoners of war. However, some of those detained include U.S. citizens and nationals of various countries who have been held without fair trial for several months and even years, thus contravening prohibitions under the International Convention on Civil and Political Rights against arbitrary and prolonged detention. Another widely reported practice that is increasingly a subject of close scrutiny is "extraordinary rendition," an extra-judicial method used by the Central Intelligence Agency (CIA) to extract information from suspected terrorists. Suspected members and supporters of terrorist organizations are extradited to other countries where they could reportedly be tortured and detained without fair trial.

The growing public scrutiny of the policies and practices of the Bush administration's "War on Terror" has generated a heated debate among scholars of international law and the U.S. Supreme Court justices as to whether combatants of non-state actors such as al-Qaeda can be accorded the same rights that the Geneva Convention on the conduct of war and the treatment of prisoners of war guarantees. This debate is as much about the proper treatment of "enemy combatants" captured abroad in battles with global non-state actors as the basic rights of suspected criminals; thus, what is at stake is the future of the Geneva Convention in particular and international human rights law in general.

The central issue of human rights is further complicated when, as in the seminal Supreme Court case of *HAMDI V. RUMSFELD*, the captive happens to be a U.S. citizen. There is no doubt that this debate will occupy the Supreme Court and legal scholars for some time to come, as it strikes at crucial intersections of international and domestic law.

For more information: Anderson, Kenneth. "Foreign Law and the U.S. Constitution." *Policy Review.* Available online. URL: http://www.policyreview.org/jun05/anderson.html. Visited 13 May 2008; Horner, Christopher. "Modern Developments In The Treaty Process." (August 1, 2002.) Available online. URL: http://www.cei.org/gencon/025,03243.cfm. Visited 24 December 2006; Huhn, Ray. "The Constitutional Jurisprudence of SANDRA DAY O'CONNOR: A Refusal to 'Foreclose the Unanticipated.'" *Akron Law Review* 39. Available online. URL: http://www.policyreview.org/jun05/anderson.html. Visited 13 May 2008; "War on Terror" Human Rights Issues. Amnesty International. Available online. URL: http://www.amnestyusa.org/waronterror/detainees/us_obligations.html. Visited 24 December 2006.

—Daniel G. Ogbaharya

International Society for Krishna Consciousness v. Lee 505 U.S. 672 (1992)

The U.S. Supreme Court, in the case of *International Society for Krishna Consciousness v. Lee*, declared publicly owned airport terminals are not free speech forums under the free speech clause of the FIRST AMENDMENT to the U.S. Constitution. In the case, a not-for-profit religious group called the International Society for Krishna Consciousness (ISKCON) wanted to distribute leaflets and solicit monetary donations inside several major public airports within the New York area. The Port Authority of New York and New Jersey, which owned the airports, adopted a regulation forbidding these actions. ISKCON eventually appealed this ban to the U.S. Supreme Court.

The Court first determined that publicly owned airport terminals are unlike traditional government-owned forums historically used for public gatherings and discussions such as parks, streets, and sidewalks. In those more traditional PUBLIC FORUMS, government must show that limiting the speaker is justified by a government interest of a compelling (very strong) nature, and the restriction on the speaker is narrowly tailored (carefully designed) to further that compelling interest rather than some other interest or no interest at all. The Court also declared that the Port Authority had not intentionally created a public forum, by the fact the airport was designed for air travel and not free speech purposes, and also by the fact the airport had a long history of trying to restrict the airport for use by air travelers only, rather than citizens who wished to distribute political or religious literature. In designated public forums, the government must also meet the same standards when restricting speech as it must meet in traditional public forums. However, because the airport terminals in the case were neither traditional public forums nor designated as public forums, the government could enact greater restrictions on speech as long as those restrictions are reasonable. The Court concluded that a total ban on solicitation of money was reasonable. Stopping people and asking them for money would delay the people who are stopped as well as other people trying to avoid the solicitation or whose paths are blocked by the pedestrian congestion caused by people stopping. This is an important problem to prevent in crowded airports where travelers are often in a hurry. In addition, there would be the possibility that the people asking for money would be lying about the reasons the money is needed. However, busy airport customers are unlikely to take the time to report this fraud when it occurs. Also, if the airports allowed one group into the airport terminals to solicit money, then the airports would have to allow all political, religious, and charitable groups to do so on an equal, nondiscriminatory basis, and the airport terminals could become too clogged by people to function as transportation terminals. Thus, the Court concluded that a complete ban on the solicitation of money inside a publicly owned airport terminal is reasonable.

In a companion case, *Lee v. ISKCON,* 505 U.S. 830 (1992), the Court held that although public airport terminals are not public forums, individuals have a right to peacefully distribute leaflets inside them. This is because the distribution of leaflets is less disruptive to the functioning of an airport, particularly pedestrian traffic flow, than is the solicitation of money, as individuals can simply walk quickly by anyone holding out a leaflet for them to take. Therefore, a complete ban on leafleting inside a public airport terminal is unreasonable, and thus violates the free speech clause of the First Amendment.

For more information: Sullivan, Kathleen, and Gerald Gunther. *Constitutional Law.* 14th ed. New York: Foundation Press, 2001; Volokh, Eugene. *The First Amendment: Problems, Cases and Policy Arguments.* New York: Foundation Press, 2001.

—Rick A. Swanson

interstate commerce

Article I, Section 8 of the Constitution provides, "Congress shall have the power . . . To regulate Commerce with foreign Nations, and among the several States, and with the Indian Tribes." This provision, known as the COMMERCE CLAUSE, is the wellspring of Congress's authority for enacting legislation in such diverse areas as criminal law, CIVIL RIGHTS, and environmental law.

The Supreme Court first interpreted the scope of the commerce clause in *GIBBONS V. OGDEN,* 22 U.S. (9 Wheat.) 1 (1824), where Chief Justice JOHN MARSHALL explained that the clause grants Congress the power to regulate "commercial intercourse" respecting "more states than one." According to Chief Justice Marshall, this "power of Congress does not stop at the jurisdictional lines of the several States" but extends to intrastate commerce if it has an impact on interstate activities (id. at 196). Moreover, "[t]his power, like all others vested in Congress, is complete in itself, may be exercised to its utmost extent, and acknowledges no limitations, other than are prescribed in the constitution" (id. at 197).

From 1887 to 1937, however, the Supreme Court espoused a more circumscribed view of Congress's commerce power. Under this view, known as dual FEDERALISM, federal and state governments are separate sovereigns with separate zones of authority, and it is the judiciary's role to demarcate and enforce these separate spheres. The Supreme Court of this era narrowly defined commerce as an element of business distinguishable from other elements such as "mining" or "manufacturing"—zones of interest reserved to the states (*UNITED STATES V. E.C. KNIGHT CO.*, 156 U.S. 1 [1895]). The Court also narrowly defined "among the several States," permitting Congress to regulate only activity having a direct effect on interstate commerce (*SWIFT & CO. V. UNITED STATES*, 196 U.S. 375 [1905]). And it interpreted the Tenth Amendment to reserve to the states certain zones of interest, such as local trade and manufacture, beyond the scope of Congress's commerce power (*HAMMER V. DAGENHART [The Child Labor Case]*, 247 U.S. 251 [1918]). Applying this framework, the Court invalidated a broad array of federal laws, including New Deal legislation enacted under President Franklin Roosevelt.

These decisions relied on formalistic distinctions that many Americans perceived as arbitrary and even inhumane in light of the Great Depression's bleak economic realities. To address this problem, President Franklin Roosevelt proposed in 1936 to increase the Supreme Court's size from nine to 15 justices. The president abandoned this "court packing" proposal after Justice Owen Roberts changed his vote in *NLRB V. JONES & LAUGHLIN STEEL CORP.*, 301 U.S. 1 (1937), forming the fifth member of a new majority willing to expand Congress's commerce power. The change is aptly known as "the switch in time that saved nine." *Jones & Laughlin* upheld Congress's authority to regulate intrastate activities that "have such a close and substantial relation to interstate commerce that their control is essential or appropriate to protect that commerce from burdens and obstructions" (id. at 37).

The Court fully retreated from its narrow interpretation of the commerce power in *UNITED STATES V. DARBY LUMBER CO.*, 312 U.S. 100 (1941), and *WICKARD V. FILBURN*, 317 U.S. 111 (1942). *Darby* explicitly rejected the view that production was a zone of interest reserved to the states, and it expressly overruled *Hammer v. Dagenhart*'s holding that the Tenth Amendment affirmatively limits Congress's commerce power. "The [Tenth] amendment states but a truism that all is retained which has not been surrendered" (*Darby*, 312 U.S. at 124). *Wickard*, in turn, expressly rejected earlier distinctions between direct and indirect effects on interstate commerce (317 U.S. at 124).

This broad interpretation survived for almost 60 years: between 1937 and 1995, the Supreme Court did not invalidate a single federal law as exceeding Congress's commerce power. (See, e.g., *Hodel v. Virginia Surface Mining & Reclamation Assn., Inc.*, 452 U.S. 264 [1981], upholding Congress's authority to regulate strip mining on intrastate land not part of interstate commerce, even though such regulation historically had been the province of the states, and *HEART OF ATLANTA MOTEL INC. V. UNITED STATES*, 379 U.S. 241 [1964], upholding Congress's authority to prohibit discrimination in places of public accommodation.)

Then, in *UNITED STATES V. LOPEZ*, 514 U.S. 549 (1995), the Court shocked many by invalidating a provision of the Gun-Free School Zones Act of 1990 criminalizing the possession of a handgun within 1,000 feet of a school. The Court explained that the interstate commerce clause authorizes Congress to regulate three categories of activities: 1) the use of the channels of interstate commerce; 2) instrumentalities of interstate commerce, or persons or things in interstate commerce, even though the threat may come only from intrastate activities; and 3) intrastate activities having a substantial relation to interstate commerce (514 U.S. at 558–59). Only the third category was relevant in *Lopez*. The Court held that because the criminalization of mere possession of a handgun "has nothing to do with commerce or any sort of economic enterprise, however broadly one might define those terms," the act "cannot, therefore, be sustained under our cases upholding regulations of activities that arise out of or are connected with a commercial transaction, which viewed in the aggregate, substantially affects interstate commerce" (id. at 561).

The Court confirmed in *UNITED STATES V. MORRISON,* 529 U.S. 598 (2000), that *Lopez* was no aberration. *Morrison* held that Congress had exceeded its commerce power in enacting the Violence Against Women Act of 1994, which created a federal civil remedy for victims of gender-motivated crimes of violence. As in *Lopez,* the *Morrison* Court "reject[ed] the argument that Congress may regulate noneconomic, violent criminal conduct based solely on that conduct's aggregate effect on interstate commerce" (529 U.S. at 617). The Court explained, "The regulation and punishment of intrastate violence that is not directed at the instrumentalities, channels, or goods involved in interstate commerce has always been the province of the States. Indeed, we can think of no better example of the POLICE POWER, which the Founders denied the National Government and reposed in the States, than the suppression of violent crime and vindication of its victims" (id. at 618).

The Supreme Court's most recent decision construing Congress's commerce power is *GONZALES V. RAICH,* 545 U.S. 1 (2005). There, the Court considered whether Congress may prohibit, via the Controlled Substances Act, "the local cultivation and use of marijuana in compliance with California law" (id. at 5). The Court upheld Congress's regulation of the intrastate, non-economic activity of growing and using marijuana for medicinal purposes. It reasoned that when a comprehensive regulatory scheme itself is "within the reach of federal power, the courts have no power to excise, as trivial, individual instances of the class" (id. at 23; internal quotation marks omitted). In such instances, courts "need not determine whether [the regulated] activities, taken in the aggregate, substantially affect interstate commerce in fact, but only whether a 'rational basis' exists for so concluding" (id. at 22). Although *Raich* expressly distinguished *Lopez* and *Morrison* on the ground that the regulations at issue in those cases were not enacted pursuant to a comprehensive regulatory scheme, the extent to which the presently constituted Supreme Court will further constrict the scope of Congress's commerce power in the name of dual federalism remains to be seen.

For more information: Barnett, Randy E. "The Original Meaning of the Commerce Clause." *University of Chicago Law Review* 68 (2001): 101–147; Clark, Bradford R. "Translating Federalism: A Structural Approach." *George Washington Law Review* 66 (1998): 1,161–1,197; Lessig, Lawrence. "Translating Federalism: *United States v. Lopez.*" *Supreme Court Review* 192 (1995): 125–215; Rotunda, Ronald D. "The Commerce Clause, the Political Question Doctrine, and *Morrison.*" *Constitutional Commentary* 18 (June 22, 2001): 319.

—Andre Mura

Interstate Commerce Commission (ICC)

Interstate Commerce Commission (ICC) was one of the first federal regulatory bodies and was the first independent agency, nicknamed the Fourth Branch by some in reference to the three branches affirmed by the Constitution.

The ICC was enacted through the Interstate Commerce Act of 1887 and signed into existence by President Grover Cleveland. The agency lasted more than 100 years, finally being closed in 1995. The Constitution's Tenth Amendment gives rise to the federal government's power to regulate only matters that are specifically delegated to it by the Constitution. In the late 1880s, the emergence of the railroads, coupled with the national reliance upon the railroads, pushed the government to attempt to regulate the unfair advantages that a few select and very powerful private railroad company owners wielded.

The challenges to the government, as elaborated through the enforcement of the Sherman Anti-trust Act regulation of the Rockefeller family, suggested that a railroad company could corner the markets and control pricing, supply quality, and concessions for transport into several markets and therefore constrain the development of smaller business. This ability to impact both the markets and the government power through market manipulation created a ripe atmosphere for the ICC to be established. The enduring impact upon regulatory bodies and future federal agencies was represented through the adoption by these agencies of similar structure and independence standards. The seven-member board of the ICC and the demand that no one on the board could retain economic ties within an industry that they regulated amounted to a belief in the agencies that at times suggested that there was more honor in regulation than politics. The ICC also drove the idea of independence by staggering appointments so that political impact could be avoided and the operations of major endeavors would continue without compromise.

In the late 1800s, anti-rail sentiment began to become a social rallying point and a political issue. The use of discriminatory political influence practices, the lack of pricing regulation, and the concern for the western producers of goods and livestock were all overt practices that spurred the call for reform of the rail systems. The emergence of the trucking industry changed the voracity of the ICC as the agency picked up other concerns over time, and in the late 1920s, it was believed that the railroads' impact on the economy was on a downward spiral which would never be recovered. By the mid- to late '20s, the Ripley plan for railroad consolidation was established as a way to reduce the competition that threatened to cause some train carriers to go bankrupt. The ICC became an early proxy for southern business rights against the rights of southern blacks as these blacks rode on trains through the South. The impact of the CIVIL RIGHTS ACT and the Freedom Riders took the ICC into unfamiliar places, and the leadership of the ICC agreed to support the Civil Rights legislation.

For more information: Hoogenboom, Ari, and Olive Hoogenboom. *A History of the ICC: From Panacea to Palliative.* New York: W.W. Norton, 1976; Stone, Richard D. *The Interstate Commerce Commission and the Railroad Industry: a History of Regulatory Policy.* Westport, Conn.: Praeger, 1991.

—Ernest Gomez

Iroquois Indian League and the Constitution

There are some who argue that the Iroquois Indian League had an impact upon the framers of the Constitution. The support for this influence is not great, even though there are some apparent parallels between the way the Iroquois organized themselves and how the Constitution structured the idea of FEDERALISM and the relationship of power between the states and the national government.

Long before the end of the colonial era, five Iroquoian-speaking tribes in Upstate New York had formed a military and economic alliance among themselves. At first only the Cayuga, Mohawk, Oneida, Onondaga, and the Seneca belonged to the Iroquois League. In 1772, the Tuscarora tribe migrated from North Carolina to New York to escape their enemies. They were given land and representation at League Conference meetings, thereby making the Iroquois the Six Indian Nations.

The word *Iroquois* is a French pronunciation of the Algonquian word *ireohkwa,* which means "real adders" (snakes). The Algonquian word was a derogatory term for their Iroquoian-speaking enemies. The Iroquois called themselves collectively the *Haudenosaunee,* which means "the people of the Longhouse." Iroquois towns were protected by wooden palisades, behind which the people lived in longhouses made of poles covered with elm bark. The Iroquois longhouse was a symbol of the Iroquois League. It was a great longhouse with the Seneca guarding the Western Door and the Mohawks guarding the Eastern Door.

Iroquois tradition reports that they were organized into a political organization about 1570 by two Indians into the Iroquois League (or Iroquois Confederacy). The Cayuga, Mohawk, Oneida, Onondaga, and Seneca were brought together by a Huron prophet, Deganawida (the Peacemaker), and by Hiawatha, a Mohawk. Together they traveled throughout Iroquois lands preaching a message of peace and unity. Deganawida and Hiawatha were active at a time of internecine warfare between the clans that was rendering the tribes into dysfunctional remnants.

Deganawida preached his vision of the tribes united under the sheltering branches of a Tree of Great Peace. Hiawatha and he carried a wampum belt to symbolize the Great Law of Peace. Opposition was overcome when the principal opponent of their plan was made the head of the League. Studies of the oral traditions of the Iroquois suggest that the Gayaneshakgowa (Great Law of Peace) founding the impressive Confederacy may have begun several centuries earlier.

Some historians have claimed that the Founding Fathers of the United States modeled the democratic self-government of the original 13 states after the Iroquois Confederacy. The different states were compared to the different tribes of the Iroquois. The members of the HOUSE OF REPRESENTATIVES and the SENATE were like the 50 sachems or chiefs chosen by clan mothers to represent the tribes. The president and his cabinet were like the honorary Pine Tree Sachems. Washington, D.C., was like the village of Onondaga, the main village of the Onondaga tribe where the Grand Council was held every year.

Historians today are less supportive of the claim that the Iroquois League influenced the Constitution. In fact the evidence is thin. Moreover, given the bias and discrimination that many held against Indians, viewing them as uncivilized savages, it is unlikely that the framers would have turned to them for constitutional ideas.

For more information: Fenton, William Nelson. *The Great Law and the Longhouse: A Political History of the Iroquois Confederation.* Norman: University of Oklahoma Press, 1998; Morgan, Lewis Henry. *League of the Iroquois.* Secaucus, N.J.: Carol Publishing Group, 1996.

—Andrew J. Waskey

Jacobellis v. Ohio 378 U.S. 184 (1964)
Jacobellis v. Ohio was an important Supreme Court case seeking to define OBSCENITY.

Nico Jacobellis was a theater manager in Cleveland Heights who showed the movie *Les Amants* (The Lovers) and was subsequently convicted for possessing and displaying an obscene film in violation of Ohio law. That conviction was upheld by Ohio's highest court but was overturned by the U.S. Supreme Court on June 22, 1964.

In the wake of the Supreme Court's 1957 opinion in *ROTH V. U.S.*, 354 U.S. 476 (decided together with *Alberts v. California*), the justices found themselves increasingly immersed in the murky waters of obscenity. In *Roth,* the Court directly held that obscenity was not covered by the FIRST AMENDMENT's umbrella that protects freedom of speech and of the press. At the same time, the *Roth* opinion, written by Justice WILLIAM J. BRENNAN, JR., limited the reach of obscenity statutes under the Constitution. The constitutional test would be "whether to the average person, applying contemporary community standards, the dominant theme of the material, taken as a whole, appeals to prurient interest," and further, that the material lacks "the slightest redeeming social importance." Writing for the 6-3 majority in *Jacobellis,* Brennan utilized the *Roth* standard while recognizing its limits. Since obscenity was a constitutional issue, Brennan noted, the Court simply could not avoid the difficult and unpleasant decisions "involved in every obscenity case" that emerged.

Importantly, in *Jacobellis,* Brennan clarified the meaning of "contemporary community standards," stating that such standards had to be national, not local, in scope. On this point, Chief Justice Earl Warren, in dissent, argued for the local approach to community standards (a view eventually adopted by the Court in its 1973 *MILLER V. CALIFORNIA,* 413 U.S. 49, decision).

Based on *Roth,* Brennan concluded that the film in question was a serious undertaking that received considerable critical praise. Obscene material was excluded from First Amendment protection (a protection applied to the states through the DUE PROCESS clause of the FOURTEENTH AMENDMENT) only because it was "utterly without redeeming social importance" in going "substantially beyond customary limits of candor." And this was not the case with *Les Amants.*

Justice HUGO BLACK (joined by Justice WILLIAM O. DOUGLAS), Justice Potter Stewart and Justice Arthur J. Goldberg wrote concurring opinions in the case, while Justice JOHN MARSHALL HARLAN, along with Warren (joined by Justice Tom Clark), dissented, arguing that Ohio had acted "within permissible limits."

In his brief concurring opinion, Stewart stated that obscenity laws under the Constitution were limited to hard-core pornography. He then wrote, "I shall not today attempt further to define the kinds of material I understand to be embraced within that shorthand description, and perhaps I could never succeed intelligibly doing so. But I know it when I see it, and the motion picture involved in this case is not that." Stewart's "I know it when I see it" comment, in many ways, would become the signature feature of *Jacobellis* and one that indicated just how far the Supreme Court still had to go in search of constitutional clarity regarding obscenity.

For more information: Friedman, Leon, ed. *Obscenity: Oral Arguments Before the Supreme Court.* New York: The Confucian Press, 1980.

—Norman Provizer

Jay, John (1745–1829) *first chief justice of the United States*

John Jay was the first chief justice of the U.S. Supreme Court and a well-known political leader. Jay was born in New York City, December 12, 1745, the youngest of eight children of Mary Van Cortlandt Jay and Peter Jay, a prosperous merchant. Jay's mother taught him English and Latin grammar until he left home to be formally instructed. At age 14, Jay entered King's College (later renamed Columbia University) and received his diploma with honors. Jay clerked in a law office and was admitted to bar in 1768. Jay became one of the most successful attorneys in New York, first in partnership with an old college classmate, Robert R. Livingston, Jr., and then on his own. Jay married the cousin of his former law partner, Sarah Van Brugh Livingston, in 1774. The Jays had six children.

In 1774, Jay committed himself to the cause of independence by representing his state at the First Continental Congress. He did not sign the DECLARATION OF INDEPENDENCE because of duties drafting the state constitution of New York. In 1777, Jay was appointed chief justice of New York's newly formed Supreme Court of Judicature. His judicial activities ended when he was sent by New York to the Second Continental Congress in November 1778. Jay helped with the establishment of the fledgling republic. Jay, as a peace commissioner, along with Benjamin Franklin, negotiated the Peace Treaty of 1783, which ended the Revolutionary War with favorable terms for the United States. Once the Constitution had been drafted, Jay contributed five essays of those that became known as *THE FEDERALIST PAPERS.* They were intended to persuade the citizens of New York to ratify the Constitution.

President George Washington was reportedly willing to consider Jay for any number of high posts in the new government, and on September 24, 1789, he nominated the 43-year-old New Yorker to be the nation's first chief justice. As chief justice, Jay's most notable case was *CHISHOLM V. GEORGIA*, 2 U.S. (2 Dall.) 419 (1793). The holding of the Court established the right of citizens of one state to sue another state in federal court, affirming that some of the state's sovereignty was subordinate to the U.S. Constitution. Because of the unfavorable reaction to the decision, Congress quickly proposed the ELEVENTH AMENDMENT, which reversed the Court's decision, denying federal courts authority in suits by citizens against a state and barring such suits unless the defendant state consented.

Jay resigned from the Supreme Court on June 29, 1795, to serve as governor of New York for two three-year terms. He then retired from public life in 1801. President JOHN ADAMS sent Jay's name, without his knowledge, to the SENATE in hopes of reappointing him chief justice. The Senate confirmed him, but Jay declined the position because of his dislike of circuit court riding and his disappointment that the Supreme Court was not vested with sufficient authority. He spent his unusually

Chief Justice John Jay *(Library of Congress)*

long retirement at his 800-acre estate in Westchester County, until his death on May 17, 1829.

For more information: Casto, William R. *The Supreme Court in the Early Republic: The Chief Justiceships of John Jay and Oliver Ellsworth.* Columbia, S.C.: University of South Carolina Press, 1995; Kelly, Alfred H., Winfred A. Harbison, and Herman Belz. *The American Constitution: Its Origins and Development.* New York: W.W. Norton & Company, 1991.

—Randy W. Hagedorn

J.E.B. v. Alabama 511 U.S. 127 (1994)

In *J.E.B. v. Alabama,* the U.S. Supreme Court decided that PEREMPTORY CHALLENGES that exclude jurors on the basis of sex violated the EQUAL PROTECTION clause of the FOURTEENTH AMENDMENT.

J.E.B. was the latest in a series of cases in which the Court determined the limits on peremptory challenges, a practice in which attorneys for either side in civil or criminal cases may excuse potential jurors without providing an explanation. The Court had held in *BATSON V. KENTUCKY,* 476 U.S. 79 (1986), that a prosecutor who uses peremptory challenges in a criminal trial to eliminate jurors based on their race violates the equal protection clause. Therefore, the question the Court had to answer in *J.E.B.* was whether to extend the principle of *Batson* to sex-based peremptory strikes.

The defendant in *J.E.B.* was on trial for charges related to his failure to pay child support for a child purported to be his. Each side used peremptory challenges to eliminate jurors on the basis of sex whom they thought would be detrimental to their side: the prosecutor used nine of his 10 peremptory challenges to strike potential male jurors; similarly, J.E.B.'s attorney used almost all his peremptory challenges to remove female jurors. The resulting jury, consisting of all women, found that he was the father of the child, and the judge ordered him to pay child support.

The Alabama courts rejected J.E.B.'s claim that the prosecutor's use of sex-based peremptory challenges violated the equal protection clause. Speaking for a 6-3 majority, Justice Harry Blackmun proclaimed that discrimination based on sex violates the equal protection clause, especially in situations in which the laws perpetuate stereotypical views of men's and women's abilities. Although the state tried to justify its practices by distinguishing racial discrimination from sex discrimination in the jury selection procedure, the Court refused to engage in a debate over whether women or racial minorities suffered more discrimination at the hands of the state. Blackmun reiterated that the nation's wide-ranging history of sex discrimination required the Court to consider the practice of allowing prosecutors to base their peremptory challenges on sex very carefully.

The Court sought to determine whether these sex-based peremptory challenges were substantially related to the state's goal of ensuring a fair trial and concluded they were not. In reaching this conclusion, the Court rejected the state's attempt to rely on studies that showed that attitudes differed by sex, thereby justifying using sex as a proxy to eliminate potential juror bias. Characterizing the state's evidence as largely gender stereotyping, Blackmun noted that the equal protection clause does not allow states to base laws on stereotypical generalizations about the sexes even though there might be some statistical evidence to support the generalizations.

Chief Justice WILLIAM HUBBS REHNQUIST dissented, arguing that the Court should maintain a distinction between the way it viewed racial and sex-based classifications. In his view, although racially-based peremptory strikes were clearly unconstitutional, the equal protection clause did not prohibit states from excluding potential jurors on the basis of sex.

For more information: Albright, Mary M. "Equal Protection and Peremptory Challenges: Reconciling the Irreconcilable." *Capital University Law Review* 25 (1996): 425–452; Grice, O. Drew, Jr. "Comment: *J.E.B. v. Alabama*: A Critical Analysis of the Supreme Court's Latest Limitation on Peremptory Challenges." *Cumberland Law Review* 25 (1995): 355–381.

—Susan Gluck Mezey

Jefferson, Thomas (1743–1826) *second U.S. vice president, third U.S. president*

Thomas Jefferson, state legislator, governor, Republican Party co-founder and leader, congressman, minister to France, secretary of state, VICE PRESIDENT, and third president of the United States, was one of the most significant figures in American constitutional history.

Jefferson first burst into the consciousness of American political leaders at large with the publication of his 1774 pamphlet *A Summary View of the Rights of British America.* In that pamphlet, Jefferson developed the view of the British Constitution that would mark his thinking through the balance of his life. Building on the views of his mentor Richard Bland, Jefferson claimed that every man had a natural right to emigrate, that Virginia had been founded by émigrés through their own efforts and with their own money, that King George III served Virginia at Virginia's pleasure, and that in case he should cease to fulfill the role they had assigned him, Virginians could rightfully replace George with someone else. In short, Virginia stood on a par with Great Britain itself in the international system.

Thomas Jefferson. Painting by Thomas Sully *(National Archives)*

His draft of the Declaration of American Independence in 1776 amounted to a simple restatement of that position—and one that Jefferson did not consider particularly significant at the time. In fact, in the weeks leading up to his appointment to the congressional committee charged with producing a declaration, Jefferson repeatedly asked to be relieved of his congressional duties so that he could participate in the key event of the Revolution: writing a constitution for the new Virginia republic. To his chagrin, Jefferson's imprecations went unheeded, and he had to be satisfied with crafting the first draft of the Declaration.

The Declaration's chief claim was that in case government's performance failed to satisfy the people, they were entitled to replace it with one more to their liking. In the context of 1776, this was a justification of secession—of Virginia's decision, already implemented by July 4, to withdraw from King George III's empire. Jefferson would remain committed to the notion that Virginia and its fellow states formed the primary elements of the North American political system to the day of his death.

Jefferson was in France while the constitutional reform movement of the 1780s crescendoed, and he played no part in drafting the Constitution in 1787. He did, however, have thoughts about it late in that year. Sent a copy by his friend JAMES MADISON, Jefferson said that he admired the compromises between large and small states, between producing and carrying states, and so on, but that he had two powerful objections: first, he said, the president should be subject to a TERM LIMIT. Otherwise, so august an officer likely would use the appointment power to build up a significant faction in each state, and thus to ensure himself lifetime tenure.

Jefferson's second objection was to the absence of a bill of rights. Virginia in 1776, like England in 1688, had preceded establishment of its new regime by adoption of a declaration of rights, and Jefferson thought the federal government ought to be introduced similarly. When Madison responded with a series of objections to this idea, Jefferson finally cut him off with the assertion that "A bill of rights is what the people are entitled to against every government in the world." Partly because of Jefferson's insistence, Madison ultimately shepherded 12 proposed amendments—11 of which ultimately became the first ten and the 27th amendments—through the first federal Congress.

Jefferson agreed to join George Washington's cabinet as secretary of state in 1789. He no doubt expected to have the leading voice in the formulation of executive policy, but things did not work out that way. Instead, Washington proved sympathetic to the incisive proposals and analyses, both in regard to matters domestic and to foreign policy, of Secretary of the Treasury ALEXANDER HAMILTON.

Jefferson and Hamilton came into notable conflict for the first time in 1791, when Congress passed the bank bill Hamilton had proposed. Washington, aware that Madison had criticized the bill as unconstitutional in the HOUSE OF REPRESENTATIVES, requested that his cabinet members provide written appraisals of the bill. In response, Jefferson and Hamilton each produced one of the most notable state papers in American history.

Jefferson took as his jumping-off point the language of the soon-to-be-ratified Tenth Amendment, which said that all powers not delegated to the federal government via the Constitution or denied by it to the states were reserved to the states or to the people. This, for Jefferson, was the key assumption of American FEDERALISM: that all powers lay in the states except those few carefully and—to borrow a word used by Virginia Federalists in the Virginia Ratification Convention of 1788—"expressly" delegated to the federal government.

Jefferson's reading of Article I, Section 8 of the Constitution did not disclose authorization to Congress to charter any corporation, much less to charter a bank. Therefore, his fall-back principle meant that that power lay solely where it had before the Constitution's ratification: in the state governments. Here we have one of the two classic positions on CONSTITUTIONAL INTERPRETATION. It is usually known as the "state's rights" or "strict construction" reading of the Constitution—but one might as well call it the "respectful" reading. Hamilton made a contrary argument to contrary effect, and thus established the other classic position on constitutional interpretation—the "liberal" or "broad" position.

In 1793, Washington responded to the dangerous international situation by issuing his Neutrality Proclamation. From his—and Hamilton's—perspective, the proclamation amounted simply to informing American citizens of the legal jeopardy they faced in case they actively took sides in the Wars of the French Revolution. Jefferson, however, considered the proclamation to be a usurpation of the power of Congress to set American foreign policy: if America was to move from friend of France to neutral, it should be for the legislature, not the chief executive, to make that determination. Perhaps the king of England could make foreign policy, but the federal Constitution, Jefferson insisted, gave that power to Congress.

Through the rest of the 1790s, Jefferson and a growing body of like-minded Republicans would wage political warfare on Hamilton and his fellow Federalists, chiefly on the basis of their diverging views concerning foreign policy and concerning the Constitution. As Jefferson understood things, Hamilton was a not-so-secret monarchist bent on destroying the Constitution, which any republican (read: patriotic American) would read Jefferson's way; Hamiltonians favored the president over Congress within the federal government and the federal government over the state governments, while Republicans stood for the opposite priorities. In 1798 and 1799, Jefferson authored two sets of Kentucky Resolutions laying out his state's-rights position—and claiming the rights both of nullification and of secession. This threat to resist the federal government forcibly was never acted upon in Jefferson's lifetime, however, because his party swept to victory in 1800.

Jefferson counseled in 1798 that his party would win the next presidential election because his opponents' military program required so many taxes. From the time of his victory, however, which he called the "Revolution of 1800," Jefferson attributed Republican success to the people's sympathy for his state's-rights constitutional views. When, at his presidential inauguration in 1801, it came time for him to address the party combat of the 1790s, Jefferson said that he thought party contention was past. It seemed to him that his views were the self-evident views of the Revolution and that Hamilton had skillfully manipulated Washington's great popularity to near-disastrous effect. Now, consensus had arrived.

Jefferson's constitutional position entailed the abrupt dismantlement of the army and navy, the elimination of virtually all federal taxes, and a pacifist foreign policy. It meant the death of Hamilton's bank. Ultimately, it resulted in the nigh disastrous War of 1812. Jefferson's presidential successor, James Madison, recanted much of the Republican position—even going so far as to ask Congress to charter a second Bank of the United States and to declare war on Great Britain.

In retirement, Jefferson worked unsuccessfully to thwart that second bank bill. He also maintained his commitment to state's rights. For example, Jefferson labored during the Missouri Crisis of 1819–20 to thwart northerners' efforts to exclude slavery from Missouri. His constitutional position was that new states must be admitted to the Union on an equal footing with the old, and that Missouri could not be equal to Massachusetts and Virginia unless it, like them, got to decide on its domestic institutions for itself. He went so far as to counsel Missourians to declare their independence in case Congress would not let them join the Union with a pro-slavery constitution.

Jefferson also encouraged other Virginians in their campaign against the nationalizing course of the U.S. Supreme Court, headed by his cousin, Chief Justice JOHN MARSHALL. Jefferson and Marshall developed a strong mutual loathing because of their contrary constitutional views. When Spencer Roane, chief judge of Virginia's highest court, wrote incisive newspaper columns criticizing Marshall's poorly reasoned opinion in *MCCULLOCH V. MARYLAND* (1819), Jefferson greeted them with great enthusiasm. He grew increasingly unhappy with the Court's behavior of those years and lamented that the Supreme Court constituted a corps of sappers and miners working stealthily to grind the states into one great, consolidated mass. This vision, of course, stood directly at odds with the vision Jefferson had first developed in *A Summary View* a half-century before.

For more information: Gutzman, Kevin R. Constantine. "Jefferson's Draft DECLARATION OF INDEPENDENCE, Richard Bland, and the Revolutionary Legacy: Giving Credit Where Credit Is Due." *The Journal of the Historical Society* 1 (2001): 137–154; Gutzman, Kevin R. Constantine. "The Virginia and Kentucky Resolutions Reconsidered: 'An Appeal to the *Real Laws* of Our Country.'" *The Journal of Southern History* 66 (2000): 473–496; Mayer, David N. *The Constitutional Thought of Thomas Jefferson.* Charlottesville: University Press of Virginia, 1994.

—Kevin R. C. Gutzman

Johnson v. Transportation Agency of Santa Clara, California 480 U.S. 616 (1987)

In *Johnson v. Transportation Agency of Santa Clara,* the Supreme Court clarified the standard for evaluating voluntary AFFIRMATIVE ACTION plans under Title VII of the CIVIL RIGHTS ACT OF 1964, clearly distinguishing it from the far stricter standard required for such plans to meet constitutional muster under the EQUAL PROTECTION clause.

Paul Johnson was an employee with the Santa Clara County Transportation Agency. In December 1979, the agency announced a vacancy for a road dispatcher, and Johnson applied for the promotion along with 11 other candidates, including co-worker Diane Joyce. Both Johnson and Joyce were deemed well qualified for the position, but ultimately the agency director chose Joyce pursuant to an affirmative action plan (AAP) which the agency had voluntarily adopted the year before. Under the terms of the AAP, the agency was authorized to consider the sex of a qualified applicant as one factor when making promotions to positions within a traditionally segregated job classification in which women had been significantly underrepresented. At the time of Joyce's selection, none of the 238 positions in the relevant Skilled Craft Worker job classification, including that of dispatcher, was occupied by a woman.

Johnson filed suit under Title VII in federal district court; in spite of the fact that the defendant was a public employer, no constitutional challenge was raised. The district court found that Joyce's sex was a determining factor in her promotion and that the AAP was invalid under the requirement articulated in *UNITED STEELWORKERS V. WEBER*, 443 U.S. 193 (1979), that the plan be temporary. The Ninth Circuit reversed, holding, inter alia, that the lack of a specific end date in the AAP was not dispositive in light of the express plan objective of attaining, not maintaining, a labor force that mirrored the local work force. The Supreme Court granted certiorari.

Justice WILLIAM J. BRENNAN, JR., writing for the majority, affirmed the court of appeals's judgment and held that the agency appropriately took Joyce's sex into account as one factor in the promotion decision. Compliance with an affirmative action plan constitutes a nondiscriminatory reason for a gender- or race-conscious promotion, and the burden of proof rests with the challenger to demonstrate that the plan is invalid and, thus, a violation of Title VII. In contrast to the more exacting constitutional standards for evaluating AAP validity, a private employer need only show "a conspicuous imbalance in traditionally segregated job categories" in general, not its own prior discriminatory practices. Thus, under Title VII, employers may take proactive steps in eliminating societal discrimination, rather than merely addressing their own history of job segregation.

The Court found that the county's AAP took into consideration a variety of factors and did not require blind adherence to numerical standards. The plan did not unnecessarily trammel the rights of male employees nor did it constitute an absolute bar to their career advancement. Rather, Johnson had no entitlement to the dispatcher position since the agency director was authorized to promote any of the seven applicants deemed qualified. The plan, although not expressly temporary, adopted a "moderate, gradual approach" to elimination of the work force imbalance, and the explicit goal of attaining, rather than maintaining, balance demonstrates that the plan is not intended to be of indefinite duration. The *Johnson* decision is important for distinguishing between Title VII's goal of eliminating the impact of societal discrimination in employment versus constitutional requirements that suspect classifications such as race or national origin or suspicious classifications such as sex receive heightened judicial scrutiny, even if for remedial purposes. Thus, private employers have far more leeway to engage in voluntary affirmative action efforts than governmental employers.

For more information: Anderson, Terry H. *The Pursuit of Fairness: A History of Affirmative Action.* New York: Oxford University Press, 2005; Urofsky, Melvin. *Affirmative Action on Trial.* Lawrence: University of Kansas Press, 1997.

—Virginia Mellema

judicial review

Judicial review is the power of the Supreme Court of the United States and other federal courts to refuse to enforce federal laws they find contrary to the Constitution. The term is often used more broadly to include the power of federal or state courts to declare unconstitutional any decisions taken by federal or state officials, whether in the form of law or not. Laws or other actions declared unconstitutional are unenforceable in the courts and are generally regarded as void.

The justification for judicial review is usually traced to Chief Justice JOHN MARSHALL's opinion in *MARBURY V. MADISON*, which declared unconstitutional a minor provision of federal law defining the jurisdiction of the Supreme Court. Marshall's most persuasive justifications were based in ARTICLE III OF THE U.S. CONSTITUTION, which provides that "the judicial power shall extend to all cases . . . arising under the Constitution" and the declaration in Article VI that the Constitution "shall be the supreme law of the land." Marshall reasoned that "it is emphatically the province and duty of the judicial department to say what the law is," and therefore if any action of the other branches violates the Constitution, it is "the province and duty" of the judges to uphold the "supreme law of the land" by rejecting that action.

Marshall's justification of judicial review has been strongly criticized throughout the nation's history. The "supreme law of the land" clause refers to federal laws and treaties as well as the Constitution, and it is followed by the phrase that "the judges in every state shall be bound thereby." Critics of judicial review argue that the SUPREMACY CLAUSE was intended only to compel states to follow all forms of federal law by requiring state judges to enforce it, but not to authorize any judges, state or federal, to say whether federal laws are unconstitutional. The framers, they argue, would have explicitly stated a power for appointed judges serving unlimited terms to undo the work of the elected Congress and president if they intended a power of judicial review. In fact, the CONSTITUTIONAL CONVENTION rejected a proposal for a Council of Revision, including judges, to disapprove laws that did not conform to the Constitution.

Neither JAMES MADISON's notes on the Constitutional Convention, the most complete record of those proceedings, nor the correspondence of any of the framers during the Convention or immediately afterward state that the courts shall have authority to strike down federal laws. Later statements by some framers are both for and against judicial review, and many of those statements appear to be dictated by the politics of later times. During the state conventions to ratify the Constitution, only five references to judicial review by members of the Constitutional Convention can be found, and two of them opposed ratification.

Judicial review, critics note, was unknown in England, from which American law was largely derived. Indeed, when the chancellor of England, the highest judicial official, attempted in 1603 in Dr. Bonham's Case to declare an act of Parliament contrary to higher law, he was immediately overruled and was soon replaced by the king. No other case from English judges overrules a law adopted by Parliament. The British Privy Council, a judicial body, did review acts of the legislative assemblies in the American colonies to determine whether they conformed to English law and colonial charters, and one scholar has said the Privy Council vetoed about 5 percent of colonial laws. But those vetoes were heatedly criticized by colonial political leaders, newspapers, and the public, suggesting that judicial review of legislative actions was not widely accepted.

There is also little support for judicial review in the period between the Revolution and the adoption of the Constitution. The Articles of Confederation, which created the first national government, had no judicial branch and therefore no judicial review. Scholars have found only two instances during this period where state supreme courts attempted to strike down state laws, and both cases were met with overwhelming opposition from state legislatures, the press, and the public.

The most important statement in the constitutional period supporting judicial review is found in *Federalist* 78, written by ALEXANDER HAMILTON, a member of the Convention, as part of a series of editorials arguing for RATIFICATION OF THE CONSTITUTION. Hamilton described the "limited Constitution . . . which contains specified exceptions to the legislative authority" that "can be preserved . . . no other way than through the medium of courts of justice, whose duty must be to declare all acts contrary to the manifest tenor of the Constitution void." But Hamilton's own plan in the Constitutional Convention had no provision for judicial review. And Hamilton himself played little role in the Convention, although he was an important figure in the struggle for ratification.

President THOMAS JEFFERSON and his Republican majorities were outraged by the decision in *Marbury.* A year later, they attempted to impeach Federalist Justice Samuel Chase, who narrowly escaped removal by a close vote in the SENATE. John Marshall kept alive the concept of judicial review only by striking down a series of state laws, which could be justified under the Article VI supremacy clause and which found defenders in Congress and the presidency because they enhanced the power of the national government. The Supreme Court did not void another federal law until 1857, in *DRED SCOTT V. SANDFORD,* which struck down the MISSOURI COMPROMISE of 1820 that prohibited slavery in the Louisiana Purchase territory north of Missouri. The hostile reaction in the North was soon overshadowed by ABRAHAM LINCOLN's election in 1860 and the onset of the Civil War, which overturned *Dred Scott*'s approval of slavery.

Despite the disastrous decision in *Dred Scott,* the Supreme Court's judicial review has expanded, with two short exceptions, throughout American history. One study put the number of federal laws struck down by the Supreme Court as 160 through June, 2005. By one scholar's count, the Court considered 116 constitutional challenges to federal statutes from 1865 to 1900 (an average of 3.22 challenges per year) and struck down 21 laws (an annual average of .58). In the period from *Marbury* until the end of the Civil War, the Court had heard only 13 constitutional challenges to federal law and had struck down only two. From 1901 to 1937, the Court reviewed numerous laws regulating economic activities. The Court heard 347 challenges to federal law (9.38 per year) and struck down 57 (1.54 per year). After Franklin Roosevelt's effort in 1937 to pack the Court with new justices, eight justices retired in just four years and were replaced by Roosevelt appointees. Judicial review ebbed for two decades: from 1937 to 1957, the Court heard only 148 cases challenging federal laws (6.73 per year) and struck down only five (.03 per year). However, from 1957 to 2001, the Court returned to an active role, striking down 74 federal laws (1.68 per year, its highest annual rate in history) in 299 (6.8 per year) challenges.

Judicial review has been controversial throughout American history for two distinct reasons. First, the specific policies struck down reflect majority views as expressed by Congress and the president. Second, judicial review itself is countermajoritarian: it substitutes the will of judges who are not elected and who serve indefinite terms for the will of recently elected officials who must regularly stand for reelection. Attorney General Robert H. Jackson, who later served on the Court, characterized judicial review as "the check of a preceding generation on the present one; . . . and nearly always the check of a rejected regime on the one in being."

While defenders of judicial review characterize it as only carrying out the words of the Constitution, its critics point out that the justices often strike down laws under broad constitutional language that does not have clear meaning. Such phrases as "DUE PROCESS of law," "EQUAL PROTECTION of the laws," "commerce . . . among the several states," or "all laws which shall be necessary and proper for carrying into execution" the other provisions of the Constitution allow justices broad latitude to read their own views into the Constitution. Even provisions that appear to be specific leave wide room for interpretation because of changing times and conditions: protections of free speech and press, for example, were written when electronic media and the Internet were unimagined, and prohibitions against "unreasonable searches" did not anticipate interception of electronic communications or technology allowing detection of objects or persons from outside the walls of buildings.

Judicial review is defended as a protection of individual rights. However, by one count, only about a third of the cases striking down federal laws related to due process for individuals, FIRST AMENDMENT freedoms, PRIVACY, or criminal defendants' rights. About 50 percent struck down federal laws defining relations with the states, regulating the economy, or taxation. About 5 percent involved the separation of powers, and 8 percent involved judicial power, issues relating to the respective authority of the branches of the federal government. Another 18 percent may have diminished individual rights by striking down federal laws related to CIVIL RIGHTS. While these categories are not sharply defined, it appears that protection of civil rights and liberties were protected by substantially fewer than half the Supreme Court decisions striking down federal laws.

The countermajoritarian character of judicial review is heightened because Congress and the president have few tools to overturn Court decisions. Constitutional amendments require approval of extraordinary majorities in Congress and among the states: only four have been approved to directly overturn decisions of the Supreme Court. The justices serve indefinite terms, and on average only one vacancy occurs every two years, so that it may take many years to appoint enough new justices to bring the Court into line with the public will. Some presidents have had few opportunities to appoint justices: President Jimmy Carter, for example, appointed none during his four-year term, and President Bill Clinton appointed only two in eight years. Moreover, after appointment, justices' decisions are often at odds with the presidents who appointed them.

Congress can change the size of the Court; and it has done so at least six times for political or policy reasons. But the last change, to nine members, was made in 1869, and that number has apparently become settled in the public mind. After his landslide reelection in 1936, President Franklin Roosevelt sought to reverse the Court's decisions striking down much of his economic program by adding new justices, but that was overwhelmingly opposed by the public and in Congress. Occasional efforts by Congress to prevent judicial review of specific issues by limiting the Court's jurisdiction have been accepted by the justices, but in each case they have warned that they still have jurisdiction under other provisions of law. In short, there are few means to curb the Court, and efforts to do so rarely succeed.

Judicial review is therefore a broad power of appointed judges serving indefinite terms to overturn as unconstitutional decisions of the elected president and Congress. It contradicts the democratic ideal that the public controls the decisions of government through the election of its officials. But judicial review has become an accepted feature of American constitutionalism, because for more than two centuries the people and Congress have acquiesced by not AMENDING THE CONSTITUTION to curb it.

For more information: Bickel, Alexander. *The Least Dangerous Branch.* Indianapolis, Ind.: Bobbs-Merrill, 1962; Bishin, William. "Judicial Review in Democratic Theory." *Southern California Law Review* 50 (1977): 1,099–1,156; Choper, Jesse. *Judicial Review and the National Political Process.* Chicago: University of Chicago Press, 1980; Dahl, Robert H. "Decision-Making in a Democracy: The Supreme Court as a National Policy-Maker." *Journal of Public Law* 6 (1958): 279–295; Keith, Linda Camp. "The United States Supreme Court and Judicial Review of Congress, 1803–2001." *Judicature* 90 (2007): 166–176; Levy, Leonard W. *Judicial Review and the Supreme Court: Selected Essays.* New York: Harper & Row, 1967.

—David Adamany

Judiciary Act of 1789

The Judiciary Act of 1789 established the structure of federal courts in the United States. Judicial power was vested in one Supreme Court (with a chief justice and five associate justices) and 13 district courts. The act stemmed from ARTICLE III OF THE U.S. CONSTITUTION, which vested judicial power in "one Supreme Court, and in such inferior courts as Congress may from time to time ordain and establish." Unlike Article I, which clearly delineates Congress's power, Article III is vague on exactly what judicial power entails, hence the need for further articulation.

The Judiciary Act was at the center of a number of controversies between the states and the federal government in the pre–Civil War era. At issue were the 13th and 25th Sections of the Judiciary Act, both of which provided for federal review of state actions. Article III, Section 2 of the Constitution provides that the judicial power extends to all cases under the Constitution and to "controversies between a state and citizens of another state." Section 13 gave the Supreme Court "exclusive jurisdiction" of all cases of a civil nature, but in cases between a state and citizens of other states, the Supreme Court had original, but not exclusive jurisdiction. The Supreme Court's decision in *CHISHOLM V. GEORGIA*, 2 U.S. 419 (1793), reaffirmed the Court's jurisdiction over disputes between a state and a citizen of another state, irrespective of whether the state was a plaintiff or a defendant in the suit.

Section 13 was also at issue in *MARBURY V. MADISON*, 5 U.S. 137 (1803), a case famous for the establishment of JUDICIAL REVIEW (and VETO) over federal legislation. At issue was whether

William Marbury was entitled to his commission as a justice of the peace. And if so, was the Court obligated under Section 13 to issue a writ of mandamus ordering the delivery of the commission? Chief Justice JOHN MARSHALL answered the first question in the affirmative but ruled the Court could not afford Marbury a remedy, since Section 13 was an unconstitutional interference with the Court's ORIGINAL JURISDICTION set forth in the Constitution.

One of the most controversial sections of the Judiciary Act was Section 25, which provided for review of state supreme court decisions by the U.S. Supreme Court in cases where a federal law or the Constitution was involved. In *MARTIN V. HUNTER'S LESSEE*, 1 Wheaton U.S. 304 (1816) and *COHENS V. VIRGINIA*, 6 Wheaton U.S. 264 (1821), the MARSHALL COURT tried to resolve these questions in favor of the federal courts—both decisions resting on the authority of the Court to hear appeals from state courts—but to no avail.

Section 25 was at the center of a number of divisive battles between the Supreme Court and various state supreme courts. States argued that Article III allowed for federal appellate review of only inferior federal courts, not state courts. The Ohio Supreme Court repeatedly clashed with the Supreme Court on whether state taxation of state-chartered banks violated the CONTRACT CLAUSE of the Constitution. Ohio argued that the Supreme Court had no jurisdiction over the state courts and therefore, any state court decision on the validity of the bank tax should be final. In response, the U.S. Supreme Court not only affirmed the sanctity of the contract clause, but in doing so, affirmed its authority under Section 25 to hear appeals from and reverse the decision of state courts.

In *Craig v. Missouri*, 29 U.S. 410 (1830), the Court invoked its jurisdiction under Section 25 to strike down a Missouri law it felt interfered with the constitutional ban on bills of credit. Section 25 came under immediate attack, as Congress was determined to repeal it and do away once and for all with the Court's jurisdiction over the state courts. This movement to repeal Section 25 also came on the heels of two other federal-state controversies—the NULLIFICATION CONTROVERSY, in which South Carolina claimed it had the right to nullify federal laws, and the Cherokee Indian affair, where the Court clashed with Georgia's claim that it had the right to legislate over the Cherokee Indians. Section 25 was spared, thanks in part to Pennsylvania Representative (and later President of the United States) James Buchanan, who defended Section 25 as essential to the survival of the Union. In *Worcester v. Georgia*, 31 U.S. 515 (1832), John Marshall reasserted the Court's power to review state court decisions under Section 25 and, in doing so, voided all laws passed by Georgia concerning the Cherokee Indians. This, however, did not stop the states from continuing to defy federal judicial authority.

For more information: Marcus, Maeva, ed. *Origins of the Federal Judiciary: Essays on the Judiciary Act of 1789*. New York: Oxford University Press, 1992; Warren, Charles. "Legislative and Judicial Attacks on the Supreme Court of the United States: A History of the Twenty-Fifth Section of the Judiciary Act." *The American Law Review* 47 (1913): 1–47 and 161–189.

—Randa Issa

jurisdiction, power of Congress to control

The U.S. Constitution provides Congress with the power to determine jurisdiction of federal courts that are not provided for constitutionally. It provides original and appellate jurisdictional rules under ARTICLE III, and Congress has several important jurisdictional powers.

In Article III, Section 1, the Constitution states: "In all Cases affecting Ambassadors, other public Ministers and Consuls, and those in which a State shall be Party, the supreme Court shall have ORIGINAL JURISDICTION. In all the other Cases before mentioned, the Supreme Court shall have appellate Jurisdiction, both as to Law and Fact, with such Exceptions, and under such Regulations as the Congress shall make." Under this ordain and establish clause, jurisdictional authority for appellate cases not excepted by Congress are determined as under the regulations provided by Congress.

While the Constitution provides some guaranteed jurisdiction for federal courts under Article III, the federal courts are subject to Congress for the scope of all other jurisdiction. This raises important questions regarding the extent to which Congress can restrict the jurisdiction of federal courts. The Constitution gives Congress some power regarding creating and presumably abolishing federal courts. *MARBURY V. MADISON*, on the other hand, clearly states that the structural principle of the rule of law requires that there be judicial remedies for violation of rights. "The Constitution . . . provides for only the barest minimum of the American judicial system, with all else left for Congress to determine," as noted by constitutional commentator James Burnham.

The ordain and establish clause of Article III, Section 1 also provides Congress with the power for deciding whether to create lower federal courts and the power to determine their jurisdiction. While there are cases that provide relatively broad power for Congress, there are others which show that congressional power is not unlimited.

The JUDICIARY ACT OF 1789 was the first step which Congress took to ordain the lower courts which were prescribed by the Constitution. It was also the basis of the landmark case *Marbury v. Madison*, in which the Supreme Court established the principle of JUDICIAL REVIEW, making the Court the constitutional authority and arbiter in the nation. This case also decided against the provision in the Judiciary Act of 1789 that enlarged the original jurisdiction of the Supreme Court.

Sheldon v. Sill, 49 U.S. (8 How.) 441 (1850) dealt with the power of Congress to decide the jurisdiction of lower courts, specifically the circuit courts. The 11th section of the Judiciary Act kept circuit courts from taking a case "to recover the contents of any promissory note of other chose of action, in favor of an assignee, unless a suit might have been prosecuted in such court to recover the contents, if no assignment had been made, except in cases of foreign bills of exchange." The court found that the Constitution ordained that there be lower courts and defined the Supreme Court's specific jurisdiction while addressing the jurisdiction of the judicial branch as a whole. Thus the Constitution does not specify the jurisdiction of the lower courts, leaving it to Congress to decide.

Similarly, the Court decided in *EX PARTE MCCARDLE*, 74 U.S. (7 Wall.) 506 (1868), that it was well within the power of Congress to direct jurisdiction, where allowed by the Constitution. The Court's APPELLATE JURISDICTION in regard to HABEAS CORPUS was repealed, and the Congress had the power to do so because of their Constitutional authority to grant jurisdiction.

In the ruling in *United States v. Klein*, 80 U.S. (13 Wall.) 128 (1871), the U.S. Supreme Court allowed that Congress's ability to constitutionally govern the judicial branch is limited. After the Civil War, presidential pardons were given to Southerners who took an oath of allegiance. One V. F. Wilson did so, and upon his death, the administrator of his estate, Klein, applied to have the proceeds from the sale of Wilson's effects given back to the estate. Congress then passed a law denying such proceeds to be given to those who had accepted the presidential pardon, the acceptance being an admission of guilt. The Court found that Congress had overstepped its bounds in the area of judicial independence and in the executive's ability to grant pardons. Congress could not give and remove power in the courts to affect the outcome that it would see as best for the government. Likewise, the Congress has no power to stipulate the effect of the presidential pardon, which is under the purview of the executive branch. The presidential pardon is both a pardon and amnesty, and to assign an admission of guilt to the acceptance of such a pardon shrinks the power of the executive branch given in the Constitution.

Though Congress possesses constitutional powers with regard to jurisdictional determination and regulation, the U.S. common law tradition and judicial precedents have provided federal courts delimitation in the scope of congressional jurisdictional prerogatives.

For more information: Bloom, Allan, ed. *Confronting the Constitution*. Washington, D.C.: AEI Press, 1990; Burnham, James. *Congress and the American Tradition*. Washington, D.C.: Regnery Publishing, 1996; Marbach, Joseph R., Ellis Katz, and Troy E. Smith, eds. *Federalism in America*. Westport, Conn.: Greenwood Publishing, 2005; Wood, Gordon. *The Creation of the American Republic 1776–1787*. New York: W.W. Norton & Co., 1969.

—Aaron Jones and Michael W. Hail

just compensation

The Fifth Amendment to U.S. Constitution guarantees that private property shall not be "taken for public use, without just compensation." Known as the just compensation clause, the amendment recognizes the federal government's authority to seize property under EMINENT DOMAIN, but the property owner has a constitutional right to be compensated for the loss. The purpose of the just compensation clause is to ensure that individual property owners do not suffer financial harm when the government seizes land for a public use.

The principle of just compensation derives from early 15th-century English law. Many American colonial governments, however, did not follow the practice of paying for the taking of land for a public purpose, and none of the first state constitutions after independence contained a just compensation requirement. Legislative supremacy to seize land for roads and other public purposes soon gave way to more protection for property rights. A just compensation clause was adopted for the Vermont Constitution in 1777 and the Massachusetts Constitution in 1780, and the Northwest Ordinance of 1787 contained a provision requiring compensation for a governmental taking of private property. Today, most state constitutions contain language similar to the Fifth Amendment. In *Chicago, Burlington, and Quincy Railroad Company v. Chicago*, 166 U.S. 226 (1897), the U.S. Supreme Court ruled that the just compensation requirement was binding not only upon the federal government but also upon state and local governments.

Ordinarily, the government first attempts to buy land from the owners. If the government is unable to negotiate a sale, the government may assert the power of eminent domain and seize the property, offering the owners what it deems to be a fair price. In some cases, the property owners find the compensation inadequate and the amount is contested in court. In *Kirby Forest Industries, Inc. v. United States*, 467 U.S. 1 (1984), the Supreme Court decided that the Fifth Amendment required that the owner be paid a fair market value for property taken. Fair market value is determined by the courts, and the amount is based on the value of the property at the time of the taking. Fair market value is the sum that a willing buyer would pay a willing seller in the open market. No precise formula exists, however, by which the elements of just compensation can be calculated, and there is much debate over what should be considered in the valuation of the property.

The Supreme Court has provided some guidelines as to what factors should be considered in determining fair market value. For example, the sentimental value of the property to the owner is not a factor in calculating fair market value. The owner has a right to recover the monetary equivalent of the property taken and is entitled to be put in as good a financial position as he or she would have been in if the property had not been taken. Fair market value does not have to be based on the current use of the property if the land has other potential uses, but the Court has said that property owners need not be compensated for future uses that are considered speculative. In some situations, the owner is entitled to additional compensation for severance damages. In *United States v. Miller*, 317 U.S. 369 (1943), the Court held that if the government takes a portion of a larger piece of property and the taking reduces the value of the land retained by the owner, the calculation of just compensation will include the "severance damage" resulting from the taking. Conversely, if a taking increases the property value of land retained by the owner, the value of the offsetting benefits may be deducted from the amount owed the landowner.

Temporary takings of land do not always require compensation. In *Tahoe-Sierra Preservation Council, Inc. v. Tahoe Regional Planning Agency*, 535 U.S. 302 (2002), the Supreme Court examined the issue of whether a 32-month ban on all real estate construction around Lake Tahoe required the government to pay compensation to the land owners. In a 6-3 opinion delivered by Justice JOHN PAUL STEVENS, the Court held that the development moratorium did not constitute a taking of the landowners' property. The Court concluded that the adoption of a categorical rule that any deprivation of all economic use, no matter how brief, constituted a compensable taking would impose unreasonable financial obligations upon governments.

For more information: Mercuro, Nicholas. *Taking Property and Just Compensation.* Boston: Kluwer, 1992; Treanor, William Michael. "The Origins and Original Significance of the Just Compensation Clause of the Fifth Amendment." *The Yale Law Journal* 94, no. 3 (1985): 694–716.

—John Fliter

justiciability

Justiciability refers to the question of whether or not a case presented to a court is capable of judicial resolution. In other words, federal courts do not necessarily have the authority, or jurisdiction, to decide every case presented to them, since limits are placed on their power by the U.S. Constitution. Article III, Section 2 of the Constitution permits federal courts to render judgments only on real "cases" and "controversies." The Constitution, however, does not clearly define these terms, and therefore, it has been left up to federal judges to define them.

Over the course of history, United States Supreme Court justices have developed guidelines for determining if a case is justiciable. When determining the justiciability of a constitutional issue, judges must first decide if the case exhibits adverseness. They also must determine if the parties in the case have STANDING to bring suit. Finally, judges must make sure that the constitutional issue in the case is ripe and is neither moot nor a political question.

Adverseness requires that the two parties involved in the dispute are seeking opposing outcomes. Moreover, adverseness prohibits the Court from deciding hypothetical or abstract questions that do not arise out of an actual dispute.

The standing requirement demands that the parties in the case be personally injured and have a personal stake in the outcome. In other words, if a person believes that an existing law violates the Constitution, he or she cannot bring the case to a federal court unless he or she has personally been affected by the law he or she wishes to challenge.

The timing for when a case is brought to the Court also is important in determining if judges can rule on the issue. If a case is brought to the Court too early, it will be dismissed for not being ripe. Typically, RIPENESS problems occur when either the individual in the case has not yet been injured by the law he or she is challenging or when the case has not gone through the proper appellate process. On the other hand, if a case is brought to the Court too late, it will be considered moot. Problems of mootness arise when the constitutional issue challenged in the case has already been resolved or no longer exists.

Finally, a case may be deemed incapable of judicial resolution because of its subject matter. Federal courts can rule only on constitutional questions that are of a legal nature and are forbidden from ruling on political questions. Separation of powers requires political questions to be decided by the elected branches of government.

However, the Court explained in *BAKER V. CARR*, 369 U.S. 186 (1962), that seeking protection of a political right does not necessarily mean the issue presents a political question. Courts can still rule on political rights as long as the issue also is a violation of an individual's legal right. While the ruling in *Baker* expanded the Court's ability to decide more constitutional questions, Justice WILLIAM J. BRENNAN, JR., nevertheless, reiterated that certain issues exist that should never be decided by the federal judiciary. For example, the Court should not decide "when and whether a war has ended" nor should it decide whether American Indian tribes should be recognized by the United States. Likewise, the Court should not interfere with the formalities of the legislative process, such as how long a proposed amendment to the Constitution should be open for ratification. Finally, the Court should not determine if a "republican form of government" is being guaranteed to citizens as the Constitution requires under Article IV, Section 4.

In sum, the Court has decided that cases and controversies that do not meet the above requirements should not be decided by federal judges, and thus, are considered nonjusticiable. However, the biggest criticism of these justiciability requirements is that they are self-defined and self-imposed limitations. Hence, while the requirement of justiciability is designed to constrain the powers of the courts, the courts are asked to police themselves on this issue.

For more information: O'Brien, David M. *Storm Center: The Supreme Court in American Politics.* 7th ed. New York: W.W. Norton, 2005; Strum, Philippa. *The Supreme Court and 'Political Questions': A Study in Judicial Evaluation.* Birmingham: University of Alabama Press, 1974.

—Francene M. Engel

Kansas-Nebraska Act

The Kansas-Nebraska Act, officially An Act to Organize the Territories of Nebraska and Kansas, is as its title suggests a set of congressionally approved conditions under which two Plains Territories might move from being part of "Indian Country," organize, write their own constitutions, elect state and federal officials, and enter the union as full-fledged states. It was signed into law by President Franklin Pierce in May of 1854. These were the last two areas of the original Louisiana Purchase to make the transition from territory to statehood.

The circumstances of, and the consequences that followed, the passage of this bill make the Kansas-Nebraska Act a landmark piece of legislation. It tore the nation apart and set the stage for the American Civil War.

With Kansas-Nebraska, a series of delicate compromises that for more than five decades had been fashioned between free states and slave states suddenly came crashing to an end. Specifically repealed was the MISSOURI COMPROMISE of 1820 that had barred slavery from most of the Louisiana Purchase Territory. That ban was replaced with the notion of popular sovereignty, mandating self-determination on whether a territory would enter the Union slave or free, based on a plebiscite of its citizens.

Manifest Destiny—westward expansion, and the gradual settlement of territories beyond the Appalachians that flourished in the land of the Louisiana Purchase (1803)—had been a bright and shining beacon of American development in the early 1800s. However glorious, this movement carried with it an unstated and far more ambiguous question. Would these newly settled lands welcome or exclude slavery? Every new acquisition—from the Northwest Territory to the Louisiana Purchase to that received at the conclusion of the Mexican War—renewed the tension between the North and the South that the Three-Fifths Compromise at the CONSTITUTIONAL CONVENTION had set in motion. Throughout its early years, deals had been struck that balanced slave state interests with those of free states. Former territories were allowed to enter the Union only in tandem: one slave, one free. Thus, when Kansas and Nebraska were organized, southerners in Congress refused to allow their entry unless the slavery question was altered to permit slavery's expansion into an area where formerly it had been excluded.

The Kansas-Nebraska Act ignited a firestorm of chaos in the state of Kansas and political fireworks throughout the nation. In Kansas, two separate legislatures met to write two competing constitutions. Each represented a different set of settlers: those who desired a free state and those who wanted one where slavery could exist. Bands of ruffians and thugs took up arms and began a guerrilla war over the controversy. With its assassinations, ambushes, and raids, "Bleeding Kansas," as it was popularly known, represents the first shooting battleground of the Civil War.

Beyond Kansas itself, which was eventually pacified and entered the Union as a free state in 1861, the Kansas-Nebraska Act destroyed long-held party loyalties. The explicit abrogation of the Missouri Compromise that Kansas-Nebraska proposed radically altered a tenuously balanced political landscape in the United States. An ailing and weak Whig political party collapsed. Democrats split into northern and southern factions. A completely new party, the Republicans, was born and quickly attracted former Whigs, Free-Soilers, Abolitionists, Know-Nothings, and others who were "anti-Nebraska men." This dramatic party realignment set the stage for the presidential election of 1860, southern secession, and the beginnings of the full-fledged Civil War in 1861.

Democrat Steven A. Douglas, the senior senator from Illinois, is credited as the author of Kansas-Nebraska. As chairman of the Senate Territories Committee, he was instrumental in pushing it through Congress, in approving its controversial provisions, and in allying himself with its overall principles. Historians and scholars have debated Douglas's motives for sponsoring a bill so controversial as this, but their complexity and interrelatedness mirrored the national tensions and competing agendas of the mid-1850s. Douglas, a well-known northern Democrat with presidential aspirations, recognized he had to strengthen his credentials with southerners in order to fashion a credible candidacy for the 1856 or 1860 nomination. Repealing the Missouri Compromise restrictions on slavery achieved this. A transcontinental railroad in the United States was becoming a likely possibility, and the central route, one that would have Chicago serve as the primary midwestern hub, as opposed to a more southerly site, was from Douglas's perspective a very desirable public works project. In order to have this to succeed, however, it was necessary for Nebraska to be organized and on its way to statehood. Further, Douglas believed citizens should determine the political landscape in which they lived and felt that the Compromise of 1850 that first enshrined "popular sovereignty" after the Mexican War had superseded the slavery ban of the Missouri Compromise, and would, if applied to Kansas and Nebraska, avoid a constitutional crisis.

In an opposing microcosm, Kansas-Nebraska was an outrage for ABRAHAM LINCOLN. His abandonment of the lack-luster Whig Party and his decision to challenge Douglas in the 1858 SENATE campaign in Illinois as a newly-minted Republican (the one that generated the Lincoln-Douglas debates) gave evidence of emerging Republican cohesion on limiting the extension of slavery into the territories and a clear theme against Democrats. The bill suffused Lincoln's "House Divided" speech with galvanizing metaphors of the "timbers" (one of which was this act) being secretly put in place by Democrats: Douglas, the last two Democratic presidents and, in the aftermath of the *Dred Scott* decision, the chief justice of the Supreme Court.

The Kansas-Nebraska Act, whatever its objectives during its debate and passage through Congress, is a wonderful example of unintended consequences. The United States was a far different country after Kansas-Nebraska than before it. It may be simplistic to say, but without something like the novel *Uncle Tom's Cabin*, the *Dred Scott* decision, and the Kansas-Nebraska Act, the defining events of the 1860s in the United States might have turned out very differently.

Americans on the losing side of this act recognized that the issues of slavery, citizenship and CIVIL RIGHTS ultimately could never be guaranteed without explicit constitutional protections. They formed the core group that championed those goals. At the end of the Civil War, in a burst of amending energy unique in American history, they spearheaded the passage of the THIRTEENTH, FOURTEENTH, and FIFTEENTH AMENDMENTS. Their persistence and clarity in the face of adversity thus led to dramatically changing the Constitution and forever altering the nature of government in the United States.

For more information: Foner, Eric. *Free Soil, Free Labor, Free Men: The Ideology of the Republican Party Before the Civil War.* New York: Oxford University Press, 1970; Goodwin, Doris Kearns. *Team of Rivals: The Political Genius of Abraham Lincoln.* New York: Simon & Schuster, 2005.

—George Peery

Katzenbach v. McClung 379 U.S. 294 (1964)

In *Katzenbach v. McClung*, the Supreme Court ruled that Congress had the authority under the COMMERCE CLAUSE to regulate discrimination in a local restaurant.

The passage of the 1964 CIVIL RIGHTS ACT was supposed to remedy discrimination. Previous efforts by Congress to remedy discrimination in commercial establishments had been invalidated by the Supreme Court. Most notably, the Court had declared unconstitutional in the *CIVIL RIGHTS CASES*, 109 U.S. 3 (1883), the Civil Rights Act of 1875 which banned discrimination in inns and other public accommodations. Given this decision and pre–New Deal Court decisions restricting the scope of Congress's commerce power, there were some who questioned whether the 1964 act was constitutional. The owner of a restaurant that has since been closed refused to serve persons of color in Birmingham, Alabama. This violation was in direct affront to Title II of the Civil Rights Act of 1964.

The restaurant was owned by Ollie McClung and named Ollie's Barbecue. It was traditionally Southern in its offerings, in that they served barbecued style meals and pies. The large size of the restaurant, which staffed almost 40 and sat almost 250, allowed it to reasonably serve many patrons at once at a location that was more than a mile away from an interstate and even farther from train stations. However, the owner refused to seat African Americans.

Justice Clark delivered the opinion of the Court. The Supreme Court found that the discrimination in restaurants posed significant burdens on "the interstate flow of food and upon the movement on products generally" to such a degree that although not horribly material in impact, the discrimination furthered a restriction upon blacks, thereby restricting their interstate travel and freedom of movement.

Katzenbach, along with the *HEART OF ATLANTA V. UNITED STATES*, 379 U.S. 241 (1964), affirmed the power of Congress under the commerce clause to regulate discrimination. These two cases were thus important constitutional victories of opponents of discrimination during the Civil Rights movement of the 1960s.

For more information: Schwartz, Bernard. *A History of the Supreme Court.* New York: Oxford University Press, 1993.

—Ernest Gomez and David Schultz

Kelo v. City of New London 545 U.S. 469 (2005)

In *Kelo v. City of New London*, the U.S. Supreme Court affirmed a decision of the Connecticut Supreme Court that held that the taking of private property for economic development purposes constituted a valid public use under both the state and federal constitutions. The *Kelo* decision was seen by many as a significant erosion of property rights, and it resulted in many state and local governments' restricting the power of EMINENT DOMAIN.

At issue in *Kelo* was an attempt by the City of New London, a municipal corporation, and the New London Development Corporation, to use a state law to take unblighted land to build and support economic revitalization of the city's downtown. In its plan, New London divided the development into seven parcels, with some of these parcels including public waterways or museums. However, one parcel, known as Lot 3, would be a 90,000 square feet high technology research and development office space and parking facility for the Pfizer Pharmaceutical Company. Several plaintiffs in Lot 3 challenged the taking of their property, claiming that the condemnation of unblighted land for economic development purposes violated both the state and federal constitutions.

They argued that the taking of private property under Chapter 132 and the handing it over to another private party did not constitute a valid public use, or at least the public benefit was incidental to the private benefits generated. The Connecticut Supreme Court rejected their claims under both the state and federal constitutions, and the U.S. Supreme Court granted certiorari to the federal question of whether the taking of private property for economic development purposes, when it involved the transferring of the land from one private owner to another, constituted a valid public use under the Fifth and FOURTEENTH AMENDMENTS. Writing for a divided Court, Justice JOHN PAUL STEVENS ruled that the taking did not violate the public use requirement of the Fifth Amendment.

In reaching his holding, Stevens first noted how the case pitted two propositions against one another—"the sovereign may not take the property of *A* for the sole purpose of transferring it to another private party *B*, even though *A* is paid JUST COMPENSATION. On the other hand, it is equally clear that a State may transfer property from one private party to another if future 'use by the public' is the purpose of the taking; the condemnation of land for a railroad with common-carrier duties is a familiar example." However, he contended that neither of these rules resolved the case. Instead, drawing upon past precedents, Stevens first reaffirmed the proposition that a taking for a purely private benefit would be unconstitutional. But in this case, this was not a private taking, because the decision to acquire the property was part of a "'carefully considered' development plan" that revealed that neither the real nor hidden motive was to convey a private benefit.

Second, the Court rejected arguments that because the property would eventually be used and transferred to a private party it failed the public use requirement because the land would not be used by the public. Here Stevens stated that the "Court long ago rejected any literal requirement that condemned property be put into use for the general public" and that instead this narrow reading of public use had been rejected in favor of a broader public purpose reading of the public use doctrine. Thus, as Stevens defined the issue, the case turned on whether the taking served a valid public purpose, and he ruled that the Court should adhere to the long established judicial tradition of deferring to legislative determinations on this matter, as evidenced by its decisions in *Berman v. Parker*, 348 U.S. 26 (1956), and *HAWAII HOUSING AUTHORITY V. MIDKIFF*, 467 U.S. 229 (1984). Given the broad and flexible meaning attached to the public use stipulation and past judicial deference to legislative determinations of what is considered a public purpose (use), Stevens and the majority concluded that the taking of private property for economic development purposes was a valid public use.

Finally, Stevens rejected arguments that the Court carve out an economic development exception to the broad public use doctrine that it had created. He rejected this new rule as unworkable, stating it would be impossible principally to distinguish economic development from other valid public purposes. He also rejected assertions that the taking for economic development purposes blurred the distinction between a public and a private taking.

In many ways, *Kelo* really did not make new law in terms of taking private property for economic development purposes. As Stevens pointed out, the city could not take private property for a private benefit for a private party. He also noted that the more narrow conception of public use had long since been abandoned, and governments have long had the power to take property for a variety of public welfare purposes, including economic development. *Kelo* really simply reaffirmed a trend that already existed in the law. Overall, *Kelo* seemed to cap a recent line of jurisprudence, giving governments broad authority to take private property, even for economic development purposes.

Concurring, Justice ANTHONY M. KENNEDY argued that he agreed that so long as a taking was rationally related to a public purpose, it should be upheld, whether it is condemnation for economic development purposes or not. However, he also contended that "a rational-basis standard of review is appropriate does not, however, alter the fact that transfers intended to confer benefits on particular, favored private entities, and with only incidental or pretextual public benefits, are forbidden by the Public Use Clause." Kennedy noted how pretextual takings which really are meant to benefit a private party have long been forbidden and that in situations involving these types of takings—especially those involving a transfer of property from one private individual to another—a more heightened standard of review might be needed. However, because the trial judge in this case did not find that the taking was primarily for a primary benefit, the heightened scrutiny was not required.

Dissenting, Justice SANDRA DAY O'CONNOR, joined by Justices WILLIAM HUBBS REHNQUIST, ANTONIN GREGORY SCALIA, and CLARENCE THOMAS, acknowledged that there are three situations when the Court has upheld the taking of private property under a broad public use doctrine. The first is when this property is transferred to public ownership to construct a hospital, road, or military base. Second, transfers of private property to another private owner are permitted when common carriers such as railroads take possession because ultimately the public does get to use the property.

O'Connor also identifies a third category of takings, when property is being used in a harmful manner, as being sanctioned by the Court as a valid public use. In reaching this claim, O'Connor examines both *Berman* and her opinion in *Midkiff*, arguing that in the former blight and in the latter concentrated ownership skewing the real estate market were the bads that the legislatures were seeking to abate and which the Court was willing to affirm. O'Connor did not see the New London condemnation as one seeking to alleviate some bad that the Kelo property was inflicting on others. Instead, the Court argued that what the majority opinion had done was to move "from our decisions sanctioning the condemnation of harmful property use, the Court today significantly expands the meaning of public use." Hence, because the taking of the Kelo property did not fit into one of these three categories, it should not be permitted.

O'Connor's dissent is notable for a couple of other points. First, she does acknowledge the broad deference that generally should be given to legislatures when it comes to making public use decisions. Second, notably absent from her opinion is a clear indication that she wished to increase the level of scrutiny for public use decisions. Granted that O'Connor would carve out three types of takings as permitted public uses, while excluding others, nowhere does her opinion really suggest heightened scrutiny of legislative motives.

The lone justice willing to move toward offering property more substantive protection was Thomas. In his solo dissent, he argued for a return to the original meaning of the public use clause. For Thomas, public use is not the same as public welfare or purpose, and property may be taken only to further an expressly enumerated power. Singularly among the justices, he would not afford deference to legislatures to define what is a public use; contrary to what the Court has previously held, *Berman* and *Midkiff* are wrong, and the Constitution imposes a substantive limit on the power of the government to take private property.

As a result of the *Kelo* decision, many of its critics worried that property rights were no longer adequately protected from a government taking. Many state and local governments thus adopted legislation that either banned or made it more difficult to take private property for economic development purposes.

For more information: Schultz, David. "What's Yours Can Be Mine: Are There Any Private Takings After *City of New London v. Kelo*?" *UCLA Journal of Environmental Law and Policy* 24 (2006): 195–234.

—David Schultz

Kennedy, Anthony M. (1936–) *Supreme Court justice*

Anthony M. Kennedy has served as an associate justice of the Supreme Court since his nomination by President Ronald Reagan in 1988. With the recent retirement of Justice Sandra Day O'Connor, Kennedy is now the Court's lone swing voter in many controversial cases. This position has given him great power to shape the Court's decisions in key areas of constitutional jurisprudence.

Kennedy, the second of three children, was born in Sacramento, California, on July 23, 1936. His father was a lobbyist with a reputation for influence in the California legislature, and his mother was involved in various civic activities. In 1958, Kennedy graduated Phi Beta Kappa from Stanford University with a B.A. in Political Science. He then enrolled in Harvard Law School, where he graduated cum laude in 1961.

After Harvard, Kennedy went to work as an associate for a law firm in San Francisco. Then, with the unexpected death of his father in 1963, he returned to Sacramento to take over his father's practice. That same year Kennedy wed Mary Davis, whom he had known for many years.

Together they would have three children. Kennedy continued to run his father's practice until 1975, when President Gerald Ford appointed him to the Court of Appeals for the Ninth Circuit.

On June 26, 1987, Justice LEWIS POWELL announced his retirement from the Supreme Court. President Reagan's first nominee was ROBERT BORK, a judge on the court of appeals for the DISTRICT OF COLUMBIA circuit. Bork was met with fierce opposition in the SENATE for his conservative views and ultimately failed to win confirmation. Next Reagan nominated Douglas Ginsburg, also from the D.C. circuit. Ginsburg soon withdrew himself from consideration, however, amid allegations of substantial prior marijuana use. Finally, Reagan turned to Kennedy to fill the vacancy. He was confirmed unanimously by the Senate on February 3, 1988, and he took his seat 15 days later.

Kennedy's voting pattern is a blend of mostly pragmatic-conservativism coupled with a strong libertarian streak. In some areas, such as criminal procedure and AFFIRMATIVE ACTION, he has usually voted with the conservative bloc. For example, Kennedy provided the critical fifth vote in *Hudson v. Michigan,* 547 U.S. 586 (2006), a case which held that a "violation of the 'knock-and-announce' rule does not require suppression of evidence found in a search."

In other areas, Kennedy has frustrated many conservatives. He has generally been protective of free speech. In *TEXAS V. JOHNSON,* 491 U.S. 394 (1989), Kennedy voted with the majority to strike down flag desecration laws. Later, in *MADSEN V. WOMEN'S HEALTH CENTER, INC.*, 512 U.S. 753 (1994), and *Hill v. Colorado,* 530 U.S. 703 (2000), Kennedy dissented from the majority's opinion that states could prohibit "unpopular speech" of protesters outside ABORTION clinics. However, Kennedy's support of free speech is not without its limits. In *Garcetti v. Ceballos,* 547 U.S. 410 (2006), Kennedy wrote the majority opinion which held that the FIRST AMENDMENT does not protect public employees from being disciplined for speech made pursuant to their professional duties.

One of the cases which has caused Kennedy to incur great ire from conservatives is *LAWRENCE V. TEXAS,* 539 U.S. 558 (2003). Kennedy, writing for the majority, held that laws prohibiting homosexual sodomy were unconstitutional. This decision reversed the precedent set in *BOWERS V. HARDWICK,* 478 U.S. 186 (1986). In doing so, he emphatically noted, "*Bowers* was not correct when it was decided, and it is not correct today. It ought not to remain binding precedent. *Bowers v. Hardwick* should be and now is overruled." If the outcome were not enough of an outrage to critics, Kennedy cited foreign cases in support of his decision. This practice, widely done outside the United States, has been criticized by some, particularly in Congress.

Another contentious issue for Kennedy is the death penalty. In the case of *ATKINS V. VIRGINIA,* 536 U.S. 304 (2002), Kennedy voted with the majority to rule executions of the mentally handicapped unconstitutional. Then, in *Roper v. Simmons,* 543 U.S. 551 (2005), Kennedy, writing for the majority, ruled that minors are not eligible to be executed. In *Roper,* as in *Lawrence,* Kennedy quoted cases from other countries, much to the chagrin of many in his party.

Kennedy's abortion jurisprudence has been very nuanced. Kennedy was one of the authors of the plurality decision in *Planned Parenthood v. Casey,* 505 U.S. 833 (1992). In this case, the Court upheld a constitutional right to an abortion but did allow states to pass certain restrictions as long as they did not create an "undue burden." In contrast, Kennedy dissented from the Court's opinion in *Sternberg v. Carhart,* 530 U.S. 914 (2000), where the Court had struck down laws banning late-term abortions.

Particularly since O'Connor's departure, Kennedy can be seen as trying to build consensus whenever possible. For example, in *LEAGUE OF UNITED LATIN AMERICAN CITIZENS V. PERRY,* 548 U.S. 399 (2006), Kennedy wrote a majority opinion, which held that Texas's redistricting plan of 2003 was not unconstitutional but that District 23 must be redrawn to comply with the VOTING RIGHTS ACT OF 1965. At least in part, each justice either joined the opinion or filed a concurrence.

Although when nominated he was seen as a solid vote for the conservative bloc, Kennedy has often frustrated many conservatives. Justices Kennedy and O'Connor had served as a moderating force on the Court for over 15 years. Now with O'Connor's departure, Kennedy is the lone swing justice. This gives him great opportunity to shape the Court's decision and thus the law of the land.

For more information: Simon, James F. *The Center Holds: The Power Struggle Inside the Rehnquist Court.* New York: Simon and Schuster, 1995; Yarbrough, Tinsley. *The Rehnquist Court and the Constitution.* New York: Oxford University Press, 2000.

—Raymond V. Carman, Jr.

Kent, James (1763–1847) *American jurist and legal scholar*

James Kent, one of the first American constitutional scholars of note, was born on July 31, 1763, in Fredericksburgh, Connecticut, the eldest of seven children of Elisha and Abigail Kent. Although of military age during part of the conflict, Kent played no role in the Revolution. In 1781, he graduated from Yale University. Kent sought to establish a legal practice but struggled in poverty for years.

As the new nation debated the new Constitution, Kent placed himself strongly on the side of the Federalists. A conservative, he expected government to vigorously protect property rights and to guard against the excesses of the masses. Kent's political connections eventually helped him acquire a professorship of law at Columbia University in 1794. Dissatisfied with the lackluster reception of his lectures, Kent resigned in 1797. By this time, he had been elected to the New York Assembly and then received an appointment as Master in Chancery in 1796. While continuing his lucrative chancery position, Kent became the recorder of New York City in 1797. The position, the most distinguished in the state judicial system below a judgeship in the supreme court, brought the leading attorneys in the state before Kent. As a result, his legal reputation grew. In 1798, Kent joined the New York Supreme Court. He became chief justice in 1804 and remained on this bench until 1814. More frequently than any of his colleagues, Kent delivered the opinions of the court. His opinions were written out and filled with citations, a practice that the other justices eventually adopted. The opinions, at Kent's urging, were recorded and occasionally published for the benefit of the bar in New York and other states. Kent soon acquired a national reputation.

Kent, as one of the first American justices, played a critical role in the development of the American legal system. Like his peers, he struggled with the issue of whether the law should emphasize English tradition or American originality. Along with his Federalist peers, Kent favored English law. Kent found that the Constitution gave Congress the power to regulate commerce and that the states had a similar right. As long as Congress did not enter a field, the state is free to act. Further, since English common law permitted monopolies, the state of New York possessed the power to permit monopolies.

In 1814, Kent became chancellor of New York. In this position, he not only respected English legal decisions handed down before the Revolution, but those issued after independence. Kent warned against the dangers of universal suffrage as tending to jeopardize the rights of property and the principles of liberty. Upon reaching the mandatory retirement age of 60, Kent resigned as chancellor. After teaching again at Columbia, he died in New York City on December 12, 1847.

For more information: Horton, John Theodore. *James Kent: A Study in Conservatism.* New York: D. Appleton Century, 1939.

—Caryn E. Neumann

Kimel v. Florida Board of Regents 528 U.S. 62 (2000)

In *Kimel v. Florida Board of Regents,* the U.S. Supreme Court ruled that the ELEVENTH AMENDMENT shields states from having to pay damages in suits brought under the Age Discrimination in Employment Act (ADEA).

The ADEA, ratified in 1798, bars federal court judges from enforcing certain kinds of lawsuits against states. Congress's power to abrogate, that is, revoke, a state's Eleventh Amendment immunity is derived from its authority to enact legislation under Section 5 of the FOURTEENTH AMENDMENT. For over a decade, the Supreme Court has construed it to declare states immune from money damages in lawsuits brought against them for violating laws related to unfair labor practices, EMPLOYMENT DISCRIMINATION, patent protection, and unfair trade practices.

The ADEA, enacted in 1967 under Congress's authority to regulate INTERSTATE COMMERCE, prohibits discrimination in employment on the basis of age. Initially limited to private employees, it was amended in 1974 to include state employees. However, although it is likely that in amending the statute, Congress intended to allow suits against states for money damages in federal court, the law did not specify that Congress abrogated the state's Eleventh Amendment immunity. In 1994, on behalf of a group of faculty members and librarians, plaintiffs J. Daniel Kimel and Roderick MacPherson filed suit against the state university systems of Florida and Alabama for age discrimination, claiming they were denied pay increases and promotions. Wellington Dickson, a prison guard, sued the Florida Department of Corrections, alleging discrimination on the basis of age and disability. The states sought to dismiss the monetary claims, citing their immunity under the Eleventh Amendment. The lower courts were divided, and on appeal, the Eleventh Circuit ruled in favor of the states.

When the case reached the Supreme Court, the outcome of the case depended on two factors: first, whether Congress intended to allow age discrimination suits against states for money damages; and second, whether its authority to do so, derived from its power to enforce the equal rights provisions of the Fourteenth Amendment, was sufficient. Writing for a majority seven justices, Justice SANDRA DAY O'CONNOR determined that Congress clearly intended to allow individuals to sue states for money damages. In addressing the second issue, O'Connor now spoke for five justices. She conceded that Congress had broad authority to legislate under Section 5 of the Fourteenth Amendment, but such legislation must not exceed the bounds of the Fourteenth Amendment's guarantee of equality. She concluded that although the Fourteenth Amendment allows states to pass laws related to age as long as they are rational, the ADEA punishes states even when they act rationally. Moreover, because there was insufficient evidence to show that states were guilty of age discrimination in employment, the ADEA was a disproportionate remedy and exceeded the bounds of Congress's authority under the Fourteenth Amendment.

With its broad interpretation of the protection offered states by the Eleventh Amendment, *Kimel* reinforced state sovereignty at the expense of Congress's authority to guarantee equal rights under the Fourteenth Amendment.

For more information: Brown, Charles. "Congressional Abrogation of Eleventh Amendment Immunity by Passing the ADEA and the ADA." *Baylor Law Review* 51 (1999): 340–372; Durham, Lisa M. "Protection from Age Discrimination for State Employees: Abrogation of Eleventh Amendment Sovereign Immunity in the Age Discrimination in Employment Act." *Georgia Law Review* 33 (1999): 541–601.

—Susan Gluck Mezey

Korematsu v. United States 323 U.S. 214 (1944)

In *Korematsu v. United States,* the Supreme Court upheld the relocation of over 120,000 Japanese Americans to camps during World War II. This case questioned the extent of the powers of the executive and the legislative branches.

After the surprise attack on Pearl Harbor on December 7, 1941, and the entrance of the United States into World War II with a declaration of war, the president and Congress took action to prevent espionage and enhance national security. These actions forced many Americans, about 120,000, to leave their homes and move to an internment camp for the remainder of the war.

President Franklin D. Roosevelt issued Executive Order 9066, and Congress created statutes

This 1942 photograph shows the Mochida family awaiting the evacuation bus to an internment camp. *(National Archives)*

that allowed the military to exclude Japanese-American citizens from areas deemed critical to national defense during World War II. Japanese-American citizens were forced to leave their homes on the West Coast and move to relocation camps. Fred Korematsu refused to leave his home in San Leandro, California, and was arrested and convicted for violating Civilian Exclusion Order No. 34. He appealed his conviction to the circuit court of appeals, who confirmed his conviction. Then, he appealed to the Supreme Court, questioning whether the president and Congress went too far in restricting the rights of American citizens of Japanese descent.

By the time of Fred Korematsu's appeal, the Supreme Court had heard many cases relating to the internment camps and the power of the government to detain citizens in a time of war. *Yasui v. United States,* 30 U.S. 115 (1943), and *Hirabayashi v. United States,* 320 United States 81 (1943), held that it was constitutional to impose curfews based on a person's ancestry.

The Supreme Court upheld Korematsu's conviction and sided with the government in a 6-3 decision. The opinion of the court was written by Justice HUGO BLACK and joined by Chief Justice Harlan Fiske Stone, Justice Stanley Reed, Justice WILLIAM O. DOUGLAS, Justice Wiley Rutledge, and Justice Felix Frankfurter. The Court found that the need to protect the national security of the country during a time of war and protect against espionage outweighed the individual rights and liberties of Korematsu and American citizens of Japanese descent, though the Court did acknowledge the hardships and racial discrimination associated with moving Japanese-American citizens to internment camps. In this case, pressing public needs justified racial discrimination since there was a military purpose. The fact that the country was engaged in a war played a major role in this decision. Justice Owen Roberts and Justice Frank Murphy dissented.

The decision in *Korematsu v. United States* has been very controversial, although it has not been overturned. Petitioner Fred Korematsu later had his conviction overturned in 1983 before his death in 2006. At the end of World War II, the Japanese-American citizens could return to their homes, even though many had lost their property, which the federal government compensated them for in 1948. The U.S. government officially apologized for the internment, issued by President Ronald Reagan in 1988, and beginning in 1990 compensation was paid to surviving detainees.

In addition to upholding the relocation, *Korematsu* is also important for another reason. In that case, the Court for the first time established the concept of suspect classification. Justice Black contended that the use of race as a form of classification was suspect and that it would be subject to increased or heightened scrutiny. Hence, even though the Court declared race suspect in this case, it found a COMPELLING GOVERNMENTAL INTEREST to impose internment based on race and affirmed its use. In subsequent cases the Court would eventually find other classifications either to be suspect or semi-suspect.

For more information: Alonso, Karen. Korematsu v. United States*: Japanese-American Internment Camps.* Springfield, N.J.: Enslow Press, 1998; Tushnet, Mark, ed. *The Constitution in Wartime.* Durham, N.C.: Duke University Press, 2005.

—Carol Walker

Kovacs v. Cooper 336 U.S. 77 (1949)

In *Kovacs v. Cooper,* the U.S. Supreme Court voted 5-4 to deny the FIRST AMENDMENT claim of Kovacs that the City of Trenton, New Jersey's ordinance to ban the use of any sound system emitting "loud and raucous" noises on its public streets violated the First and FOURTEENTH AMENDMENTS including the violation of his DUE PROCESS. The conviction in the City of Trenton was upheld by the New Jersey Supreme Court. The U.S. Supreme Court upheld the lower courts' decision.

The City of Trenton's ordinance No. 430 made it unlawful to "play, use or operate . . . on or upon the public streets, alleys and or thoroughfares . . . , any device known as a soundtruck, loud speaker or sound amplifier, or any vehicle operated or standing upon said streets or public places." In question was the City of Trenton's ordinance. Was it a violation of a person's right of expression and participation?

The appellant was found guilty by police judge Cooper of the City of Trenton of violating Ordinance No. 430 of the City of Trenton, New Jersey. At the trial in the Trenton Police Court, a patrolman testified that he heard loud music coming from a broadcasting truck. Once the truck was located on a public street near a public building, the patrolman no longer heard music. He heard a man's voice, which was later identified as the appellant's, being broadcast from the truck. The appellant even admitted that he was the individual that was broadcasting the music and speaking into the amplifier. Although there was no real known reason for the broadcast cited in the police court, the Supreme Court's opinion was that the appellant was broadcasting his views about a labor dispute that was going on in the City of Trenton at the time.

The majority opinion and judgment of the court was announced by Justice Stanley Reed, and joined by Chief Justice Fred Vinson, and Justice Harold Burton.

The Supreme Court decided that it was not a violation of the Fourteenth Amendment regarding his freedom of speech, assemblage, or freedom to communicate. And the Court found that it was a far cry to claim that the ordinance violated his due process because its language was too obscure and vague to be able to interpret its true meaning of the words "loud and raucous." The Court felt that a regular person would be able to determine that "loud and raucous" noises would be found unacceptable in a public place.

In upholding the city's ordinance, it was pointed out that it specifically applied to only vehicles that were being operated on the city's streets with sound amplifiers or some type of device that could "emit loud and raucous noises." The ordinance specifically targeted the use of sound trucks and other sound amplification devices. The Supreme Court stated that the city of Trenton should have the right to bar or ban sound trucks that broadcast a loud noise on behalf of its public's interest. Such a vehicle can blare such a loud noise as to "rise above other street noises," which can intrude or interfere with the daily business or any activity on or near the public streets.

The ban itself does not infringe on the right of free speech, and the Court feels that the ordinance is justified. The city barred sound trucks, but there is no other restriction on communications such as "the human voice, by newspapers, by pamphlets," etc. to elicit a "willing audience." It was also mentioned that a public street is an accepted place for some form of speech and communication but not without some limitation referring to "loud and raucous" noises.

The concurring opinion was held by Justice Felix Frankfurter and Justice Robert H. Jackson.

Justice Frankfurter concluded that nothing in the Constitution prevents the state of New Jersey from approving the city of Trenton to pass laws that they feel appropriate to deal with certain matters such as sound trucks.

A concern Justice Frankfurter addressed was the "preferred position of freedom of speech." In other words, the power of state should refrain from passing laws limiting freedom of speech, as a matter of the "exception not the rule."

He also stated that the Constitution protects freedom of speech, which includes the right to communicate by whatever means necessary. Sound trucks are a form of communication and should be protected just like any other form of communication.

In Justice Jackson's opinion, he agreed that the Trenton ordinance was legal. He said that such a device does disrupt the "quiet enjoyment of home and park and with safe and legitimate use of street and market place." Freedom of speech should not include such use of a device as to "drown out the natural speech of others." Therefore, it should be under the regulation of the local authorities to maintain order in the interest of the community.

He also stated that it was not a violation of Kovacs's due process, because the ordinance was not "censoring" his broadcast. But Justice Jackson also agreed with Justice HUGO BLACK when it came to the definition of "loud and raucous" noises.

The dissenting opinion was held by Justices Frank Murphy, Black, WILLIAM O. DOUGLAS, and Wiley B. Rutledge. Justice Black's main contention was that the appellant was not charged or convicted for operating a sound truck that emits "loud and raucous" noises, but was charged with playing, operating, and using a device known as a sound truck, which violated the city ordinance. There was no proof offered that the truck even emitted noise considered "loud and raucous."

If he was convicted of "operating a machine that emitted loud and raucous noises" then "he was convicted on a charge for which he was never tried." His due process was violated. The New Jersey Supreme Court confirmed only the version of the city of Trenton's ordinance that he was originally found guilty of.

Justice Black also made reference to the *Saia v. New York*, 334 U.S. 558 (1948), case inasmuch as it pertained to "censorship." In that case, the Court struck down a city ordinance which required anyone who wanted to use a sound truck within the city limits to obtain permission from the chief of police. In short, the Court's decision was not based on the all-out ban of amplifying devices but the fact that one had to obtain permission from the chief of police to use such a device. That left the discretion solely up to the chief of police which could lead to a form of censorship. The chief of police had "arbitrary power" over who could and could not have use of such a device in or upon public property.

When deciding that case, Justice Black said loud speakers were put on "the same constitutional level as freedom to speak on streets without such devices, freedom to speak over radio, and freedom to distribute literature." He also stated that all forms of communication, present and future, should be protected by the First Amendment and free from censorship.

Justice Black concluded by saying that some forms of communication can be abused and be "an intolerable nuisance." But a city could provide alternatives, such as certain hours of the day where one could use such a device, which would be better than completely banning said devices altogether.

Justice Rutledge's dissent was based more on the fact that a majority upheld a conviction where what actually constituted the crime was still unclear. There were too many differing views. He conceded that "state power" is capable of balancing the right to free speech and "freedom from public nuisances," but to forbid it altogether is unacceptable.

For more information: Kelly, Alfred H., Winfred A. Harbison, and Herman Belz. *The American Constitution: Its Origins and Development.* New York: W.W. Norton & Company, 1991.

—Thomas Caiazzo

Kyllo v. United States 533 U.S. 27 (2001)

In *Kyllo v. United States,* the U.S. Supreme Court held that the use of a thermal-imaging device aimed at the outside of a private home to detect relative amounts of heat inside the home was a search within the meaning of the FOURTH AMENDMENT to the U.S. Constitution.

Federal agents suspected that Kyllo was growing marijuana inside his house. Knowing that the grow lights necessary for indoor cultivation produce significant amounts of heat, the agents scanned the outside of the house with a thermo-imaging device for the purpose of detecting amounts of heat that would be indicative of such lamps. The scan showed that portions of the exterior of Kyllo's house were warmer than other portions and substantially warmer than adjacent homes. With this imaging information, along with tips from informants and utility bills, the agents obtained a search warrant from a federal magistrate. In the search, the agents found a growing operation with more than 100 plants. After Kyllo attempted unsuccessfully to have the seized evidence excluded from the case, the case was eventually appealed to the U.S. Supreme Court.

The central issue for the Court was whether scanning Kyllo's home with this device constituted a search. If it did, then the absence of a warrant authorizing its use would make the search illegal, and the information it provided could not be used to obtain a search warrant or otherwise be used against Kyllo. Although Anglo-American law has traditionally given heightened protection to the PRIVACY associated with a home, the visual surveillance of a home has never been considered to be a search. Over the course of the last century, the Court has had to consider the constitutionality of law enforcement officers' using various kinds of technology in surveillance activities. In 1986, the Court held that low-flying aerial surveillance of private homes and surrounding areas does not constitute a search. In that same year, the Court also held that enhanced aerial photography of an industrial complex was a search, but made it clear that the case did not involve a home. The Court saw Kyllo's case as an opportunity to determine what limits, if any, should be put on the use of sense-enhancing technology not in general use to search a home. The Court held that the use of such technology to obtain information regarding the interior of a home (that could not have been obtained without physical intrusion into the home) constitutes a search. The Court argued that to hold otherwise would erode an important area of privacy, one that was protected from government intrusion under the original intent of the Fourth Amendment.

Inasmuch as the agents had not obtained a warrant prior to searching Kyllo's house with the thermo-imaging device, it followed that the information obtained from it could not be used against him. After reaching this conclusion, the Court sent the case back to the trial court to determine if the other evidence presented to the magistrate who issued the search warrant was sufficient to constitute probable cause. Without probable cause, the warrant would have been invalid and the marijuana plants that were discovered during the search would have been inadmissible under the EXCLUSIONARY RULE.

For more information: LaFave, Wayne R., Jerold H. Israel, and Nancy J. King. *Criminal Procedure.* 4th ed. St. Paul, Minn.: Thomson/West, 2004; McKenzie, Daniel. "What Were They Smoking?: The Supreme Court's Latest Step in a Long Strange Trip Through the Fourth Amendment: *Kyllo v. United States,* 533 U.S. 27 (2001)." *Journal of Criminal Law & Criminology* 93 (2002): 153–194.

—Steven B. Dow

labor unions

The Constitution influences labor regulation both in the private sector and in the public sector. The Supreme Court has often limited the reach of private-sector labor laws so as to avoid confronting constitutional issues.

The National Labor Relations Act (NLRA) is the primary federal law governing labor relations in the private sector. The NLRA is administered by the National Labor Relations Board (NLRB). In *NLRB v. JONES & LAUGHLIN STEEL CORP.*, 301 U.S. 1 (1937), the Supreme Court upheld the NLRA as a valid exercise of Congress's power under the COMMERCE CLAUSE of the Constitution.

The NLRA limits the expression of both employers and unions. Under Section 8(a)(1) of the NLRA, it is a prohibited unfair labor practice for an employer to "interfere with, restrain, or coerce employees" in the exercise of their organizational rights, including their right to be represented by a union. One way in which an employer can violate the organizational rights of its employees is by communicating with its employees. However, Section 8(c) of the NLRA provides that the "expressing of any views, argument, or opinion . . . shall not constitute or be evidence of an unfair labor practice . . . if such expression contains no threat of reprisal or force or promise of benefit." The Supreme Court has stated that section 8(c) "merely implements the FIRST AMENDMENT" (*NLRB v. Gissel Packing Co.*, 395 U.S. 575, 617 [1969]).

In *Gissel*, an employer facing an organizational campaign predicted that the election of a union would result in a strike, which in turn "could lead to the closing of the plant" (*Gissel*, 395 U.S at 588). The NLRB determined that this and similar statements were threats of reprisal and constituted an unfair labor practice. The Court in *Gissel* upheld the determination of the NLRB and further held that the employer's statements were not protected by the First Amendment. The Court observed that "an employer's rights cannot outweigh the equal rights of the employees to associate freely. . . . And any balancing of those rights must take into account the economic dependence of the employees on their employers, and the necessary tendency of the former, because of that relationship, to pick up intended implications of the latter that might be more readily dismissed by a more disinterested ear" (*Gissel*, 395 U.S. at 617).

The NLRA regulates union expression as well as employer expression. Section 8(b)(4) of the NLRA, the secondary boycott provision, limits the ability of unions to exert pressure on those not directly involved in a labor dispute. Among other things, section 8(b)(4) makes it an unfair labor practice for a union to "threaten, coerce, or restrain any person" to "cease doing business with any another person."

Several Supreme Court cases address the relationship between section 8(b)(4) of the NLRA and the First Amendment. In *NLRB v. Fruit Packers*, 377 U.S. 58 (1964) *(Tree Fruits)*, the union had a dispute with fruit packing companies that sold Washington State apples. The union picketed supermarkets, asking patrons not to buy Washington State apples. The NLRB determined that the union had engaged in an unlawful secondary boycott. The Supreme Court, however, expressed the concern that "a broad ban against peaceful picketing might collide with the guarantees of the First Amendment" (*Tree Fruits*, 377 U.S. at 63). As the union asked only patrons to boycott the struck product (apples) rather than the secondary business (the supermarket), the Court determined that the union's peaceful picketing was not prohibited by the NLRA.

Tree Fruits's protection for peaceful picketing that merely "followed" the struck product was limited in *NLRB v. Retail Store Employees,* 447 U.S. 607 (1980) (*Safeco*). The Court in *Safeco* announced that picketing a struck product at a secondary site is prohibited by the NLRA if, by "encouraging customers to reject the struck product, the secondary appeal is reasonably likely to threaten the neutral party with ruin or substantial loss" (*Safeco,* 447 U.S. at 615 n. 11). The Court also decided, through fractured opinions, that such picketing was not protected by the First Amendment.

In *Edward J. DeBartolo Corp. v. Florida Gulf Coast Building & Constr. Trades Council,* 485 U.S. 568 (1988), the Court drew a sharp distinction between picketing and handbilling (leafleting), announcing that handbilling receives more First Amendment protection. In *DeBartolo,* the union had a dispute with a construction company that was building a store in a shopping mall. The union distributed handbills at all mall entrances, asking customers not to shop at any stores in the mall until the mall owner (DeBartolo) promised that all construction at the mall would be done by "contractors who pay their employees fair wages and fringe benefits" (*DeBartolo,* 485 U.S. at 570). There was no picketing at all.

The NLRB found that the union's handbilling was an illegal secondary boycott, but the Court overturned this decision. To avoid the "serious constitutional problems" that would otherwise be raised (*DeBartolo,* 485 U.S. at 575), the Court held that peaceful handbilling such as the union conducted was not prohibited by the NLRA. The Court distinguished its decision in *Safeco* on the ground that picketing (as was present in *Safeco*) is "qualitatively different from other modes of communication" (*DeBartolo,* 485 U.S. at 580).

The First Amendment has also shaped the Supreme Court's interpretation of the NLRA in other ways. To avoid confronting constitutional issues involving the First Amendment's RIGHT TO PETITION THE GOVERNMENT, the Supreme Court has limited the NLRB's authority to take action against a party to a labor dispute that files a retaliatory lawsuit (*BE & K Constr. Co. v. NLRB,* 536 U.S. 516 [2002]; *Bill Johnson's Restaurants, Inc. v. NLRB,* 461 U.S. 731 [1983]). To avoid raising issues under the First Amendment's religion clauses, the Court has limited the jurisdiction of the NLRB over religiously affiliated institutions (*NLRB v. Catholic Bishop of Chicago,* 440 U.S. 490 [1979]).

Because there is pervasive federal regulation of private-sector labor relations, state and local regulation is often found to be preempted (overridden) under the SUPREMACY CLAUSE in Article VI of the Constitution. One often repeated rule, drawn from *San Diego Building Trades Council v. Garmon,* 359 U.S. 236 (1959), is that state regulation of labor matters is preempted if the regulated conduct is either arguably protected or arguably prohibited by the NLRA. Another often repeated rule, drawn from *Machinists v. Wisconsin Employment Relations Comm'n,* 427 U.S. 132 (1976), is that states may not regulate conduct that Congress intended to be unregulated.

In both the private sector and the public sector, unions are held to have a duty to represent their members fairly. The development of the duty of fair representation in the private sector was influenced by constitutional considerations. The Court first imposed a duty of fair representation on unions in *Steele v. Louisville & Nashville R. Co.,* 323 U.S. 192 (1944), a case involving alleged racial discrimination by a railway union. The Court in *Steele* stated that "constitutional questions arise" if a union is authorized by statute to be the exclusive representative of employees "without any commensurate statutory duty toward its members" (*Steele,* 323 U.S. at 198). In *Teamsters Local 391 v. Terry,* 494 U.S. 558 (1990), the Court held that the SEVENTH AMENDMENT guarantees the right of jury trial in an action for breach of the duty of fair representation.

For more information: Higgins, John E. *The Developing Labor Law.* Washington, D.C: BNA Books, 2006.

—Mark S. Stein

Laird v. Tatum 408 U.S. 1 (1972)

Laird v. Tatum is a case that called to question the constitutionality of military intelligence units' collecting data on civilians and civilian social and political organizations.

In this case, Arlo Tatum, executive secretary of the Central Committee for Conscientious Objectors, sued Melvin Laird, the secretary of defense and other individuals. Ultimately, the Supreme Court ruled that the individuals who brought suit lacked STANDING to do so, because there was no evidence that they had been negatively affected by the gathering of intelligence data gathered about their actions.

This case began with the public revelation, in an article by Christopher H. Pyle in the *Washington Monthly*, that military intelligence units had been gathering information on civilians and civilian organizations through newspaper clippings, but also by active surveillance and by breaching the membership of these organizations. Several of the individuals and organizations that had been surveilled, with the assistance of the AMERICAN CIVIL LIBERTIES UNION, filed a class action challenging the constitutionality of the military's actions. The case was dismissed in federal district court. DISTRICT OF COLUMBIA Court of Appeals heard the case, and remanded the case to trial court for an evidentiary hearing.

The Supreme Court then agreed to hear the case, upon the defendant's petition, to decide the issues of justiciablity and standing. The government argued that the plaintiffs failed to describe a genuine injury to their rights and also that the case was moot because, according to the military, the programs had ceased. The plaintiffs asked the Supreme Court to affirm the ruling of the appellant court, allowing for an evidentiary hearing. Before oral arguments began, the Court received an amicus brief from 29 former military intelligence officers and enlisted personnel who stated that the data collection efforts of the military went beyond merely clipping newspaper articles, but also included clandestine operations such as: agents posing as news reporters during protests to gather information from willing, though unsuspecting civilian participants; personnel who penetrated peace organizations; and staking out Martin Luther King's grave to discover who visited the site.

Despite the supporting amicus brief, the Supreme Court, in a 5-4 decision written by Chief Justice WARREN BURGER, reversed the appellate court's decision, affirming the dismissal of the case. The Supreme Court supported the government's view that the data collection was of public actions that had potential to lead to civil unrest. The Court also found the case to be nonjusticiable because there was no injury due to the military's actions. Without injury, the case amounted to a political question.

It is also worth noting that Justice WILLIAM HUBBS REHNQUIST arguably should have recused himself from this decision. As the assistant attorney general, Office of Legal Counsel, Rehnquist appeared before a congressional subcommittee to defend the military's program. Had Rehnquist recused himself, the decision would have been a 4-4 affirmation of the Court of Appeals decision, allowing for an evidentiary trial.

For more information: N.A. "*Laird v. Tatum*: The Supreme Court and a First Amendment Challenge to Military Surveillance of Lawful Civilian Political Activity." *Hofstra Law Review* 1 (1973): 244–275; Shaffer, Karen A. "*Tatum v. Laird*: Military Encroachment on First Amendment Rights." *American University Law Review* 21 (1971): 262–280.

—Tobias T. Gibson

Lamb's Chapel v. Center Moriches Union Free School District 508 U.S. 384 (1993)

In *LAMB'S CHAPEL V. CENTER MORICHES UNION FREE SCHOOL DISTRICT*, the Supreme Court held that a school district's decision to refuse a church's request to use school facilities to show religious films violated the free speech clause of the FIRST AMENDMENT. This principle was later upheld in *GOOD NEWS CLUB V. MILFORD CENTRAL SCHOOL*, 533 U.S. 98 (2001).

In accordance with New York law, a local school district issued regulations allowing access to school grounds for certain social, civic, and recreational uses, but prohibiting use of school facilities for religious purposes. After the school district refused the request of Lamb's Chapel to use school facilities for a religious film series about family values and child-rearing, the church filed suit, claiming that the school district's actions violated its free speech rights.

The Supreme Court held that denying the church access to school premises to exhibit the film series violated the free speech clause of the First Amendment. In his opinion for the Court, Justice Byron White explained that the school had created a nonpublic forum. Although access to a nonpublic forum can be based on subject matter or speaker identity, the distinctions drawn must be reasonable and may not discriminate based on the speaker's viewpoint. Justice White explained that the school district's prohibition applied equally to all religions, but it discriminated on the basis of viewpoint by permitting school property to be used for the presentation of all views about family issues except those dealing with the subject from a religious viewpoint. Therefore, the school district's regulations denied the request of Lamb's Chapel solely to suppress its point of view on an otherwise permissible subject.

Furthermore, the Court held that permitting the school district's property to be used to exhibit the religious film series would not have constituted an establishment of religion. Because the film series would not have been shown during school hours, it would not have been sponsored by the school, and it would have been open to the public, there was no realistic danger that the community would think the school district was endorsing religion in general or Christianity in particular.

For more information: Hitchcock, James. *The Supreme Court and Religion in American Life.* Vol. 1, *The Odyssey of the Religion Clauses.* Princeton, N.J.: Princeton University Press, 2004.

—Winston E. Calvert

Lawrence v. Texas 539 U.S. 558 (2003)

In its six to three decision in *Lawrence v. Texas,* the Supreme Court declared that Texas's homosexual sodomy law violates the DUE PROCESS clause that permits adults the liberty to engage in consensual intimate conduct in private. Justice ANTHONY M. KENNEDY's majority opinion explicitly overturned the Court's earlier sodomy case, *BOWERS V. HARDWICK,* 478 U.S. 186 (1986), while Justice SANDRA DAY O'CONNOR's concurrence focused attention on the Texas statute's EQUAL PROTECTION violation because it was directed against a group, same-sex couples, rather than an act. *Lawrence* is an example of a later generation's looking afresh at enduring social issues and laws in the light of constitutional principles.

The Court found that the history of sodomy regulations presented in *Bowers* misrepresented the facts and was misconstrued by the majority in that case to ground their shrunken view of the liberty and PRIVACY interests at stake both then and now. The Court also noted that sodomy laws, especially those directed at only homosexual conduct, were rarely enforced except in cases of predatory acts, their main purpose being to demean a group of people, such as the Court found was true of the state constitutional amendment it struck down in *ROMER V. EVANS,* 517 U.S. 620 (1996).

The dissent by Justice ANTONIN GREGORY SCALIA conjectured that as many of the nation's laws rested on a moral basis alone as understood by the people, they were in danger of being overturned, and argued that as a constitutional right to engage in sexual intercourse outside of marriage is not rooted in the nation's history or traditions, it is a misapplication of the doctrine of SUBSTANTIVE DUE PROCESS to have applied any standard other than rational basis scrutiny. Scalia expressed fear that in the wake of *Lawrence* no traditional morals offense could be sustained and that this is a dangerous decision with the potential to upset the American social order itself given the legitimate state interest in furthering the moral choices of the people, including majority opinion regarding permissible sexual behavior, which in *Bowers* provided the rational basis for the Georgia sodomy statute that withstood constitutional challenge. Justice CLARENCE THOMAS's individual dissent labeled the Texas law, and all others similar to it, "uncommonly silly" and stated that were he a legislator, he would vote to repeal it, the legislature being the appropriate branch to provide such relief for the petitioners, which Justice Scalia had also argued.

Lawrence is significant in at least two ways. First, as a GAY AND LESBIAN RIGHTS case, it completes the work begun by *Romer* in articulating that non-heterosexual Americans are equal citizens with equal rights, including in that area where they are deemed most different, their sexual behavior. Whether *Lawrence* will affect SAME-SEX MARRIAGE cases can only be speculated, and both sides of this constitutional argument find comfort in it. Secondly, with its overturning of the reasoning in *Bowers*, *Lawrence* seems finally to express the conviction at the heart of liberal constitutionalism that moral disapproval alone does not provide a rational basis sufficient to legitimate a statute, including one that would infringe on the liberty interests of a group of Americans whom the majority has traditionally viewed with disdain, and that the classic criterion of a showing of harm must be present to justify any such statute.

For more information: Schwartz, Bernard. *A History of the Supreme Court.* New York: Oxford University Press, 1993.

—Gordon A. Babst

League of United Latin American Citizens (LULAC) v. Perry 548 U.S. 399 (2006)

In *LULAC v. Perry*, 548 U.S. 399 (2006), the Supreme Court held that a portion of the Texas congressional redistricting plan enacted in 2003 violated the Voting Rights Act. The Court declined, however, to declare a clear legal standard for a claim of political gerrymandering. Six of the nine justices authored opinions, demonstrating the lack of consensus on the issues presented in the case.

The dispute at the heart of the *LULAC* case began when the Republican-controlled Texas Senate and Democratic-controlled Texas House of Representatives could not agree on a redistricting plan following the 2000 census. As a result, a three-judge federal district court created a redistricting plan for the 2002 elections. In those elections, Texas Republicans gained control of the state House of Representatives. During the next legislative session, the Texas Republicans sought to enact a new redistricting plan to replace the court-drawn one. A heated political dispute ensued, with a group of Democratic legislators briefly fleeing the state to deny the quorum required to pass new laws. Eventually the Republican legislators prevailed and passed a new redistricting plan that substantially altered several congressional districts, including District 23, represented by Republican incumbent Henry Bonilla.

Multiple plaintiffs challenged the new redistricting plan, arguing that it was an improper partisan gerrymander and violated the Voting Rights Act, the FIRST AMENDMENT, and the EQUAL PROTECTION clause of the FOURTEENTH AMENDMENT. Following a judgment in favor of the defendants, the Supreme Court remanded the case back to the district court for reconsideration in light of *Vieth v. Jubelirer*, 541 U.S. 267 (2004), where the Court addressed the issue of the JUSTICIABILITY of PARTISAN GERRYMANDERING claims but failed to announce a clear precedent. On remand, the three-judge panel again found in favor of the defendants, and the plaintiffs appealed to the Supreme Court for a second time.

In *LULAC*, Justice ANTHONY M. KENNEDY authored a majority opinion with regard to the political gerrymandering and VOTING RIGHTS ACT claims. The majority found that the plaintiffs failed to present a "manageable, reliable measure of fairness" for determining the constitutionality of an alleged gerrymander. Thus, the divided opinion from the *Vieth v. Jubelier* decision continues to govern political gerrymandering claims.

The majority found that the redrawn District 23 violated Section 2 of the Voting Rights Act because it diluted the votes of the Latino population. Although District 23 contained a narrow Latino majority in voting age population, it did not have a Latino majority of citizen voting age population. Additionally, the plan diluted the Latino vote because the majority Latino population was composed of two communities separated by 300 miles and possessing diverging "needs and interests." The Court refuted the state's argument that the newly created District 25, which also contained a Latino majority, met its requirements under the Voting Rights Act. Because the new redistricting plan contained one less "reasonably compact" Latino majority or "opportunity" district than the previous plan, it violated the Voting Rights Act. Justices ANTONIN GREGORY SCALIA, CLARENCE THOMAS, SAMUEL ALITO, and Chief Justice JOHN G. ROBERTS, JR., argued that the lower court's ruling should be upheld because the redistricting plan did not violate the Voting Rights Act. As a result of the Supreme Court's decision, a three-judge district court panel adjusted the boundaries of District 23 and neighboring districts to comply with the Voting Rights Act in time for the 2006 elections.

For more information: Grofman, Bernard, and Gary King. "The Future of Partisan Symmetry as a Judicial Test for Partisan Gerrymandering after *LULAC v. Perry*." *Election Law Journal* 6 (2007): 2–34; Ortiz, Daniel R. "Cultural Compactness." *Mich. Law Review First Impressions* 105 (2006): 48–52.

—Joshua A. Kimsey

Lebron v. National Railroad Passenger Corporation 513 U.S. 374 (1995)

In *Lebron v. National Railroad Passenger Corporation,* the Supreme Court addressed the constitutional status of Amtrack for the purposes of the FIRST AMENDMENT. Although *Lebron* is nominally a First Amendment case, its significance rests primarily with the Supreme Court's findings regarding the constitutional obligations of a corporation created for a public purpose and over which the government retains permanent control.

At issue in *Lebron* was a photomontage that the petitioner, artist Michael Lebron, had contracted to display on a large billboard known as the "Spectacular" in New York City's Penn Station. The proposed montage was a send-up of a popular advertising campaign by the Coors Brewing Company of Colorado for its Coors Light product that featured the tagline "It's the right beer now." The montage proposed by the petitioner portrayed a group of smiling Coors beer drinkers set against the image of Nicaraguan villagers threatened by a fire-emitting can of Coors beer above the caption, "Is it the Right's Beer Now?" Text on both sides of the image sharply criticized the Coors family for supporting various political positions and groups, including the Contra rebels fighting the leftist government in Nicaragua. National Railroad Passenger Corporation (Amtrak), which owned the billboard, refused to display the ad, citing its political nature. Lebron filed suit in district court in 1993, claiming that the refusal was a violation of his First Amendment rights.

The district court found that Amtrak's refusal to display the montage violated Lebron's right to free speech and directed the company to display the ad. Amtrak appealed to the U.S. Court of Appeals for the Second Circuit, which subsequently ruled against Lebron, finding in its decision that Amtrak was, in effect, a private corporation and therefore was not obligated to uphold liberties guaranteed in the Constitution. Lebron appealed to the Supreme Court in 1994, and the high Court reversed the lower court's decision regarding Amtrak's status as a private body, but took no position on the First Amendment issue, electing instead to remand that decision back to the court of appeals. Lower court decisions that had found Amtrak to be a private body did so in large measure because the original statute that created the rail line had provided that the corporation would "not be an agency or establishment of the United States Government." Writing on behalf of an 8-1 majority (only Justice SANDRA DAY O'CONNOR dissented), Justice ANTONIN GREGORY SCALIA argued in *Lebron* that while Congress could classify agencies as public or private for administrative purposes, "it is not for Congress to make the final determination of Amtrak's status as a government entity for purposes of determining the constitutional rights of citizens affected by its actions." Justice Scalia went on to conclude that when government creates a corporation by special law for the furtherance of governmental objectives and retains for itself permanent authority to appoint a majority of that corporation's directors, the corporation is part of the government for purposes of the First Amendment.

Per the remand from the Supreme Court, the appeals court once again ruled against Lebron on the First Amendment claim, maintaining in its October 1995 decision that "Amtrak's historical refusal to accept political advertisements such as Lebron's . . . is a reasonable use of that forum that is neutral as to viewpoint." The appeals court denied a rehearing, and Lebron's second appeal to the Supreme Court was rejected in May 1996.

For more information: Froomkin, Michael. "Reinventing the Government Corporation." *Illinois Law Review* 543, no. 3 (1995): 543–634; Smith, Catherine. "*Lebron v. National Railroad Passenger Corp. (Amtrak)*: Another Misapplication of the Public Forum Doctrine." *St. John's Law Review* 70 (Summer 1996): 609–628.

—Gregory Baldi

Lee v. Weisman 505 U.S. 577 (1992)

In *Lee v. Weisman*, the Court ruled that prayers at public school graduation ceremonies violate the ESTABLISHMENT CLAUSE. This case is important because it uses the coercion test to determine the meaning of the establishment clause.

For many years, the Providence, Rhode Island, school district had a policy of allowing school principals to invite local clergy members to offer nonsectarian prayers at graduation ceremonies. Daniel Weisman, the father of two public school students, objected to this practice to no avail. Consequently, he sought a permanent INJUNCTION against the school system from allowing prayers as a violation of the FIRST AMENDMENT's establishment clause. The district court agreed and the First Circuit and Supreme Court affirmed.

Writing for a narrow five-justice majority, Justice ANTHONY M. KENNEDY held that according to *LYNCH V. DONNELLY*, 465 U.S. 668 (1984), the "government may not coerce anyone to support or participate in religion or its exercise, or otherwise act in a way that establishes a [state] religion." The school district, by its control of the graduation ceremony, and the theoretically required nature of this once-in-a-lifetime opportunity, places public and peer pressure on students to stand and maintain silence which may signify their participation or approval.

Concurring in the judgment, Justices Harry Blackmun, JOHN PAUL STEVENS, and SANDRA DAY O'CONNOR believe that the establishment clause prevents more than coercion. Rather, it prevents government from endorsing any religious activity because government sponsorship makes participation relevant to one's standing in the community. In a separate concurrence, Justice DAVID H. SOUTER maintained that the establishment clause requires neutrality between religion and disbelief and that state-sponsored prayer impermissibly crosses the line to support.

Dissenting, Justice ANTONIN GREGORY SCALIA, writing for Justices WILLIAM HUBBS REHNQUIST, Byron White, and CLARENCE THOMAS, claimed historical analysis and a proper understanding of coercion would lead the Court to uphold prayers at graduations. Using history, he showed that prayer has been a tradition at public ceremonies from the DECLARATION OF INDEPENDENCE to George Washington's inauguration to the present. Invocations at high school graduation ceremonies simply continue this tradition, and the Court should accommodate this.

Justice Scalia also claimed that no coercion occurs because students are not forced to pray or even to stand in respect. Furthermore, it is illogical to assume that because someone stands in respect that one is participating in the prayer or supports prayer. If anything, standing indicates respect for the religious observances of others, which is a civic virtue that government has and should promote. Finally, the coercion that the establishment clause is meant to prevent is the state's imposing its religious beliefs on others, and the state does not do this with prayers at graduation ceremonies. This case shows the division on the court in regard to how to interpret the establishment clause. While *LEMON V. KURTZMAN*, 403 U.S. 602 (1971), is the controlling precedent, the justices are unhappy with the *Lemon* test because of its vagueness, the difficulty in applying it, and the fear, depending upon their ideology, that it allows religion too much or too little a role in the public square. Unable to find a substitute that can command five votes, the Court debates tests, from the more restrictive neutrality and endorsements test to the less restrictive coercion and ACCOMMODATION tests.

For more information: Feldman, Stephen. *Law and Religion: A Critical Anthology*. New York: New York University Press, 2000; McConnell, Michael W. "Coercion: The Lost Element of Establishment." *William & Mary Law Review* 27 (1986): 933–941; Sherry, Suzanna. "*Lee v. Weisman*: Paradox Redux." *Supreme Court Law Review* 1992 (1993): 123–153; Witte, John. *America and the Constitutional Experiment*. 2nd ed. Boulder, Colo.: Westview Press, 2005.

—Frank J. Colucci and Sean Evans

Legal Services Corporation v. Velazquez

531 U.S. 533 (2001)

In *Legal Services Corporation v. Velazquez*, the U.S. Supreme Court ruled 5-4 that Congress violated the FIRST AMENDMENT's protection against viewpoint discrimination by restricting legal services attorneys' abilities to challenge the constitutionality of existing welfare laws. This case is significant in that the Court rejected Congress's attempt to limit the First Amendment rights of legal services providers, not directly, but indirectly, by placing "unconstitutional conditions" on the receipt of federal funds.

Federally funded legal assistance for the poor emerged in the mid-1960s as part of Johnson's War on Poverty programs. Opposition to this assistance became intense in the early 1970s, as federally funded attorneys successfully litigated challenges to federal and state law. The Nixon administration initially attempted to dismantle the existing programs, but changed its position in the face of aggressive lobbying efforts by the American Bar Association. In response, Congress established a new, politically independent Legal Services Corporation (LSC) in 1974. In exchange for independence from the executive branch, LSC-funded attorneys had to accept restrictions on the types of law reform activities they could pursue, including litigation involving ABORTION, school DESEGREGATION, and redistricting, among others. The restrictions at issue in *Legal Services Corporation v. Velazquez* were similarly aimed at limiting the law reform activities of these attorneys.

In 1996, Congress passed the Omnibus Consolidated Rescissions and Appropriations Act, which, among other things, prohibited federally funded legal services attorneys from challenging welfare laws. In addition, if the legal services providers received federal funds, they were restricted from engaging in the proscribed actions even if they were using private funds to do so.

Writing for the majority, Justice ANTHONY M. KENNEDY found that "[b]y seeking to prohibit the analysis of certain legal issues and to truncate presentation to the courts, the enactment under review prohibits speech and expression upon which the courts must depend for the proper exercise of the judicial power." As a result, "the restriction operates to insulate current welfare laws from constitutional scrutiny and certain other legal challenges, a condition implicating central First Amendment concerns."

Those concerns require that the Court "must be vigilant when Congress imposes rules and conditions which in effect insulate its own laws from legitimate judicial challenge." Here, the Court distinguishes this case from *RUST V. SULLIVAN*, 500 U.S. 173 (1991), by noting that viewpoint-based funding decisions may be upheld when government is the speaker or, as in *Rust*, when "government 'used private speakers to transmit information pertaining to its own program,'" but "where private speech is involved, even Congress' antecedent funding decision cannot be aimed at the suppression of ideas thought inimical to the Government's own interest."

Insofar as the challenged provisions of the 1996 Appropriations Act would allow federally funded legal services attorneys to argue a particular view (that welfare statutes and regulations are constitutional) but disallow litigation aimed at another view (that welfare statutes and regulations are unconstitutional or unlawful), the restrictions unconstitutionally violated the First Amendment protections afforded legal services providers and their clients.

The dissent, written by Justice ANTONIN GREGORY SCALIA and joined by Chief Justice WILLIAM HUBBS REHNQUIST and Justices SANDRA DAY O'CONNOR and CLARENCE THOMAS, argued that "[t]he LSC subsidy neither prevents anyone from speaking nor coerces anyone to change speech." Thus, the "statutory scheme" decided by the Court in *Rust* "is in all relevant aspects indistinguishable from" the provisions at issue in *LSC v. Velazquez.* The dissenters recognized that the prohibition at issue might lead LSC-funded attorneys to withdraw from challenges to welfare laws, but "[s]o what?" Scalia wrote. "Courts must consider only those questions of statutory validity *that are presented by litigants,* and if the Government chooses not to subsidize the presentation of some such questions, that in no way 'distorts' the court's role." The decision of the Court, in the view of the dissenters, reflects "the making of innumerable social judgments through judge-pronounced constitutional imperatives—that prompted Congress to restrict publicly funded litigation of this sort" in the first place.

Overall, *Legal Services Corporation v. Velazquez* is an important case, drawing limits upon the ability of the government to use its funding to restrict free speech rights.

For more information: Cole, David. "Beyond Unconstitutional Conditions: Chartering Spheres of Neutrality in Government-Funded Speech." *New York University Law Review* 67 (1992): 675–749; Johnson, Earl, Jr. "Justice and Reform: A Quarter Century Later." In *The Transformation of Legal Aid.* Oxford: Oxford University Press, 1999; Rhode, Deborah. *Access to Justice.* New York: Oxford University Press, 2004.

—Brian M. Harward

legislative veto

Legislative veto is the popular name for a device granting Congress the power to disapprove, or VETO, proposed executive branch or agency actions. The device originated in the 1932 Legislative Appropriations Act. This instrumental piece of New Deal legislation gave the president sweeping new powers to reorganize federal agencies and functions by executive order, provided that neither House adopted a resolution disapproving of any such order during a 60-day period before the order could take effect. Similar legislative veto provisions became increasingly common in congressional delegations of authority to federal agencies in the 1970s, until in the 1983 case of *Immigration and Naturalization Service v. Chadha,* 462 U.S. 919 (1983), the U.S. Supreme Court declared the device unconstitutional. Nevertheless, Congress retains alternative means of conditioning executive branch action on its approval.

In essence, a legislative veto operated on the premise that because the assent of both Houses of Congress is necessary to enact laws that delegate authority in the first place, Congress could condition these delegations on both Houses' continuing assent to how that authority is used. Some legislative veto provisions permitted either House (or even a particular committee) acting alone to veto executive branch action, while other provisions required both Houses to act jointly. Yet in contrast to the Constitution's explicit grant of a presidential veto power, by which the president may disapprove congressional enactments, no constitutional provision expressly gives Congress the power to exercise continuing authority over its legislative delegations.

The story of the legislative veto therefore is a story about separation of powers. Accompanying the rise of a vast federal bureaucracy during and since the New Deal has been a concern about the proper relationships among the legislative, executive, and judicial branches of government, including concern about the loss of congressional responsibility over the specific contours of federal law. One manifestation of this concern is the nondelegation doctrine, a judicial tool that purports to prohibit Congress from delegating its lawmaking authority to departments and agencies unless Congress itself has established an "intelligible principle" that properly guides the exercise of that delegated authority. In practice, however, the nondelegation doctrine has been largely toothless in constraining congressional delegations of lawmaking authority.

The legislative veto offered a different kind of check on congressional delegations of lawmaking authority, a check lodged exclusively in the legislative branch itself. A legislative veto allows Congress to delegate broad authority up front, while reserving the ability to oversee and disapprove specific exercises of this authority after the fact. Yet even from its first appearance in the 1932 Legislative Appropriations Act, concerns arose about the constitutionality of this reservation of authority. As a result, Congress omitted a legislative veto provision when it renewed the president's reorganization authority in 1933.

The device reappeared in 1939 in a similar executive branch reorganization act, and thereafter appeared, on average, several times a year for the next three decades. Then, in the 1970s, partly because of increased distrust of the executive branch, Congress rapidly multiplied the number of legislative veto provisions, including them in a variety of contexts, from war powers to emergency petroleum allocations to expenditure controls to regulating presidential papers. Congress even considered adopting a generic legislative veto that would have applied to all agency actions.

Accordingly, in *Immigration and Naturalization Service v. Chadha,* the Supreme Court squarely addressed the question of whether the Constitution permitted Congress to retain this form of control over agency activities. Directly at issue was a provision in the Immigration and Naturalization Act that allowed either House of Congress to override the Justice Department's exercise of its statutory authority to suspend the deportation of a deportable alien and allow the alien to obtain permanent residence status. Indirectly at issue was the constitutionality of some 200 legislative veto mechanisms then present in a variety of federal laws.

As authorized by statute, an immigration judge had granted Jagdish Chadha a suspension of deportation on the grounds that deportation would cause Chadha extreme hardship. The HOUSE OF REPRESENTATIVES adopted a resolution disapproving this suspension, however, with the result that the INS was required to deport Chadha. Chadha then sought federal court review of the INS's deportation order. Because the INS agreed with Chadha's position that the House's disapproval of his suspension was unconstitutional, Congress accepted the invitation to participate in the case to defend the constitutionality of the legislative veto.

Notwithstanding Congress's arguments that the legislative veto was both consistent with the Constitution's lawmaking processes and a significant tool for facilitating legislative responsibility in an increasingly complex government, the Supreme Court found the veto unconstitutional. The Court took a formalistic approach, reasoning that because the House's resolution of disapproval altered legal rights, it was an exercise of lawmaking power and therefore must conform with the two fundamental lawmaking requirements set forth in Article I, Section 7, Clauses 2 and 3 of the Constitution: 1) bicameralism, or passage by both Houses of Congress, and 2) presentment, or approval by the President (or the override of a presidential veto). The disapproval resolution was unconstitutional because it satisfied neither requirement.

In response to the *Chadha* decision, Congress replaced many of the 200 now invalidated legislative veto provisions with "report-and-wait" provisions. These devices require agencies to inform Congress ahead of time how they intend to use their delegated authority and then give Congress a defined interval to withdraw or modify the agency's authority through the ordinary lawmaking processes of bicameralism and presentment, if Congress (and the president) so chooses. In addition, Congress continues to use a number of informal, nonstatutory "legislative veto" devices to control executive action, particularly through demands that agencies get approval from the relevant appropriations committees or subcommittees for certain uses of appropriated funds, demands that agencies are loath to ignore because of Congress's power of the purse.

Among the many pieces of legislation that include a legislative veto is the WAR POWERS ACT, a law meant to limit the power of the president to deploy troops. However, given that it operates with a two-house veto, its constitutionality is in question.

For more information: Bruff, Harold, and Ernest Gellhorn. "Congressional Control of Administrative Regulation: A Study of Legislative Vetoes." *Harvard Law Review* 90 (1977): 1,369–1,440; Craig, Barbara. *Chadha: The Story of an Epic Constitutional Struggle.* New York: Oxford University Press, 1988; Fisher, Louis. "The Legislative Veto: Invalidated, it Survives." *Law and Contemporary Problems* 56, (1993): 273–292; Korn, Jessica. *The Power of Separation: American Constitutionalism and the Myth of the Legislative Veto.* Princeton, N.J.: Princeton University Press, 1996.

—Steven F. Huefner

Lemon v. Kurtzman 403 U.S. 602 (1971)

In *Lemon v. Kurtzman,* the Supreme Court developed the Lemon test, a tool for determining if government funding or actions constitute a violation of the FIRST AMENDMENT ESTABLISHMENT CLAUSE.

The relationship between church and state has changed over the course of history. In ancient times, government and religion were inextricably intertwined and there was no separation. For example, Roman emperors were treated with utmost reverence and respect and were considered religious officials; medieval monarchs ruled the people, and it was believed that they did so with God's authority. Even today, some countries continue to have tight connections between state and religion. The world's greatest conflicts have arisen from the people's refusal to acknowledge a state religion or to recognize a political leader as a religious authority.

In the United States, the separation of church and state has its roots in the First Amendment of the Constitution which states "Congress shall make no law respecting an establishment of religion, or prohibiting the free exercise thereof." This amendment, also known as the establishment clause, has been the springboard for a great deal of litigation.

Lemon v. Kurtzman was one of many First Amendment cases. In that case, the State of Pennsylvania enacted a law that provided aid to many religious schools, most of which were Roman Catholic, in the form of direct reimbursement for teachers' salaries and textbooks. The primary plaintiff, Alton Lemon, a taxpayer and parent of a child attending a Pennsylvania public school, was displeased by the thought of state funds being used for religious purposes and filed suit against Kurztman, Superintendent of Public Instruction, and others. The plaintiffs alleged that the law fostered religion and was a violation of the establishment clause.

This litigation gave birth to a three-part constitutionality analysis applicable to any establishment of religion challenge, known as the Lemon test or the neutrality doctrine: 1) the primary purpose of the law must not be to advance religion and there must be a legitimate secular purpose; 2) the primary effect of the law must be one that neither advances or inhibits the practice of religion; 3) the challenged law must not result in excessive government entanglement with religion.

In applying the first leg of the analysis, the Court did not find a basis to conclude that the primary legislative intent was to advance religion. The statute clearly stated that it was intended to enhance secular (nonreligious) education in all schools and conditioned reimbursement on instructors' teaching only courses offered at the public schools, using the same materials as public schools, and a tacit agreement not to teach religion courses.

The *Lemon* Court did not reach the second step of the analysis, "primary effect," recognizing a clear violation of the third prong. The justices agreed that the detailed process for reimbursement dealt the final blow to the statute, which by its very nature would inevitably require "comprehensive, discriminating, and continuing state surveillance to ensure that the restrictions were obeyed" and that "these prophylactic contacts will involve excessive and enduring entanglement between state and church."

The Lemon test remains a source of controversy with some justices on the Supreme Court advocating different tools, such as the coercion test, to determine if there is an establishment clause violation.

For more information: Kritzer, Herbert M., and Mark J. Richards. "Jurisprudential Regimes and Supreme Court Decisionmaking: The *Lemon* Regime and Establishment Clause Cases." *Law and Society Review* 37, no. 4 (2003): 827–840.

—Loretta M. Young

letters of marque and reprisal

Letters of marque and reprisal provide a legal mechanism for waging war while sparing the public great expenses. Letters of marque were commissions from a government to a private person authorizing military operations beyond the boundaries of the nation (marque) in order to search, seize, or destroy property of the enemy. Usually letters of marque were issued to those who would arm a ship for use in seizing enemy shipping.

The Continental Congress issued letters of marque and reprisal during the Revolutionary War, which brought many prize cases into the courts. Letters of marque and reprisal were addressed in the Articles of Confederation at Article VI, Para. 5, which says that states could issue letters of marque only after a declaration of war by the Congress. The "letters of marque or reprisal" could be issued only against the kingdom or state and citizens against whom Congress had declared war. However, the states could issue letters of marque if the waters of the state were so infested with pirates that it could brook no delay.

Article IX, Para. 1 of the Articles of Confederation granted to Congress the sole and exclusive power to issue letters of marque and reprisal during time of peace. Issuing letters of marque and reprisal in either war or peace required the affirmative vote of nine states (Article IX, Para. 6).

The authors of the Constitution carried the practice of issuing letters of marque into the new constitution. However, the power was limited to the Congress alone, giving it a greater control over foreign policy and war powers. The Constitution forbids the states (Article I, Section 8, Para. 11) from granting letters of marque.

James Madison briefly discussed letters of marque in Federalist Papers No. 44. As president, he issued them during the War of 1812.

The Republic of Texas issued at least six letters of marque in its fight against Mexico. However, when Mexico issued letters of marque in the Mexican-American War (1846–48), President Polk declared that privateering would be treated as piracy.

The Declaration of Paris in 1856 banned the use of letters of marque by civilized nations. The United States did not sign this document, but during the War Between the States and the Spanish-American War (1898) it issued statements that it would not issue such letters. However, between 1861 and 1865, the Confederate States of America issued almost a hundred letters of marque and reprisal.

Following the September 11, 2001, terrorist attack, Congressman Ron Paul of Texas proposed legislation (H.R. 3074) to authorize the granting of letters of marque and reprisal in the war on terrorism. The United States is not a party to Protocol I of the Geneva Convention which forbids reprisals against civilians and their property. This allows reprisals against non-state actors including terrorists.

For more information: Marley, David. *Pirates and Privateers of the Americas.* Santa Barbara, Calif.: ABC-CLIO, 1994; Rodin, David. *War and Self-Defense.* Oxford: Oxford University Press, 2002.

—Andrew J. Waskey

liberty of contract

Liberty of contract was an important constitutional doctrine of the late 19th and early 20th centuries that was often invoked by the Supreme Court to limit government regulation. The doctrine is often linked or related to substantive due process under the Fourteenth Amendment.

In 1897 in the case of *Allgeyer v. Louisiana,* 165 U.S. 578 (1897), the U.S. Supreme Court established a new constitutional right under the rubric of liberty of contract. Ostensibly a constitutional protection from government interference with the freedom to enter into contractual agreements for all individuals, the new right principally served the interests of business and significantly reduced the authority of government to enact worker protective measures.

In *Allgeyer,* the Supreme Court struck down a statute enacted by the state of Louisiana that limited the sale and purchase of insurance contracts. A more controversial use of the concept of liberty of contract came in 1905 with the case of *LOCHNER V. NEW YORK,* U.S. 45, 25 S. Ct 539 (1905). In *Lochner,* the Supreme Court ruled that because individuals had a constitutional liberty to contract freely, statutes that interfered with this liberty must be shown to protect a public interest that outweighs the individual right. This case challenged the power of the state of New York to enact a law limiting the number of hours a week that a baker could work to 10 hours a day, six days a week. The state defended the law as a health code allowable under the state's POLICE POWERS.

However, the Supreme Court rejected this argument, contending instead that the measure was a patronizing overreaching by the state and could not be a health code since the number of hours a baker worked had no impact on the quality of the bread produced and then later consumed by the public. Beginning with *Lochner,* the Supreme Court consistently framed its analysis of state and federal laws that claimed to be health and safety codes as unconstitutional "protectionist" measures.

Lochner marked the zenith of the doctrine of substantive due process analysis that had given birth to the concept of liberty of contract as a new constitutional right against which statutes regulating private property could be challenged. Beginning with only the seed of the idea's being planted by dissenting justices in the *Slaughterhouse Cases,* 83 U.S. 16 Wall. 36 (1873), the Supreme Court had been cultivating the thought that the Fourteenth Amendment's due process clause could be used to provide constitutional protection for markedly unfettered capitalism.

In the year previous to handing down *Allgeyer,* the Supreme Court had determined in an otherwise unremarkable case that business corporations are "legal persons" for constitutional purposes, pulling them under the constitutional umbrella of protections of the BILL OF RIGHTS and the Fourteenth Amendment (*SANTA CLARA COUNTY V. SOUTHERN PACIFIC RAILROAD COMPANY,* 118 U.S. 398 [1886]). Hence, the liberty of contract that applied to individuals traditionally understood as individual human beings now also applied to business corporations. With its power to review the substance of economic legislation to determine its constitutionality under the doctrine of substantive due process together with the doctrine of liberty of contract, which recognized business corporations and individual persons as equals in contractual negotiations, the Supreme Court had two constitutional tools with which it could strike down legislation that regulated business.

The Supreme Court continued its use of the concept of liberty of contract under substantive due process analysis to protect economic interests against state and federal worker protective legislation for 40 years, finally abandoning the concept in the case of *WEST COAST HOTEL V. PARRISH,* 300 U.S. 379, 57 S. Ct. 578 (1937). Although the Supreme Court emphatically repudiated the concept of liberty of contract in this case, the Court did not reject the doctrine of substantive due process, which stands as a constitutional doctrine today and continues to enable the Supreme Court to play a significant role in the American constitutional and political debate over rights.

For more information: Breyer, Stephen. *Active Liberty: Interpreting Our Democratic Constitution.* New York: Knopf Publishers, 2005; Van Geel, T. R. *Understanding Supreme Court Opinions.* 4th ed. New York: Pearson Longman Publishers, 2005.

—Phyllis Farley Rippey

Lincoln, Abraham (1809–1865) *16th U.S. president*

America's greatest president, according to the polls of scholars, and the subject of more books than any other democratic leader in world history, Abraham Lincoln in his performance in the presidency (1861–65) turned into one of the greatest surprises of all time. The frontier lawyer literally saved the Union and preserved the idea of self-government in the world during an age of monarchs, ended slavery, and promulgated the first code in international law regarding the conduct of soldiers and treatment of prisoners of war during wartime. Remarkably, this was accomplished in the midst of a great civil war.

The Great Commoner's biography was a classic rags-to-riches story of a self-made person. Born February 12, 1809, in Kentucky, Abraham was the only son of Tom and Nancy Hanks Lincoln who survived infancy. The family moved to Indiana, where he grew up on a farm, and he moved to Illinois immediately after turning legal age. His border-state origins and frontier background made him an outsider by New England and aristocratic Southern standards. He "married up" when he wed Mary Todd, the politically ambitious daughter of one of the most prominent families in Lexington, Kentucky. She literally dusted him off to make him more socially acceptable. Having rejected his father's preference of working with his back, Lincoln became a self-taught lawyer, allowing him to enter Mary Todd's world.

In 1832, he ran for the Illinois statehouse but lost. More important than the outcome is that the youthful Lincoln ran for public office long before he became a lawyer—earlier than any other lawyer who became president. After bouts as a storekeeper, surveyor, postmaster, and other positions, he had discovered the perfect match for his interests and abilities. He ran for the statehouse again in 1834, winning the first of four terms. In an extremely short time, Lincoln emerged from nowhere to become the Whig floor leader in the state legislature. It was the first of two transforming moments in his political life; the second was his presidency. Between those two periods, he spent time seeking or serving in political office, except for a seemingly dormant five-year hiatus between his single term in the U.S. HOUSE OF REPRESENTATIVES (1846–48) and the seminal Lincoln-Douglas debates that dealt with the spread of slavery into the territories, marking his active return to the political arena.

Other than his single term in Congress, Lincoln spent seventeen years in Springfield, Illinois, practicing law and developing his political views and jurisprudence. Enjoying a highly active practice with three separate law partners, he became one of Illinois's best-known lawyers. With the demise of the Whigs, the lawyer-politician became the Republican candidate for the U.S. SENATE, representing the new anti-slavery party that he had helped to organize in Illinois. He engaged in the seven famous debates with "the Little Giant," incumbent Democratic senator Stephen A. Douglas, who advocated the amoral concept of "popular sovereignty" in dealing with slavery. Lincoln countered with a Golden Mean approach, by opposing the spread of slavery into the new territories but upholding protection of the institution in the South, as guaranteed by the U.S. Constitution. Though Douglas won that battle in the short term by retaining his Senate seat, two years later Lincoln emerged as the dark-horse compromise candidate of the Republican Party and defeated Douglas for president after the Democratic Party split over the slavery issue. However, the first successful Republican ticket only won 39.8 percent of the popular vote.

To the surprise of many, the former Whig lawyer demonstrated a willingness to act to meet the secession crisis after Southern extremists fired first at Ft. Sumter, triggering the outbreak of the Civil War. Lincoln was unwilling for a minority to overturn the results of the 1860 election. While Congress was in recess, the consummate politician and skillful lawyer saw the crisis in constitutional terms. He instinctively transformed JOHN LOCKE's "prerogative power" of the executive as a means to guide his actions, unlike his much more experienced yet befuddled Democratic Party predecessor, James Buchanan. Using his war powers, Lincoln blockaded Southern ports, raised funds to finance the war, suspended HABEAS CORPUS, initiated the draft, and issued paper money. These bold initiatives and others made Lincoln the chief executive who governed the most extra-constitutionally until World War II. Nonetheless, he understood that his actions would be subject eventually to congressional and judicial scrutiny.

PROCLAMATION OF EMANCIPATION

1861 1863

By the President of the United States of America.

Whereas, On the Twenty-Second day of September, in the year of our Lord one thousand eight hundred and sixty-two, a Proclamation was issued by the President of the United States, containing, among other things the following, to wit:

"That on the first day of January, in the year of our Lord one thousand eight hundred and sixty-three, all persons held as Slaves within any State or designated part of a State, the people whereof shall then be in rebellion against the United States, shall be then, thenceforth, and **FOREVER FREE,** and the EXECUTIVE GOVERNMENT OF THE UNITED STATES, including the military and naval authorities thereof, WILL RECOGNIZE AND MAINTAIN THE FREEDOM of such persons, and will do no act or acts to repress such persons, or any of them, in any efforts they may make for their actual freedom.

"That the Executive will, on the first day of January aforesaid, by proclamation, designate the States and parts of States, if any, in which the people thereof respectively shall then be in rebellion against the United States, and the fact that any State, or the people thereof shall on that day be in good faith represented in the Congress of the United States by members chosen thereto at elections wherein a majority of the qualified voters of such State shall have participated, shall, in the absence of strong countervailing testimony be deemed conclusive evidence that such State and the people thereof are not then in rebellion against the United States."

Now, therefore, I, ABRAHAM LINCOLN, PRESIDENT OF THE UNITED STATES, by virtue of the power in me vested as **Commander-in-Chief of the Army and Navy** of the United States in time of actual armed Rebellion against the authority and government of the United States, and as a fit and necessary war measure for suppressing said Rebellion, do, on this first day of January, in the year of our Lord one thousand eight hundred and sixty-three, and in accordance with my purpose so to do, publicly proclaim for the full period of one hundred days from the day of the first above-mentioned order, and designate, as the States and parts of States wherein the people thereof respectively are this day in rebellion against the United States, the following, to wit: ARKANSAS, TEXAS, LOUISIANA (except the Parishes of St. Bernard, Plaquemines, Jefferson, St. John, St. Charles, St. James, Ascension, Assumption, Terre Bonne, La Fourche, St. Mary, St. Martin, and Orleans, including the City of Orleans), MISSISSIPPI, ALABAMA, FLORIDA, GEORGIA, SOUTH CAROLINA, NORTH CAROLINA, AND VIRGINIA (except the forty-eight counties designated as West Virginia, and also the counties of Berkeley, Accomac, Northampton, Elizabeth City, York, Princess Ann, and Norfolk, including the cities of Norfolk and Portsmouth), and which excepted parts are for the present left precisely as if this Proclamation were not issued.

And by virtue of the power and for the purpose aforesaid, I do order and declare that **ALL PERSONS HELD AS SLAVES** within said designated States and parts of States ARE, AND HENCEFORWARD **SHALL BE FREE!** and that the Executive Government of the United States, including the Military and Naval Authorities thereof, will RECOGNIZE AND MAINTAIN THE FREEDOM of said persons.

And I hereby enjoin upon the people so declared to be free, to abstain from all violence, UNLESS IN NECESSARY SELF-DEFENCE, and I recommend to them that in all cases, when allowed, they LABOR FAITHFULLY FOR REASONABLE WAGES.

And I further declare and make known that such persons of suitable condition will be received into the armed service of the United States, to garrison forts, positions, stations, and other places, and to man vessels of all sorts in said service.

And upon this act, SINCERELY BELIEVED TO BE AN ACT OF JUSTICE, warranted by the Constitution, upon military necessity, I invoke the considerate judgment of mankind, and the gracious favor of ALMIGHTY GOD.

In testimony whereof I have hereunto set my name, and caused the seal of the United States to be affixed.

[L. S.] Done at the CITY OF WASHINGTON, this first day of January, in the year of our Lord one thousand eight hundred and sixty-three, and of the Independence of the United States the eighty-seventh.

A. Lincoln

By the President.

William H. Seward
Secretary of State.

Proclamation of Emancipation *(Library of Congress)*

Unlike the British, who postponed national elections during World War II, Lincoln held the 1864 election, despite his conviction that he would be defeated for reelection.

As most former presidents, Lincoln had supported voluntary colonization of American slaves abroad. Yet his views evolved. After meeting resistance to his support for compensated emancipation, he finally used his war power to issue the Emancipation Proclamation on January 1, 1863, which he followed with active support of the THIRTEENTH AMENDMENT to permanently abolish slavery. Moreover, the Great Emancipator took steps to free the entire emerging middle class by signing into law three of the most important pieces of legislation in American history. The first was the Homestead Act of 1862, which James Buchanan had vetoed previously. The second, which Buchanan also had vetoed as unconstitutional, was the Land Grant College Act of 1862, which transformed higher education in the nation. That same year, Lincoln signed the Pacific Railroad Act, which led to the building of the transcontinental railroad.

Despite his stunning leadership, the Lincoln presidency raised a host of constitutional issues: 1) whether presidents must obey Supreme Court decisions, e.g., *DRED SCOTT* (1857); 2) whether states have a right to secede from the Union; 3) whether part of a state may secede from an existing state, e.g., West Virginia from Virginia; 4) whether presidents have the right to act when Congress is not in session; 5) whether the Emancipation Proclamation was constitutional; 6) whether the president's suspension of habeas corpus was constitutional; and 7) whether the president or Congress should determine reconstruction, i.e., the extent of the president's pardoning power. The outcome of the Civil War itself answered some of these questions, as did the passage of the so-called Civil War amendments to the Constitution, as well as the decisions of the Supreme Court during and after the Civil War.

To appreciate Lincoln's philosophy of the law requires considering his role in preserving the Union and the idea of democratic government during an autocratic age; how he emancipated not only the slaves but the entire middle class and the nation as a whole; and how "the Great Reconciler" implemented a non-Marxian "people's jurisprudence" through his "with malice toward none" philosophy.

For more information: Farber, Daniel. *Lincoln's Constitution*. Chicago: University of Chicago Press, 2003; Neely, Mark. E., Jr. *The Fate of Liberty: Abraham Lincoln and Civil Liberties.* New York: Oxford University Press, 1991; Pederson, William D. "The Impact of Abraham Lincoln's Constitutional Legacy: A Global Outlook." *Lincoln Lore* 1885 (Summer 2006): 18–22.

—William D. Pederson

line-item veto

The line-item veto is a proposal that would allow the president to VETO certain items from a budget bill, rather than requiring the president to veto the entire bill. This type of veto power has been requested by several presidents, and at least all since Ronald Reagan was in office.

The most recent iteration of the attempt to gain the line-item veto is by the George W. Bush administration. The version that was considered by Congress was different from ideas that have previously been considered. Like the previous versions, the current version would allow the president to veto a single budgetary item from a larger bill. However, rather than seek a two-thirds majority vote, as is required by the Constitution, the vetoed item would be sent back to Congress for a simple majority vote for override. President Bush believed that this would help to alleviate major concerns that prior administrations and the Supreme Court have had with the line-item veto. However, until legislation passes in both chambers of Congress and passes what would likely be an imminent challenge in the federal judicial system, it is impossible to be sure of the success of this, or any other, legislative attempt to give the president the power of the line-item veto.

The most public rebuke of the presidential power of line-item veto occurred in the Supreme Court case *CLINTON V. CITY OF NEW YORK*, 524

U.S. 417 (1998). Congress granted the president the power of the line-item veto in 1996. President Clinton used that power about 80 times before this case was heard. In this case, President Clinton vetoed part of the Balanced Budget Act of 1997. New York sued to return a provision that allowed the state to raise taxes on hospitals and use the tax revenue to solicit federal Medicaid payments. The Supreme Court ruled that the Line-Item Veto Act violated the PRESENTMENT CLAUSE of the Constitution (Article I, Section 7, Clause 2.). In the decision, written by Justice JOHN PAUL STEVENS, the Supreme Court stated that "[i]f there is to be a new procedure in which the president will play a different role in determining the text of what may become a law, such change must come not by legislation but through the amendment procedures set forth in Article V of the Constitution."

The finding of the Supreme Court is not surprising, however. On at least two separate occasions, President Reagan's own administration noted that the line-item veto was unconstitutional. During the latter part of the Reagan administration, there was a public attempt to argue that the line-item veto would be a constitutional exercise of presidential power. The most vocal advocate was Stephen Glazier of the *Wall Street Journal*. Because of the public support for Glazier's argument, the Office of Legal Counsel was asked to prepare an opinion discussing the probability that the line-item veto was, in fact, constitutional. OLC's opinion stated that it was not. The opinion, penned by the head of OLC, Charles Cooper, stated categorically that "Article I of the Constitution does not vest the President with the inherent power to veto portions of a bill while signing the remainder of it into law." Cooper received severe criticism for this decision from conservative pundits. However, what many of these critics might not have realized was that OLC had already stated that the line-item veto was unconstitutional.

In 1985, Congress was preparing to give the president the power of line-item veto. However, OLC was asked to give its legal opinion on the proposed bill, and OLC decided that it was unlikely that the bill would pass constitutional muster. According to the decision, "[a] bill that purports to the President a line-item veto by providing that each item of the appropriation in an appropriation bill be enrolled, although not voted on, as a separate bill raises serious constitutional questions under Article I, § 7, cl. 2 of the Constitution." In other words, in two separate instances, with two differing ideas of what might constitute a constitutional provision to give the president the power of the line-item veto, President Reagan's own legal advisors stated that a legislatively mandated power of this type was unconstitutional. It is not surprising that the Supreme Court came to the same decision.

Despite several failed previous attempts to give the president the power of the line-item veto through legislative action, the idea continues to appeal to both the president, who tends to desire more power generally, and Congress, which seems to need assistance in curbing its own spending power. The outcome of the president's power of the line-item veto will continue to be watched closely by many people. Ultimately, the power seems to lie in the Supreme Court's interpretation of the Constitution, especially Article I.

For more information: N.A. "Constitutionality of Line-Item Veto Proposal." *Opinions of the Office of Legal Counsel* 9 (1985): 28; N.A. "The President's Veto Power." *Opinions of the Office of Legal Counsel* 12 (1988): 128.

—Tobias T. Gibson

living constitution

The "living constitution" refers to the notion that in order to be viable, a constitution must not be static but rather must be able to adapt to changing values and circumstances, just as a living creature grows and changes. The term is most popularly associated with a continuing debate among constitutional scholars and jurists triggered by writings and speeches by then-Justice WILLIAM J. BRENNAN, JR., and then-Attorney General Edwin Meese in the 1980s, although the dispute traces back to the American founding and even earlier.

It would seem that a living constitution must surely be better than the apparent alternative—a dead constitution—but the issue is not so simple, and it may be that the only good constitution is a dead constitution. On its face, it is hard to see what could be wrong with a living constitution, especially in a democracy. If we are to govern ourselves, there should not be unnecessary structural or substantive obstacles to achieving the public will. But taken to the extreme, a living constitution would be no constitution at all, because it would impose no constraints upon modern politics. Like Ulysses strapped to the mast, "we the people" have bound ourselves to constitutional constraints that precede and are superior to ordinary politics. The American constitution, with its division of authority between federal and state levels, separation of the national government into three branches, and substantive rights limitations on government, throws obstacles in the way of self-rule. That, at least in theory, is how we secure rights against majority tyranny and preserve some role for the states. These restrictive clauses—mostly ratified long before anyone alive today was born—create a certain "tyranny of the dead."

On the other hand, rigid adherence to old text and principles may be suffocating, preventing adaptation to changing circumstances and perceived needs. As Brennan wrote, "the genius of the Constitution rests not in any static meaning it might have had in a world that is dead and gone, but in the adaptability of its great principles." The trick, then, is to find a balance, so that CONSTITUTIONAL INTERPRETATION is not too lively, but not comatose. Conservative critics of the living constitution approach say the answer is simple: Apply the enduring principles of the Constitution consistently, and if you don't like them, amend the Constitution. But AMENDING THE CONSTITUTION is a long and difficult process, making it hard to bring in modern constitutional principles. More important, how to identify and apply basic constitutional principles and textual meaning is not clear.

For example, the FOURTEENTH AMENDMENT forbids denial by the states of EQUAL PROTECTION of the law. The amendment was passed on the heels of the Civil War and intended to secure the rights of newly freed slaves, yet the language is simple and sweeping. Does the amendment forbid or tolerate—or even require—AFFIRMATIVE ACTION programs to eradicate effects of past or present discrimination? Should women's rights be enforced just as strongly as those of racial minorities, even though the amendment came decades before women even gained the RIGHT TO VOTE? And what about business corporations? They are persons in the eyes of the law, so should they be able to claim protection against state discrimination? There are no simple answers even at this level of generality, and more uncertainties arise as principles are applied to specific circumstances.

Some guidance, then, is needed to apply the text. Critics of the living constitution advocate immersion in the meanings and understanding of language at the time constitutional text was written and ratified and the then-prevailing political theories. Some argue, for example, that the DECLARATION OF INDEPENDENCE must be central to informed constitutional interpretation. Skeptics of this approach argue that going beyond the text in this way is only an obsolete version of living constitutionalism, but proponents say it is at least better moored to the Constitution than modern judicial journeys into fundamental values. They argue that living constitutionalism easily becomes a vehicle for substituting the personal preferences of the judge or justice for the will of the people. In his exchange with Justice Brennan, Edwin Meese emphasized that adhering to the Constitution promotes democracy: "The Constitution is the fundamental will of the people. . . . To allow the courts to govern simply by what it [sic] views at the time as fair and decent, is a scheme of government no longer popular; the idea of democracy has suffered."

It is easy to exaggerate the differences between proponents and critics of the living constitution, in part because of the inherently evolving character of constitutional doctrine, which has developed in the pattern that judges in Anglo-American common law have followed for centuries: developing, articulating, and applying rules in a sequence of cases in very specific fact situations. It is these doctrines, rather than the text itself, that most determine the outcomes of cases and the development of the law. So in a sense all constitutional law is living law, gradually developing into a form quite different from the original document. Even conservative jurists and scholars, who are frequently critics of living constitutionalism, have led the development of new doctrines, such as in FEDERALISM and property rights cases.

On the other hand, it is difficult to find a scholar, and probably impossible to find a judge, who is so enthused with living constitutionalism that he or she would advocate entirely abandoning text and doctrine to strike out in bold new directions. Even in these post-modern days, there is no significant dispute over the meaning of many clauses, such as the age requirement to serve as president or the allocation of two SENATE seats per state. The sparks start to fly more over the substantive powers of the national government and the rights that limit both state and federal governments. But even here, it is still prudent to root constitutional arguments in text and tradition, even if that is no more than a jumping-off point. In response to the success of the Federalist Society in nurturing an intellectual base in the courts and universities in support of dead originalism, liberal jurists and scholars, who have been most commonly associated with living constitutionalism, have in turn created the American Constitution Society as a way to remind the public, and perhaps themselves, that they as well recognize the primacy of the Constitution.

So it is probably fair to say that, paraphrasing THOMAS JEFFERSON, we are all living constitutionalists, and we are all dead constitutionalists. There is virtually universal recognition that interpretation should be rooted in the Constitution and that fundamental principles embedded in the document are enduring yet adaptable to changing circumstances. But just what those principles are and how they should be ranked and applied is disputed. That debate is both healthy and constructive, arguably improving the quality of constitutional development. Many liberal jurists and scholars, for example, have been critical of the death penalty, even suggesting that it should be unconstitutional under the CRUEL AND UNUSUAL PUNISHMENT clause of the Eighth Amendment. Conservatives counter that the Constitution includes specific references to CAPITAL PUNISHMENT, so it would be nonsensical to strike it down under that same document. The courts have effectively split the difference, upholding the constitutionality of the death penalty but looking more closely at how it is applied, holding that an arbitrary or discriminatory application would be unconstitutional.

We are back to where we began, and that is to suggest that a constitution is inescapably living, changing in its meaning as judges and justices struggle to understand and apply its principles in changing circumstances, yet also essentially dead, embodying a set of principles superior to the day-to-day whims of politics, and effective only when interpretation is conscientiously constrained by text. When it comes to protecting rights, federalism, and separation of powers, the "cold hand of the dead" may be inescapable. The controversy over the living constitution will go on, because it embodies the inescapable tensions between rights and democracy, and between our rich legacy and future aspirations.

For more information: Belz, Herman. *A Living Constitution or Fundamental Law?: American Constitutionalism in Historical Perspective.* Lanham, Md.: Rowman & Littlefield, 1998; Marshall, Thurgood. "The Constitution: A Living Document." *Howard Law Journal* 30 (1987): 623–628; Wolfe, Christopher. *How to Read the Constitution.* Lanham, Md.: Rowman & Littlefield, 1996.

—Christopher Wolfe

lobbying and the First Amendment

Lobbying is a constitutionally protected activity. Accountability and integrity in representative government are achieved through the ability of the public to access and petition those elected to represent their interests. Justice HUGO BLACK observed, "The whole concept of representation depends upon the ability of the people to make their wishes known to their representatives" (*Eastern Railroad Presidents Conference v. Noerr Motors, Inc.*, 365 U.S. 127, 137 [1961]). To this end, the FIRST AMENDMENT guarantees that no law shall abridge "the right of the people . . . to petition the Government for a redress of grievances."

Lobbying is advocacy of a point of view, either by groups or individuals, who may be paid, independent, or volunteers. In addition to direct communication with government officials, lobbyists research, analyze, and draft legislation; build coalitions around issues; and educate government officials, employees, and corporate officers as to the implications of legislative proposals.

Public officials must consider information from a broad range of interested parties in order to reach fair and informed decisions. The U.S. Supreme Court has recognized that "[p]resent-day legislative complexities are such that the individual members of Congress cannot be expected to explore the myriad pressures to which they are regularly subjected" (*United States v. Harriss,* 347 U.S. 612, 625 [1954]). While the U.S. Constitution protects freedom of speech for those speaking on behalf of both institutional and personal interests, courts have recognized that these rights may be regulated to protect the public interest.

In 1928, the SENATE enacted a bill requiring lobbyists to register with the secretary of the Senate and the clerk of the House, but the House failed to pass the legislation. The issue did not go away, and members of Congress were concerned that concentrated lobbying efforts by a vocal minority could distort legislation of national impact. Eventually, Congress enacted the Federal Regulation of Lobbying Act (repealed by the Lobbying Disclosure Act of 1995) as part of the Legislative Reorganization Act of 1946. For the first time, lobbyists were required to register and file quarterly reports with the House and Senate. In 1954, the Supreme Court upheld registration requirements in *United States v. Harriss,* but defined the legislation narrowly to exclude individuals who spent their own money to lobby Congress directly from the act's requirements. Individual scandals led to calls to strengthen lobbying laws. In 1976, the Senate passed such a measure. Notably, concerns that the legislation would violate the First Amendment rights of lobbyists prevented the measure from gaining traction in the House.

Even a right as basic as free speech can be regulated in certain instances. The Supreme Court has upheld campaign contribution legislation where it was found to "serve the basic government interest in safeguarding the integrity of the electoral process without directly impinging upon the rights of individual citizens and candidates to engage in political debate and discussion" (*BUCKLEY V. VALEO,* 424 U.S. 1 [1976]). Appropriate regulation in this area is regulation which acts as a shield, protecting the public and integrity of the institution, not regulation that seeks to act as a sword by carving out exceptions to basic First Amendment rights. Lobbying need not be an equal opportunity activity. It makes no difference that some groups are more effective than others in gaining support for their positions. Rather, through appropriate disclosure, lobbyists themselves become subject to the same pressures they place on legislators. Such disclosure may implicate political and ethical considerations which may prevent legislators from undertaking certain interactions with lobbyists. The First Amendment requires *regulation* rather than *prohibition.* Indeed, "[b]ecause First Amendment rights need breathing space to survive, government may regulate the area only with narrow specificity" (*Cantwell v. Connecticut,* 310 U.S. 296, 311 [1940]).

Congress has been unable to substantially amend the substance of the provisions at issue in *Harriss.* A series of amendments that would have required disclosure by certain grassroots organizations was defeated in 1993. New technologies have presented new challenges for regulators. In 2007, the Senate struck a provision in pending lobbying reform legislation that would have required individuals involved in certain grassroots efforts, including blogging, to register as lobbyists. The effect of the *Harriss* decision was to regulate only those who lobby directly. Ironically, the very decision which upheld certain regulations on lobbyists acts to prevent further legislation. Any additional legislation would likely require certain interests to disclose their activities for the first time. Some fear that such legislation could chill citizen involvement in the legislative process.

Lobbying is a tradition nearly as old as Congress itself. Indeed, it would be difficult for Congress to complete its work without lobbyists. Laws regulating lobbying must strike a balance between disclosure in the public interest and the First Amendment rights of those who speak on behalf of issues and interests.

For more information: Nowak, John E., and Ronald D. Rotunda. *Principles of Constitutional Law.* St. Paul, Minn.: Thomson/West, 2005.

—Mark A. McGinnis

Lochner v. New York 198 U.S. 45, 25 S.Ct. 539 (1905)

In *Lochner v. New York,* the Supreme Court invalidated a state law restricting the number of hours a bakery employee could work. The state argued that the law was in place to protect the health of employees and the general public, but the Court held that the state was unconstitutionally interfering with each individual's liberty to contract as protected by the DUE PROCESS clause of the FOURTEENTH AMENDMENT.

A New York law prohibited employers from requiring or permitting employees to work more than 10 hours in a day or 60 hours in a week. Joseph Lochner, the owner of a bakery in Utica, New York, was convicted on two separate occasions for overworking an employee. He appealed the second conviction, giving rise to this case.

The state of New York contended that the law was designed to protect workers from health hazards related to long and odd hours in bakeries, which are often hot and void of clean air. The state also argued that overworking bakers results in a poorer quality product, affecting the health of the public consumers. Justice Peckham responded in his majority opinion by stating that bakers were fully capable of negotiating their own work hours and that if an individual baker felt he needed to work more to, for example, support his family, it should be his prerogative. He pointed out that plenty of other legislation was passed to ensure the bakery was clean and also noted that there is no quantifiable evidence that a loaf of bread made in a baker's 11th hour of work is any less clean or wholesome than a loaf made in his 10th hour. Finally, he hypothesized that a contrary decision would render economic protections provided by the substantive element of the due process clause meaningless.

Justice JOHN HARLAN dissented, arguing that the majority underestimated the hazardous effects of working in a bakery. Justice OLIVER WENDELL HOLMES, JR., also dissented, arguing that the judiciary had no right to supplant the judgment of the New York state legislature on the issue and that governments have restrained the public's right of contract for centuries. He listed Sunday laws and usury laws as examples. Holmes's dissent is most famous for the statement that the "Constitution did not enact Spencer's *Social Stats,"* a reference to the notion that the Constitution did not embody a specific economic philosophy to be enforced by the Court.

The Supreme Court used the precedent set in *Lochner* to invalidate economic regulations for over 30 years. However, by the end of the 1930s *Lochner* had lost most of its influence. If the Court had left any doubt over its stance on *Lochner,* it made itself clear in 1955, in *Williamson v. Lee Optical,* 348 U.S. 483, when Justice WILLIAM O. DOUGLAS explained that the days were over when the Court uses the due process clause to strike down a state's business and industry regulations because it deems them unwise or improvident. Today, the Supreme Court uses its RATIONAL BASIS TEST to analyze challenges to most economic regulations.

For more information: Bernstein, David E. "Lochner Era Revisionism, Revised: Lochner and the Origins of Fundamental Rights Constitutionalism." *Georgetown Law Journal* 92 (November 2003): 1–58; Cox, Archibald. *The Court and the Constitution.* Boston: Houghton Mifflin, 1987.

—Dylan R. Kytola

Locke, John (1632–1704) *English political philosopher*

John Locke was an important British political thinker who influenced many of the framers and founders of the American Constitution.

The British philosopher John Locke is often referred to as the American political philosopher because his political thought arguably influenced the nation's founders more than any other political theorist. Locke's major political writings include his *Two Treatises of Government* (published in 1689) and *A Letter Concerning Toleration* (first published anonymously in 1685), each reflecting the political conflicts of the times and especially the rivalries between crown and Parliament and between religious denominations. Locke crystallized the central elements of liberalism in his day into a coherent political regime dedicated to the protection of "life, liberty, and estate," with the state playing largely the role of umpire or protective nightwatchman. Locke's social contract argument provides a modern statement to show how government is made legitimate and also how revolt is legitimate when government ceases to be.

Locke's political philosophy is based in his empiricist and rationalist inclinations, which dictate that all knowledge originally is grounded in sensory perception and that while ideas may have non-arbitrary, agreed-upon meanings, there are no knowable innate or pure ideas to give humankind objective answers. An innate idea must be believed in, such as an article of religious faith, and the mind is such that it cannot be compelled to believe that to which it has not on its own assented. It is no indication of actual assent to a proposition or a particular understanding if it is given under threat of compulsion. Hence, compulsion in matters of faith is a fruitless attempt to overpower a person's natural liberty to willingly form his or her own ideas, and submission to an enforced orthodoxy reflects more the (illegitimate) power of the enforcer than it does voluntary assent to an idea. Locke argues that application of the principle of toleration is a prudent response to divergent, sincerely held beliefs and a better way to manage and maintain a stable society than for the state to side with one or other religious truth. Any agent, however, is welcome to try to persuade others of the superiority of its understandings through persuasive arguments or good works.

Locke's notion of consent to be governed is roughly parallel to assent in knowledge, as consent grants legitimacy to the state and cannot be compelled, and any attempt at coercion relies on force, not reason, and so is unjust. Locke's version of the social contract described a rather idyllic state of nature in which people enjoyed natural equality and had sufficient resources to meet their needs, provided they worked with nature to secure them, whereby a property claim was created to any goods produced. In addition, the people recognized a moral law, the Law of Nature, which requires that the plenty that is available to them be preserved so as much and as good should remain for others and the next generation. When the inevitable disputes arose regarding property claims, disputes which need not be presumed hostile, it became necessary first to establish some collective mechanism to deal with these inconveniences, something people individually could not do nearly as well despite their "executive power" to enforce their justifiable claims based in the Law of Nature.

People would move out of the state of nature and into civil society primarily in order to interpret and enforce the Law of Nature more fairly and evenly, especially as regards conflicting property claims. Locke understood property as more than merely material belongings or assets, and extended this concept to include anything—especially, one's person and one's rights—that a person may have an interest in, contributes to a person's independence from others, and provides the basis for claims against others who violate them. Eventually, however, as society and the issues people confronted or raised regarding property became more complex, the community would need to establish some overarching binding authority—a government—entrusted with the power to enforce the Law of Nature and arbitrate disputes in an impartial way, making judgments based in promulgated law and constrained to serve the interests of the people.

Locke presents the classical liberal argument that the State is established through the consent of the majority of the people to secure their interests through the use of duly constituted civil power. Should the government betray the trust placed in it through a series of abuses by either its executive or legislative branch, then the people can regard it as having revolted from them and may exercise their right to recall their trust through, if necessary, an armed rebellion. Locke's arguments in favor of individual rights, property, limited government, and the right of the people to hold their governors accountable to them, including through the threat of rebellion, appealed to the American founding generation, influencing not only the drafting of the DECLARATION OF INDEPENDENCE, but also the Constitution.

For more information: Hartz, Louis. *The Liberal Tradition in America: An Interpretation of American Political Thought since the Revolution.* New York: Harcourt Brace, 1965; Pangle, Thomas L. *The Spirit of Modern Republicanism: The Moral Vision of the American Founders and the Philosophy of Locke.* Chicago: Chicago University Press, 1988.

—Gordon A. Babst

Locke v. Davey 540 U.S. 712 (2004)

In *Locke v. Davey,* the U.S. Supreme Court held that the state of Washington did not violate the U.S. Constitution by excluding a student from a publicly funded scholarship program.

In 1999, the Washington legislature created the Promise Scholarship, a program designed to assist academically gifted students with postsecondary education expenses. After satisfying various academic and financial conditions, Joshua Davey received the scholarship funding and enrolled at Northwest College, a church-affiliated institution. When Davey chose to major in both pastoral ministries and business administration, however, Washington withdrew Davey's funding, because Promise Scholarship funding was not available to students attending religious colleges who studied religion from a devotional perspective. Washington placed this limitation on Promise Scholarship funding to comply with its state constitution's prohibition on public funding of clergy training. Davey challenged this limitation, claiming that Washington's exclusion of him from the Promise Scholarship on the basis of his desire to use the funding for religious purposes violated the free exercise, free speech, and EQUAL PROTECTION clauses in the U.S. Constitution.

In a 7-2 opinion, the Court rejected all of Davey's claims. The Court found that Davey's burden was akin to being denied the scholarship funding in the first place—a burden that the Court found minimal since the scholarship's financial and academic conditions prevented many people from ever being eligible to receive the funding. The Court ruled that Davey's minimal burden could not defeat Washington's substantial interest in enforcing the separation of church and state required by its own state constitution.

Justice ANTONIN GREGORY SCALIA wrote a dissenting opinion, in which Justice CLARENCE THOMAS joined, declaring that because the free exercise clause categorically prohibits the government from ever discriminating on the basis of religion, the majority wrongly focused on the weight of Davey's burden. Moreover, Justices Scalia and Thomas claimed that because the withdrawn funding cost Davey almost $3,000, the majority would still be wrong even if the weight of Davey's burden were relevant.

Davey is an important case because it permits states to require a greater degree of church-state separation than the U.S. Supreme Court has interpreted the ESTABLISHMENT CLAUSE to require. It is quite likely, for example, that the *Davey* rule permits those states that implement school-voucher programs to limit the use of the funding to secular purposes, even though the U.S. Supreme Court has expressly held that the establishment clause does not compel this limitation. Many scholars have noted, however, that the discretion that *Davey* grants the government must be limited because at some point a state's attempt to enforce a strict separation between church and state will violate the free exercise clause's guarantee of religious liberty. Many believe, for instance, that the free exercise clause deprives states of the authority to prohibit state employees from using their income for private religious purposes, but it is not clear why states lack this authority under the *Davey* rationale.

The ultimate scope of the *Davey* holding, and how it will mediate the tension between the religion clauses, remains to be seen.

For more information: Berg, Thomas, and Douglas Laycock. "Davey's Mistakes and the Future of State Payments for Services Provided by Religious Institutions." *Tulsa Law Journal* 40, no. 2 (2005): 227–253; Brown, Stephen P. *Trumping Religion: The New Christian Right, the Free Speech Clause, and the Courts.* Tuscaloosa, Ala.: University of Alabama Press, 2002; Merriam, Jesse R. "Finding a Ceiling in a Circular Room: *Locke v. Davey,* Federalism, and Religious Neutrality." *Temple Political & Civil Rights Law Review* 16 (2006): 103–143.

—Jesse R. Merriam

Loretto v. Teleprompter Manhattan CATV Corp. 458 U.S. 419 (1982)

In *Loretto v. Teleprompter Manhattan CATV Corp.*, the U.S. Supreme Court held that any government regulation that authorizes a permanent physical occupation of private property will always constitute a compensable taking pursuant to the Fifth and FOURTEENTH AMENDMENTs of the U.S. Constitution.

In 1973, the state of New York adopted a statute that prohibited landlords from interfering with the installation of cable television facilities on their property by local cable companies. The statute also limited the compensation that cable companies were required to pay landlords for this right to an amount set by the state's Commission on Cable Television. At the time, the commission set this amount at $1.

Jean Loretto was the owner of a five-story apartment building in New York City that had cable television equipment installed by Teleprompter Manhattan CATV. She brought a class action lawsuit on behalf of all landlords serviced by Teleprompter Manhattan CATV and alleged that the installation of cable equipment was a physical invasion of private property that amounted to a taking for which the plaintiffs were entitled to JUST COMPENSATION.

The New York trial court found for the cable company, and the appellate division affirmed. The New York Court of Appeals affirmed the lower court's decisions, finding that the statute was a legitimate exercise of the legislature's POLICE POWERs that did not constitute a taking under the balancing test articulated in *Penn Central Transportation Co. v. New York City,* 438 U.S. 104 (1978). The U.S. Supreme Court reversed, holding that the cable equipment effected a permanent physical occupation of Loretto's private property and was thus a per se compensable taking. In so doing, the Court reaffirmed its precedents that had established this per se rule.

The Court pointed to prior cases involving telegraph and telephone lines, underground pipes, and wires. The Court noted that even though a permanent physical occupation—such as the cable equipment—may not seriously interfere with an owner's use and enjoyment of their property, a regulation requiring a permanent physical occupation is qualitatively more severe than any regulation of property use. The owner has lost, among others, the rights to possess, use, dispose, and exclude with regard to the area of such occupation. Accordingly, the Court rejected a de minimus exception for minor permanent physical occupations reasoning that no matter how small or insignificant, such occupations deprive an owner of all of their property rights to that area. However, the Court noted that the extent of the occupation is relevant in determining just compensation. Ironically, on remand, the New York Court of Appeals found that just compensation for the cable equipment occupation was $1—the amount originally set by the commission.

The Court's ruling was narrow, as it applied only to permanent physical occupations—whether by the government or by a third party with government authorization. Any temporary physical occupations, such as overflights, and regulations that restrict use are instead subject to the *Penn Central* balancing test. However, this case was significant for reviving the per se rule that lower courts had ignored in favor of the *Penn Central* test, which did not guarantee the finding of a taking or the payment of just compensation.

For more information: Pick, Randall J. "*Loretto v. Teleprompter*: A Restatement of the Per Se Physical Invasion Test for Takings." *Baylor Law Review* 35 (1983): 373–386.

—Matthew J. Parlow

Loving v. Virginia 388 U.S. 1 (1967)

In *Loving v. Virginia,* the Supreme Court overturned Virginia's law banning interracial marriage. In making this decision, citing Virginia's violations to both the EQUAL PROTECTION and the DUE PROCESS clauses of the FOURTEENTH AMENDMENT, the Court also struck down similar antimiscegenation laws that punished and prohibited such marriages in 15 other states.

Loving v. Virginia marked the first time the tribunal addressed the question whether state laws governing marriage could utilize race as the sole criteria in banning them.

The case reached the Supreme Court nine years after two residents of Virginia wed. Mildred Jeter, an African-American female, and Richard Loving, a Caucasian male, married each other in Washington, D.C. The District had no antimiscegenation prohibitions, and Jeter and Loving were legally joined. The Lovings returned to their home in Virginia where subsequently they were charged with violating the statute that prohibited marriages like theirs. Pleading guilty to the charge, they were sentenced to a year in jail, which was suspended on the condition that they leave and not return to the state for 25 years. They then moved to D.C., where they filed a suit requesting that Virginia's law that banned interracial marriage be declared unconstitutional and that the state be restrained from enforcing its sentence on them.

Antimiscegenation statutes had their roots in colonial slavery codes, but their passage and codification was a result of Jim Crow–era laws that in increasing and more exacting ways separated whites and blacks. The Virginia law that the Lovings tested was typical. The Racial Integrity Act, passed in 1924, specifically prohibited whites from marrying blacks. In the words of the Supreme Court of Appeals of Virginia that upheld the Lovings' original conviction, the legitimate intent of these laws was to "'preserve the racial integrity of its citizens,' and to prevent 'the corruption of blood,' 'a mongrel breed of citizens,' and 'the obliteration of racial pride.'"

Since the founding of the republic, domestic relations—and the policies associated with them, marriage, divorce, survivor rights, child custody—remained the responsibility of the states. Thus from state to state a wide array of laws regarding these matters was enforced. At one time or another, 30 states had approved interracial marriage bans like Virginia's, though by the time Loving was heard, 14 had repealed them. Although the full faith and credit clause of Article IV, Section 1 acknowledges federal interest in this area of law, it was not until *Loving* that the Court squarely addressed this question.

Employing a benchmark that had emerged in *McLaughlin v. Florida,* 379 U.S. 184 (1964), where the Court had struck down a statute that had punished interracial cohabitation, Chief Justice Earl Warren wrote for a unanimous Court and concluded that STRICT SCRUTINY of the Virginia ban revealed discrimination that ran counter to the "clear and central purpose of the Fourteenth Amendment [which] was to eliminate all official state sources of invidious racial discrimination in the States."

In one of the strongest statements in this decision, Warren went on to say that such bans were "designed to maintain White Supremacy," and were therefore unconstitutional. He concluded, "Under our Constitution the freedom to marry, or not marry, a person of another race rests on the individual and cannot be infringed by the state" and reversed the Lovings' convictions.

Loving v. Virginia was one in a series of cases that the WARREN COURT tackled that, taken together, mark an important shift in the constitutional protections of individual CIVIL RIGHTS, especially for African Americans. Four decades later, the case remains a significant precedent for the Court's decisions relative to gay and lesbian relationships. (See especially *LAWRENCE V. TEXAS,* 539 U.S. 558 [2003].)

For more information: Moran, Rachel F. *Interracial Intimacy: The Regulation of Race and*

Romance. Chicago: University of Chicago Press, 2001; Woodward, C. Vann. *The Strange Career of Jim Crow.* New York: Oxford Press, 1966.

—George Peery

loyalty oaths

Loyalty oaths have been a source of significant constitutional litigation, raising questions to whether they violate the FIRST AMENDMENT. During the 1950s and the McCarthy era, loyalty oaths were popular tools to root out communists.

Loyalty oaths do two things: declare allegiance to the government and its institutions and disavow support for ideologies or associations that oppose the government and its institutions. Loyalty oaths are common in the United States. To assume office, government officials like the president, members of Congress, or of the judiciary take loyalty oaths. Similarly, state employees (including teachers, professors, police officers, etc.) often must affirm their allegiance and repudiate incitement of revolution. Armed forces members and national security workers also take loyalty oaths as conditions of employment. Even school children traditionally pledge allegiance at the start of the school day.

Early in the nation's history, the Puritans required that members pledge their support to the commonwealth and report dissent. The Continental Congress had members swear their loyalty. The original state legislatures invoked citizen loyalty oaths to reflect the covenant between the state and its citizens. Even now, the oath of allegiance is considered the most important part of the naturalization process for potential citizens. Customarily, new citizens first take the oath of naturalization and then pledge allegiance as their first act as citizens.

Courts have held that loyalty oaths as conditions of employment are constitutional so long as they are narrow and achieve a legitimate government purpose, even if they infringe on an individual's constitutional rights. Oaths must be reasonably related to the position. Oaths considered too vague may be deemed unconstitutional.

Loyalty oaths are frequently invoked when there is the perception of a security threat. Following the Civil War, some states enacted statutes excluding people from certain professions based on previous sympathy with the Confederacy. In *Ex parte Garland,* 71 U.S. 333 (1866), the Supreme Court held that mandating an oath of prior loyalty as a prerequisite for admission to the bar was unconstitutional, as it punished, without trial, an act performed before the imposition of the statute. After World War II, fear of Communist infiltration of the public education system led to state establishment of loyalty oaths as a condition of employment for educators. In many jurisdictions, those refusing to sign could be discharged. Most statutes required of educators pledge of allegiance to state and U.S. constitutions, assertion not to incite revolution, and declaration that they did not belong to the Communist Party. Many jurisdictions still continue the practice.

The Court has repeatedly struck down oaths considered broad, as they violate DUE PROCESS and infringe on freedom of speech (*Baggett v. Bullitt,* 377 U.S. 360 [1964]). In *Keyishian v. Board of Regents,* 385 U.S. 589, 605–606 (1967), the Court declared a New York loyalty oath threatened academic freedom by limiting teacher speech. In *Wieman v. Updegraff,* 344 U.S. 183 (1952), the Court held the oath infringed on freedom of association because it indiscriminately penalized innocent association with the Communist Party or other groups. The Court generally disallows attempts to condition benefit eligibility on loyalty declaration, as it would have a chilling effect on free speech (*Speiser v. Randall,* 357 U.S. 513 [1958]). In contrast, the Court ruled that loyalty oaths that infringed on constitutional rights to religious freedom were not acceptable but that employers could make reasonable accommodations (*Bessard v. California Community College,* 867 F. Supp. 1454 [E.D. Cal. 1994]).

For more information: Levinson, Sanford. "Constituting Communities through Words That Bind: Reflections on Loyalty Oaths." *Michigan Law Review* 84, no. 7 (June 1986): 1,440–1,470.

—Robin A. Harper

Lujan v. Defenders of Wildlife 504 U.S. 555 (1992)

In *Lujan,* the Supreme Court ruled that environmental groups lacked STANDING to challenge a regulation of the Secretary of the Interior. A rule promulgated by the Secretary of the Interior interpreted the Endangered Species Act as applicable only within the boundaries of the United States and on the high seas. The previous regulation had extended this act to include actions taken in foreign nations. The district court dismissed the lawsuit for lack of standing, but the court of appeals reversed. On remand, and in response to a motion for summary judgment, the district court entered judgment in favor of the environmental groups.

The case ultimately reached the U.S. Supreme Court, where Justice ANTONIN GREGORY SCALIA provided the opinion of the court. He began by noting that standing cases are typically analyzed through the injury in fact standard. Specifically, to bring suit in federal court, plaintiffs must suffer a concrete, discernible injury which is neither conjectural nor hypothetical. Furthermore, the injury must be fairly traceable to the conduct of the defendant state.

To help meet this standard, plaintiffs filed two affidavits describing their foreign trips to the traditional habitats of endangered species. Each document disclosed past travel to the habitat as well as a general statement of intent to return to these locations. The affidavits claimed an injury in fact, arguing the American role in these allegedly environmentally detrimental projects would reduce the population of the species within these habitats. Defenders of Wildlife pressed a series of arguments including their eco-system nexus theory arguing that "any person who uses any part of a 'contiguous ecosystem' adversely affected by a funded activity has standing even if the activity is located a great distance away" (id. at 565).

The court of appeals previously found standing based upon a citizen-suit provision. However, the Supreme Court disagreed. Justice Scalia stated the judiciary branch cannot, consistent with ARTICLE III OF THE U.S. CONSTITUTION, allow judicial proceedings to proceed based upon a generalized grievance. Specifically, he argued a general intent to return to previously visited sites was not sufficient for standing purposes. Without concrete travel plans, there was no showing of actual or imminent injury to the plaintiffs. Parties may not assert standing by merely emphasizing the connection of all ecosystems. Instead, the injury must be in the actual location currently in use by complaining party. Likewise, the Court noted the plaintiff's professional interest in animal survival did not provide a factual showing of actual injury. Specifically, to have standing, the plaintiff should submit specific facts that the protective species living in foreign nations were threatened and that the "Respondents members would thereby be 'directly' affected" (id. at 563).

For more information: Nowak, John E., and Ronald D. Rotunda. *Principles of Constitutional Law.* St. Paul, Minn.: Thomson/West, 2005.

—Daniel M. Katz

Luther v. Borden 48 U.S. 1, 39 (1849)

Luther v. Borden is an important political case where the Supreme Court refused to decide a case, citing the political question doctrine.

Luther rose from the Dorr Rebellion and resulting constitutional crisis in Rhode Island, in which political reformers attempted to create a new constitution (the People's Constitution) in the face of resistance from the existing Charter government. On June 29, 1842, Luther Borden, a militiaman under the Charter government acting under the authority of martial law, broke into the home of Rachel Luther looking for her son, Dorrite sympathizer Martin Luther. Rachel Luther sued on the grounds that the Charter government was no longer the legal government of Rhode Island since it was superseded by the People's Constitution, which was ratified by the people in 1841. The defense argued that the Charter government was the legal government of Rhode Island at the time, that it had the authority to declare martial law, and that Borden was acting as an agent of the government.

There were three main points of contention in *Luther v. Borden.* First, did the Court have jurisdiction to hear the matter or was it a political question? Second, which government, the Charter government or the People's Constitution, was the legal government of the State? Finally, did the State have the authority to declare martial law? The Court was unanimous on the first two points, but disagreed on the third.

In order to determine which law governed this case, the Court was asked to identify which government was in force at the time—the People's Constitution or the Charter government. The Court refused to enter this area since the Court felt that the case posed a political question, which was out of its purview. Justice ROGER TANEY, who wrote the opinion for the Court, argued that the determination of the validity of the People's Constitution was not a judicial question. Taney made it clear that under Article IV, Section 4 of the Constitution (the GUARANTEE CLAUSE), which guaranteed to every state a "Republican Form of Government," it rested with Congress to decide what government is the established one in a state and it is the president who decides when to interfere in civil disturbances within a state. Justice Levi Woodbury agreed with Taney that the Court could not be called upon to serve as an umpire in political matters.

Although the Court extolled the virtues of the political questions doctrine as an impediment to ruling on the matter, the doctrine did not prevent the Court from taking a position on a political controversy that it felt was out of its jurisdiction. Taney and Woodbury agreed that courts were not superior to a constitution and the people who created it. Judicial power, they argued, commences after a constitution is created and derives its power from it. Accordingly, courts should not be in the business of determining which government/constitution is valid. However, the Court made it clear that its power derived from an "established government capable of enacting laws and enforcing their execution, and of appointing judges to expound and administer them" (40). Therefore, only when a constitution is changed through the established institutional structures set up by an existing government will the Court consider interpreting it.

For more information: Dennison, George Marshel. *The Constitutional Issues of the Dorr War: A Study in the Evolution of American Constitutionalism, 1776–1849.* Ph.D. Thesis. University of Washington, 1967; Dennison, George Marshel. "The Dorr War and Political Questions." *Supreme Court Historical Society Yearbook* (1979): 44–62; Magrath, Peter C. "Optimistic Democrat: Thomas W. Dorr and the Case of *Luther v. Borden.*" *Rhode Island History* 27 (1970): 94–112; Schuchman, John S. "The Political Background of the Political-Question Doctrine: The Judges and the Dorr War." *The American Journal of Legal History* 16 (1972): 111–125.

—Randa Issa

Lynch v. Donnelly 465 U.S. 668 (1984)

In *Lynch v. Donnelly,* a majority of the Supreme Court, in a 5-4 vote, found no constitutional problems with a government-owned crèche (Nativity scene) as part of a larger holiday display including a Santa, reindeer, and other items, in Pawtucket, Rhode Island. The city argued that Christmas was so secularized that even biblical elements such as the crèche were no longer purely religious symbols, and defended the display as both long-standing tradition and a way to lure holiday shoppers downtown. The AMERICAN CIVIL LIBERTIES UNION, on behalf of a Jewish resident, argued that the crèche, unlike other seasonal images, remained a religious symbol, inappropriate in a government-sponsored display.

In ruling against Pawtucket, the district court judge said the Nativity scene's original meaning had not disappeared and its placement in the context of secular items did not have the effect of secularizing it. Applying the three-part Lemon test that had guided the Supreme Court's ESTABLISHMENT CLAUSE rulings for the previous two decades, he found no secular purpose served by the crèche, while its primary effect implied official government recognition of Christianity as a favored religion. He also thought the display risked fostering political divisiveness, thus failing the third part of the test. Two of the three appeals court judges upheld this ruling. The lone dissenter agreed with Pawtucket that Christmas, and all its symbols, had become entrenched in American secular tradition. He also thought the passive nature of the crèche kept it from violating the establishment clause.

The split lower court decision in this case along with similar controversies brewing in other cities led the Supreme Court to agree to hear the case. One reason for the uncertainty among the lower courts was that the facts in this case differed significantly from earlier establishment clause cases. Most major cases thus far had addressed education, and the Court had developed a consistent pattern of applying the Lemon test and disallowing religious practices in public schools. However, in 1983, in a non-school-related case, *Marsh v. Chambers,* 463 U.S. 783, the Court had taken a different direction, upholding legislative prayers on the basis of tradition; and it was this line of thought that the Lynch majority chose to follow.

Chief Justice WARREN BURGER, writing for the majority, provided a litany of instances in which government acknowledged America's religious heritage, asserted that the line of church-state separation was not rigid, and concluded that in the context of the secular display the crèche passed the Lemon test. In contrast, the four dissenters thought the display failed all parts of the Lemon test and disagreed with the idea that public celebrations of Christmas had always been an American tradition.

This case left many questions unanswered. It addressed only a government-owned display and not private displays on government property. Also, the emphasis on the "secularizing" effect of the broader display led to lighthearted but real queries as to how many reindeer were needed to secularize a Nativity scene. It also raised doubts about the continuing value of the Lemon test as a meaningful criterion for judging establishment clause cases. And for some Christians, rather than helping to "keep Christ in Christmas," it served only to trivialize the religious nature of this holiday.

For more information: Pfeffer, Leo. *Religion, State, and the Burger Court.* Buffalo, N.Y.: Prometheus Books, 1984; Swanson, Wayne R. *The Christ Child Goes to Court.* Philadelphia, Pa.: Temple University Press, 1990.

—Jane G. Rainey